Kickstart IoT Systems Engineering

Build Intelligent IoT Systems from Embedded Devices to Cloud and Edge AI

Mr. Pavan Bendre R
Mr. Sandeep Telkar R
Dr. Likewin Thomas
Mrs. Akhila CV

www.orangeava.com

Copyright © 2026, Orange Education Pvt Ltd, AVA®

All rights reserved. No part of this book may be reproduced, stored in a retrieval system, or transmitted in any form or by any means, without the prior written permission of the publisher, except in the case of brief quotations embedded in critical articles or reviews.

Every effort has been made in the preparation of this book to ensure the accuracy of the information presented. However, the information contained in this book is sold without warranty, either express or implied. Neither the author nor **Orange Education Pvt Ltd** or its dealers and distributors, will be held liable for any damages caused or alleged to have been caused directly or indirectly by this book.

Orange Education Pvt Ltd has endeavored to provide trademark information about all of the companies and products mentioned in this book by the appropriate use of capital. However, **Orange Education Pvt Ltd** cannot guarantee the accuracy of this information. The use of general descriptive names, registered names, trademarks, service marks, etc. in this publication does not imply, even in the absence of a specific statement, that such names are exempt from the relevant protective laws and regulations and therefore free for general use.

First Published: April 2026

Published By: Orange Education Pvt Ltd, AVA®

Address: 9, Daryaganj, Delhi, 110002, India

275 New North Road Islington Suite 1314 London,
N1 7AA, United Kingdom

ISBN (PBK): 978-93-49887-24-4

ISBN (E-BOOK): 978-93-49887-09-1

Scan the QR code to explore our entire catalogue

www.orangeava.com

Get a Free eBook

We hope you're enjoying your recent book purchase! Your feedback is incredibly valuable to us and helps other readers discover books that truly make a difference.

If you found this book useful or enjoyable, we'd greatly appreciate it if you could leave a short review with a 5-star rating on Amazon. Your review supports our work and allows us to reach more learners worldwide.

As a thank-you, we're happy to offer you a **free digital copy of this book** plus a **30% discount code** for your next purchase on our official websites:

www.orangeava.com

www.orangeava.in (For the Indian Subcontinent).

☑ **How it works:**

Leave your review on Amazon, take a screenshot of the confirmation or use the following link to submit the claim and email it to **info@orangeava.com.** Once received the required detail, we will send your rewards within 24 hours, **along with one month free subcription to the book on AVA SkillShelf!**

Claim Form
https://rebrand.ly/4d2477

Thank you for your support—it truly means a lot to us.

Enjoy 1 Month of Free Access to AVA SkillShelf!

The future belongs to lifelong learners. With AVA SkillShelf, you go beyond reading books and start building real, job-ready skills curated by industry experts.

Your membership unlocks **200+ learning products** covering AI, Cloud, Python, Cybersecurity, Data Science, DevOps, and more—all in one platform. Our bestselling technical books are transformed into structured courses designed for practical, real-world application.

Learn directly from experienced professionals and published authors, with no filler—just actionable insights. Earn **verified digital certifications** to strengthen your CV, LinkedIn profile, and professional credibility.

Learn anytime, anywhere, on any device, at your own pace. Ideal for students, professionals, career switchers, and tech leaders.

For full access to all current and future courses, choose our **Annual Membership**. Simply scan the QR to get started!

For 1 month Free access, simply refer to the steps on the previous page titled: Get a Free ebook!

https://www.avaskillshelf.com/

Downloading the code bundles and colored images

Please follow the links or scan the QR codes to download the
Code Bundles and Images of the book:

https://github.com/ava-orange-education/Kickstart-IoT-Systems-Engineering

The code bundles and images of the book are also hosted on
https://rebrand.ly/e5c398

In case there's an update to the code, it will be updated on the existing GitHub repository.

Errata

We take immense pride in our work at **Orange Education Pvt Ltd,** and follow best practices to ensure the accuracy of our content to provide an indulging reading experience to our subscribers. Our readers are our mirrors, and we use their inputs to reflect and improve upon human errors, if any, that may have occurred during the publishing processes involved. To let us maintain the quality and help us reach out to any readers who might be having difficulties due to any unforeseen errors, please write to us at :

errata@orangeava.com

Your support, suggestions, and feedback are highly appreciated.

Dedicated to

My Beloved Parents:

Mr. B. A. Raju

And

Late Smt. Jyothi B. R

For Their Unwavering Support, Values, and Encouragement That Shaped My Journey.

And

To My Sister,

Meghana B. R

for Her Constant Motivation, Belief, and Support throughout This Endeavor.

--Mr. Pavan Bendre R

My Beloved Parents:

Late Smt Nagarathna GR

And

Mr. Ramachandra RT.

My Wife, Mrs. Rashmi PK,

My Lovely Daughter, Ms. Sirisha ST and My Son, Ujjwal ST.

-- Mr. Sandeep Telkar R

My Beloved Parents:

Maj (Retd.) T C Thomas and Mrs. Mary Kutty Thomas.

And

My Wife, Dr. Evelyn M. M, and My Children, Alfy and Kia.

--Dr. Likewin Thomas

My Dear Students,

Who Inspire Me to Learn, Grow, and
Teach Better Every Day.

My Beloved Husband,

Mr. Gururaja B

For His Constant Support, Patience, and Encouragement.

--Mrs. Akhila CV

About the Authors

Mr. Pavan Bendre R is an AI and Machine Learning Engineer as well as Data Engineer with expertise in Artificial Intelligence, Machine Learning, IoT systems, Data Engineering, and intelligent automation. He currently works as a Data Engineer at Saturam, where he builds scalable data pipelines and cloud-integrated intelligent solutions for real-world applications.

Pavan is a recipient of the Institute of Electrical and Electronics Engineers (IEEE) Best Paper Award for his research in Healthcare AI. He has also served as Vice Chairperson of GeeksforGeeks PESITM, and is an active member of IEEE and Google Developer Student Clubs.

Mr. Sandeep Telkar R is an Assistant Professor in the Department of Artificial Intelligence and Machine Learning at PES Institute of Technology & Management, Shivamogga. He holds an M. Tech. in Digital Communication and Networking and a B.E. in Information Science and Engineering, with expertise in programming, machine learning, deep learning, and emerging AI technologies.

He is the author of internationally published textbooks including Kickstart to Compiler Design Fundamentals, Python for Machine Learning, and Conquering C Programming, known for their clear concepts and practical approach. A recipient of Best Paper and Best Research Awards, he has published research in reputed IEEE, Springer, and Scopus-indexed journals.

Dr. Likewin Thomas is a Professor and Head of the Department of Artificial Intelligence and Machine Learning at PES Institute of Technology and Management, Shivamogga. He holds a Ph.D. and M. Tech. in Computer Science and Engineering from NITK Surathkal, and brings over two decades of experience spanning academia, industry, and research.

A Senior Member of IEEE and former Secretary of the IEEE Mangalore Sub-Section, he has played key roles in academic governance with VTU and other institutions. Dr. Thomas has led and organized several prestigious IEEE conferences and flagship events, served as Principal Investigator for multiple AICTE and VGST-funded projects, and is the license holder of TEDx PESITM.

An accomplished researcher and author, he holds two patents, has authored eight books, and published extensively in IEEE, Springer, ACM, Scopus, and SCI-indexed venues.

Mrs. Akhila CV is an Assistant Professor at the PES Institute of Technology and Management (PESITM), VTU, with academic qualifications in Computer Science and Engineering (B.E., M. Tech.) and is currently pursuing her doctoral research. Her core areas of interest include Artificial Intelligence (AI), Machine Learning, Data Science, and Database Management Systems.

With a strong professional background of 9 years in the industry, and about 3 years in academia, she brings valuable practical perspectives into the classroom as well as her academic writing. Her work focuses on making complex technical concepts accessible and application-oriented, thereby supporting learners in developing strong conceptual foundations and industry-relevant competencies.

About the Technical Reviewers

Krunal Ajaybhai Patel is a Technical Program Manager with experience across three Fortune 500 hardware companies in consumer electronics, semiconductors, and electric vehicle industries. He has led cross-functional hardware programs from ideation to high-volume production exceeding one billion dollars in product impact, and pioneered IoT-based vehicle access systems. An IEEE Senior Member, Krunal drives innovation in connected hardware and advanced manufacturing.

Avichal Chum is a technologist and thought leader specializing in Internet of Things (IoT) and cloud computing, with deep expertise in designing scalable solutions across AWS, Microsoft Azure, and GCP. His experience spans IoT architecture, cloud infrastructure optimization, and developing connected device ecosystems.

As an active contributor, Avichal publishes articles on cloud computing best practices and IoT implementations, bridging traditional infrastructure with modern connected device workloads. His expertise includes building device state management systems, telemetry streaming architectures using IoT Hubs and Event Hubs, and integrating smart devices including thermostats with platforms such as Amazon Alexa, Google Home, and IFTTT, while ensuring scalability for demanding IoT workloads.

Shrey Tyagi is an enterprise technology architect with extensive experience in designing, evaluating, and governing complex CRM and data platforms at scale. His career has been centered on solving high-impact architectural challenges for large organizations operating in regulated, data-intensive environments, where technical decisions carry long-term operational and financial consequences.

He is recognized for his ability to assess sophisticated technical systems across dimensions of architecture, data quality, security, and platform extensibility, and is frequently entrusted with responsibilities that require independent technical judgment.

In addition to hands-on architectural leadership, Shrey contributes to the profession as a technical reviewer and advisor, evaluating advanced manuscripts and practitioner-focused content for accuracy, rigor, and enterprise relevance. His work reflects a sustained record of influence within the field of modern cloud and enterprise systems.

Acknowledgments

First and foremost, I express my heartfelt gratitude to my parents, Mr. B. A. Raju and Late Smt. Jyothi B. R., whose unwavering love, values, and sacrifices have been the foundation of my academic and professional journey.

I sincerely thank my teachers and mentors for their guidance, insight, and encouragement, which shaped my understanding of engineering, IoT systems, and emerging technologies.

I am deeply grateful to my sister, Meghana B. R., for her constant support and motivation, and to my co-authors for their dedication and collaborative efforts that made this work possible.

I extend my sincere thanks to all who supported and believed in this endeavor, directly or indirectly.

--Mr. Pavan Bendre R

We express our sincere gratitude to our parents for their unwavering support, encouragement, and belief, which have been a constant source of motivation throughout our academic journey.

We gratefully acknowledge the PES Institute of Technology and Management (PESITM), Shivamogga, for providing a conducive academic environment, and essential resources that enabled the successful completion of this work.

We extend our respectful thanks to the faculty members and non-teaching staff of the Department of Artificial Intelligence and Machine Learning (AIML) for their valuable guidance, academic support, and cooperation. Their collective efforts significantly contributed to the successful completion of this book, Kickstart IoT Systems Engineering.

Finally, we remain thankful to all individuals who, directly or indirectly, supported and inspired this endeavor.

-- Mr. Sandeep Telkar R

--Dr. Likewin Thomas

--Mrs. Akhila CV

Preface

The Internet of Things (IoT) is a driving force behind modern computing, connecting physical devices to the digital world to sense, communicate, and act intelligently. From smart homes to industrial automation and smart cities, every IoT solution relies on a well-designed architecture that integrates hardware, software, networks, cloud platforms, and data intelligence.

This book provides a comprehensive yet practical guide to IoT systems—from core device level fundamentals to advanced cloud-based and intelligent architectures. Designed for students, engineers, and professionals, it simplifies complex concepts across embedded systems, networking, cloud computing, security, and AI through clear explanations and real-world examples.

Thus, with a strong hands-on approach, practical exercises, and real-world case studies, this book equips readers to design, build, deploy, and scale complete IoT solutions. By the end, you will not just understand IoT—you will be ready to create it!

Chapter-wise Summary

Chapter 1: Introduction to IoT

This chapter introduces the fundamental concept of the Internet of Things (IoT), tracing its evolution from early embedded systems to today's connected, data-driven ecosystems. It explains the core building blocks of IoT—devices, sensors, connectivity, data, and applications—while highlighting real-world use cases across smart homes, healthcare, agriculture, and industrial automation. The chapter establishes the motivation and scope of IoT in modern technology.

Chapter 2: IoT Architecture and Ecosystem

This chapter explores the architectural foundations of IoT systems. Readers learn about layered IoT architectures, including perception, network, and application layers, and how data flows across devices, gateways, and cloud platforms. The chapter also introduces common hardware platforms, communication technologies, and cloud services, helping readers understand how complete IoT ecosystems are designed and integrated.

Chapter 3: Sensor Technologies and Actuators

This chapter focuses on the physical interface between IoT systems and the real world. It explains different types of sensors (analog, digital, smart sensors) and actuators, their operating principles, signal characteristics, and use cases. Practical examples demonstrate how sensors collect the environmental data, and how actuators respond to control signals in automated systems.

Chapter 4: Networking and Communication Protocols

This chapter introduces the networking fundamentals that enable IoT connectivity. Readers learn about LAN, WAN, IP addressing, and ports, followed by IoT-specific communication protocols such as MQTT, HTTP, BLE, Zigbee, and LoRa. The chapter emphasizes protocol selection based on bandwidth, latency, power consumption, and scalability requirements.

Chapter 5: Getting Started with Arduino, NodeMCU, and ESP32

This chapter provides a hands-on introduction to popular IoT development boards. It explains microcontroller fundamentals, GPIO usage, programming workflows, and development environments. Readers learn how to write, upload, and debug their first programs, gaining confidence in working with embedded hardware platforms.

Chapter 6: Interfacing Sensors and Modules

This chapter demonstrates practical sensor and module interfacing using Arduino and ESP32 platforms. Readers learn wiring techniques, signal reading, calibration, and debugging methods, while working with commonly used sensors such as temperature, gas, ultrasonic, and relay modules. A mini-project reinforces real-world integration skills.

Chapter 7: Real-Time Control with GPIO, PWM, and Interrupts

This chapter explores real-time hardware control techniques. It covers GPIO input/output handling, PWM for analog-like control, servo and motor operation, as well as interrupt-driven programming. Readers learn how to build responsive and efficient IoT systems that react immediately to real-world events.

Chapter 8: Serial Communication and Data Transmission between Devices

This chapter introduces serial communication protocols such as UART, SPI, and I2C. Readers learn how devices exchange data, debug communication using serial monitors, and implement cross-device communication between microcontrollers. In fact, the chapter establishes a foundation for multi-device IoT systems.

Chapter 9: Firebase, Blynk, and Google Sheets

This chapter transitions IoT systems from local operation to cloud connectivity. It explains how to send, store, visualize, and retrieve sensor data using Firebase, Google Sheets, and Blynk dashboards. Readers also learn how cloud platforms enable remote monitoring and control of IoT devices.

Chapter 10: MQTT, REST APIs, and Webhooks for Device Communication

This chapter introduces professional communication mechanisms used in real-world IoT systems. It explains the client–server model, publish–subscribe architecture, RESTful APIs, and Webhooks. Practical examples demonstrate how devices communicate reliably with cloud services, and trigger automated workflows.

Chapter 11: Encryption, Device Hardening, and Authentication

This chapter addresses IoT security fundamentals. Readers learn about data encryption, authentication mechanisms, secure communication, and device hardening practices. The chapter emphasizes building IoT systems that are resilient to attacks and safe for real-world deployment.

Chapter 12: Data Logging, Alert Systems, and Notification Integration

This chapter focuses on data logging strategies and real-time alerting systems. It explains local and cloud-based logging, structured data formats, threshold-based alerts, and notification services such as email, mobile alerts, and automation platforms. Readers learn how logging supports monitoring, analytics, and system reliability.

Chapter 13: Cloud-Backed End-to-End Projects and Enterprise IoT Integration

This chapter introduces enterprise-scale IoT architectures using platforms such as AWS IoT Core and Azure IoT Hub. Readers learn about secure device provisioning, serverless processing, rule-based message routing, and professional dashboards. End-to-end projects demonstrate how large-scale IoT systems operate in production environments.

Chapter 14: Introduction to ML with Sensor Data

This chapter marks the entry into intelligent IoT systems. It introduces Edge AI and TinyML, explaining how sensor data is collected, preprocessed, and used to train lightweight Machine Learning (ML) models. Readers deploy ML models directly on microcontrollers, enabling local decision-making and intelligent automation.

Chapter 15: Deployment, Testing, and Scaling

This chapter prepares readers for real-world IoT deployment. It covers firmware versioning, OTA updates, remote configuration, testing strategies, rollback mechanisms, and scalability planning. Practical checklists and workflows reflect industry best practices for building reliable, long-term IoT products.

Chapter 16: The Future of IoT

This chapter provides a forward-looking view of IoT evolution. Topics include Industrial IoT, digital twins, 5G connectivity, sustainability, and emerging trends such as swarm systems and self-healing networks. The chapter also highlights future career paths and certifications in IoT and Edge AI.

Chapter 17: Applied IoT with Edge AI and Vision

This final chapter explores advanced IoT applications combining edge computing, computer vision, and AI. Readers are introduced to platforms like Raspberry Pi and Jetson Nano as well as examine real-world industry case studies across manufacturing, agriculture, logistics, and energy. Thus, this chapter serves as a practical and inspirational conclusion to the book.

DID YOU KNOW

Did you know that Orange Education Pvt Ltd offers eBook versions of every book published, with PDF and ePub files available? You can upgrade to the eBook version at **www.orangeava.com** and as a print book customer, you are entitled to a discount on the eBook copy. Get in touch with us at: **info@orangeava.com** for more details.

At **www.orangeava.com**, you can also read a collection of free technical articles, sign up for a range of free newsletters, and receive exclusive discounts and offers on Print Books and eBooks.

PIRACY

If you come across any illegal copies of our works in any form on the internet, we would be grateful if you would provide us with the location address or website name. Please contact us at **info@orangeava.com** with a link to the material.

ARE YOU INTERESTED IN AUTHORING WITH US?

If there is a topic that you have expertise in, and you are interested in either writing or contributing to a book, please write to us at **business@orangeava.com**. We are on a journey to help developers and tech professionals to gain insights on the present technological advancements and innovations happening across the globe and build a community that believes Knowledge is best acquired by sharing and learning with others. Please reach out to us to learn what our audience demands and how you can be part of this educational reform. We also welcome ideas from tech experts and help them build learning and development content for their domains.

REVIEWS

Please leave a review. Once you have read and used this book, why not leave a review on the site that you purchased it from? Potential readers can then see and use your unbiased opinion to make purchase decisions. We at Orange Education would love to know what you think about our products, and our authors can learn from your feedback. Thank you!

For more information about Orange Education, please visit **www.orangeava.com**.

Table of Contents

Chapter 1
Introduction to IoT

Introduction

In this section, we will discuss the Internet of Things (IoT) — one of the most revolutionary technologies of the 21st century. IoT is transforming the way humans, machines, and systems interact by connecting everyday devices to the internet, enabling them to sense, communicate, and act intelligently. The IoT is arguably one of the most foundational and transformative technologies of the 21st century. As of 2026, IoT is no longer a futuristic concept but the silent infrastructure that underpins modern global commerce, smart living, and industrial operations. It is fundamentally transforming the way humans, machines, and systems interact by connecting billions of everyday devices to the internet, enabling them to sense, communicate, and act intelligently.

In today's world, we live surrounded by billions of connected devices — from smartphones, wearables, and smart home assistants to industrial sensors, medical monitoring devices, and smart city infrastructure. Without IoT, managing this vast ecosystem of devices and data would be inefficient, error-prone, and disconnected. IoT provides a structured way to integrate sensors, controllers, communication networks, and cloud platforms, allowing seamless flow of data and automated decision-making. The core idea of IoT is simple: physical objects become *smart* by embedding sensors and connectivity that allow them to send and receive data. For example, a fitness tracker monitors heart rate, communicates with a smartphone over Bluetooth, and uploads the data to the cloud for analysis. Similarly, in agriculture, soil moisture sensors send real time data to an IoT gateway, which then triggers irrigation systems only when needed.

The evolution of IoT is deeply rooted in earlier computing paradigms — starting from basic embedded systems, progressing to smart devices with wireless communication, and today, advancing to AI-powered IoT systems running on the edge and cloud. Almost every modern application — whether in healthcare, agriculture, industry, or transportation — now leverages IoT to improve efficiency, reduce costs, and enhance decision-making.

Evolution of IoT

Embedded Systems: (Foundation) Basic, single-purpose computing in devices.

- **Smart Devices with Wireless Communication:** (Progression) Devices with connectivity and richer functionality.

- **AI-powered IoT Systems (Edge and Cloud):** (Current State) Sophisticated systems using AI for enhanced efficiency and decision-making at the device level, and in the cloud.

Understanding IoT is the first step toward mastering smart systems, automation, and intelligent decision-making in the modern digital economy. In this chapter, we will explore the fundamentals of IoT, its core components, architecture, and applications, along with practical exercises to help you visualize how IoT systems are built in the real world.

Structure

In this chapter, we will cover the following topics:

- Introduction to IoT and Its Importance
- Core components of an IoT system
    - Sensors and actuators
    - Controllers (microcontrollers and processors)
    - Connectivity and networks
    - Cloud platforms and applications
- Evolution of IoT
    - Embedded systems → Smart devices → Edge AI and IoT
- IoT Architecture Overview
    - Device layer
    - Network layer
    - Application layer
- Real-world IoT Applications
    - Smart homes
    - Precision agriculture
    - Healthcare and fitness
    - Industrial automation
    - Smart cities and transport
- Practical Exercises
    - Exercise 1: IoT System Breakdown
    - Exercise 2: Architecture Mapping
    - Exercise 3: Explore Real IoT Projects

Introduction to IoT and Its Importance

The Internet of Things (IoT) is one of the most significant technological revolutions of the modern era. At its core, IoT refers to the idea of connecting everyday physical objects – such as appliances, vehicles, machines, or even wearable devices – to the internet so that they can collect, share, and act upon data. These objects are no longer passive; instead, they become *smart*, capable of sensing their environment, communicating with other devices, and taking actions automatically.

Think of a smart home assistant that adjusts the room temperature when you arrive, or a fitness tracker that records your steps and sends the data to your phone for analysis. On a larger scale, IoT powers industrial automation, smart agriculture, and intelligent transportation systems. With billions of connected devices worldwide, IoT is shaping the way we live, work, and interact with technology.

IoT Example	Domain	Sensor(s)	Connectivity	Outcome/Action
Smart Home Assistant	Consumer	Temperature, Presence/Motion	Wi-Fi, Cloud	Adjusts room temperature upon user arrival
Fitness Tracker	Consumer	Accelerometer, Heart Rate Monitor	Bluetooth, Internet/Cloud	Records steps and heart rate, sends data for analysis
Industrial Automation	Enterprise	Proximity, Pressure, Vibration	Wired/Wireless (e.g., LoRaWAN, Cellular)	Automated machine control, predictive maintenance alerts
Smart Agriculture	Enterprise	Soil Moisture, Light, Temperature	Cellular, Satellite, LoRaWAN	Automated irrigation, pest monitoring, yield optimization
Intelligent Transportation	Enterprise/ Public	GPS, Radar, Vision	Cellular (4G/5G), Dedicated Short Range (DSRC)	Real-time traffic management, dynamic route guidance, vehicle safety

Table 1.1: *Common IoT Components and Examples*

The Importance of IoT in Today's World

We live in a time where data has become as valuable as oil once was. Every second, enormous amounts of data are being generated — by machines in factories, by sensors in cars, by monitoring systems in hospitals, and even by simple devices like your smartphone. Without IoT, most of this data would remain unutilized and isolated.

IoT provides a structured way to connect devices, meaningful data, and enable real-time decision-making. This makes systems more efficient, responsive, and intelligent.

Some practical examples:

- In healthcare, wearable devices monitor heart rate, blood oxygen, and sleep patterns, alerting doctors in case of emergencies.
- In agriculture, IoT sensors track soil moisture and weather conditions, ensuring that crops are watered only when necessary, saving water and increasing yield.
- In smart cities, connected streetlights adjust brightness, depending on traffic or pedestrians, reducing energy costs and improving safety.

Without IoT, these use cases would require manual intervention, and would be slow, costly, and less effective.

Key Benefits of IoT

The importance of IoT lies in its ability to transform the raw data into meaningful insights and automated actions. Its benefits can be grouped into several dimensions:

- **Seamless Connectivity:** Devices talk to each other and to central systems in real time, creating a unified ecosystem.
- **Data-Driven Decisions:** Information collected from devices helps organizations predict failures, improve efficiency, and reduce costs.
- **Automation and Efficiency:** Many systems operate without human input — for example, irrigation systems that activate only when the soil is dry.

- **Enhanced Quality of Life:** IoT enables safer homes, personalized healthcare, smarter transportation, and improved convenience.
- **Foundation for Advanced Technologies:** IoT lays the groundwork for AI, edge computing, and machine learning, which depend on real-time data to function.

IoT as the Nervous System of the Digital World

Just as the nervous system in the human body collects signals from sensory organs, processes them in the brain, and triggers actions in muscles, IoT works in a similar way:

- Sensors act as the sensory organs (detecting temperature, motion, pressure, and so on).
- Controllers and networks act as the nerves (carrying information).
- Cloud platforms and applications act as the brain (analyzing and making decisions).
- Actuators act as the muscles (performing actions like turning on a fan or unlocking a door).

This analogy helps us understand why IoT is so crucial — it essentially gives the digital world a "nervous system," enabling intelligence and responsiveness at scale.

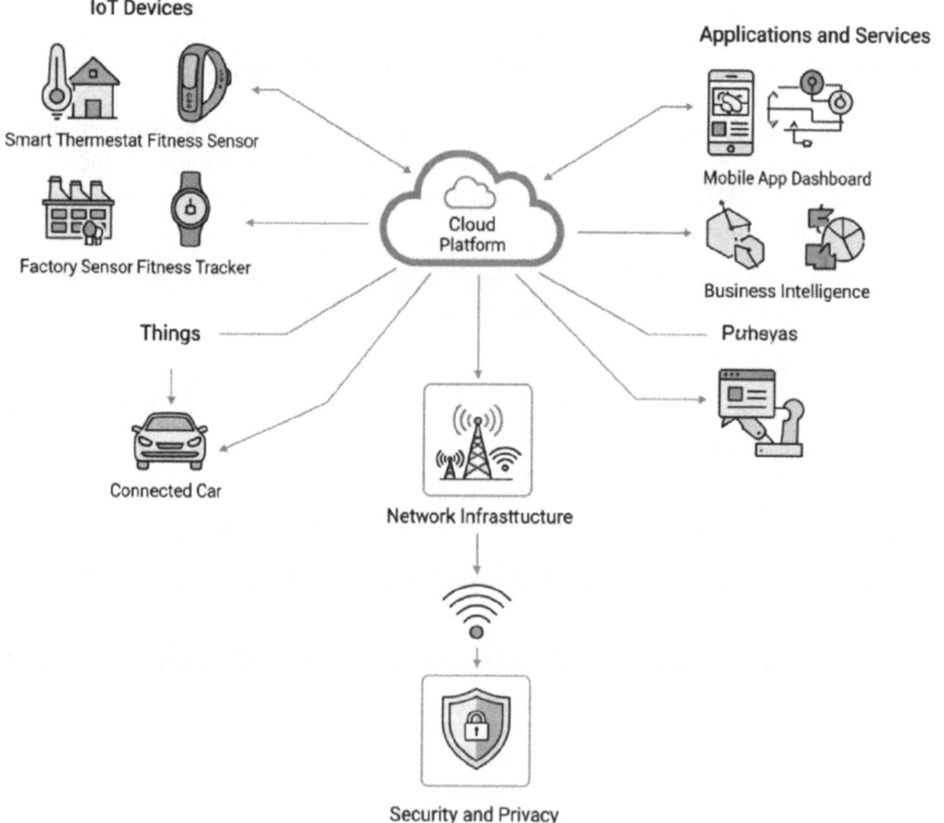

Figure 1.1: *Internet of Things (IoT) Ecosystem*

Figure 1.1 illustrates the concept of the Internet of Things (IoT), where multiple devices and smart objects are connected through a central cloud platform. Each device—such as smartphones, tablets, laptops, or sensors—communicates via networks to exchange data in real time. The cloud acts as the integration layer, enabling data storage, analysis, and intelligent decision-making. This interconnected ecosystem allows applications such as smart homes, healthcare monitoring, industrial automation, and smart cities to function efficiently, providing seamless interaction between the physical and digital worlds.

Core Components of an IoT System

Every IoT solution, no matter how small or large, is built using a set of fundamental building blocks. These components work together to capture data, process it, transmit it, and finally, turn it into meaningful actions. Without these components, the Internet of Things would remain just an idea, instead of a working ecosystem.

The five essential components of an IoT system are:

- Sensors and Actuators
- Controllers (Microcontrollers and Processors)
- Connectivity and Networks
- Cloud Platforms and Storage
- Applications and Services

Each of these plays a unique role in the IoT pipeline.

Smart Thermostat is a common example used to illustrate the components of an IoT system. It is a connected device that learns your heating and cooling preferences, adjusts the temperature automatically based on occupancy, time of day, or weather, and can be controlled remotely via a mobile application or web service. It acts as an excellent reference to understand the five essential components of an IoT system:

1. **Sensors and Actuators:** It uses temperature and humidity sensors to collect data (for example, the current room temperature). It uses an actuator (like a relay) to turn the HVAC (Heating, Ventilation, and Air Conditioning) system on or off.
2. **Controllers (Microcontrollers and Processors):** An embedded processor manages the sensors, runs the local control algorithms (like maintaining a set temperature), and handles communication protocols.
3. **Connectivity and Networks:** It connects to the home Wi-Fi network to send data to the cloud, and receive commands from the user's phone.
4. **Cloud Platforms and Storage:** The collected temperature data and user preferences are stored, analyzed, and processed on a remote server (the cloud).

Applications and Services: The mobile app or web interface allows the user to monitor the current temperature, change settings, view energy usage reports, and receive alerts.

Sensors

In every IoT system, sensors play the role of data collectors. They detect changes in the physical environment – such as heat, light, sound, motion, or chemical presence – and transform these changes into signals that can be measured and processed. Without sensors, the Internet of Things would lack awareness of its surroundings. A sensor essentially acts as the bridge between the physical and digital worlds. It converts raw environmental information into digital form so that microcontrollers, processors, and cloud platforms can analyse and respond.

A sensor is a device or material that responds to a specific physical property (such as temperature, pressure, or light) and produces an output signal. This output may be in the form of voltage, current, resistance, or digital pulses.

For example:

- A thermistor changes its resistance when the temperature changes.

- A microphone converts sound waves into electrical signals.
- A proximity sensor generates a signal when an object comes near.

Thus, sensors give IoT systems the ability to *feel* the environment in the same way our sense organs allow us to perceive the world.

Classification of Sensors

Sensors are at the heart of every IoT ecosystem. They detect real-world changes, and translate them into signals that can be processed by controllers and applications. Because sensors come in many forms and serve different purposes, it is important to classify them in an organized manner. Proper classification helps engineers and learners understand how sensors work, where to use them, and what their limitations are.

The following are the most common ways sensors are classified:

Classification Based on Power Requirement

Sensors differ in whether they need an external energy source to function.

- **Active Sensor:** Active sensors require an external power supply or excitation signal to operate. They send out a stimulus (like sound or electromagnetic waves) and measure the response from the environment.

  Example: An ultrasonic parking sensor (emits sound waves and measures the echo). *Application Example*: Used in automotive parking assist systems to measure distance to obstacles.

- **Passive Sensors:** Passive sensors do not need an external energy source. Instead, they detect naturally occurring signals such as light, heat, or radiation.

  Example: A thermistor or thermocouple (measures ambient temperature/heat). *Application Example*: Used in smart thermostats to monitor and regulate the room temperature.

The following are the most common ways sensors are classified:

Sensor Type	Best Suited For	Key Consideration
Active Sensor	Measuring properties where a natural stimulus is absent or too weak (e.g., radar, sonar, motion detection).	Requires a power source; generates its own signal.
Passive Sensor	Measuring naturally occurring phenomena (e.g., ambient temperature, visible light, infrared radiation).	Does not require external power; relies entirely on the environment.

Table 1.2: *Comparison of Sensors*

Classification Based on Detection Method

Sensors can also be grouped according to the type of property they detect.

- Electrical Sensors → Measure electrical variables like voltage, current, or resistance.
- Biological Sensors → Detect biological processes or molecules.
- Chemical Sensors → Measure concentration or presence of gases or liquids.
- Radiation Sensors → Detecting ionizing radiation such as alpha, beta, and gamma particles.

Classification Based on Conversion Phenomenon

Every sensor works by converting one form of energy or signal into another form of energy or signal, this is known as the transduction principle.

- Photoelectric Sensors → They will convert light into electrical signals.
- Thermoelectric Sensors → They will convert heat differences into voltage.
- Electrochemical Sensors → They will convert chemical reactions into signals.
- Electromagnetic Sensors → Detects magnetic fields, and convert them into electrical output.

Classification Based on Output Type

- **Analog Sensors:** Produce a continuous output signal proportional to the measured property. The signal varies smoothly, and requires an ADC (Analog-to-Digital Converter) to be understood by microcontrollers.
- **Digital Sensors:** Provide discrete output values in binary form (0s and 1s). They interface directly with digital controllers without needing extra conversion.

Common Sensors in IoT

Let us now look at some of the most widely used sensors across IoT applications.

- **Temperature Sensors** → Used in smart thermostats, industrial boilers, and cold chain logistics.
- **Motion and PIR Sensors** → Control lighting in smart homes, and detect intruders in security systems.
- **Proximity Sensors** → Used in cars for parking, in smartphones to turn off screens during calls, and in robotics for collision avoidance.
- **Soil Moisture Sensors** → Help farmers optimize irrigation, and improve crop yield.
- **Gas and Smoke Sensors** → Crucial in mining safety, pollution monitoring, and fire detection.
    - **Biometric Sensors** → Power fitness trackers (heart rate, SpO_2), and fingerprint authentication in smartphones.

Image and Camera Sensors → Enable face recognition, smart surveillance, and cashier-less retail stores.

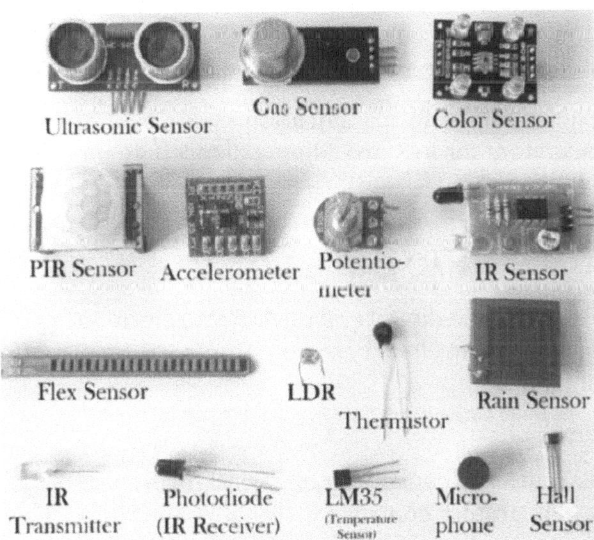

Figure 1.2: *Sensors*

The following diagram illustrates the critical role that sensors play in an IoT ecosystem. It shows how sensors detect changes in the physical environment—such as temperature, motion, or light—and convert these changes into signals that can be processed by controllers. These signals allow IoT systems to interact intelligently with the environment, enabling automated actions or decisions based on real-time data. For example, in a smart home, motion sensors can trigger lights or adjust climate control, while temperature sensors regulate heating and cooling. This seamless integration of sensors with IoT systems bridges the physical and digital worlds, providing IoT devices the ability to sense, analyze, and respond to their surroundings.

Applications of Sensors in IoT

Sensors are embedded in almost every industry such as:

- **Automotive Industry** → Engine monitoring, tire pressure sensors, and speed detection.
- **Smart Homes** → Motion detection, HVAC control, smart lighting.
- **Healthcare** → Vital sign monitoring (heart rate, oxygen, glucose, and so on).
- **Robotics** → Object detection, navigation, and force feedback.
- **Transportation** → GPS tracking, load sensors in logistics, and smart traffic systems.
- **Agriculture** → Soil and weather monitoring, automated irrigation systems.

Actuators

Actuators are the action-oriented components of Internet of Things (IoT) systems, serving as the "hands and legs" that translate digital instructions into physical outcomes. While sensors act as the "eyes and ears" by collecting environmental data, actuators close the perception-action loop by executing commands from controllers. These commands result in tangible effects such as motion, sound, heat, or fluid control, enabling IoT systems to interact with the physical world. Actuators are essential for transforming the intelligence of IoT systems into real-world responses, making them crucial for applications, ranging from smart homes to industrial automation.

For example:

- In a smart irrigation system, soil moisture sensors detect low moisture levels, and a controller sends a signal to an actuator-operated valve to release water, ensuring that crops are adequately watered.
- In a smart home, a motion sensor detects activity, prompting a controller to activate an actuator that switches on lights or locks a door automatically.

This expanded content explores the role, classification, types, applications, technical considerations, and emerging trends in actuators for IoT, providing a detailed guide to their significance in modern IoT ecosystems.

Role of Actuators in IoT

Actuators are the bridge between the digital and physical realms in IoT systems. Their primary role is to execute commands issued by controllers based on processed sensor data, enabling IoT systems to interact with their environment.

The key functions include:

- **Physical Action Execution** – converting electrical, hydraulic, or thermal signals into actions like movement or temperature control.
- **Automation Enablement** – enabling automated responses without human intervention.

- **Feedback Integration –** working with sensors for closed-loop precision.
- **Real-Time Responsiveness –** ensuring rapid reactions to changes.
- **System Integration –** working seamlessly with controllers and communication networks.

Thus, without actuators, IoT would be limited to data collection, unable to make real-world changes.

Classification of Actuators in IoT

Actuators can be classified by the source of energy, motion type, or control mechanism.

- **Based on Source of Energy**
  - **Electrical Actuators:** Use electricity. Examples: DC motors, stepper motors, relays, solenoids. Common in smart homes, drones, and automation.
  - **Hydraulic Actuators:** Use pressurized liquids. Examples: hydraulic cylinders. Suitable for heavy machinery, robotics, and automotive brakes.
  - **Thermal/Magnetic Actuators:** Use heat or magnetic fields. Examples: SMA actuators, solenoids. Found in wearables, medical devices, haptics, and so on.
- **Based on Motion Produced**
  - **Linear Actuators**: Create straight-line motion. Used in hospital beds, adjustable furniture, and conveyor systems.
  - **Rotary Actuators:** Create rotational motion. Examples: DC motors, servo motors. Used in drones, robotic joints, and HVAC vents.
- **Based on Control Mechanism**
  - **Open-Loop Actuators:** No feedback, simple, less accurate. Examples: DC motors, and relays. Used in fans, basic smart devices.
  - **Closed-Loop Actuators:** Use sensor feedback for precision. Examples: servo motors, stepper motors with encoders, and so on.

Types of Actuators in IoT

Actuators play a crucial role in the Internet of Things (IoT) by converting electrical signals into physical actions. These devices are necessary for making IoT systems interactive and responsive, enabling everything from motion to sound and temperature control. The following are the key types of actuators used in IoT:

- **Motors (DC, Stepper, Servo) –** convert electricity into motion, widely used in robotics, drones, and smart appliances.
- **Relays and Switches –** enable remote electrical control, common in smart plugs and lighting.
- **Valves –** regulate fluids or gases, used in irrigation, HVAC, and water treatment.
- **Speakers and Buzzers –** produce sound for alarms, notifications, or voice output.
- **Heating Elements –** generate heat, found in ovens, heaters, and coffee machines.
- **Electromagnets –** magnetic force for locking or gripping, common in smart locks and sorting systems.

Applications of Actuators in IoT

Actuators are the driving force behind many of the most innovative and practical IoT applications. They transform digital commands into physical actions, enabling systems to operate autonomously and intelligently across various industries. The following are some key areas where actuators are making a significant impact:

- **Smart Homes:** Automated blinds, locks, and HVAC vents.
- **Healthcare:** Infusion pumps, prosthetics, and robotic surgery.
- **Industrial Automation:** Robotic arms, conveyor belts, CNC machines.
- **Transportation:** Electric propulsion, adaptive headlights, braking systems.
- **Agriculture:** Irrigation valves, greenhouse vents, and automated harvesters.

Key Considerations for Selecting Actuators

Choosing the right actuator for an IoT application involves careful evaluation of several factors to ensure optimal performance, efficiency, and cost-effectiveness. Each use case demands specific actuator characteristics, from power needs to environmental durability. The following considerations are crucial when selecting actuators for IoT systems:

- **Power requirements** – balance between low-power wearables and high-power industrial actuators.
- **Precision** – open-loop for basic tasks, closed-loop for precision robotics.
- **Size and weight** – micro-actuators for wearables, hydraulic for heavy machinery.
- **Response time** – electromagnets for fast responses, and thermal actuators for slower needs.
- **Environmental durability** – rugged actuators for outdoor/agricultural use.
- **Cost** – low-cost for scalable smart homes, high-cost for critical healthcare/robotics.

Emerging Trends and Challenges

The field of actuators in IoT is rapidly evolving, driven by technological advancements, and growing demand for smarter, more efficient solutions. As new trends shape the future of IoT, challenges arise that require innovative solutions. The following highlights the key trends emerging in actuator technology, as well as the challenges that must be addressed to ensure sustainable growth and adoption.

- **Miniaturization** – MEMS and SMAs for wearables and micro-robotics.
- **Energy Efficiency** – low-power actuators with energy harvesting.
- **Smart and Adaptive Actuators** – AI-driven, self-calibrating designs.
- **Security** – preventing cyberattacks on smart locks or industrial systems.
- **Interoperability** – adoption of standards like Matter and OPC UA.
- **Challenges** – managing power, ensuring reliability, and addressing cost barriers.

Actuators are indispensable for IoT, turning data into real-world action. From motors and relays to valves and electromagnets, they power smart homes, healthcare, factories, vehicles, and farms. As IoT advances, actuators are becoming smaller, smarter, and more energy-efficient. However, challenges remain in power management, security, reliability, and cost. Choosing the right actuator ensures robust, scalable, and effective IoT systems that truly bridge the digital and physical worlds.

If sensors are the eyes and ears of IoT, then actuators are the hands and legs. While sensors collect data from the environment, actuators perform physical actions based on processed information. They take commands from controllers, and transform them into motion, sound, heat, or other real-world effects.

For example:

- A smart irrigation system uses soil moisture sensors to detect dryness, and then an actuator-operated valve to release water.
- In a smart home, motion detected by sensors may trigger actuators to switch on lights or lock doors automatically.

Thus, actuators close the perception-action loop of IoT, turning digital intelligence into real-world responses.

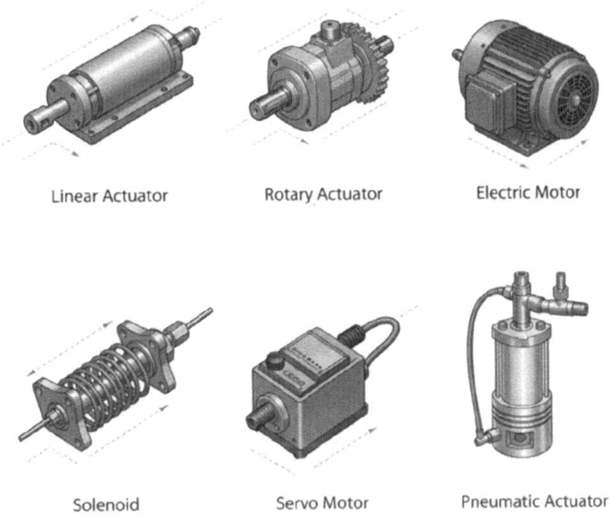

***Figure 1.3**: Actuators*

This diagram illustrates the critical role of actuators in an IoT system. It shows how data from various sensors is processed by controllers and then translated into physical actions by actuators. For instance, in a smart home, the sensors detect motion or changes in temperature, and the controller processes this information to trigger actuators like lights, thermostats, or door locks. The diagram highlights the seamless flow of information from sensors to actuators, demonstrating how IoT systems bridge the gap between the digital and physical worlds. This interaction ensures automation, responsiveness, and efficiency in applications ranging from smart homes to industrial automation.

Controllers

While sensors are responsible for collecting data from the environment, controllers form the brain of an IoT system. Controllers receive input from sensors, process this information, make decisions based on predefined logic or algorithms, and then send commands to actuators or other devices. Essentially, a controller converts raw data into actionable intelligence, bridging the gap between sensing and actuation.

A controller is an embedded device or microprocessor that manages the operations of an IoT system. It interprets sensor data, applies decision-making logic, and orchestrates the response of actuators, communication modules, and connected devices. Controllers can range from simple microcontrollers for basic tasks to complex processors capable of running AI models locally.

Example Controllers:

- **Arduino** → Popular microcontroller used in prototyping and small IoT projects.
- **Raspberry Pi** → Single-board computer capable of running full operating systems and complex processing.
- **ESP32/ESP8266** → Low-cost Wi-Fi-enabled microcontrollers ideal for smart home devices.
- **Industrial PLCs (Programmable Logic Controllers)** → Used in manufacturing automation for controlling machinery.

Characteristics of Controllers

Controllers form the backbone of IoT systems by acting as the central unit for processing, decision-making, and communication. They handle everything from data collection and filtering to real-time decision-making, and ensuring secure, efficient communication. The following characteristics highlight the necessary functions of controllers in an IoT ecosystem:

- **Data Acquisition:** Controllers are tasked with collecting, aggregating, and preprocessing data from a variety of sensors within an IoT system. These sensors may monitor environmental parameters (for example: temperature, humidity, light), physical states (for example: motion, pressure), or operational metrics (for example: voltage, current).
- **Sensor Interfacing:** Controllers interface with sensors using protocols like I2C, SPI, or Analog-to-Digital Converters (ADCs). For instance, a temperature sensor like the DS18B20 uses a 1-Wire protocol to communicate with a microcontroller such as an ESP32.
- **Data Filtering and Preprocessing:** Raw sensor data is often noisy or redundant. Controllers apply filters (for example: Kalman filters or moving averages) to remove noise and ensure only relevant data is processed. This advanced filtering can be implemented either directly on the controller or on an upstream edge gateway, depending on system constraints such as processing power and latency requirements. For example, in a smart agriculture system, a controller might filter soil moisture readings to eliminate outliers caused by transient environmental changes.
- **Data Aggregation:** In systems with multiple sensors, controllers aggregate data to reduce redundancy, and optimize bandwidth usage. For instance, in a smart building, a controller might combine temperature, occupancy, and air quality data into a single packet for transmission.
- **Real-Time Processing:** Some controllers perform real-time data processing to ensure low-latency responses, which is critical in applications like autonomous vehicles or industrial automation.

  Example Application: In a smart home, a controller such as the Texas Instruments CC2650 gathers data from motion sensors, door/window sensors, and temperature sensors, filters the data to eliminate false positives, and prepares it for further processing or transmission.
- **Decision-Making:** Controllers make intelligent decisions based on the data they collect, using predefined algorithms, rule-based thresholds, or advanced machine learning models. This function is critical for enabling autonomous or semi-autonomous operations in IoT systems.
- **Rule-Based Decision-Making:** Simple controllers use predefined thresholds or logic to make decisions. For example, in a smart thermostat, the controller compares the room temperature (for example: 22°C) with a user-defined setpoint (for example: 20°C) and activates the heater if the temperature falls below the setpoint.
- **Algorithm-Driven Decisions:** More advanced controllers use algorithms to process complex data streams. For instance, in a traffic management system, a controller might analyze vehicle

density data from cameras and sensors to optimize traffic light timings using algorithms like fuzzy logic or reinforcement learning.

- **AI and Machine Learning Integration:** Advanced controllers, such as those based on NVIDIA Jetson Nano or Google Coral, can run lightweight machine learning models for predictive analytics or anomaly detection. For example, in predictive maintenance, a controller might analyze vibration data from industrial machinery to predict potential failures before they occur.
- **Data Transmission:** Controllers package data into formats suitable for transmission, such as JSON or binary payloads, and ensure reliable delivery using error-checking mechanisms like CRC or retransmission.
- **Security:** Controllers implement encryption (for example: TLS/SSL) and authentication mechanisms to secure data during transmission. For example, in a smart lock system, the controller encrypts communication with a mobile app to prevent unauthorized access.
- **Interoperability:** Controllers often bridge different protocols or ecosystems, enabling heterogeneous devices to communicate. For instance, a controller might translate Zigbee messages from a smart light to MQTT for cloud integration.

  Example Application: In a smart city, a controller like the ESP32 transmits air quality data from sensors to a cloud platform via MQTT, enabling real-time monitoring and visualization on a city dashboard.

Classification of Controllers in IoT

Controllers in IoT systems can be classified based on their processing capabilities, functionality, or connectivity. This classification helps in selecting the right controller for specific IoT applications, balancing factors such as cost, performance, and scalability.

Based on Processing Power

The processing power of a controller determines its ability to handle tasks ranging from simple sensor reading to complex data analytics.

- **Simple Controllers**
  - **Characteristics**:
    - Limited processing power (for example: 8-bit or 16-bit microcontrollers).
    - Low memory and storage (for example: a few KB of RAM and flash).
    - Designed for basic tasks such as reading sensor data, performing simple logic, and controlling actuators.
    - Low power consumption, making them ideal for battery-operated devices.
  - **Examples**:
    - **Arduino Uno**: Based on the ATmega328P microcontroller, with 32 KB of flash memory and 2 KB of SRAM. Suitable for simple IoT projects like temperature monitoring or basic home automation.
    - **ESP8266**: A Wi-Fi-enabled microcontroller with 80–160 MHz processing speed, commonly used in low-cost IoT devices like smart plugs.
  - **Use Cases**:
    - Smart lighting systems, where the controller reads ambient light levels and toggles LEDs.

        - Wearable devices, such as fitness trackers, that monitor basic metrics like steps or heart rate.
    - **Limitations**:
        - Cannot handle complex algorithms or large datasets.
        - Limited multitasking capabilities.
    - **Example Application**: In a smart irrigation system, an Arduino Uno reads soil moisture sensor data and activates a water pump when moisture levels drop below a threshold.
- **Advanced Controllers**
    - **Characteristics**:
        - High processing power (for example: 32-bit or 64-bit processors, often with clock speeds above 1 GHz).
        - Larger memory and storage (for example: several MB of RAM and GB of flash).
        - Capable of running complex algorithms, machine learning models, or Real-Time Operating Systems (RTOS) like FreeRTOS or Linux.
        - Support for multi-sensor fusion and advanced analytics.
    - **Examples**:
        - **Raspberry Pi 4**: A single-board computer with a quad-core 1.5 GHz processor, 2–8 GB of RAM, and support for running Linux-based IoT platforms like Node-RED.
        - **NVIDIA Jetson Nano**: A powerful controller with a quad-core ARM Cortex-A57 CPU and GPU, designed for AI-driven IoT applications.
    - **Use Cases**:
        - Smart surveillance systems that process video feeds for facial recognition or motion detection.
        - Industrial IoT applications requiring predictive maintenance or real-time analytics.
    - **Advantages**:
        - High computational capacity for edge computing.
        - Support for advanced communication protocols and operating systems.
    - **Limitations**:
        - Higher power consumption compared to simple controllers.
        - Increased cost and complexity.
    - **Example Application**: In a smart retail system, a Raspberry Pi 4 analyzes customer footfall data from cameras, predicts peak hours, and adjusts lighting and HVAC systems to optimize energy usage.

Based on Functionality

Controllers in IoT systems can be categorized based on their functionality, depending on whether they are designed for specific tasks or for broader applications. These classifications help in understanding the unique capabilities and limitations of different controllers, allowing engineers to choose the most suitable one for a given use case. In the following paragraph, we explore two key categories of controllers:

- **Dedicated Controllers**
  - **Characteristics**:
    - Designed for a specific application or task, with optimized hardware and firmware.
    - Often non-programmable or limited in flexibility to ensure reliability and efficiency.
    - Compact and cost-effective for their specific use case.
  - **Examples**:
    - Thermostat Controllers: Devices like the Honeywell T6 Pro are dedicated to controlling HVAC systems, with pre-programmed logic for temperature regulation.
    - Smart Meter

Applications of Controllers in IoT

Controllers enable intelligent automation across industries:

- **Smart Homes:** Automate lighting, HVAC, and security systems based on occupancy, environmental conditions, and user preferences.
- **Industrial Automation:** PLCs and embedded controllers monitor production lines, detect faults, and optimize manufacturing processes.
- **Healthcare:** Controllers in wearable devices track heart rate, detect anomalies, and alert medical personnel, if needed.
- **Agriculture:** Irrigation controllers process soil moisture and weather data to optimize watering schedules, conserving water, and improving crop yields.
- **Transportation:** Controllers in smart traffic systems regulate traffic lights, monitor congestion, and coordinate vehicle-to-infrastructure communication.

Connectivity

Connectivity is the lifeblood of the Internet of Things (IoT), enabling seamless communication between devices, sensors, controllers, actuators, and cloud platforms. It serves as the nervous system of an IoT ecosystem, ensuring that data flows efficiently, commands are delivered accurately, and real-time interactions are possible. Without robust and reliable connectivity, IoT devices would be isolated, rendering even the most advanced systems ineffective. Connectivity facilitates the exchange of sensor data, enables real-time decision-making, and supports remote monitoring and control, making it a critical component of any IoT deployment.

Connectivity Type	Typical Range	Power Consumption	Latency	Relative Cost
Wired (Ethernet)	Up to 100m (standard)	High	Very Low	Moderate to High (installation)
Wired (CAN Bus)	Up to 1000m (low data rate)	Moderate	Low	Moderate
Wireless (Wi-Fi)	Medium (up to 50-100m)	High	Low	Low to Moderate
Wireless (Bluetooth)	Short (up to 10-100m)	Very Low	Low	Low
Wireless (LoRa)	Long (Kilometers)	Very Low	High	Low to Moderate (device), Moderate (infrastructure)
Wireless (Cellular: 4G/5G)	Very Long (Kilometers)	Moderate	Low	High (service plan)

Table 1.3: *Different Types of Connectivity*

IoT connectivity can be wired (such as Ethernet, CAN bus) or wireless (such as Wi-Fi, Bluetooth, LoRa, cellular), with the choice depending on factors such as range, data rate, power consumption, latency, reliability, and security requirements. Each IoT application demands a tailored connectivity solution to balance performance and efficiency, from short-range protocols for personal devices to long-range networks for industrial or smart city applications.

Note: *These are general comparisons. Actual values depend heavily on specific implementations, hardware, and environment.*

Thus, this section explores the purpose, types, protocols, considerations, applications, and emerging trends in IoT connectivity, providing a detailed guide to understanding its role in modern IoT ecosystems.

Purpose of Connectivity in IoT

Connectivity in IoT serves multiple critical functions, enabling the ecosystem to operate as a cohesive unit:

- **Data Transmission:** Connectivity allows sensors to send the raw or processed data to controllers, gateways, or cloud platforms for analysis. For example, in a smart agriculture system, soil moisture sensors transmit data to a cloud dashboard for irrigation planning.
- **Command Delivery:** Controllers use connectivity to send instructions to actuators, such as turning on a motor or opening a valve. In a smart home, a Wi-Fi-enabled controller sends commands to smart lights to adjust brightness.
- **Real-Time Coordination:** Connectivity enables real-time interactions between devices, ensuring timely responses to events. For instance, in an autonomous vehicle, sensors and controllers communicate via CAN bus to adjust speed or avoid obstacles instantly.
- **Remote Monitoring and Control:** Connectivity allows users to monitor and manage IoT systems remotely via mobile apps or web interfaces. In healthcare, wearables send patient data to doctors for remote diagnostics.
- **Interoperability:** Connectivity bridges heterogeneous devices and protocols, enabling seamless integration across ecosystems. For example, a smart home hub may use Zigbee to communicate with lights and Wi-Fi to connect to a cloud server.

Thus, without reliable connectivity, these functions would fail, leading to delays, data loss, or system inefficiencies. Connectivity ensures that IoT systems are responsive, scalable, and capable of delivering actionable insights.

Types of Connectivity in IoT

IoT connectivity can be broadly classified into wired and wireless modes, each with distinct advantages, limitations, and use cases. The choice of the type of connectivity depends on the application's requirements, such as range, power constraints, and environmental factors.

Wired Connectivity

Wired connectivity uses physical connections to transmit data, offering high reliability and low latency but limited flexibility.

- **Characteristics:**
  - High data rates and stability, ideal for environments requiring consistent performance.
  - Immune to wireless interference, and typically more secure than wireless options.
  - Requires physical infrastructure, limiting mobility and increasing installation costs.

- **Examples:**
    - **Ethernet:** Provides high-speed, reliable connectivity for fixed IoT devices like smart building controllers or industrial PLCs. For example, a Siemens SIMATIC controller in a factory uses Ethernet to connect to a SCADA system.
    - **CAN Bus:** A robust protocol for real-time communication in automotive and industrial applications, such as in-vehicle networks or robotic systems.
    - **RS-485/Modbus:** Used in industrial automation for connecting sensors and actuators over long distances with minimal wiring.
    - **Serial Interfaces (UART, SPI, I2C):** Common in microcontroller-based systems for short-range communication between sensors and controllers.
- **Use Cases:**
    - Industrial IoT (IIoT) systems, such as manufacturing lines, where Ethernet or CAN bus ensures reliable data exchange.
    - Smart buildings, where wired connections link HVAC systems, lighting, and security cameras.
- **Advantages:**
    - High reliability and low latency, critical for mission-critical applications.
    - Less susceptible to interference or hacking compared to wireless.
- **Limitations:**
    - Limited scalability and mobility due to physical cabling.
    - Higher installation and maintenance costs in large or remote deployments.

  Example Application: In a smart factory, Ethernet connects a network of sensors, controllers, and actuators to monitor production metrics and coordinate machinery, ensuring high-speed and reliable communication.

Key Considerations for Choosing IoT Connectivity

Selecting the appropriate connectivity solution requires evaluation of the following factors:

- **Range**: Short-range (Bluetooth, Zigbee) for localized use; long-range (LoRa, NB-IoT) for distributed systems.

  Example: Smart parking uses LoRaWAN, while a thermostat uses Wi-Fi.
- **Data Rate**: High-bandwidth (Wi-Fi, 5G) for video; low-bandwidth (LoRa, Sigfox) for sensor readings.

  Example: Security cameras use Wi-Fi; soil sensors use LoRa.
- **Energy Efficiency**: Battery devices need low-power (BLE, Zigbee, LoRa); mains-powered devices can use Wi-Fi or Ethernet.

  Example: Remote environmental sensors use LoRaWAN to last for years.
- **Latency**: Real-time (5G, CAN bus) for critical systems; tolerant (Sigfox, NB-IoT) for periodic data.

  Example: Self-driving cars use 5G; smart meters use NB-IoT.
- **Reliability**: Wired (Ethernet) for stable environments; wireless (LoRa, NB-IoT) for challenging terrains.

  Example: Factories use Ethernet; farms use LoRaWAN.

Evolution of IoT: From Embedded Systems to Smart Devices to Edge AI

The Internet of Things (IoT) has transformed how devices interact with the physical world, enabling a connected ecosystem that drives automation, efficiency, and intelligence across industries. Far from being an overnight innovation, IoT is the culmination of decades of advancements in computing, electronics, networking, and artificial intelligence. Understanding its evolution—from early embedded systems to connected smart devices and now intelligent edge AI systems—provides critical insight into its current capabilities and future potential. This section traces the historical and technical progression of IoT, highlighting key milestones, examples, and the transformative impact of each phase.

Embedded Systems: The Foundation (1970s–1990s)

Embedded systems laid the groundwork for IoT by introducing the concept of specialized computing for dedicated tasks. These systems are purpose-built computers integrated into larger devices, designed to perform specific functions with high reliability and minimal resources.

Characteristics of Embedded Systems

Before diving into the world of IoT, it is important to understand the foundation it builds upon—embedded systems. These systems are the unsung heroes inside everyday devices, quietly ensuring they work as intended. Their defining traits set them apart from general-purpose computers, and highlight why they are so crucial in specialized applications.

- **Tightly Integrated Hardware and Software:** Embedded systems combine dedicated hardware (for example: microcontrollers) with tailored firmware to execute specific tasks efficiently.
- **Resource-Constrained:** They typically operate with limited memory (for example: a few KB of RAM), simple 8-bit or 16-bit processors, and low power consumption.
- **Real-Time Operation**: Many embedded systems are designed for real-time performance, ensuring immediate responses in critical applications such as automotive control or industrial automation.
- **Standalone Functionality**: Unlike modern IoT devices, early embedded systems lacked network connectivity, operating in isolation.

Role in IoT Evolution

Embedded systems introduced the idea of automated, machine-driven control without human intervention. By embedding intelligence into everyday devices, they set the stage for IoT's core principle such as: enabling machines to sense, process, and act on environmental data. For example, early embedded systems in appliances like washing machines used timers and sensors to automate wash cycles, while automotive Engine Control Units (ECUs) optimized fuel injection based on sensor inputs.

Examples

- **Microwave Controllers:** Used microcontrollers such as the Intel 8051 to manage cooking time and power levels.
- **Programmable Logic Controllers (PLCs):** Devices like the Modicon 084 (introduced in 1969) automated factory processes, replacing mechanical relays with digital control.
- **Car Engine Control Units:** Managed ignition timing and fuel efficiency in vehicles, improving performance and emissions.

Limitations

- Lack of network connectivity restricted data sharing and remote control.
- Limited processing power constrained complex computations or multitasking.
- Fixed functionality made upgrades or reprogramming challenging.

Case Example

In the 1980s, PLCs like the Allen-Bradley PLC-5 revolutionized industrial automation by controlling machinery with programmable logic. These systems used embedded microprocessors to monitor sensors and control actuators, laying the foundation for IoT's automation capabilities but without the ability to connect to external networks.

Smart Devices: Adding Connectivity (2000s–2010s)

The transition to smart devices marked the true birth of IoT, as embedded systems gained the ability to communicate over networks. This era saw devices evolve from standalone units to connected systems capable of exchanging data with other devices, cloud platforms, and users, enabling remote monitoring, control, and data-driven insights.

Key Drivers

The rapid growth of IoT didn't happen in isolation—it was fueled by a convergence of technological breakthroughs. From shrinking hardware to the rise of global networks, several forces came together to make connected devices practical, affordable, and scalable. These drivers collectively laid the groundwork for today's IoT ecosystem.

- **Miniaturization of Communication Modules:** Advances in Wi-Fi (for example: IEEE 802.11 standards) and Bluetooth modules made it feasible to integrate connectivity into compact devices.
- **Mobile Network Growth:** The rollout of 3G and 4G networks provided high-speed, reliable connectivity for mobile and remote IoT applications.
- **Low-Cost Microcontrollers:** Affordable platforms like the Arduino (introduced in 2005) and ESP8266 (2014) democratized IoT development, offering integrated Wi-Fi and GPIO for sensor/actuator control.
- **Cloud Computing:** The rise of cloud platforms like AWS and Azure enabled scalable data storage and processing, supporting the influx of data from connected devices.

Characteristics of Smart Devices

While embedded systems laid the foundation, smart devices take things a step further by adding intelligence and connectivity. These devices are not just task-oriented—they actively communicate, share data, and interact with users. Their defining characteristics highlight how they bridge the physical and digital worlds, making them central to modern IoT applications.

- **Network Connectivity:** Smart devices use protocols such as Wi-Fi, Bluetooth, Zigbee, or cellular networks to communicate locally or with cloud servers.
- **Data Exchange:** They collect the sensor data, transmit it for analysis, and receive commands for actuation.
- **User Interaction:** Many smart devices offer user interfaces via mobile apps or web dashboards for remote control and monitoring.

- **Scalability**: Connectivity enabled ecosystems where multiple devices could interoperate, forming the backbone of smart homes and cities.

Examples of Smart Devices

The impact of smart devices is best understood through real-world examples that demonstrate their capabilities. From managing energy at home to monitoring personal health, these devices showcase how connectivity and intelligence transform ordinary products into powerful tools.

- **Smart Thermostats**: Devices such as the Nest Thermostat (launched in 2011) learn user preferences, connect to Wi-Fi for remote control, and integrate with cloud services for energy analytics.
- **Fitness Bands**: Wearables like Fitbit track activity and sync data to smartphones via Bluetooth for health monitoring.
- **Smart TVs**: Devices such as Samsung Smart TVs connect to the internet for streaming and app-based services.
- **Connected Cars**: Vehicles with GPS and cellular connectivity enable real-time navigation and diagnostics.

Edge AI and IoT: Intelligence at the Edge (2015–Present)

The proliferation of smart devices led to an explosion of data, overwhelming cloud infrastructure and raising concerns about latency, bandwidth, and privacy. This challenge spurred the development of edge computing and edge AI, where data processing and artificial intelligence occur closer to the data source—on devices or local gateways—rather than relying solely on the cloud. This phase represents IoT's shift from connected to intelligent systems.

- **Edge Computing**: Edge computing involves processing data locally on IoT devices or nearby gateways, reducing the need to send all data to the cloud. This approach minimizes latency, optimizes bandwidth, and enhances system reliability by enabling operation during network disruptions.
- **Edge AI:** Edge AI refers to the deployment of artificial intelligence algorithms (for example: machine learning models) on IoT devices or edge nodes. Specialized hardware such as GPUs, TPUs, or AI accelerators (for example: Google Coral, NVIDIA Jetson Nano) enables lightweight AI frameworks (for example: TensorFlow Lite) to run locally. Edge AI refers to the deployment of artificial intelligence algorithms (for example: machine learning models) on IoT devices or edge nodes. Specialized hardware such as GPUs, TPUs, or AI accelerators (for example: Google Coral, NVIDIA Jetson Nano) enables lightweight AI frameworks (for example: TensorFlow Lite) to run locally.

Feature	Edge AI	Cloud AI
Processing Location	Locally on device/edge node	Remote data centers (Cloud)
Latency	Low (Near real-time)	Higher (Dependent on network)
Bandwidth Needs	Low (Only necessary data uploaded)	High (Raw data often uploaded)
Cost	Upfront hardware cost	Ongoing subscription/usage fees
Privacy/Security	Data stays local (Higher privacy)	Data is transferred to the cloud
Computational Power	Limited by device hardware	Virtually unlimited

Table 1.4: *Comparison of Edge AI and Cloud AI*

- **Key Drivers:** The rise of intelligent IoT was not driven by connectivity alone—it required a new wave of innovation in processing, software, and networks. Recent advances in hardware, edge AI frameworks, and communication standards have accelerated the shift from simple connected devices to truly smart, autonomous systems. At the same time, stricter privacy regulations have guided how and where data is processed, shaping the way modern IoT solutions are designed.
    - **Advancements in Hardware:** Powerful yet compact processors such as ARM Cortex-A series and AI accelerators enabled on-device computation.
    - **AI Frameworks:** Lightweight frameworks such as TensorFlow Lite and ONNX Runtime made AI accessible for resource-constrained devices.
    - **5G Networks:** Ultra-low-latency and high-bandwidth 5G networks supported real-time edge-to-cloud communication.
    - **Privacy Regulations:** Laws like GDPR and CCPA emphasized local data processing to protect user privacy.

Benefits of Edge AI and IoT

As IoT devices became smarter, the need to process data closer to where it is generated gave rise to Edge AI. By combining local intelligence with connectivity, this approach unlocks several advantages that traditional cloud-only models cannot match. Hence, from faster decision-making to stronger privacy safeguards, Edge AI enhances both performance and reliability in modern IoT ecosystems.

- **Reduced Latency:** Local processing enables near-instantaneous responses, critical for applications like autonomous vehicles or real-time monitoring.
- **Bandwidth Efficiency:** Only critical or aggregated data is sent to the cloud, reducing network congestion and costs.
- **Enhanced Privacy:** Sensitive data (for example: medical or video feeds) can be processed locally, minimizing exposure to external networks.
- **Offline Capability:** Edge devices can operate independently during network outages, ensuring reliability.
- **Scalability:** Hybrid edge-cloud architectures distribute processing, enabling large-scale IoT deployments.

Examples

The power of Edge AI and IoT becomes most evident when looking at real-world applications. Across industries—transportation, healthcare, manufacturing, and consumer electronics—devices are leveraging local intelligence to deliver faster, smarter, and more reliable outcomes. These examples illustrate how theory translates into impactful solutions.

- **Autonomous Vehicles:** Tesla vehicles use on-board AI to process sensor data (for example: cameras, LIDAR) for real-time navigation, sending only diagnostic logs to the cloud.
- **Smart Cameras:** Devices such as the Google Nest Cam use edge AI to detect faces or objects locally, reducing cloud dependency, and enhancing privacy.
- **Industrial IoT**: Edge gateways like the Siemens SIMATIC IoT2050 perform predictive maintenance by analyzing sensor data on-site, minimizing downtime.
- **Healthcare Wearables**: Devices such as smart insulin pumps use edge AI to adjust dosages based on real-time glucose readings.

Emerging Trends and Challenges

As IoT continues to evolve, several trends and challenges are shaping its future such as:

Trends

The IoT landscape is evolving rapidly, driven by innovations in AI, connectivity, and energy solutions. While these advancements open exciting opportunities, they also introduce new challenges around interoperability, scalability, and privacy. Understanding both the trends and hurdles is essential for designing robust, future-ready IoT systems.

- **AI-Driven Autonomy:** Edge AI is enabling devices to make autonomous decisions, such as predictive maintenance in industrial IoT or adaptive navigation in drones.
- **5G Integration**: 5G's ultra-low latency and high bandwidth are enhancing edge-to-cloud communication, critical for applications like smart cities and autonomous vehicles.
- **Energy Harvesting**: Technologies such as solar or kinetic energy harvesting are powering edge devices, reducing reliance on batteries (for example: EnOcean's energy-harvesting sensors).
- **Interoperability Standards**: Protocols like Matter and OPC UA are ensuring seamless integration across diverse IoT ecosystems.
- **Federated Learning**: Distributed AI training across edge devices (for example: Google's federated learning) improves models, while maintaining privacy.

Challenges

While emerging trends are pushing IoT to new heights, they also bring significant challenges that cannot be ignored. Thus, from ensuring robust security to managing large-scale deployments, and maintaining energy efficiency, these issues must be addressed to fully realize the potential of connected, intelligent devices.

- **Security:** Edge devices are vulnerable to cyberattacks, requiring robust encryption, and secure boot mechanisms.
- **Scalability:** Managing thousands of edge devices for OTA updates or AI model deployment is complex and resource-intensive.
- **Interoperability:** Integrating devices from different manufacturers remains challenging despite emerging standards.
- **Power Efficiency:** Balancing computational power with energy constraints in edge AI devices is critical for battery-powered applications.

Thus, the evolution of IoT from embedded systems to smart devices to edge AI reflects a journey from reactive, isolated automation to proactive, intelligent, and connected systems. Embedded systems laid the foundation with task-specific control, smart devices introduced connectivity and cloud integration, and edge AI has brought intelligence to the edge, enabling faster, more private, and scalable IoT solutions. Moreover, as technologies like 5G, AI accelerators, and energy harvesting advance, IoT will continue to transform industries and daily life, creating smarter, more autonomous systems.

IoT Architecture Overview: Device Layer, Network Layer, Application Layer

The Internet of Things (IoT) is a sophisticated ecosystem of interconnected devices, networks, and applications that work together to collect, transmit, and process data, enabling automation, monitoring, and intelligent decision-making. Rather than a haphazard collection of devices, IoT systems are built on a structured, layered architecture that ensures modularity, scalability, and manageability. This architecture is commonly divided into three core layers: The Device Layer (also known as the Perception Layer), the Network Layer (Transmission Layer), and the Application Layer. Each layer plays a distinct role in transforming raw environmental data into actionable insights, forming a cohesive pipeline from physical interaction to user-facing services. This section provides a detailed exploration of each layer, including their components, functions, examples, challenges, and real-world applications, along with a practical exercise to reinforce understanding.

Device Layer (Perception Layer)

The Device Layer, often referred to as the Perception Layer, is the physical foundation of an IoT system. It encompasses the hardware components that interact directly with the physical world, enabling IoT systems to "perceive" their environment through data collection and execute actions through physical outputs. This layer includes sensors, actuators, and controllers, which work together to gather data, process it locally, and perform tasks such as turning on a motor or opening a valve.

Characteristics

Edge devices form the backbone of modern IoT systems, bringing computation and sensing closer to where data is generated. Their defining characteristics—from energy efficiency to real-time operation—highlight how these devices balance performance, cost, and versatility to support diverse applications in dynamic environments.

- **Edge Operation:** Operates at the network's edge, closest to the physical environment, enabling real-time interaction.
- **Data Generation:** Sensors collect raw data (for example: temperature, motion, light) from the environment, while actuators translate commands into physical actions (for example: motion, sound, and so on.).
- **Energy Efficiency:** Devices are often designed for low power consumption to support battery-operated or remote deployments.
- **Cost-Effectiveness:** Components like microcontrollers and sensors are optimized for affordability to enable large-scale IoT deployments.
- **Heterogeneity:** Includes a wide variety of devices, from simple temperature sensors to complex robotic actuators.

Components

Edge devices rely on a combination of sensors, actuators, and controllers to sense, process, and interact with their environment. Understanding these components is essential, as they form the building blocks that enable IoT systems to function effectively and respond intelligently to real-world conditions.

- **Sensors:** Devices that measure environmental parameters, such as temperature (for example: DS18B20), humidity (for example: DHT22), motion (for example:, PIR sensors), or biometric data (for example: heart rate sensors).

- **Actuators:** Devices that perform physical actions such as motors (for example: servo, stepper), relays, valves, or buzzers.
- **Controllers:** Microcontrollers (for example: Arduino, ESP32) or single-board computers (for example: Raspberry Pi) that process sensor data and control actuators locally.

Functions

- **Data Acquisition:** Sensors collect environmental data such as soil moisture in agriculture or air quality in smart cities.
- **Local Processing:** Controllers pre-process data (for example: filtering noise) to reduce bandwidth usage, and improve response times.
- **Actuation**: Actuators execute commands such as opening a valve or adjusting a robotic arm's position.
- **Device Management:** Controllers handle device configuration, power management, and basic error handling.

Network Layer (Transmission Layer)

The Network Layer, also known as the Transmission Layer, serves as the nervous system of IoT, enabling seamless communication between the Device Layer and the Application Layer. It is responsible for transmitting sensor data to cloud platforms, gateways, or other devices and delivering commands to actuators. Without robust connectivity, IoT devices would remain isolated, unable to share data or coordinate actions.

Functions

Beyond their physical components, edge devices perform a variety of critical functions that ensure seamless operation within IoT ecosystems. From secure data transmission to protocol management and error handling, these functions enable devices to communicate reliably, maintain interoperability, and operate securely in diverse environments.

- **Data Transmission:** Securely and reliably transfers sensor data to cloud servers, gateways, or local networks.
- **Protocol Selection:** Chooses appropriate communication technologies based on range, bandwidth, power, and application needs.
- **Interoperability:** Bridges heterogeneous devices and protocols, ensuring seamless communication across ecosystems.
- **Security:** Implements encryption (for example: TLS/SSL) and authentication to protect data during transmission.
- **Error Handling:** Uses mechanisms like CRC or retransmission to ensure data integrity.

Connectivity Options

The Network Layer supports a variety of wired and wireless technologies, each suited to specific IoT applications:

Short-Range Technologies

- Bluetooth Low Energy (BLE):
- Wi-Fi:

- Zigbee/Z-Wave:
- Thread:

Long-Range Technologies

- LoRaWAN:
- Sigfox:
- Cellular (3G, 4G, 5G, NB-IoT, LTE-M):

Wired Options

- Ethernet:
- CAN Bus/Modbus:

Challenges

While edge devices and IoT systems offer remarkable capabilities, they also face significant operational challenges. Issues such as scalability, latency, security, network interference, and power consumption must be carefully managed to ensure reliable, efficient, and secure performance in real-world deployments.

- **Scalability:** Managing millions of devices in large-scale deployments such as smart cities require robust network infrastructure.
- **Latency:** Time-critical applications (for example: healthcare, autonomous vehicles) demand low-latency protocols like 5G.
- **Security:** Data interception risks necessitate encryption and secure protocols (for example: MQTT with TLS).
- **Interference:** Wireless networks face challenges from signal degradation in dense or remote environments.
- **Power Consumption:** Low-power protocols (for example: LoRaWAN, BLE) are critical for battery-operated devices.

Application Layer

The Application Layer is the user-facing component of IoT, where data from the Device and Network Layers is transformed into meaningful services, analytics, and automation. This layer delivers value to end users through dashboards, mobile apps, and advanced analytics, enabling decision-making, visualization, and integration with business systems.

Functions

IoT platforms extend beyond mere data collection by offering a range of intelligent functions that turn raw information into actionable insights. From visualization and analytics to automation and integration with business systems, these functions empower users to monitor, control, and optimize processes efficiently, enhancing both operational performance and user experience.

- **Data Visualization:** Provides user-friendly interfaces (for example: dashboards, mobile apps) to display IoT data.

  Example: A factory manager views a real-time dashboard showing the temperature and energy consumption of all machines on the production line.
- **Advanced Analytics:** Uses AI, machine learning, or statistical models to derive insights, such as predictive maintenance or user behavior analysis.

Example: An industrial IoT platform uses machine learning to predict a pump failure a week in advance based on vibrations and temperature anomalies, prompting a scheduled maintenance order.

- **Automation and Decision Support:** Implements rules or AI-driven decisions to automate tasks, such as adjusting thermostat settings or scheduling irrigation.

  Example: A smart building platform automatically adjusts the HVAC (Heating, Ventilation, and Air Conditioning) system based on occupancy data from sensors to maintain optimal temperature and save energy.

- **Integration with Business Systems:** Connects IoT data to enterprise systems like ERP (for example: SAP) or CRM (for example: Salesforce) for operational efficiency.

  Example: When a smart vending machine reports low stock (IoT data), the platform automatically creates a restocking work order in the company's ERP system.

- **User Interaction:** Enables remote control and monitoring via web or mobile interfaces.

  Example: A homeowner uses a mobile app to remotely lock their smart door and check the live feed from their security camera, while away from home.

Role of Cloud and Edge

Modern IoT systems rely on a combination of cloud and edge computing to balance scalability, performance, and responsiveness. While cloud platforms offer massive storage, analytics, and device management capabilities, edge computing brings processing closer to the source of data, reducing latency and bandwidth demands. Hybrid architectures leverage the strengths of both approaches, enabling efficient and intelligent IoT deployments across diverse applications.

- **Cloud Platforms:** Services like AWS IoT Core, Microsoft Azure IoT Hub, and Google Cloud IoT provide scalable storage, processing, and analytics. They host applications, manage device fleets, and support big data analytics.
- **Edge Computing:** Edge devices (for example: Raspberry Pi, NVIDIA Jetson) process data locally to reduce latency and bandwidth usage, critical for applications like real-time surveillance or autonomous vehicles.
- **Hybrid Architectures:** Combine edge and cloud processing for optimal performance, with edge devices handling time-sensitive tasks and clouds managing long-term analytics.

Examples

The combined power of cloud and edge computing is best illustrated through real-world applications. From smart homes and healthcare to industry, agriculture, and transportation, these examples demonstrate how IoT systems leverage both local and cloud-based processing to deliver intelligent, efficient, and responsive solutions.

- **Smart Homes:** Mobile apps (for example: Google Home) control lights, locks, and HVAC systems based on sensor data.
- **Healthcare:** Remote patient monitoring dashboards display real-time biometric data from wearables.
- **Industry 4.0:** Predictive maintenance platforms (for example: Siemens, Mind Sphere) analyze machine data to prevent failures.
- **Agriculture:** Crop monitoring apps schedule irrigation based on soil and weather data.
- **Transportation:** Fleet management systems optimize routes using GPS and traffic data.

Emerging Trends and Challenges

The IoT landscape continues to evolve rapidly, with new technologies and practices shaping its future. From Edge AI and 5G integration to interoperability standards and digital twins, these trends are enhancing real-time analytics, connectivity, and system modeling.

Trends

IoT technologies are advancing at a remarkable pace, driven by innovations that enhance intelligence, connectivity, and interoperability. From Edge AI and 5G networks to digital twins and robust security measures, these trends are shaping smarter, faster, and more reliable IoT systems across industries.

- **Edge AI Integration:** The Application Layer increasingly leverages edge AI for real-time analytics, reducing cloud dependency (for example: smart cameras with on-device object detection).
- **5G and Low-Power Networks:** 5G's low latency and high bandwidth, combined with LPWANs like NB-IoT, enhance the Network Layer's capabilities for real-time and remote applications.
- **Interoperability Standards:** Protocols like Matter ensure seamless Device and Network Layer integration across ecosystems.
- **Privacy and Security:** End-to-end encryption and secure boot mechanisms protect data across all layers, especially in sensitive applications like healthcare.
- **Digital Twins:** The Application Layer uses digital twins—virtual models of physical systems—for real-time monitoring and simulation in industries like manufacturing.

Challenges

Despite the rapid advancements in IoT technologies, several critical challenges must be addressed to ensure effective deployment. From handling scalability across millions of devices to maintaining security, minimizing latency, optimizing power consumption, and ensuring interoperability, these challenges span all layers of IoT systems, and are crucial for reliable and resilient operations.

- **Scalability:** Managing millions of devices across layers requires robust infrastructure and device management systems.
- **Security:** Protecting data from interception (Network Layer) and ensuring device integrity (Device Layer) are critical.
- **Latency:** Time-sensitive applications (for example: autonomous vehicles) demand low-latency communication and processing across all layers.
- **Power Efficiency:** Battery-powered devices in the Device Layer must balance functionality with energy constraints.
- **Interoperability:** Ensuring heterogeneous devices and protocols work together seamlessly across layers remains a challenge.

The IoT architecture, comprising the Device, Network, and Application Layers, provides a structured framework for building scalable, efficient, and intelligent systems. The Device Layer perceives and interacts with the physical world, the Network Layer ensures seamless data transmission, and the Application Layer delivers user-facing services and insights. Together, these layers enable IoT applications in smart homes, healthcare, agriculture, and beyond. Thus, as technologies such as edge AI, 5G, and interoperability standards evolve, the IoT architecture will continue to advance, addressing challenges like security, scalability, and latency to create more robust and user-centric systems.

Real-World IoT Applications

The Internet of Things (IoT) has transcended its initial hype to become a transformative force embedded in everyday life and across industries. From enhancing home convenience to revolutionizing agriculture, healthcare, industrial processes, and urban infrastructure, IoT applications leverage sensors, connectivity, and analytics to deliver efficiency, automation, and intelligence. This section explores five key IoT application domains—Smart Homes, Precision Agriculture, Healthcare and Fitness, Industrial Automation (Industry 4.0), and Smart Cities and Transport—detailing their components, benefits, challenges, and real-world impact. Each domain illustrates how IoT's layered architecture (Device, Network, and Application Layers) creates tangible value for users and organizations.

Smart Homes

Smart homes represent one of the most accessible and consumer-driven applications of IoT, transforming residences into interconnected, automated ecosystems. IoT-enabled devices, equipped with sensors, actuators, and connectivity, allow homeowners to monitor and control lighting, heating, security, and appliances remotely or automatically, enhancing comfort, efficiency, and safety.

Components and Functionality

IoT systems are built on a layered architecture that integrates devices, networks, and applications to deliver seamless functionality. Each layer—from the Device Layer with sensors and actuators, to the Network Layer enabling communication, and the Application Layer providing user interfaces and analytics—plays a critical role in ensuring that IoT solutions are intelligent, responsive, and user-friendly.

- **Device Layer:** Includes sensors (for example: motion, temperature, light), actuators (for example: smart locks, motorized blinds), and controllers (for example: ESP32, Raspberry Pi). For example, a PIR motion sensor detects movement, triggering a relay actuator to turn on lights.
- **Network Layer:** Utilizes short-range protocols like Wi-Fi (for example: for smart cameras), Zigbee/Z-Wave (for example: for smart lights), or Bluetooth (for example: for smart locks). Smart home hubs bridge these protocols for interoperability.
- **Application Layer:** Mobile apps (for example: Google Home, Amazon Alexa) or web dashboards provide user interfaces for remote control, automation rules, and data visualization. Cloud platforms like AWS IoT Core enable integration and analytics.

Benefits

Smart home technologies offer more than just novelty—they improve daily life by enhancing efficiency, safety, and convenience. From reducing energy consumption and lowering utility costs to providing real-time security alerts and seamless automation, these systems demonstrate how IoT can make homes smarter, safer, and more responsive to user needs.

- **Energy Efficiency:** Automated lighting and HVAC systems reduce energy usage by 15–20%, lowering utility bills.
- **Safety and Security:** Real-time alerts and remote monitoring enhance protection against intrusions or hazards like smoke.
- **Convenience:** Remote control and automation (for example: scheduling coffee makers) simplify daily tasks.
- **Scalability:** Smart home ecosystems support integration of new devices such as smart plugs or sensors.

Challenges

While smart home systems offer numerous benefits, they also face practical hurdles that affect adoption and usability. Interoperability issues, security vulnerabilities, and high initial costs are key challenges that users and developers must address to ensure safe, reliable, and seamless smart home experiences.

- **Interoperability:** Devices from different manufacturers may use incompatible protocols, requiring hubs like SmartThings.
- **Security:** Vulnerabilities in Wi-Fi or cloud connections risk hacking (for example: unauthorized camera access).
- **Cost:** High initial investment for devices and installation can deter adoption.
- **User Complexity:** Non-technical users may struggle with setup or integration.

Emerging Trends

Smart home technology continues to evolve rapidly, driven by innovations that improve interoperability, efficiency, and intelligence. From unified standards such as the Matter protocol to energy-harvesting devices and Edge AI for local processing, these trends are shaping the next generation of connected, responsive, and sustainable homes.

- **Matter Protocol:** A unified standard (supported by Google, Amazon, and Apple) ensures interoperability across smart home devices.
- **Energy Harvesting:** Devices such as EnOcean's solar-powered sensors eliminate battery dependency.
- **Edge AI:** Local processing (for example: on-device motion detection) enhances privacy, and reduces latency.

Precision Agriculture

Precision agriculture leverages IoT to optimize farming practices, enabling data-driven decisions that enhance crop yield, reduce resource waste, and promote sustainability. By integrating sensors, drones, and connected systems, farmers monitor soil, weather, and crop conditions in real time, automating tasks like irrigation and fertilization.

Components and Functionality

Smart agriculture systems rely on a layered IoT architecture to monitor, analyze, and automate farming operations. From sensors and actuators in the Device Layer to long-range connectivity in the Network Layer and cloud-based dashboards in the Application Layer, each component works together to optimize resource usage, improve crop health, and enable data-driven decision-making.

- **Device Layer:** Soil moisture sensors (for example: YL-69), temperature/humidity sensors (for example: DHT22), and actuators like solenoid valves or fertilizer dispensers. Controllers (for example: Arduino Mega) process data locally.
- **Network Layer:** Long-range, low-power protocols like LoRaWAN or NB-IoT connect remote sensors to gateways, with cellular (4G/5G) for cloud connectivity. Drones use Wi-Fi or cellular for data transmission.
- **Application Layer:** Cloud-based dashboards (for example: John Deere Operations Center) or mobile apps provide real-time insights, irrigation schedules, and crop health analytics.

Benefits

Implementing IoT in agriculture delivers measurable advantages that enhance both productivity and sustainability. By leveraging real-time data from sensors and automated systems, farmers can make informed decisions that increase crop yield, optimize the use of water and fertilizers, and reduce labor costs.

- **Increased Yield:** Data-driven decisions boost crop productivity by up to 20%.
- **Resource Efficiency:** Smart irrigation reduces water usage by 30–40%, and precise fertilization minimizes waste.
- **Sustainability:** Optimized resource use lowers environmental impact, supporting eco-friendly farming.
- **Cost Savings:** Automation reduces labor and resource costs.

Challenges

Despite its many benefits, IoT adoption in agriculture faces several practical obstacles. Limited connectivity in remote areas, high upfront costs, large-scale data management, and the need for durable devices capable of withstanding harsh environmental conditions, all pose significant challenges for farmers and technology providers, alike.

- **Connectivity:** Remote farms may lack reliable cellular or LoRaWAN coverage.
- **Cost:** High upfront costs for sensors, drones, and gateways can be prohibitive for small farms.
- **Data Management:** Processing large datasets from sensors requires robust analytics platforms.
- **Durability**: Devices must withstand harsh outdoor conditions (for example rain, dust, and so on).

Emerging Trends

The future of smart agriculture is being shaped by innovations that combine IoT with advanced analytics and automation. AI-driven models, satellite data integration, and autonomous equipment are enabling more precise, efficient, and scalable farming practices, transforming how crops are monitored, maintained, and harvested.

- **AI Analytics:** Machine learning models predict crop diseases or optimize planting schedules.
- **Satellite Integration:** Combining IoT with satellite imagery enhances large-scale monitoring.
- **Autonomous Equipment:** IoT-enabled robots perform tasks like weeding or harvesting.

Healthcare and Fitness

IoT has revolutionized healthcare through the Internet of Medical Things (IoMT), enabling continuous monitoring, remote diagnostics, and personalized care. Wearable fitness devices and connected medical equipment collect real-time health data, improving patient outcomes, and reducing healthcare costs.

Components and Functionality

The future of smart agriculture is being shaped by innovations that combine IoT with advanced analytics and automation. AI-driven models, satellite data integration, and autonomous equipment are enabling more precise, efficient, and scalable farming practices, transforming how crops are monitored, maintained, and harvested.

- **Device Layer:** Sensors (for example: heart rate, SpO_2, ECG) and actuators (for example: haptic vibrators, and insulin pumps). Controllers like STM32 process data locally.
- **Network Layer:** Bluetooth Low Energy (BLE) for wearables, NB-IoT or 5G for remote monitoring devices, and Wi-Fi for hospital equipment.
- **Application Layer:** Mobile apps or cloud platforms (for example: Medtronic CareLink) display health trends, issue alerts, and integrate with Electronic Health Records (EHRs).

Benefits

IoT technologies in healthcare provide significant advantages by enabling continuous, real-time monitoring and proactive care. Wearables and connected devices allow early detection of health anomalies, support remote care for chronic or elderly patients, encourage patient engagement through interactive feedback, and ultimately help reduce the overall healthcare costs through timely interventions.

- **Continuous Monitoring:** Real-time data enables early detection of anomalies (for example: irregular heartbeats).
- **Remote Care:** Reduces hospital visits, especially for the elderly or chronic patients.
- **Patient Engagement:** Wearables encourage healthier lifestyles through gamified goals.
- **Cost Reduction:** Early interventions and remote monitoring lower healthcare costs.

Challenges

While IoT brings transformative benefits to healthcare, it also introduces critical challenges that must be carefully managed. Ensuring patient privacy, maintaining sensor accuracy, achieving interoperability across diverse EHR systems, and optimizing battery life for wearables are necessary for delivering safe, reliable, and effective healthcare solutions.

- **Privacy:** Sensitive health data requires strict compliance with regulations such as HIPAA or GDPR.
- **Accuracy:** Sensor errors can lead to incorrect diagnoses or alerts.
- **Interoperability:** Integrating devices with diverse EHR systems is complex.
- **Battery Life:** Wearables must balance functionality with power efficiency.

Emerging Trends

Healthcare IoT continues to evolve through innovations that enhance real-time monitoring, diagnostics, and patient care. AI-driven wearables, high-speed 5G connectivity, and IoT-enabled implantable devices are enabling proactive, data-driven healthcare, transforming how patients are monitored and treated both remotely, and in clinical settings.

- **AI-Driven Diagnostics:** Edge AI in wearables predicts health risks (for example: heart attacks).
- **5G Connectivity:** Enables real-time telemedicine with high bandwidth data.
- **Implantable Devices:** IoT-enabled implants monitor internal conditions (for example: glucose levels).

Industrial Automation (Industry 4.0)

Industrial IoT (IIoT) drives Industry 4.0, transforming factories into smart, interconnected systems where machines communicate, optimize processes, and predict maintenance needs. IoT enables real-time monitoring, automation, and data-driven decision-making, enhancing productivity and reducing costs.

Components and Functionality

Modern manufacturing leverages IoT to create intelligent, connected production environments. Sensors and actuators in the Device Layer, robust wired or wireless connectivity in the Network Layer, and advanced analytics platforms in the Application Layer work together to enable predictive maintenance, real-time monitoring, and optimization of industrial processes.

- **Device Layer:** Vibration, temperature, and pressure sensors; actuators like robotic arms or conveyor motors; controllers like Siemens SIMATIC PLCs.
- **Network Layer**: Ethernet or Modbus for wired systems, Wi-Fi or 5G for wireless connectivity, and MQTT for efficient data exchange.
- **Application Layer**: Cloud platforms (for example: Siemens MindSphere) or edge gateways provide predictive analytics, digital twins, and real-time dashboards.

Benefits

IoT-enabled manufacturing systems deliver tangible improvements across productivity, quality, and cost efficiency. By leveraging real-time monitoring and predictive maintenance, factories can reduce unplanned downtime, optimize operations, ensure consistent product quality, and achieve significant cost savings.

- **Reduced Downtime**: Predictive maintenance cuts unplanned outages by 20–30%.
- **Increased Productivity**: Automation and real-time monitoring boost efficiency.
- **Quality Control**: Sensors ensure consistent product quality.
- **Cost Savings**: Optimized operations reduce energy and maintenance costs.

Challenges

Despite the advantages of IoT in manufacturing, several hurdles must be addressed for successful implementation. Integrating legacy equipment, ensuring cybersecurity, managing large volumes of sensor data, and training a skilled workforce are critical challenges that industrial organizations must navigate to fully realize the benefits of connected manufacturing.

- **Integration:** Retrofitting legacy equipment with IoT is costly and complex.
- **Security:** Industrial networks are prime targets for cyberattacks.
- **Data Overload:** Managing massive sensor data requires robust analytics.
- **Skilled Workforce:** Implementing IoT requires trained personnel.

Emerging Trends

The future of manufacturing is being reshaped by innovations that enhance efficiency, flexibility, and intelligence. Digital twins allow real-time simulation of factory processes, Edge AI provides low-latency analytics for critical tasks, and 5G connectivity enables precise coordination of robotics and automated systems, driving the next generation of smart factories.

- **Digital Twins:** Real-time simulation of factory processes improves planning.
- **Edge AI:** Local analytics reduce latency for critical tasks like quality control.
- **5G in Factories:** High-speed connectivity enables real-time robotics coordination.

Smart Cities and Transport

Smart cities and transportation systems leverage IoT to enhance urban infrastructure, reduce congestion, and improve citizen services. IoT-enabled smart mobility solutions optimize traffic, parking, and public transport, creating safer and more sustainable cities.

Components and Functionality

Smart cities rely on IoT to create efficient, safe, and responsive urban environments. Sensors and actuators in the Device Layer, robust connectivity in the Network Layer, and cloud- or app-based platforms in the Application Layer work together to monitor traffic, optimize energy use, manage public services, and provide real-time information to citizens.

- **Device Layer:** Sensors (for example: traffic counters, air quality monitors), actuators (for example: smart streetlights, traffic signals), and controllers (for example: Raspberry Pi).
- **Network Layer**: LoRaWAN for long-range sensors, 5G for high-bandwidth applications like traffic cameras, and Ethernet for fixed infrastructure.
- **Application Layer**: Cloud platforms (for example: IBM Watson IoT) or mobile apps provide traffic dashboards, parking guidance, and public transport schedules.

Benefits

IoT-enabled smart city solutions offer significant advantages for urban living. By enabling dynamic traffic management, reducing environmental impact, improving safety through accident detection, and providing real-time transit updates, these technologies enhance both the efficiency of city operations, and the overall experience for citizens.

- **Reduced Congestion:** Dynamic traffic management cuts travel times by 10–15%.
- **Environmental Impact:** Lower emissions through optimized transport and lighting.
- **Safety:** Accident detection and emergency response improve road safety.
- **Citizen Experience:** Real-time transit updates enhance convenience.

Challenges

While smart city initiatives offer numerous benefits, they also face significant obstacles. Managing large-scale deployments, funding infrastructure upgrades, safeguarding citizen privacy, and ensuring reliable connectivity across urban and rural areas are key challenges that must be addressed for successful implementation.

- **Scalability:** Managing thousands of devices across a city is complex.
- **Cost:** Infrastructure upgrades require significant investments.
- **Privacy:** Surveillance systems raise concerns about data misuse.
- **Connectivity:** Ensuring reliable coverage in urban and rural areas.

Emerging Trends

The evolution of smart cities is being driven by technologies that enhance connectivity, efficiency, and sustainability. Vehicle-to-Everything (V2X) communication, AI-based traffic prediction, and IoT-enabled smart grids are enabling real-time coordination, optimized resource usage, and the integration of renewable energy into urban infrastructure, shaping the cities of the future.

- **V2X Communication:** Vehicle-to-Everything (V2X) systems use 5G for real-time traffic coordination.
- **AI Traffic Prediction:** Machine learning optimizes signal timings, and predicts congestion.
- **Smart Grids:** IoT integrates renewable energy into city infrastructure.

IoT applications are reshaping industries and daily life by enabling automation, efficiency, and data-driven decision-making. Smart homes enhance comfort and energy savings, precision agriculture boosts sustainability, healthcare improves patient outcomes, Industry 4.0 optimizes manufacturing, and smart cities streamline urban living. Each domain leverages IoT's layered architecture—Device, Network, and Application Layers—to deliver value. As technologies like 5G, edge AI, and interoperability standards evolve, IoT applications will continue to expand, addressing challenges such as security, scalability, and cost to create smarter, more connected systems.

Practical Exercises for IoT Learning

To solidify understanding of IoT systems and their layered architecture (Device, Network, and Application Layers), practical exercises are essential for bridging theoretical concepts with real-world applications. These exercises encourage learners to analyze, design, and explore IoT systems by breaking down components, mapping architectures, and investigating real projects. Below are three expanded exercises designed to enhance comprehension of IoT ecosystems through hands-on and analytical tasks: IoT System Breakdown, Architecture Mapping, and Explore Real IoT Projects. Each exercise includes detailed instructions, examples, tools, expected outcomes, and tips for success, ensuring learners gain practical insights into IoT system design and implementation.

Exercise 1: IoT System Breakdown

Objective: This exercise helps learners understand how IoT components—sensors, controllers, communication methods, cloud platforms, and actuators—interconnect to form a functional system. Thus, by analyzing a real-world IoT use case, learners categorize components and visualize their roles across the IoT architecture layers.

Task: Choose one real-world IoT use case (for example: Smart Street Light, Smart Thermostat, or Smart Irrigation System) and create a detailed breakdown, categorizing the following:

- **Sensors Used:** Identify the sensors that collect environmental data.
- **Controllers:** Specify the microcontroller or processor handling local data processing.
- **Communication Method:** Determine the wired or wireless protocol used for data transmission.
- **Cloud or Platform Used:** Identify the cloud platform or local server for data storage and analytics.
- **Output/Action Performed:** Describe the physical actions or outputs triggered by the system.

Instructions

1. **Select a Use Case:** Choose a familiar IoT application, such as a Smart Street Light, to analyze. Alternatively, consider other examples like a Smart Doorbell or Smart Parking System.
2. **Research Components:** Use online resources, datasheets, or IoT project repositories (for example: Hackster.io, Arduino Project Hub) to identify typical components for the chosen use case.
3. **Categorize Components**: Create a table or mind map (using tools such as XMind, Miro, or paper) to organize components under the specified categories.
4. **Explain Interactions:** Describe how sensors, controllers, communication methods, platforms, and actuators work together to achieve the system's goal.

5. **Visualize**: Optionally, sketch a simple diagram showing data flow from sensors to cloud to actuators.

Example: Smart Street Light

- **Sensors Used:**
  - **Light Sensor (for example: LDR or BH1750):** Measures ambient light levels to determine when to activate the streetlight.
  - **Motion Sensor (for example: PIR HC-SR501):** Detects nearby vehicles or pedestrians to adjust brightness.
- **Controllers:**
  - **ESP32:** A Wi-Fi-enabled microcontroller that processes sensor data and controls actuators. It supports low-power modes for energy efficiency.
- **Communication Method:**
  - **LoRaWAN:** Used for long-range, low-power communication to transmit sensor data to a gateway.
  - **Wi-Fi:** Connects the gateway to a cloud platform for broader network access.
- **Cloud or Platform Used:**
  - **The Things Network (TTN):** A LoRaWAN-based platform for managing streetlight data.
  - **AWS IoT Core:** Processes and stores data, enabling analytics and remote control.
- **Output/Action Performed:**
  - **LED Actuator:** Adjusts streetlight brightness (for example: dimming when no motion is detected).
  - **Relay:** Switches the streetlight on or off based on light sensor data.

Tools

- **Mind Mapping:** XMind, Miro, or Lucidchart for digital mind maps; paper and pen for manual sketches.
- **Research:** Websites like Hackster.io, Arduino.cc, or manufacturer datasheets (for example: Adafruit, SparkFun).
- **Templates:** Use a table format or a radial mind map to categorize components clearly.

Outcome

- **Learning Objectives:**
  - Understand how IoT components map to the Device, Network, and Application Layers.
  - Gain insight into the interplay between sensing, processing, communication, and actuation.
  - Develop skills in analyzing real-world IoT systems.
- **Deliverable:** A completed mind map or table detailing the components and their roles, with a brief explanation of data flow.

Challenges and Tips

- **Challenge:** Identifying specific hardware for niche applications may require research.

  Tip: *Start with well-documented use cases on platforms like Hackster.io or Instructables.*

- **Challenge:** Understanding communication protocols may be complex for beginners.

  Tip: *Focus on common protocols like Wi-Fi, LoRaWAN, or Bluetooth for initial analysis.*

- **Example Deliverable:** A mind map for a Smart Street Light showing sensors (LDR, PIR) connected to an ESP32, using LoRaWAN to send data to TTN, which integrates with AWS IoT Core to control LED brightness.

Exercise 2: Architecture Mapping

Objective: This exercise focuses on visualizing the three-layer IoT architecture (Device, Network, Application) by creating a block diagram for a chosen IoT system. Learners will map the flow of data from perception (sensing) to transmission (networking) to service delivery (application), reinforcing understanding of IoT's modular design.

Task: Create a block diagram (on paper or using a tool like Fritzing, draw.io, or Lucidchart) for one of the following IoT systems:

- **Smart Fan**
- **Soil Moisture Monitoring System**
- **Home Security System:** The diagram should illustrate the Device Layer (sensors, actuators, controllers), Network Layer (communication protocols), and Application Layer (user interface, analytics).

Instructions

1. **Choose a System:** Select one of the provided IoT systems (for example: Home Security System) or propose another with instructor approval.
2. **Identify Components**:
   - **Device Layer:** List sensors, actuators, and controllers.
   - **Network Layer:** Specify the communication protocol (for example: Wi-Fi, Zigbee, LoRaWAN).
   - **Application Layer:** Describe the user interface or platform (for example: mobile app, cloud dashboard).
3. **Create the Diagram:**
   - Use a tool like draw.io (free, web-based) or Fritzing (for hardware schematics) to create a block diagram.
   - Show data flow with arrows from sensors to controllers, controllers to network, and network to application.
   - Label each component clearly, including specific hardware (for example: ESP32) or platforms (for example: Google Cloud IoT).
4. **Annotate the Diagram**: Add brief descriptions of each layer's role and how data flows between them.
5. **Validate the Design**: Ensure that the diagram reflects a realistic IoT system, considering power, connectivity, and scalability.

Example: Home Security System

- **Device Layer:**
  - **Sensors:** PIR motion sensor (HC-SR501), door/window contact sensor (magnetic reed switch), glass-break sensor.

  - **Actuators:** Siren (buzzer), smart lock (solenoid), PTZ camera motor.
  - **Controller:** Raspberry Pi 4 (processes sensor data, controls actuators).
- **Network Layer:**
  - **Protocol:** Zigbee for low-power sensor communication; Wi-Fi for camera streaming and cloud connectivity.
  - **Gateway:** A Zigbee hub (for example: SmartThings) aggregates sensor data and connects to the cloud via Wi-Fi.
- **Application Layer:**
  - **Platform:** Mobile app (for example: Ring Home) or web dashboard displaying live camera feeds, motion alerts, and lock status.
  - **Cloud:** AWS IoT Core for data storage and analytics, with integration to Alexa for voice control.
- **Diagram Description:** The block diagram shows PIR sensors detecting motion, sending data via Zigbee to a Raspberry Pi 4, which triggers a siren and locks. The Pi uses Wi-Fi to upload alerts and video to AWS IoT Core, displayed on a mobile app.

Tools

- **Fritzing**: For hardware-focused diagrams showing sensor/controller connections.
- **`draw.io`:** For web-based, professional block diagrams with customizable templates.
- **Lucidchart:** For collaborative diagramming with IoT-specific shapes.
- **Paper and Pen:** For quick sketches, using boxes for components and arrows for data flow.

Outcome

- **Learning Objectives**:
  - Visualize the three-layer IoT architecture in a practical context.
  - Understand data flow from perception to application.
  - Gain experience with diagramming tools for system design.
- **Deliverable:** A block diagram (digital or hand-drawn) with labeled components and annotations explaining the data flow.

Challenges and Tips

- **Challenge:** Beginners may struggle with diagramming software.

  Tip: *Start with draw.io's free templates or hand-draw a draft before digitizing.*
- **Challenge:** Ensuring realistic connectivity choices (for example: Wi-Fi vs. LoRaWAN).

  Tip: *Refer to datasheets or IoT project guides to select appropriate protocols.*
- **Example Deliverable:** A draw.io diagram for a Home Security System showing PIR sensors → Raspberry Pi 4 → Zigbee/Wi-Fi → AWS IoT Core → mobile app, with arrows indicating data flow.

Exercise 3: Explore Real IoT Projects

Objective: This exercise exposes learners to real-world IoT implementations by analyzing open-source projects on platforms like Hackster.io. By summarizing a project's components, goals, and outcomes, learners gain insight into practical IoT system design, and identify areas for improvement, moving beyond theoretical concepts.

Task: Visit **Hackster.io** and search for a project using "ESP32 + Firebase" or "IoT dashboard." Select one project, and summarize the following:

- **Project Goal:** What problem does the project solve or what functionality does it provide?
- **Hardware Used:** List the sensors, actuators, and controllers.
- **Communication Protocol:** Identify the protocol used (for example: Wi-Fi, MQTT).
- **Cloud/Dashboard Platform:** Specify the platform for data storage or visualization.
- **What You Liked/Would Change:** Reflect on the project's strengths and potential improvements.

Instructions

1. **Find a Project:**
    a. Go to Hackster.io and use search terms like "ESP32 Firebase" or "IoT dashboard."
    b. Choose a project with clear documentation, including hardware, code, and outcomes (for example: "Smart Home Monitoring with ESP32 and Firebase").
2. **Analyze the Project**:
    a. Read the project description, code, and schematics to understand its components and functionality.
    b. Note how the project aligns with the three-layer IoT architecture.
3. **Summarize Components**:
    a. Goal: Describe the project's purpose (for example: monitoring temperature in a greenhouse).
    b. Hardware: List specific components (for example: DHT11 sensor, ESP32, relay).
    c. Protocol: Identify the communication method (for example: Wi-Fi to Firebase).
    d. Platform: Note the cloud or dashboard (for example: Google Firebase, Blynk).
    e. Reflection: Highlight innovative features and suggest improvements (for example: adding LoRaWAN for longer range).
4. **Document Findings**: Write a 300–500-word summary or create a presentation slide summarizing the project, using bullet points or a table for clarity.
5. **Share Insights:** Optionally, discuss findings with peers or instructors to compare different projects.

Example: Smart Home Monitoring with ESP32 and Firebase

- **Project Goal:** Monitor temperature, humidity, and smoke levels in a home, sending alerts to a mobile app, if thresholds are exceeded.
- **Hardware Used:**
    - **Sensors:** DHT11 (temperature/humidity), MQ-2 (smoke).
    - **Controller:** ESP32 DevKitC (processes sensor data, handles Wi-Fi).
    - **Actuator:** Buzzer (alerts for smoke detection).
- **Communication Protocol:** Wi-Fi (ESP32 connects to Firebase via HTTP/MQTT).
- **Cloud/Dashboard Platform:** Google Firebase Real-time Database for data storage; Firebase-hosted web app for visualization.
- **What You Liked/Would Change:**
    - **Liked:** Simple setup, real-time alerts, and integration with Firebase's scalable database.

    - **Would Change:** Add LoRaWAN for larger homes or offline capability with edge processing to reduce cloud dependency.

Tools

- **Hackster.io:** Primary platform for finding IoT projects.
- **Google Firebase:** For understanding cloud integration in selected projects.
- **Text Editor:** For summarizing findings (for example: Microsoft Word, and Google Docs).
- **Presentation Tools**: PowerPoint or Canva for creating slides (optional).

Outcome

- **Learning Objectives**:
    - Gain exposure to real-world IoT implementations, and their practical challenges.
    - Understand how open-source projects apply IoT architecture principles.
    - Develop critical thinking by evaluating and proposing improvements.
- **Deliverable**: A written summary or slide deck detailing the project's components, functionality, and personal reflections.

Challenges and Tips

- **Challenge**: Projects may lack detailed documentation.

  Tip: *Choose projects with clear schematics, codes, and community comments.*
- **Challenge:** Understanding cloud platforms like Firebase may be complex.

  Tip: *Watch tutorials on YouTube or read Firebase documentation for basics.*
- **Example Deliverable:** A 400-word summary of a "Smart Greenhouse" project, detailing DHT11 sensors, ESP32, Wi-Fi, Firebase, and a suggestion to add edge AI for local anomaly detection.

Emerging Trends and Challenges in IoT Exercises Trends

The Internet of Things (IoT) landscape is rapidly evolving, driven by advancements in connectivity, processing power, and data analytics. Key emerging trends include the rise of edge computing, which processes data closer to the source to reduce latency; the proliferation of 5G networks, enabling massive device connectivity and high-speed data transfer; and the increasing integration of Artificial Intelligence (AI) and Machine Learning (ML) to derive actionable insights from the vast amounts of IoT data. Furthermore, the focus on sustainable and green IoT solutions, along with the development of sophisticated digital twins for real-time monitoring and simulation, are shaping the future of the field.

- **Open-Source Ecosystems:** Platforms like Hackster.io and Arduino Project Hub foster collaborative IoT development, providing accessible resources for learners.
- **Edge AI Integration:** Projects increasingly incorporate edge AI (for example: TensorFlow Lite on ESP32) for local processing, as seen in smart cameras or wearables.
- **Low-Code Platforms:** Tools like Blynk or Node-RED simplify IoT prototyping, making exercises more accessible to beginners.
- **Simulation Tools:** Virtual prototyping with tools such as Tinkercad Circuits allows learners to test IoT designs without hardware.
- **Interoperability Standards:** Projects using Matter or MQTT ensure compatibility across devices, reflected in modern Hackster.io examples.

Challenges

- **Hardware Access:** Learners may lack access to components like ESP32 or sensors.

  Solution: Use simulation tools such as Wokwi or Tinkercad for virtual prototyping.

- **Technical Complexity:** Beginners may struggle with coding or protocol setup.

  Solution: Start with well-documented projects, and use beginner-friendly platforms like Arduino IDE.

- **Cost:** Building physical IoT systems can be expensive.

  Solution: Focus on paper-based or simulation exercises initially.

- **Security:** Real projects must address vulnerabilities like unencrypted data transmission.

  Solution: Encourage learners to explore secure protocols (for example: MQTT with TLS).

These practical exercises—IoT System Breakdown, Architecture Mapping, and Explore Real IoT Projects—provide hands-on opportunities to understand IoT's layered architecture and real-world applications. Thus, by categorizing components, visualizing data flow, and analyzing open-source projects, learners gain practical skills in IoT system design, from sensing to cloud integration. These exercises bridge theory and practice, preparing learners to design, critique, and improve IoT systems. As IoT evolves with trends like edge AI and low-code platforms, such exercises will remain critical for fostering innovation and problem-solving in IoT development.

Conclusion

The Internet of Things (IoT) is a transformative technology connecting physical devices to the internet, enabling them to sense, communicate, and act intelligently. IoT's fundamentals, emphasizing its role in creating efficient, automated, and data-driven systems across industries like healthcare, agriculture, and smart cities. IoT integrates sensors, controllers, networks, and cloud platforms to facilitate seamless data flow and decision-making, exemplified by fitness trackers syncing health data or smart irrigation systems optimizing water use.

IoT's importance lies in its ability to harness data for automation, efficiency, and enhanced quality of life. It enables seamless device connectivity, data-driven decisions, and automation, serving as the digital world's nervous system — sensors as sensory organs, controllers and networks as nerves, and cloud platforms as the brain.

IoT's evolution traces from standalone embedded systems (1970s–1990s) to connected smart devices (2000s–2010s) and now edge AI-driven systems, reducing latency and enhancing privacy. The three-layer IoT architecture — Device (sensing/actuation), Network (data transmission), and Application (analytics/services) — ensures modularity and scalability.

In fact, practical exercises reinforce learning IoT System Breakdown categorizes components, Architecture Mapping visualizes data flow, and Explore Real IoT Projects analyzes open-source implementations. These exercises bridge theory and practice, preparing learners to design IoT systems. Thus, as IoT advances with 5G, edge AI, and interoperability standards, it continues to reshape industries, addressing challenges like security and scalability.

Having established the foundational principles, core components, and extensive applications of IoT, the next chapter will transition from the "what" and "why" to the "how." The following chapters will dive into the specifics of IoT device programming, network protocols, and cloud integration, beginning with an in-depth exploration of widely used microcontrollers and development boards essential for building practical IoT solutions.

Chapter 2

IoT Architecture and Ecosystem

Introduction

In *Chapter 1*, we explored the fundamentals of the Internet of Things (IoT), establishing its significance as a transformative technology that connects physical devices to the internet, enabling them to sense, communicate, and act intelligently. We examined its core components—sensors, actuators, controllers, connectivity, and cloud platforms—and how they work together to transform the raw environmental data into meaningful insights and automated actions. We also introduced the three-layer IoT architecture (Device, Network, and Application layers) and explored real-world applications, such as smart homes, precision agriculture, healthcare, industrial automation, and smart cities, supported by practical exercises to bridge theory and practice.

Building upon that foundation, this chapter takes a deeper dive into the IoT architecture and ecosystem, providing a comprehensive understanding of how its layers and components interact to create scalable, modular, and efficient systems. The goal is to explore how data travels from the physical environment—captured by sensors—to cloud dashboards for visualization and analysis, and how developers can design robust IoT solutions that meet real-world demands. Building upon that foundation, this chapter takes a deeper dive into the IoT architecture and ecosystem, providing a comprehensive understanding of how its layers and components interact to create scalable, modular, and efficient systems.

This architectural focus becomes critical when scaling, as poor design significantly amplifies issues such as device failure rates, security vulnerabilities, and cost overruns. The goal is to explore how data travels from the physical environment—captured by sensors—to cloud dashboards for visualization and analysis, and how developers can design robust IoT solutions that meet real-world demands.

A robust architecture is essential because IoT is not a random collection of devices; it is a carefully structured ecosystem where each component plays a specific role. Sensors collect environmental data, controllers process it locally, communication networks transfer it securely, gateways bridge heterogeneous protocols, and cloud applications provide analytics and user interfaces. This layered approach ensures modularity, scalability, and efficiency, preventing the chaos and inefficiencies that would arise in poorly designed systems. For example, a smart city traffic system relies on sensors to detect vehicle flow, gateways to aggregate data, and cloud platforms to optimize traffic signals, all orchestrated through a well-defined architecture.

Structure

In this chapter, we will discuss the following topics:

- Foundations of IoT Architecture and Ecosystem
- Significance of IoT Architecture in System Design
- Three-Layer IoT Architecture
- IoT Component Categories and Roles
- Introduction to Data Flow in IoT Systems
- Scalability, Modularity, and Low-Power Design
- Common IoT Design Considerations
- Approach to Evaluating IoT System Performance
- Preparing the IoT Development Environment
- Hands-On with IoT Projects

By the end of this chapter, you will have a complete mental model of how IoT systems are structured, and how each component contributes to the ecosystem. This understanding will serve as the technical groundwork for upcoming chapters on hardware integration, cloud dashboards, and advanced IoT applications.

The Three-Layer IoT Architecture

The Internet of Things (IoT) is a complex ecosystem that connects physical devices to digital services, enabling data-driven automation, monitoring, and decision-making. To manage this complexity, IoT systems are typically organized using a layered architectural model, which provides clarity, modularity, and scalability. The most widely adopted framework is the three-layer IoT architecture, consisting of:

- **Perception Layer (Device Layer):** Responsible for sensing the environment and performing physical actions.
- **Network Layer (Transmission Layer):** Facilitates secure and reliable data communication between devices and applications.
- **Application Layer:** Delivers user-facing services, analytics, and control through dashboards, apps, and integrations.

Each layer has distinct roles, technologies, and challenges, working together to create a cohesive IoT ecosystem. This structured approach ensures that IoT systems are scalable, interoperable, and efficient, whether deployed in a smart home in Japan, a precision agriculture system in India, or a smart city in Singapore. Thus, this section explores each layer in depth, providing technical details, global examples, and practical considerations for designing IoT systems that meet international standards and diverse application needs.

To further drive the point regarding scalability and security, the exploration of each layer will be framed around its specific challenges:

- **Perception Layer (or Device Layer):** Focus on Scalability (managing billions of diverse, low-power devices) and Security (physical tampering, device authentication, and securing constrained endpoints).
- **Network Layer (or Communication Layer):** Focus on Scalability (handling massive, diverse data traffic from various protocols) and Security (securing communication channels, preventing Man-in-the-Middle attacks, and ensuring network reliability).

- **Application/Service Layer (or Platform Layer):** Focus on Scalability (processing, analyzing, and storing exabytes of data efficiently, and supporting complex services) and Security (data privacy, access control, and ensuring the integrity of business logic and algorithms).

Perception Layer (Device Layer)

The Perception Layer, also known as the Device Layer, is the foundation of any IoT system, serving as the interface between the physical world and the digital ecosystem. This layer encompasses all hardware components that interact directly with the environment, collecting data through sensors, processing it locally with controllers, and executing actions via actuators. Often referred to as the *eyes, ears, and hands* of IoT, the Perception Layer enables systems to sense conditions (for example: temperature, motion) and respond (for example, turning on a pump or sounding an alarm). As initially specified in *Chapter 1* for a better flow of information, its importance lies in its ability to bridge the physical and digital realms, making IoT systems aware of and responsive to their surroundings.

Key Functions of the Perception Layer

The Perception Layer performs several critical functions that enable IoT systems to interact with the physical world:

- **Data Collection:** Sensors measure environmental parameters, such as temperature, humidity, light intensity, motion, or biometric data (for example, heart rate). Another example is a soil moisture sensor in an Indian smart farming system that monitors water levels to optimize irrigation.
- **Local Data Processing:** Microcontrollers or edge nodes preprocess raw sensor data to filter noise, aggregate readings, or apply simple logic. For instance, an ESP32 in a smart thermostat may average temperature readings to eliminate outliers before transmission. This is distinct from the more complex, higher-level aggregation and protocol translation performed by an edge gateway, which often handles data from multiple local devices before sending it to the cloud.
- **Actuation:** Actuators translate digital commands into physical actions such as opening a valve, rotating a motor, or activating a lock. In a European smart home, a motion sensor triggers a relay actuator to turn on lights automatically.
- **Device Management:** Controllers handle power management, error correction, and device configuration, ensuring reliable operation in diverse environments, such as a Brazilian rainforest monitoring system or a German industrial plant.

Common Components

The Perception Layer comprises a variety of hardware components, each tailored to specific tasks:

- **Sensors:** Devices that detect and measure physical properties, converting them into electrical or digital signals.
- **Microcontrollers:** Embedded devices that process sensor data and control actuators.
- **Edge Nodes:** More powerful devices capable of running lightweight AI models or complex algorithms.
- **Actuators:** Devices that perform physical actions based on controller commands.

Global Examples

The Internet of Things (IoT) is transforming industries worldwide through intelligent sensing, data-driven decision-making, and automation. The following real-world implementations highlight how IoT technologies are applied across different sectors and regions:

- **Smart Agriculture in India:** Capacitive soil moisture sensors (YL-69) measure water content in rice fields, processed by an ESP32, which controls solenoid valve actuators to optimize irrigation, reducing water usage by 30–40%.
- **Smart Home Security in Germany:** PIR motion sensors (HC-SR501) detect intruders, triggering a buzzer actuator via a Raspberry Pi, with data sent to a cloud platform for homeowner alerts.
- **Healthcare Wearables in Australia**: MAX30102 sensors in fitness trackers monitor heart rate and SpO_2, processed by an STM32 microcontroller, with haptic actuators providing user notifications.

These diverse examples illustrate that while the specific sensor and actuator technologies, as well as the application domains, vary significantly across regions, the fundamental architectural principles of IoT—sensing, processing, communication, and actuation—remain universally consistent.

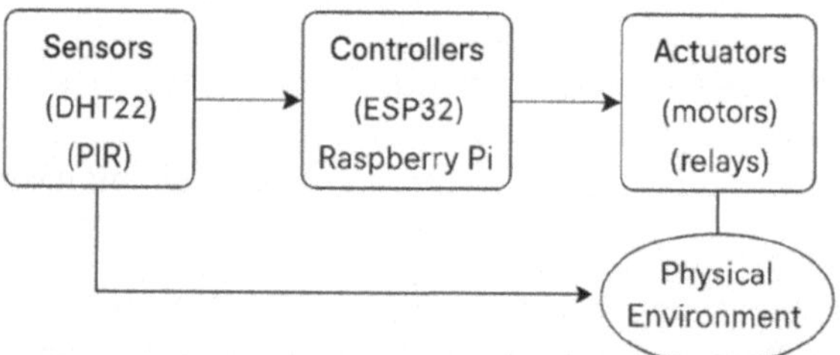

Figure 2.1: *Perception Layer*

Figure 2.1 illustrates the interaction between sensors, controllers, and actuators forms the backbone of modern embedded and IoT systems. Sensors collect data from the physical environment, controllers (such as microcontrollers or single-board computers) process this information, and actuators perform the required actions in response. This diagram illustrates this relationship, showing how components like DHT22 (temperature and humidity sensor) and PIR (motion sensor) provide input, which is processed by controllers such as ESP32 or Raspberry Pi, and then translated into actions through actuators such as motors and relays.

Network Layer (Transmission Layer)

The Network Layer, often called the Transmission Layer, acts as the nervous system of IoT, enabling seamless communication between the Perception Layer and the Application Layer. It is responsible for transmitting sensor data to cloud platforms or gateways, delivering commands to actuators, and ensuring secure, reliable, and efficient data exchange. The core health indicators of this system are its latency, reliability, and security. This layer is critical for connecting devices across diverse environments, from urban smart cities in Singapore to remote agricultural fields in Brazil. The Network Layer leverages a variety of wired and wireless technologies and protocols, each suited to a specific range, bandwidth, power, and scalability requirements.

Responsibilities of the Network Layer

The Network Layer performs several key functions to ensure robust IoT connectivity:

- **Secure and Reliable Data Transmission:** Ensures that the data is delivered without loss or corruption, using encryption (TLS) and error-checking mechanisms (CRC). For example, a smart meter in the UK sends usage data securely to a cloud platform.

- **Protocol Management and Interoperability:** Translates between protocols (Zigbee to Wi-Fi) at the **Gateway** to enable communication across heterogeneous devices, critical in smart homes.
- **Routing and Addressing:** Assigns unique identifiers (IP addresses) and routes data through networks, as seen in smart city routers.
- **Error Detection and Correction:** Uses techniques like retransmission or forward error correction to handle packet loss, vital in industrial IoT.
- **Network Management:** Balances bandwidth, latency, and power to optimize performance, such as prioritizing real-time traffic in autonomous vehicles.

Communication Technologies in the Network Layer

The Network Layer supports a range of wired and wireless technologies, each tailored to specific IoT applications and global deployment scenarios.

Wired Technologies

Wired communication technologies provide reliable, high-speed, and interference-free data transmission, making them ideal for industrial, automotive, and large-scale IoT deployments.

Feature	Wired Communication	Wireless Communication
Latency	Very Low and Predictable	Higher and More Variable
Reliability	High (Less susceptible to interference)	Moderate (Susceptible to interference, signal blockage, and range)
Deployment Cost	Higher (Cost of cabling, routing, and infrastructure)	Lower (Infrastructure typically limited to access points/base stations)

Table 2.1: *Comparison of Wired and Wireless Communication*

The following examples illustrate their practical applications across different domains:

- **Ethernet:** Offers high-speed (up to 1 Gbps), low-latency connectivity for fixed installations. Used in German factories for Siemens SIMATIC PLCs to connect to the SCADA systems.
- **CAN Bus:** A robust, real-time protocol for automotive and industrial applications, used in Japanese vehicle ECUs for sensor communication.
- **Modbus:** A simple, widely-used protocol for industrial automation, connecting sensors and actuators in Brazilian manufacturing plants.

Wireless Technologies

Wireless communication forms the backbone of modern IoT systems, enabling flexibility, scalability, and remote connectivity without physical cabling. Depending on range, power consumption, and data requirements, wireless technologies are categorized into **short-range** and **long-range** systems. The following examples demonstrate their diverse real-world applications:

- **Short-Range (10–100m):**
  - **Bluetooth Low Energy (BLE):** Low-power (1–10 mW), 1 Mbps data rate, ideal for wearables and smart homes. Used in Australian fitness trackers.
  - **Wi-Fi (802.11):** High-bandwidth (up to 1 Gbps), short-range, used in Singaporean smart homes for video streaming.

- **Zigbee/Z-Wave:** Low-power (10–100 mW), mesh networks with 20–250 kbps data rate, used in Japanese smart homes (Philips Hue lights).
- **Thread:** An IPv6-based, low-power mesh protocol, emerging in smart homes globally (Google Nest devices).

- **Long-Range (1–15 km)**

  LoRaWAN: Ultra-low-power (10 mW), long-range (up to 15 km), low-bandwidth (0.3 -- 50 kbps), used in Indian smart agriculture for soil sensor networks.

  - **NB-IoT:** Cellular-based, low-bandwidth (200 kbps), and long-range (10 km), used in Chinese smart meters for utility monitoring.
  - **5G:** High-bandwidth (up to 10 Gbps), and ultra-low latency (1 ms), used in Singaporean smart cities for real-time traffic management.

Application-Layer Protocols

Application-layer protocols define how IoT devices exchange data with servers, applications, and users. These protocols ensure efficient communication across networks with varying bandwidth, latency, and power constraints. The following are widely used application-layer protocols in IoT systems:

- **MQTT (Message Queuing Telemetry Transport):** Lightweight, publish-subscribe protocol for low-bandwidth, unreliable networks. Used in German smart factories for real-time sensor data transmission.
- **CoAP (Constrained Application Protocol):** Lightweight, REST-like protocol for constrained devices, used in Indian smart energy systems.
- **HTTP/REST:** Web-based, high-bandwidth protocol for cloud integration, used in Australian smart home apps.

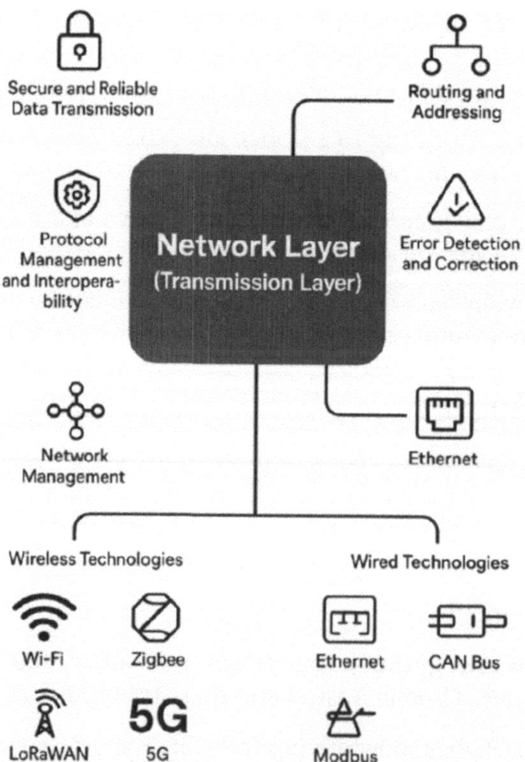

Figure 2.2: *IoT Connectivity Options Comparison*

Figure 2.2 illustrates when designing IoT systems, different communication technologies offer trade-offs in terms of range, power consumption, data rate, and deployment cost. For example, Wi-Fi provides high data rates but consumes more power, making it suitable for smart homes, while LoRaWAN and NB-IoT enable long-range communication with low power usage, ideal for agriculture and smart city applications. The following chart compares popular IoT connectivity options such as Wi-Fi, Bluetooth Low Energy (BLE), Zigbee, LoRaWAN, NB-IoT, and 5G, highlighting their strengths and typical use cases.

Application Layer

The Application Layer is the user-facing component of the IoT architecture, where data from the Perception and Network Layers is transformed into meaningful insights, automation, and control. This layer delivers value through dashboards, mobile apps, and integrations with business systems, enabling users to visualize data, make decisions, and interact with IoT devices. Critically, a poorly designed or implemented Application Layer can negate the benefits of a robust device and network infrastructure, as it is the point where the system's value is ultimately delivered (or fails to be delivered) to the user. From a farmer in Brazil monitoring crop health to a city planner in Singapore optimizing traffic, the Application Layer bridges IoT systems with end users, making it critical for delivering tangible benefits globally.

Functions of the Application Layer

The Application Layer performs several key functions to provide value to the users and organizations:

- **Data Visualization:** Presents data through graphs, dashboards, and alerts, making it accessible to non-technical users. For example, a smart home app in the US displays energy usage trends.
- **Advanced Analytics:** Uses AI, machine learning, or statistical models to derive insights, such as predicting equipment failures in German factories or crop yields in India.
- **Automation:** Implements rule-based or AI-driven triggers to automate tasks, like turning on irrigation in Australian farms when soil moisture drops below 30%.

The core idea is that connecting "things" (like machines or sensors) to big company systems helps things run smoother and faster.

Use Cases for Connecting IoT Data to Systems (Simplified for non-ERP/CRM Users):

- **Manufacturing/Maintenance:**
    - **Instead of:** A machine breaking down unexpectedly, stopping the whole factory.
    - **With Integration:** Sensors on a machine detect unusual vibration or heat (IoT data). This data is automatically sent to the company's **Maintenance System** (like an ERP function). The system then automatically creates a **work order** for a technician *before* the machine fails.
- **Supply Chain/Inventory:**
    - **Instead of:** An unexpected rush on a product causing an "out-of-stock" situation.
    - **With Integration:** A smart shelf or sensor (IoT) detects that the stock of a popular item is low. This triggers an alert in the company's **Inventory and Ordering System** (part of ERP) to automatically re-order the item from a supplier, ensuring that shelves stay full.
- **Customer Service/Field Operations:**
    - **Instead of:** A customer having to call in to report that their appliance (for example, smart HVAC, water heater) is malfunctioning.

  - **With Integration:** The appliance itself (IoT) detects an error and sends a diagnostic code to the company's **Customer Service System (CRM).** A support agent can then proactively call the customer with a fix, or the system can automatically dispatch a repair technician with the right parts, leading to a much better customer experience.
- **Sales and Marketing:**
  - **Instead of:** Sales staff guessing which customers are interested in a new service.
  - **With Integration:** A company's connected product (IoT) shows that a customer is frequently using a certain feature but not another. This usage data is sent to the **Sales and Marketing System** (CRM), which then suggests a specific add-on service or product to the sales team to pitch to that customer.
- **User Interaction**: Enables remote control and monitoring via mobile apps, web interfaces, or voice assistants.

Popular Cloud Platforms

The Application Layer in IoT systems relies on cloud and edge computing platforms to store, process, and analyze massive streams of sensor data. These platforms provide services ranging from real-time communication and analytics to device management and AI integration. The following are some of the most widely used cloud platforms across academic, industrial, and enterprise IoT deployments:

The Application Layer relies on cloud platforms and edge computing solutions to store, process, and analyze data. These platforms cater to different needs, from academic projects to enterprise-grade deployments:

- **ThingSpeak:** A beginner-friendly platform for academic projects, used in Indian universities for IoT prototyping.
- **Firebase:** A real-time database platform by Google, ideal for mobile app integration, used in Australian smart home apps.
- **Blynk:** A low-code platform for building IoT mobile apps, popular in South African smart home projects.
- **AWS IoT Core**: An enterprise-grade platform for scalable IoT deployments, used in Singaporean smart cities.
- **Microsoft Azure IoT Hub**: Enterprise platform with strong integration for business systems, used in US healthcare IoT.
- **Google Cloud IoT:** Offers advanced AI/ML capabilities, used in South Korean autonomous vehicle systems.

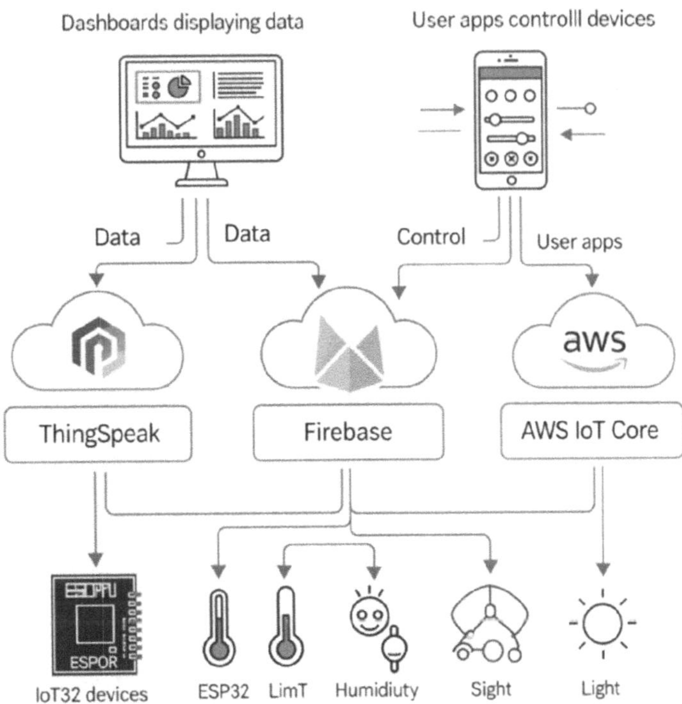

Figure 2.3: *Cloud Platforms in IoT Application Layer*

Figure 2.3 illustrates the IoT architecture, the application layer plays a vital role in enabling interaction between devices and the end users. Once the data is collected by IoT devices such as ESP32 and sensors, it is transmitted to cloud platforms like ThingSpeak, Firebase, or AWS IoT Core for storage, analysis, and visualization.

Role of Devices in IoT Ecosystem

In *Chapter* 1, we introduced the core components of IoT—sensors, actuators, and controllers—as the foundational building blocks that enable IoT systems to interact with the physical world. *Chapter* 2: *IoT Architecture and Ecosystem*, explored the three-layer IoT architecture (Perception, Network, and Application Layers), providing a framework for understanding how these components fit into a structured ecosystem. In this section, we place sensors, actuators, and controllers within the broader IoT ecosystem, examining their roles, interactions, and contributions for creating intelligent and responsive systems. Thus, by leveraging analogies—sensors as the eyes and ears, controllers as the brain, and actuators as the hands and legs—we illustrate how these devices work together to sense, process, and act, enabling IoT applications from smart homes.

The IoT ecosystem is a dynamic network of interconnected devices, networks, and applications that collaborate to collect data, make decisions, and perform actions. Devices in the Perception Layer form the critical interface between the physical and digital worlds, enabling real-world interaction. This section explores the roles of sensors, controllers, and actuators in detail, their integration across the three-layer architecture, and their impact on global IoT applications, supported by examples, technical considerations, and challenges.

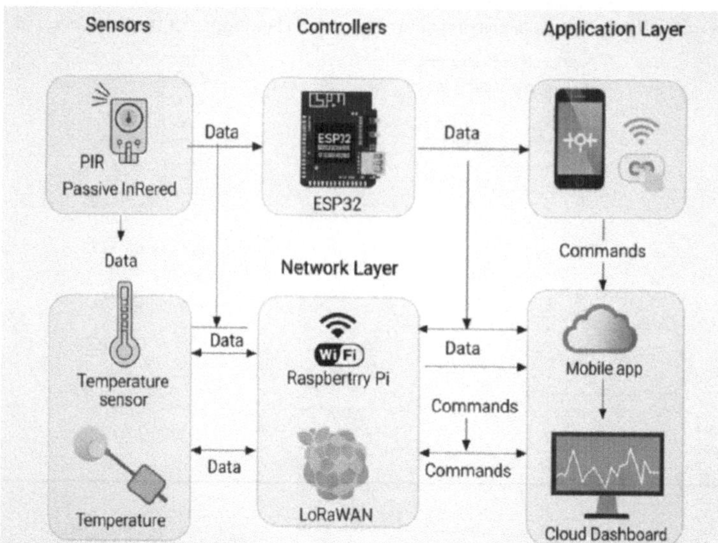

Figure 2.4: *Role of Devices in IoT Ecosystem*

Figure 2.4 illustrates IoT devices operate in layers, where sensors collect data, controllers such as ESP32 or Raspberry Pi process it, and networks such as Wi-Fi or LoRaWAN transmit it. At the application layer, cloud dashboards and mobile apps allow users to monitor and control devices. The above diagram shows this flow of data and commands across the IoT ecosystem.

Role of Sensors: The Eyes and Ears of IoT

Sensors are the sensory organs of IoT systems, acting as the *eyes and ears* that perceive and measure environmental conditions. They collect raw data from the physical world—such as temperature, humidity, motion, light, or biometric signals—and convert it into electrical or digital signals for processing. As the primary components of the Perception Layer, sensors enable IoT systems to monitor and respond to real-world changes, forming the foundation for applications like smart agriculture, healthcare wearables, and environmental monitoring.

Functions of Sensors

Sensors are the fundamental building blocks of IoT systems, responsible for perceiving the physical environment, and converting real-world phenomena into actionable digital data. They enable monitoring, event detection, and timely responses across diverse applications.

- **Environmental Monitoring:** Sensors detect physical parameters such as temperature in a smart thermostat or soil moisture in an irrigation system.
- **Data Acquisition:** Convert analog phenomena (for example, light intensity) into digital signals for controllers to process.
- **Event Detection:** Identify specific conditions, such as motion in a security system or heart rate anomalies in a wearable.
- **Real-Time Feedback:** Provide continuous or periodic data to enable timely responses, critical in applications like industrial IoT in Germany.

Types of Sensors

Sensors are classified based on their function, power requirements, or output type, with each suited to specific IoT applications:

- **Environmental Sensors:**
    - Temperature Sensors
    - Humidity Sensors
    - Light Sensors
- **Motion and Proximity Sensors:**
    - Passive Infrared (PIR)
    - Ultrasonic Sensors
- **Biometric Sensors:**
    - Heart Rate and SpO_2 Sensors
    - Fingerprint Sensors
- **Chemical and Gas Sensors:**
    - Air Quality Sensors
    - Soil Moisture Sensors

Role of Controllers: The Brain of IoT

Controllers serve as the *brain* of IoT systems, processing sensor data, making decisions, and coordinating actions within the Perception Layer. They range from simple microcontrollers for basic tasks to powerful edge nodes capable of running complex algorithms or AI models. Controllers bridge sensors and actuators, enabling local decision-making, data preprocessing, and communication with the Network Layer, making them essential for applications like smart homes in Japan, industrial automation in Germany, and healthcare in Canada.

Functions of Controllers

Sensors are the foundation of IoT systems, responsible for perceiving real-world conditions and converting them into digital data for intelligent decision-making. They enable accurate monitoring, event detection, and control across diverse applications. The primary functions of sensors include:

1. **Data Processing:** Filter, aggregate, or analyze the sensor data to reduce noise or extract insights.
2. **Decision-Making:** Apply logic or AI models to trigger actions, such as activating a pump when soil moisture is low in Indian agriculture.
3. **Device Coordination:** Manage communication between sensors, actuators, and networks, ensuring seamless operation.
4. **Power Management:** Optimize energy usage, critical for battery-powered devices such as wearables in Australia.
5. **Error Handling:** Detects and corrects issues, such as retrying failed sensor reads in industrial IoT systems in China.

Types of Controllers

Controllers in IoT systems vary in complexity and capability, from simple microcontrollers to powerful edge-computing devices. Selecting the appropriate controller depends on processing needs, connectivity, and the application environment. The common types of controllers include:

- **Microcontrollers:**
    - Arduino Uno
    - ESP32
    - STM32
- **Single-Board Computers (Edge Nodes):**
    - Raspberry Pi 4
    - NVIDIA Jetson Nano
- **Programmable Logic Controllers (PLCs)**

Role of Actuators: The Hands and Legs of IoT

Actuators are the *hands and legs* of IoT systems, translating digital commands into physical actions to interact with the environment. They execute decisions made by controllers, enabling automation and control in applications like smart homes in the UK, industrial systems in China, and irrigation in Brazil. Actuators complete the IoT feedback loop, turning data-driven insights into tangible outcomes.

Functions of Actuators

Actuators are the effectors in IoT systems, translating digital commands from controllers into physical actions. They enable automation, feedback, and direct interaction with the environment or users. **The main functions of actuators include:**

- **Physical Action:** Perform tasks like turning on lights, opening valves, or moving robotic arms based on controller commands.
- **Automation:** Execute rule-based or AI-driven actions, such as watering crops when the soil moisture is low.
- **Feedback Provision:** Some actuators (motors with encoders) provide feedback to controllers, ensuring precise control.
- **User Interaction:** Deliver notifications or responses, like haptic feedback in wearables or alarms in security systems.

Types of Actuators

Actuators come in various forms, each suited to specific tasks and application requirements. They can produce motion, force, or signals, depending on the system's needs. Some of the common types of actuators include:

- **Mechanical Actuators**
- **Electrical Actuators**
- **Auditory/Notification Actuators**
- **Hydraulic/Pneumatic Actuators**

Integration in the IoT Ecosystem

Sensors, controllers, and actuators work together within the three-layer IoT architecture to create a cohesive ecosystem. Their integration enables real-world interaction, data-driven decisions, and automation across diverse applications. The following example illustrates their roles and interactions:

Example: Smart Lighting System

- **Perception Layer:**
  - **Sensor:** A PIR sensor (HC-SR501) detects motion in a room, generating a digital signal when a person enters.
  - **Controller:** An ESP32 microcontroller processes the PIR signal, applying logic to determine if lights should turn on (only during nighttime).
  - **Actuator:** A 5V relay actuator switches on the connected LED lights.
- **Network Layer:**
  - The ESP32 uses Wi-Fi to send motion data to a cloud platform (for example, AWS IoT Core) and receives user commands (override automation).
  - A home router acts as a gateway, ensuring secure data transmission with TLS encryption.
- **Application Layer**:
  - A mobile app (Blynk) displays motion events and light status, allowing users to override automation or set schedules.
  - The cloud platform logs data for analytics such as energy usage trends.
- **Data Flow**:
  - The PIR sensor detects motion, sending a signal to the ESP32.
  - The ESP32 processes the signal, activates the relay, and sends data via Wi-Fi to AWS IoT Core.
  - The Blynk app visualizes motion events, and allows remote control, sending commands back to the ESP32 to adjust the relay.

Sensors, controllers, and actuators are the backbone of the IoT ecosystem, enabling real-world interaction through the Perception Layer. Sensors act as the *eyes and ears*, collecting data from the environment, as seen in Indian agriculture with soil moisture sensors. Controllers serve as the *brain*, processing data and making decisions, like ESP32s in Japanese smart homes. Actuators function as the *hands and legs*. Together these devices integrate with the Network and Application Layers to create cohesive IoT systems, as illustrated by the smart lighting example, where a PIR sensor, ESP32, and relay interact via Wi-Fi and a mobile app. Global applications, from Singaporean smart cities to European healthcare, highlight their versatility, while challenges like power efficiency, security, and interoperability underscore the need for careful design. Thus, emerging trends like edge AI, 5G, and Matter are shaping the future of IoT devices, enabling smarter, more scalable systems.

Gateways and Routers

In the Internet of Things (IoT), Gateways and Routers serve as critical intermediaries in the IoT ecosystem, bridging the gap between the Perception Layer (devices like sensors and actuators) and the Application Layer (cloud platforms and user interfaces). Building on introduction to IoT components, three-layer architecture, and exploration of device roles, this section examines how gateways and routers enable seamless connectivity, data aggregation, and protocol translation in the Network Layer.

Gateways aggregate data from multiple devices, translate protocols, perform edge computing, and enhance security, acting as the glue that connects heterogeneous devices to cloud platforms. Gateways are often the very first line of defense for security. Routers manage network traffic, ensuring reliable data delivery across local and external networks. Together, they enable IoT systems to scale globally, supporting applications like precision agriculture in India, healthcare in Europe, and smart grids in Brazil. This section explores their functions, technologies, challenges, and real-world applications, providing technical depth and practical insights for an international audience.

Role of Gateways

Gateways are pivotal in the IoT ecosystem, acting as *translators* and *coordinators* that connect resource-constrained devices in the Perception Layer to the broader Network and Application Layers. They aggregate data, translate protocols, perform edge computing, and enforce security, enabling interoperability and efficiency in IoT systems. Gateways are essential in scenarios where devices use low-power protocols that cannot directly connect to the internet, such as in smart homes, industrial plants, or remote agriculture deployments.

Functions of Gateways

Gateways perform several critical functions to ensure seamless IoT operation:

- **Data Aggregation:** Collect and consolidate data from multiple devices to reduce network traffic, and improve efficiency. For example, a gateway in a Singaporean smart city aggregates traffic sensor data before sending it to the cloud.
- **Protocol Translation**: Convert between incompatible protocols (Zigbee to Wi-Fi, BLE to MQTT) to enable communication across devices and networks. This is vital in Japanese smart homes where diverse devices interoperate.
- **Edge Computing**: Process data locally to reduce latency, filter noise, or run lightweight AI models, critical for real-time applications like autonomous vehicles in South Korea.
- **Security Enforcement**: Implement encryption, authentication and firewalls to protect data, especially in European healthcare IoT systems.
- **Device Management**: Monitor device health, manage firmware updates, and handle connectivity issues, ensuring reliability in large-scale deployments like Brazilian smart grids.
- **Load Balancing:** Distribute data traffic to prevent network congestion, as seen in German industrial IoT systems with thousands of sensors.

Feature	Gateway-Based Edge Computing	Device-Level Edge AI
Primary Location of Processing	Dedicated physical device (gateway) located near the data sources (devices) but often managing multiple devices.	Directly on the end-device itself (e.g., sensor, camera, phone, vehicle).
Scope of Data Processed	Aggregated data from multiple connected devices. Often handles pre-processing, filtering, and running larger, more complex AI models than individual devices could manage.	Data generated by that specific device (and sometimes very limited data from close neighbors). Focuses on immediate, lightweight AI tasks.
Processing Power/ Resources	Generally higher processing power, memory, and storage compared to individual end-devices. Can support more resource-intensive AI and analytics.	Limited by the device's battery, size, and cost constraints. Typically supports lightweight, optimized AI models (TinyML).
Latency	Low latency compared to the cloud, as processing occurs locally. However, there is still communication overhead between the device and the gateway.	Extremely low (near-zero) latency, as processing is instantaneous and local to the data generation.
Communication Need	Requires reliable, low-latency communication between end-devices and the gateway. Gateway then communicates with the cloud (often less frequently).	Often runs completely offline or only communicates with the cloud periodically to send processed insights or receive model updates.

Feature	Gateway-Based Edge Computing	Device-Level Edge AI
Scalability	Scalable by deploying more gateways to cover new physical areas or groups of devices. Each gateway can handle many devices.	Scalability is inherently tied to the number of individual devices deployed. Management and update of thousands of devices can be complex.
Cost	Higher initial cost per gateway unit, but potentially lower total cost of ownership when managing a large number of simple end-devices.	Lower cost per individual device, but the cumulative cost for large deployments can be significant, especially if specialized hardware is needed.
Use Cases	Industrial IoT (IIoT), smart city infrastructure (traffic light control), remote monitoring of large sites, data aggregation for fleet management.	Autonomous vehicle control (immediate object recognition), smart camera image analysis, wearable health monitors, predictive maintenance on individual machines.
Key Advantage	Centralized management, more powerful processing, ability to run complex models, and aggregate data from diverse sources.	Real-time decision-making, maximum privacy (data stays on the device), works reliably offline, and minimal network bandwidth usage.
Key Limitation	Introduces a physical point of failure (the gateway). Requires an intermediate communication step.	Limited processing power restricts the complexity of AI models. Harder to centrally manage and update models across a massive fleet of diverse devices.

Table 2.2: *Comparison of Gateway- based Edge Computing and Device- level Edge AI*

Types of Gateways

Gateways act as bridges between IoT devices and networks, enabling communication, protocol translation, and local data processing. Different types of gateways are used depending on the environment, connectivity requirements, and application complexity:

- **Home Automation Gateways:** SmartThings Hub and Philips Hue Bridge, used in UK smart homes to connect Zigbee/Z-Wave devices to Wi-Fi networks.
- **Industrial Gateways:** Cisco IR1101, used in Chinese factories for Ethernet-to-cloud connectivity.
- **IoT Edge Gateways:** Raspberry Pi 4 with custom software, used in Indian agriculture for LoRaWAN-to-Wi-Fi translation.
- **Cellular Gateways:** Sierra Wireless Air Link, used in Australian smart utilities for NB-IoT connectivity.

Role of Routers

Routers are the *traffic directors* of the IoT ecosystem, managing data flow between local networks and external networks. Operating primarily in the Network Layer, routers ensure reliable, efficient, and secure data transmission, enabling IoT systems to scale across diverse applications.

Functions of Routers

Routers are essential components of IoT networks, directing data, managing traffic, and ensuring secure and reliable communication between devices, gateways, and cloud platforms. Their primary functions include:

- **Data Routing**: Direct data packets between devices, gateways, and cloud platforms using IP addresses, ensuring efficient delivery.
- **Network Management**: Assign IP addresses (via DHCP), manage bandwidth, and prioritize traffic using Quality of Service (QoS) protocols, critical for real-time applications like autonomous vehicles in South Korea.
- **Security**: Implement firewalls, VPNs, and intrusion detection to protect IoT networks, especially in European healthcare systems.
- **Connectivity Bridging**: Connect local networks to external networks ensuring seamless communication.
- **Error Handling**: Detects and corrects transmission errors using protocols like TCP, vital in industrial IoT in Germany.

Types of Routers

Routers in IoT networks vary based on their application environment, performance requirements, and connectivity options. Selecting the appropriate router ensures reliable communication and efficient network management. The common types of routers include:

- Home Routers
- Industrial Routers
- Cellular Routers
- Edge Routers

Integration in the IoT Ecosystem

Gateways and routers work together to ensure seamless connectivity and data flow in the IoT ecosystem, bridging the Perception, Network, and Application Layers. Gateways aggregate and process data locally, translate protocols, and enforce security, while routers manage network traffic, and ensure reliable delivery to cloud platforms or external networks. Their integration is crucial for scalable, secure, and efficient IoT systems.

Example: Smart Home System

- **Perception Layer**: Zigbee-enabled light bulbs with PIR sensors (HC-SR501) detect motion, and send data to a controller (ESP32).
- **Network Layer:**
    - **Gateway:** A Zigbee hub aggregates data from multiple Zigbee devices, translates it to Wi-Fi, and performs edge computing to filter motion events.
    - **Router**: A TP-Link Archer router connects the hub to AWS IoT Core via Wi-Fi, ensuring secure data transmission with TLS.
- **Application Layer:** A mobile app displays motion events, and allows users to control lights remotely, with AWS IoT Core logging data for analytics.
- **Data Flow**:
    a. The PIR sensor detects motion, sending data to the ESP32.
    b. The ESP32 forwards data to the Zigbee hub, which aggregates and translates it to Wi-Fi.
    c. The router sends data to AWS IoT Core, which updates the mobile app.
    d. User commands follow the reverse path to the actuator.

Gateways and routers are essential intermediaries in the IoT ecosystem, enabling connectivity, data aggregation, and secure communication between the Perception, Network, and Application Layers. Thus, Gateways act as *translators*, aggregating data, translating protocols performing edge computing, and enforcing security, as seen in Japanese smart homes where Zigbee hubs connect to AWS IoT Core. Routers serve as *traffic* directors, managing data flow and ensuring reliable delivery, as in Singaporean smart cities using 5G routers. Global examples, from Indian agriculture to European healthcare, highlight their versatility, while challenges such as interoperability, security, and scalability underscore the need for careful design. Emerging trends like 5G, edge computing, and Matter are shaping their future, enabling smarter, more scalable IoT systems.

Data Flow in IoT Systems

Understanding how data flows through an IoT system is essential for designing efficient, scalable, and secure solutions. This section examines the data flow process, tracing data from sensors to dashboards or actuators. Think of data flow as a *postal system*: sensors send letters (data), controllers package them, networks deliver them, and applications open or respond with actions. We will cover the typical data flow, key protocols (HTTP, MQTT), global examples, and challenges, ensuring relevance for an international audience. Think of data flow as a *postal system*: sensors send letters (data), controllers package them, networks deliver them, and applications open or respond with actions.

Typical Data Flow in IoT Systems

Data flows through IoT systems in a structured pipeline across the Perception, Network, and Application Layers, transforming raw measurements into insights or actions. The following are the key stages, illustrated with a smart agriculture example:

- **Data Acquisition (Perception Layer):**
  - **Function:** Sensors capture environmental data.
  - **Example:** A YL-69 soil moisture sensor in an Indian farm measures 25% moisture.
  - **Components:** Sensors
  - **Process:** Sensors convert physical signals into digital data.
- **Data Formatting and Processing (Perception Layer):**
  - **Function:** Controllers format data into payloads, and process it locally.
  - **Example:** An ESP32 formats soil moisture data: {"sensor"; "soil_1", "value": 25 }.
  - **Components:** Microcontrollers
  - **Process:** Controllers aggregate data or apply logic.
- **Data Transmission (Network Layer):**
  - **Function:** Data is sent to gateways, routers, or cloud platforms via wired or wireless protocols.
  - **Example:** The ESP32 sends JSON via MQTT to a LoRaWAN gateway, then to The Things Network.
  - **Components:** Gateways (for example, Raspberry Pi), routers (for example, TP-Link).
  - **Process:** Protocols like MQTT ensure secure, and reliable transmission.
- **Cloud Storage and Processing (Application Layer):**
  - **Function:** Cloud platforms store and analyze data for insights or automation.
  - **Example:** The Things Network stores soil moisture data, and predicts irrigation needs.

- **Components:** Cloud platforms (for example, ThingSpeak, AWS IoT Core).
- **Process:** Data is stored in databases, and processed with analytics tools.

- **Visualization and Automation (Application Layer):**
  - **Function:** Applications display data or trigger actions via dashboards or actuators.
  - **Example:** A ThingSpeak dashboard shows moisture trends, triggering a solenoid valve if moisture < 30%.
  - **Components:** Dashboards (for example, Blynk), actuators (for example, relays).
  - **Process:** Dashboards render data, and automation rules or user commands activate actuators.

Protocols for Data Transmission

Protocols manage data transmission in the Network Layer, balancing efficiency, power, and reliability. HTTP and MQTT are the most common, with others like CoAP used for specific needs.

Guiding Principles and Decision Logic for Choosing Network Layer Protocols (HTTP, MQTT, CoAP)

Protocol	Primary Use Case / Environment	Key Characteristics	Decision Logic / When to Use
HTTP (Hypertext Transfer Protocol)	Web services, traditional client-server communication, high-bandwidth networks, and applications requiring robust security (with HTTPS).	Synchronous, stateless (often uses session management), relatively high overhead, universally supported, reliable, request-response model.	**Use when:** High bandwidth is available, the application is request-response driven (e.g., fetching large data/web pages, standard API calls), real-time low-latency is not critical, or robust, standard web security (TLS/SSL) is mandatory.
MQTT (Message Queuing Telemetry Transport)	IoT, constrained networks, unreliable links, applications requiring low power consumption and high throughput of small messages.	Asynchronous, publish-subscribe model, low overhead, low power consumption, built-in Quality of Service (QoS 0, 1, 2) for reliability, requires a central broker.	**Use when:** Devices have limited power/memory/bandwidth (e.g., sensors), many devices need to communicate with a central service, the communication pattern is event-driven or broadcast (one-to-many), and efficient resource utilization is paramount.
CoAP (Constrained Application Protocol)	Highly constrained devices and networks (e.g., 6LoWPAN), where power and processing resources are extremely limited.	RESTful architecture over UDP (low overhead), supports resource discovery, asynchronous messages, includes basic reliability (re-transmissions).	**Use when:** The network or device constraints are too severe for MQTT (e.g., extremely low power budget, need to run on UDP only), and a lightweight, REST-like interaction model is desired for accessing resources on the device.

Table 2.3: *Network Layer Protocols*

HTTP (Hypertext Transfer Protocol)

- **Description:** A request-response protocol for web applications, using TCP/IP.
- **Characteristics:** JSON/XML payloads, high bandwidth (100 KB–1 MB), HTTPS for security, and moderate latency (100–500 ms).
- **Pros:** Easy for web apps, widely supported (for example, Japanese smart home dashboards).

- **Cons:** Power-intensive, less scalable for constrained devices.
- **Use Case:** Smart home apps in Australia using HTTP to fetch data from Firebase.

MQTT (Message Queuing Telemetry Transport)

- **Description:** A lightweight publish-subscribe protocol for low-bandwidth, unreliable networks.
- **Characteristics:** Binary/JSON payloads, low bandwidth (1–10 KB), TLS for security, and low latency (10–50 ms).
- **Pros:** Power-efficient, scalable for large deployments (for example, Indian agriculture).
- **Cons:** Needs a broker (for example, Mosquitto).
- **Use Case:** A German industrial IoT, publishing sensor data to Azure IoT Hub.

Other Protocols

- **CoAP:** Lightweight, REST-like, UDP-based for constrained devices, used in Brazilian smart grids.
- **AMQP:** Robust for enterprise IoT, used in Chinese factories for SAP integration.
- **WebSocket:** Bidirectional for real-time apps, used in US smart homes.

Thus, data flows through IoT systems from sensors to dashboards or actuators, following a pipeline across the Perception, Network, and Application Layers. Sensors collect data (for example, soil moisture), controllers format it (for example, JSON), networks transmit it via HTTP/MQTT, clouds process it, and applications visualize or automate actions. Global examples like Indian agriculture and Singaporean smart cities, show its impact. MQTT's lightweight design suits low-power IoT, while HTTP fits web apps. Challenges such as scalability and security, and trends like 5G and edge computing, shape efficient data flow in IoT ecosystems.

Real-World IoT Architecture Examples

The Internet of Things (IoT) transforms industries and daily life through interconnected systems that sense, process, and act on data. Previous sections—*Chapter* 1's fundamentals, three-layer architecture, device roles, gateways and routers, and data flow—laid the groundwork for understanding IoT ecosystems. This section illustrates how these concepts come together in real-world applications, specifically a **Smart Irrigation System** and a **Home Automation System**. Think of IoT systems as *orchestras*: sensors play the notes, controllers conduct, networks carry the sound, and applications deliver the performance to the audience. We will explore these systems through the three-layer architecture, highlighting components, protocols, automation, and global applications in regions like India, Singapore, Europe, and Brazil, ensuring relevance for an international audience.

Smart Irrigation System

The **Smart Irrigation System** optimizes water usage in agriculture by monitoring soil conditions and automating irrigation, crucial in water-scarce regions like India and Brazil. This system integrates the three-layer IoT architecture to collect data, transmit it over long distances, and enable remote monitoring and control.

Architecture Breakdown

IoT architectures are typically organized into layers, each responsible for specific tasks—from sensing the environment to delivering actionable insights. The three-layer model consists of the Perception Layer, Network Layer, and Application Layer.

- **Perception Layer**:
    - **Components**:
        - **Soil Moisture Sensor:** YL-69 sensor measures soil moisture (0–100% RH, ±5% accuracy), detecting water content in soil.
        - **ESP32 Microcontroller:** Dual-core, 520 KB SRAM, processes sensor data, and controls actuators.
        - **Solenoid Valve:** 12V valve actuator opens/closes to regulate the water flow.
    - **Function:** The YL-69 sensor collects moisture data (e.g., 25% RH), the ESP32 formats it and decides if irrigation is needed, and the solenoid valve acts on commands.
    - **Example:** In an Indian rice field, the ESP32 reads moisture every 10 minutes, triggering the valve if moisture < 30%.
- **Network Layer:**
    - **Components:** The LoRaWAN module (for example: SX1276, 10–15 km range, 0.3–50 kbps), LoRaWAN gateway (for example: Kerlink Wirnet), a cellular router (for example: Sierra Wireless Air Link).
    - **Function:** The ESP32 sends JSON payloads (`{"sensor": "soil_1", "value": 25 }`) via LoRaWAN to a gateway, which translates to Wi-Fi or 4G for cloud connectivity.
    - **Example:** A LoRaWAN gateway in rural Brazil aggregates data from multiple sensors, forwarding it to The Things Network.
- **Application Layer**:
    - **Components:** ThingSpeak cloud platform, mobile/web dashboard.
    - **Function:** ThingSpeak stores data, visualizes moisture trends, and triggers automation (for example, valve opens if moisture < 30%).
    - **Example**: A farmer in India uses a ThingSpeak dashboard to monitor fields remotely, reducing water usage by 30%.

Automation Logic

Automation in IoT systems allows devices to respond intelligently to sensor data without human intervention. The logic is typically implemented on controllers, such as microcontrollers or edge devices such as:

- **Rule**: If soil moisture < 30%, the ESP32 sends a command to open the solenoid valve for 10 minutes, and then rechecks the moisture.

Challenges

Implementing IoT systems in real-world environments comes with several technical and operational challenges. These factors must be addressed to ensure reliable, scalable, and cost-effective deployments:

- **Power**: Battery-powered sensors in remote fields need low-power LoRaWAN (10 mW).
- **Range**: LoRaWAN's 10–15 km range suits rural deployments but requires gateway placement.
- **Cost**: Affordable sensors ($2–5) and gateways are critical for large-scale farms in India.

Home Automation System

The **Home Automation System** enhances comfort, security, and energy efficiency in homes by automating devices such as lights and fans, widely adopted in urban areas like Japan and the UK. This system leverages the three-layer architecture to integrate sensors, local networks, and user-friendly apps.

Architecture Breakdown

IoT architectures are typically organized into layers that handle sensing, communication, and application-level processing. In a smart home setup, the three-layer model—Perception Layer, Network Layer, and Application Layer—demonstrates how devices interact seamlessly.

- **Perception Layer:**
    - **Components:**
        - **PIR Sensor:** HC-SR501 detects motion (5–7 m range, <100 µA power).
        - **Temperature Sensor:** DHT22 measures temperature/humidity (±0.5°C, 2–5% RH accuracy).
        - **Relays:** 5V single-channel relays control lights and fans.
        - **ESP32 Microcontroller:** Manages sensor data and relay actuation.
    - **Function:** The PIR sensor detects motion, the DHT22 monitors temperature, and the ESP32 controls relays based on sensor inputs or user commands.
    - **Example:** In an apartment, the ESP32 turns on lights when motion is detected at night.
- **Network Layer:**
    - **Components:** Zigbee module (for example, CC2530, 10–100 m range, and 250 kbps), Wi-Fi router (for example, TP-Link Archer), and Zigbee gateway (for example, SmartThings Hub).
    - **Function:** Zigbee enables local mesh networking for sensors and relays; the gateway translates to Wi-Fi for cloud connectivity.
    - **Example:** In a UK home, Zigbee sensors send data to a SmartThings Hub, which uses Wi-Fi to connect to the Blynk cloud.
- **Application Layer:**
    - **Components:** Blynk mobile app, cloud platform.
    - **Function:** The Blynk app displays temperature and motion data, allowing users to control lights/fans remotely.
    - **Example:** A homeowner in Singapore uses Blynk to adjust fan speed based on temperature, saving 15% energy.

Automation Logic

Automation in IoT systems enables devices to respond intelligently to environmental conditions without manual intervention. Controllers such as microcontrollers or edge devices, execute predefined rules or AI-driven logic to manage connected actuators.

- **Rule:** If motion is detected and temperature > 25°C, the ESP32 activates the fan and light relays.

Challenges

Implementing smart home IoT systems introduces several practical challenges that affect performance, reliability, and security:

- **Interoperability:** Zigbee and Wi-Fi integration requires robust gateways, critical in European smart homes.
- **Security:** Encryption (TLS) is needed to protect the user data, especially in UK homes.
- **Power:** Battery-powered sensors need low-power Zigbee (10 mW) for longevity.

Thus, real-world IoT architectures like smart irrigation and home automation systems, demonstrate the three-layer model in action. The smart irrigation system uses YL-69 sensors, ESP32, LoRaWAN, and ThingSpeak to optimize water use in India, while the home automation system leverages PIR/DHT22 sensors, Zigbee, Wi-Fi, and Blynk for energy-efficient control in Japan. Global examples in healthcare and smart cities highlight IoT's versatility. Challenges like scalability and security, and trends like 5G and Matter, shape real-world IoT deployments.

Integration of Hardware and Cloud Services

Integrating hardware with cloud services is where the Internet of Things (IoT) unlocks its true potential, transforming the raw sensor data into actionable insights, and remote control capabilities. Building on Chapter 1's introduction to IoT components, real-world examples, this section explores how hardware (sensors, microcontrollers) connects to cloud platforms to enable real-time monitoring, analytics, and automation. Think of hardware-cloud integration as a *relay race*: sensors pass data to controllers, which hand it off to networks, and cloud services cross the finish line with visualizations or actions. We will focus on connecting an ESP32 microcontroller with ThingSpeak, detailing each step, and extend the discussion with global examples, technical insights, and challenges, ensuring relevance for an international audience of students, educators, and professionals.

Steps to Connect ESP32 with ThingSpeak

The ESP32, a versatile, Wi-Fi-enabled microcontroller, integrates seamlessly with cloud platforms like ThingSpeak to enable real-time data monitoring and control. In the following paragraph, we outline the steps to connect an ESP32 with ThingSpeak, using a temperature sensor (DHT22) as an example, followed by global applications and technical considerations.

1. **Program ESP32 in Arduino IDE**
   a. **Function:** Write firmware to configure the ESP32 for sensor data collection, formatting, and cloud communication.
   b. **Process:**
      i. Install the Arduino IDE and ESP32 board support (via Boards Manager).
      ii. Include libraries: DHT.h for sensor interfacing, WiFi.h for connectivity, and HTTPClient.h for ThingSpeak communication.
      iii. Configure Wi-Fi credentials and ThingSpeak API keys.
   c. **Technical Details:** The ESP32 (dual-core, 520 KB SRAM, 240 MHz) supports Wi-Fi (802.11 b/g/n, up to 150 Mbps) and interfaces with sensors via GPIO pins (I2C, SPI).
2. **Collect Sensor Data**
   a. **Function:** Read the environmental data from sensors connected to the ESP32.

   b. **Process:** The ESP32 polls the DHT22 sensor every 15 seconds to measure the temperature and humidity (±0.5°C, ±2–5% RH accuracy).

   c. **Technical Details:** The DHT22 uses a single-wire protocol, connected to a GPIO pin (for example, pin 4), with pull-up resistors for stable readings.

3. **Format Data in JSON**

   a. **Function:** Structure the sensor data into a JSON payload for cloud transmission.

   b. **Process:** The ESP32 formats temperature and humidity data into a JSON string, **e** `{"field1": 22.5, "field2": 60 }`.

   c. **Technical Details**: JSON is lightweight and interoperable, widely supported by cloud platforms like ThingSpeak, ensuring compatibility across global IoT systems.

4. **Send to ThingSpeak Channel Using HTTP POST**

   a. **Function:** Transmit the JSON payload to a ThingSpeak channel via HTTP POST.

   b. **Process:** The ESP32 sends data to ThingSpeak's REST API (api.thingspeak.com/update) using the HTTPClient library, authenticated with an API key.

   c. **Technical Details:** HTTP POST uses HTTPS (TLS encryption) for security, with payloads limited to 8 fields per ThingSpeak channel (free tier).

5. **Visualize in Real-Time Dashboard**

   a. **Function:** Display data on a ThingSpeak dashboard for monitoring or trigger automation.

   b. **Process:** ThingSpeak stores data in a time-series database, rendering it as graphs or gauges on a web/mobile dashboard.

   c. **Example:** A dashboard shows temperature and humidity trends, with alerts if temperature > 30°C.

   d. **Technical Details:** ThingSpeak supports MATLAB analytics for advanced processing (for example, trend prediction) and integrates with the mobile apps via APIs.

Challenges in Hardware-Cloud Integration

- **Interoperability:** Ensuring hardware (for example, ESP32) supports cloud protocols (HTTP, MQTT) in multinational systems, critical in European smart homes.
- **Security:** GDPR-compliant encryption (TLS) is vital for healthcare IoT in Europe to prevent data breaches
- **Scalability:** Managing thousands of devices in Singapore smart cities requires robust cloud platforms.
- **Power:** Battery-powered ESP32s in remote Brazilian farms need low-power protocols like MQTT.
- **Cost:** Affordable hardware and cloud services are key for deployments in India.

Thus, integrating hardware with cloud services empowers IoT systems to deliver real-time insights and automation. Connecting an ESP32 to ThingSpeak involves programming in Arduino IDE, collecting sensor data, formatting it as JSON, sending via HTTP POST, and visualizing on a dashboard. Global examples like smart agriculture in India and smart homes in Japan, show its impact. Challenges such as security and scalability, and trends like 5G and edge computing, shape effective hardware-cloud integration for international IoT deployments.

Importance of Scalability, Modularity, and Low-Power Design

For IoT systems to thrive in diverse applications—from smart cities in Singapore to remote agriculture in Brazil—three design principles are critical: **scalability**, **modularity**, and **low-power design**. These principles ensure that IoT ecosystems can handle massive deployments, adapt to changing needs, and operate efficiently in resource-constrained environments. Thus, building on Chapter 1's fundamentals, Chapter 2.1's three-layer architecture, Chapter 2.2's device roles, Chapter 2.3's gateways, Chapter 2.4's data flow, Chapter 2.5's real-world examples, and Chapter 2.6's hardware-cloud integration, this section explores how these principles enable robust IoT systems. Think of an IoT system as a *city*: scalability supports growing populations (devices), modularity allows infrastructure upgrades, and low-power design ensures sustainable energy use. Next, we will examine each principle with technical details, global examples, challenges, and future trends, ensuring relevance for an international audience.

Scalability

This ensures IoT systems can handle thousands or millions of devices without compromising performance, critical for large-scale deployments like smart cities or industrial IoT. It involves designing networks, protocols, and cloud infrastructure to manage increasing data volumes, device connections, and processing demands efficiently. Other key scalability concerns include Device Provisioning (the ability to onboard new devices quickly and securely), and Fleet Management (efficiently monitoring, updating, and maintaining a large, dispersed set of devices).

Key Aspects

- **Network Scalability:** Use protocols like LoRaWAN or MQTT to handle high device counts with low bandwidth (for example, 0.3–50 kbps for LoRaWAN).
- **Cloud Scalability:** Leverage platforms like AWS IoT Core or Azure IoT Hub to manage massive datasets and device fleets.
- **Device Management:** Implement Over-the-Air (OTA) updates and dynamic addressing (DHCP) to support the growing networks.

Example: Smart City Streetlights in Singapore

- **Context**: A smart city deploys 10,000 LoRaWAN-enabled streetlights to optimize energy use.
- **Implementation**:
  - **Perception Layer:** Each streetlight has a light sensor and ESP32 microcontroller.
  - **Network Layer:** LoRaWAN gateways (for example, Kerlink Wirnet) aggregate data from thousands of lights, forwarding it via 5G to AWS IoT Core.
  - **Application Layer:** A dashboard adjusts brightness based on ambient light, reducing energy costs by 20%.
- **Scalability Features:** LoRaWAN's low-bandwidth mesh topology supports thousands of devices as well as AWS IoT Core scales to millions of messages per second.
- **Impact:** Saves 15–20% energy across Singapore's urban areas.

Modularity

This allows IoT systems to be flexible, with components (hardware, software, or protocols) that are easily replaceable or upgradable without overhauling the entire system. This ensures adaptability to new technologies, vendor changes, or application requirements, critical for long-term IoT deployments.

Key Aspects

- **Hardware Modularity:** Use standard interfaces (I2C, SPI) for swapping sensors or modules (Wi-Fi to LoRa).
- **Software Modularity:** Adopt open-source platforms (OpenHAB) for protocol flexibility.
- **Interoperability:** Support standards like Matter to integrate diverse devices.

Example: Replacing Wi-Fi with LoRa in a Smart Home

- **Context:** A UK smart home upgrades from Wi-Fi to LoRa for longer-range connectivity.
- **Implementation:**
  - **Original System:** ESP32 with Wi-Fi connects DHT22 sensors to a Blynk app.
  - **Upgrade:** Replace Wi-Fi module with a LoRa module (SX1276) without changing the ESP32 or sensors, using I2C for compatibility.
  - **Network Layer:** A LoRaWAN gateway (The Things Indoor Gateway) connects to ThingSpeak via 4G.
  - **Application Layer:** The Blynk app continues to visualize data seamlessly.
- **Modularity Features:** I2C interface ensures sensor compatibility; open-source firmware supports both Wi-Fi and LoRa.
- **Impact:** Extends range from 100 m (Wi-Fi) to 10 km (LoRa) for rural homes.

Technical Considerations

- Use standard interfaces (for example, I2C, SPI, and UART) for hardware compatibility.
- Adopt open-source platforms (for example, Home Assistant) for protocol flexibility.
- Implement Matter or Thread for seamless device integration.

Low-Power Design

It ensures that IoT devices operate for months or years on battery power, critical for remote or resource-constrained applications like agriculture or environmental monitoring. It minimizes energy consumption, while maintaining functionality, often by sacrificing some processing latency to achieve greater power savings.

Key Aspects

- **Sleep Modes:** Devices enter low power states (for example, ESP32 deep sleep at <10 µA) between tasks.
- **Efficient Protocols:** Use low-bandwidth protocols such as LoRaWAN or BLE (1–10 mW).
- **Energy Harvesting:** Leverage solar or vibration energy to extend the battery life.

Example: Soil Sensors in Agriculture

- **Context:** Soil moisture sensors in Brazilian farms use LoRaWAN and sleep modes.
- **Implementation:**
  - **Perception Layer:** YL-69 sensor (1 mW) and ESP32 in deep sleep mode collect moisture data every 30 minutes.
  - **Network Layer:** LoRaWAN (10 mW, 10 km range) sends data to a gateway.
  - **Application Layer:** ThingSpeak visualizes data, triggering irrigation if needed.
- **Low-Power Features:** ESP32's deep sleep consumes <10 µA; LoRaWAN's low bandwidth minimizes transmission energy.

- **Impact:** Sensors last 2–3 years on a single AA battery, reducing maintenance costs by 25%.

Thus, scalability, modularity, and low-power design are critical for successful IoT systems. Scalability supports thousands of devices, as in Singapore's 10,000 streetlights. Modularity enables upgrades, like swapping Wi-Fi for LoRa in UK smart homes. Low-power design ensures long battery life, as in Brazilian soil sensors lasting 2 years. Global examples highlight their impact, while challenges such as cost and security, and trends like 5G and energy harvesting, shape future IoT deployments.

Practical Exercises

Practical exercises are essential for mastering IoT concepts by applying theoretical knowledge from Chapter 1 (fundamentals), Chapter 2.1 (three-layer architecture), Chapter 2.2 (device roles), Chapter 2.3 (gateways), Chapter 2.4 (data flow), Chapter 2.5 (real-world examples), Chapter 2.6 (hardware-cloud integration), and Chapter 2.7 (design principles). These exercises—**Architecture Mapping with Real Devices**, **Protocol Debug Lab**, and **Cloud Platform Playground**—enable students to explore IoT systems hands-on, from designing architectures to simulating protocols and interacting with cloud platforms. Think of IoT as a *pipeline*: sensors collect water (data), networks channel it, and cloud platforms process and display it.

Exercise 1: Architecture Mapping with Real Devices

Task: Select a real IoT system (Smart Home, Precision Farming, or Smart Healthcare) and map its three-layer architecture (Perception, Network, Application) to understand how components interact.

Steps:

1. **Identify Perception Layer:** Select sensors (DHT22 for temperature, YL-69 for soil moisture, MAX30102 for heart rate) and controllers (ESP32, Arduino).

   Example: For a Smart Home in Japan, use a PIR sensor (HC-SR501, 5–7 m range) and ESP32 (dual-core, 520 KB SRAM).

2. **Identify Network Layer:** Specify connectivity protocols (Wi-Fi, Zigbee, LoRaWAN) and gateways/routers (SmartThings Hub, TP-Link Archer).

   Example: Use Zigbee for local communication and Wi-Fi for cloud connectivity in a Smart Home.

3. **Identify Application Layer**: Choose a cloud platform (Firebase, Blynk, ThingSpeak) or app for visualization/control.

   Example: Blynk app for real-time control of lights in a Smart Home.

4. **Create a Block Diagram**:

   a. Draw a diagram showing data flow: sensors → controller → gateway/router → cloud → dashboard/actuator.

   b. Use tools like draw.io or Lucidchart for professional diagrams.

5. **Annotate Key Points**: Mark data collection (sensor readings), transfer (MQTT payload), processing (for example, cloud analytics), and visualization (dashboard graphs).

Exercise 2: Protocol Debug Lab

Task: Simulate HTTP and MQTT protocols without hardware to compare request-response (HTTP) and publish-subscribe (MQTT) models, understanding their roles in IoT data transmission (Chapter 2.4).

Steps:

1. **HTTP Simulation**:
    a. Use Postman or ReqBin to send a JSON payload to a test endpoint (e.g., https://webhook.site).
    b. **Payload**: `{"sensor_id": "101", "temp": 28.7 }`.
    c. Configure an HTTP POST request with the URL and payload.
    d. Observe the response (status code 200) and note request-response latency (~100–500 ms).
2. **MQTT Simulation**:
    a. Use HiveMQ Web Client (client.hivemq.com) to simulate MQTT communication.
    b. **Subscribe**: Connect to the public broker (broker.hivemq.com, port 1883) and subscribe to iot/test/temp.
    c. **Publish**: Send a message: {"humidity": 55 } to iot/test/temp.
    d. Observe real-time message delivery and note low latency (~10–50 ms).
3. **Compare HTTP and MQTT**:
    a. **Analyze differences:** HTTP's request-response model (higher bandwidth, synchronous) vs. MQTT's publish-subscribe model (low bandwidth, asynchronous).
    b. **Document trade-offs**: HTTP for web apps (for example, dashboards in Japan), MQTT for low-power IoT (agriculture in India).

Exercise 3: Cloud Platform Playground

Task: Explore ThingSpeak and Firebase to understand how IoT cloud platforms structure, store, and visualize data, reinforcing hardware-cloud integration.

Steps:

1. **ThingSpeak Exploration:**
    a. Create a free ThingSpeak account (**`thingspeak.com`**) and set up a channel.
    b. Add fields: Temperature (**`field1`**) and Humidity (**`field2`**).
    c. Simulate data: Use ThingSpeak's REST API to send **`{ "field1": 22.5, "field2": 60 }`** via a tool like Postman Visualize data on a dashboard with line graphs or gauges.
2. **Firebase Exploration:**
    a. Create a Firebase project (**`console.firebase.google.com`**) and enable the Real-time Database.
    b. Manually add objects: **`{"sensor_id": "101", "temp": 22.5, "humidity": 60, "timestamp": "2025-09-10T11:43:00Z" }`**.
    c. Observe real-time updates in the Firebase console.
3. **Compare Platforms:**
    a. Note ThingSpeak's focus on time-series data and visualization vs. Firebase's flexible NoSQL structure for real-time apps.
    b. Document the ease of setup, scalability, and use cases (ThingSpeak for agriculture, Firebase for mobile apps).

Learning Outcomes

- **Exercise 1**: Master the three-layer IoT architecture by mapping real systems, applicable to global contexts like Japanese smart homes.
- **Exercise 2**: Understand HTTP versus: MQTT trade-offs, preparing for protocol selection in Indian agriculture or German industrial IoT.
- **Exercise 3**: Gain hands-on experience with cloud platforms, enabling hardware-cloud integration for Brazilian farming or European healthcare.

These practical exercises reinforce IoT concepts through hands-on tasks. Architecture Mapping maps real systems (Smart Farming) to the three-layer model. Protocol Debug Lab compares HTTP and MQTT using Postman and HiveMQ, highlighting their roles in IoT. Cloud Platform Playground explores ThingSpeak and Firebase for data visualization. Global contexts, from India to Europe, ensure relevance, while challenges like accessibility and trends such as cloud scalability enhance learning for IoT system design.

Conclusion

The Internet of Things (IoT) evolves from individual components to a dynamic ecosystem, seamlessly integrating hardware, networks, and cloud services to create intelligent, data-driven solutions across global industries. Chapter 2 builds on Chapter 1's fundamentals, presenting IoT as a *digital nervous system*—sensors and actuators as sensory organs, controllers and networks as nerves, and cloud platforms as the brain. This chapter explored the **three-layer architecture** (Perception, Network, Application), detailing such as:

- **Perception Layer:** Sensors (YL-69 for soil moisture) and actuators (solenoid valves) collect data and perform actions, as seen in Indian agriculture.
- **Network Layer:** Gateways (SmartThings Hub) and routers (TP-Link Archer) enable connectivity via protocols like LoRaWAN and Wi-Fi, supporting Singapore's smart cities.
- **Application Layer:** Cloud platforms (ThingSpeak and AWS IoT Core) and apps (for example, Blynk) provide analytics and visualization, driving automation in European healthcare.

We examined device roles—sensors as eyes and ears, controllers as brains, and actuators as hands—illustrated by smart irrigation systems saving 30% water in Brazil. Gateways and routers bridge devices to clouds, translating protocols (Zigbee to Wi-Fi) for Japanese smart homes. Data flow was traced from sensors to dashboards using HTTP and MQTT, with MQTT's lightweight design powering low-power applications in India. Real-world examples, like smart irrigation (India) and home automation (Japan), showcased practical implementations, while hardware-cloud integration connected ESP32s to ThingSpeak for real-time monitoring. Scalability, modularity, and low-power design ensure robust systems, supporting 10,000 streetlights in Singapore or 2-year battery life for Brazilian sensors. Practical exercises such as architecture mapping, protocol debugging, and cloud platform exploration—bridged theory and practice, preparing learners to design IoT systems.

In fact, IoT's importance lies in its ability to scale, adapt, and optimize resources, enhancing efficiency in agriculture, healthcare, and smart cities worldwide. As IoT advances with 5G, edge AI, and standards like Matter, it addresses challenges like security and interoperability, reshaping industries. This chapter equips learners to design and implement IoT solutions that integrate hardware, software, and cloud services, paving the way for innovative, scalable, and sustainable systems globally.

The next chapter will focus on sensor technologies, covering analog, digital, and smart sensors, their datasheets, voltage levels, and signal formats. You will learn calibration and reading techniques for accurate data collection, and practice interfacing sensors (temperature, motion, gas, light, and sound) and actuators (relays, motors, servos, buzzers, and displays) with ESP32 or Arduino. Key topics like power handling, voltage requirements, and protection will be included, with real-world examples such as intrusion detection and automatic fan control to provide hands-on IoT experience.

Chapter 3
Sensor Technologies and Actuators

Introduction

The Internet of Things (IoT) transforms the physical world into a responsive digital ecosystem, with the Perception Layer as its cornerstone, where sensing and action converge. In *Chapter* 2, we explored the IoT ecosystem through the three-layer architecture—Perception, Network, Application—detailing how devices like sensors and controllers interact with gateways and routers to enable data flow via protocols such as HTTP and MQTT. We examined real-world systems, such as smart irrigation and home automation, and emphasized hardware-cloud integration, scalability, modularity, and low-power design through practical exercises like architecture mapping and protocol debugging. This chapter dives deeper into the Perception Layer, where sensors, acting as the *eyes and ears* of an IoT system, detect environmental changes such as temperature, motion, or light, and actuators, the *muscles*, execute actions such as switching relays or rotating motors. Reliable sensors ensure accurate data for decision-making, while actuators complete the loop by effecting physical change.

This chapter explores sensor types—analog, digital, and smart and how sensors work, covering data sheets, voltage levels (3.3V–5V), and signal formats (I2C, analog). Sensor calibration and reading techniques include offset correction and polling or interrupt methods for accuracy. We will work with specific sensors: temperature, motion, gas, light, and sound, interfacing sensors with ESP32 or Arduino involves GPIO, ADC, or I2C, using libraries in Arduino IDE, with pull-up/pull-down resistors and debouncing to stabilize signals. For actuators, we will cover types and classifications, and interfacing relays, motors, servos, buzzers, and displays via PWM or GPIO. Power handling, voltage requirements, and protection address safe operation with diodes and regulators. Real-world examples, like intrusion detection and automatic fan control, illustrate practical applications.

By the end of this chapter, you will have a clear understanding of how sensors capture real-world data, how actuators respond to control signals, and how both interact with microcontrollers like the ESP32 and Arduino. This foundation will equip you with the practical and theoretical knowledge needed to design reliable IoT systems, and prepare you for deeper explorations into connectivity, data processing, and full-scale IoT deployments.

Structure

In this chapter, we will cover the following topics:

- Classification of Sensors
- Working of Sensors
- Sensor Calibration and Reading Techniques
- Common IoT Sensors
- Pull-up, Pull-down Resistors and Debouncing
- Actuators in IoT
- Power Handling and Protection
- Real-World Sensor-Actuator Loops
- Tips for Wiring, Debugging, and Best Practices
- Practical Exercises

Classification of Sensors: Digital, Analog, Smart Sensors

Sensors are the sensory organs of IoT systems, acting as the *eyes, ears, and nerves* that detect environmental changes like temperature, motion, light, or gas levels, enabling data-driven decisions in the Perception Layer. Building on Chapter 2's exploration of the IoT ecosystem – where the three-layer architecture (Perception, Network, Application) orchestrates data flow via protocols such as HTTP and MQTT – this section dives into sensor classification: digital, analog, and smart sensors. Each type differs in output, interfacing, calibration, and application, impacting their suitability for tasks like monitoring soil moisture in agriculture or detecting motion in security systems. This section details their characteristics, interfacing with controllers such as ESP32 or Arduino, and practical applications, with examples spanning global industries. By understanding these sensor types, readers will learn to select and integrate sensors for robust IoT designs, ensuring accurate data collection for automation and analytics.

Digital Sensors

Digital sensors are devices that provide discrete electrical signals to represent a physical phenomenon. Unlike analog sensors, which produce continuously varying voltages, digital sensors output data in the form of binary signals – usually HIGH/LOW or 1/0. This makes it extremely straightforward to integrate with microcontrollers and digital systems, as no Analog-to-Digital Conversion (ADC) is required.

These sensors are widely used in IoT applications where the requirement is to detect clear, threshold-based conditions such as motion detection, obstacle presence, or button presses. Their inherent resistance to noise and minimal calibration needs make them reliable and efficient for real-world deployments.

Example Wiring: A common digital sensor is the **HC-SR501 PIR Motion Sensor**. To connect it to an Arduino (a microcontroller), you would typically use three wires:

- **VCC** (Power): Connected to the Arduino's 5V pin.
- **GND** (Ground): Connected to the Arduino's GND pin.
- **OUT** (Signal): Connected to any digital input pin on the Arduino (for example, Digital Pin 2). When motion is detected, the **OUT** pin sends a HIGH (5V) signal to the Arduino.

Key Characteristics

Digital sensors are devices that provide discrete electrical signals to represent physical phenomena. They are widely used in IoT applications due to their simplicity, low power consumption, and ease of interfacing with microcontrollers. The key characteristics of digital sensors include output type, power requirements, resolution, interface options, and calibration.

- **Output**:
  - **Binary signal**: typically, **HIGH = 3.3V/5V**, **LOW = 0V**.
  - Some digital sensors provide **multi-bit data streams** through communication protocols.
- **Power Requirements**:
  - Operate on standard logic levels, usually **3.3V–5V**.
  - Extremely low power consumption, often less than **100 µA in standby mode**, making them suitable for battery-operated devices.
- **Resolution**:
  - Basic digital sensors provide a **1-bit resolution.**
  - Advanced digital sensors embed internal ADCs and output higher-resolution digital data.
  - **Threshold Tuning**: Refers to setting a specific analog voltage level that, when crossed, triggers a change in a basic digital sensor's 1-bit output (from 0 to 1, or vice-versa). This only defines the *point* at which the simple digital state changes, but does not increase the *precision* (resolution) of the measurement itself.
- **Interface**:
  - Connect directly to GPIO pins of microcontrollers.
  - Communication can be:
    - Simple HIGH/LOW signals
    - 1-Wire protocol
    - Other digital buses like I²C or SPI
- **Calibration**:
  - Generally, factory-calibrated and include internal signal conditioning.
  - Output is processed internally, so external calibration is rarely required.

Advantages

- **Noise immunity:** Less susceptible to signal degradation compared to analog outputs.
- **Ease of use:** Directly readable by digital pins without ADC.
- **Consistency:** Minimal variation in output due to built-in processing.
- **Compact design:** Often combine sensing elements, ADC, and signal conditioning in one package.

Analog Sensors

Analog sensors are devices that generate continuous electrical signals—typically in the form of voltages or currents—that vary in proportion to a physical quantity such as light intensity, temperature, or pressure. Unlike digital sensors that output discrete states, analog sensors provide fine-grained information that captures subtle variations in the measured environment. A key consideration, however, is that the final precision of the measurement is often limited more by the quality of the Analog-to-Digital Converter (ADC) and system noise than the sensor's inherent capability.

Because microcontrollers like the ESP32 and Arduino primarily operate in the digital domain, analog signals must be converted into digital values using an Analog-to-Digital Converter (ADC). This introduces challenges such as noise sensitivity, calibration requirements, and ADC resolution limits, but also allows richer and more detailed measurements.

Key Characteristics

Analog sensors provide a continuous stream of data, capturing subtle variations in the physical world. Their design allows for detailed measurements, but requires careful interfacing, calibration, and signal conversion to ensure accurate readings.

- **Output:**
  - Continuous voltage (for example, **0–5V**, **0–3.3V**).
  - Continuous current (for example, **4–20 mA** in industrial-grade sensors).
- **Power Requirements:**
  - Typically operate on **3.3V–5V supplies**.
  - Draw moderate current (for example: **1–5 mA** for an LDR circuit).
- **Resolution:**
  - Depends entirely on the **ADC resolution** of the controller.
  - **Example**: ESP32's **10-bit ADC** produces **1024 discrete steps**, meaning the analog range (0–3.3V) is quantized into 3.2 mV increments.
- **Interface:**
  - Connect to **analog input pins (A0, A1, and so on)**.
  - Often require **voltage divider or scaling circuits** to map sensor voltage to measurable ranges.
- **Calibration:**
  - Essential to handle **offset errors, noise, drift, and non-linearities**.
  - Often requires mapping raw ADC values into **physical units** (lux, °C, and so on) via calibration curves.

Advantages

- **High Granularity:** Can capture **fine variations** in environmental conditions.
- **Cost-Effective:** Simple sensor designs, widely available and inexpensive.
- **Versatile:** Suitable for diverse physical measurements (light, pressure, temperature, and sound).

Smart Sensors

Smart sensors represent the next level of sensing technology, integrating not only the sensing element but also signal conditioning circuits, microcontrollers, and communication interfaces within the same package. This means they can directly provide processed, calibrated, and ready-to-use digital data, reducing the burden on external microcontrollers. However, for extremely simple IoT applications with minimal processing needs, the complexity and cost of smart sensors can be overkill.

Unlike simple digital or analog sensors, smart sensors often include onboard ADCs, filters, and compensation algorithms, making their data more accurate and consistent across different environments. However, these benefits come with trade-offs in cost, power consumption, and complexity of communication protocols.

Key Characteristics

Smart sensors combine sensing elements with onboard processing and communication capabilities, delivering pre-processed, accurate digital data. Their integrated design simplifies interfacing, and enhances reliability, though it may require careful consideration of power, cost, and communication protocols.

- **Output**:
    - Digital data streams, often transmitted as multi-byte packets.
    - Uses standardized serial protocols like I²C, SPI, or UART for communication.
- **Power Requirements**:
    - Operates at 3.3V–5V.
    - Consumes more current than basic sensors (1–5 mA active for DHT22).
- **Resolution:**
    - High-resolution data, often 12–16 bits or more.
    - **Example**: BME280 provides 16-bit pressure measurements with excellent granularity.
- **Interface:**
    - Communicates via I²C (SDA/SCL lines), SPI (MISO/MOSI/CLK/CS), or UART.
    - Typically requires software libraries (`Adafruit_DHT`, `Adafruit_BME280`) for easy use.
- **Calibration:**
    - Most are factory-calibrated or include self-calibration routines.
    - Greatly reduces the need for user-side calibration or manual compensation.

Advantages

- **High Accuracy:** Onboard compensation algorithms ensure reliable measurements (for example, ±0.5 °C for DHT22).
- **Ease of Integration**: Communication protocols like I²C and SPI are standardized and well-supported by libraries.
- **Multi-Sensing Capability:** Many smart sensors can measure multiple parameters simultaneously (for example, BME280 measures temperature, humidity, and pressure).

Considerations

- **Selection Criteria:**
    - **Digital**: Choose for simplicity and noise resistance (for example, PIR for security).
    - **Analog:** Use for cost-sensitive, high-granularity applications (for example, LDR for lighting).
    - **Smart:** Opt for precision and multi-sensing (for example, DHT22 for climate control).

- **Interfacing Tips:**
  - Use pull-up resistors (10 kΩ) for digital/smart sensors to stabilize signals.
  - Add capacitors (0.1 µF) for analog sensors to filter noise.
- **Power Management:**

  vDigital: Low-power modes (for example, PIR's 65 µA standby) for battery-powered IoT.
  - **Analog**: Minimize ADC sampling frequency to save power.
  - **Smart**: Use sleep modes (for example, DHT22's 40 µA standby) for efficiency.

Digital, analog, and smart sensors form the backbone of IoT's Perception Layer, each offering unique strengths. Digital sensors provide simple, noise-resistant binary outputs, ideal for motion detection. Analog sensors deliver continuous, high-granularity signals but require calibration and ADC interfacing. Smart sensors offer processed, high-accuracy data via I2C/SPI, simplifying integration at higher cost and power. By understanding their characteristics, interfacing (GPIO, ADC, I2C), and applications, learners can select sensors for IoT systems, from security to climate control, ensuring accurate data collection for automation and analytics.

Sensor Type	Relative Cost	Accuracy	Complexity (Integration)
Digital	Low	Low to Medium	Low (Simple binary output/GPIO)
Analog	Medium	High (Continuous signal)	High (Requires ADC and calibration)
Smart	High	Very High (Processed data)	Low (I2C/SPI output, pre-calibrated)

***Table 3.1**: Comparison of Sensors*

Working of Sensors

Sensors are the sensory organs of IoT systems, acting as the *eyes, ears, and nerves* that capture physical stimuli—such as heat, motion, light, pressure, gas, or sound—and convert them into electrical signals for processing. Building on *Chapter 2*'s exploration of the IoT ecosystem and Section classification of sensors (digital, analog, smart), this section delves into the mechanisms behind sensor operation. Understanding data sheets, voltage levels and signal formats, and reading sensor outputs is critical for selecting and integrating sensors into IoT systems, ensuring accurate data collection for applications like climate control or security monitoring. This section provides a comprehensive guide to sensor functionality, interfacing with controllers like ESP32 or Arduino, and practical considerations, with global examples from agriculture, healthcare, and smart cities. By mastering these concepts, readers can design reliable IoT systems that effectively bridge the physical and digital worlds.

Data Sheets

Data sheets are the technical blueprints for sensors, providing essential specifications for operation, interfacing, and performance. They guide developers in selecting sensors, configuring circuits, and ensuring compatibility with controllers like ESP32 or Arduino.

Key Information in Data Sheets

- **Operating Voltage**: Range for powering the sensor (for example: 3.3–5V for DHT22, 5V for HC-SR501 PIR).
- **Current Consumption**: Active and standby currents (for example: DHT22: 1 mA active, 40 µA standby; MQ-135: 150 mA active).
- **Output Format**: Analog (0–5V), digital (HIGH/LOW), or protocol-based (I2C, SPI, UART).
- **Accuracy**: Precision of measurements (for example: DHT22: ±0.5°C temperature, ±2–5% RH).

- **Range**: Measurable limits (for example: HC-SR501 PIR: 3–7 m detection; MQ-135: 10–10,000 ppm CO2).
- **Calibration Requirements**: Factory or user calibration needs (for example: LDR requires manual scaling).
- **Pinout**: Pin assignments (for example: DHT22: VCC, GND, Data; BME280: SDA, SCL for I2C).
- **Timing**: Sampling rate or response time (for example: DHT22: 2-second sampling; PIR: <1 s response).

Example: DHT22 Data Sheet

- **Specs:** 3.3–5V, 1 mA active, single-wire digital output, ±0.5°C accuracy, 0–100% RH, -40°C to 80°C.
- **Key Details:** Uses a single-wire protocol, requires a 10 kΩ pull-up resistor, 2-second minimum sampling interval.
- **Application:** Reading temperature/humidity for climate control, interfaced with ESP32 pin 4.

Practical Use

- **Selection:** Choose sensors based on voltage compatibility (for example, 3.3V for ESP32) and accuracy needs.
- **Configuration**: Use data sheet pinouts for wiring (for example: MQ-135's analog output to ESP32 A0).
- **Debugging**: Check timing specs to avoid errors (for example: DHT22's 2-second delay prevents data corruption).

Voltage Levels and Signal Formats

Sensors convert physical stimuli into electrical signals, defined by voltage levels and signal formats, which determine how they interface with controllers and transmit data. A mismatch in voltage levels between the sensor and the controller's General-Purpose Input/Output (GPIO) pins poses a significant risk, and can lead to permanent damage to the controller's hardware.

Voltage Levels

- **TTL Logic (Digital Sensors)**:
  - **LOW**: 0V (or <0.8V for 3.3V systems).
  - **HIGH**: 3.3V or 5V, depending on the controller (for example: ESP32 uses 3.3V, Arduino Uno 5V).
  - **Example**: HC-SR501 PIR outputs HIGH (3.3V/5V) on motion, LOW (0V) otherwise.
- **Analog Output**:
  - Ranges from 0–3.3V or 0–5V, proportional to the stimulus (for example, LDR outputs 0–5V based on light intensity).
  - Requires ADC with resolution (for example: ESP32's 10-bit ADC yields 1024 levels for 0–3.3V).
- **Smart Sensors**:
  - Often 3.3V for I2C/SPI (for example: BME280), compatible with modern controllers like ESP32.

  - May require level shifters for 5V systems (common examples include modules based on MOSFETs like the BSS138, or dedicated ICs like the TXS0108E) (for example: Arduino Uno).

Signal Formats

- **Analog Signals**: Continuous voltage or current (for example: MQ-135 outputs 0–5V for 10–10,000 ppm CO_2).

  Example: LDR in a voltage divider outputs 0.5V (dark) to 4.5V (bright).
- **Digital Signals**: Binary pulses (HIGH/LOW) or encoded data (for example, DS18B20's 1-Wire protocol sends 12-bit temperature data).

  Example: PIR sends HIGH pulse on motion detection.
- **Protocol-Based (Smart Sensors)**:
  - **I2C**: Two-wire (SDA, SCL) for multi-device communication (for example: BME280 sends temperature/humidity).
  - **SPI**: Four-wire (MOSI, MISO, SCK, CS) for high-speed data (for example: VL53L0X distance sensor).
  - **UART**: Serial communication (TX, RX) for simple data transfer (for example: some GPS modules).
  - **Single-Wire**: Proprietary protocols (for example: DHT22's single-wire for temperature/humidity).

Practical Considerations

- **Voltage Matching**: Ensure sensor voltage matches controller (for example: 3.3V ESP32 for BME280; use level shifters for 5V sensors).
- **Signal Conditioning**: Analog sensors need pull-up/pull-down resistors (for example: 10 kΩ for LDR) or capacitors (0.1 µF) for noise filtering.
- **Protocol Setup**: Configure I2C/SPI addresses or baud rates in Arduino IDE for smart sensors.

Reading Sensor Outputs

Reading sensor outputs involves capturing their electrical signals using appropriate controller functions and libraries, ensuring accurate data for IoT applications.

Techniques for Reading Outputs

- **Analog Sensors (`analogRead`)**: Use `analogRead(pin)` to capture voltage levels (0–1023 for 10-bit ADC on ESP32).

  Example: Read LDR on ESP32 A0 to measure light intensity.
- **Digital Sensors (`digitalRead`)**: Use `digitalRead(pin)` to detect HIGH/LOW states (for example, PIR's motion trigger).

  Example: Read HC-SR501 on ESP32 GPIO 5.
- **Smart Sensors (Libraries):** Use libraries like `DHT.h`, `Adafruit_Sensor`, or Wire for protocol-based sensors (I2C, SPI, UART).

  Example: Read DHT22 temperature/humidity using `DHT.h` on ESP32.

- **Advanced Techniques:**
    - **Polling:** Periodically read sensor data (for example: every 2 seconds for DHT22).
    - **Interrupts**: Use pin interrupts for fast response (for example: PIR triggers interrupt on ESP32).
    - **Averaging**: Take multiple readings to reduce noise (for example: average 5 LDR samples).
    - **Filtering**: Apply software filters (for example: moving average, Kalman) for smoother data.

Practical Considerations

- **Timing:** Respect sensor sampling rates (for example: DHT22's 2-second minimum interval).
- **Noise Reduction**: Use capacitors (0.1 µF) for analog sensors or pull-up resistors (10 kΩ) for digital/I2C.
- **Error Handling**: Check for invalid readings (for example: `isnan()` for DHT22) to avoid crashes.
- **Controller Compatibility**: ESP32 (3.3V, 10-bit ADC) vs. Arduino Uno (5V, 10-bit ADC).

Thus, sensors convert physical stimuli into electrical signals, guided by data sheets that detail voltage (3.3–5V), current, accuracy, and protocols. Voltage levels (TTL for digital, 0–5V for analog, I2C/SPI for smart) and signal formats (analog, digital, protocol-based) determine interfacing with controllers like ESP32. Reading outputs involve analogRead for analog sensors, `digitalRead` for digital, and libraries (for example: `DHT.h`) for smart sensors, with techniques like polling, interrupts, and filtering for accuracy. These principles enable reliable data collection for IoT applications, from climate control to security, paving the way for robust system design.

Sensor Calibration and Reading Techniques

Sensors, often called the "eyes and ears" of IoT systems, are essential for accurate and reliable data delivery to the Perception Layer, enabling effective decision-making. Building on the IoT ecosystem and concepts from Chapter 2, specifically 'Sensor types' and 'Sensor Operation,' this section focuses on two crucial processes for ensuring measurement accuracy and reliable data capture: calibration and reading techniques.

Calibration corrects errors like baseline offsets or scaling issues, thereby guaranteeing measurement accuracy. Reading techniques, which include polling, interrupts, averaging, and filtering, are used to minimize noise and optimize the data collection process. Both processes are critical for applications like motion detection or temperature monitoring, as inaccurate data can lead to faulty automation.

This section will detail various calibration methods (such as offset, scaling, reference devices, and software filtering) and reading techniques. Practical examples using the ESP32 and Arduino IDE will be provided. The impact of these concepts is illustrated through their global applications in agriculture, healthcare, and smart cities, ultimately equipping readers to design robust and effective IoT systems.

Calibration Techniques

Calibration ensures that sensors provide accurate measurements by correcting systematic errors and aligning outputs with real-world values. Without calibration, sensors may produce misleading data, such as a gas sensor reporting non-zero values in clean air, or a temperature sensor deviating from actual conditions.

Offset Calibration

- **Definition:** Adjusts for baseline errors where a sensor's output deviates from the expected zero-point in the absence of a stimulus.
- **Example:** MQ-135 gas sensor may output 0.2V in clean air (expected 0V). Subtract this offset (0.2V) from readings.
- **Process:**
    - Measure output in a controlled environment (for example, clean air for MQ-135).
    - Record baseline value (for example, 0.2V = 40 ADC units on ESP32's 10-bit ADC).
- **Application:** Ensures that MQ-135 accurately detects CO2 increases in air quality monitoring.

Scaling Calibration

- **Definition:** Maps raw sensor outputs (for example: ADC values) to meaningful physical units (for example: voltage, lux, °C).
- **Example:** LDR outputs 0–1023 (ESP32 10-bit ADC, 0–3.3V), mapped to 0–1000 lux.
- **Process:** Measure sensor output at known points (for example: LDR at 100 lux = 200 ADC, 800 lux = 900 ADC).
- **Application:** Converts raw ADC values to meaningful units for light-based automation.

Reference Devices

- **Definition:** Cross-check sensor outputs against calibrated instruments (for example: thermometers, multimeters, and so on) to verify accuracy.
- **Example:** Calibrate DHT22 against a reference thermometer (for example: Fluke 62 MAX, ±1°C).
- **Process:**
    - Place sensor and reference device in the same environment (for example, 25°C room).
    - Compare readings (for example: DHT22 reads 26°C, reference 25°C).
- **Application:** Ensures DHT22 accuracy for climate control systems.

Software Filtering

- **Definition:** Reduces noise in sensor readings using algorithms like moving averages or median filters.
- **Caution:** Over-filtering can introduce latency and potentially mask real, significant events.
- **Moving Average:** Average multiple readings to smooth fluctuations (for example: 5 samples for LDR).
- **Median Filter:** Sort multiple readings, and select the middle value to eliminate outliers.

  Example: For MQ-135, take 5 readings, sort, and use the median.
- **Application:** Reduces noise in analog sensors like MQ-135 in noisy industrial environments.

Reading Techniques

Reading sensor outputs involves capturing electrical signals using appropriate controller functions and techniques to ensure reliable data collection. Techniques vary by sensor type (analog, digital, smart) and application requirements.

- **Polling**: In sensor-based systems, one of the most common strategies for acquiring data is polling. This approach involves the controller actively checking sensor values at regular intervals, ensuring timely updates, while keeping the implementation simple. Periodically, read the sensor data at fixed intervals using **`analogRead`** or **`digitalRead`**.

  Example: Read DHT22 every 2 seconds (per data sheet) to monitor temperature.

- **Interrupts**: Beyond polling, another powerful method for sensor interaction is interrupt-driven acquisition. Instead of continuously checking sensor values, the controller responds instantly when an event occurs, saving power and processing time. Use hardware interrupts to trigger readings on specific events (for example: PIR motion detection).

  Example: HC-SR501 PIR triggers an interrupt on ESP32 GPIO 5 when motion is detected.

- **Averaging:** Raw sensor data, especially from analog sources, often contains small fluctuations. Averaging techniques help smooth these variations, providing more stable and reliable measurements. Take multiple readings, and compute the average to reduce noise, especially for analog sensors.

  Example: Average 5 LDR readings to smooth light intensity fluctuations.

- **Filtering:** When simple averaging is not enough, more advanced filtering methods can be applied. These use mathematical models or algorithms to reduce noise, reject outliers, and extract the true signal from noisy sensor data. Apply software algorithms (for example: moving average, Kalman, median) to smooth data and remove outliers.

- **Kalman Filter:**
  - Uses predictive modeling to estimate true values, ideal for noisy sensors like MQ-135.
  - **Example**: Simple Kalman filter library (for example, **`SimpleKalmanFilter`**) for gas readings.

Practical Considerations

- **Wiring**:
  - **Analog**: Use 0.1 μF capacitors to filter noise (for example: MQ-135 to ESP32 A0).
  - **Digital/Smart**: Add pull-up resistors (4.7–10 kΩ) for I2C (for example: BME280 SDA/SCL).
- **Timing**:
  - Respect sensor sampling rates (for example: DHT22's 2-second minimum).
  - Use delays sparingly in polling to avoid blocking code.
- **Error Handling**:
  - Check for invalid data (for example: **`isnan()`** for DHT22).
  - Handle ADC saturation (for example: LDR exceeding 3.3V on ESP32).
- **Power Management**:
  - Reduce polling frequency (for example: 1 Hz for DHT22) to save power.
  - Use interrupts for event-driven sensors (for example: PIR) to minimize CPU usage.

Calibration ensures sensor accuracy through offset correction (for example: subtracting MQ-135's baseline), scaling (for example: mapping LDR ADC to lux), reference devices (for example: DHT22 vs. thermometer), and software filtering (for example: moving averages). Reading techniques include polling for periodic data, interrupts for event-driven responses, averaging to smooth noise, and filtering (for example: Kalman) for reliability. These methods, implemented on ESP32/Arduino, enable precise data collection for IoT applications like climate control and security, addressing challenges like noise and power efficiency, while leveraging trends like auto-calibration and advanced filtering.

Common IoT Sensors

Sensors are the *eyes, ears, and nerves* of IoT systems, capturing physical stimuli like temperature, motion, gas, light, and sound to enable data-driven decisions in the Perception Layer. Building on Chapter 2's IoT ecosystem, which covered sensor types, operation, and calibration, this section explores specific sensor categories: **temperature**, **motion**, **gas**, **light**, and **sound sensors**. Each category plays a unique role in applications like climate control, security, environmental monitoring, and automation. This section details their operating principles, specifications, interfacing with ESP32/Arduino, calibration, and real-world applications across global industries, such as agriculture, healthcare, smart homes, and smart cities. With code snippets, wiring guides, and practical considerations, readers will learn to integrate these sensors into IoT systems, ensuring accurate data for automation and analytics.

Temperature Sensors

Temperature sensors measure environmental or object temperature, critical for applications requiring precise climate control or monitoring. They are widely used in IoT for their reliability and versatility.

Examples and Specifications

- **DHT22**:
    - **Type**: Smart, digital output (single-wire protocol).
    - **Specs**: ±0.5°C accuracy, -40°C to 80°C range, 0–100% RH, 3.3–5V, 1 mA active, 40 μA standby.
    - **Operation**: Capacitive humidity sensor and thermistor, processed by onboard microcontroller.
- **LM35**:
    - **Type**: Analog, outputs 10 mV/°C.
    - **Specs**: ±0.5°C accuracy, 0°C to 100°C range, 4–30V, 60 μA.
    - **Operation**: Linear voltage output proportional to temperature (250 mV at 25°C).
- **DS18B20**:
    - **Type**: Digital, 1-Wire protocol.
    - **Specs**: ±0.5°C accuracy, -55°C to 125°C range, 3–5V, 1 mA active, 12-bit resolution.
    - **Operation**: Digital temperature data via 1-Wire interface.

Interfacing

- **DHT22**: Connect to ESP32 pin 4 (single-wire), use DHT.h library, 10 kΩ pull-up resistor.
- **LM35**: Connect to ESP32 A0 (ADC), scale 0–3.3V to 0–330°C.
- **DS18B20**: Connect to ESP32 GPIO 5 (1-Wire), use `DallasTemperature.h`.

Calibration

- **DHT22**: Compare with reference thermometer, apply offset (-0.5°C).
- **LM35**: Scale ADC values (0–1023 to 0–330°C), verify with multimeter.
- **DS18B20**: Factory-calibrated, minimal user calibration needed.

Applications

- **HVAC**: DHT22 adjusts room temperature in smart thermostats.

- **Weather Stations**: DS18B20 monitors outdoor conditions.
- **Healthcare**: LM35 tracks patient temperature in wearables.

Motion Sensors

Motion sensors detect movement or distance, enabling automation and security in IoT systems. They are critical for event-driven applications.

Examples and Specifications

- **HC-SR501 PIR (Passive Infrared)**:
  - **Type:** Digital, outputs HIGH/LOW.
  - **Specs:** 3–7 m range, 3–5V, 65 μA standby, <1 s response, adjustable sensitivity/delay.
  - **Operation:** Detects infrared changes from moving objects (for example, human body heat).
- **HC-SR04 Ultrasonic:**
  - **Type:** Digital, outputs pulse width.
  - **Specs:** 2 cm–4 m range, 5V, 15 mA, ±3 mm accuracy.
  - **Operation**: Emits ultrasonic waves, measures echo time for distance.

Interfacing

- **HC-SR501 PIR**: Connect to ESP32 GPIO 5, read with `digitalRead`.
- **HC-SR04**: Connect trigger/echo to ESP32 GPIO 12/13, use `pulseIn`.

Calibration

- **PIR**: Adjust sensitivity/delay via onboard potentiometers, verify with motion tests.
- **Ultrasonic**: Calibrate echo timing with known distances (1 m).

Applications

- **Intrusion Detection**: PIR triggers alarms in security systems.
- **Automation**: Ultrasonic sensors open doors or adjust conveyor belts.

Gas Sensors

Gas sensors detect harmful or environmental gases (CO, LPG, methane), critical for safety and monitoring in IoT systems. **Note on MQ-series Sensors:** Sensors such as the MQ series require a warm-up period (often 20 minutes or more) to achieve accurate readings. They also exhibit long-term drift, meaning recalibration may be necessary over time to maintain accuracy.

Examples and Specifications

- **MQ-2**:
  - **Type**: Analog, outputs 0–5V.
  - **Specs**: 300–10,000 ppm (smoke, LPG, methane), 5V, 150 mA, 2–5 min preheat.
  - **Operation**: Gas-sensitive material changes resistance with concentration.
- **MQ-7**:
  - **Type**: Analog, outputs 0–5V.
  - **Specs**: 10–10,000 ppm CO, 5V, 150 mA, cyclic heating (high/low voltage).
  - **Operation**: Similar to MQ-2, optimized for carbon monoxide.

Interfacing

- **MQ-2**: Connect to ESP32 A0, scale 0–1023 to ppm.
- **MQ-7**: Similar to MQ-2, requires cyclic heating (5V for 60 s, 1.4V for 90 s).

Calibration

- **MQ-2/MQ-7**: Measure in clean air for baseline offset, scale with known gas concentrations.

Applications

- **Safety Systems**: MQ-2 detects gas leaks in homes.
- **Industrial Monitoring**: MQ-7 monitors CO in factories.

Light Sensors

Light sensors measure ambient light or specific wavelengths, enabling automation in lighting and environmental monitoring.

Examples and Specifications

- **LDR (Light Dependent Resistor)**:
  - **Type**: Analog, outputs 0–5V via voltage divider.
  - **Specs**: 10 kΩ (dark) to 1 kΩ (bright), 0–1000 lux, 500 μA, 5V.
  - **Operation**: Resistance decreases with light intensity.
- **TSL2561**:
  - **Type**: Smart, I2C digital output.
  - **Specs**: 0.1–40,000 lux, 3.3–5V, 0.6 mA, 16-bit resolution.
  - **Operation**: Photodiodes with onboard ADC and I2C interface.

Interfacing

- **LDR**: Connect to ESP32 A0 with 10 kΩ pull-down resistor.
- **TSL2561**: Connect to ESP32 I2C (SDA 21, SCL 22), use Adafruit_TSL2561.

Calibration

- **LDR**: Scale ADC to lux using known light sources.
- **TSL2561**: Factory-calibrated, adjustable gain for low/high light.

Applications

- **Automatic Brightness Control**: LDR adjusts display brightness.
- **Solar Tracking**: TSL2561 optimizes solar panel alignment.

Sound Sensors

Sound sensors detect audio signals or noise levels, enabling voice-activated systems or environmental monitoring. Note that these sensors typically measure sound amplitude (volume/intensity) and are not designed to analyze specific frequencies or speech content. Examples and Specifications:

- **KY-037**:
  - **Type**: Analog, outputs 0–5V.
  - **Specs**: Detects sound intensity, 5V, 4 mA, adjustable sensitivity.
  - **Operation**: Microphone with amplifier, outputs voltage proportional to sound.

- **MAX9814**:
  - **Type**: Analog, outputs 0–3.3V/5V.
  - **Specs**: 20 Hz–20 kHz, 3–5V, 3 mA, adjustable gain.
  - **Operation**: Electret microphone with automatic gain control.

Interfacing

- **KY-037**: Connect to ESP32 A0, adjust sensitivity via potentiometer.

Calibration

- **KY-037**: Adjust potentiometer for threshold, verify with known sound levels.
- **MAX9814**: Calibrate gain for specific audio ranges.

Applications

- **Voice-Activated Systems**: Trigger commands with sound detection.
- **Noise Monitoring**: Measure environmental noise levels.

Temperature sensors (DHT22, LM35, DS18B20) monitor climate and health, using digital or analog outputs. Motion sensors (PIR, ultrasonic) enable security and automation with digital signals. Gas sensors (MQ-2, MQ-7) ensure safety by detecting harmful gases. Light sensors (LDR, TSL2561) optimize lighting, and sound sensors (KY-037, MAX9814) support voice and noise monitoring. Interfacing with ESP32/Arduino, calibration, and noise handling ensure reliable data, driving IoT applications from HVAC to smart cities.

Pull-up, Pull-down Resistors and Debouncing

In IoT systems, sensors act as the *eyes and ears*, delivering critical environmental data to controllers like ESP32 or Arduino. However, unstable or noisy inputs can lead to unreliable data, undermining the Perception Layer's effectiveness. Building on Chapter 2's IoT ecosystem, which covered sensor types, operation, calibration, and interfacing, this section explores pull-up resistors, pull-down resistors, and debouncing to ensure stable sensor signals. Pull-up and pull-down resistors prevent floating pins, ensuring predictable HIGH or LOW states, while debouncing eliminates false triggers from noisy inputs like mechanical switches or sensors. This section provides detailed guidance on circuit design, code implementation, and troubleshooting, with practical examples using ESP32 and Arduino IDE. Global applications in agriculture, smart homes, and industrial automation illustrate real-world impact, equipping readers to build robust IoT systems with reliable data inputs.

Pull-up Resistors

These ensure a digital input pin reads a stable HIGH (3.3V/5V) when not actively driven by a sensor or switch, preventing undefined or "floating" states that can cause erratic behavior in IoT systems.

Functionality

- **Purpose:** Connects an input pin to VCC (3.3V for ESP32, 5V for Arduino) via a resistor (typically 4.7–10 kΩ), defaulting the pin to HIGH unless grounded by the sensor/switch.
- **Mechanism:** When the input is unconnected or in a high-impedance state, the resistor pulls the pin to VCC, ensuring a consistent HIGH state. When the sensor/switch grounds the pin, it reads LOW.
- **Example:** DHT22's single-wire protocol uses a 10 kΩ pull-up resistor to stabilize the data line, ensuring reliable communication.

Circuit Design

- **Components:** 4.7–10 kΩ resistor (common values for I2C or single-wire protocols).
- **Wiring:**
    - Connect one end of the resistor to the input pin (ESP32 GPIO 4).
    - Connect the other end to VCC (3.3V for ESP32, 5V for Arduino).
    - Connect the sensor/switch between the input pin and GND.
- **Example with DHT22:**
    - Data pin to ESP32 GPIO 4.
    - 10 kΩ resistor between Data and 3.3V.
    - VCC to 3.3V, GND to GND.

Note: *The pull-up resistor ensures stable HIGH signals during DHT22's single-wire communication.*

Practical Considerations

- **Resistor Value:** 4.7–10 kΩ balances current draw (low enough for signal stability, high enough to minimize power loss).
- **Internal Pull-ups**: ESP32 and Arduino offer internal pull-up resistors (for example, `pinMode(pin, INPUT_PULLUP)`), but external resistors (10 kΩ) are more reliable for sensors like DHT22.
- **Power Consumption**: Pull-up resistors draw minimal current (3.3V / 10 kΩ = 0.33 mA).
- **Troubleshooting**:
    - **Erratic Readings**: Verify resistor value and connection to VCC.
    - **No Signal**: Check sensor pin for proper grounding.

Pull-down Resistors

These ensure a digital input pin reads a stable LOW (0V) when not actively driven, preventing floating states that could misinterpret as HIGH signals.

Functionality

- **Purpose:** Connects an input pin to GND via a resistor (typically 10 kΩ), defaulting the pin to LOW unless actively driven HIGH by the sensor/switch.
- **Mechanism:** When unconnected, the resistor pulls the pin to GND (0V). When the sensor/switch connects to VCC, the pin reads HIGH.
- **Example:** A button switch uses a 10 kΩ pull-down resistor to ensure the pin reads LOW when not pressed, avoiding false triggers.

Circuit Design

- **Components**: 10 kΩ resistor.
- **Wiring**:
    - Connect one end of the resistor to the input pin (Arduino D2).
    - Connect the other end to GND.

    - Connect the sensor/switch between the input pin and VCC.
- **Example with Button:**
    - Button between Arduino D2 and 5V.
    - 10 kΩ resistor between D2 and GND.

Note: *The pull-down resistor ensures the pin reads LOW when the button is not pressed.*

Practical Considerations

- **Resistor Value:** 10 kΩ is standard to minimize current while ensuring stability.
- **Internal Pull-downs:** Less common than pull-ups; external resistors are preferred for reliability.
- **Power Consumption:** Negligible (for example, 0 mA when LOW).
- **Troubleshooting:**
    - **False Triggers:** Verify resistor connection to GND.
    - **No Response:** Check switch connection to VCC.

Debouncing

Debouncing eliminates false triggers from noisy inputs, such as mechanical switches or sensors with unstable signals (buttons, PIR sensors), ensuring reliable data in IoT systems.

Functionality

- **Purpose:** Filters out rapid voltage fluctuations caused by mechanical switch bouncing or sensor noise.
- **Mechanism:** Uses hardware (capacitors) or software (delays, timers) to ensure only intentional state changes are registered.
- **Example:** A button press may generate multiple HIGH/LOW transitions within milliseconds; debouncing ensures only one trigger is recorded.

Hardware Debouncing

- **Components:** 0.1 µF capacitor across the switch, 10 kΩ pull-up/pull-down resistor.
- **Wiring:**
    - Connect the capacitor in parallel with the switch (between Arduino D2 and GND).
    - Use pull-up resistor to VCC for stable HIGH state.
- **Effect:** The capacitor smooths voltage transitions, reducing bounce noise.
- **Example:** Button with 0.1 µF capacitor and 10 kΩ pull-up resistor on ESP32 GPIO 5.

Software Debouncing

- **Techniques:**
    - **Delay-Based:** Wait for a stable state (e.g., 50 ms) after a state change.
    - **Timer-Based:** Use `millis()` to track time since the last state change.

Note: *The code waits 50 ms to confirm a stable button state, preventing false triggers.*

Advanced Debouncing: Interrupt-Based

- **Use Case:** Fast response to sensor events (PIR motion detection).
- **Note:** *Debouncing ensures that only valid motion triggers are processed.*

Practical Considerations

- **Hardware vs. Software:**
  - **Hardware:** Simple, low CPU overhead, but adds components.
  - **Software:** Flexible, no extra components, but requires careful timing.
- **Timing:** Use 20–50 ms debounce delay for switches, 100–200 ms for sensors such as PIR.
- **Power:** Minimize interrupt frequency to reduce power consumption in battery-powered systems.
- **Troubleshooting:**
  - **Multiple Triggers:** Increase debounce delay or add capacitor.
  - **No Response:** Verify pull-up/pull-down resistor and pin configuration.

Pull-up resistors (for example, 10 kΩ to VCC) ensure stable HIGH inputs for sensors like DHT22, while pull-down resistors (for example, 10 kΩ to GND) prevent false triggers in switches. Debouncing, via hardware (0.1 µF capacitors) or software (50 ms delays), eliminates noise from mechanical inputs or sensors like PIR. These techniques, implemented on ESP32/Arduino, ensure reliable data for IoT applications, from smart homes to agriculture. With proper wiring, code, and troubleshooting, readers can build robust systems that avoid floating pins and false triggers, enhancing IoT reliability.

Actuators in IoT

Actuators are the muscles of IoT systems, transforming digital commands from sensors and controllers into physical actions like switching appliances, moving motors, or displaying data. Building on *Chapter* 2's IoT ecosystem (Perception, Network, Application layers) which covered sensors and their interfacing, this section explores actuator types—electrical (relays, buzzers, LEDs), mechanical (motors, servos, solenoids), and displays (LCD, OLED, TFT screens). Actuators enable automation in applications like smart homes, agriculture, and industrial systems. This section details their operating principles, specifications, and interfacing with ESP32 and Arduino, providing wiring diagrams and examples. Thus, by mastering actuator integration, readers can create responsive IoT systems that act on sensor data, bridging the digital and physical worlds.

Types of Actuators

Actuators are categorized by their energy source or motion type, each suited to specific IoT tasks. This subsection details electrical, mechanical, and display actuators, their specifications, interfacing techniques, and applications.

Electrical Actuators

Electrical actuators use electrical energy to produce simple actions such as switching, signaling, or alerting, making them ideal for low-power IoT applications.

Relays:

- **Specs:** 5V coil, 10A/250V AC contacts, 50 mA coil current, 5–12V operation.

- **Operation:** Electromagnetic coil closes/opens contacts to control high-power loads (for example, appliances).
- **Interfacing:** Coil to ESP32 GPIO via transistor (for example, BC547), VCC to 5V, GND to GND.
- **Applications:** Control lights, fans, or pumps in smart homes.

Buzzers:

- **Specs:** Piezoelectric, 3–5V, 1–5 kHz frequency, 10–30 mA.
- **Operation:** Oscillates to produce sound for alerts or notifications.
- **Interfacing:** Positive to ESP32 GPIO, negative to GND.
- **Applications:** Alarms in security systems or feedback in IoT devices.

LEDs:

- **Specs:** 2–3.3V forward voltage, 20 mA, various colors (for example, red, green).
- **Operation:** Emits light for status indicators or visual feedback.
- **Interfacing:** Anode to ESP32 GPIO via 220 Ω resistor, cathode to GND.
- **Applications:** Indicate system status (for example, power ON, error).

Mechanical Actuators

Mechanical actuators produce physical motion (rotational or linear), enabling dynamic IoT applications like robotics or automation.

DC Motors:

- **Specs:** 6–12V, 100–500 mA, bidirectional with H-bridge (for example, L298N).
- **Operation:** Rotates to drive fans, pumps, or wheels.
- **Interfacing:** Connect to L298N H-bridge, control via ESP32 PWM pins.
- **Applications:** Ventilation systems, robotic wheels.

Servos (for example, SG90):

- **Specs:** 4.8–6V, 0–180° rotation, 100–500 mA, 9 g weight.
- **Operation:** Precise angular control via PWM signals.
- **Interfacing:** Signal to ESP32 GPIO, VCC to 5V, GND to GND.

  Note: *For multiple servos or higher torque servos, a separate, dedicated power supply is recommended to avoid brownouts on the main board.*

- **Applications:** Robotic arms, camera gimbals.

Solenoids:

- **Specs:** 12V, 100–300 mA, linear motion (5–10 mm stroke).
- **Operation:** Electromagnetic push/pull for locking or valve control.
- **Interfacing:** Connect to ESP32 GPIO via MOSFET (for example, IRLZ44N).
- **Applications:** Door locks, irrigation valves.

Display Actuators

Display actuators provide visual output for user interaction or data presentation, critical for IoT dashboards and feedback systems.

LCD (16x2):

- **Specs:** 5V, I2C interface, 20 mA backlight, 16 characters × 2 lines.
- **Operation:** Displays text using liquid crystals.
- **Interfacing:** I2C (SDA to ESP32 GPIO 21, SCL to GPIO 22), 4.7 kΩ pull-up resistors.
- **Applications:** Display sensor data (for example, temperature).

OLED (SSD1306):

- **Specs:** 3.3–5V, I2C, 128×64 pixels, 10 mA.
- **Operation:** Organic LEDs for high-contrast monochrome display.
- **Interfacing:** SDA to ESP32 GPIO 21, SCL to GPIO 22.
- **Applications:** Compact dashboards for IoT devices.

TFT Screens (for example, ILI9341):

- **Specs:** 3.3V, SPI, 320×240 pixels, 50 mA, color display.
- **Operation:** High-resolution color visuals for complex data.
- **Interfacing:** SPI (MOSI to ESP32 GPIO 23, MISO to GPIO 19, SCK to GPIO 18, CS to GPIO 5).
- **Applications:** Display real-time sensor graphs.

Practical Considerations

- **Power Management:**
  - Relays and motors require external power (for example, 12V supply, not ESP32's 3.3V).
  - Use low-power modes (for example, OLED's 10 mA) for battery-powered systems.
- **Driver Circuits:**
  - Use transistors (for example, BC547) for relays.
  - Use H-bridges (for example, L298N) for motors.
  - Use MOSFETs (for example, IRLZ44N) for solenoids.
- **Wiring:**
  - Add flyback diodes for inductive loads (for example, relays, motors).
  - Use 4.7 kΩ pull-up resistors for I2C displays.
- **Troubleshooting:**
  - **No Response:** Verify pin mappings and power supply.
  - **Noise:** Add capacitors (0.1 µF) for stable signals.
  - **Overheating:** Ensure current limits (for example, 20 mA for LEDs).

Thus, Actuators enable IoT systems to act on sensor data, serving as the muscles for automation. Electrical actuators (relays, buzzers, LEDs) control appliances or signal alerts, mechanical actuators (motors, servos, solenoids) produce motion, and displays (LCD, OLED, TFT) present data. Interfacing with ESP32/Arduino involves GPIO, PWM, or I2C/SPI, with driver circuits for high-power loads. Applications in smart homes, agriculture, and healthcare highlight their impact, while proper wiring and power management ensure reliability.

Power Handling and Protection

Actuators, the muscles of IoT systems, often demand significantly more electrical power than microcontrollers such as ESP32 or Arduino can directly supply. While sensors generally operate at low current (tens of microamps to a few milliamps), actuators such as relays, motors, and solenoids draw much higher currents, sometimes hundreds of milliamps or even several amps. This creates a challenge: microcontroller GPIO pins are designed only for logic-level control signals (for example, 3.3V at 20–40 mA per pin on ESP32), not for powering heavy loads.

To safely and efficiently operate actuators, developers must design power handling circuits that can amplify signals, and protect components from electrical stress. This involves using driver circuits (transistors, MOSFETs, ICs), protection devices (flyback diodes, fuses, regulators), and a datasheet-driven design process to ensure that actuator voltage, current, and switching requirements are fully met.

Power Requirements and Challenges

IoT actuators such as relays, motors, solenoids, and displays have unique voltage and current requirements. Since GPIO pins cannot provide sufficient power, an external circuit must be added.

Power Characteristics of Controllers

- **ESP32**
  - **GPIO output**: 3.3V, up to 40 mA per pin
  - **Input supply**: 3.3–5V (USB or external)
  - **Total current capacity (with external supply)**: ~1.1 A
- **Arduino Uno**
  - **GPIO output**: 5V, up to 20 mA per pin
  - **5V rail capacity**: ~500 mA
  - **Input voltage**: 7–12V via barrel jack, 5V via USB

Power Characteristics of Actuators

- **Relays:** 5V coil, 50–70 mA, contacts rated for up to 10A/250V AC
- **DC Motors:** 6–12V, 100–500 mA (stall currents can exceed 2A)
- **Solenoids:** 12V, 100–300 mA (short pulses or continuous hold)
- **Buzzers and LEDs:** 3–5V, 10–20 mA (safe for direct GPIO control)
- **Displays (OLED/TFT):** 3.3–5V, 10–50 mA

Challenges in Power Delivery

- **Current Limitations:** A GPIO pin cannot directly supply 70 mA for a relay or 500 mA for a motor. Attempting this risks permanent damage to the microcontroller.
- **Voltage Mismatch:** Many actuators operate at 12V, while ESP32 and Arduino output only 3.3V or 5V. Voltage step-up and level shifting are required.
- **Inductive Spikes:** Relays, motors, and solenoids are inductive loads that generate reverse voltage spikes when switched off, potentially damaging sensitive electronics.
- **Power Stability:** High-current actuators can cause voltage drops, leading to unstable operation or microcontroller resets, if power is not isolated and regulated.

Datasheet Analysis: A Critical Step

Actuator datasheets contain specifications that guide design decisions. Developers must carefully check:

- **Voltage Range:** The operating voltage window (for example, motor: 6–12V).
- **Current Rating:** Active, standby, and peak currents (for example, relay coil: 70 mA).
- **Switching Time:** How fast the actuator responds (for example, relay: 10 ms).
- **Power Dissipation:** Heat produced during operation (for example, motor drivers may reach 70°C).

Example – 5V Relay Datasheet Highlights

- **Coil voltage**: 5V, 70 mA
- **Contact capacity**: 10A at 250V AC
- **Switching time**: 10 ms
- **Design Recommendation**: Must be driven via a transistor or MOSFET for safe isolation

Driver Circuits

These bridge the gap between low-power GPIO signals and high-power actuator needs. They act as electronic switches that use a small control signal to handle much larger voltages and currents.

Transistor Drivers

- **Purpose:** Switch moderate loads like relays or buzzers.
- **Example Device:** BC547 NPN transistor (supports ~100 mA).
- **Operation:** GPIO drives transistor base via resistor; transistor completes the circuit for the actuator.
- **Protection:** A flyback diode is required across inductive loads (relays, solenoids).
- **Advantages:** Simple, low-cost, reliable.
- **Limitations:** Not suitable for motors with high stall current.

MOSFET Drivers

- **Purpose:** Handle higher current loads (hundreds of mA to several amps).
- **Example Device:** IRLZ44N logic-level MOSFET.
- **Operation:** Gate voltage from GPIO switches motor or solenoid connected at drain-source path.
- **Advantages:** High efficiency, can switch large loads quickly.
- **Limitations:** Must select logic-level MOSFETs (3.3V compatible) for ESP32.

Driver ICs

- **Purpose:** Provide multi-channel, robust driver capability for multiple relays, stepper motors, or displays.
- **Example Device:** ULN2003 (seven-channel Darlington transistor array).
- **Operation:** GPIO pins feed IC inputs, outputs drive actuators directly.
- **Advantages:** Compact, multiple channels in one IC, built-in protection.
- **Limitations:** Larger footprint, and higher cost.

Protection Techniques

Power-handling circuits must include protection mechanisms to shield microcontrollers and actuators from electrical hazards.

- **Flyback Diodes**
    - **Purpose:** Absorb reverse voltage spikes from inductive loads.
    - **How It Works:** When current is cut, the collapsing magnetic field in a coil generates a surge. The diode provides a safe discharge path.
    - **Example:** 1N4007 diode across a relay coil ensures ESP32 safety.
- **Fuses**
    - **Purpose:** Prevent damage from short circuits or excessive current draw.
    - **How It Works:** Fuse wire melts when current exceeds rated capacity.
    - **Example:** A 500 mA fuse in a motor circuit protects against stalls.
- **Voltage Regulators**
    - **Purpose:** Provide a stable supply voltage to microcontrollers and actuators.
    - **Types:**
        - Linear regulators (for example, LM7805) – simple, but less efficient.
        - Switching regulators (for example, LM2596) – efficient, suitable for high-current loads.
    - **Use Case:** Step down 12V supply to 5V for relays or to 3.3V for ESP32.

Datasheet-Driven Design

Proper design begins with datasheet interpretation. A methodical approach ensures compatibility and longevity of IoT systems.

Steps in Datasheet-Driven Design

1. **Identify Requirements:** Check voltage and current ratings of the actuator.
2. **Select Driver:** Choose transistor, MOSFET, or IC based on current demands.
3. **Add Protection:** Always include diodes for inductive loads, fuses for current control, and regulators for stable voltage.
4. **Verify Compatibility:** Ensure that microcontroller GPIO logic matches actuator driver thresholds (for example, ESP32 at 3.3V).

Example: Relay Interfacing

- Datasheet shows: 5V coil, 70 mA, 10A contacts
- Design choice: BC547 transistor driver, flyback diode, 100 mA fuse
- External power supply: 5V for relay, isolated from ESP32 logic

Actuators draw far more power than microcontrollers can directly provide. For example, a motor may require 500 mA, while an ESP32 GPIO pin can only supply 40 mA. To safely bridge this gap, driver circuits (transistors, MOSFETs, ICs) amplify control signals. Protection mechanisms (flyback diodes, fuses, voltage regulators) prevent damage from spikes, short circuits, or unstable power. A datasheet-driven design approach ensures correct voltage, current, and protection choices for each actuator.

With proper power handling, IoT systems can reliably operate relays, motors, solenoids, and displays in applications ranging from smart homes to industrial automation.

Real-World Sensor-Actuator Loops

Sensor-actuator loops are the heartbeat of IoT systems. Sensors act as the *eyes and ears*, detecting environmental changes such as motion or temperature, while actuators serve as the muscles, performing physical actions such as sounding alarms or switching on fans. These loops form the foundation of real-world automation, where environmental data is sensed, processed by microcontrollers, and converted into meaningful actions.

Building on Chapter 2's IoT ecosystem (Perception, Network, and Application layers) and Sections which covered sensors, interfacing, actuators, and power handling, this section demonstrates how sensors and actuators can be practically integrated into closed feedback loops. Such loops are central to applications in security, climate control, and agriculture.

Intrusion Detection System

The Intrusion Detection System (IDS) provides a practical example of how IoT can enhance security. Using a PIR (Passive Infrared) sensor, the system detects human movement, and immediately triggers a buzzer for a local alert, while also sending notifications to a mobile application. This dual-alert mechanism makes it highly suitable for homes, offices, and small businesses. It is important to note that mobile notifications, relying on cloud services, may experience slight latency compared to the instant local buzzer.

System Overview

- **Sensor:** HC-SR501 PIR, detects motion in the 3–7 m range with HIGH/LOW digital output.
- **Actuator:** Piezo buzzer, operating at 5V with low current draw (about 10 mA).
- **Controller:** ESP32, providing both GPIO-level control and Wi-Fi connectivity.
- **Communication:** Alerts transmitted via MQTT to mobile apps or cloud dashboards.
- **Logic:** When the PIR output goes HIGH, the buzzer is activated for a fixed duration (for example, 5 seconds), while an intrusion message is published to the app.

Hardware Setup

- **PIR Sensor:**
  - `VCC → ESP32 5V`
  - `GND → ESP32 GND`
  - `OUT → ESP32 GPIO 5`
  - `Optional: 10 kΩ pull-down resistor to reduce false triggers`
- **Buzzer:**
  - `Positive terminal → ESP32 GPIO 8`
  - `Negative terminal → ESP32 GND`
- **Power:**
  - 5V external supply for the buzzer and PIR
  - ESP32 powered via USB or 3.3V regulator
- **Protection:** Flyback diode across buzzer terminals (to absorb voltage spikes).

Calibration and Error Handling

- PIR sensors allow **sensitivity adjustment** (range between 3–7 m) and **delay adjustment** (5–200 seconds) through onboard potentiometers.
- To reduce **false alarms**, a pull-down resistor or small debounce delay can be applied.
- Wi-Fi and MQTT connection status should be continuously monitored for reliable alert delivery.

Automatic Fan Control

The Automatic Fan Control system demonstrates how environmental monitoring can improve comfort and efficiency. A temperature sensor continuously monitors ambient temperature, and when it exceeds a threshold (for example, 30°C), the controller switches on a fan via a relay.

System Overview

- **Sensor:** DHT22, measuring temperature between 0–80°C with ±0.5°C accuracy.
- **Actuator:** 5V relay module driving a 12V DC fan.
- **Controller:** Arduino Uno, chosen for its simplicity and 5V compatibility.
- **Logic:** If the sensed temperature is greater than the threshold, the fan is turned on; otherwise, it remains off.

Hardware Setup

- **DHT22 Sensor:**
  - `VCC → Arduino 5V`
  - `GND → Arduino GND`
  - `Data → Arduino digital pin D4 (with 10 kΩ pull-up resistor)`
- **Relay Circuit:**
  - Driven through a BC547 transistor connected to Arduino D7
  - Flyback diode (1N4007) across relay coil for protection
  - Relay contacts wired to control a 12V DC fan using an external 12V supply
- **Power:**
  - Arduino powered via USB (5V)
  - External 12V power supply for the fan
- **Protection:**
  - Flyback diode across relay coil
  - 1A fuse in fan circuit to protect against short circuits or stalls

Calibration and Error Handling

- The DHT22 sensor should be compared with a reference thermometer to account for offsets.
- If faulty readings occur, software must handle invalid or "NaN" values.
- Relay activation issues are commonly caused by incorrect transistor wiring or insufficient current supply.

Soil Moisture-Based Irrigation

This system automates irrigation by using a soil moisture sensor to detect dry conditions and activating a solenoid valve to release water. Such loops are widely applied in precision agriculture to conserve water, and improve crop yields.

System Overview

- **Sensor:** YL-69 soil moisture sensor, providing an analog output proportional to soil wetness.
- **Actuator:** 12V solenoid valve, typically drawing about 200 mA.
- **Controller:** ESP32, reading analog values and supporting Wi-Fi for monitoring.
- **Logic:** If moisture percentage falls below a threshold (for example, 40%), the solenoid opens for a fixed time (for example, 10 seconds) before shutting off.

Hardware Setup

- **Soil Moisture Sensor (YL-69):**
    - `VCC → ESP32 3.3V`
    - `GND → ESP32 GND`
    - `Analog Output → ESP32 A0 pin`
- **Solenoid Valve:**
    - Controlled via an IRLZ44N MOSFET connected to ESP32 GPIO 15
    - Flyback diode across solenoid coil
    - Powered by an external 12V supply
- **Power:**
    - 12V supply for solenoid
    - ESP32 powered by 3.3V regulator or USB
- **Protection:**
    - 500 mA fuse in solenoid circuit
    - Flyback diode to suppress inductive spikes

Calibration and Error Handling

- Moisture sensor values must be **calibrated** by testing in dry (0%) and fully wet (100%) soil, mapping raw ADC values (0–1023) into percentages.
- Sensor noise can be reduced by **averaging multiple samples** or adding a small capacitor.
- Valve activation issues usually stem from incorrect MOSFET wiring or inadequate 12V power supply.

Practical Considerations

- **Wiring:**
    - Use 22 AWG or thicker wires for actuators such as fans and solenoids.
    - Always include flyback diodes across inductive loads (relays, solenoids, motors, and so on).
    - Use pull-up resistors (4.7–10 kΩ) for sensors like DHT22.

- **Power Management:**
  - Actuators such as fans or solenoids should always use external supplies, rather than being powered directly from the controller.
  - To conserve battery life, sensor sampling should be kept minimal (for example, 2 seconds for DHT22).
- **Error Handling:**
  - Validate all sensor readings (for example, check for invalid temperature values).
  - Use software debounce on digital sensors such as PIR modules to avoid false triggers.
  - Continuously check Wi-Fi/MQTT connectivity when app alerts are involved.
- **Troubleshooting:**
  - If actuators fail to respond, check driver circuits (transistors, MOSFETs, and relays).
  - Apply filtering techniques for noisy sensor data.
  - Verify communication settings for MQTT-based alerts.

Sensor–actuator loops bring IoT systems to life by converting environmental sensing into meaningful action. The Intrusion Detection System (PIR sensor → buzzer and app alert) illustrates IoT security applications. The Automatic Fan Control system (DHT22 → relay → fan) highlights climate regulation. The Soil Moisture Irrigation system (YL-69 → MOSFET → solenoid) demonstrates agricultural automation. With proper wiring, calibration, and protection, such loops can be reliably implemented on microcontrollers like ESP32 or Arduino, forming the backbone of smart homes, smart cities, and precision farming.

Tips for Wiring, Debugging, and Best Practices

In IoT systems, sensors act as the eyes and ears of the device, while actuators serve as the muscles that execute actions. Together, they form the foundation of perception and interaction in the IoT ecosystem. However, the reliability of these components is not just about selecting the right sensor or actuator — it depends heavily on correct wiring, systematic debugging, and adherence to sound engineering practices.

This section builds on earlier concepts from Chapter 2 (the IoT ecosystem layers: Perception, Network, Application) and previous sections in this chapter (3.1–3.9 on sensors, actuators, and interfacing). It focuses on practical, real-world techniques which ensure that your IoT systems remain robust, efficient, and scalable.

Thus, by learning how to wire properly, debug systematically, and follow the best practices, you can avoid many of the common pitfalls that cause inaccurate readings, unstable operation, or even permanent hardware damage.

Wiring Tips

Proper wiring is fundamental to ensuring stable signal transmission, preventing interference, and protecting microcontrollers, sensors, and actuators from electrical issues.

Use Short Wires to Minimize Noise

- **Purpose:** Long wires can behave like antennas, picking up Electromagnetic Interference (EMI) from nearby power lines, motors, or electronic devices. This interference can distort sensor signals or actuator commands, leading to erratic performance.

- **Guideline:** Keep wires less than 30 cm for digital sensors and less than 15 cm for analog sensors. Shorter connections reduce the surface area exposed to interference.
- **Implementation:**
    - Use 22–24 AWG wires for most sensor and actuator connections.
    - When routing, avoid placing signal wires near power cables, especially those driving motors or relays.
- **Practical Note:** If interference still occurs, adding a small capacitor close to the sensor's signal pin can stabilize the readings by filtering out high-frequency noise.

Keep Analog and Digital Grounds Common

- **Purpose:** A reliable ground connection is the backbone of any circuit. If analog and digital grounds are not tied together, small voltage differences may develop, which can cause unpredictable sensor readings or actuator failures.
- **Guideline:** Always connect all GND points — sensors, actuators, and the microcontroller — to a single ground reference.
- **Implementation:**
    - On breadboards or PCBs, use a shared ground rail.
    - When using external power supplies (for example, a 12V motor supply), connect their ground to the microcontroller's ground to maintain consistency.
- **Troubleshooting Tip:** Use a multimeter in continuity mode to verify that all ground connections are linked properly.

Use Shielded Cables for Long-Distance Analog Signals

- **Purpose:** Analog signals are highly susceptible to interference, especially when transmitted over long wires. Using shielded cables helps reduce the impact of electromagnetic noise.
- **Guideline:** For analog signals traveling more than 30 cm, use coaxial cables or twisted-pair shielded wires.
- **Implementation:** Connect the shielding layer to the system ground on one side only. This drains away interference without creating ground loops.
- **Additional Measure:** If interference persists, consider adding a simple RC low-pass filter (resistor and capacitor) to smooth the signal before it reaches the microcontroller.

Additional Wiring Tips

- **Color Coding:** Assign consistent colors to wires — for example, red for VCC, black for GND, blue for data — to make circuits easier to troubleshoot.
- **Secure Connections:** For prototypes, breadboards are acceptable, but permanent setups should use soldered joints or crimped connectors. Loose wires are a major source of intermittent faults.
- **Labeling:** Mark wires and components with small labels to avoid confusion, especially in multi-sensor systems.

Debugging Techniques

Even with perfect wiring, IoT systems can misbehave due to noise, software errors, or faulty components. Debugging techniques allow engineers to isolate and solve problems quickly.

Serial Monitor for Real-Time Diagnostics

- **Purpose:** The Serial Monitor provides a simple, direct way to check system behavior by displaying sensor readings, actuator states, or error messages in real time.
- **Implementation:** Configure the microcontroller to output status messages at an appropriate baud rate (for example, 115200 for ESP32).
- **Usage Example:** Regularly outputting temperature readings or actuator switching states helps confirm that data is being captured and processed as expected.
- **Troubleshooting Tip:** Look for unexpected values (for example, "NaN" or zeroes) that may indicate wiring or timing issues.

Multimeter for Hardware Verification

- **Purpose:** A multimeter is an indispensable tool for verifying electrical conditions. It allows you to measure voltage, current, resistance, and continuity.
- **Implementation:**
    - Confirm that sensors and actuators receive the correct supply voltage (for example, 3.3V for ESP32).
    - Check signal lines to verify they fall within the expected ranges.
    - Use continuity mode to test for broken connections or miswiring.
- **Practical Note:** A multimeter can often identify problems before powering up the entire system, preventing potential damage.

Logic Analyzer for Signal Analysis

- **Purpose:** Some problems involve timing, rather than simple wiring. Logic analyzers capture and display signal waveforms, making it possible to inspect communication protocols such as I2C, SPI, or UART.
- **Implementation:** By probing GPIO pins, you can confirm whether digital protocols are operating correctly, or if noise is causing missed pulses.
- **Use Case:** When a sensor using I2C (for example, BME280) does not respond, a logic analyzer can reveal whether the clock and data lines are functioning properly.

Simulation Tools for Pre-Hardware Testing

- **Purpose:** Before committing to physical assembly, simulation platforms allow you to test circuit logic and code.
- **Implementation:** Use online simulators to model microcontrollers, sensors, and actuators, adjusting parameters to replicate real-world scenarios.
- **Benefit:** Early detection of logic errors in software reduces the time wasted on debugging of the hardware.

Best Practices

Best practices are habits and design standards that ensure your IoT systems are reliable, maintainable, and scalable over time.

Apply Software Filtering to Smooth Noisy Signals

- **Purpose:** Raw sensor data often contains noise, especially from analog sensors. Filtering improves accuracy and stability.
- **Techniques:**
  - **Moving Average:** Collect several consecutive readings, and calculate the average to smooth out spikes.
  - **Low-Pass Filtering:** Remove high-frequency noise, while preserving slower changes in sensor values.
- **Benefit:** By filtering data, decisions made by actuators (for example, turning on a pump) are based on stable inputs, rather than random fluctuations.

Always Cross-Check Wiring with Datasheets

- **Purpose:** Datasheets provide authoritative details on voltage levels, pin assignments, and operating conditions. Ignoring them risks damaging components.
- **Implementation:**
  - Verify supply voltage requirements before connecting (for example, confirm whether a sensor tolerates 3.3V or requires 5V).
  - Confirm resistor values for pull-up or pull-down configurations.
  - Ensure current requirements of actuators match driver circuit capabilities.
- **Practical Note:** Even small mistakes, such as omitting a pull-up resistor, can cause sensors to behave unpredictably.

Additional Best Practices

- **Modular Design:** Structure projects into reusable modules, both in code and hardware. This makes debugging and upgrading simpler.
- **Power Management:** Implement energy-saving techniques like sleep modes for battery-powered projects. Reducing consumption increases deployment lifetime.
- **Documentation:** Maintain clear notes on pin mappings, component specifications, and wiring diagrams. This reduces confusion during upgrades or repairs.
- **Incremental Testing:** Test each part of the system individually – first the sensor, then the actuator, and finally the combined loop. This approach makes it easier to isolate issues.

Practical Considerations

- **Wiring:** Use breadboards for prototypes, but switch to soldered PCBs for production. Protect connections with heat-shrink tubing to prevent accidental shorts.
- **Debugging:** Add small status indicators, such as LEDs, that signal when an error occurs. Maintain logs with timestamps for easier fault analysis.
- **Calibration Storage:** Save calibration values (for example, baseline readings from a gas sensor) in non-volatile memory so that they remain consistent after power cycles.
- **Regular Updates:** Keep libraries and firmware up to date to ensure compatibility, and take advantage of performance improvements.

Reliable IoT systems depend on more than just choosing the right sensors and actuators — they require disciplined wiring, careful debugging, and consistent best practices. Short wires minimize noise, common grounds prevent erratic readings, and shielded cables protect long analog signals. Debugging with tools such as the Serial Monitor, multimeters, and logic analyzers helps diagnose both hardware and timing issues. Software filtering improves data quality, while cross-checking wiring with datasheets prevents costly mistakes.

Thus, by applying these principles, readers can design IoT systems that are not only functional but also robust, accurate, and long-lasting — whether for agriculture, smart homes, healthcare, or industrial automation.

Practical Exercises

Practical exercises bridge theory and application, enabling readers to internalize IoT concepts by working with sensors (*eyes and ears*) and actuators (*muscles*). Building on Chapter 2's IoT ecosystem (Perception, Network, Application layers) and Sections which covered sensors, actuators, interfacing, power handling, and wiring/debugging, this section presents three hands-on exercises: Sensor Identification Challenge, Simulate Sensor Readings, and Sensor-to-Actuator Loop Demo. These exercises reinforce sensor categorization, simulation, and sensor-actuator integration using ESP32/ Arduino and tools like Arduino IDE and Wokwi simulator. Detailed instructions, code snippets, wiring diagrams, and global applications (for example: agriculture, smart homes, and security) ensure practical learning. By completing these exercises, readers will gain confidence in designing reliable IoT systems.

Exercise 1: Sensor Identification Challenge

Task: Identify the sensor type, voltage range, use-case, and ESP32 pin type for four real-world scenarios, internalizing sensor categorization and applications.

Scenarios:

1. Temperature reading for room automation.
2. Detecting gas leakage.
3. Motion sensing in corridors.
4. Ambient light for display brightness control.

Instructions

- For each scenario, research and identify:
    - **Sensor Type:** Digital, analog, or smart (based on output).
    - **Voltage Range:** Operating voltage (for example: 3.3–5V).
    - **Use-Case:** Practical application in IoT systems.
    - **ESP32 Pin Type:** GPIO, ADC, or I2C/SPI.
- Use datasheets or online resources (for example: manufacturer websites) to verify specifications.
- Document findings in a table, and explain the rationale for each choice.

Implementation

- **Steps:**
    1. Research each sensor's datasheet (for example: DHT22: ±0.5°C, 3.3-5V; MQ-2: 300–10,000 ppm, 5V).
    2. Match scenarios to applications (for example: PIR for security, LDR for displays).
    3. Identify ESP32 pins (for example: GPIO 4 for DHT22, A0 for MQ-2).
- **Deliverable:** Complete the table, and justify choices in 100–150 words per scenario.

Exercise 2: Simulate Sensor Readings (No Hardware Required)

Task: Use Arduino IDE or Wokwi simulator to simulate analog sensor readings, and practice sensor logic without hardware.

Steps:

1. Load analogRead () code with dummy data.
2. Manually change simulated values.
3. Print to Serial Monitor: "Temperature = XX °C".

Instructions

- Use Wokwi (wokwi.com) or Arduino IDE to simulate an analog temperature sensor (for example, mimicking LM35).
- Write the code to read dummy values (0–1023, simulating ADC output) and map to temperature (0–100°C).
- Output results to Serial Monitor for debugging.

Implementation

- **Steps:**
  1. Open Wokwi (wokwi.com), select ESP32.
  2. Add a potentiometer (simulating analog sensor) to A0.
  3. Load the code above.
  4. Adjust the potentiometer slider to simulate ADC values (0–1023).
  5. Open Serial Monitor (115200 baud) to view output: "Temperature = XX °C".

Exercise 3: Sensor-to-Actuator Loop Demo

Task: Write a program for a motion-activated buzzer, simulating a complete sensor–actuator loop.

Steps:

1. Simulate motion input (digital toggle).
2. Trigger buzzer output (`digitalWrite`).
3. Add delay/reset logic.

Instructions

- Use Wokwi to simulate an HC-SR501 PIR sensor (digital input) triggering a buzzer (digital output) on ESP32.
- Write code to detect motion (HIGH), activate the buzzer for 2 seconds, and reset with a delay to prevent rapid retriggering.
- Output status to Serial Monitor for debugging.

Hardware Setup (Simulated in Wokwi)

- **Components**:
  - **HC-SR501 PIR**: OUT to ESP32 GPIO 5, VCC to 5V, GND to GND.
  - **Buzzer**: Positive to ESP32 GPIO 8, negative to GND.

- **Wokwi Setup**:
    1. Add ESP32, PIR sensor, and buzzer to Wokwi canvas.
    2. Connect PIR OUT to GPIO 5, buzzer to GPIO 8.
    3. Use Wokwi's PIR toggle to simulate motion.

Practical Considerations

- **Exercise 1**:
    - Use online resources (for example: Adafruit, SparkFun) for datasheet specs.
    - Cross-check ESP32 pinout (GPIO for digital, A0–A5 for analog).
- **Exercise 2**:
    - Experiment with different map () ranges (for example: 0–50°C for LM35).
    - Add error handling (for example, check for invalid ADC values).
- **Exercise 3**:
    - Add debouncing (200 ms) for PIR to avoid false triggers.
    - Test with physical hardware after simulation to validate results.
- **Tools**:
    - Arduino IDE for coding and Serial Monitor debugging.
    - Wokwi for no-hardware simulation, ideal for prototyping.

Conclusion

This chapter has provided a comprehensive exploration of the sensory and reactive components that form the backbone of Internet of Things (IoT) systems, equipping readers with the practical skills to design, implement, and troubleshoot IoT projects. By treating sensors as the eyes and ears and actuators as the muscles of a living organism, this chapter has illuminated how these components work together in the Perception Layer to sense environmental changes, and execute intelligent responses. From classifying sensors to interfacing actuators, managing power, and building real-world automation loops, this chapter has laid a solid foundation for creating responsive IoT systems using platforms like ESP32 and Arduino. Through hands-on exercises, readers have internalized these concepts, preparing them to bridge the physical and digital worlds. This summary recaps the key topics covered, and sets the stage for Chapter 4, which will delve into communication protocols and middleware layers for scalable IoT ecosystems.

Sensors are the sensory organs of IoT systems, capturing environmental data such as temperature, motion, gas, light, and sound. They can be categorized into digital sensors (for example, HC-SR501 PIR, outputting HIGH/LOW), analog sensors (for example, MQ-2 gas sensor, producing continuous voltages), and smart sensors (for example, DHT22, with onboard processing and protocols like I2C). This classification helps developers choose sensors based on application needs, whether for binary event detection, high-granularity measurements, or processed data. Their operation is rooted in physical principles such as thermistors for temperature, resistive changes for gas detection, or infrared sensing for motion, highlighting how environmental changes are translated into electrical signals. Calibration techniques, including offset adjustments (for example, -0.5°C for DHT22) and scaling ADC values (for example, MQ-2's 0–1023 to 300–10,000 ppm), ensure measurement accuracy. Common IoT sensors such as temperature (DHT22), motion (HC-SR501), gas (MQ-2), light (LDR), and sound (KY-038) play key roles in applications ranging from smart homes to industrial monitoring.

Practical interfacing with ESP32 and Arduino further demonstrates how these sensors can be deployed. Digital sensors such as PIR modules connect to GPIO pins for simple HIGH/LOW readings, requiring little calibration. Analog sensors such as MQ-2 connect through ADC pins, and often require noise filtering (for example, 0.1 μF capacitors) alongside calibration to map voltage ranges to meaningful values. Smart sensors like DHT22 use single-wire or I2C communication, supported by libraries (for example, DHT.h), but require precise timing, such as a two-second sampling interval. Code snippets illustrate how to read sensor values (for example, digitalRead for PIR, analogRead for MQ-2), and wiring provide reliable connection references. Ensuring stable signals, and integrating actuators are equally critical for building reliable IoT systems. Pull-up and pull-down resistors prevent floating pins, ensuring stable HIGH (for example, 10 kΩ to VCC for DHT22) or LOW (for example, 10 kΩ to GND for buttons) states. Debouncing techniques, whether hardware-based (for example, 0.1 μF capacitors) or software-based (for example, 50 ms delays), eliminate false triggers caused by noisy inputs such as mechanical switches or PIR modules. Such practices are essential for robust system performance, as demonstrated in India's irrigation systems where pull-down resistors ensure stable switch inputs.

Actuators serve as the muscles of IoT systems, executing actions in response to sensor inputs. Electrical actuators such as relays, buzzers, and LEDs manage appliances or provide alerts, with relays (5V, 70 mA) handling high-power switching and LEDs (3.3V, 20 mA) serving as status indicators. Mechanical actuators, including DC motors, servo motors, and stepper motors, enable motion and precise control, making them indispensable in robotics, automation, and industrial machinery. Displays such as LCD and OLED modules function as feedback actuators, conveying system states directly to users. Choosing actuators based on voltage, current capacity, and intended application ensures reliable operation within IoT projects.

Overall, this chapter has shown how sensors and actuators work in harmony to create intelligent and responsive IoT systems. By understanding their principles, classifications, calibration methods, interfacing techniques, and integration challenges, readers are well prepared to design IoT solutions that seamlessly connect the physical and digital realms.

In the next chapter, we will dive into IoT communication protocols and middleware, including MQTT, HTTP/REST, BLE, and LoRa, and learn hands-on techniques to connect ESP32 devices to cloud platforms and public brokers, building real-world sensor-to-cloud applications.

CHAPTER 4

Networking and Communication Protocols (MQTT, HTTP, LoRa, BLE)

Introduction

In the preceding chapters, we laid a robust foundation for understanding the Internet of Things (IoT) by delving into its architectural framework, as outlined in *Chapter 2*, and exploring the core components of the Perception Layer—sensors and actuators—in *Chapter 3*. *Chapter 2* introduced the three-layer IoT architecture (Perception, Network, and Application), elucidating how devices, gateways, and routers collaborate to enable data flow across protocols like HTTP and MQTT, with real-world examples ranging from smart homes to industrial automation. *Chapter 3* then deepened this knowledge by classifying sensors into digital (for example, PIR motion sensors), analog (for example, MQ-2 gas sensors), and smart (for example, DHT22 temperature sensors), detailing their interfacing with microcontrollers such as ESP32 and Arduino, and exploring actuators (for example, relays, motors) that translate digital commands into physical actions. These chapters collectively demonstrated how sensors act as the eyes and ears—detecting environmental changes like temperature, motion, or gas levels—while actuators serve as the muscles, executing responses such as turning on a fan or sounding an alarm.

However, an IoT system becomes truly powerful, and reaches its scaling inflection point, only when devices can communicate across networks. Without connectivity, a temperature sensor remains an isolated device, limited to local data collection and basic actuation. With networking, it transforms into a dynamic component of a smart home ecosystem—automatically adjusting air conditioning based on real-time readings, logging historical data to the cloud for long-term analysis. This seamless communication is the lifeblood of IoT, often employing distinct protocol families to manage data exchange: request-response (like a web browser asking for a page), publish-subscribe (where sensors publish data and applications subscribe to it, such as MQTT), and device-to-device (direct, low-latency communication between two devices). These protocols enable scalability, remote monitoring, and intelligent automation across diverse applications, from precision agriculture in rural India to smart city traffic management in Singapore. It transforms isolated components into a cohesive ecosystem, where data flows from sensors through networks to applications, driving decisions and actions in real time.

This chapter on IoT Communication Protocols and Networking, shifts the focus to the Network Layer, where devices transcend physical boundaries to exchange data efficiently and securely. We will begin by revisiting fundamental networking concepts—IP addresses, ports, Local Area Networks (LAN), and Wide Area Networks (WAN)—to establish a common vocabulary essential for IoT developers. This will pave the way for a detailed exploration of networking models such as the Open Systems Interconnection (OSI) model and the Transmission Control Protocol/Internet Protocol (TCP/IP) stack, adapted to the unique demands of IoT systems, including low power consumption, intermittent connectivity, and massive device scaling. These models provide a structured framework for understanding how data packets traverse networks, from the physical layer (for example, cables, wireless signals) to the application layer (for example, user interfaces).

Next, we will dive into the most widely adopted IoT communication protocols, each designed to address specific use cases and constraints. MQTT (Message Queuing Telemetry Transport), a lightweight publish/subscribe protocol, excels in resource-constrained environments like smart meters, offering low bandwidth usage, reliable message delivery, and Quality of Service (QoS) levels for guaranteed transmission. HTTP/REST (HyperText Transfer Protocol/Representational State Transfer), a request-response model, powers web-based IoT applications such as weather stations uploading data to cloud platforms, leveraging JSON for structured payloads and endpoints for API interactions. BLE (Bluetooth Low Energy) provides short-range, energy-efficient communication for wearables and home automation devices, with features like advertising packets and GATT profiles for data exchange. LoRa (Long Range) enables long-distance, low-power connectivity, ideal for remote sensor networks in agriculture or environmental monitoring, using spread-spectrum modulation for robust signal penetration.

The chapter will also address critical considerations such as security (for example, TLS encryption for MQTT, secure pairing in BLE), power optimization (for example, duty cycling in LoRa, low-energy advertising in BLE), and scalability (for example, broker load balancing for MQTT, edge gateways for LoRa). Global examples will illustrate practical deployments: MQTT in Japan's smart factories for real-time machine monitoring and predictive maintenance, HTTP/REST in Brazil's weather forecasting systems for seamless cloud integration, BLE in Australia's healthcare wearables for continuous vital sign tracking, and LoRa in India's rural irrigation networks for low-cost, long-range crop monitoring. By the end, you will possess a comprehensive understanding of how networking and protocols enable IoT systems to communicate effectively, preparing you for advanced topics in cloud integration, edge computing, and large-scale deployments in the subsequent chapters.

Structure

In this chapter, we will cover the following topics:

- Fundamentals of IoT Networking
- OSI Model and TCP/IP for IoT
- MQTT Protocol
- HTTP and REST APIs
- Bluetooth Low Energy (BLE)
- LoRa: Long-Range, Low-Power Communication
- Setting up ESP32 for Wi-Fi and Cloud
- Connecting to Public MQTT Brokers
- Sending Sensor Data via HTTP POST
- BLE Scanning and Device-to-Device Communication
- LoRa Transmission Use Cases
- Common Pitfalls in IoT Networking
- Choosing the Right Protocol
- Practical Exercises

Fundamentals of IoT Networking

Networking serves as the backbone that enables IoT devices to connect, share data, and interact seamlessly, transforming isolated sensors and actuators into a cohesive ecosystem. Furthermore, networking failures are among the most common causes of IoT system instability and downtime. This section lays the groundwork by exploring the vital concepts that underpin IoT communication, ensuring that devices can communicate effectively across local and global scales. Hence, understanding these fundamentals is critical for designing reliable IoT systems, whether for smart homes, industrial automation, or environmental monitoring.

LAN and WAN

The foundation of IoT networking lies in the distinction between LAN (Local Area Network) and WAN (Wide Area Network), which define the scope and reach of device connectivity.

- **LAN (Local Area Network):** A LAN connects devices within a confined geographical area, such as a home, office, or factory floor. For instance, smart bulbs, thermostats, and security cameras in a home Wi-Fi network form a LAN, enabling real-time interaction via protocols like Wi-Fi or Ethernet. LANs offer high bandwidth (up to 1 Gbps with modern Wi-Fi 6) and low latency, making them ideal for applications requiring immediate response, such as a smart doorbell alerting a user instantly. ESP32-based projects initially operate within a LAN before scaling outward.
- **WAN (Wide Area Network):** A WAN extends connectivity across larger distances, linking devices across cities, countries, or continents. Examples include sensors sending data via GSM networks to a central server or LoRaWAN-enabled devices monitoring remote agricultural fields in rural India. Gateways often act as the bridge, receiving data from local, short-range LAN technologies (such as Wi-Fi or Bluetooth) and forwarding it to the wider WAN using technologies like cellular or satellite. WANs rely on technologies such as cellular (4G/5G), satellite, or LoRa, offering lower bandwidth but greater range (up to tens of kilometers for LoRa), suitable for applications like smart grid monitoring or disaster management.

IP Address

Every device on a network requires a unique IP address to identify and communicate with other devices, acting as a digital address in the vast IoT landscape.

IP addresses are categorized as either **Private** or **Public**.

- **Private IP addresses** are used within a private network (like your home or office LAN) to allow devices to communicate with each other. These addresses are not routable on the public internet.
- **Public IP addresses** are unique, globally routable addresses assigned to your network by your Internet Service Provider (ISP). This is the address that identifies your network to the outside world, allowing your devices to access the internet.
- **IPv4:** The traditional 32-bit addressing scheme supports approximately 4.3 billion unique addresses, commonly used in home and small office networks. However, with the explosive growth of IoT devices, IPv4 is nearing its limit, often supplemented by Network Address Translation (NAT) to reuse addresses.
- **IPv6:** The next-generation 128-bit addressing scheme offers an almost limitless number of addresses (2^128), future-proofing IoT deployments by accommodating billions of devices. For example, IPv6 enables every sensor in a smart city like Singapore to have a unique address, enhancing scalability and simplifying network management. However, many existing IoT

deployments still rely on IPv4 with Network Address Translation (NAT) for connectivity, even as the industry moves toward IPv6 readiness.

Ports and MAC Address

Ports and MAC addresses provide additional layers of identification and service management within IoT networks.

- **Port Numbers:** Ports are virtual endpoints that identify specific services or applications on a device. *Caution: Exposing ports directly to the internet without proper firewalls and security controls can pose significant security risks.* For instance, HTTP traffic uses port 80 for web access, while MQTT leverages port 1883 for messaging. These ports allow multiple services to coexist on a single IP address, such as an ESP32 hosting both a web server and an MQTT client simultaneously.
- **MAC Address:** The Media Access Control (MAC) address is a unique 48-bit identifier assigned to a device's network adapter, ensuring that no two devices share the same hardware identity. For example, an ESP32's Wi-Fi module has a MAC address like 24:6F:28:12:34:56, used for local network identification and device tracking, distinct from its IP address which may change dynamically. (*Advanced Aside: Modern operating systems often employ MAC address randomization when scanning or connecting to Wi-Fi networks to enhance user privacy by making it more difficult to track a device's movements based on a static hardware identifier.*)

OSI Model and TCP/IP for IoT

The ability of IoT devices to communicate effectively relies on structured networking models that define how data is transmitted across layers. This section introduces the OSI (Open Systems Interconnection) model, a seven-layer framework that provides a comprehensive blueprint for network communication, and the TCP/IP model, a more streamlined four-layer approach widely adopted in IoT systems. Understanding these models is essential for designing efficient, interoperable IoT networks, whether for local smart home setups or global industrial deployments.

OSI Model (7 Layers)

The OSI model breaks down network communication into seven distinct layers, each with specific functions tailored to IoT applications:

- **Physical Layer:** This layer deals with the physical transmission of raw signals over hardware mediums. In IoT, this includes LoRa radio waves for long-range communication, Wi-Fi RF signals for high-speed local connectivity, or Ethernet cables in industrial settings. It defines voltage levels, signal types, and connector specifications, ensuring that devices like ESP32 transceivers can interface with the network.
- **Data Link Layer:** Responsible for node-to-node data transfer and error detection, this layer manages MAC addressing to uniquely identify devices (an ESP32's Wi-Fi MAC) and facilitates processes such as BLE pairing for secure short-range connections. It also handles frame synchronization and collision avoidance in Wi-Fi networks.
- **Network Layer:** This layer handles IP addressing and routing, enabling devices to find paths across networks. For instance, an IoT sensor in a WAN uses IPv6 to route data to a cloud server, ensuring scalability in smart city deployments.
- **Transport Layer:** This layer manages end-to-end connections and data reliability using protocols like TCP (for guaranteed delivery) and UDP (for low-latency, best-effort delivery). In IoT, TCP ensures that critical data (health monitor readings) reaches its destination, while UDP suits real-time applications like video streams.

- **Session Layer:** This layer establishes, manages, and terminates communication sessions. In IoT, it is rarely customized, as protocols like MQTT handle session management implicitly, though it can support persistent connections in industrial gateways.
- **Presentation Layer:** Focused on data formatting and encryption, this layer translates data into a common format (for example: JSON for MQTT payloads, XML for HTTP responses) and ensures compatibility between devices and applications, such as formatting sensor data for cloud analytics.
- **Application Layer:** The top layer interfaces with IoT applications, hosting protocols like MQTT for messaging, HTTP for web services, and CoAP for constrained devices. It enables end-user interactions, such as controlling a smart thermostat via a mobile app.

TCP/IP in IoT

IoT systems predominantly rely on the TCP/IP model, a simplified four-layer framework that aligns with the OSI model but is optimized for practical implementation:

- **Link Layer:** Equivalent to OSI's Physical and Data Link layers, this layer handles hardware-specific communication, including MAC addressing, Wi-Fi, and BLE pairing. It ensures that data frames are transmitted reliably over the physical medium.
- **Internet Layer (IP):** Corresponding to the OSI Network Layer, this layer manages IP addressing (IPv4 or IPv6) and routing, allowing devices to communicate across LANs and WANs, such as a LoRa sensor sending data to a remote server.
- **Transport Layer (TCP/UDP):** Mapping to the OSI Transport Layer, this layer provides TCP for reliable, ordered data delivery (HTTP requests) and UDP for lightweight, real-time transmission (IoT sensor updates), balancing reliability and efficiency.
- **Application Layer:** Aligning with OSI's Session, Presentation, and Application layers, this layer supports IoT protocols such as MQTT, HTTP, and CoAP, enabling applications such as publishing sensor data to ThingSpeak or subscribing to MQTT topics for device control.

MQTT Protocol

MQTT (Message Queuing Telemetry Transport) stands out as the most widely adopted IoT communication protocol due to its lightweight design, high efficiency, and robust reliability, making it ideal for resource-constrained devices and unreliable networks. Developed in 1999 by IBM for oil pipeline monitoring, MQTT has evolved into a cornerstone of modern IoT applications, powering everything from smart homes to industrial automation. Its simplicity and low bandwidth usage (often less than 2 bytes overhead per message) allow devices like ESP32 microcontrollers to transmit data efficiently, even in remote or low-power environments.

Core Concepts

The MQTT protocol operates on a set of core principles that enable flexible and scalable communication:

- **Publish/Subscribe Model:** Unlike traditional request-response protocols, MQTT uses a publish/subscribe architecture. Devices, known as publishers, send messages to specific topics (home/room/temperature), while other devices, or subscribers, receive these messages by subscribing to the same topics. This decoupling allows for one-to-many communication such as a temperature sensor publishing data that updates multiple dashboards or triggers an actuator, enhancing system flexibility in applications like smart agriculture.

- **Broker:** The central hub of an MQTT system, the broker manages message distribution between publishers and subscribers. It authenticates devices, routes messages to the appropriate topics, and ensures delivery based on Quality of Service (QoS) levels. Popular brokers include HiveMQ (a cloud-based solution), Mosquitto (an open-source option), and Adafruit IO (ideal for prototyping). For instance, a Mosquitto broker running on a local server can handle real-time updates from sensors in a Japanese smart factory.
- **Topics:** These are hierarchical strings that categorize messages, functioning like channels or addresses. This structure allows fine-grained control, enabling subscribers to receive only relevant data. For example, a smart home system might use to control a specific light bulb, while subscribing to all home-related updates.
- **QoS (Quality of Service):** MQTT offers three QoS levels to balance reliability and performance:
    - **QoS 0 (At Most Once):** Fire-and-forget delivery with no guarantee, suitable for non-critical data like weather updates, minimizing overhead.
    - **QoS 1 (At Least Once):** Ensures delivery with acknowledgments, ideal for sensor readings where duplicates are tolerable but loss is not.
    - **QoS 2 (Exactly Once):** Provides guaranteed, duplicate-free delivery using a four-step handshake, critical for financial or health-related data. For example, an ESP32 publishing heart rate data to a medical IoT system might use QoS 2 for accuracy.

      Note: *This level of service introduces the highest overhead and latency compared to* QoS 0 *and* QoS 1.

These concepts collectively make MQTT a versatile protocol, widely adopted in global IoT deployments such as smart grids in Europe, environmental monitoring in Australia, and industrial IoT in India, where reliable, low-bandwidth communication is paramount.

HTTP and REST APIs

HTTP (HyperText Transfer Protocol) and REST (Representational State Transfer) APIs are foundational technologies for IoT systems that require web-based communication, enabling devices to interact with cloud platforms, databases, and user interfaces. Known for their widespread adoption in web development, these protocols have been adapted for IoT to facilitate data exchange between sensors, actuators, and remote services. Their robustness and compatibility with the existing internet infrastructure make them ideal for applications like weather monitoring, smart home dashboards, and industrial data logging, where structured data delivery is essential.

HTTP Basics

HTTP operates on a request-response model, where a client sends a request to a server, which processes it and returns a response. This model underpins RESTful communication, making it suitable for IoT devices interacting with cloud platforms.

- **Request-Response Model:** The client initiates communication with a request (asking for sensor data), and the server replies with a response (the latest temperature reading). This stateless nature ensures simplicity but requires careful session management for continuous IoT tasks.
- **Common Methods**:
    - **GET:** Retrieves data from a server, such as querying a ThingSpeak channel for historical temperature values.
    - **POST:** Sends data to a server, like uploading sensor readings to Firebase.

  - **PUT:** Updates the existing data, useful for modifying a device's configuration on a cloud platform.
  - **DELETE:** Removes data, such as clearing old logs from a server.
- **Payload Format**: Data is typically formatted in JSON (JavaScript Object Notation), a lightweight, human-readable structure. JSON's compatibility with web services and ease of parsing make it the preferred choice for IoT payloads, enabling seamless integration with platforms such as ThingSpeak or Google Cloud.

Example: Sending Data to ThingSpeak via HTTP POST

To demonstrate HTTP in action, consider sending temperature data from an ESP32 to ThingSpeak, a popular IoT analytics platform. ThingSpeak requires an API key and a channel ID for authentication and data routing. The following is a step-by-step example:

1. **Setup:** Connect a DHT22 sensor to an ESP32, and obtain a ThingSpeak API key as well as channel ID.
2. **Code Outline:** Use the ESP32's Wi-Fi and HTTP client libraries to send the data.
3. **HTTP POST Request:** Construct a request to https://api.thingspeak.com/update with a payload like **`field1=25.5&api_key=YOUR_API_KEY`**, where field1 represents the temperature value.
4. **Execution:** The ESP32 reads the sensor, sends the POST request every 15 seconds (per ThingSpeak's rate limit, *which may vary by platform, and should always be verified*), and receives a response to confirm data upload.

Result: The temperature data appears on the ThingSpeak dashboard, accessible globally for monitoring or analysis, such as tracking climate conditions in a Brazilian smart farm.

This example highlights HTTP's role in bridging IoT devices with cloud services, a common practice in applications ranging from weather stations in Australia to industrial sensors in Germany.

Bluetooth Low Energy (BLE)

Bluetooth Low Energy (BLE) is a power-efficient wireless communication protocol designed for short-range IoT applications, distinguishing itself from Classic Bluetooth by prioritizing low power consumption over high data throughput. making it a go-to choice for wearables, smart home devices, and healthcare monitors. Introduced as part of the Bluetooth 4.0 specification in 2010, BLE consumes significantly less power than classic Bluetooth enabling devices to operate for months or even years on a single coin-cell battery. Its widespread adoption in devices such as fitness trackers and smart locks highlights its importance in creating responsive, low-power IoT ecosystems, particularly in scenarios requiring frequent data updates with minimal energy drain.

Key Concepts

BLE's design revolves around efficient, secure, and low-bandwidth communication, defined by the following core concepts:

- **Advertising:** BLE devices broadcast small packets of data, and the advertising intervals directly impact power consumption. To announce their presence, allowing nearby devices to detect and connect. For example, a BLE-enabled temperature sensor might advertise its service UUID enabling a smartphone to discover it without an initial connection, a process critical for applications like asset tracking in warehouses.

- **Pairing:** This process establishes a secure connection between two BLE devices, often using encryption to protect data. Pairing involves exchanging keys during a handshake, ensuring that only authorized devices can communicate, enhancing security in healthcare wearables, and monitoring sensitive data.
- **Data Exchange:** BLE transfers small data packets (typically 20–250 bytes) with low power consumption, optimized for infrequent updates, rather than continuous streams. This suits IoT use cases like sending heart rate readings every few seconds from a fitness tracker to a mobile app, balancing efficiency and functionality in low-power environments.

ESP32 BLE Example

To illustrate BLE in practice, consider using an ESP32 microcontroller to create a BLE peripheral that advertises temperature data, and connects to a smartphone.

1. **Setup:** Connect a DHT11 sensor to an ESP32, and install the Arduino BLE library.
2. **Code Outline:** Configure the ESP32 as a BLE server, defining a service and characteristic for temperature data.
3. **Advertising:** Set the ESP32 to broadcast its presence with a device name and service UUID, detectable by a BLE scanner app.
4. **Pairing:** Implement a simple pairing process where a smartphone app requests a connection, authenticated via a pre-shared key.
5. **Data Exchange:** Read the DHT11 every 5 seconds, update the characteristic value and notify the connected app, which displays the data in real-time.
6. **Result:** The smartphone app successfully monitors temperature, useful for a smart home system in India, with the ESP32 operating efficiently on minimal power.

LoRa: Long-Range Low-Power Communication

LoRa (Long Range) is a revolutionary wireless communication technology tailored for long-distance, low-power IoT applications, making it an ideal choice for rural or large-scale deployments such as agriculture, environmental monitoring, and disaster management. Developed by Semtech and standardized under the LoRaWAN specification, LoRa leverages Chirp Spread Spectrum (CSS) modulation to achieve exceptional range and penetration through obstacles like buildings or foliage, where traditional Wi-Fi or cellular networks falter. Its ability to operate on minimal power—extending battery life to 5–10 years for end nodes—positions it as a game-changer for remote IoT ecosystems, from Indian farmland irrigation systems to flood detection networks in Southeast Asia.

LoRa Basics

LoRa's design is optimized for efficiency and reliability in challenging environments, defined by the following key characteristics:

- **Operates in sub-GHz frequency bands:** These unlicensed bands offer long-range communication with low interference, though specific frequencies vary by region. This allows LoRa devices such as ESP32-LoRa modules to connect in areas with limited infrastructure.
- **Coverage:** Up to 10–15 km: In rural settings with line-of-sight, LoRa can extend up to 15 km, and even 2–5 km in urban environments, making it suitable for sprawling applications like smart cities or forest monitoring.
- **Low data rate, high reliability:** With data rates ranging from 0.3 to 50 kbps, LoRa prioritizes reliability over speed, using Forward Error Correction (FEC) to ensure data integrity over long distances, ideal for periodic updates like soil moisture readings.

Example Applications

LoRa's strengths shine in real-world IoT deployments, particularly in resource-constrained or remote areas:

- **Smart Farming (Soil Moisture Data):** In rural India, LoRa-enabled sensors monitor soil moisture levels, transmitting data to a gateway every hour. This data guides irrigation systems, reducing water waste by 30–40% and boosting crop yields, demonstrating LoRa's role in sustainable agriculture.
- **Disaster Management (Flood Sensors):** In flood-prone regions like Bangladesh, LoRa sensors detect water levels and send alerts to a network server, enabling early warnings to communities. The long range and low power ensure continuous operation during power outages or network disruptions.

Setting up ESP32 for Wi-Fi and Cloud

The ESP32 microcontroller is a powerhouse for IoT networking, offering greater memory and processing capabilities than simpler microcontrollers, though this comes with a slightly higher power consumption profile. Featuring built-in Wi-Fi and Bluetooth capabilities that make it ideal for connecting to the internet and cloud services, this section provides a step-by-step guide to setting up the ESP32 for Wi-Fi connectivity and cloud integration, enabling devices to send sensor data and receive commands. With its dual-core processor (up to 240 MHz), 520 KB SRAM, and support for 802.11 b/g/n Wi-Fi, the ESP32 facilitates seamless communication with platforms like ThingSpeak or Firebase, powering applications from smart agriculture to home automation.

Steps

1. **Connect ESP32 to Wi-Fi using SSID and Password:**
   a. **Purpose:** Establish internet connectivity for data transmission.
   b. **Process:** Use the WiFi.h library in Arduino IDE to scan networks and connect.
   c. **Configuration:** Enter SSID and password in code; ESP32 supports WPA2 security.
   d. **Testing:** Monitor Serial output for connection status and IP address
2. **Configure MQTT Client or HTTP Client:**
   a. **MQTT Client:** For publish/subscribe messaging, use **PubSubClient** library to connect to a broker.
   b. **HTTP Client:** For request-response, use **HTTPClient** library for GET/POST to services like ThingSpeak.
   c. **Configuration:** Set broker URL/port for MQTT; API endpoints for HTTP.
3. **Test Connectivity with Public Brokers or APIs:**
   a. **MQTT Test:** Publish to HiveMQ public broker (broker.hivemq.com:1883), and subscribe to a topic using a client like MQTT Explorer.
   b. **HTTP Test:** Send a POST to a public API, and verify response (status 200).
   c. **Verification:** Use Serial Monitor for ESP32 logs; tools like Wireshark for packet inspection.
   d. **Example:** ESP32 sends DHT22 temperature to ThingSpeak via HTTP POST, visible on the dashboard.

Connecting to Public MQTT Brokers

Public MQTT brokers provide a convenient way for IoT developers to test and deploy MQTT-based applications without setting up private servers, making them invaluable for prototyping and learning. MQTT (Message Queuing Telemetry Transport), with its lightweight publish/subscribe model, thrives in such environments, enabling devices like ESP32 microcontrollers to share data efficiently, connecting to public brokers such as HiveMQ, Adafruit IO, and Eclipse Mosquitto allows real-time communication for projects ranging from smart classrooms to environmental monitoring. This section explores these brokers, their configurations, and practical usage, using a sample topic like iot/classroom/temperature to illustrate data exchange.

- **HiveMQ Public Broker:** The HiveMQ Public Broker is a cloud-hosted MQTT broker offered by HiveMQ, designed for testing and educational purposes. It operates on broker.hivemq.com at port 1883 (non-SSL) or 8883 (SSL), supporting unauthenticated connections for public use. Its global availability ensures low latency, making it suitable for international IoT projects. To connect an ESP32, configure it with the broker address, and publish to iot/classroom/temperature with a payload such as 24.5°C. Subscribers (using MQTT Explorer) can monitor this topic, ideal for a classroom temperature dashboard. Security is limited due to public access, so it is the best for non-sensitive data or development phases.
- **Adafruit IO:** Adafruit IO is a cloud platform tailored for IoT, offering an MQTT broker integrated with its dashboard and data visualization tools. Accessible via io.adafruit.com at port 1883, it requires an Adafruit IO username, and an active key for authentication, ensuring a secure connection. This broker supports feeds (username/feeds/temperature) that align with the sample topic iot/classroom/temperature when mapped accordingly. An ESP32 can publish DHT11 sensor data (`{"value": 23.8}`) every 15 seconds, adhering to Adafruit's rate limits. The platform's user-friendly interface allows real-time plotting, making it perfect for educational settings or hobbyist projects in regions like India or Australia.
- **Eclipse Mosquitto:** Eclipse Mosquitto is an open-source MQTT broker with public instances available for testing, such as test.mosquitto.org on port 1883. Known for its reliability and lightweight footprint, Mosquitto is widely used in both development and production environments. Connecting an ESP32 involves setting the broker address and publishing to iot/classroom/temperature with a payload like 25.0°C. Subscribers can use tools such as Node-RED to visualize data, supporting applications like smart classroom monitoring in Japan. While public instances lack authentication, local Mosquitto setups can be secured with TLS, making it versatile for global IoT deployments from Europe to Southeast Asia.

Practical Example with ESP32

Using the sample topic iot/classroom/temperature, configure an ESP32 with the PubSubClient library. Connect to HiveMQ (broker.hivemq.com, port 1883), publish a DHT22 reading (24.7°C) every 5 seconds, and subscribe to receive updates. For Adafruit IO, use io.adafruit.com, your username, and key, mapping the topic to a feed. With Mosquitto, test on test.mosquitto.org similarly. Monitor via Serial output or a client like MQTTLens, ensuring connectivity with ping responses. This setup supports real-time temperature tracking, enhancing classroom comfort or remote learning systems, worldwide.

Considerations

- **Security:** Public brokers lack encryption; use SSL ports or private servers for sensitive data.
- **Rate Limits:** Adafruit IO limits to 30 requests/minute; adjust intervals accordingly.
- **Reliability:** Test connectivity; public servers may face downtime.

- **Global Use:** Brokers such as HiveMQ suit wide-area tests, while Adafruit IO excels in integrated dashboards.

This exploration equips you to leverage public MQTT brokers effectively, bridging IoT devices to global networks.

Sending Sensor Data via HTTP POST

The ability to send sensor data from IoT devices to cloud platforms is a cornerstone of modern IoT applications, enabling real-time monitoring, data analysis, and remote control. HTTP POST, a method within the HyperText Transfer Protocol (HTTP), allows devices to upload data to a server in a structured format, making it ideal for integrating IoT systems with cloud services. This section focuses on using an ESP32 microcontroller to send sensor data via HTTP POST to the Firebase Real-time Database, a popular NoSQL cloud database that provides real-time data synchronization and a user-friendly dashboard. By storing data as JSON objects, this approach supports diverse applications, from smart home temperature monitoring to industrial sensor networks, offering scalability and accessibility across global deployments.

Overview of HTTP POST in IoT

HTTP POST is a request-response method where a client, such as an ESP32, sends data to a server, which processes and stores it. Unlike GET, which retrieves data, POST is designed to submit data—making it perfect for uploading sensor readings like temperature, humidity, or motion detection. In IoT, this data is typically formatted as a JSON (JavaScript Object Notation) object, a lightweight and human-readable structure that cloud platforms like Firebase can easily parse and display. The process involves establishing a Wi-Fi connection, crafting the HTTP request with the appropriate endpoint and payload, and handling the server's response to confirm successful data transmission. This method's compatibility with RESTful APIs ensures seamless integration with platforms that support web-based data exchange, a standard in today's connected world.

Firebase Real-time Database

The Firebase Real-time Database, offered by Google, is a cloud-hosted database that stores data as JSON and synchronizes it in real-time across all connected clients. Its REST API allows IoT devices to interact with it using HTTP requests, making it an excellent choice for projects requiring immediate data updates. Each Firebase project has a unique URL (*https://your-project-id.firebaseio.com/*) and requires an authentication token or secret key for secure access. Once the data is posted, it becomes instantly available on the Firebase dashboard or any connected app, supporting use cases like monitoring environmental conditions in a smart classroom or tracking equipment status in a factory. Its global infrastructure, with servers in multiple regions, ensures low latency and high availability, benefiting users from India to the United States.

Example: ESP32 Posts Sensor Data to Firebase Real-time Database

This example demonstrates how to configure an ESP32 to read data from a DHT11 temperature and humidity sensor, and send it to Firebase via HTTP POST combining it with hardware setup, coding, and testing to create a functional IoT solution.

Step-by-Step Implementation

1. **Hardware Setup:**

    a. Connect a DHT11 sensor to the ESP32: VCC to 3.3V, GND to ground, and data pin (GPIO 4) to a digital pin with a 10kΩ pull-up resistor.

   b. Ensure that the ESP32 is powered and connected to a computer via USB for programming.

2. **Software Prerequisites:**
   a. Install the Arduino IDE and add the ESP32 board support package.
   b. Include the WiFi.h, HTTPClient.h, and DHT.h libraries for Wi-Fi, HTTP requests, and sensor reading, respectively.
   c. Obtain Firebase project credentials: a database URL (https://your-project-id.firebaseio.com/) and a secret key from the Firebase Console.

3. **Code Development:**
   a. Initialize Wi-Fi and DHT11 in the setup () function.
   b. Read sensor data (temperature and humidity) in the loop () function every 15 seconds (to respect rate limits).
   c. Construct an HTTP POST request with a JSON payload.
   d. Explanation: The code connects to Wi-Fi, reads DHT11 data, creates a JSON payload ({"temperature": 24.5, "humidity": 60.2}), and sends it to Firebase. The response code (200 for success) confirms delivery.
   e. Note: Robust code should include a check for valid sensor readings (not NaN) before creating the JSON payload and attempting to send the data.

4. **Testing and Verification:**
   a. Upload the code to the ESP32, and open the Serial Monitor to check connection status as well as response codes.
   b. Log into the Firebase Console, navigate to the Real-time Database, and observe the data under the sensor node ({ "temperature": 24.5, "humidity": 60.2 }).
   c. Access the Firebase dashboard to visualize the data in real-time, adjustable with custom widgets for temperature trends or humidity alerts.

BLE Scanning and Device-to-Device Communication

Bluetooth Low Energy (BLE) is a cornerstone of short-range IoT communication, enabling devices to detect and interact with one another efficiently, while conserving power. This section explores how the ESP32 microcontroller can function as a BLE scanner to detect nearby devices, and facilitate device-to-device communication, unlocking innovative applications such as smart locks, proximity-based alerts, and peer-to-peer data sharing. Introduced with Bluetooth 4.0 in 2010, BLE's low energy consumption (0.01–0.5 W) and ability to operate on coin-cell batteries for years, make it ideal for wearable devices, smart home gadgets, and industrial sensors. This section provides a detailed guide to leveraging ESP32's BLE capabilities, with a focus on a practical example: a smart lock that unlocks only when a paired smartphone is nearby.

BLE Scanning Fundamentals

BLE scanning allows a device, such as an ESP32, to passively listen for advertising packets broadcast by nearby BLE peripherals. These packets contain essential information like device names, service UUIDs, and signal strength (RSSI), enabling the scanner to identify and potentially connect to other devices. The ESP32, equipped with a dual-mode Bluetooth module, supports both central (scanner) and peripheral (advertiser) roles, making it versatile for IoT projects. Scanning operates in the 2.4 GHz

ISM band, using 40 channels, with three dedicated advertising channels to minimize interference. This process is power-efficient, consuming minimal energy during idle scanning (<50 μA), which suits battery-powered applications like asset tracking or presence detection.

- **Advertising Packets:** Devices broadcast packets every 20–10,000 ms (configurable), including a device address and optional data (a smartwatch advertising its battery level).
- **RSSI (Received Signal Strength Indicator):** Measures signal strength in dBm, helping estimate proximity (-60 dBm indicates a device within 1–2 meters).
- **Filtering:** The ESP32 can filter by UUID or name, focusing on relevant devices such as a specific smartphone model.

Device-to-Device Communication

Once a device is detected, BLE enables secure device-to-device communication through pairing and data exchange. Pairing establishes a connection using encryption (AES-CCM), ensuring that only authorized devices interact. Data exchange occurs via characteristics within GATT (Generic Attribute Profile) services, allowing small packets (20–250 bytes) to be sent bidirectionally. This is ideal for applications requiring low-latency responses, such as a smart lock verifying a smartphone's identity or a fitness tracker syncing data with a phone.

- **Pairing Process:** Involves a handshake exchanging keys, often initiated by the scanner (ESP32) requesting a connection from the advertiser (smartphone).
- **GATT Services:** Define data structures; for example, a lock service might include an unlock characteristic.
- **Security:** Uses bonding to store keys, preventing unauthorized access in scenarios like healthcare device pairing.

Example: Smart Lock with ESP32

This example illustrates an ESP32 acting as a BLE scanner and central device to control a smart lock, unlocking it only when a paired smartphone is detected nearby. This setup, tested combines hardware, coding, and testing to create a secure IoT solution.

Step-by-Step Implementation

1. **Hardware Setup:**
   a. Connect a relay module to the ESP32 (GPIO 5) to control the lock mechanism.
   b. Power the ESP32 via USB or a 3.7V LiPo battery for portable use.
   c. Ensure a smartphone with BLE (Android/iOS with Bluetooth 4.0+) is available for pairing.
2. **Software Prerequisites:**
   a. Install the Arduino IDE with ESP32 board support.
   b. Include the BLEDevice.h, BLEUtils.h, and BLEScan.h libraries for BLE functionality.
   c. Pair the smartphone with the ESP32 beforehand using a Bluetooth settings menu or app.
3. **Code Development:**
   a. Configure the ESP32 as a BLE scanner to detect the smartphone's advertising packet.
   b. Check RSSI and UUID to verify the paired device.
   c. Trigger the relay to unlock, if conditions are met.

d. **Explanation**: The ESP32 scans for 5 seconds, filters by the smartphone's name, and unlocks the relay if the RSSI exceeds -70 dBm (indicating proximity). The active scan mode enhances detection but increases power use.

4. **Testing and Verification:**
   a. Upload the code, and open the Serial Monitor to log detected devices and actions.
   b. Move the smartphone closer (within 2 meters) and confirm the relay activates, simulating the lock opening.
   c. Test with an unpaired device to ensure no unauthorized access.

LoRa Transmission Use Cases

LoRa (Long Range) technology, with its long-distance, and low-power communication capabilities, has emerged as a transformative solution for IoT deployments in remote and resource-constrained environments. Operating in sub-GHz frequency bands (868 MHz in Europe, 915 MHz in North America), LoRa leverages Chirp Spread Spectrum (CSS) modulation to achieve ranges of 10–15 km in rural areas and 2–5 km in urban settings, all while consuming minimal power—enabling battery-powered devices to operate for 5–10 years. This section explores two key use cases for LoRa transmission: Smart agriculture, where soil moisture readings are sent to a central gateway. It also contains remote monitoring, where environmental stations track temperature, humidity, and air quality as these applications demonstrate LoRa's potential to revolutionize rural development, environmental conservation, and disaster preparedness across the globe.

LoRa Technology Overview

LoRa, standardized under the LoRaWAN protocol, is designed for low-bandwidth, high-reliability data transmission, making it ideal for IoT devices in areas with limited infrastructure. Its architecture includes end nodes (sensors), gateways, network servers, and application servers, forming a star-of-stars topology. End nodes transmit data packets (0.3–50 kbps) to gateways, which relay them to a network server via standard IP networks. The use of Forward Error Correction (FEC) ensures data integrity over long distances, while Adaptive Data Rate (ADR) optimizes power and range based on signal conditions. This efficiency suits applications where frequent, high-speed communication is unnecessary, such as periodic environmental updates or agricultural telemetry.

Feature	LoRa (Physical Layer)	LoRaWAN (Protocol)
Definition	The physical layer (PHY) technology; the actual chirp spread spectrum modulation.	The Media Access Control (MAC) layer and the network architecture.
Function	Enables long-range, low-power data transmission.	Defines network communication, security, and scalability.
Scope	Point-to-point communication link technology.	Full star-of-stars network topology and communication management.
Key Components	Chirp Spread Spectrum, Forward Error Correction (FEC).	End nodes, gateways, network servers, application servers, Adaptive Data Rate (ADR).
Standardized As	Physical Layer Technology	Protocol for Wide Area Networks

Table 4.1: *Comparison of LoRa and LoRaWAN*

Use Case 1: Smart Agriculture – Transmitting Soil Moisture Readings

Smart agriculture leverages LoRa to monitor and manage farmland resources, particularly in rural regions with poor cellular coverage. Soil moisture sensors, deployed across fields, transmit data to a central gateway, enabling farmers to optimize irrigation and improve crop yields. This use case is critical in water-scarce areas, where efficient resource use can reduce waste by 30–40%.

Implementation

- **Hardware Setup:** Use an ESP32-LoRa module with a soil moisture sensor (capacitive sensor on GPIO 34). Power the setup with a solar panel and 3.7V LiPo battery.
- **Configuration:** Set the LoRa module to 915 MHz (adjust for region), with a spreading factor (SF) of 7 for a balance of range and data rate.
- **Process:** The ESP32 reads moisture levels (0–4095 ADC range), encodes them into a payload (soil/moisture:1200), and transmits via LoRa to a gateway 10 km away.
- **Gateway and Server:** The gateway forwards data to a network server (The Things Network), which stores it in a database or triggers irrigation commands.
- **Testing:** Verify transmission with a LoRa receiver or TTN Console, checking for packet loss (<5% with FEC).

Use Case 2: Remote Monitoring – Environmental Stations

Remote monitoring uses LoRa to deploy environmental stations that track temperature, humidity, and air quality in inaccessible areas like forests, mountains, or disaster zones. This data supports climate research, wildlife conservation, and early warning systems, providing critical insights where traditional networks fail.

Implementation

- **Hardware Setup:** Equip an ESP32-LoRa with a BME280 sensor (temperature, humidity, pressure) and an MQ-135 sensor (air quality) on GPIOs 32, 33, and 35.
- **Configuration:** Use 868 MHz, SF 9 for extended range, and a 1% duty cycle to comply with regional regulations.
- **Process:** The ESP32 collects the sensor data (env/data:25.3,60.1,150), transmits it to a gateway 12 km away, and updates a network server.
- **Testing:** Use a LoRa gateway and The Things Network to log data, verifying accuracy with a local BME280 reader.

Common Pitfalls in IoT Networking

As IoT deployments grow in scale and complexity, navigating potential pitfalls becomes essential to ensure reliable, secure, and efficient systems. Networking challenges can undermine the performance of devices such as ESP32s, gateways, and cloud platforms, affecting applications from smart homes to industrial automation. This section examines three critical pitfalls—security, power consumption, and latency—that developers frequently encounter when implementing IoT communication protocols such as MQTT, HTTP, LoRa, and BLE, understanding and mitigating these issues is key to designing robust IoT ecosystems, drawing from real-world examples and technical insights to guide the best practices across diverse global contexts.

Security: Protecting the Sensitive Data

Security is a paramount concern in IoT networking, where devices often handle sensitive data such as personal health metrics, home security statuses, or industrial process controls. Unsecured communication can expose data to interception, unauthorized access, or manipulation, leading to privacy breaches or system failures. The proliferation of connected devices—estimated at 30 billion by 2025—amplifies this risk, making encryption a non-negotiable requirement.

Common Issues

- **Unencrypted Transmission:** Public MQTT brokers (HiveMQ) or HTTP endpoints without TLS (Transport Layer Security) leave data vulnerable. For instance, an unencrypted MQTT payload like home/alarm: enabled could be intercepted by a malicious actor.
- **Weak Authentication:** Default credentials or lack of key rotation on devices such as ESP32s can be exploited, especially in smart lock systems.
- **Device Vulnerabilities:** Outdated firmware or lack of updates in remote LoRa nodes can create entry points for attacks.

Mitigation Strategies

- **Encryption:** Use TLS for MQTT (port 8883) and HTTPS for HTTP to encrypt data in transit. For example, an ESP32 posting temperature data to Firebase should use https://your-project-id.firebaseio.com/ with a secret key.
- **Authentication:** Implement strong passwords, client certificates, or OAuth tokens. Pairing BLE devices with bonding ensures that only authorized smartphones unlock a smart lock.
- **Secure Boot:** Enable secure boot on ESP32 to prevent unauthorized code execution.
- **Example:** In a German smart home, TLS-encrypted MQTT messages (home/light: off) protect against eavesdropping, ensuring that only authorized users control devices.

Power Consumption: Optimizing Battery Life

Power consumption is a critical factor for battery-operated IoT devices, especially in remote or mobile applications. Protocols and hardware choices significantly impact battery life, with Wi-Fi draining more power than LoRa or BLE due to continuous connectivity and higher transmit power.

Common Issues

- **Wi-Fi Drain:** An ESP32 using Wi-Fi for HTTP POST to ThingSpeak consumes 70–120 mA during active transmission, reducing battery life to days or weeks without sleep modes.
- **Frequent Transmissions:** Continuous BLE advertising or MQTT publishing exhausts power, unsuitable for sensors in remote monitoring.
- **Inefficient Sleep Modes:** Failing to implement deep sleep on ESP32 (<10 μA) leads to rapid battery depletion in agriculture nodes.

Mitigation Strategies

- **Protocol Selection:** Use LoRa for long-range, low-power needs or BLE for short-range, intermittent data, Wi-Fi suits high-bandwidth, and infrequent tasks like firmware updates.

- **Sleep Modes**: Enable ESP32 deep sleep between readings, waking only for scheduled transmissions. For instance, a LoRa node can sleep for 4 minutes and transmit for 1 second, extending life to years.
- **Duty Cycling**: Limit transmission duty cycles to conserve energy.
- **Example:** In Australia's bushfire monitoring, LoRa nodes with deep sleep transmit temperature data every 10 minutes, lasting 5 years on a 2000 mAh battery, unlike Wi-Fi nodes that last for months.

Latency: Managing Communication Delays

Latency, the time delay between data transmission and reception, affects the responsiveness of IoT systems. Different protocols exhibit inherent delays, impacting real-time applications like industrial control or emergency alerts.

Common Issues

- **HTTP Latency:** The request-response model of HTTP introduces delays (100–500 ms) due to server processing and network hops. For example, posting sensor data to Firebase may lag during peak usage.
- **MQTT Variability:** While MQTT is faster (20–100 ms) due to its publish/subscribe model, unreliable networks or broker overload can cause delays, as seen in smart factory deployments.
- **LoRa Delays:** Low data rates (0.3–50 kbps) and spreading factors (SF 7–12) result in transmission times of seconds per packet, unsuitable for time-critical tasks like flood alerts.

Mitigation Strategies

- **Protocol Choice:** Use MQTT for low-latency, real-time needs (classroom temperature control) and HTTP for less urgent data logging (weekly reports).
- **Network Optimization:** Reduce hops by placing gateways closer to end nodes; use edge computing to preprocess data before transmission.
- **QoS Tuning:** Set MQTT QoS 0 for speed (at most once) in non-critical cases or QoS 1 for reliability with minimal delay in health monitoring.
- **Example:** In Japan's smart factories, MQTT with QoS 0 ensures machine status updates within 50 ms, while HTTP logs historical data with acceptable 200 ms delays.

Best Practices

- **Holistic Design:** Assess security, power, and latency together; a secure system with high latency may fail in emergencies.
- **Testing:** Simulate network conditions (packet loss, low battery) to identify weaknesses.
- **Documentation:** Maintain logs of encryption keys, sleep schedules, and latency benchmarks for troubleshooting.

Addressing these pitfalls ensures that IoT networks are secure, energy-efficient, and responsive, supporting global innovation from urban smart cities to rural agricultural hubs.

Choosing the Right Protocol

Selecting the appropriate communication protocol is a pivotal decision in IoT development, directly impacting the performance, power efficiency, and scalability of a system. Protocols like MQTT (Message Queuing Telemetry Transport), HTTP (HyperText Transfer Protocol), BLE (Bluetooth Low Energy), and LoRa (Long Range), each offer unique strengths tailored to specific use cases, ranging from real-time messaging to long-distance rural monitoring. This section provides a comprehensive guide to choosing the right protocol based on application requirements, drawing from technical characteristics, practical examples, and global deployment insights. The goal is to equip developers with the knowledge to optimize ESP32-based IoT projects, whether for smart homes, industrial automation, or environmental sensing.

MQTT: Best for Frequent, Small Messages

MQTT is a lightweight, publish/subscribe protocol designed for efficient data exchange in resource-constrained environments. Operating over TCP/IP, it uses a broker to manage message distribution, making it ideal for frequent, small-message scenarios where real-time updates are critical.

Strengths

- **Low Overhead:** With a header size of 2 bytes, MQTT minimizes bandwidth usage, perfect for sending sensor data (0–100 bytes) every few seconds.
- **Real-Time:** QoS levels (0, 1, 2) ensure timely delivery, with latencies as low as 20–100 ms, suitable for dynamic applications.
- **Scalability:** Supports thousands of devices via topics (iot/classroom/temperature), as seen in smart building management.

Use Cases

- **Smart Homes:** An ESP32 publishes temperature updates (home/room1/temp:24.5) to a Mosquitto broker every 5 seconds, triggering HVAC adjustments.
- **Health Monitoring:** Wearables send heart rate data to a central server, ensuring immediate alerts for anomalies.

HTTP: Best When Working with Web APIs

HTTP, a request-response protocol, is the backbone of the web and a standard for interacting with RESTful APIs. Its robustness and compatibility with cloud platforms make it a go-to choice for IoT applications requiring structured data exchange.

Strengths

- **Web Integration:** Seamlessly connects to APIs like Firebase or ThingSpeak, supporting JSON payloads (`{"temp": 25.3}`).
- **Reliability:** Uses TCP for guaranteed delivery, with response codes (200 OK) confirming success.
- **Flexibility:** Supports GET, POST, PUT, DELETE methods, ideal for data logging or configuration updates.

Use Cases

- **Environmental Logging:** An ESP32 posts DHT11 data to Firebase every 15 seconds, viewable on a dashboard for climate research.
- **IoT Dashboards:** HTTP updates a web app with sensor readings from a smart farm, enabling remote management.

Considerations

- **Latency:** Delays of 100–500 ms due to server processing suit non-real-time tasks but may lag in emergencies.
- **Power:** Wi-Fi-based HTTP consumes 70–120 mA, necessitating sleep modes for battery devices.

BLE: Best for Short-Range, Low-Power Device-to-Device

BLE is a short-range, low-power protocol optimized for device-to-device communication, leveraging the 2.4 GHz band with advertising and GATT profiles. Its energy efficiency (0.01–0.5 W) suits battery-powered wearables and proximity-based systems.

Strengths

- **Low Power:** Deep sleep modes (<10 μA) extend battery life to years, ideal for coin-cell devices.
- **Proximity: RSSI-b**ased detection enables location-aware features, like unlocking a smart lock within 2 meters.
- **Simplicity:** No internet required, facilitating peer-to-peer interactions.

Use Cases

- **Smart Locks:** An ESP32 scans for a paired smartphone, unlocking a door when RSSI exceeds -70 dBm, enhancing home security in Germany.
- **Wearables:** A fitness tracker syncs step counts with a phone via GATT characteristics, conserving power in daily use.

LoRa: Best for Long-Range, Low-Bandwidth Rural Deployments

LoRa, operating in sub-GHz bands, excels in long-range, low-power communication, standardized under LoRaWAN. Its chirp spread spectrum modulation achieves 10–15 km ranges, perfect for rural or remote settings.

Strengths

- **Long Range:** Covers vast areas without repeaters, ideal for agriculture or environmental monitoring.
- **Low Power:** Transmits 0.3–50 kbps with duty cycles (1%), enabling 5–10 yearbattery life.
- **Penetration:** Navigates obstacles like foliage, suited for rugged terrains.

Use Cases

- **Smart Agriculture:** An ESP32-LoRa node sends soil moisture data (soil/moisture:1200) to a gateway 12 km away, optimizing irrigation in rural Maharashtra.
- **Environmental Stations:** LoRa nodes in Australia's outback transmit temperature and air quality data, supporting bushfire prevention.

Decision Framework

- **Data Size and Frequency:** MQTT and BLE for small, frequent messages; HTTP for larger, occasional uploads; LoRa for sparse and long-range data.
- **Range:** BLE for short-range (<100 m), LoRa for long-range (10–15 km), HTTP/MQTT over Wi-Fi for local networks.
- **Power:** Prioritize BLE or LoRa for battery devices; use Wi-Fi with sleep for HTTP/MQTT.
- **Latency:** MQTT for real-time, HTTP for delayed, and LoRa for tolerant applications.
- **Infrastructure:** HTTP/MQTT need internet; BLE is standalone, and LoRa requires gateways.

Best Practices

- **Prototyping:** Test multiple protocols (ESP32 with BLE, LoRa, and Wi-Fi) to match use case.
- **Hybrid Approach:** Combine protocols (BLE for local, and HTTP for cloud) for versatility.
- **Documentation:** Log protocol choices, configs, and performance metrics for future scaling.
- **Global Adaptation:** Adjust frequencies (868 MHz vs. 915 MHz) and regulations per region.

Thus, choosing the right protocol aligns technical capabilities with application needs, ensuring efficient and sustainable IoT solutions, worldwide.

Practical Exercises

Hands-on practice is essential for mastering IoT development, bridging theoretical knowledge with real-world application. This section introduces two practical exercises designed to build foundational skills using the ESP32 and Arduino Uno microcontrollers. These exercises—flashing the classic blink sketch and creating a GPIO mapping chart—equip learners with the ability to upload code, understand pin functionality, and debug hardware setups. These tasks are accessible to beginners and scalable for advanced projects, fostering confidence in IoT prototyping across diverse applications like smart lighting or sensor networks.

Exercise 1: Flash the Classic Blink Sketch

Task: Upload the classic LED blink program to an ESP32 or Arduino Uno to illuminate the onboard LED, introducing basic programming, hardware interaction, and debugging.

Steps

1. **Open Arduino IDE:**
    a. Download and install the Arduino IDE (latest version, 2.3.2) from arduino.cc.
    b. Launch the IDE on your computer (Windows, macOS, or Linux).
2. **Select Board:**
    a. **For ESP32**: Go to `Tools` > `Board` > `ESP32` > `ESP32` Dev Module (ensure ESP32 board support is added via Board Manager).

  b. **For Arduino Uno**: Select `Tools` > `Board` > `Arduino AVR Boards > Arduino Uno`.
  c. This configures the IDE for the microcontroller's architecture.

3. **Choose COM Port:**
   a. Connect the ESP32 or Uno to your computer via USB.
   b. In `Tools` > `Port`, select the appropriate COM port (COM3 on Windows or /dev/ttyUSB0 on Linux).
   c. Verify connection with a device manager or terminal (LED lights up on Uno).

4. **Write Code for Onboard LED (GPIO 2):**

   Note: *For Arduino Uno, change ledPin to 13, as its onboard LED is on pin 13. Adjust based on your board's schematic.*

5. **Upload and Observe Blink:**
   a. Click the upload button (right arrow) or press Ctrl+U.
   b. Monitor the IDE's output window for compilation and upload status ("Done uploading").
   c. Observe the onboard LED blinking every second. If it fails, check the COM port, board selection, or USB cable.

6. **Learn Uploading:** Understand the process of compiling and flashing code to a microcontroller.
7. **Pin Mapping:** Grasp how GPIO 2 (ESP32) or 13 (Uno) controls the LED, introducing hardware-software interaction.
8. **Debugging Basics:** Identify the common issues (wrong port, loose connection) using Serial Monitor or LED behavior.

Exercise 2: GPIO Mapping Chart

Task: Create a reference chart of GPIO pins for the ESP32 and Arduino Uno, documenting their functions, restrictions, and safe usage for sensors and actuators.

Goal

- **Build Confidence:** Enable informed pin selection, avoiding conflicts with boot processes or reserved functions.
- **Reference Tool:** Provide a quick guide for future projects, enhancing efficiency in sensor-actuator integration.

Steps

1. **Research Pin Specifications:**
   a. **ESP32:** Refer to the ESP32 DevKit V1 pinout (Express if documentation).
   b. **Note 34 GPIOs, with restrictions:**
      i. GPIO 0, 2, 15: Boot mode pins (avoid during setup).
      ii. GPIO 6–11: Reserved for flash.
      iii. ADC pins (34–39): Input-only, 12-bit resolution.
   c. **Arduino Uno:** Check the official pinout (14 digital, 6 analog).
   d. **Note:**
      i. **Pin 13**: Onboard LED.
      ii. **Pin 0, 1**: Serial RX/TX (avoid for other uses during upload).

2. **Create the Chart:**
    a. Use a table format (for example, in a text editor or spreadsheet) to list pins, functions, and notes.
    b. Validate with Hardware.
    c. Connect a sensor (for example, DHT11 on GPIO 4 for ESP32, pin 2 for Uno) and an actuator (for example, LED on GPIO 5 for ESP32, pin 3 for Uno).
    d. Test with a blink sketch, ensuring no conflicts (for example, boot pins and remain free).
3. **Document and Share:**
    a. Save the chart as a PDF or image for reference.
    b. Note safe pins for I2C (for example, ESP32 GPIO 21, 22; Uno A4, A5) or SPI.

These exercises lay a solid foundation for IoT development, preparing learners for advanced topics such as protocol implementation or cloud integration.

Conclusion

This chapter has provided a comprehensive exploration of the networking and communication protocols that form the backbone of Internet of Things (IoT) systems, equipping readers with the practical skills to design, implement, and troubleshoot connected IoT projects. By treating protocols as the nervous system and middleware as the brain of a living organism, the chapter illuminated how these components work together to enable seamless data exchange and scalable ecosystems. From understanding fundamental networking concepts like LAN, WAN, IP, and ports, to mastering models such as OSI and TCP/IP, a solid foundation was laid for creating responsive IoT networks using platforms like ESP32. We examined essential IoT protocols—MQTT, HTTP/REST, BLE, and LoRa—highlighting their unique strengths based on range, power, and data needs, and demonstrated their practical interfacing with the ESP32, including necessary security, power management, and optimization techniques. Communication middleware, such as public MQTT brokers and cloud platforms like Firebase, was shown to be the decision-making hub, coordinating data flow and responses.

Overall, this chapter has shown how networking protocols and middleware work in harmony to create intelligent, connected IoT systems. By understanding their principles, classifications, optimization methods, interfacing techniques, and integration challenges, readers are well prepared to design IoT solutions that seamlessly connect the physical and digital realms. In the next chapter, readers will step into the world of physical computing, getting a hands-on knowhow with widely used IoT boards like Arduino Uno, NodeMCU, and ESP32, learning about their architectures, programming, and debugging to select the right microcontroller for their projects.

CHAPTER 5

Getting Started with Arduino, NodeMCU, and ESP32

Introduction

In *Chapter 4, IoT Communication Protocols and Networking*, we laid a robust foundation for understanding how devices exchange data efficiently and securely within the Network Layer. We revisited fundamental networking concepts and explored models like the OSI and TCP/IP stack, adapting them to meet the unique IoT demands of low power, intermittent connectivity, and massive device scaling.

We then dove into widely adopted IoT communication protocols, each tailored to specific use cases. MQTT (Message Queuing Telemetry Transport), a lightweight publish/subscribe protocol, excelled in resource-constrained environments like smart meters, offering low bandwidth usage, reliable message delivery, and Quality of Service (QoS) levels. HTTP/REST (HyperText Transfer Protocol/ Representational State Transfer), a request-response model, powered web-based IoT applications such as weather stations uploading data to cloud platforms, leveraging JSON for structured payloads and API endpoints. BLE (Bluetooth Low Energy) provided short-range, energy-efficient communication for wearables and home automation, utilizing advertising packets and GATT profiles for data exchange. LoRa (Long Range) enabled long-distance, low-power connectivity ideal for remote sensor networks in agriculture or environmental monitoring, employing spread-spectrum modulation for robust signal penetration. The chapter addressed critical considerations like security (for example, TLS encryption for MQTT, secure pairing in BLE), power optimization (for example, duty cycling in LoRa, low-energy advertising in BLE), and scalability (for example, broker load balancing for MQTT, edge gateways for LoRa). Global examples illustrated practical deployments: MQTT in smart factories for real-time machine monitoring, HTTP/REST in weather forecasting systems, BLE in healthcare wearables, and LoRa in rural irrigation networks. By the end, you gained a comprehensive understanding of how networking and protocols enable effective IoT communication, preparing you for advanced topics in subsequent chapters.

This chapter, *Getting Started with Arduino, NodeMCU, and* ESP32, shifts the focus to physical computing, serving as your gateway to bringing IoT systems to life. Building on the networking foundation, we now explore the microcontroller boards that act as the brain of an IoT system, without which sensors cannot process data, actuators cannot be triggered, and network communication cannot occur. We will introduce three widely used development boards: Arduino Uno, a simple and beginner-friendly option; NodeMCU (ESP8266), a compact board with built-in Wi-Fi; and ESP32, a powerful, feature-rich, dual-core microcontroller. You will learn their architecture, specifications, GPIO pin configurations, and use cases, while gaining hands-on experience with installing the Arduino IDE, writing your first program, uploading it to a board, and debugging with the Serial Monitor. This chapter also compares 8-bit versus 32-bit boards, highlights differences in Wi-Fi and peripheral support, and provides troubleshooting guides for common errors, equipping you to integrate the sensory, reactive, and communicative elements of IoT into cohesive, real-world solutions.

Structure

In this chapter, we will cover the following topics:

- Introduction to Microcontrollers
- Development Boards and Their Role in IoT
- Overview of Arduino Uno, NodeMCU, and ESP32
- Installing and Configuring the Arduino IDE
- Understanding GPIO Pins
- Using the Serial Monitor for Debugging
- Choosing the Right Development Board
- Best Practices for Wiring and Flashing Boards
- Safety and Grounding Considerations
- Common Errors and Troubleshooting
- Handling Board Resets and Power Stability
- Practical Exercises

Microcontroller

A microcontroller is a compact, self-contained computer on a single Integrated Circuit (IC), often referred to as a *system on a chip* (SoC). Designed to perform dedicated tasks with minimal external components, it serves as the heart of embedded systems, powering applications ranging from IoT devices and automation to robotics and consumer electronics, microcontrollers are indispensable in modern technology, bridging the physical and digital worlds by processing data from sensors, controlling actuators, and managing communication protocols. Unlike general-purpose computers, microcontrollers are optimized for efficiency, low power consumption, and real-time operation, making them ideal for resource-constrained environments.

At its core, a microcontroller integrates several key components into a single chip:

- **CPU (Central Processing Unit)**: The processor executes instructions stored in memory, performing computations and controlling the flow of data. Depending on the architecture—8-bit, 16-bit, or 32-bit—the CPU processing power varies, with 32-bit options like the ESP32 offering dual-core capabilities for multitasking.

- **Memory**: This includes **RAM (Random Access Memory)** for storing temporary variables and data during execution, and **Flash memory** for holding the program code and constants even when power is off. For instance, the Arduino Uno provides 32 KB of flash and 2 KB of SRAM, while the ESP32 boasts 520 KB SRAM and 4 MB flash, catering to more complex applications.

- **I/O Pins (Input/Output Pins)**: These versatile pins connect the microcontroller to the external world, interfacing with sensors (for example, DHT22 temperature sensors), actuators (for example, relays), and communication modules (for example, Wi-Fi or LoRa transceivers). Configurable as digital or analog inputs/outputs, they enable tasks like reading a button press or driving an LED.

Distinction from Microprocessors

Microcontrollers differ significantly from microprocessors, their close relatives in the computing family. A microprocessor, found in PCs and smartphones, is a general-purpose CPU that requires external memory, I/O devices, and peripherals to function, relying on a complex motherboard ecosystem. In contrast, a microcontroller is an all-in-one solution, embedding memory, I/O ports, and often timers, ADCs (Analog-to-Digital Converters), and communication interfaces (for example, UART, SPI, I2C) on the chip. This integration reduces size, cost, and power consumption, making microcontrollers suited for embedded applications where space and energy are at a premium.

For example, a Raspberry Pi, based on a microprocessor, needs external storage and modules to operate as a mini-computer, consuming 700–1000 mA. Conversely, an ESP32 microcontroller, with built-in Wi-Fi and Bluetooth, operates on 20–150 mA in active mode and drops to under 10 µA in deep sleep, ideal for battery-powered IoT nodes. This distinction highlights why microcontrollers dominate in embedded systems like smart thermostats or robotic arms, where a full-fledged computer would be overkill.

Role in Embedded Applications

Microcontrollers are engineered for specific, repetitive tasks, distinguishing them from the versatile but power-hungry microprocessors. Their design prioritizes real-time processing, low latency, and deterministic behavior, critical for applications like automation (for example, controlling a factory conveyor), robotics (for example, navigating a drone), and IoT (for example, monitoring soil moisture in rural areas). The embedded nature means they are often invisible to users, silently managing tasks within devices like washing machines, car engine control units, or wearable fitness trackers.

In IoT, microcontrollers act as the brain, orchestrating the Perception Layer (sensors and actuators) and Network Layer (communication protocols). For instance, an ESP32 can read data from a PIR motion sensor, process it to detect movement, and trigger a relay to turn on a light—all while sending an MQTT message to a smart home hub. This integration of sensing, actuation, and networking, built on the foundations from Chapters 2 to 4, underscores the microcontroller role as a central hub.

Architectural Variations

Microcontroller architectures vary based on bit width, influencing performance and application suitability:

- **8-bit Microcontrollers (for example, ATmega328P in Arduino Uno):** With a 16 MHz clock and limited memory (32 KB flash, 2 KB RAM), they handle simple tasks like LED blinking or basic sensor reading, ideal for educational projects or low-cost deployments.
- **32-bit Microcontrollers (for example, ESP8266 in NodeMCU, ESP32):** Offering 80–240 MHz clocks and larger memories (4 MB flash, 520 KB SRAM for ESP32), they support multitasking, wireless communication, and complex algorithms, fitting advanced IoT use cases like environmental monitoring.

The transition from 8-bit to 32-bit architectures reflects the growing demands of IoT, where data processing and connectivity (for example, Wi-Fi on ESP32) require greater computational power. This evolution is evident in global deployments: 8-bit Arduinos power classroom projects, while 32-bit ESP32s drive smart irrigation in outback.

Practical Components and Features

Beyond the core CPU, memory, and I/O pins, microcontrollers often include:

- **Timers and Counters**: For precise timing in PWM (Pulse Width Modulation) to control motor speed or LED brightness.
- **ADCs and DACs**: For converting analog sensor signals (for example, MQ-2 gas sensor voltages) to digital data or generating analog outputs, enhancing versatility.
- **Communication Interfaces**: UART for serial communication, SPI and I2C for multi-device connectivity, and integrated Wi-Fi/Bluetooth on ESP32 for network access.
- **Power Management**: Sleep modes and voltage regulators ensure energy efficiency, critical for battery-operated devices in remote areas.

These features enable microcontrollers to interface with a wide range of peripherals. For example, ESP32 I2C pins can connect to a BME280 sensor, while its PWM outputs drive a servo motor, all coordinated by a single program uploaded via the Arduino IDE.

Use Cases and Global Impact

Microcontrollers power diverse applications worldwide. ESP32s manage smart factory automation, leveraging dual-core processing for real-time machine monitoring. NodeMCUs with Wi-Fi track deforestation, uploading data to cloud platforms. Arduino Uno teaches students physical computing, fostering innovation in rural schools. These examples highlight how microcontrollers transform raw data into actionable insights, from precision agriculture to urban smart grids.

Getting Started

To harness a microcontroller, developers use tools like the Arduino IDE to write code (for example, C/C++), upload it via USB, and debug with the Serial Monitor. This hands-on process, detailed in later sections, turns theoretical knowledge into practical skills, preparing you to build IoT projects that integrate sensors, actuators, and networks seamlessly, a microcontroller is more than a chip—it the intelligent core that brings IoT systems to life, blending processing power, memory, and connectivity into a compact package. Its design for embedded applications ensures efficiency and reliability, making it the foundation for innovative solutions across the globe.

Development Board

A development board is a pre-assembled platform designed to simplify the process of prototyping, testing, and developing embedded systems, serving as an accessible entry point into the world of microcontrollers and IoT. A development board is not the same as a microcontroller. At its core, a development board integrates a microcontroller chip—the computational brain—along with essential supporting components, making it an all-in-one solution for engineers, hobbyists, and students, these boards have become indispensable tools in the rapid evolution of IoT, enabling the creation of smart devices ranging from home automation systems to environmental monitoring networks. By providing a ready-to-use hardware platform, development boards eliminate the need for complex circuit design, allowing users to focus on coding and application development.

The key features of a development board include:

- **Microcontroller Chip**: The heart of the board, containing a CPU, memory, and I/O capabilities. Examples include the ATmega328P on the Arduino Uno, the ESP8266 on the NodeMCU, and the dual-core ESP32 on its respective board, each tailored to different performance needs.

- **USB Programming Interface**: A built-in USB port facilitates code uploading from a computer to the microcontroller, using software like the Arduino IDE, and often doubles as a power source or debugging channel via the Serial Monitor.
- **Power Supply Regulation**: Onboard voltage regulators and connectors (for example, USB or barrel jack) ensure stable power delivery, typically converting 5V USB input to 3.3V or 5V as required by the microcontroller and connected peripherals.
- **Headers for Connecting Sensors and Actuators**: Pin headers or breakout pads allow easy connection of external components like sensors (for example, DHT22 temperature sensors), actuators (for example, relays), and communication modules (for example, LoRa transceivers), enabling rapid prototyping.

Examples of Development Boards

Prominent examples include the Arduino Uno, NodeMCU, and ESP32, each offering unique strengths:

- **Arduino Uno**: Based on the ATmega328P 8-bit microcontroller, it features 14 digital I/O pins (6 PWM), 6 analog inputs, 32 KB flash memory, and a 16 MHz clock, its simplicity and extensive community support make it a favorite for beginners learning physical computing, such as controlling classroom lights.
- **NodeMCU (ESP8266)**: Powered by the ESP8266 32-bit microcontroller with built-in Wi-Fi, it offers 11 digital I/O pins (1 analog), 4 MB flash memory, and an 80 MHz clock (overclockable to 160 MHz). At approximately $5, its compact design suits IoT projects like remote temperature monitoring, connecting to cloud platforms via HTTP.
- **ESP32**: A dual-core 32-bit microcontroller with Wi-Fi, Bluetooth, 34 GPIO pins (18 analog), 520 KB SRAM, 4 MB flash, and a 240 MHz clock, costing around $10. Its advanced peripherals—ADC, DAC, touch sensors—support complex applications like smart locks or environmental stations using BLE and LoRa.

Role in Prototyping and Development

Development boards serve as a sandbox for innovation, allowing users to experiment with hardware and software without the need to design custom circuits. The integrated USB interface simplifies programming, enabling rapid iteration—write a code, upload it, and test in minutes. The regulated power supply ensures compatibility with a wide range of peripherals, while headers provide flexibility to connect sensors and actuators, mirroring the Perception Layer concepts from *Chapter 2, IoT Architecture and Ecosystem*. For instance, an ESP32 can interface with a PIR motion sensor and a relay, forming a security system that activates lights when movement is detected, all manageable through a single board.

This accessibility is particularly valuable in educational settings and rapid prototyping. Students use Arduino Uno to learn basic electronics, while the makers leverage ESP32s for smart home prototypes. The boards' design reduces the barrier to entry, making embedded development approachable for novices and professionals alike.

Architectural and Functional Details

The microcontroller chip dictates the board capabilities. The Arduino Uno 8-bit architecture suits simple tasks, with limited memory constraining complex operations, but its robustness supports long-term educational use. The NodeMCU ESP8266 adds Wi-Fi, enabling wireless projects like IoT dashboards, though its single-core design limits multitasking. The ESP32, with dual cores and extensive peripherals, handles advanced applications, such as simultaneous BLE scanning and LoRa transmission, aligning with the networking insights from *Chapter 4, Networking and Communication Protocols* (MQTT, HTTP, LoRa, BLE).

Power regulation is critical, especially for IoT devices. The Arduino Uno supports 5V operation with a 3.3V option via a regulator, while NodeMCU and ESP32 operate at 3.3V, optimizing for low-power modes (for example, ESP32 <10 µA deep sleep). Headers are standardized (for example, 0.1-inch spacing), accommodating shields (Arduino) or breadboard connections, enhancing modularity. For example, an ESP32 GPIO pins can drive a servo motor via PWM, while reading an analog LDR sensor, showcasing versatility.

Global Applications and Use Cases

Development boards power diverse IoT solutions worldwide. ESP32s manage smart factory automation, using dual cores for real-time monitoring and predictive maintenance. NodeMCUs track deforestation, uploading data to cloud platforms via Wi-Fi. ESP32s monitor bushfires with LoRa, leveraging long-range connectivity in remote areas. In rural, Arduino Uno teach coding in schools, fostering innovation for local challenges like irrigation control

Overview of Arduino Uno, NodeMCU, and ESP32

This section provides a detailed overview of three widely used development boards—Arduino Uno, NodeMCU (ESP8266), and ESP32—each tailored to specific needs within the IoT ecosystem. These boards serve as the backbone for physical computing, enabling beginners and advanced users alike to prototype and deploy IoT solutions. Building on the networking and communication foundations from *Chapter 4, Networking and Communication Protocols* (MQTT, HTTP, LoRa, BLE), where protocols like MQTT, HTTP, BLE, and LoRa were explored, this section highlights how these boards integrate sensors, actuators, and connectivity into practical applications. Let dive into the specifications, features, and use cases of each board.

Arduino Uno

The Arduino Uno is a beginner-friendly development board based on the ATmega328P, an 8-bit microcontroller renowned for its simplicity and reliability. Operating at a 16 MHz clock speed, it delivers sufficient processing power for basic tasks, making it an ideal choice for those new to embedded programming. Its memory configuration includes 2 KB of SRAM for runtime data and 32 KB of flash memory for storing programs, providing a modest yet functional capacity for small-scale projects. The board features 14 digital I/O pins, of which 6 support PWM (Pulse Width Modulation) for controlling devices like LEDs or motors, and 6 analog input pins for reading sensors such as potentiometers or LDRs. However, it lacks built-in Wi-Fi or Bluetooth, requiring external modules (for example, ESP-01) for wireless connectivity, which aligns it with offline projects or those using wired communication.

Ideal for beginners, the Arduino Uno shines in educational environments and simple automation tasks. Its extensive community support, with thousands of tutorials and libraries, simplifies learning curves—students use it to master blinking LEDs or reading button inputs in rural classrooms. Offline projects, like a standalone temperature logger with a DHT22 sensor, leverage its robust pinout and ease of use. The board operating voltage of 5V, with a current draw of about 50 mA, suits battery-powered setups with careful power management. Crucially, the logic level of the board is also 5V. This is an important consideration as many modern sensors and modules operate at a 3.3V logic level, requiring a level shifter for safe interconnection (as will be detailed in the Safety Considerations section). Limitations include its memory constraints, which may bottleneck complex code, and the absence of wireless features, necessitating add-ons for IoT integration. Nonetheless, its affordability (around $20) and durability make it a staple for foundational IoT exploration.

NodeMCU (ESP8266)

The NodeMCU, built around the ESP8266 32-bit microcontroller, represents a significant leap into IoT with its integrated Wi-Fi capability. With a clock speed adjustable from 80 MHz to 160 MHz, it offers enhanced processing power compared to 8-bit boards, supported by 160 KB of SRAM and 4 MB of flash memory for storing larger programs and data. Its GPIO configuration is more limited, providing 11 digital I/O pins (with 1 analog input), which suits compact designs but requires careful pin management. The standout feature is its built-in Wi-Fi, enabling wireless communication for IoT applications without additional hardware, a direct evolution from the networking concepts in *Chapter 4, Networking and Communication Protocols (MQTT, HTTP, LoRa, BLE)*, where HTTP and MQTT were implemented.

This low-cost board, priced at approximately $5, is excellent for budget-conscious IoT projects. Its Wi-Fi support facilitates remote monitoring, such as uploading temperature data from a BME280 sensor to ThingSpeak, a common use case in smart homes or environmental tracking. NodeMCUs monitor deforestation by sending data to cloud platforms, showcasing its global utility. The board operates at 3.3V with a current draw of about 70 mA, and its deep sleep mode (around 20 µA) optimizes power for battery-operated devices. However, the limited GPIO pins and single-core architecture may hinder multitasking or projects requiring extensive peripherals. Its compact size and affordability make it a go-to for hobbyists and small-scale deployments, bridging traditional microcontrollers with wireless IoT.

ESP32

The ESP32, featuring a dual-core Tensilica 32-bit processor, is a powerhouse designed for advanced IoT applications. With a clock speed scalable up to 240 MHz, it delivers robust performance for multitasking and real-time processing, supported by 520 KB of SRAM and 4 MB of flash memory. This board offers 34 GPIO pins, with 18 configurable as analog inputs, providing ample connectivity for complex projects. It includes built-in Wi-Fi and dual-mode Bluetooth (Classic and BLE), aligning with *Chapter 4, Networking and Communication Protocols (MQTT, HTTP, LoRa, BLE)* exploration of BLE for short-range communication and Wi-Fi for MQTT/HTTP. Additional features like ADCs (which often require calibration/attenuation settings due to inherent noise for accurate readings), DACs, touch sensors, and PWM channels enhance its versatility, making it suitable for AI at the edge, such as running lightweight machine learning models on-device.

Priced around $10, the ESP32 is ideal for sophisticated IoT projects requiring connectivity and processing power. It manages smart factory automation, using its dual cores for real-time machine monitoring and predictive maintenance. ESP32s track bushfires with LoRa integration, leveraging long-range capabilities. The board operates at 3.3V, with a current draw of 20–150 mA (dropping to <10 µA in deep sleep), supporting energy-efficient designs. Its extensive GPIO and peripheral support allow integration of multiple sensors (for example, MQ-2 gas sensor) and actuators (for example, servo motors) simultaneously. Challenges include a steeper learning curve for beginners and potential GPIO conflicts if not managed properly, but its feature-rich nature positions it as a leader for cutting-edge IoT innovations.

Comparative Insights

Comparing these boards reveals their distinct roles. The Arduino Uno 8-bit architecture and offline focus suit educational and simple projects, while the NodeMCU 32-bit design and Wi-Fi cater to cost-effective IoT. The ESP32 dual-core, multi-connectivity approach targets advanced, scalable solutions. Memory and GPIO differences—2 KB SRAM and 14 pins for Uno, 160 KB SRAM and 11 pins for NodeMCU, 520 KB SRAM and 34 pins for ESP32—guide project selection. Power consumption varies, with Uno at 50 mA, NodeMCU at 70 mA, and ESP32 adaptive range, influencing battery-powered designs. These factors, combined with global use cases, underscore their complementary strengths.

Practical Applications

These boards bridge theory and practice. The Arduino Uno teaches pin mapping in classrooms, NodeMCU enables remote sensing in forests, and ESP32 powers smart systems in cities and homes. Hands-on projects—like blinking an LED on Uno, uploading data with NodeMCU, or running BLE on ESP32—reinforce learning, preparing users for IoT challenges, the Arduino Uno, NodeMCU, and ESP32 offer a spectrum of capabilities, from beginner-friendly basics to advanced IoT innovation, empowering developers to build connected, intelligent systems worldwide.

Installing Arduino IDE and Configuring Boards

This section guides you through the essential steps to set up the Arduino Integrated Development Environment (IDE) and configure it for the Arduino Uno, NodeMCU (ESP8266), and ESP32 development boards, enabling you to start programming and prototyping IoT projects, as these steps form the foundation for leveraging the hardware capabilities explored in previous sections, connecting the theoretical networking insights from *Chapter 4, Networking and Communication Protocols (MQTT, HTTP, LoRa, BLE)*, (for example, MQTT, HTTP, BLE, LoRa) with hands-on coding. Hence, whether you are a beginner or an advanced user, this process ensures that your development environment is ready to bring sensors, actuators, and communication modules to life. Let us dive into the installation and configuration details.

Installing Arduino IDE

The Arduino IDE is the primary software tool for programming microcontroller boards, offering a user-friendly interface for writing, compiling, and uploading code. To get started, visit the official website at arduino.cc and download the latest version available for Windows, macOS, and Linux operating systems. The download page provides installers tailored to your platform: an .exe file for Windows, a .dmg for macOS, and a .tar.xz for Linux. Select the appropriate version, ensuring compatibility with your system (for example, 64-bit Windows 10 or Ubuntu 20.04).

The installation process is straightforward. On Windows, run the .exe file, follow the wizard to choose the installation directory (default is fine), and install any additional drivers (for example, for USB communication). On macOS, open the .dmg, drag the Arduino icon to the Applications folder, and grant necessary permissions. For Linux, extract the .tar.xz file, navigate to the folder, and run the **`install.sh`** script or move it to /opt. After installation, launch the IDE to confirm it opens, displaying a blank sketch window with options like File, Sketch, and Tools menus. This step, taking about 5-10 minutes, sets the stage for configuring boards and writing your first program, such as the classic blink sketch, as explored in *Chapter 4, Networking and Communication Protocols (MQTT, HTTP, LoRa, BLE)*, practical exercises.

Configuring Arduino Uno

The Arduino Uno is natively supported by the Arduino IDE, requiring no additional setup beyond installation. To configure it, connect the board to your computer via a USB cable, typically a USB-B or USB-C depending on the version. Open the IDE, and from the top menu, navigate to **`Tools → Board.`** Scroll through the list and select **Arduino Uno** (under Arduino AVR Boards). This action tells the IDE to compile code compatible with the ATmega328P microcontroller 8-bit architecture, 16 MHz clock, and 32 KB flash memory.

Next, select the correct **COM port** under **`Tools → Port`**, which appears once the board is connected (for example, COM3 on Windows or /dev/ttyUSB0 on Linux). Verify the connection by checking the onboard LED (pin 13) lights up. If the port does not appear, ensure that drivers are installed (downloadable from arduino.cc) or try a different cable. Once configured, you can upload a test sketch—

go to **File → Examples → 01.Basics → Blink**, click the upload button (right arrow), and watch the LED blink every second. This process, taking about 2-3 minutes, leverages the Uno beginner-friendly design, making it ideal for offline projects like a classroom timer, as seen in an educational setting.

Configuring NodeMCU (ESP8266)

To program the NodeMCU (ESP8266), additional board support must be added to the Arduino IDE due to its 32-bit architecture and Wi-Fi capabilities. Start by opening the IDE and going to **File → Preferences**. In the *Additional Boards Manager* URLs field, paste the following URL : http://arduino.esp8266.com/stable/package_esp8266com_index.json. Click **OK** to save. This URL points to the ESP8266 community board package, enabling support for the ESP8266 microcontroller with its 80-160 MHz clock and 4 MB flash.

Next, navigate to **Tools → Board → Boards Manager**. In the search bar, type esp8266 and find the **esp8266 by ESP8266 Community** package. Click **Install** to download and install it (about 5-10 minutes depending on internet speed). Once installed, under **Tools → Board**, select **NodeMCU 1.0 (ESP-12E Module)** or a similar variant based on your board labeling. Connect the NodeMCU via USB, choose the **COM port** under **Tools → Port**, and verify with the onboard LED. Upload a Wi-Fi test sketch (such as, connect to a network and print the IP address via Serial Monitor) to confirm setup. This configuration, used globally for low-cost IoT like deforestation trackers, takes about 15 minutes and unlocks wireless projects.

Configuring ESP32

Configuring the ESP32 follows a similar process but requires a different board package due to its dual-core, Wi-Fi, and Bluetooth features. Open the Arduino IDE, go to **File → Preferences**, and add the ESP32 board manager URL: `https://dl.espressif.com/dl/package_esp32_index.json` in the Additional Boards Manager URLs field. Click OK to save. This URL, provided by Espressif, supports the ESP32 advanced capabilities, including 240 MHz clock and 520 KB SRAM.

Proceed to **Tools → Board → Boards Manager**, search for esp32, and install the esp32 by Espressif Systems package (approximately 10-15 minutes). After installation, under **Tools → Board**, select **ESP32 Dev Module** (or match your board variant, for example, ESP32-WROOM-32). Connect the ESP32 via USB, select the COM port, and verify connectivity. Upload a test sketch, such as a BLE scanner, to leverage its dual-mode Bluetooth, aligning with *Chapter* 4, *Networking and Communication Protocols* (MQTT, HTTP, LoRa, BLE), BLE examples. This setup, used in smart factories and bushfire monitors, takes about 20 minutes and prepares the board for advanced IoT tasks.

Troubleshooting Tips

Common issues include Board not found errors (check COM port or drivers), Upload failed (ensure correct board selection), or slow installs (verify internet stability). Use the Serial Monitor (**Tools → Serial Monitor**) to debug, checking for error codes or boot loops. For ESP8266/ESP32, ensure the latest package version to avoid compatibility issues. These steps are refined through global use and ensure a smooth setup.

Practical Applications

With the IDE configured, you can program the Uno for offline LED projects, NodeMCU for Wi-Fi data logging, and ESP32 for BLE automation, bridging *Chapters* 2–4 *sensor-actuator-network* concepts. This setup empowers global innovation, from n classrooms to n IoT deployments, installing the Arduino IDE and configuring that these boards equip you to unlock their full potential, turning ideas into functional IoT systems worldwide.

Understanding GPIO Pins

GPIO (General Purpose Input/Output) pins are the vital connection points on microcontroller development boards like the Arduino Uno, NodeMCU, and ESP32, enabling interaction between the board and the external world. These pins serve as the interface for connecting sensors, actuators, and communication modules, forming the bridge between the digital logic of the microcontroller and the physical environment, mastering GPIO pins is essential for building IoT systems that leverage the sensory and reactive components explored in *Chapter 2, IoT Architecture and Ecosystem*, as well as the networking capabilities from *Chapter 4, Networking and Communication Protocols* (MQTT, HTTP, LoRa, BLE). Whether reading data from a temperature sensor or triggering a relay, GPIO pins are the foundation of physical computing. This section delves into their types, functions, and practical usage within the Arduino IDE.

Types of GPIO Pins

GPIO pins are categorized based on their functionality, catering to different input and output requirements:

- **Digital Pins**: These pins operate in a binary state, toggling between HIGH (1, typically 3.3V or 5V depending on the board) and LOW (0, 0V). They are ideal for controlling devices that require on/off signals, such as LEDs, buttons, or relays. Caution: Never feed 5V into a 3.3V GPIO.On the Arduino Uno, 14 digital pins are available, with 6 supporting PWM (Pulse Width Modulation) for variable output control, like dimming an LED. The ESP32, with 34 GPIO pins, offers even greater flexibility, including multiple PWM channels.
- **Analog Pins**: These pins read continuous voltage signals, converting them into digital values through an Analog-to-Digital Converter (ADC). On Arduino boards, analog inputs range from 0 to 1023, corresponding to 0V to 5V (or 3.3V on ESP32/NodeMCU), allowing precise measurements from sensors like potentiometers or MQ-2 gas sensors. The Arduino Uno has 6 analog pins, while the ESP32 provides 18, enhancing its capability for multi-sensor projects.

Functions in Arduino IDE

The Arduino IDE provides a set of built-in functions to manage GPIO pins, simplifying programming for beginners and experts alike. These functions, written in C/C++, are essential for configuring and manipulating pin behavior:

- **`pinMode(pin, INPUT/OUTPUT)`**: This function sets the mode of a specified pin. Use **`pinMode(pin, INPUT)`** to configure a pin to read data from a sensor (for example : a PIR motion sensor), or **`pinMode(pin, OUTPUT)`** to send signals to an actuator (for example: an LED). For example, **`pinMode(13, OUTPUT)`** prepares pin 13 on an Arduino Uno to control an onboard LED. On the ESP32, this function also supports **`INPUT_PULLUP`** to enable internal pull-up resistors, reducing the need for external components.
- **`digitalWrite(pin, HIGH/LOW)`**: This function sets the voltage level of a digital pin. **`digitalWrite(pin, HIGH)`** turns on a connected device (for example : a relay), while **`digitalWrite(pin, LOW)`** turns it off. For instance, **`digitalWrite(12, HIGH)`** on a NodeMCU can activate a buzzer, with the state persisting until changed. Timing can be controlled with **`delay(ms)`** to create patterns, like blinking an LED every 500 ms.
- **`digitalRead(pin)`**: This function reads the current state of a digital pin, returning HIGH or LOW. It is useful for detecting button presses or sensor triggers, such as **`int state = digitalRead(2)`** to check a PIR sensor on an ESP32. The function is fast and reliable, though it requires debouncing for mechanical switches (for example, using a 50 ms delay or capacitor).

- **`analogRead(pin)`**: This function reads the analog voltage on a pin, returning a value from 0 to 1023. For example, **`int value = analogRead(A0)`** on an Arduino Uno measures a potentiometer position, which can be mapped to control a servo motor angle. On the ESP32, analog readings benefit from higher resolution (12-bit versus 10-bit on Uno), improving accuracy for sensors like LDRs. ADC is non-linear/noisy; use attenuation settings and calibration for accuracy. Calibration may be needed, such as scaling MQ-2 gas sensor values from 0–1023 to 300–10,000 ppm.

Practical Applications and Pin Mapping

GPIO pins enable a wide range of IoT applications by interfacing with hardware. Digital pins can drive a relay to control a fan based on a DHT22 temperature reading, as seen in n smart homes. Analog pins allow monitoring soil moisture with a capacitive sensor on an ESP32 for precision agriculture in. The Arduino IDE pin mapping which is accessible via **`Tools → Pinout`** or online references—helps avoid conflicts, such as reserving PWM pins (including 3, 5, 6, 9, 10, 11 on Uno) for motor control.

Global Context and Considerations

Globally, GPIO usage varies by region. ESP32 multiple GPIOs support smart factory sensors, while NodeMCU limited pins manage deforestation trackers. Arduino Uno pins teach students basic input/output in rural schools. Power constraints are key; digital pins draw minimal current (for example, 20 mA on Uno), but analog readings on ESP32 require stable 3.3V supplies. Pull-up/pull-down resistors (for example, 10 kΩ) stabilize inputs, as practiced in *Chapter 2, IoT Architecture and Ecosystem*, preventing floating states on pins like 2 or 3.

Advanced Features and Limitations

Some boards offer enhanced GPIO features. The ESP32 supports touch input on certain pins (like T0–T9), useful for capacitive buttons, and internal DACs for analog output, expanding beyond analogRead. However, limitations exist—Uno 6 analog pins may restrict multi-sensor projects, and NodeMCU fewer GPIOs (11) demand efficient pin allocation. Pin conflicts (such as ESP32 Strapping pins 0 and 15) require careful configuration during boot.

Debugging and Best Practices

Use the Serial Monitor (**`Tools → Serial Monitor`**) to debug GPIO issues, printing values like **`analogRead(A0)`** to check sensor data `Target ≤20 mA and use resistors/transistors`Label pins in code (for example, const int ledPin = 13) for clarity, enhancing maintainability, GPIO pins are the lifelines of microcontroller boards, enabling digital and analog interactions that power IoT innovation. With Arduino IDE functions, you can configure, read, and write to these pins, building responsive systems from n classrooms to n IoT networks.

Using the Serial Monitor

The Serial Monitor is a powerful tool within the Arduino IDE, enabling real-time debugging, monitoring, and interaction with microcontroller-based projects on boards like the Arduino Uno, NodeMCU, and ESP32, this feature is indispensable for IoT development, building on the GPIO and programming concepts from *Section* 5.5 and the networking insights from Chapter 4. By facilitating the display of sensor data, code outputs, and error messages, the Serial Monitor bridges the gap between hardware and software, allowing developers to verify functionality and troubleshoot issues efficiently. Whether you are tracking temperature readings or debugging a Wi-Fi connection, this tool transforms raw data into actionable insights. Let us explore its setup, usage, and practical applications in detail.

Setting up the Serial Monitor

To use the Serial Monitor, begin by initializing serial communication in your sketch. Start with a setup function where you configure the serial port with a specific baud rate—commonly 9600, though options like 115200 are available depending on your project speed requirements. For instance, you might set up the serial connection to prepare for sending messages. In the main loop, you can then send text or data periodically, such as a greeting or sensor value, with a delay to control the update frequency—say, every second—to avoid overwhelming the output.

Once the sketch is uploaded to your board (for example, via USB on an ESP32), open the Serial Monitor from the Arduino IDE by clicking the magnifying glass icon in the top-right corner or selecting `Tools → Serial Monitor`. Ensure the baud rate in the Serial Monitor matches the sketch setting (such as 9600). Upon opening, you should see the output start appearing, reflecting the board activity. This process, taking about 1-2 minutes, sets the stage for monitoring, aligning with global IoT practices.

Key Functions and Usage

The Serial Monitor relies on several core functions to manage data transmission:

- **Initialize Serial Communication**: Begin by setting up the serial port with a chosen baud rate to establish a communication channel between the board and IDE.
- **Send Text or Data**: Use a command to print messages or values, such as a welcome note or a sensor reading, to the monitor for real-time observation.
- **Add Line Breaks**: Include an option to append a newline after each message, ensuring clear separation of outputs for readability.
- **Delay Control**: Incorporate a pause between transmissions, such as a one-second interval, to regulate the flow of information and prevent buffer overflow.

For instance, you might configure the setup to start serial output and then loop to display a recurring message like "Hello, IoT World!" every second. This setup helps verify that the board is running correctly and provides a baseline for more complex debugging tasks.

Debugging and Sensor Monitoring

The Serial Monitor is a first-line tool for debugging code. If a sketch fails to behave as expected—say, an LED does not blink—print status messages at key points (such as Setup complete or Loop running) to trace execution. For GPIO-related issues from Section 5.5, monitor pin states; send the result of a digital input read or an analog value to check sensor data. For example, tracking a potentiometer position or a PIR sensor trigger can reveal wiring or logic errors.

It also excels at displaying sensor outputs, a critical aspect of IoT Perception Layer from *Chapter 2, IoT Architecture and Ecosystem*. Connect a DHT22 temperature sensor to an ESP32, read its value, and send it to the monitor—for example, Temperature: 25°C—to verify accuracy. In smart factories, engineers use this to monitor machine sensors, while in, students debug irrigation system data. The monitor scrolling log helps identify anomalies, like sudden spikes, prompting further investigation.

Advanced Features and Global Applications

The Serial Monitor supports advanced debugging with features like timestamping (via IDE settings) and variable formatting (including decimals for analog readings). It can also receive input—use a function to read user commands from the monitor, allowing runtime adjustments like changing a delay value. On the ESP32, monitor Wi-Fi status or BLE scan results, tying into Chapter 4 networking protocols. In bushfire monitors use it to log LoRa signal strength, ensuring remote reliability.

Globally, its applications are diverse. In the classrooms use it to teach output basics, while it tracks deforestation sensor data. The tool versatility shines in low-bandwidth scenarios, requiring only a USB connection and minimal processing power (like20 mA on Uno).

Best Practices and Limitations

To maximize effectiveness, label outputs clearly (for example, Light Level) and avoid excessive print frequency to prevent lag—cap updates at 1 Hz for stability. Match baud rates precisely, as mismatches (like 9600 versus 115200) causes garbled text. Limitations include a single serial port per board (use SoftwareSerial for multiple on Uno) and a 64-byte buffer, which may overflow with rapid data—mitigate with slower loops.

Troubleshooting Tips

If no output appears, check the COM port (`Tools → Port`), ensure the board is powered, and verify the baud rate. Garbled text indicates a rate mismatch, needs to be adjusted in both sketch and monitor. Using the IDE auto-scroll option to track live data, enhancing debug efficiency, the Serial Monitor is a vital tool for debugging and monitoring IoT projects, empowering developers to refine code and visualize data from sensors and networks worldwide, from n classrooms to n IoT deployments.

Board Selection Guide

Selecting the right development board—Arduino Uno, NodeMCU (ESP8266), or ESP32—is a critical decision that shapes the success of your IoT project, these boards cater to diverse needs, from beginner-friendly basics to advanced, connected applications, building on the GPIO, programming, and debugging insights from *Chapter* 4 - Networking and Communication Protocols (MQTT, HTTP, LoRa, BLE). The choice depends on factors like experience level, project requirements (including connectivity, processing power), budget, and scalability. This guide provides a detailed framework to help you match your project with the ideal board, considering specifications, use cases, and global examples to ensure informed decision-making for IoT innovation worldwide.

Choosing Arduino Uno

Opt for the Arduino Uno if you are a beginner or your project does not require Wi-Fi connectivity. Based on the ATmega328P 8-bit microcontroller, this board operates at a 16 MHz clock speed with 2 KB SRAM and 32 KB flash memory, offering 14 digital I/O pins (6 PWM) and 6 analog inputs. Its simplicity and extensive community support make it an excellent starting point for those new to physical computing. Priced around $20, it lacks built-in wireless features, making it ideal for offline projects where wired connections or external modules suffice. For example, a classroom project might use the Uno to teach LED blinking or button input, leveraging its robust pinout without the complexity of networking.

This board shines in educational settings and basic automation tasks, such as a standalone temperature logger with a DHT22 sensor or a simple robotic arm controlled by potentiometers. Its 5V operating voltage and 50 mA current draw support battery-powered setups with careful management, though memory limits (32 KB) may constrain larger codebases. Beginners benefit from its plug-and-play nature with the Arduino IDE, requiring no additional board packages, and its durability ensures long-term use. However, for projects needing real-time data transmission or wireless control—common in modern IoT—this board requires add-ons like an ESP-01 Wi-Fi module, adding cost and complexity.

Choosing NodeMCU (ESP8266)

Select the NodeMCU (ESP8266) if your project requires Wi-Fi in a low-cost setup. Powered by the ESP8266 32-bit microcontroller, it features an adjustable 80–160 MHz clock speed, 160 KB SRAM, and 4 MB flash memory, with 11 digital I/O pins (1 analog). Its built-in Wi-Fi, a significant upgrade over the Uno, enables wireless communication without extra hardware, aligning with *Chapter 4, Networking and Communication Protocols* (*MQTT, HTTP, LoRa, BLE*), exploration of HTTP and MQTT protocols. It is a budget-friendly option for IoT enthusiasts and small-scale deployments, drawing about 70 mA with a deep sleep mode of 20 μA for energy efficiency.

This board is perfect for low-cost IoT projects like remote temperature monitoring, where a BME280 sensor sends data to ThingSpeak, or smart plugs that control appliances via a mobile app. NodeMCUs track deforestation by uploading sensor data to cloud platforms, showcasing its global utility in resource-constrained environments. Its compact size suits space-limited designs, and the 3.3V operation optimizes power for battery-powered nodes. However, the limited GPIO count (11) and single-core architecture may restrict multitasking or projects with multiple peripherals. For applications needing Bluetooth or higher processing power, the NodeMCU falls short, but its affordability and wireless capability make it a go-to for cost-sensitive IoT solutions.

Choosing ESP32

Choose the ESP32 if your project demands Wi-Fi, Bluetooth, high speed, and an abundance of GPIO pins. Featuring a dual-core Tensilica 32-bit processor with a clock speed up to 240 MHz, it offers 520 KB SRAM and 4 MB flash memory, along with 34 GPIO pins (18 analog). This board includes dual-mode Bluetooth (Classic and BLE) and Wi-Fi, supporting advanced networking from the previous chapter, such as BLE for short-range device-to-device communication or MQTT for real-time updates. Priced around $10, it draws 20–150 mA (with <10 μA in deep sleep), balancing performance and power efficiency at 3.3V.

The ESP32 is ideal for advanced IoT projects and edge AI applications, such as smart locks using BLE or environmental stations with LoRa in the outback. Its dual cores manage smart factory automation, processing sensor data for predictive maintenance. The extensive GPIO and peripherals—ADCs, DACs, touch sensors—allow integration of multiple sensors (such as MQ-2 gas sensor) and actuators (like servo motors) simultaneously. This versatility supports complex workflows, like running lightweight machine learning models on-device. However, its feature-rich nature presents a steeper learning curve, and GPIO conflicts (for example, Strapping pins 0, 15) require careful configuration, making it less beginner-friendly than the Uno.

Comparative Decision Framework

To decide, evaluate your project needs:

- **Experience Level**: Beginners should start with the Uno for its simplicity, while intermediate users can handle NodeMCU Wi-Fi, and advanced users can leverage ESP32 capabilities.
- **Connectivity**: Uno lacks wireless (add-ons needed), NodeMCU offers Wi-Fi, and ESP32 provides Wi-Fi and Bluetooth.
- **Processing Power**: Uno 8-bit, 16 MHz suits basic tasks; NodeMCU 32-bit, 160 MHz handles moderate loads; ESP32 dual-core, 240 MHz excels in multitasking.
- **GPIO and Peripherals**: Uno (14 digital, 6 analog), NodeMCU (11 digital, 1 analog), and ESP32 (34 digital, 18 analog) cater to increasing complexity.
- **Budget**: Uno ($20), NodeMCU ($5), and ESP32 ($10) reflect a range of investment levels.
- **Power Consumption**: Uno (50 mA), NodeMCU (70 mA), and ESP32 (20–150 mA) influence battery life.

Practical Tips

Test with a simple sketch (for example, LED blink on Uno, Wi-Fi connect on NodeMCU, BLE scan on ESP32) to assess fit. Use the Serial Monitor (Section 5.6) to debug, ensuring compatibility. Scale up as needed—start with Uno, upgrade to NodeMCU, then ESP32 for advanced features, this guide empowers you to select the Arduino Uno for beginner offline projects, NodeMCU for cost-effective Wi-Fi IoT, or ESP32 for high-performance, connected solutions, driving innovation from classrooms to industrial deployments worldwide.

Best Practices for Wiring and Flashing

Mastering wiring and flashing techniques is essential for successfully building and programming IoT projects using development boards like the Arduino Uno, NodeMCU, and ESP32,these practices ensure reliable connections, efficient power management, and smooth code uploads, building on the GPIO usage from, Serial Monitor debugging, and board configurations . Proper wiring prevents hardware damage, while effective flashing avoids upload errors, enabling seamless integration of sensors, actuators, and networking components explored in *Chapters 2 and 4*. This section provides a comprehensive guide to best practices, incorporating tools, safety measures, and global examples to support your IoT journey.

Using a Breadboard for Prototyping

A breadboard is a cornerstone of prototyping, offering a solderless platform to connect components and test circuits. Its grid of holes, connected internally in rows, allows you to insert jumper wires, resistors, sensors (for example, DHT22), and actuators (for example, relays) without permanent soldering. Start by placing your development board, such as an Arduino Uno, on the breadboard edges, using its pin headers to access GPIO pins. COM Port Detective and black wires for ground, ensures a stable supply. Arrange sensors and actuators in the central grid, linking them to the board pins with short jumper wires to minimize interference.

This approach, taking 5–10 minutes per setup, supports iterative design; swap a potentiometer for an LDR or adjust a relay circuit without rework. In classrooms, students use breadboards to learn circuit basics, while in, hobbyists prototype irrigation monitors. Avoid overcrowding to prevent short circuits, and use a breadboard with power rails for larger projects. Its reusability saves costs, though complex designs may require a perfboard for permanence.

Check Ground Connections

Ground connections are the foundation of a stable circuit, serving as the reference point for all voltage levels. A missing or a loose ground can cause erratic behavior—for example, an ESP32 might fail to boot if its ground is not tied to the power source. Begin by connecting the board ground pin (GND) to the breadboard ground rail using a black jumper wire. Extend this connection to all components, such as sensors and actuators, ensuring a common ground. For example, a PIR motion sensor ground pin must align with the Arduino Uno GND to register movement accurately.

Use a multimeter in continuity mode to verify connections—set to the beep setting, touch probes to GND points, and listen for a continuous tone. This step, taking 1–2 minutes, prevents floating pins, which can trigger false readings or damage components. In smart factories, engineers check grounds to ensure reliable sensor data for automation. Avoid daisy-chaining grounds excessively, as resistance can build up; instead, use a star configuration from a single GND point. This practice, critical for IoT stability, aligns with *Chapter 2, IoT Architecture and Ecosystem*, signal stability lessons.

Power ESP32 via USB or Regulated 3.3V Supply

The ESP32 requires careful power management due to its 3.3V logic and higher current demands (20–150 mA). Power it via the USB port, which supplies 5V and includes an onboard regulator to step down to 3.3V, simplifying setup for programming and testing. Connect a USB cable from your computer to the ESP32 micro-USB port, ensuring a firm fit to avoid disconnections during flashing. Alternatively, use a regulated 3.3V external power supply (for example, a bench power unit or battery pack with a regulator) for standalone operation, connecting positive to the 3.3V pin and negative to GND.

Avoid applying 5V directly to 3.3V pins, as this can damage the ESP32 sensitive components—its maximum input tolerance is 3.6V. Monitor current with a multimeter in series to stay below 250 mA, the board safe limit. In, bushfire monitors power ESP32s with solar-regulated 3.3V supplies for remote reliability. This practice, taking 3–5 minutes to set up, ensures stability during uploads and runtime, especially for Wi-Fi or BLE tasks from *Chapter 4, Networking and Communication Protocols (MQTT, HTTP, LoRa, BLE)*.

Use Jumper Wires with Proper Color Coding

Jumper wires facilitate connections, and proper color coding enhances clarity and safety. Use red wires for power lines (5V or 3.3V), black wires for ground, and other colors (for example, yellow, green) for signal lines to GPIO pins. For instance, connect a red wire from the Arduino Uno 5V pin to the breadboard power rail, a black wire from GND to the ground rail, and a yellow wire from pin 2 to a button signal pin. This convention, taking 2–3 minutes to implement, reduces wiring errors—for example, mistaking a signal line for power.

Store wires organized by color in a kit, using male-to-female or male-to-male types based on your setup (for example, female for breadboard to board), deforestation trackers use color-coded wires to manage NodeMCU circuits efficiently. Avoid mixing colors haphazardly, as this can lead to shorts or confusion during debugging with the Serial Monitor (Section 5.6). Test connections with a multimeter to confirm continuity, ensuring robust IoT prototypes.

Flashing Best Practices

Flashing—uploading code to the board—requires precision. Use the Arduino IDE (*Section* 5.4) with the correct board selected (for example, ESP32 Dev Module). Press the reset button (if available) or cycle power before uploading to clear the buffer. Hold the boot button (for example, on ESP32) during upload if it fails, forcing the board into programming mode. Monitor the IDE for Done Uploading and check the Serial Monitor for boot messages.

Common issues include *Upload failed* (check COM port or drivers) or *Timeout* (ensure boot mode). In smart city projects, engineers flash ESP32s with optimized code for traffic systems. This process, taking 1–2 minutes per upload, leverages stable wiring to avoid interruptions.

Additional Tips and Global Context

Use heat-shrink tubing or electrical tape to insulate exposed wires, preventing shorts in humid climates like monsoons. Label circuits with masking tape for complex setups. Globally, these practices support IoT—Uno in education, NodeMCU in forests, ESP32 in factories—ensuring reliability, these wiring and flashing best practices—using breadboards, checking grounds, powering correctly, color-coding wires, and optimizing uploads—equip you to build and program robust IoT systems worldwide.

Safety and Grounding Tips

Ensuring safety and proper grounding is paramount when working with development boards like the Arduino Uno, NodeMCU, and ESP32, especially in IoT projects involving sensors, actuators, and power circuits, these practices protect both the hardware and the user, building on the wiring and flashing techniques and the GPIO usage , Poor safety measures can lead to component damage, inaccurate readings, or even personal injury, while effective grounding ensures stable operation, aligning with the Perception Layer stability discussed in *Chapter 2, IoT Architecture and Ecosystem*. This section provides a detailed guide to key safety and grounding tips, incorporating tools, precautions, and global examples to foster secure IoT development worldwide.

Never Connect Sensors or Actuators Directly without Checking Voltage Ratings

Connecting sensors or actuators without verifying voltage compatibility is a common mistake that can destroy components or the development board. Each board operates at specific logic levels—Arduino Uno at 5V, NodeMCU and ESP32 at 3.3V—and sensors or actuators must match these levels. For instance, a 5V relay connected to an ESP32 3.3V GPIO can overdraw current, frying the pin, while a 3.3V DHT22 sensor on a 5V Uno may fail to register data. Before connecting, consult the datasheet: a PIR motion sensor might tolerate 3.3–5V, but an MQ-2 gas sensor requires 5V with a voltage divider for analog reads.

To check, use a multimeter to measure the sensor operating voltage (for example, 3.3V across its pins) and compare it to the board supply. Add a level shifter or resistor network if needed—for example, a 10 kΩ and 20 kΩ resistor for a 5V-to-3.3V step-down. This precaution, taking 2–5 minutes, prevents damage, and ensures accurate readings. In smart factories, engineers verify voltage ratings to protect ESP32s in automation systems, while in, students learn this to safeguard classroom Uno.

Use External Power Supplies for Motors

Motors, such as DC motors or servos, draw significant current (100–500 mA or more) compared to the 20–40 mA limit per GPIO pin on most boards. Powering them directly from the Arduino Uno 5V pin (maximum 500 mA total) or ESP32 3.3V (limited by USB) can overload the regulator, causing overheating or board failure. Instead, use an external power supply—for instance, a 5V 2A adapter or a 3.7V LiPo battery with a regulator—matched to the motor voltage (including, 6V for a small DC motor).

Connect the external supply positive to the motor power pin and negative to a common ground with the board, using a black wire. Add a transistor (such as NPN like BC547) or motor driver (similar to L298N) controlled by a GPIO pin to switch the motor on/off (like pin 9 on Uno with PWM). This setup, taking 5–10 minutes, protects the board while enabling robust actuation. In bushfire monitor robots use external 12V supplies for motor-driven wheels, ensuring ESP32 stability. Avoid bypassing grounds, as this can create voltage differences, damaging components. This practice supports IoT applications like robotic arms or irrigation pumps globally.

Loose Breadboard Connections

Loose connections on a breadboard can cause intermittent failures, erratic sensor readings, or short circuits, undermining IoT project reliability. Breadboard contacts wear over time, especially with frequent use, leading to poor contact with jumper wires or components. To prevent this, insert wires and pins firmly; push until you feel resistance; and wiggle them gently to ensure a snug fit. Use fresh breadboards for critical projects, as old ones may have oxidized contacts.

Check connections with a multimeter in continuity mode—touch probes to each end of a wire (for example, from 5V to a sensor pin) and listen for a beep. Tighten setups by securing the breadboard with tape or a non-conductive base to avoid movement. This step, taking 2-3 minutes, stabilizes circuits like a NodeMCU-based deforestation tracker where loose wires could miss data uploads; and, students learn to re-seat pins to fix blinking LED issues on Uno. Avoid overloading a single row with multiple wires, as this increases resistance—distribute connections across rows. Proper grounding (Section 5.8) complements this by minimizing noise from loose contacts.

Additional Safety and Grounding Tips

- **Use Fuses or Current Limiters**: Install a 500 mA fuse between the power supply and board to prevent overcurrent, protecting against short circuits during motor tests.
- **Insulate Exposed Wires**: Apply heat-shrink tubing or electrical tape to bare ends, especially in humid climates like monsoons, to prevent accidental shorts.
- **Ground All Components**: Ensure every sensor, actuator, and power source shares a common ground with the board—for example, tie an external 5V supply GND to Uno GND—to avoid floating voltages.
- **Wear Anti-Static Wrist Straps**: Discharge static electricity before handling boards, particularly ESP32s with sensitive Wi-Fi chips, reducing ESD (electrostatic discharge) risks.
- **Label Circuits**: Use masking tape to mark power, ground, and signal lines, aiding troubleshooting during complex IoT setups like smart traffic systems.

Global Context and Troubleshooting

These tips are vital globally. In grounded ESP32s ensure factory sensor accuracy, insulated NodeMCU wires prevent rainforest humidity issues; infuses protect classroom Uno. If issues arise—for example, no sensor data—check voltages with a multimeter, re-seat breadboard connections, and verify grounds. Use the Serial Monitor (*Section* 5.6) to log errors, ensuring stability, these safety and grounding practices—checking voltage ratings, using external power for motors, avoiding loose connections, and applying additional precautions—safeguard your IoT projects, enabling reliable innovation from educational labs to industrial deployments worldwide.

Common Errors and Fixes

Encountering errors while working with development boards like the Arduino Uno, NodeMCU, and ESP32 is a natural part of the IoT learning and development process, understanding and resolving these issues is crucial for successful prototyping, building on the wiring, flashing, and safety practices, as well as the programming and GPIO insights. These errors—ranging from board detection failures to upload issues—can stem from hardware misconfigurations, driver problems, or software mismatches. This section provides a detailed guide to common errors and their fixes, incorporating troubleshooting steps, tools, and global examples to ensure smooth operation of your IoT projects worldwide.

Board Not Detected: Install Drivers (CH340/CP2102)

One frequent issue is the IDE failing to detect the board, often indicated by a grayed-out COM port or an error like Board at COMX is not available. This typically occurs due to missing or incompatible drivers, especially for boards using CH340 or CP2102 USB-to-serial chips, common in clones like some Arduino Uno or NodeMCUs. The Arduino IDE relies on these drivers to communicate via USB, and without them, the board remains invisible.

To fix this, first identify the chip. Check the board silkscreen for CH340 or CP2102 near the USB port, or consult the product documentation. Download the appropriate driver from the manufacturer website; CH340 drivers are available from WCH.cn, and CP2102 drivers from Silicon Labs, or use the Arduino IDE driver installer under **`Tools → Board → Board Manager`** after selecting the board. On Windows, run the .exe file, follow the wizard, and restart the IDE. On macOS/Linux, use the .dmg or terminal commands provided. After installation, reconnect the board, go to **`Tools → Port`**, and select the new COM port (for example, COM3 on Windows or /dev/ttyUSB0 on Linux). Students fix this in classrooms to get Uno running, hobbyists resolve it for ESP32 projects. This process, taking 5 to 10 minutes, restores detection.

COM Port Missing: Check USB Cable and Connections

A missing COM port, where no port appears under **`Tools → Port`**, often points to a faulty USB cable or loose connection. The cable might be data-only (charging cables lack data lines), or the connection might be unstable due to a damaged port or cable. This issue can halt communication, preventing code uploads or Serial Monitor use.

Start by testing with a different USB cable—preferably a high-quality one with data support (for example, a 2.0 A-to-B for Uno). Ensure the cable is securely plugged into both the board and computer, as a loose fit can interrupt power or data. Inspect the board USB port for debris or bent pins, cleaning with compressed air if needed. Try another computer USB port or machine to isolate the problem. Onboard LEDs (for example, power LED on ESP32) should light up if power is reaching the board. In, bushfire monitor developers troubleshoot NodeMCU connections this way. This fix, taking 2–5 minutes, re-establishes the COM port, enabling further work.

Upload Error: Wrong Board or COM Port Selected

An upload error, often displayed as Error compiling for board or **`stk500_getsync():`** not in sync, typically arises from selecting the wrong board or COM port in the Arduino IDE. This mismatch confuses the IDE, leading to failed code transfers to the microcontroller. For example, selecting Arduino Mega for an Uno or an incorrect COM port can trigger this.

To resolve, open the IDE and navigate to **`Tools → Board`**. Choose the exact board variant—for example, Arduino Uno for Uno, NodeMCU 1.0 (ESP-12E Module) for NodeMCU, or ESP32 Dev Module for ESP32—matching the hardware. Then, go to **`Tools → Port`** and select the active COM port, which should appear after a successful driver install (for example, COM4). Double-check with the Serial Monitor (**`Tools → Serial Monitor`**) to confirm communication. If the error persists, ensure that the board is in a reset state—press the reset button on Uno or cycle power on ESP32. In smart factories, engineers align ESP32 settings to upload control code. This adjustment, taking 1–3 minutes, clears the error and enables uploads.

ESP32 Upload Stuck: Press and Hold BOOT Button during Upload

For ESP32 boards, an upload might stall, showing *Connecting...* or timing out, due to the board not entering programming mode. This occurs because the boot process locks the flash until manually triggered, especially if GPIO0 (boot pin) is not held low during upload. This is a common issue with ESP32 variants like the DevKitC.

To fix, start the upload process in the IDE by clicking the upload button (right arrow). As soon as Connecting... appears, press and hold the BOOT button (labeled on the board) until the IDE progresses to Uploading... — typically 2–5 seconds. Release the button once uploading begins. This forces GPIO0 low, signaling the ESP32 to enter flash mode. Ensure a stable USB connection and correct COM/

port settings beforehand. In smart traffic systems, developers use this technique for ESP32 firmware updates. This fix, taking 1–2 minutes per upload, resolves the stall and ensures successful flashing.

Additional Troubleshooting Tips

- **Serial Monitor Issues**: If no data appears, verify the baud rate matches the sketch (for example, 9600) and the board is powered. Use **`Tools → Get Board Info`** to confirm detection.
- **Overheating**: If the board feels hot, disconnect immediately—check for short circuits or overcurrent from motors.
- **Firmware Mismatch**: For ESP32/NodeMCU, update board packages via **`Tools → Board → Boards Manager`** if uploads fail repeatedly.
- **Power Supply**: Use a powered USB hub if the computer port lacks sufficient current (for example, 500 mA for Uno).

Global Context and Prevention

These fixes are applied globally: deforestation trackers debug NodeMCU COM ports; classroom Uno gets driver updates; ESP32 boot issues are resolved for IoT labs. Prevent errors by labeling cables, using quality USBs, and double-checking settings before uploads, ensuring reliability, addressing board detection, COM port, upload, and ESP32 boot errors with these fixes empowers you to troubleshoot effectively, keeping your IoT projects on track from educational settings to industrial applications worldwide.

Troubleshooting Board Resets

Board resets, where a development board like the ESP32, NodeMCU, or Arduino Uno unexpectedly restarts, can disrupt IoT projects and lead to unreliable operation, addressing these resets is vital for maintaining system stability, building on the safety, wiring, and flashing practices from *Sections* 5.8–5.10, as well as the GPIO and programming foundations from *Sections* 5.5 *and* 5.6. Resets often stem from power supply issues, poor cable quality, or insufficient voltage regulation, impacting the continuous operation required for networking tasks outlined in *Chapter 4, Networking and Communication Protocols* (MQTT, HTTP, LoRa, BLE). This section provides a detailed guide to troubleshooting board resets, including causes, fixes, and global examples, ensuring your IoT setups remain robust worldwide.

ESP32 May Reset if Power Supply is Unstable

The ESP32 is particularly sensitive to power supply instability, often resetting due to voltage drops or current surges, especially during Wi-Fi or Bluetooth operations that spike power demand (20–150 mA). Symptoms include the onboard LED blinking erratically or the Serial Monitor showing *Brownout detected* or *Reset reason: Software WDT reset*. This can occur if the USB port provides insufficient current (for example, a laptop 500 mA limit) or if an external supply lacks regulation, causing voltage to dip below the 3.3V minimum.

To address this, first measure the supply voltage with a multimeter across the 3.3V and GND pins—expect 3.2–3.4V under load. If it drops (say to 2.8 V), switch to a powered USB hub (1A output) or a regulated 3.3V external supply, such as a 3.7 V LiPo battery with a buck converter. Avoid unregulated 5V sources without a step-down, as they can overshoot. In smart factories, engineers stabilize ESP32 power for real-time sensor monitoring, preventing resets during peak loads. This fix, taking 5–10 minutes, restores reliable operation by ensuring consistent voltage.

Use Quality USB Cables

A common cause of board resets is the use of low-quality or damaged USB cables, which can interrupt power or data transmission. Charging-only cables lack data lines, while worn cables may have broken wires, leading to intermittent power delivery. This triggers resets on boards like the NodeMCU or ESP32, especially during code uploads or heavy processing, with the Serial Monitor showing Connection lost or repeated boot messages.

To resolve, replace the cable with a high-quality, data-capable USB 2.0 or 3.0 cable (for example, A-to-micro-B for ESP32). Test with a multimeter for continuity between the USB plug power (VCC) and ground (GND) pins, ensuring no breaks. Avoid long cables (>1m) without boosters, as resistance increases voltage drop. In, bushfire monitor developers use shielded USB cables to prevent resets in remote ESP32 deployments. This swap, taking 2–3 minutes, stabilizes power and data flow, thereby eliminating reset triggers.

Add Capacitors for Stable Voltage Supply

For boards experiencing resets due to voltage fluctuations, especially under load from motors or multiple sensors, and adding capacitors can smooth the power supply. Capacitors act as buffers, storing charge to compensate for sudden drops, preventing the microcontroller from resetting when current demand spikes. This is particularly relevant for ESP32 projects with Wi-Fi or the Arduino Uno driving high-current peripherals.

Install a 10 μF–100 μF electrolytic capacitor across the 3.3V (or 5V for Uno) and GND pins on the breadboard, with the positive leg to the voltage pin and negative to ground. For finer filtering, add a 0.1 μF ceramic capacitor in parallel to handle high-frequency noise. Solder or secure with heat-shrink tubing if permanent. Use a multimeter to verify voltage stability before and after—expect less than 0.1V ripple. Irrigation system developers add 47 μF capacitors to NodeMCUs to prevent resets during pump cycles. This modification, taking 5–7 minutes, enhances reliability, though overcapacitance can slow response. Therefore, start with 10 μF and scale up as needed.

Additional Troubleshooting and Prevention Tips

- **Check Load Current**: Measure total current with a multimeter in series—if it exceeds the supply rating (for example, 500 mA for USB), add an external power source.
- **Monitor Temperature**: If the board heats up, disconnect immediately—overheating from poor grounding or shorts can cause resets. Use a thermal pad if needed.
- **Update Firmware**: For ESP32/NodeMCU, ensure the latest board package via `Tools → Board → Boards Manager`, as old firmware may mishandle power events.
- **Grounding Check**: Verify all components share a common ground as floating grounds can induce resets. Use a star configuration for multiple devices.
- **Serial Monitor Logs**: Enable the Serial Monitor at 115200 baud to capture reset reasons (for example, Brownout or Exception), guiding further fixes.

Advanced Considerations

For high-load IoT (for example, ESP32 with LoRa), consider a 1000 μF capacitor and a 5V-to-3.3V regulator (like AMS1117) for heavy motors, but test for overheating. Avoid capacitors near heat-sensitive Wi-Fi chips; place them near power inputs. These measures, refined through global use, support complex deployments, troubleshooting board resets by stabilizing power, using quality cables, and adding capacitors equips you to maintain reliable IoT systems, from educational labs to industrial networks worldwide.

Practical Exercises

Hands-on practice is key to mastering IoT development with boards like the Arduino Uno, NodeMCU, and ESP32, these practical exercises build on the troubleshooting, wiring, and programming skills from *Sections* 5.10, 5.8, *and* 5.5–5.6, reinforcing the theoretical networking concepts from *Chapter* 4, *Networking and Communication Protocols* (MQTT, HTTP, LoRa, BLE). Designed for beginners and intermediate users, the exercises focus on upload debugging, reset behavior, and multi-board management, subsequently, fostering confidence and problem-solving abilities. Each task includes detailed steps, goals, and global examples to inspire real-world application, ensuring you can apply these skills in diverse IoT contexts worldwide.

Exercise 1: Board Boot and Blink Debugging Drill

This exercise helps you troubleshoot and resolve common upload failures, a frequent challenge when starting with boards like the ESP32 or Arduino Uno. The goal is to build confidence in diagnosing and fixing issues, preparing you for more complex IoT projects.

Steps:

1. **Connect ESP32/Arduino Uno**: Use a quality USB cable (for example, USB-A to micro-B for ESP32) to connect the board to your computer. Ensure the cable supports data transfer, not just charging. Check that the onboard power LED lights up to confirm power.
2. **Upload Blink Sketch**: Open the Arduino IDE, go to **`File → Examples → 01.Basics → Blink`**, and click the upload button (right arrow). The sketch toggles an LED (pin 13 on Uno, onboard LED on ESP32) every second, serving as a basic test.
3. **If Fails, Check Board/Port Selection**: If you see an error like **`stk500_getsync():`** not in sync or **`Upload failed`**, verify the board and port. Navigate to **`Tools → Board`** and select Arduino Uno or ESP32 Dev Module (match your hardware). Then, go to **`Tools → Port`** and choose the correct COM port (for example, COM3 on Windows). Re-upload to test.
4. **For ESP32, Press BOOT Button During Upload**: If the ESP32 upload stalls at Connecting..., press and hold the **`BOOT`** button (labeled on the board) as soon as uploading starts. Hold for 2–5 seconds until **`Uploading...`** appears, then release. This forces the board into programming mode, resolving boot lock issues.

The successful uploading of the Blink sketch after fixing errors enhances your ability to handle hardware-software mismatches. Students use this drill in rural classrooms to debug Uno, and hobbyists apply it to ESP32s for LED projects. Expect 10 to 15 minutes per attempt, with practice reducing errors over time.

Exercise 2: Flash and Reset Race

This exercise explores how microcontrollers handle resets, teaching you to observe and control restart behavior. The goal is to understand the setup() function role and how resets re-execute it, a key concept for IoT stability.

Steps:

1. **Upload Blink**: Start by uploading the Blink sketch as in Exercise 1. Verify the LED blinks every second, confirming the code runs correctly on your ESP32 or Uno.
2. **Press `RESET/EN` Button**: Locate the **`RESET`** button on the **`Uno`** or **`EN`** (Enable) button on the ESP32. Press it briefly (1 second) to restart the board. Observe the LED turn off and resume blinking, indicating a reset.

3. **Add Serial.println(Device restarted); in `setup()`**: Open the sketch, find the `setup()` function, and add a line to print a message—for example : `Serial.begin(9600); Serial.println(Device restarted);`—before any other code. Upload again, open the Serial Monitor (`Tools → Serial Monitor`) at 9600 baud, and press RESET. Note the Device restarted message each time, showing setup() re-runs.

This exercise, taking 10–12 minutes, reveals reset triggers (for example, power dips, manual presses) and `setup()` initialization, critical for debugging IoT devices. In, smart factory engineers use this to test ESP32 reset recovery, while NodeMCU deforestation trackers monitor restart logs. Practice varying reset timing to see consistent behavior.

Exercise 3: COM Port Detective

Managing multiple boards requires identifying their COM ports, a skill for scaling IoT projects. The goal is to confidently handle multi-board setups, avoiding upload conflicts.

Steps:

1. **Connect Arduino + ESP32**: Use separate quality USB cables to connect an Arduino Uno and an ESP32 to your computer. Ensure both power LEDs light up, indicating active connections.
2. **`Open Tools → Port in Arduino IDE`**: Launch the IDE, go to `Tools → Port`, and note the listed ports (for example, COM3, COM4). Disconnect one board (for example, ESP32) and refresh the list—disappearing ports indicate the disconnected board. Ports can change after reboot, so do not treat COM numbers as permanent.
3. **Upload Test Sketch to Identify Ports**: Load a simple sketch and upload to each board, selecting ports one by one. Open the Serial Monitor for each to match the output (Test) with the port, confirming assignment.
4. **Label Boards Physically**: Use masking tape or stickers to label each board with its COM port (for example, COM3 - Uno, COM4 - ESP32). Update labels if ports change after reboots.

This exercise, taking 15–20 minutes, builds skills for multi-device IoT systems. In smart traffic developers label ESP32s for port tracking, while bushfire monitors manage NodeMCUs this way. Practice with three boards to enhance proficiency, ensuring no upload overlaps.

Conclusion

This chapter provides a comprehensive introduction to the core development boards used in IoT—Arduino Uno, NodeMCU (ESP8266), and ESP32—equipping learners with the knowledge and skills to prototype and build real-world IoT systems, the content spans board selection, setup, programming, debugging, and practical application, laying a solid foundation for integrating sensors, actuators, and cloud platforms as explored in previous chapters.

We began by comparing the architectures, specifications, and features of the Arduino Uno, NodeMCU, and ESP32, highlighting their strengths. The Arduino Uno, with its 8-bit ATmega328P, 16 MHz clock, and 32 KB flash, suits beginners and offline projects due to its simplicity and native IDE support. The NodeMCU (ESP8266), featuring a 32-bit processor, 160 MHz speed, and built-in Wi-Fi, offers a low-cost solution for wireless IoT tasks. The ESP32, with dual-core 240 MHz processing, Wi-Fi, Bluetooth, and 34 GPIO pins, excels in advanced, connected applications. A detailed board selection guide helped learners choose based on experience, connectivity needs, and budget, with global examples like educational Uno and industrial ESP32s.

Next, we covered the practical setup process. Installing the Arduino IDE and configuring boards—Arduino Uno natively, NodeMCU and ESP32 via board manager URLs—enabled coding and uploading.

We explored GPIO pins (digital HIGH/LOW, analog 0-1023), using functions like **pinMode()**, **digitalWrite()**, and **analogRead()**, and leveraged the Serial Monitor for real-time debugging of sensor data or errors. Best practices for wiring—using breadboards, checking grounds, powering ESP32 with 3.3V, and color-coding wires—ensured safe, organized circuits. Safety tips, such as verifying voltage ratings and using external power for motors, protected hardware, while grounding techniques minimized noise.

Troubleshooting was a key focus, addressing common issues like board detection (installing CH340/CP2102 drivers), missing COM ports (checking USB cables), upload errors (correcting board/port settings), ESP32 boot stalls (pressing **BOOT**), and resets (stabilizing power with capacitors). These fixes, supported by global contexts like NodeMCU trackers and ESP32 monitors, built resilience in handling hardware challenges.

The chapter has concluded with practical exercises to reinforce skills. The Board Boot and Blink Debugging Drill taught upload troubleshooting, pressing BOOT for ESP32s. The Flash and Reset Race explored reset behavior with Serial Monitor logs in **setup()**. The COM Port Detective exercise managed multiple boards by identifying and labeling ports. These tasks, practiced in settings from classrooms to traffic systems, enhanced hands-on confidence.

With this knowledge, learners are now equipped to confidently use microcontroller boards, troubleshoot issues, and move forward to *Chapter 6, Interfacing Sensors and Modules*, where they will interface essential sensors and modules such as the DHT11, Ultrasonic sensor, Relay module, and MQ-2 gas sensor, mastering wiring, coding, and calibration for real-world IoT projects with sensors, actuators, and cloud platforms, driving innovation globally.

CHAPTER 6
Interfacing Sensors and Modules

Introduction

As we step into *Chapter 6, Interfacing Sensors and Modules*, we build upon the foundational skills acquired in the previous chapter, where we explored the core development boards of IoT—Arduino Uno, NodeMCU (ESP8266), and ESP32. In that chapter, we compared their specifications and features, learning when to select each for specific projects. We installed the Arduino IDE, configured the boards, wrote our first Blink sketch, and honed debugging techniques using the Serial Monitor. By now, you should feel confident setting up your board, flashing code, and resolving basic upload errors such as board detection or COM port issues. This hands-on experience has prepared you to transition from theoretical understanding to practical application in the exciting realm of IoT development.

This chapter marks a pivotal shift toward interfacing sensors and modules, unlocking the ability to interact with the physical world through data collection and control. The essence of IoT lies in its ability to sense and actuate, bridging the digital and physical domains. Sensors are the eyes and ears of any IoT system, capturing environmental data such as temperature, humidity, distance, or gas levels, which can then be processed and acted upon. Modules, such as relays, extend this capability by enabling control over external devices such as lights, fans, or alarms.

This chapter is designed to be highly practical, guiding you through the physical connection, coding, and calibration of widely used components. You will work with the DHT11 and DHT22 for temperature and humidity monitoring, the Ultrasonic sensor for distance measurement, the Relay module for switching AC loads, and the MQ-2 gas sensor for detecting air quality metrics such as LPG, smoke, and carbon monoxide. These components are staples in IoT projects, from smart homes to industrial automation, and mastering them will empower you to create innovative solutions.

Structure

In this chapter, we will cover the following topics:

- Overview
- Understanding Digital and Analog Sensor Outputs
- Reading Environmental Data
- DHT11/DHT22 Sensors

- Ultrasonic Sensor
- Relay Module
- MQ-2 Gas Sensor
- Building a Mini Project: Smart Air Quality Monitor with Buzzer Alarm
- Visualizing SensorData
- Testing, Calibration, and Noise Reduction Techniques
- Troubleshooting Common Issues

Overview

Let us begin with the DHT11 and DHT22, popular sensors for environmental monitoring. The DHT11 offers a cost-effective solution with a temperature range of 0–50°C and humidity from 20–80% with ±5% accuracy, while the DHT22 provides higher precision (±2–5% humidity, -40–80°C) and is ideal for more demanding applications. Wiring these sensors involves connecting three or four pins (VCC, GND, data, and optionally NC) to 3.3V or 5V supply of your board, ground, and a digital pin, respectively, with a 4.7kΩ–10kΩ pull-up resistor on the data line to ensure reliable communication. You will use the DHT library in the Arduino IDE to read and parse data, a process that takes about 250ms per reading, making it suitable for real-time monitoring.

Next, the Ultrasonic sensor—typically the HC-SR04—measures distance using sound waves, calculating the time-of-flight between an emitted ping and its echo. With a range of 2cm to 400cm and ±3mm accuracy, it is perfect for applications such as obstacle avoidance or liquid level monitoring. Wiring requires four pins (VCC, Trig, Echo, GND) to 5V, a digital output, a digital input, and ground, respectively. You will write code to trigger the sensor, measure the echo time, and convert it to distance using the speed of sound (approximately 343 m/s in air).

The Relay module introduces you to controlling high-voltage AC loads, a critical skill for IoT home automation. Operating at 5V or 3.3V with a coil that switches a 250V AC/10A load, it acts as an electrically operated switch. Wiring connects the VCC, GND, and signal pin of the relay to the board, with the AC load wired to the NO (Normally Open) or NC (Normally Closed) terminals of the relay. Safety is paramount—use insulated tools, work with power off, and employ external power supplies for motors to avoid board damage.

The MQ-2 gas sensor detects combustible gases (LPG, methane, propane) and smoke, with a sensitivity range adjustable via a potentiometer. It outputs an analog signal (0–1023 on Arduino) proportional to gas concentration, requiring a 5V supply, ground, and analog pin connection, often with a load resistor (for example, 10kΩ). Calibration is key to interpreting readings accurately, a process used in many safety and monitoring systems.

The chapter culminates in a mini-project: The Smart Air Quality Monitor. This integrates the MQ-2 with a buzzer (actuator) to alert when gas levels exceed a threshold (for example, 500 ppm), using an ESP32 for Wi-Fi connectivity to log data. Wiring involves connecting the analog output of MQ-2 to A0, the buzzer to a digital pin (for example, 13), and powering both via a 5V supply with common grounding. Code will read gas levels, trigger the buzzer, and display results on the Serial Monitor, with potential cloud integration via MQTT.

Visualization is enhanced using the Serial Monitor and Serial Plotter. The Monitor logs raw data (for example, Temperature: 25°C, Hum: 60%), while the Plotter graphs trends over time, aiding in noise analysis. Testing and calibration—adjusting sensor placement, averaging readings, or adding filters—ensure accuracy. Noise reduction techniques, such as debouncing or moving averages, stabilize outputs, critical for reliable IoT data.

Troubleshooting covers incorrect values (check wiring, power), noisy output (add capacitors), and unstable readings (verify grounds, calibrate). These skills apply across many practical scenarios where sensors and modules are deployed. This hands-on approach prepares you for *Chapter 7, Real-Time Control with GPIO, PWM and Interrupts*. This introduction sets the stage for a practical journey into sensor and module interfacing, equipping you with the tools to sense the environment and control devices, paving the way for robust IoT solutions worldwide.

Understanding Digital and Analog Sensor Outputs

In the realm of IoT development, understanding the distinction between digital and analog sensor outputs is fundamental to effectively interfacing sensors with microcontroller boards such as the Arduino Uno, NodeMCU, and ESP32. This knowledge builds on the GPIO programming skills from the previous chapter, enabling you to capture and process environmental data accurately. Sensors serve as the sensory organs of IoTsystems, translating physical phenomena—temperature, distance, gas levels—into electrical signals that microcontrollers can interpret. These signals are categorized as digital or analog, each with unique characteristics, wiring requirements, and reading methods. This section delves into the nuances of digital and analog sensor outputs, providing detailed explanations, examples, and practical considerations to guide you through their implementation in real-world projects.

Digital Sensors

Digital sensors produce a binary output, typically represented as HIGH (1) or LOW (0). Some are binary (switches), others are pulse-width or serial-data, corresponding to specific voltage levels defined by the logic of the microcontroller. For Arduino Uno, HIGH is approximately 5V and LOW is 0V, while for ESP32 and NodeMCU, these levels are 3.3V and 0V, respectively. This binary nature simplifies data interpretation, as the output is a clear on/off signal, making digital sensors ideal for applications requiring discrete states, such as presence detection or threshold-based triggers.

A prime example is the Ultrasonic sensor, such as the HC-SR04, widely used for distance measurement. This sensor operates by emitting a short ultrasonic pulse (a HIGH signal) via its Trig pin and listening for the echo on its Echo pin, which returns a HIGH pulse when the sound wave reflects back. The duration of the HIGH pulse, measurable in microseconds, indicates the time-of-flight, which is then converted to distance using the speed of sound (approximately 343 m/s in air). Wiring involves connecting the Trig pin to a digital output (for example: pin 9 on Uno) and the Echo pin to a digital input (for example: pin 10), with VCC to 5V and GND to ground. The **`digitalRead()`** function in the Arduino IDE reads these HIGH/LOW states, making it straightforward to process the pulse duration.

Digital sensors are easy to interface due to their compatibility with digital pins, which are designed to handle binary signals. The simplicity extends to coding—after triggering the Ultrasonic sensor with a 10µs HIGH pulse on Trig, you use **`pulseIn()`** to measure the HIGH duration of Echo pin, calculating distance with the formula: **`distance = (duration * 0.0343) / 2 (cm)`**, accounting for the round trip. This process, taking 50–100ms per reading, suits applications such as obstacle avoidance in robotics or parking assist systems. Ultrasonic sensors are integral to automated parking garages, ensuring precise vehicle detection.

However, digital sensors have limitations. Their binary output lacks granularity, meaning they cannot capture continuous variations. For example, the Ultrasonic sensor provides a single distance value per reading, not a range of intermediate states. Noise can also affect pulse timing, requiring debouncing or averaging techniques to stabilize readings. Power consumption is typically low (5–15mA for HC-SR04), but wiring must ensure clean signals—loose connections or electromagnetic interference can cause false HIGH/LOW transitions. Troubleshooting involves checking pin assignments with a multimeter in continuity mode and verifying power stability, aligning with the safety practices from the previous chapter.

Analog Sensors

In contrast, Analog Sensors produce a continuous output, typically as a voltage that varies between 0V and the logic level of the board (0–5V for Uno, 0–3.3V for ESP32/NodeMCU), reflecting the magnitude of the measured phenomenon. This analog signal provides a rich, detailed representation of data, making these sensors suitable for applications requiring fine-grained measurements, such as gas concentration or environmental monitoring. The Analog-to-Digital Converter (ADC) of microcontroller converts this voltage into a digital value (0–1023 for a 10-bit ADC), which can then be mapped to physical units.

A quintessential example is the MQ-2 gas sensor, used to detect combustible gases such as LPG, methane, propane, smoke, and carbon monoxide. The output voltage of the sensor increases with gas concentration, ranging from near 0V in clean air to close to 5V at high concentrations (for example: 1000 ppm LPG). Wiring connects the VCC of the sensor to 5V, GND to ground, and the analog output (AO) to an analog pin (for example: A0 on Uno), often with a 10kΩ load resistor between AO and VCC to adjust sensitivity via a built-in potentiometer. The **analogRead()** function samples this voltage, returning a value that correlates with gas levels, requiring calibration to interpret accurately—for example: mapping 0–1023 to 0–1000 ppm based on a reference curve.

Analog sensors excel in capturing continuous data, offering versatility for IoT applications. The MQ-2, with a warm-up time of 1–2 minutes and a current draw of 150mA, is used in air quality monitors and industrial safety systems. In urban areas, deploy MQ-2s to alert residents of gas leaks, while in Europe, factories use them to detect methane in confined spaces. The continuous output allows for trend analysis—for example, plotting gas levels over time with the Serial Plotter—enhancing decision-making. Coding involves reading the analog value in the **`loop()`** function, applying a calibration formula (for example: **`gasLevel = (analogValue / 1023) * 1000`**), and adding thresholds for alerts.

However, analog sensors pose challenges. The resolution of ADC (10-bit on most boards) limits precision, and noise from power supply fluctuations or electromagnetic interference can skew readings—for example: a 0.1V ripple might register as a 20-unit jump on A0. Wiring requires stable power (use a regulated 5V supply) and shielded cables to minimize noise, often supplemented by a 0.1µF capacitor across VCC and GND. Calibration is critical—expose the sensor to known gas concentrations (for example: 200 ppm propane) to establish a baseline, adjusting the potentiometer for optimal sensitivity. Troubleshooting includes checking for loose connections, verifying voltage with a multimeter, and averaging multiple readings (for example, over 10 samples) to reduce noise, aligning with previous chapter grounding tips.

Practical Considerations and Comparison

Choosing between digital and analog sensors depends on the needs of your project. Digital sensors, like the Ultrasonic, are simpler to code and interface, requiring fewer resources (for example, no ADC) and offering fast response times (10–50ms). They are ideal for binary decisions—for example, obstacles present or not—but lack the detail for gradual changes. Analog sensors, like the MQ-2, provide rich data for nuanced analysis, supporting applications like environmental monitoring, but demand more complex wiring and calibration. Power consumption varies; Ultrasonic at 15mA versus MQ-2 at 150mA, consequently impacting battery-powered designs.

Wiring best practices apply to both. Use a breadboard for prototyping, color-code wires (red for VCC, black for GND), and ensure a common ground (previous chapter). For digital sensors, test pulse stability with an oscilloscope if available; for analog, add filtering capacitors (10µF) to smooth the voltage. Coding efficiency matters—digital readings use **`digitalRead()`** in tight loops, while analog requires **`analogRead()`** with delay (for example: 100ms) to avoid ADC overload. The Serial Monitor logs both outputs, aiding debug—for example, **`Distance: 50cm`** or **`Gas: 300ppm`**.

Understanding digital and analog sensor outputs equips you to select and interface the right sensor for your IoT needs. Digital sensors like the Ultrasonic offer simplicity and speed, while analog sensors like the MQ-2 provide detailed, continuous data. With proper wiring, coding, and troubleshooting, you will harness these outputs to build robust systems, setting the stage for the practical exercises ahead.

Reading Environmental Data

IoT projects thrive on the ability to monitor and respond to environmental conditions, making sensors indispensable tools for capturing real-world data. This section builds on the digital and analog sensor fundamentals, focusing on how to read and interpret environmental data using the DHT11/DHT22 for temperature and humidity, the Ultrasonic sensor for distance, and the MQ-2 gas sensor for air quality. These sensors generate raw electrical signals—pulses, voltage variations—that must be converted into meaningful values through libraries, formulas, and calibration. This hands-on exploration equips you with the skills to interface these components with Arduino Uno, NodeMCU, and ESP32 boards, laying the groundwork for practical IoT applications such as smart homes, industrial monitoring, and environmental protection. With detailed wiring, coding examples, and troubleshooting tips, you will transform raw data into actionable insights, supported by global use cases.

Temperature and Humidity: DHT11/DHT22 Sensors

The DHT11 and DHT22 sensors are go-to choices for monitoring temperature and humidity, critical parameters in applications ranging from climate control to agriculture. The DHT11, a cost-effective option, measures temperature from 0 to 50°C (±2°C accuracy) and humidity from 20% to 80% (±5% accuracy), with a sampling rate of one reading per second. The DHT22, a more precise upgrade, covers from -40°C to 80°C (±0.5°C) and 0–100% humidity (±2–5%), ideal for demanding environments. Both use a single-wire digital protocol, outputting a serialized data stream that includes humidity, temperature, and a checksum for verification.

Wiring involves connecting the VCC of the sensor to 3.3V or 5V (DHT11 tolerates both, DHT22 prefers 3.3V), GND to ground, and the data pin to a digital pin (for example, pin 2 on Uno) with a 4.7kΩ–10kΩ pull-up resistor between data and VCC to ensure reliable communication. The Adafruit DHT library simplifies coding; install it via the Library Manager of Arduino IDE. Conversion is straightforward—raw data is parsed directly into Celsius and percentage humidity. A typical output might be Temp: 25.5°C, Hum: 60% on the Serial Monitor, updated every 2 seconds (respecting the 1Hz limit). Farmers use DHT22s to optimize greenhouse irrigation, while smart thermostats rely on DHT11s for home automation. Challenges include slow response (250ms per reading) and sensitivity to humidity-induced corrosion. Use a sealed enclosure if needed. Troubleshooting involves checking the pull-up resistor, ensuring stable power (add a 10µF capacitor), and verifying pin assignments with a multimeter.

Distance: Ultrasonic Sensor

The Ultrasonic sensor, such as the HC-SR04, measures distance by emitting ultrasonic waves and calculating the time-of-flight of the echo, offering a range of 2cm to 400cm with ±3mm accuracy. This digital sensor is perfect for applications such as obstacle detection, parking assistance, or liquid level monitoring, providing a non-contact solution for physical measurements.

Wiring connects VCC to 5V, GND to ground, Trig to a digital output (for example: pin 9), and Echo to a digital input (for example: pin 10) on the board. The sensor operates by sending a 10µs HIGH pulse on Trig to trigger the ping, then measuring the HIGH pulse duration on Echo, which reflects the round-trip time. The distance formula, `distance = (duration * 0.0343) / 2`, converts microseconds to centimeters, dividing by 2 for the one-way distance (speed of sound is 343 m/s).

A sample output might be *Distance: 45cm* every 50ms, suitable for real-time tracking. Ultrasonic sensors automate parking systems in crowded cities, and they monitor water levels in outback reservoirs. Limitations include a blind spot below 2cm and angle dependency—waves scatter off uneven surfaces, requiring alignment. Noise from electrical interference can skew pulse timing—add a 0.1μF capacitor across VCC and GND, and average multiple readings (for example: 5 samples) for stability. Troubleshooting checks for loose wires, verifies Trig/Echo pin logic with an oscilloscope, and ensures power (15mA draw) does not overload the board.

Air Quality: MQ-2 Gas Sensor

The MQ-2 gas sensor detects combustible gases including LPG, methane, propane, smoke, and CO, thereby, making it essential for air quality monitoring and safety systems. As an analog sensor, it outputs a voltage (0–5V) proportional to gas concentration, with sensitivity adjustable via a built-in potentiometer. Its detection range spans 200–10000 ppm for various gases, with a warm-up time of 1–2 minutes for stable readings.

Wiring connects VCC to 5V, GND to ground, and the analog output (AO) to an analog pin (for example: A0 on Uno), often with a 10kΩ load resistor between AO and VCC to fine-tune sensitivity. The heater circuit (H pins) requires 5V separately, drawing 150mA, so use an external power supply to avoid board strain. Code uses `intgasValue = analogRead(A0);` in `loop()`, mapping the 0–1023 ADC value to a concentration range (for example : 0–1000 ppm) via calibration: `float gasLevel = (gasValue / 1023.0) * 1000`. Add a delay (for example: 100ms) to avoid ADC saturation.

Output might read *Gas Level: 350ppm* on the Serial Monitor, triggering alerts above thresholds (for example: 500ppm). In Europe, industrial sites use MQ-2s for methane detection, while urban air quality monitors track pollution. Challenges include cross-sensitivity (for example: smoke affects LPG readings) and drift over time—calibrated monthly with known gas samples (for example: 200ppm propane). Noise from power fluctuations requires a 10μF capacitor and a stable 5V supply. Troubleshooting involves checking the AO voltage with a multimeter, adjusting the potentiometer, and ensuring proper grounding to reduce interference.

Practical Implementation and Conversion

Converting raw signals to meaningful data requires libraries and formulas. The DHT library handles DHT11/DHT22 parsing, while Ultrasonic code uses `pulseIn()` with the speed-of-sound formula. For MQ-2, calibration curves (for example, from datasheets) map analog values to ppm, often requiring empirical adjustment. Wiring best practices—breadboard use, color-coded wires (red for VCC, black for GND), and common grounding ensure reliability. Test with the Serial Monitor, logging Temp: 26°C, Distance: 50cm, Gas: 300ppm every second.

Reading environmental data with DHT11/DHT22, Ultrasonic, and MQ-2 sensors transforms raw signals into actionable insights. With proper wiring, coding, and calibration, you will master temperature, humidity, distance, and gas monitoring, preparing for the mini-project ahead.

DHT11/DHT22 Sensors

The DHT11 and DHT22 sensors are cornerstone components in IoT for monitoring temperature and humidity, enabling applications from smart homes to agricultural automation. This section builds on the environmental data concepts, providing an in-depth guide to interfacing these digital sensors with Arduino Uno, NodeMCU, and ESP32 boards. These sensors deliver reliable environmental data through a single-wire protocol, requiring careful wiring and library support to convert raw signals into meaningful temperature (in Celsius) and humidity (in percentage) values. This hands-on exploration includes detailed wiring instructions, library usage, coding examples, troubleshooting tips, and global use cases, equipping you to integrate these sensors into real-world projects with confidence.

Wiring

Proper wiring is the foundation of successful DHT11/DHT22 operation, ensuring stable communication between the sensor and microcontroller. Both sensors feature a three- or four-pin configuration, with the key connections being VCC, GND, and a data pin, plus an optional NC (no connection) pin. The DHT11 operates on 3.3V or 5V, drawing about 1–2.5mA, while the DHT22 prefers 3.3V but tolerates 5V, with a slightly higher current draw of 1–1.5mA. This flexibility allows compatibility with various boards, but voltage stability is critical to avoid erratic readings.

To wire the sensor, connect the VCC pin to the 3.3V or 5V pin of the board—use 3.3V for ESP32/NodeMCU to match their logic levels, or 5V for Arduino Uno if needed. The GND pin goes to the ground of the board, ensuring a common reference. The data pin, which transmits the serialized signal, connects to a digital GPIO pin—for example, pin 2 on Uno or pin D4 on NodeMCU. A 10kΩ pull-up resistor is essential, placed between the data pin and VCC, to keep the line HIGH when idle, preventing floating states that could corrupt the signal. Use a breadboard for prototyping, with color-coded wires (red for VCC, black for GND, and any color for data) to maintain organization, aligning with previous chapter wiring best practices.

The single-wire protocol operates at a baud rate of approximately 1MHz, sending a 40-bit data packet (16-bit humidity, 16-bit temperature, 8-bit checksum) in every 1–2 seconds. The sensor requires a 250-ms stabilization period after power-on before reliable readings begin. For ESP32, where 3.3V logic is standard, ensure the data line matches this level—use a level shifter if connecting to a 5V board like Uno to avoid damaging the sensor. In humid environments, like monsoons, seal the sensor in a breathable enclosure (similar to perforated plastic) to protect against moisture while allowing air exchange.

Library Usage

To process the raw data stream of DHT11/DHT22, the Arduino IDE requires the DHT sensor library, which simplifies reading and parsing the 40-bit packets into usable temperature and humidity values. Installing and using this library is a critical step, leveraging the digital pin capabilities of the microcontroller to handle the protocol of the sensor efficiently.

Begin by opening the Arduino IDE and navigating to Sketch → Include Library → Manage Libraries. Search for the DHT sensor library by Adafruit, authored by Adafruit, and click Install. This library, compatible with Arduino Uno, NodeMCU, and ESP32, includes pre-written functions to interface with the sensor. After installation, include the library in your sketch with `#include <DHT.h>` at the top. Define the sensor type and pin in a global variable—for example: DHT dht(2, DHT11)for a DHT11 on pin 2, or DHT dht(D4, DHT22) for a DHT22 on NodeMCU's D4. The constructor accepts the GPIO pin number and sensor model as arguments.

The library automates the complex task of decoding the 40-bit packet, which includes a checksum to verify data integrity. A typical output on the Serial Monitor might be *Humidity*: 60.5%, *Temperature*: 25.3°C. For ESP32, ensure the library version (for example: 1.4.4) supports its dual-core architecture—update via the Library Manager if needed. Deforestation trackers use DHT22s with this library to monitor microclimates, and smart buildings log data for HVAC optimization.

Challenges include library conflicts—uninstall older versions if errors like DHT *not declared* occur, or slow response times, mitigated by avoiding excessive readings. Troubleshooting involves verifying the library installation (check Sketch → Include Library), ensuring the correct pin and model in the constructor, and testing with a simple sketch. Power stability is key—use a regulated supply and a capacitor. This process unlocks precise environmental monitoring.

Mastering DHT11/DHT22 wiring and library usage enables accurate temperature and humidity monitoring. With proper setup and coding, you will harness these sensors for IoT success.

Troubleshooting

- **No readings / Serial Monitor empty:** Verify the correct GPIO pin is specified in the sketch and that the DHT library is properly installed. Ensure the data line has a 10kΩ pull-up resistor.
- **Incorrect temperature or humidity values:** Check wiring (VCC, GND, data) and ensure the sensor is powered with stable 3.3V or 5V. Allow the sensor a 250 ms stabilization period after power-on.
- **Checksum errors or erratic readings:** Reduce the reading frequency to 1–2 seconds. Ensure no voltage spikes or interference are present. Adding a small capacitor (0.1–1 μF) near the sensor can stabilize the power supply.
- **Slow or delayed response:** Avoid excessive read commands in the loop. DHT sensors are not designed for high-frequency sampling.
- **Library-related errors:** Confirm that the latest version of the Adafruit DHT library is installed and remove conflicting older versions.

Applications

The DHT11 and DHT22 sensors, with their ability to measure temperature and humidity, unlock a wide array of practical applications in IoT, enhancing automation, environmental monitoring, and agricultural efficiency. This section builds on the wiring and library usage skills, exploring how these sensors are integrated into real-world scenarios such as home automation, weather monitoring, and agriculture. By leveraging the data collected—temperature in Celsius and humidity in percentage—these applications demonstrate the versatility of sensors across diverse environments. This detailed guide includes implementation strategies, coding examples, global use cases, challenges, and troubleshooting tips, empowering you to apply DHT11/DHT22 sensors effectively with Arduino Uno, NodeMCU, and ESP32 boards in your own projects.

Home Automation (Fan Control)

Home automation leverages DHT11/DHT22 sensors to create intelligent climate control systems, with fan control being a prime example. The goal is to automate fan operation based on temperature or humidity thresholds, enhancing comfort and energy efficiency. For instance, a fan might activate when the temperature exceeds 28°C or humidity surpasses 70%, conditions common in humid climates.

Implementation involves wiring the sensor—VCC to 3.3V/5V, GND to ground, and data to a digital pin (for example: pin 2 on Uno)—with a 10kΩ pull-up resistor. Connect a relay module to control the fan, wiring its signal pin to another digital pin (for example, pin 3) and the fan to the AC terminals of the relay, ensuring safety with an external power supply. For temperature-based triggering, add a 2-second delay to respect the 1Hz limit of the sensor.

A sample output on the Serial Monitor might be Temp: 29°C, Fan: ON when activated. Smart homes use DHT22s for this, integrating with Alexa for voice control, and humid climates drive DHT11-based fan systems. Challenges include relay noise (add a 0.1μF capacitor across coil terminals) and false triggers from rapid temperature swings. One can implement hysteresis (such as turn off only below 26°C) to stabilize operation. Troubleshooting checks pin logic with a multimeter, verifies relay switching, and ensures power stability, taking 30–45 minutes to set up.

Weather Monitoring

Weather monitoring stations rely on DHT11/DHT22 sensors to collect local temperature and humidity data, providing insights for personal use or integration with weather networks. These stations can log data for trends, alert on extreme conditions, or sync with cloud platforms like ThingSpeak.

Wiring follows with the sensor connected to a digital pin (for example: D4 on NodeMCU) and powered by 3.3V for ESP32 compatibility. Use the DHT library as before, enhancing the sketch with timestamp logging. Add a real-time clock (RTC) module (for example: DS3231) for accurate timestamps if offline, wiring its SDA/SCL to the I2C pins of the board (A4/A5 on Uno).

Output might show 125s *Temp*: 24.5°C *Hum*: 55%, which is updated every 2 seconds, and is viewable on the Serial Monitor or Plotter for trend analysis. Outback weather stations use DHT22s to track arid conditions, while in Europe, urban setups monitor humidity for mold prevention. Challenges include sensor drift over time, which is calibrated monthly against a reference thermometer; and, exposure to rain, which is mitigated by weatherproof enclosures with vents. Troubleshooting involves checking data integrity (ensure no NaN values), verifying RTC sync, and stabilizing power with a 10µF capacitor, taking 1–2 hours to assemble.

Agriculture

In agriculture, DHT11/DHT22 sensors optimize crop growth by monitoring greenhouse or field conditions, enabling automated irrigation or ventilation based on temperature and humidity levels. This application is vital for precision farming, improving yield and resource use.

Wiring connects the sensor to a digital pin (for example, pin 5 on Uno) with a 10kΩ pull-up resistor, powered by 5V for compatibility with irrigation controllers. Integrate with a relay or solenoid valve—for example: relay signal to pin 6—to control water flow when humidity drops below 50%. Use the DHT library, after reading t and h. Add a soil moisture sensor (analog, for example: FC-28) on A0 for combined control, mapping its 0–1023 value to a percentage.

Output might be *Temp*: 30°C, *Hum*: 45%, *Irrigation*: ON the Serial Monitor. Farmers use DHT22s in greenhouses to manage monsoon effects, and coffee plantations monitor humidity for optimal growth. Challenges include sensor fouling from dust—clean monthly with a soft brush—and power interruptions in remote areas, addressed with solar panels and batteries. Troubleshooting checks wiring continuity, calibrates against a hygrometer, and ensures relay operation, taking 1–2 hours to configure.

DHT11/DHT22 applications in home automation, weather monitoring, and agriculture showcase their IoT potential. With proper wiring, coding, and troubleshooting, you will master these use cases, preparing for further sensor integration.

Ultrasonic Sensor

The HC-SR04 Ultrasonic sensor is a versatile tool for distance measurement in IoT projects, leveraging sound waves to detect objects without physical contact. This section expands on the environmental data concepts, providing a comprehensive guide to understanding its operation and interfacing it with Arduino Uno, NodeMCU, and ESP32 boards. Known for its reliability and ease of use, the HC-SR04 measures distances from 2 to 400cm with ±3mm accuracy, making it ideal for applications such as obstacle avoidance, parking assistance, and liquid level monitoring. This detailed exploration covers how the sensor works, wiring instructions, coding examples, global use cases, challenges, and troubleshooting tips, equipping you to integrate this digital sensor into practical IoT solutions with confidence.

The HC-SR04 operates on the principle of echolocation, similar to sonar, by emitting ultrasonic pulses and measuring the time it takes for the echo to return. This process allows the sensor to calculate distance based on the speed of sound in air. The sensor features a transmitter and receiver housed in a single unit, with two key pins; Trig (Trigger) and Echo, handling the signal exchange.

The operation begins when the microcontroller sends a 10µs HIGH pulse to the Trig pin, activating the transmitter to emit eight 40kHz ultrasonic bursts. These sound waves travel through the air until they encounter an object, reflecting back to the receiver. The Echo pin then outputs a HIGH signal for the duration of the round-trip time, which the microcontroller measures using the **`pulseIn()`** function. The distance is calculated using the formula: Distance = (Time × Speed of Sound) / 2, where the speed of sound is approximately 343 m/s (or 0.0343 cm/µs) at 20°C, and dividing by 2 accounts for the round trip. For example, a 588µs echo time indicates a distance of **`10cm ((588 × 0.0343) / 2 = 10.08cm)`**.

The accuracy of the sensor depends on environmental factors such as temperature and humidity, which affects sound speed, for example, at 30°C, it increases to ~346 m/s. A typical measurement cycle takes 50–100ms, limited by the maximum range (400cm, ~23ms one-way). This makes it suitable for real-time applications but requires a minimum 2cm range due to the blind spot of the transducer. Automated parking systems use HC-SR04s to detect vehicle proximity; they monitor water levels in remote tanks, showcasing their adaptability across climates.

Challenges include angle dependency, where waves scatter off uneven surfaces, reducing accuracy beyond 30°, and interference from multiple sensors, which are mitigated by staggering Trig pulses. Noise from electrical sources can distort echo timing, necessitating filtering techniques. Understanding these dynamics, which takes 15–20 minutes to grasp through testing, is key to optimizing performance.

Wiring

Correct wiring is essential to ensure the HC-SR04 functions reliably, connecting it to the power of microcontroller and GPIO pins with precision. The sensor operates at 5V, drawing approximately 15mA, making it compatible with Arduino Uno but it requires a level shifter or voltage regulator for ESP32/NodeMCU's 3.3V logic if direct connection is considered (though 5V is standard).

The wiring process involves four connections. First, connect the VCC pin to the 5V pin of the board to power the sensor, ensuring a stable supply. Use a powered USB hub or external 5V source if the port of the board limits current (for example: 500mA on Uno). Second, connect the GND pin to the ground of the board, establishing a common reference to prevent floating signals, aligning with previous chapter grounding best practices. Third, connect the Trig pin to a digital output pin (for example, pin 9 on Uno or D5 on NodeMCU), which sends the trigger pulse. Fourth, connect the Echo pin to a digital input pin (for example, pin 10 on Uno or D6 on NodeMCU), which receives the echo signal. Use a breadboard for prototyping, with color-coded wires—red for VCC, black for GND, and distinct colors (for example: green for Trig, yellow for Echo)—to maintain clarity.

The compact design of the sensor (45mm × 20mm × 15mm) fits easily into projects, but wiring must account for noise. Add a 0.1µF ceramic capacitor across VCC and GND to filter high-frequency interference, and use shielded cables if operating near motors or power lines. Ensure pin assignments match the code, as mismatched pins cause 0cm readings. Educational robotics uses this setup with Unos, deforestation trackers secure connections with heat-shrink tubing to withstand jungle humidity.

Challenges include power instability which means that if the voltage drops below 4.5V, it can fail the sensor, so it should be monitored with a multimeter; and, loose connections, that are to be checked with continuity mode. The 15mA draw is low, but multiple sensors require a current budget (for example, 100mA for four), possibly necessitating an external 5V regulator. This wiring process, taking 10 to 15 minutes, sets the stage for accurate distance measurement.

Troubleshooting:

- **No Readings**: Check power (5V), ground, and pin connections with a multimeter.
- **Erratic Values**: Add a capacitor, average readings, or shield wire.
- **Out of Range**: Verify object distance (2–400cm) and angle (<30°).

Applications

The ability of HC-SR04 Ultrasonic sensor to measure distance with precision opens up a wide range of practical applications in IoT, revolutionizing automation, robotics, and environmental monitoring. This section builds on the operational and wiring knowledge, exploring how this sensor is deployed in smart parking systems, obstacle avoidance robots, and water level measurement. By converting echo time into actionable distance data, the HC-SR04 enhances safety, efficiency, and resource management across diverse settings. This detailed guide includes implementation strategies, coding examples, global use cases, challenges, and troubleshooting tips, empowering you to integrate this sensor into real-world projects using Arduino Uno, NodeMCU, and ESP32 boards with confidence.

Smart Parking Systems

Smart parking systems utilize the HC-SR04 to detect vehicle presence and guide drivers to available spaces, optimizing urban mobility. The sensor measures the distance to a vehicle, triggering indicators when a spot is occupied or free, typically within its 2–400cm range.

Implementation involves wiring the sensor — VCC to 5V, GND to ground, Trig to a digital output (like pin 9 on Uno), and Echo to a digital input (say pin 10)—with a 0.1µF capacitor for noise reduction. Connect an LED or buzzer (for example: to pin 11) to signal status. Use the sketch, modifying the logic to indicate a car (within 20cm) with the LED on. Add a delay of 100ms and print *Spot: Occupied or Spot: Free* on the Serial Monitor.

Output might show *Distance: 15cm, Spot: Occupied* when a vehicle is detected. Urban parking lots use multiple HC-SR04s networked via ESP32s for real-time updates; they integrate with traffic apps. Challenges include reflections from nearby walls—calibrated with an offset (for example: +5cm) or angle of the sensor (<30°)—and rain interference, mitigated by weatherproof housings. Troubleshooting checks pin continuity with a multimeter, verifies LED/buzzer response, and ensures stable 5V power, taking 45–60 minutes to set up.

Obstacle Avoidance Robots

Obstacle avoidance robots rely on the HC-SR04 to navigate environments safely, stopping or turning when objects are detected within a set distance, enhancing autonomous mobility. This application is common in educational and industrial robotics.

Wiring follows with Trig and Echo connected to digital pins (for example, D5 and D6 on NodeMCU), powered by 5V. Add a motor driver (for example, L298N) to control two DC motors, wiring its inputs to pins 12 and 13, to stop or turn right if an obstacle is within 30cm, with motors running forward otherwise. Include a 100ms delay and log *Obstacle: 25cm, Turning* on the Serial Monitor.

Output might be *Distance: 20cm, Turning* during navigation. The classrooms use HC-SR04s with Unos for robot kits. Challenges include uneven terrain scattering waves, average 5 readings for stability; and, motor noise, filtered with a 10µF capacitor on the power line. Troubleshooting involves checking motor direction with a multimeter, verifying sensor alignment, and ensuring power (15mA + motor draw).

Water Level Measurement

Water level measurement with the HC-SR04 monitors tanks or reservoirs, providing data for irrigation, flood prevention, or industrial use, operating non-invasively above the liquid surface. The sensor detects the distance to the water surface within its 400cm range.

Wiring aligns with connecting to pins 9 and 10 on the Uno, with a 5V supply and ground. Mount the sensor above the tank, ensuring no obstructions, and add an LCD (for example: 16×2 via I2C) on SDA/

SCL (A4/A5) to display levels. Use the distance code (for example: `maxHeight = 100cm`), printing *Level: 75%* on the Serial Monitor and LCD with a 200ms delay.

Output might show Distance: 25cm, Level: 75% for a 100cm tank. Outback farms use HC-SR04s to manage rainwater tanks, while rural wells employ them for irrigation. Challenges include condensation on the sensor—use a hydrophobic coating or enclosure—and temperature affecting sound speed (adjust to 346 m/s at 30°C). Troubleshooting checks mounting height with a ruler, verifies LCD display, and stabilizes power with a 10µF capacitor, taking 1–2 hours to configure.

Troubleshooting:

- **No Detection**: Check power (5V), wiring, and object range (2–400cm).
- **Inconsistent Readings**: Average samples, adjust angle, or add shielding.
- **Component Failure**: Verify the LED/motor/LCD with a multimeter.

HC-SR04 applications in smart parking, obstacle avoidance, and water level measurement highlight its IoT versatility. With proper wiring, coding, and troubleshooting, you will master these use cases, preparing for further sensor projects.

Relay Module

The relay module is a critical component in IoT, enabling microcontrollers such as Arduino Uno, NodeMCU, and ESP32 to safely control high-voltage AC appliances through low-voltage signals. This section builds on the sensor interfacing skills from previous sections, offering a detailed exploration of how relay modules work and essential safety practices for their use. Relays act as electrically operated switches, bridging the gap between the 3.3V/5V logic of microcontrollers and the 110V–240V AC loads of household or industrial devices. This comprehensive guide covers the operational principles, wiring considerations, safety tips, global applications, challenges, and troubleshooting strategies, equipping you to integrate relay modules into practical IoT projects with confidence and caution.

A relay module functions as an electrically controlled switch, allowing a low-voltage microcontroller to activate a high-voltage circuit without direct electrical connection, ensuring safety and isolation. The core component is an electromechanical relay, typically a single-pole double-throw (SPDT) or single-pole single-throw (SPST) device, comprising a coil, an armature, and contacts. When a voltage (for example, 5V) is applied to the coil via the GPIO pin of the microcontroller, it generates a magnetic field that moves the armature, closing or opening the contacts to connect or disconnect the AC load.

The process begins with the microcontroller sending a HIGH signal (for example: 5V for Arduino Uno, 3.3V for ESP32) to the signal pin of the relay, often through an optocoupler for added isolation. The optocoupler uses an LED and a phototransistor to transfer the signal without direct current flow, protecting the microcontroller from voltage spikes. When energized, the coil (rated at 5V or 3.3V, drawing 70–100mA) pulls the armature, switching the normally open (NO) contact to connect the AC load (for example: a 220V fan) or the normally closed (NC) contact to disconnect it. The common (COM) terminal serves as the pivot point. De-energizing the coil by setting the signal LOW releases the armature, reverting the switch to its default state.

This mechanism supports loads up to 250V AC and 10A, depending on the rating of the relay, making it suitable for controlling lights, motors, or heaters. A typical switching cycle takes 5–10ms, with a mechanical lifespan of 100,000 operations. In Europe, industrial automation uses relays to manage conveyor belts; they control irrigation pumps, demonstrating their robustness. Challenges include coil noise (a clicking sound) and contact arcing with inductive loads (for example: motors), mitigated by snubber circuits (for example: 0.1µF capacitor + 100Ω resistor across contacts). Understanding this, which takes 20–30 minutes through testing, is key to safe operation.

Safety is paramount when working with relay modules, given their handling of high-voltage AC power, which poses risks of electric shock, short circuits, or fire. Adhering to these guidelines protects both the user and the equipment, aligning with the best practices introduced in the previous chapter.

First, never touch AC connections directly. High-voltage terminals (COM, NO, NC) can carry 110V–240V, capable of delivering lethal shocks. Always power off the AC supply (using a switch or unplugging) before wiring, testing, or adjusting connections, and use insulated tools (for example: screwdrivers with rubber handles) to avoid accidental contact. Home automation enthusiasts follow this rule when wiring relays to outlets, reducing injury risks.

Second, use relays with optocouplers for isolation. Optocouplers create a galvanic barrier between the low-voltage control circuit (3.3V/5V) and the high-voltage AC side, preventing voltage spikes from damaging the microcontroller or endangering the user. Most relay modules (for example: 5V 1-channel modules) include this feature, indicated by an LED lighting when the coil is energized. Verify the datasheet or module markings (for example: Opto-Isolated) before use. Industrial setups prioritize optocoupled relays for machinery safety, a practice worth emulating.

Third, always double-check wiring before powering. Incorrect connections—for example, swapping COM and NO or misaligning GND—can cause short circuits or relay failure. After wiring, use a multimeter in continuity mode to confirm the circuit is open when de-energized and closed when the signal is HIGH. Label wires (red for VCC, black for GND, blue for signal) and photograph the setup for reference. Rural irrigation systems enforce this step to prevent pump damage, ensuring reliability.

Additional safety measures include working in a dry, well-lit area to avoid slips or misjudgments, using a grounded power strip for AC input, and employing external power supplies (for example: 5V/1A adapter) for the relay coil to reduce board strain. Wear rubber gloves and safety goggles when handling AC loads, especially during initial tests. Challenges include human error—for example, forgetting to power off—mitigated by a checklist, and overheating with high currents, addressed by ensuring the 10A rating of the relay matches the load. This safety setup, taking 15–20 minutes to review and implement, is critical before proceeding.

Wiring

Before powering the relay module, proper wiring is crucial to ensure both functionality and safety. Connect the VCC pin to the 5V (or 3.3V for ESP32) supply, GND to the microcontroller ground, and the signal pin to a GPIO pin on the microcontroller. For AC loads, wire the device through the COM (Common) and NO (Normally Open) terminals for standard switching, or NC (Normally Closed) if the default on state is required. Use color-coded wires (for example, red for VCC, black for GND, blue for signal) to reduce errors, and verify all AC connections are powered off before testing. Optionally, include an opto-isolator if your relay module has one, which separates the high-voltage AC circuit from the low-voltage control side.

Troubleshooting:

- **No Switching**: Check power (5V), signal (HIGH), and AC connection with a multimeter.
- **Clicking but No Load**: Verify wiring (COM/NO) and load compatibility (<10A).
- **Overheating**: Reduce load, add a heat sink, or use a higher-rated relay.

Understanding how relay modules work and following safety tips enables safe control of AC loads in IoT. With proper wiring and coding, you will master this component, preparing for advanced projects.

Applications

The capability of the relay module to control high-voltage AC devices with low-voltage signals makes it a cornerstone of IoT automation, enabling smart and efficient systems across various domains. This section builds on the operational and safety knowledge, delving into its practical applications in smart home appliance control, automated lighting systems, and industrial machine control. By interfacing relays with microcontrollers such as Arduino Uno, NodeMCU, and ESP32, these applications transform environmental data into actionable control, enhancing comfort, energy efficiency, and productivity. This detailed guide includes implementation strategies, coding examples, global use cases, challenges, and troubleshooting tips, empowering you to deploy relay modules effectively in real-world IoT projects.

Smart Home Appliance Control

Smart home appliance control uses relay modules to automate devices such as fans, heaters, or coffee makers based on sensor inputs, improving convenience and energy savings. For example, a fan might turn on when the temperature exceeds 28°C, detected by a DHT11 sensor.

Implementation involves wiring the relay -- VCC to 5V, GND to ground, and signal to a digital pin (for example: pin 3 on Uno)—with a 10kΩ resistor if not optocoupled. Connect the appliance (for example: a 220V fan) to the COM and NO terminals, using an external 5V/1A supply for the coil to avoid board strain. Wire a DHT11 (data to pin 2, 10kΩ pull-up) and use the DHT library, adding a 2-second delay. Output on the Serial Monitor might be Temp: 29°C, Fan: ON.

Smart homes integrate relays with Alexa for voice control, and rural households automate pumps. Challenges include power surges—use a varistor across contacts—and false triggers from sensor noise, mitigated by averaging 5 readings. Troubleshooting checks wiring with a multimeter, verifies relay click, and ensures AC isolation, taking 45–60 minutes to set up.

Automated Lighting Systems

Automated lighting systems employ relay modules to control lights based on time, occupancy, or ambient light levels, enhancing energy efficiency and security. Lights might turn on at dusk or when motion is detected by a PIR sensor.

Wiring connects the signal of the relay to pin 4 on the Uno, VCC to 5V, and GND to ground, with the light (for example: 110V bulb) to COM and NO. Add a PIR sensor (VCC to 5V, GND to ground, OUT to pin 5) to detect motion, logging Motion: Detected, Light: ON every 100ms on the Serial Monitor.

Office buildings use relays for occupancy-based lighting, which sync with smart grids. Challenges include relay arcing with inductive loads—add a snubber (0.1µF + 100Ω)—and false positives from PIR noise, filtered with a 10µF capacitor. Troubleshooting verifies PIR output with an LED, checks relay contacts with a multimeter, and ensures power stability, taking 1–2 hours to configure.

Industrial Machine Control

Industrial machine control leverages relay modules to automate machinery such as conveyor belts or pumps based on sensor thresholds, boosting productivity and safety. A pump might activate when the water level drops below 20%, detected by an HC-SR04.Smart homes lead adoption, while irrigation systems use them for water management. Challenges include voltage spikes (use surge protectors), contact corrosion (clean annually), and power outages—backup with UPS. Remote setups address this with solar power, enhancing IoT control.

Troubleshooting:

- **No Switching**: Check signal (HIGH), power (5V), and AC wiring with a multimeter.
- **Intermittent Operation**: Clean contacts, add a snubber, or replace the relay.
- **Overheating**: Reduce load, add a heat sink, or use a higher-rated module.

Relay applications in smart homes, lighting, and industrial control showcase their IoT potential. With proper wiring, coding, and safety, you will master these use cases, preparing for advanced projects.

MQ-2 Gas Sensor

The MQ-2 gas sensor is a vital tool in IoT for detecting combustible gases, playing a crucial role in air quality monitoring, safety systems, and industrial applications. This section builds on the environmental data concepts, offering an in-depth exploration of how the MQ-2 operates and how to interface it with Arduino Uno, NodeMCU, and ESP32 boards. Capable of detecting gases such as LPG, methane, carbon monoxide (CO), and smoke, the MQ-2 provides both analog and digital outputs, making it versatile for continuous monitoring and threshold-based alerts. This comprehensive guide covers its working principles, wiring instructions, coding examples, global use cases, challenges, and troubleshooting tips, equipping you to integrate this analog sensor into practical IoT projects with precision and reliability.

The MQ-2 gas sensor operates on the principle of gas-sensitive resistance, detecting combustible gases through a chemical reaction on its sensing element. The sensor features a tin dioxide (SnO_2) semiconductor layer heated by an internal heater, which lowers its resistance when exposed to target gases. This change in resistance is translated into electrical signals, providing both analog and digital outputs for versatile data interpretation.

The sensing element of the sensor consists of a heater coil (operating at ~5V, 150mA) and a sensing resistor, housed in a stainless-steel mesh to protect against dust while allowing gas diffusion. When exposed to gases such as LPG (200–10000 ppm), methane, CO, or smoke, the SnO_2 layer's resistance decreases due to the oxidation reaction, altering the voltage across a load resistor (typically 10kΩ). The Analog Output (AO) provides a continuous voltage (0–5V) proportional to gas concentration, which the ADC of the microcontroller converts to a 0–1023 value. The Digital Output (DO) compares this voltage against a preset threshold (adjusted via an onboard potentiometer), outputting HIGH (for example: 5V) when the threshold is exceeded, serving as an alert.

A warm-up period of 1–2 minutes is required for the heater to stabilize, ensuring accurate readings. Sensitivity varies by gas—for example, 200–5000 ppm for LPG, 300–10000 ppm for methane—requiring calibration with known concentrations (for example: 200 ppm propane) to map ADC values to ppm. In Europe, industrial plants use MQ-2s to monitor methane leaks, while urban air quality stations track smoke levels, highlighting its global utility. Challenges include cross-sensitivity (for example, smoke affecting LPG readings), mitigated by filtering with activated charcoal, and baseline drift over time, addressed by periodic recalibration. Understanding this process, which takes 20–30 minutes through experimentation, is essential for effective use.

Wiring

Proper wiring is critical to harness the dual-output capability of MQ-2, ensuring stable power and accurate signal transmission to the microcontroller. The sensor operates at 5V, drawing significant current (150mA for the heater, plus 10–20mA for the circuit), necessitating a robust power supply to avoid board overload.

The wiring process involves four connections. First, connect the VCC pin to the 5V pin of the board to power the heater and circuit—use an external 5V/1A adapter or powered USB hub, as the 500mA limit of Arduino Uno may suffice for short tests but struggles with prolonged use. Second, connect the GND pin to the board's ground, establishing a common reference to prevent noise, aligning with previous chapter grounding practices. Third, connect the analog output (AO) pin to an analog pin (for example, A0 on Uno or A0 on NodeMCU), which provides the continuous voltage for gas concentration data. Fourth, connect the digital output (DO) pin to a digital pin (for example, pin 2 on Uno or D4 on NodeMCU), which signals threshold breaches. Use a breadboard for prototyping, with color-coded wires—red for VCC, black for GND, green for AO, and yellow for DO—to maintain clarity.

The onboard potentiometer adjusts the DO threshold, typically set by rotating it while exposing the sensor to a target gas concentration (for example: 500 ppm LPG) until the DO LED lights, indicating the trigger point. Add a 10kΩ load resistor between AO and VCC if not pre-installed, and include a 10μF electrolytic capacitor across VCC and GND to filter power supply ripple, enhancing signal stability. Educational labs wire MQ-2s with Unos for gas experiments, and remote monitoring systems use shielded cables to reduce electromagnetic interference.

Challenges include power instability—voltage drops below 4.5V can cause erratic readings, so monitor with a multimeter—and heater overheating, mitigated by ensuring adequate ventilation. Loose connections or incorrect pin assignments (for example, AO to a digital pin) result in no data—verify with continuity mode.

Troubleshooting:

- **No Readings**: Check power (5V), GND, and pin assignments with a multimeter.
- **Erratic Analog Values**: Add a capacitor, stabilize power, or average 10 readings.
- **DO Not Trigger**: Adjust the potentiometer or verify threshold gas exposure.

Applications

The ability of MQ-2 gas sensor to detect combustible gases such as LPG, methane, CO, and smoke makes it a cornerstone of safety and environmental monitoring in IoT systems. This section builds on the operational and wiring insights, exploring its practical applications in gas leakage detection, smart kitchens, and air quality monitoring. By converting analog voltage and digital threshold signals into actionable data, the MQ-2 enhances safety, automation, and health awareness across diverse settings. This detailed guide includes implementation strategies, coding examples, global use cases, challenges, and troubleshooting tips, empowering you to integrate this sensor into real-world projects using Arduino Uno, NodeMCU, and ESP32 boards with confidence.

Gas Leakage Detection

Gas leakage detection uses the MQ-2 to identify hazardous gas escapes, such as LPG or methane, triggering alerts to prevent explosions or poisoning. This application is critical in homes, factories, and storage facilities where gas is prevalent.

Implementation involves wiring the sensor —VCC to 5V, GND to ground, AO to A0, and DO to pin 2 on the Uno—with an external 5V/1A supply for the 150mA heater. Connect a buzzer (to pin 3) and an LED (to pin 4) for alerts, logging every 100ms. Adjust the potentiometer to trigger DO at a safe threshold (for example, 500 ppm LPG).

Output might show Analog: 600, Gas Level: 600 ppm, Digital: Alert on the Serial Monitor when gas is detected. Rural households use MQ-2s to monitor LPG cylinders, while in Europe, industrial plants detect methane leaks in pipelines. Challenges include false positives from cooking fumes—filter with a vented enclosure—and sensor drift, requiring monthly calibration with a 200-ppm standard. Troubleshooting checks DO logic with a multimeter, verifies buzzer/LED operation, and ensures power stability with a 10μF capacitor, taking 45–60 minutes to set up.

Smart Kitchens

Smart kitchens integrate the MQ-2 to automate safety and efficiency, detecting gas levels to control stoves, ventilators, or alarms based on cooking activities. This enhances safety by mitigating risks from unattended gas usage.

Wiring connects the sensor to A0 and pin 2, with a relay (signal to pin 5, COM/NO to a ventilator) for control, powered by an external 5V supply. Add a DHT11 (data to pin 6, 10kΩ pull-up) to monitor humidity, indicating cooking intensity. Use the MQ-2 code, logging Gas: 300 ppm, Hum: 72%, Vent: ON every 200ms. Calibrate the potentiometer for a 400 ppm LPG threshold.

Output might be Analog: 450, Gas Level: 450 ppm, Digital: Normal, Hum: 65%, Vent: OFF. Smart kitchens use MQ-2s with ESP32s for integrated control sync with smart hubs. Challenges include humidity interference—use a desiccant—and relay arcing with inductive loads, mitigated by a snubber (0.1µF + 100Ω). Troubleshooting verifies relay switching, checks DHT readings, and stabilizes power, taking 1–2 hours to configure.

Air Quality Monitoring

Air quality monitoring employs the MQ-2 to assess indoor or outdoor environments for smoke, CO, or other pollutants, providing data for health safety or ventilation decisions. This is vital in urban areas or industrial zones, with AO to A0 and DO to pin 2, using an external 5V supply. Add an LCD (16×2 via I2C on A4/A5) to display levels and a fan relay (pin 7, COM/NO to fan) for ventilation. Use the MQ-2 code, displaying Gas: 350 ppm, Fan: ON the LCD and Serial Monitor every 200ms. Calibrate against a 300 ppm CO standard.

Output might show Analog: 700, Gas Level: 700 ppm, Digital: Alert, Fan: ON. Urban offices monitor air with MQ-2s, outback stations track bushfire smoke. Challenges include cross-sensitivity to humidity—use a weather shield—and baseline drift, requiring quarterly recalibration. Troubleshooting checks the LCD, verifies fan operation, and ensures sensor exposure, taking 1–2 hours to set up.

Troubleshooting:

- **No Response**: Check power (5V), wiring, and sensor warm-up with a multimeter.
- **False Alerts**: Adjust potentiometer, filter air, or recalibrate.
- **Component Failure**: Verify buzzer/relay/LCD with a multimeter.

Building a Mini Project: Smart Air Quality Monitor with Buzzer Alarm

The Smart Air Quality Monitor is a practical IoT project that combines environmental sensing and automation to enhance indoor safety and comfort. This section leverages the skills, guiding you through building a system using DHT11/DHT22, MQ-2 sensor, buzzer, and relay module with Arduino Uno, NodeMCU, or ESP32. This project monitors temperature, humidity, and gas levels, triggering a buzzer and relay (for example: to control a ventilator) when conditions exceed safe thresholds, while displaying real-time data on the Serial Plotter. This detailed guide covers component integration, logic implementation, coding examples, global applications, challenges, and troubleshooting tips, empowering you to create a functional air quality solution.

Components

The Smart Air Quality Monitor relies on a carefully selected set of components, each contributing to its sensing, alerting, and control capabilities. These components are wired and programmed to work seamlessly with a microcontroller, forming a robust system.

- **DHT11/DHT22**: This temperature and humidity sensor provides critical environmental data, with the DHT11 offering ±2°C and ±5% accuracy (0–50°C, 20–80% RH) and the DHT22 providing higher precision (±0.5°C, ±2% RH, -40–80°C). Wired with VCC to 3.3V/5V, GND to ground, and data to a digital pin (for example: pin 2 on Uno), it uses a 10kΩ pull-up resistor. The DHT11 suits budget projects, while the DHT22 excels in precision applications like industrial monitoring.

- **MQ-2 Sensor**: This gas sensor detects LPG, methane, CO, and smoke, offering analog (AO) and digital (DO) outputs. Wired with VCC to 5V, GND to ground, AO to an analog pin (for example: A0), and DO to a digital pin (for example: pin 3), it requires an external 5V/1A supply for its 150mA heater. Its potentiometer sets the DO threshold, making it ideal for gas alerts.
- **Buzzer**: A simple active buzzer provides audible alerts, wired with VCC to 5V, GND to ground, and signal to a digital pin (for example: pin 4). Drawing minimal current (~10mA), it emits a 2–3kHz tone when activated, signaling unsafe conditions effectively.
- **Relay Module**: This module controls a high-voltage device (for example: a 220V ventilator) via a low-voltage signal. Wired with VCC to 5V, GND to ground, and signal to a digital pin (for example, pin 5), it connects the ventilator to the COM and NO terminals. An optocoupled 5V/10A relay ensures safe isolation, requiring an external power supply for the coil.

These components, assembled on a breadboard with color-coded wires (red for VCC, black for GND, and so on), create a compact system. Hobbyists use this setup for home safety. It monitors rural kitchens, reflecting its adaptability. Challenges include power demands—plan for 200mA total—mitigated by external supplies, and component compatibility, ensured by matching pin logic (5V for Uno, 3.3V with level shifters for ESP32). This assembly, taking 20–30 minutes, forms the hardware backbone of the project.

Logic

The logic of the Smart Air Quality Monitor defines its decision-making process, activating the buzzer and relay based on temperature or gas thresholds, while continuously displaying data for analysis. This ensures timely responses to hazardous conditions.

The system operates on a simple conditional rule: if the temperature exceeds 35°C OR the gas level surpasses 400 ppm, the buzzer and relay activate. The DHT11/DHT22 measures temperature (in °C), while the analog output of MQ-2, calibrated to ppm, assesses gas concentration. When either condition is met, the buzzer emits a continuous alert, and the relay switches on the ventilator to improve air circulation. Otherwise, both remain off. Data—temperature, humidity, gas level, and digital status—is sent to the Serial Plotter every 200ms, allowing visual tracking of trends over time.

Implementation begins with wiring as described, ensuring a 1–2-minute warm-up period for the MQ-2. The sketch initializes the DHT library, sets pin modes, and continuously reads sensor values in the `loop()`. Temperature is read using `dht.readTemperature()`, gas levels are measured (after calibration), and the digital threshold is checked. The logic is then applied, with results updated on the Serial Plotter.

Office buildings use this logic for climate control, and rural homes monitor bushfire risks. Challenges include sensor lag—allow 2 seconds between reads—and false triggers from cooking fumes, mitigated by adjusting the MQ-2 threshold or adding a vent. Troubleshooting verifies sensor outputs with a multimeter, checks buzzer/relay response, and ensures Serial Plotter scaling (for example, 0–1000 for gas)

Open the Serial Plotter, and observe temperature (y-axis left) and gas level (y-axis right) trends. Test by heating the DHT11 (for example: with a lamp) or exposing the MQ-2 to smoke, triggering alerts.

Troubleshooting:

- **No Alerts**: Check power (5V), wiring, and sensor thresholds with a multimeter.
- **Erratic Plotter**: Verify delay, calibrate sensors, or adjust Serial scaling.
- **Relay/Buzzer Failure**: Test components individually with a multimeter.

Visualizing Sensor Data

Visualizing sensor data is a key skill in IoT development, transforming raw numerical outputs into actionable insights for debugging, analysis, and optimization. This section builds on the sensor projects, focusing on using the Serial Monitor and Serial Plotter in the Arduino IDE to interpret data from sensors such as DHT11/DHT22, MQ-2, and HC-SR04. These tools enable text-based logging and graphical trending, respectively, helping identify anomalies such as spikes, noise, or unstable signals. This detailed guide covers the functionality of each tool, practical implementation, coding examples, global applications, challenges, and troubleshooting tips, empowering you to enhance your IoT projects with effective data visualization.

Serial Monitor: Text Output of Sensor Readings

The Serial Monitor provides a text-based interface to display real-time sensor readings, offering a straightforward way to verify data and debug code. It logs values such as temperature, humidity, gas levels, or distances as they are read by the microcontroller.

The tool is accessed via the Arduino IDE under **Tools → Serial Monitor**, setting the baud rate (for example: 9600) to match the `Serial.begin(9600)` of the sketch. For example, a DHT11 might output Temp: 25.3°C, Hum: 60.5% every 2 seconds, while an MQ-2 could show Gas: 350 ppm, Digital: Normal. Each reading is printed using `Serial.print()` or `Serial.println()`, with commas or tabs for readability. This format is ideal for quick checks during development, such as confirming a warm-up of the sensor (for example: 2-minute stabilization of MQ-2) or testing threshold triggers.

Students use the Serial Monitor to debug classroom weather stations with DHT22s, and farmers monitor irrigation sensors like HC-SR04. Challenges include data overflow—limit updates to 100ms intervals—or garbled text, caused by mismatched baud rates, fixed by syncing `Serial.begin()` and the monitor. Troubleshooting involves checking the baud rate, verifying `Serial.begin()` placement in `setup()`, and ensuring stable power, taking 10–15 minutes to master.

Serial Plotter: Graphical Visualization of Data Trends over Time

The Serial Plotter offers a graphical representation of sensor data over time, plotting values on a dynamic graph to reveal trends, patterns, or anomalies. It is particularly useful for spotting spikes, noise, or unstable signals that text alone might miss.

Accessed via **Tools → Serial Plotter** in the Arduino IDE, it operates at the same baud rate as the sketch (for example: 9600). Data is sent as comma-separated values, plotting each variable on a separate y axis (for example: temperature on the left, gas level on the right, ranging 0–1023 for analog or calibrated units). For instance, a Smart Air Quality Monitor might show temperature rising to 36°C or gas spiking to 450 ppm, triggering alerts. The x-axis represents time, auto-scaling with each update (for example: every 200ms).

Engineers use the Serial Plotter to analyze factory sensor stability with MQ-2s, and outback stations track HC-SR04 water levels. Challenges include overlapping plots—use distinct ranges (for example, 0–50°C, 0–1000 ppm)—or flat lines, indicating stalled data, addressed by checking sensor connections. Troubleshooting verifies `Serial.print()syntax`, adjusts delay timing, and ensures that plotter compatibility with the sketch, taking 15–20 minutes to optimize.

Useful for Spotting Spikes, Noise, or Unstable Signals

Visualizing data with these tools is essential for diagnosing sensor behavior. Spikes—sudden peaks like a gas reading jumping from 300 to 600 ppm—might indicate real events (for example: a leak) or noise (for example: electrical interference), distinguishable by their duration. Noise appears as random fluctuations (for example: ±10°C on DHT11), often from power instability or poor shielding, while unstable signals show inconsistent trends (for example: oscillating distances on HC-SR04), suggesting wiring issues or environmental factors like temperature affecting sound speed.

Practical use involves comparing Serial Monitor logs with Plotter graphs. For example, a DHT22 might log Temp: 35.1°C normally but spike to 40°C on the Plotter during a lamp test, confirming heat sensitivity. Averaging 5 readings (for example: total / 5) or adding a 10µF capacitor can stabilize noise. In urban air quality systems, use this to filter traffic-related spikes. Jungle monitors detect unstable smoke signals from the wind. Challenges include misinterpreting spikes as errors—cross-check with a reference sensor—and plotter lag with high update rates, mitigated by increasing delays. This analysis, taking 20–30 minutes, enhances project reliability.

Troubleshooting:

- **No Serial Output**: Check baud rate, cable, and `Serial.begin()`
- **Flat Plotter Line**: Verify sensor data, delay, and `Serial.print()` format
- **Spikes/Noise**: Add averaging, capacitors, or shield wiring

Testing, Calibration, and Noise Reduction Techniques

Testing, calibration, and noise reduction are essential steps to ensure the reliability and accuracy of IoT sensor systems, particularly for sensors such as DHT11/DHT22, MQ-2, HC-SR04, and relay modules, providing a comprehensive guide to preparing sensors, applying software and hardware filters, and calibrating with reference instruments using Arduino Uno, NodeMCU, or ESP32. These techniques enhance data integrity, reduce errors, and optimize performance for real-world applications. This detailed guide covers warm-up procedures, filtering methods, calibration strategies, global use cases, challenges, and troubleshooting tips, empowering you to refine your IoT projects with precision.

Warm-up Sensors

Warming up sensors is a critical initial step to stabilize their internal components, ensuring accurate readings from the outset. Most sensors, especially those with heaters like the MQ-2, require a brief stabilization period after power-on.

The MQ-2 gas sensor, for instance, needs 1–2 minutes for its tin dioxide (SnO_2) layer and 150mA heater to reach operating temperature (typically 200–300°C), stabilizing its resistance baseline. During this time, readings may fluctuate—for example, gas levels might show 0 ppm initially before settling. Add a `delay(120000)` or `delay(60000)` in the `setup()` function after `Serial.begin(9600)` to allow this warm-up. Other sensors, such as DHT11 (30–60 seconds) or HC-SR04 (no significant warm-up), benefit from shorter delays to account for microcontroller boot time. Monitor the Serial Monitor during this period to observe stabilization.

Industrial MQ-2 setups enforce a 2-minute warm-up for methane detection, and Rural DHT11 systems use 1-minute delays for weather monitoring. Challenges include impatience leading to premature readings—wait the full duration—or power strain from the current draw of MQ-2, mitigated by an external 5V/1A supply. Troubleshooting involves checking the delay timing with a stopwatch, verifying sensor response post-warm-up with a multimeter, and ensuring stable voltage, taking 5–10 minutes to implement.

Software Filtering: Moving Average or Median Filter

Software filtering processes sensor data to smooth out noise and stabilize readings, using algorithms such as the moving average or median filter. These methods reduce random fluctuations without requiring additional hardware.

A moving average filter calculates the average of the last n readings (for example, 5) to dampen noise. For example, with an MQ-2, store values in an array (`intreadings[5];`) and update with `readings[i] = analogRead(A0); i = (i + 1) % 5;` then compute `int total = 0; for(int j = 0; j < 5; j++) total += readings[j]; intavg = total / 5`. A median filter sorts the same n readings and selects the middle value, effectively removing outliers (for example, a spike from interference). Both require a 100–200ms delay between samples to avoid overlap.

Classrooms use moving averages on HC-SR04 data to filter ultrasonic noise, and median filters stabilize MQ-2 readings in urban air quality systems. Challenges include lag—larger n (for example: 10) slows response, so limit to 5—and computational load on low-memory boards like Uno, mitigated by optimizing loop efficiency. Troubleshooting checks filter output on the Serial Plotter, adjusts n based on noise level, and verifies data consistency, taking 15–20 minutes to tune.

Hardware Filtering: Capacitors across Power Supply

Hardware filtering uses capacitors to suppress electrical noise on the power supply lines, stabilizing sensor performance by smoothing voltage fluctuations. This is especially effective for analog sensors such as MQ-2 and HC-SR04.

Add a 10µF electrolytic capacitor (positive to VCC, negative to GND) across the power pins of the sensor to filter ripple from the 5V supply, reducing noise by 10–20mV. For high-current devices like the MQ-2 (150mA), include a 0.1µF ceramic capacitor in parallel for high-frequency noise. Place these close to the sensor pins on the breadboard, using short wires to minimize inductance. This setup grounds transient spikes, improving analog readings (for example, reducing MQ-2 jitter from 50 to 10 ADC units).

Outback HC-SR04 systems use capacitors to counter motor interference, and MQ-2 setups filter jungle humidity effects. Challenges include capacitor polarity—reverse connection can damage the circuit, so double-check with a multimeter—or insufficient capacitance, requiring a 100µF upgrade for noisy environments. Troubleshooting verifies voltage stability with a multimeter, tests noise reduction on the Serial Plotter, and ensures proper soldering, taking 10–15 minutes to install.

Calibration: Comparing with Reference Instruments

Calibration aligns sensor readings with known standards using reference instruments, ensuring accuracy for critical applications. This process adjusts raw data to match real-world values, compensating for drift or environmental factors.

For the DHT11, compare temperature readings with a calibrated thermometer (for example: ±0.1°C accuracy) in a controlled setting (for example: 25°C). For the MQ-2, expose it to a certified gas source (for example: 200 ppm propane) and adjust the potentiometer until the DO output toggles, then refine the analog-to-ppm formula based on the reference. The HC-SR04 can be calibrated with a ruler, measuring a fixed distance (for example: 50cm) and adjusting the speed of sound (for example: 0.0343 cm/µs at 20°C) for temperature effects.

In Europe, industrial HC-SR04s are calibrated monthly with laser rangefinders, MQ-2s use gas standards for kitchen safety. Challenges include reference inaccuracy—use high-quality tools—or environmental drift (for example: humidity on MQ-2), mitigated by regular recalibration (for example: weekly). Troubleshooting compares Serial Monitor data with the reference, adjusts calibration factors, and retests.

Troubleshooting:

- **Unstable Readings**: Check warm-up delay, add filters, or recalibrate.
- **No Improvement**: Verify capacitor value, filter algorithm, or reference accuracy.
- **Power Issues**: Test voltage with a multimeter, upgrade supply if needed.

Testing, calibrating, and reducing noise with warm-ups, filters, and references enhances IoT sensor reliability. With proper setup and coding, you will master these techniques, preparing for advanced projects.

Troubleshooting Common Issues

Troubleshooting is a vital skill for resolving issues in IoT projects involving sensors such as DHT11/ DHT22, MQ-2, HC-SR04, and relay modules, ensuring reliable operation with Arduino Uno, NodeMCU, or ESP32. This section builds on the practical experience from addressing common problems such as incorrect values, noisy output, unstable readings, and board resets. By systematically identifying and fixing these issues, you can maintain the integrity of your projects. This detailed guide covers each problem, diagnostic steps, solutions, global applications, challenges, and additional tips, empowering you to debug effectively and enhance your IoT systems.

Incorrect Values: Check Power Supply and Wiring

Incorrect values occur when sensor readings deviate significantly from expected results, often due to power instability or faulty connections. This can lead to misleading data, such as a DHT11 reporting 0°C or an MQ-2 showing 0 ppm despite gas presence.

Start by checking the power supply with a multimeter—ensure 5V ±0.5V for sensors such as MQ-2 (150mA draw) or 3.3V for ESP32-compatible devices. A dropping voltage (for example: 4.5V) indicates insufficient current, requiring an external 5V/1A adapter or powered USB hub. Next, verify wiring using continuity mode on the multimeter—confirm VCC to 5V, GND to ground, and signal pins (for example: AO to A0, DO to pin 2) are secure. Loose connections or swapped pins (for example: AO to a digital pin) are common culprits. Re-seat wires on the breadboard and use color-coded cables (red for VCC, black for GND) for clarity.

Students troubleshoot HC-SR04 distance errors by checking 5V stability, farmers fix DHT11 temperature issues with better wiring. Challenges include intermittent faults—wiggle wires to replicate—or power noise, mitigated by adding a 10µF capacitor across VCC and GND. Troubleshooting takes 10–15 minutes, involving re-wiring and re-testing on the Serial Monitor.

Noisy Output: Add Filters and Shielded Wires

Noisy output manifests as random fluctuations in sensor data, such as an HC-SR04 reporting 50±10cm or an MQ-2 showing 300±50 ppm, often due to electrical interference or poor signal quality. This can obscure true readings and trigger false alerts.

Apply hardware filtering by adding a 0.1µF ceramic capacitor in parallel with a 10µF electrolytic capacitor across the power pins of the sensor to suppress high-frequency and ripple noise. For analog signals (for example: MQ-2 AO), place a 10kΩ resistor and 0.1µF capacitor in a low-pass filter configuration between the output and the microcontroller pin. Use shielded wires or twisted pairs for long runs (for example,>30cm) to reduce electromagnetic interference from motors or power lines, grounding the shield at one end.

Industrial MQ-2 systems use shielded cables to counter factory noise, and HC-SR04 setups add capacitors for outback motor interference. Challenges include insufficient filtering—upgrade to 100µF if noise persists—or capacitor polarity, checked with a multimeter to avoid damage. Troubleshooting involves observing noise on the Serial Plotter, adjusting filter values, and re-testing, taking 15–20 minutes.

Unstable Readings: Warm up the Sensor and Avoid Rapid Sampling

Unstable readings, such as oscillating DHT11 temperatures (for example: 25–27°C) or erratic MQ-2 gas levels, often result from insufficient sensor warm-up or overly frequent sampling, causing inconsistent data that undermines reliability.

Ensure proper warm-up by adding a delay in **`setup()`**—for example: delay(120000); for 1 to 2-minute heater stabilization or delay(30000) of MQ-2; for' 30–60 seconds of DHT11. Avoid rapid sampling by setting a minimum delay (for example: 200ms) in **`loop()`** to match sensor response times, preventing overlap or overheating. For example, HC-SR04 measurements every 50ms can jitter due to echo interference—increase to 100ms. Average multiple readings (for example: 5 samples) with total / 5 to smooth outliers.

In Europe, factory HC-SR04s stabilize with 2-minute warm-ups, MQ-2s avoid rapid sampling in jungle humidity. Challenges include forgetting warm-up—monitor Serial Monitor during delay—or excessive averaging causing lag, adjusted by limiting samples to 5. Troubleshooting checks stability on the Serial Plotter, adjusts delays, and verifies warm-up completion, taking 10–15 minutes.

Board Reset: Use a Stable USB Cable and Power Supply

Board resets, where the microcontroller restarts unexpectedly (for example: Serial Monitor shows repeated **`setup()`** logs), stem from unstable power delivery or faulty USB connections, disrupting sensor operation and data logging.

Use a high-quality USB cable with thick wires (for example: 24 AWG) and minimal resistance, avoiding cheap or data-only cables that limit current (for example: 500mA). Connect to a powered USB hub or external 5V/2A supply instead of a computer port, which may drop below 4.5V under load (for example: MQ-2 + relay). Add a 100µF capacitor across the VIN and GND of the board to buffer power dips. Avoid long USB extensions, which increase resistance—keep within 1 meter.

Urban ESP32 projects use stable hubs for relay control, while in Africa, Arduino Unos rely on solar-powered supplies. Challenges include cable wear—replace if frayed—or insufficient current, requiring a 2A upgrade. Troubleshooting tests reset with a multimeter on voltage, swap cables/supplies, and monitor stability, taking 10–15 minutes.

Conclusion

In this chapter, we moved from foundational microcontroller concepts to practical sensor and module interfacing, forming the Perception Layer in IoT systems. You gained hands-on experience designing, implementing, and troubleshooting IoT projects using Arduino Uno, NodeMCU, and ESP32 platforms. Through structured exercises, we explored sensor technology, data handling, and system integration, culminating in a Smart Air Quality Monitor mini-project.

We began with the distinction between digital and analog sensors: digital sensors like DHT11 and HC-SR04 provide binary outputs, while analog sensors like MQ-2 deliver continuous voltage requiring ADC conversion. This knowledge laid the groundwork for effective sensor interfacing.

Next, we interfaced key components—DHT11/DHT22, HC-SR04, relay modules, and MQ-2—covering wiring, pin configurations, power requirements, and practical tips such as using pull-up resistors or external supplies for stability. We explored data visualization and calibration, using the Serial Monitor and Serial Plotter to monitor readings, applying software filters and hardware solutions to reduce noise.

Troubleshooting addressed common issues including incorrect readings, noisy output, unstable values, and board resets, teaching systematic diagnostics with multimeters and Serial Tools.

Practical exercises reinforced these skills: Exercise 1 classified sensor outputs; Exercise 2, the Cable Chaos challenge, simulated miswiring; Exercise 3 tested sensor stability across environments; and Exercise 4 integrated all components into a full-loop Smart Air Quality Monitor that senses, decides, and acts automatically.

Chapter 7, Real-Time Control with GPIO, PWM and Interrupts, dives into real-time hardware control, focusing on how microcontrollers like Arduino, NodeMCU, and ESP32 interact with external devices through digital and analog signals. Readers will learn to use GPIO (General Purpose Input/Output) pins to read inputs from switches or buttons and control outputs such as LEDs, buzzers, and relays.

Practical Exercises

This section contains Exercises 1-3.

Exercise 1: Sensor Signal Detective – Digital or Analog

This exercise helps you develop the ability to identify whether a sensor provides digital or analog outputs by testing with `analogRead()` and `digitalRead()` functions using Arduino Uno, NodeMCU, or ESP32. This task builds on sensor interfacing skills from using examples such as DHT11, MQ-2, and HC-SR04. The goal is to train your instinct to recognize sensor types, enhancing your IoT troubleshooting and design capabilities. This guide provides step-by-step instructions, a coding example, global applications, challenges, and troubleshooting tips.

Task: Test Sensors with `analogRead()` and `digitalRead()` to Classify Their Output

This task encourages learners to actively engage with both the hardware and software aspects of IoT systems. By performing hands-on readings from multiple sensor types, you gain practical experience in observing how different sensors communicate with microcontrollers. It also helps develop a systematic approach to data collection, enabling you to notice patterns, anticipate potential issues, and lay the groundwork for more complex IoT applications in the future.

Goal: Train the Instinct to Recognize Sensor Types

Achieving this goal equips learners with a foundational skill for IoT troubleshooting and design. Being able to quickly distinguish between analog and digital outputs allows for faster circuit integration, more efficient coding, and effective debugging. Over time, this instinctive understanding of sensor behavior becomes a critical tool, enabling the development of reliable, scalable, and responsive IoT solutions across diverse real-world applications.

Steps

Step 1: Gather Materials

a. Collect an Arduino Uno (or compatible board), a breadboard, jumper wires, and sensors: DHT11 (digital), MQ-2 (analog and digital), and HC-SR04 (digital).

b. Ensure a USB cable, a 5V power supply, and a computer with the Arduino IDE are ready.

This step ensures that you start the experiment with complete readiness and clarity. Gathering and checking each component beforehand prevents wiring errors, missing parts, or unexpected delays later in the process.

Step 2: Set up the Breadboard

a. Place the DHT11 on the breadboard, connecting VCC to 5V, GND to ground, and data to pin 2 with a 10kΩ pull-up resistor.

b. Connect the MQ-2 with VCC to 5V, GND to ground, AO to analog pin A0, and DO to digital pin 3.

c. Wire the HC-SR04 with VCC to 5V, GND to ground, Trig to pin 4, and Echo to pin 5.

d. Use color-coded wires (red for VCC, black for GND) for clarity.

This step focuses on building clean, logical wiring connections that mirror real-world IoT circuit design practices. Paying attention to pin alignment, resistor placement, and consistent color coding not only prevents short circuits but also improves readability during troubleshooting.

Step 3: Write the Sketch

a. Open the Arduino IDE and create a new sketch.

b. Include the necessary setup.

c. In the `loop()`, add reading code.

d. Log results.

This step transitions the exercise from hardware setup to software implementation, where logic meets electronics. Writing the sketch allows you to translate physical sensor signals into readable digital data, reinforcing the connection between code and circuit behavior.

Step 4: Upload and Observe

a. Upload the sketch to the board.

b. Open the Serial Monitor (set to 9600 baud) and observe the output every 200ms.

c. Note that DHT11 and HC-SR04 (via duration) return 0 or 1 (digital), while MQ-2's AO shows 0–1023 (analog), and DO shows 0 or 1 based on the potentiometer.

This step emphasizes the importance of real-time monitoring and validation. Observing sensor outputs immediately after uploading the sketch allows you to confirm proper wiring and correct functioning of your code.

Step 5: Analyze and Classify

a. Compare outputs: DHT11 is digital (binary), HC-SR04 is digital (pulse-based), MQ-2 AO is analog (continuous), and MQ-2 DO is digital (threshold-based).

b. Record findings in a notebook to build intuition for future sensor identification.

This step reinforces critical analytical skills by encouraging you to interpret sensor behavior and classify signal types. Documenting observations helps create a reference for future projects and strengthens pattern recognition, which is vital when integrating multiple sensors into complex IoT systems.

Troubleshooting

- **No Serial Output:** Ensure the correct board and COM port are selected in the Arduino IDE. Reconnect the USB cable and check that Serial.begin(9600) is placed in the `setup()` function.
- **Sensor Not Responding:** Double-check wiring connections. Verify that VCC and GND are properly connected — reversed polarity can damage sensors.

- **Unstable or Fluctuating Analog Values (MQ-2):** Allow the MQ-2 sensor to preheat for at least 20 seconds. Use stable power and avoid touching the sensing element during testing.
- **Incorrect Digital Readings (DHT11 or HC-SR04):** Make sure the correct pins are defined in the code. The DHT11 requires a library (DHT.h) and a small delay between readings (~1 second). For HC-SR04, confirm that `pulseIn()` is used correctly for Echo pin readings.
- **All Readings Show Zero:** Check the common ground connection between the board and sensors. Use a multimeter to verify power at the VCC pin of each sensor.

This process not only ensures accurate readings for the current exercise but also cultivates habits that are essential for reliable, real-world IoT development, where quick identification and resolution of problems can save time and prevent system failures.

Exercise 2: Cable Chaos Troubleshooting Challenge

This exercise simulates real-world wiring mistakes to sharpen your debugging skills using an Arduino Uno, NodeMCU, or ESP32 with a sensor like the MQ-2. This task builds on troubleshooting techniques, encouraging you to intentionally miswire a sensor and systematically resolve the issue. The goal is to practice debugging under real-world conditions, enhancing your ability to handle unexpected hardware problems in IoT projects. This guide provides step-by-step instructions, a coding example, global applications, challenges, and troubleshooting tips.

Task: Intentionally Miswire a Sensor and Troubleshoot

This task puts learners in a realistic debugging scenario, helping them practice identifying and correcting wiring errors methodically. By simulating mistakes, you learn to observe how incorrect connections affect sensor outputs and microcontroller behavior, building both confidence and problem-solving skills that are essential for handling real-world IoT hardware setups.

Goal: Practice Debugging under Real-World Conditions

Achieving this goal equips learners with a systematic approach to troubleshooting, fostering the ability to resolve unexpected hardware problems efficiently. Developing this skill is critical for reliable IoT system design, as it ensures that sensors, microcontrollers, and circuits operate correctly even in complex or fault-prone environments. Over time, these exercises cultivate intuition for detecting issues quickly and maintaining robust, functional systems.

Steps

Step 1: Gather Materials

a. Prepare an Arduino board, a breadboard, jumper wires, an MQ-2 sensor, a USB cable, a 5V power supply, and a multimeter.

b. Ensure that the Arduino IDE is installed on your computer.

Step 2: Correct Wiring Setup

a. Place the MQ-2 on the breadboard, connecting VCC to 5V, GND to ground, AO to analog pin A0, and DO to digital pin 3.

b. Use an external 5V/1A supply for the 150mA heater of MQ-2 to avoid board overload.

c. Verify connections with a multimeter in continuity mode.

Step 3: Intentionally Miswire

a. Disconnect AO from A0 and connect it to a digital pin (for example: pin 3) instead, leaving DO unconnected.

b. Alternatively, swap VCC and GND to simulate a power reversal.

c. Note the expected behavior: AO on a digital pin will read 0 or 1023 (no analog range), and swapped power may show no output.

Step 4: Write and Upload the Sketch

a. Open the Arduino IDE and create a sketch.

b. Upload the sketch and open the Serial Monitor (set to 9600 baud).

c. Observe the output—expect a constant 0 or 1023 due to the digital pin limitation.

Step 5: Troubleshoot the Issue

a. Use a multimeter to check the voltage at VCC (should be ~5V) and the continuity of AO to pin 3.

b. Identify the miswiring (AO on digital pin) and rewire it correctly to A0.

c. Test again, expecting a 0–1023 range reflecting gas levels.

d. Repeat with VCC/GND swap—check for 0V output, then correct and verify.

Step 6: Document Findings

a. Record the symptoms (for example, 0 reading on digital pin) and fixes (for example: rewired AO to A0).

b. Reflect on how miswiring affects sensor behavior to build debugging intuition.

The objective is to develop a systematic approach to diagnosing faults, rather than relying on guesswork. This hands-on challenge mirrors real-world IoT issues where faulty wiring, loose jumpers, or incorrect pin mapping cause unexpected behavior.

Troubleshooting:

- **No Output**: Check USB connection, baud rate (9600), and power supply with a multimeter.
- **Constant Value**: Verify pin type (analog versus digital) and rewire accordingly.
- **Unstable Readings**: Ensure MQ-2 warm-up (delay 60000) and stable 5V supply.

Exercise 3: Sensor Sensitivity Tuner – Reading Stability Test

This exercise explores how environmental changes affect the readings of an MQ-2 gas sensor and a DHT11 temperature/humidity sensor, using an Arduino Uno, NodeMCU, or ESP32. This task builds on sensor operation, aiming to help you observe and understand sensor noise and stability under varying conditions. By testing in different environments, you will gain insights into how external factors influence data accuracy, a critical skill for IoT development. This guide provides step-by-step instructions, a coding example, global applications, challenges, and troubleshooting tips.

Task: Observe MQ-2/DHT Values under Different Environments

This task involves setting up the MQ-2 gas sensor and the DHT-series temperature and humidity sensor. The primary objective is to collect and record the sensor readings—specifically gas concentration (from MQ-2) and temperature/humidity (from DHT)—across a variety of distinct environmental conditions. This hands-on exercise will allow for direct observation of how these sensor values fluctuate when exposed to different ambient environments.

Goal: Understand Sensor Noise and Stability

The Goal for this section is to develop a thorough Understanding of Sensor Noise and Stability.

This involves exploring different types of noise that affect sensor readings, such as random noise and systematic errors. Furthermore, we will analyze the various factors that influence sensor stability over time, including drift and environmental effects.

Steps

Step 1: Gather Materials

a. Collect an Arduino board, a breadboard, jumper wires, an MQ-2 sensor, a DHT11 sensor, a 10kΩ pull-up resistor, a 10μF capacitor, a USB cable, a 5V power supply, and a multimeter.

b. Prepare a notebook to record observations.

Step 2: Set up the Breadboard

a. Place the MQ-2 on the breadboard, connecting VCC to 5V, GND to ground, AO to analog pin A0, and DO to digital pin 2.

b. Wire the DHT11 with VCC to 5V, GND to ground, and data to digital pin 3 with a 10kΩ pull-up resistor.

c. Add a 10μF capacitor across VCC and GND of MQ-2 to reduce noise.

d. Use an external 5V/1A supply for the heater of MQ-2 and verify connections with a multimeter.

Step 3: Write the Sketch

a. Open the Arduino IDE and create a new sketch.

b. Include the setup // Warm-up for MQ-2.

c. In the `loop()`, add the reading code.

d. Log results

Step 4: Test in Different Environments

a. Start in normal room air, noting baseline readings (for example, Gas: 300, Temp: 25°C) on the Serial Monitor or Plotter.

b. Move the setup near a smoke source (for example, incense or candle smoke) and observe MQ-2 spikes (for example: 400–600).

c. Apply heat (for example, a lamp or hairdryer) near the DHT11 and note temperature increases (for example, 25–35°C).

d. Record variations and stability over 5 minutes per environment.

Step 5: Analyze Stability and Noise

a. Identify noise as random fluctuations (for example, ±50 on MQ-2) and stability as consistent trends.

b. Note how smoke increases MQ-2 readings and heat affects DHT11, documented in your notebook.

c. Consider applying a moving average (for example, an average of 5 readings) if noise is significant.

Troubleshooting:

- **No Readings**: Check power (5V), wiring, and warm-up delay with a multimeter.
- **Erratic Values**: Add a capacitor, increase the delay to 500ms, or shield from interference.
- **Failed DHT**: Verify pull-up resistor and pin connection.

Chapter 7
Real-Time Control with GPIO, PWM and Interrupts

Introduction

In the previous chapter, we had laid a strong foundation by interfacing practical sensors and modules such as the DHT11 for temperature and humidity, the HC-SR04 ultrasonic sensor for distance measurement, relay modules for high-voltage control, and the MQ-2 gas sensor for detecting gases like LPG and smoke. Through these exercises, we mastered the art of sensing and interpreting environmental data, transforming raw inputs into actionable insights. We now elevate our IoT journey to the next level, shifting from passive data collection to active, real-time hardware interaction. This chapter focuses on harnessing the power of General Purpose Input/Output (GPIO), Pulse Width Modulation (PWM), and Interrupts—three cornerstone techniques that enable responsive and dynamic control in IoT systems.

The ability to control the real world in real time is what distinguishes a truly interactive IoT device from a static sensor setup. GPIO serves as the versatile backbone, allowing microcontrollers such as the Arduino Uno, NodeMCU, or ESP32 to send and receive digital signals to and from external components such as LEDs, buttons, and relays. This bidirectional communication forms the basis for turning ideas into physical actions, from lighting up an LED to toggling a relay for appliance control. PWM takes this a step further by introducing analog-like control through digital means, enabling precise adjustments such as dimming LEDs or varying motor speeds with a series of pulses. Interrupts, meanwhile, revolutionize responsiveness by allowing the microcontroller to react instantly to events, such as a button press or sensor trigger, without being bogged down by continuous polling loops, ensuring timely actions even in complex systems.

Together, these techniques form the core of responsive IoT applications, bridging the gap between software logic and hardware behavior. Imagine a smart home where an LED blinks to signal a door opening, a fan motor adjusts speed based on temperature, or a security system instantly locks down upon detecting motion—all made possible through GPIO, PWM, and interrupts. This chapter will guide you through the principles, practical implementation, and optimization of these methods, starting with basic GPIO control and progressing to advanced interrupt-driven designs.

Structure

In this chapter, we will cover the following topics:

- Understanding General Purpose Input/Output and its Role in Digital Control

- Pin Configuration Modes: Input, Output, and Pull-Up/Pull-Down Settings
- Driving External Components such as LEDs, Buzzers, and Relays Using GPIO
- Fundamentals of Pulse Width Modulation: Duty Cycle, Frequency, and Analog Signal Simulation
- Controlling LED Brightness and Motor Speed using PWM
- Servo Motor Control with PWM using the ESP32 or Arduino Servo library
- Interrupts versus Polling: Implementing Event-Driven Programming
- Common Edge Triggers: RISING, FALLING, and CHANGE
- Power and Timing Considerations for Reliable GPIO Handling
- Mini projects:
    - Touchless Switch using Interrupts
    - Smart Lighting System with PWM-Based Brightness Control

Understanding GPIO and Digital Control

In the previous chapter, we mastered the art of interfacing sensors such as the DHT11, HC-SR04, relay modules, and MQ-2 to collect environmental data, marking our entry into the Perception Layer of IoT. We now advance to *Chapter 7*, where we shift our focus to real-time hardware interaction, starting with the foundational concept of General Purpose Input/Output (GPIO) and digital control. This section introduces GPIO as the essential bridge between microcontrollers, such as Arduino Uno, NodeMCU, or ESP32, and the physical world, enabling us to both sense inputs and drive outputs. By understanding and applying GPIO, you will unlock the ability to create responsive systems, from simple LED blinks to complex relay-based automation, setting the stage for the advanced techniques of PWM and Interrupts explored later in this chapter.

General Purpose Input/Output

GPIO pins are the basic interface between a microcontroller and the outside world, serving as versatile gateways for digital communication. These pins can be programmatically configured to perform two primary functions, forming the backbone of hardware interaction in IoT projects. This flexibility makes GPIO indispensable for both input and output tasks, tailored to the needs of your application.

- **Input**: When configured as an input, a GPIO pin reads external signals from devices such as buttons, switches, or digital sensors (for example: the data line of DHT11). This mode allows the microcontroller to detect high (for example, 3.3V or 5V) or low (0V) logic levels, translating physical actions into digital data. For instance, pressing a button might send a HIGH signal, triggering a program response. To ensure reliable input, techniques such as pull-up or pull-down resistors (for example: 10kΩ) are often used to define a default state, preventing floating voltages that could cause erratic readings.

- **Output**: When set as an output, a GPIO pin drives external devices such as LEDs, buzzers, or relays by sending HIGH or LOW signals. A HIGH output (typically 3.3V or 5V, depending on the board) can light an LED or activate a relay, while a LOW output (0V) turns them off. This mode is ideal for controlling hardware, with current limits (for example, 20mA per pin on Arduino Uno) dictating the need for external drivers like transistors for high-power devices. Proper current-limiting resistors (for example: 220Ω for LEDs) protect both the pin and the component.

The configuration of GPIO pins is handled through simple code, making it accessible even for beginners. For example, on an Arduino, `pinMode(pin, MODE)` sets a pin as `INPUT` or `OUTPUT`, while `digitalWrite(pin, VALUE)` controls the output state (`HIGH` or `LOW`), and `digitalRead(pin)` retrieves the input state. This programmability allows a single pin to serve multiple purposes, adapting to project requirements with minimal hardware changes.

Globally, GPIO is a universal tool that farmers use GPIO inputs to monitor soil moisture switches, while manufacturers leverage GPIO outputs to control robotic assembly line LEDs. In Europe, smart homes rely on GPIO to toggle relays for lighting, and in remote weather stations, use it to read button inputs for manual resets. Challenges include electrical noise—mitigated by debouncing circuits or shielded wires—and pin limitations, addressed by multiplexing or using expansion boards. Troubleshooting involves checking voltage with a multimeter, verifying pin modes, and ensuring stable power (for example: 5V ±0.5V).

Configuring Pins

Building on our introduction to GPIO and digital control, we now dive deeper into the process of configuring pins on microcontrollers such as the Arduino Uno, NodeMCU, or ESP32. This section explores the critical steps and considerations for setting up GPIO pins as inputs or outputs, ensuring they function reliably in real-time IoT applications. Pin configuration is the foundation of hardware interaction, enabling you to tailor the behavior of each pin to suit specific devices, whether reading a button press or driving an LED.

Configuring Pins: The Basics

Configuring a GPIO pin involves defining its role—input or output—using software commands, a process that transforms a versatile pin into a specialized interface. On Arduino platforms, this is achieved with the **`pinMode(pin, mode)`** function, where **`pin`** specifies the PIN (for example: 2, 13, A0) and **`mode`** is set to **`INPUT`**, **`OUTPUT`**, or **`INPUT_PULLUP`**. The choice of mode dictates how the pin interacts with the external circuit, and proper configuration is crucial to avoid damage or erratic behavior.

- **Setting Pins as Outputs**: When a pin is configured as **`OUTPUT`**, it can source or sink current to drive devices such as LEDs, buzzers, or relays. For example, **`pinMode(13, OUTPUT)`** prepares pin 13 to control the built-in LED on an Arduino Uno. The pin then uses **`digitalWrite(pin, HIGH)`** or **`digitalWrite(pin, LOW)`** to send 5V or 0V, respectively, with a typical current limit of 20mA. This mode requires careful current management—adding a 220Ω resistor in series with an LED prevents overloading the pin, while high-power devices like relays need external transistors or modules to handle currents beyond 40mA.

- **Setting Pins as Inputs**: Configuring a pin as **`INPUT`** allows it to read voltage levels from external sources, such as buttons or digital sensors. For instance, **`pinMode(2, INPUT)`** sets pin 2 to detect a button press. However, inputs are susceptible to floating states—undefined voltages when no signal is present—leading to unreliable readings. To address this, **`INPUT_PULLUP`** activates an internal pull-up resistor (typically 20kΩ–50kΩ), pulling the pin to HIGH (5V) by default, with a button to ground triggering LOW. Alternatively, an external 10kΩ pull-down resistor can be used to set a LOW default, pulled HIGH by a switch.

- **Pin Numbering and Mapping**: Each microcontroller has a unique pin layout. On Arduino Uno, pins 0–13 are digital, with A0–A5 as analog inputs convertible to digital. NodeMCU uses D0–D8, mapped to ESP8266 GPIO numbers (for example: D1 is GPIO 5), requiring careful reference to datasheets. ESP32 offers up to 34 GPIO pins, but some (for example, GPIO 6–11) are input-only due to flash connections. Misidentifying pins can lead to errors, so always consult the pinout diagram of the board.

Programming Techniques

Configuration is implemented in the **`setup()`** function, executed once at startup, ensuring pins are ready before the **`loop()`** function runs. Here is a structured approach:

- Initialize Pins
- Control Outputs

- Read Inputs
- Debouncing

Advanced configurations may involve libraries or direct register manipulation for efficiency, though this is less common for beginners. For instance, `ledcAttachPin()` of ESP32 can repurpose GPIO for PWM, hinting at future sections.

Hardware Considerations

Proper hardware setup enhances pin reliability:

- **Voltage Levels**: Ensure compatibility. Arduino Uno uses 5V logic, while ESP32 uses 3.3V. Level shifters or resistors (for example: 1kΩ series) protect pins when interfacing mismatched devices.
- **Current Limits**: Respect per-pin limits (for example: 20mA on Arduino) and total limits (for example: 200mA on Uno). Use external power for high-current devices.
- **Protection**: Add diodes or optocouplers to shield pins from voltage spikes, especially with relays or motors.
- **Wiring**: Use short, color-coded wires (red for VCC, black for GND) and a breadboard for secure connections.

Pull-Up and Pull-Down Resistors

Following our exploration of GPIO pin configuration, we now delve into a critical aspect of digital input management: pull-up and pull-down resistors. This section expands on how these resistors stabilize GPIO inputs on microcontrollers such as the Arduino Uno, NodeMCU, or ESP32, preventing the unpredictable behavior caused by floating inputs. Floating inputs occur when a pin is left unconnected or in an indeterminate state, leading to erratic readings that can derail IoT projects. Pull-up and pull-down resistors provide a reliable default voltage, ensuring consistent operation whether you are reading a button press, a switch, or a digital sensor. This comprehensive guide covers their purpose, implementation, hardware, and software options.

The Role of Pull-Up and Pull-Down Resistors

GPIO pins configured as inputs are highly sensitive to voltage levels, interpreting anything above a threshold (for example: 2.5V on a 5V Arduino) as HIGH and below as LOW. However, when an input pin is not actively driven by a device, such as a button in its open state, it can "float," picking up stray electrical noise or electromagnetic interference. This floating state result in random HIGH/LOW transitions, causing unpredictable readings that might falsely trigger actions such as turning on a LED or misinterpreting sensor data.

- **Preventing Floating Inputs:** Pull-up and pull-down resistors address this by providing a defined default voltage. A pull-up resistor connects the pin to VCC (for example: 5V), keeping it HIGH until grounded, while a pull-down resistor connects it to GND (0V), keeping it LOW until pulled to VCC. This ensures that the pin has a stable state when no active signal is present, eliminating the chaos of floating inputs.

- **Pull-up Resistors:** A pull-up resistor keeps the input pin at HIGH (for example: 5V) by default. When a switch or button connected to ground is closed, it overrides the pull-up by pulling the pin LOW. Internally, microcontrollers like Arduino offer `INPUT_PULLUP` mode, activating a built-in 20kΩ–50kΩ resistor. Externally, a 10kΩ resistor is commonly used between VCC and the pin, with the switch to GND. This configuration is ideal for active-low circuits, where a LOW signal indicates an action.

- **Pull-down Resistors:** A pull-down resistor maintains the pin at LOW (0V) by default. When a switch connected to VCC is closed, it pulls the pin HIGH. An external 10kΩ resistor between the pin and GND, with the switch to VCC, is typical. This setup suits active-high circuits, where a HIGH signal triggers an event. Pull-downs are less common with internal options, but are useful when external control or a higher current is needed.

Implementation and Hardware Considerations

Implementing pull-up or pull-down resistors requires careful design:

- **Resistor Selection:** A 10kΩ resistor is a standard choice, balancing current draw (for example: 0.5mA at 5V) and response speed. Values from 1kΩ to 100kΩ can work, but 1kΩ risks excessive current, while 100kΩ may slow response or be noise-prone. Use a multimeter to verify voltage drops.
- **Wiring:** For a pull-up, connect the resistor from VCC to the pin, with a switch or sensor output to GND. For a pull-down, connect from the pin to GND, with the switch to VCC. Ensure short wire runs to minimize interference.
- **Internal versus External:** The `INPUT_PULLUP of Arduino` eliminates the need for an external resistor, simplifying circuits. However, for high-noise environments or specific resistance values, external resistors provide flexibility. ESP32 and NodeMCU also support internal pull-ups, typically 45kΩ, adjustable via registers for advanced users.
- **Power and Protection:** Excessive current through a pulled pin (for example, short to VCC/GND) can damage the microcontroller. Add a 1kΩ series resistor as a safeguard, and use a 5V regulator to stabilize the supply.

Programming Techniques

Configuration is straightforward with the API of Arduino:

- Using Internal Pull-Up
- Reading the State
- External Resistor Setup

Driving LEDs, Buzzers, and Relays Using GPIO

Building on our mastery of GPIO fundamentals, pin configuration, and pull-up/pull down resistors, we now apply these concepts to drive real world devices, where we explore how GPIO enables the control of LEDs, buzzers, and relays—key components in responsive IoT systems. This section kicks off with LED control, demonstrating how to toggle an LED ON and OFF every 0.5 seconds, laying the groundwork for more complex applications such as sound alerts with buzzers and high-power switching with relays.

LED Control

LED control is one of the simplest yet most illustrative ways to understand GPIO output functionality. By toggling an LED ON and OFF every 0.5 seconds using a microcontroller such as the Arduino Uno, NodeMCU, or ESP32, you gain hands-on experience with digital output, timing, and circuit design. This exercise not only introduces basic GPIO programming but also serves as a building block for more sophisticated projects, such as status indicators or visual feedback systems in IoT devices. Let us break down the process, hardware setup, coding, and optimization to ensure that a blinking LED becomes a reliable part of your toolkit.

The Concept of LED Toggling

A Light Emitting Diode (LED) is a low-power device that emits light when current flows from its anode (positive) to cathode (negative). When connected to a GPIO pin configured as an output, the microcontroller can switch the LED ON by setting the pin to HIGH (for example: 5V on Arduino), allowing current to flow, and OFF by setting it to LOW (0V), stopping the flow. The 0.5-second interval, equivalent to a 1Hz frequency with a 50% duty cycle, creates a noticeable blink, making it ideal for testing and demonstration. This timing is controlled using the `delay()` function, which pauses execution, though we will explore more efficient methods later with Interrupts.

Hardware Setup

To toggle an LED, a proper circuit is essential to protect both the LED and the microcontroller:

- **Components:** Gather an Arduino Uno, a breadboard, jumper wires, an LED (for example: 5mm red), a 220Ω current-limiting resistor, and a USB cable.
- **Wiring:** Insert the LED into the breadboard, with the longer anode leg connected to a GPIO pin (for example, pin 13, which has a built-in LED on Arduino Uno, or pin 9 for an external LED). Connect the shorter cathode leg to one end of the 220Ω resistor, and the other end to GND. For an external LED, use pin 9 instead of 13, ensuring the anode goes to pin 9. Use color-coded wires (red for positive, black for ground) to avoid confusion.
- **Power Considerations:** The 5V pin of Arduino or USB power supplies the circuit, with the GPIO pin sourcing up to 20mA. The 220Ω resistor limits current to ~15mA (per Ohm's Law: $I = V/R = 5V/220\Omega \approx 0.023A$, adjusted by LED forward voltage ~2V), preventing burnout.

Programming the Toggle

The Arduino sketch uses a loop to alternate the LED state every 0.5 seconds:

- **Setup:** Configure the pin as an output using `pinMode(pin, OUTPUT)`. Example is `pinMode(9, OUTPUT);` for an external LED.
- **Loop:** Use `digitalWrite(pin, HIGH)` to turn the LED ON and `digitalWrite(pin, LOW)` to turn it OFF, with `delay(500)` for a 0.5-second pause. This creates a continuous blink.
- **Monitoring:** Add `Serial.println()` to log states for debugging, enhancing visibility.

Buzzer Control

Buzzer control introduces the use of GPIO to generate audible signals, transforming a silent microcontroller into an interactive device. A buzzer is an electromechanical or piezoelectric component that produces sound when an electrical signal is applied, making it ideal for alerts, notifications, or user feedback in IoT projects. By toggling a GPIO pin to drive a buzzer ON and OFF—similar to the LED blinking, you can create beeps, patterns, or continuous tones. This section explores how to control a buzzer with a microcontroller such as the Arduino Uno, NodeMCU, or ESP32, starting with a basic ON/OFF cycle and expanding to timed sequences, offering a stepping stone to more advanced audio applications using PWM in later sections.

Understanding Buzzer Operation

Buzzers come in two main types: active (with built-in oscillators) and passive (requiring an external signal). Active buzzers produce a fixed tone (like 2kHz) when powered, responding directly to a HIGH/LOW signal on a GPIO pin. Passive buzzers, conversely, require a square wave (for example: 1-5kHz) to generate variable pitches, often driven by PWM or timed pulses. For this section, we focus on an active buzzer, which simplifies initial learning by needing only a digital signal to produce a steady beep. The current draw of the buzzer (typically 10 to 30mA) and voltage rating (3.3V–5V) must match the output of the microcontroller to avoid damage.

Hardware Setup

A well-designed circuit ensures safe and effective buzzer operation:

- **Components**: Gather an Arduino Uno, a breadboard, jumper wires, an active buzzer, a 100Ω current-limiting resistor (optional for safety), and a USB cable.
- **Wiring**: Place the buzzer on the breadboard, aligning the positive (+) leg (often marked) to a GPIO pin (for example, pin 8) and the negative (-) leg to GND. Add a 100Ω resistor in series with the positive leg to limit current to ~40mA (I = 5V/100Ω ≈ 0.05A, adjusted by buzzer drop ~2V). Use red wire for the positive connection and black for GND to maintain clarity. For an Arduino with a 5V logic level, ensure the buzzer is rated for 5V; use a 3.3V buzzer with ESP32 and adjust accordingly.
- **Power Considerations**: The 5V pin of Arduino or USB supply powers the circuit, but exceeding the 20mA limit of pin requires an external transistor (for example: NPN like BC547) for higher currents. A 10μF capacitor across the buzzer terminals can reduce noise.

Programming the Buzzer

The Arduino sketch uses GPIO to toggle the buzzer, creating a simple beep pattern:

- **Setup**: Configure the pin as an output with `pinMode(pin, OUTPUT)`. Example: `pinMode(8, OUTPUT);`.
- **Loop**: Use `digitalWrite(pin, HIGH)` to turn the buzzer ON and `digitalWrite(pin, LOW)` to turn it OFF, with `delay(milliseconds)`to control duration. A 1-second ON/OFF cycle (for example: `delay(1000)`) produces a steady beep pattern.
- **Monitoring**: Add `Serial.println()` to log states, aiding debugging and timing verification.

Advanced Techniques and Variations

The basic operation of a buzzer using simple digital HIGH and LOW signals, you can take your project a step further by experimenting with timing, tone, and pattern control. These advanced techniques not only make buzzer outputs more dynamic but also allow the design distinctive alert systems, notification tones, or interactive feedback for IoT applications. By tweaking delay intervals, duty cycles, and frequencies, you can transform a basic beep into a meaningful signal – much like how different tones indicate specific actions or warnings in real-world devices.

- **Multiple Beeps**: Create a sequence with shorter delays; for example, `delay(200)` for three beeps: `for (int i = 0; i < 3; i++) { digitalWrite(8, HIGH); delay(200); digitalWrite(8, LOW); delay(200); }`.
- **Custom Patterns**: Mimic Morse code or alerts with variable ON/OFF times, for example: `delay(500)` for a long beep, `delay(100)` for short.
- **PWM for Passive Buzzers**: For a passive buzzer, use `analogWrite(pin, duty)` (0–255) with a frequency (for example: 1000Hz via `tone(pin, frequency)`). For now, stick to digital control for active buzzers.

Relay Switching

Relay switching allows a microcontroller to control high-power devices, such as fans, pumps, or lights, by using a low-power GPIO signal to activate an electromechanical or solid-state relay. Unlike LEDs and buzzers, which operate at the voltage of the microcontroller (for example: 5V) and current (for example: 20mA), relays handle voltages up to 240V AC or 30V DC and currents up to 10A or more, making them indispensable for real-world automation. However, the direct connection of AC to a microcontroller board poses a severe safety hazard, risking damage or electrocution. To mitigate this, optocoupled relay modules are recommended, isolating the control circuitry from the high-voltage load using an optocoupler, a device that transfers signals via light to prevent electrical feedback.

Understanding Relay Operation

A relay is essentially a switch controlled by an electromagnet. When a GPIO pin sends a HIGH signal (for example: 5V), it energizes the relay coil, closing the switch to connect the load (for example: a lamp) to its power source. A LOW signal de-energizes the coil, opening the switch and disconnecting the load. Optocoupled relay modules enhance this process by using an optocoupler, typically a phototransistor and LED pair, to isolate the 3.3V/5V logic of microcontroller from the 5V coil of the relay or higher-voltage load. This isolation protects the board from voltage spikes, noise, or shorts, making it a standard choice for safe IoT projects. Never connect the AC directly to your board; always use a relay module with proper terminals for load connection.

Hardware Setup

Safety and precision are paramount when wiring a relay circuit:

- **Components:** Gather an Arduino Uno, a breadboard, jumper wires, an optocoupled 5V relay module (for example: 1-channel with 10A rating), a 12V DC load (for example: small motor or LED strip), a 12V power supply, and a USB cable. Avoid AC loads for initial testing due to complexity.
- **Wiring:** Connect the VCC of the relay module to the 5V pin of Arduino, GND to GND, and signal (IN) to a GPIO pin (for example: pin 7). For the load, attach the COM (common) terminal to the 12V positive, NO (normally open) to the positive of the load, and the negative of the load to the 12V negative. Ensure the relay module has an onboard optical isolator and diode to protect against back-EMF from the coil.
- **Power Considerations:** Use a separate 12V supply for the load to avoid overloading the 5V/500mA limit of Arduino. Verify that the coil voltage (5V) of relay matches with the output of Arduino, and that it never bridges AC mains directly. Use the screw terminals of the module for load connection. A multimeter can confirm voltage and continuity.

Programming the Relay

The Arduino sketch toggles the relay to switch the load ON and OFF:

- **Setup:** Configure the pin as an output with **`pinMode(pin, OUTPUT)`**.
- **Loop:** Use **`digitalWrite(pin, HIGH)`** to activate the relay (closing the switch) and **`digitalWrite(pin, LOW)`** to deactivate it (opening the switch), with a **`delay(milliseconds)`** to control duration. A 2-second ON/OFF cycle (for example: **`delay(2000)`**) provides a clear test pattern.
- **Monitoring:** Add **`Serial.println()`** to log states, aiding verification.

Understanding Pulse Width Modulation

Having mastered GPIO-driven control of LEDs, buzzers, and relays, Pulse Width Modulation (PWM), is a powerful technique that extends the capabilities of digital pins on microcontrollers such as the Arduino Uno, Node MCU, or ESP32. PWM allows us to simulate analog voltage levels using rapid ON/OFF switching, enabling precise control over devices such as dimmable LEDs, variable-speed motors, and tone-generating buzzers. For example, a 50% duty cycle means the signal is HIGH half the time and LOW the other half, producing a medium brightness in an LED or a moderate speed in a motor. By adjusting this duty cycle, you can smoothly vary intensity, speed, or sound—achieving analog-like control using purely digital means. This makes PWM an essential technique for creating energy-efficient, responsive, and user-friendly IoT applications.

Concept

Pulse Width Modulation (PWM) is a technique that simulates an analog voltage by rapidly switching a digital pin between HIGH and LOW states at a controlled rate. Unlike traditional digital output, which provides only full ON (for example: 5V) or OFF (0V) signals, PWM creates an average voltage that appears analog to connected devices by varying the proportion of time the pin is ON versus OFF within a cycle. This method leverages the inertia or filtering properties of hardware, such as the human eye for LEDs or motor windings, to interpret the average voltage, making PWM a cornerstone of efficient and flexible control in IoT systems. Understanding the core components of PWM, including duty cycle and frequency, unlocks a world of precision beyond simple toggling.

The Mechanics of PWM

At its heart, PWM operates by generating a square wave, a digital signal that alternates between HIGH and LOW. The timer hardware of microcontroller modulates this wave, adjusting the ON time (pulse width) and OFF time within a fixed period, known as the cycle. The average voltage across this cycle is calculated as (Duty Cycle% % × Supply Voltage), allowing a 5V pin to effectively deliver 0V to 5V in steps. For example, a 50% duty cycle on a 5V system produces an average of 2.5V, perceivable as dimmed light or reduced motor speed. This simulation is seamless because many devices respond to the average rather than the rapid switching, which occurs too fast for human perception (typically >100Hz).

Duty Cycle: The Proportion of ON Time

The duty cycle is the percentage of one cycle during which the pin is HIGH, directly determining the effective voltage and output intensity. Expressed as a value from 0% (always OFF, 0V average) to 100% (always ON, 5V average), the duty cycle is the key to the versatility of PWM:

- **Definition:** If a cycle lasts 10ms (100Hz frequency), a 25% duty cycle means the pin is HIGH for 2.5ms and LOW for 7.5ms, yielding an average voltage of 1.25V on a 5V system.
- **Applications:** A 10% duty cycle dims an LED to 10% brightness, while 75% drives a motor at three-quarters speed. On Arduino, duty cycle is set using `analogWrite(pin, value)`, where `value` ranges from 0 (0%) to 255 (100%), corresponding to 8-bit resolution.
- **Precision:** The granularity depends on the PWM resolution of the microcontroller. The 8-bit PWM of Arduino offers 256 levels, while the 10-bit mode of ESP32 provides 1024, allowing finer control.

Frequency: The Rate of Repetition

Frequency, measured in Hertz (Hz), defines how many cycles occur per second, influencing the smoothness and responsiveness of the PWM output. It is the inverse of the cycle period (Frequency = 1/Period) and determines how quickly the pin switches:

- **Definition**: A 500Hz frequency means 500 cycles per second, with each cycle lasting 2ms (1/500s). At 50% duty cycle, the pin is HIGH for 1ms and LOW for 1ms per cycle.
- **Impact**: Low frequencies (for example: 100Hz) may cause visible LED flicker or audible motor whine, while high frequencies (for example: 10kHz) smooth out the effect but may strain the timer resources of the microcontroller. Typical PWM frequencies range from 100Hz to 1kHz for general use, with Arduino defaulting to ~490Hz or ~980Hz depending on the pin.

- **Adjustability**: On Arduino, frequency is fixed per timer (for example: Timer0, Timer1), but ESP32 allows dynamic adjustment via `ledcSetup(channel, frequency, resolution)`, offering flexibility for specific applications such as audio or motor control.

Hardware and Software Integration

PWM is implemented using the hardware timers of microcontrollers, which generate the square wave autonomously once configured. On Arduino, PWM-capable pins are marked with a ~ symbol (for example, 3, 5, 6, 9, 10, 11 on Uno), limiting its use to these pins. The `analogWrite(pin, value)` function sets the duty cycle, while the timer handles the switching. For devices like motors or LEDs, a low-pass filter (for example, an RC circuit with a 10µF capacitor) can smooth the PWM into a true analog signal, though this is optional for most applications.

Controlling Brightness and Speed with PWM

Building on our understanding of the concepts and applications of PWM, we now dive into practical implementations. This section focuses on leveraging Pulse Width Modulation (PWM) to control brightness and speed, starting with an LED fade effect using the Arduino Uno. The ability of PWM to simulate analog voltage through duty cycle adjustments makes it ideal for creating smooth transitions, enhancing IoT projects with dynamic visual feedback, or precise motor control.

LED Brightness (Fade Effect) - Arduino Uno

The LED fade effect is a classic PWM application that demonstrates how to gradually increase and decrease brightness, creating a smooth breathing or pulsating effect. Using the Arduino Uno, this technique leverages PWM-capable pins to adjust the duty cycle from 0% (off) to 100% (full brightness) and back, mimicking analog dimming. This effect is not only visually appealing but also serves practical purposes, such as ambient lighting or status indicators in IoT devices. Let us explore the process step-by-step, ensuring that you can replicate and customize this effect with confidence.

Mechanics of the Fade Effect

The fade effect relies on PWM to incrementally change the perceived brightness of LED by adjusting the duty cycle over time. The 8-bit PWM resolution of Arduino provides 256 levels (0-255 via `analogWrite()`), allowing fine-grained control. The process involves:

- **Increasing Brightness:** Starting at 0 (off), the duty cycle increases (for example: from 0 to 255) in small steps (for example, 5 units), with a delay (for example, 30ms) between steps to create a gradual rise.
- **Decreasing Brightness:** Once reaching 255 (full brightness), the duty cycle decreases back to 0, reversing the process for a fade-out.
- **Looping:** This cycle repeats, producing a continuous breathing effect. The delay determines the speed, while the step size controls smoothness—smaller steps (for example, 1) yield finer transitions but take longer.

The human eye perceives this as a smooth change due to its integration over time, with frequencies above 100Hz (default ~490Hz or ~980Hz of Arduino) eliminating flicker.

Hardware Setup

A safe and functional circuit is the key to achieving the fade effect:

- **Components**: Gather an Arduino Uno, a breadboard, jumper wires, a 5mm LED (for example: red or white), a 220Ω current-limiting resistor, and a USB cable.

- **Wiring**: Place the LED on the breadboard, connecting the longer anode leg to a PWM pin (for example: pin 9, marked with ~) via the 220Ω resistor. Connect the shorter cathode leg to GND. Use red wire for the positive path and black for ground to avoid confusion. Pin 9 is chosen for its Timer1 association, ensuring reliable PWM.
- **Power Considerations**: The 5V pin of Arduino or USB supply (maximum 500mA) powers the circuit. The 220Ω resistor limits current to ~15mA (`I = (5V - 2V)/220Ω ≈ 0.0136A`, accounting for the LED's ~2V drop), protecting both the LED and pin (20mA limit).

Programming Techniques

The Arduino sketch uses a loop with a variable to adjust the PWM value:

- **Setup:** Configure the pin as an output with `pinMode(pin, OUTPUT)`. Example: `pinMode(9, OUTPUT);`.
- **Fade Logic:** Use a `for` loop to increment (`brightness++`) and decrement (`brightness--`) a variable from 0 to 255, applying it with `analogWrite(pin, brightness)`. A `delay(milliseconds)` controls the fade speed.
- **Direction Control:** Use an `if` statement to switch between fading up and down when limits (0 or 255) are reached, often with a `fadeAmount` variable to track direction.

Optimization and Variations

After implementing the basic LED fading operation using PWM, it becomes important to explore how subtle changes in timing, duty cycle increments, and signal handling can significantly influence performance and visual output. By optimizing these parameters, learners can fine-tune fade speed, smoothness, and responsiveness, creating more polished and efficient control effects.

- **Speed Adjustment:** Reduce `delay(30)` to 10ms for a faster fade (5s cycle) or increase to 50ms for a slower one (25s cycle).
- **Step Size:** Lower `fadeAmount` to 1 for smoother transitions (255 × 30ms ≈ 7.65s per direction) or raise to 10 for coarser but quicker changes (~1.5s per direction).
- **Multiple LEDs**: Extend to pins 9, 10, and 11 with an array, creating a synchronized fade.
- **Non-blocking Fade**: Use `millis()` instead of `delay()` for multitasking,
- **Controlling Brightness and Speed with PWM**

Expanding on our exploration of PWM applications, and following the Arduino Uno LED fade effect in the previous context, we now shift focus to the ESP32 microcontroller. This section details how to control LED brightness with a fade effect using the `ledcAttachPin()` function of ESP32, a powerful PWM implementation that leverages its advanced hardware timers. The flexible PWM capabilities of ESP32, with up to 16 channels and configurable frequency/resolution, offer greater precision and versatility compared to the Arduino Uno, making it ideal for sophisticated IoT projects.

LED Brightness (Fade Effect) - ESP32

The LED fade effect on the ESP32 creates a smooth transition in brightness, emulating a breathing or pulsating light by incrementally adjusting the PWM duty cycle. The LEDC peripheral of ESP32, accessed via `ledcAttachPin()`, provides a robust framework for PWM control, and also supports frequencies from 1Hz to 40MHz and resolutions up to 16 bits (65,536 levels), far surpassing the 8-bit limit of Arduino Uno. This allows for finer granularity and smoother fades, making the ESP32 a preferred choice for applications requiring high precision, such as ambient lighting or dynamic status indicators in IoT devices. Let us dive into the setup and coding to harness this capability effectively.

Mechanics of the Fade Effect on ESP32

The fade effect on the ESP32 operates by modulating the duty cycle of a PWM signal generated by the LEDC module. Unlike the fixed-timer approach of Arduino, the ESP32 allows independent channel assignment and frequency tuning.

- **Increasing Brightness:** The duty cycle starts at 0 (off) and increases in small steps (for example, 500 units) up to the maximum (for example: 8191 for 13-bit resolution), with a delay (for example: 20ms) between steps for a gradual rise.
- **Decreasing Brightness:** Upon reaching the maximum, the duty cycle decreases back to 0, creating a fade-out effect.
- **Looping:** The cycle repeats continuously, with the delay and step size determining the speed and smoothness of the fade. The default frequency of ESP32 (~1kHz) ensures no visible flicker, while its high resolution minimizes stepping artifacts.

The LEDC module uses hardware timers, freeing the CPU for other tasks, and supports up to 16 channels, enabling multiple simultaneous fades.

Hardware Setup

A well-constructed circuit ensures safe and effective PWM control on the ESP32:

- **Components**: Gather an ESP32 (for example, ESP32 DevKit V1), a breadboard, jumper wires, a 5mm LED (for example, white or blue), a 220Ω current-limiting resistor, and a USB cable.
- **Wiring**: Place the LED on the breadboard, connecting the longer anode leg to a GPIO pin (for example, GPIO 18, a versatile choice) via the 220Ω resistor. Connect the shorter cathode leg to GND. Use red wire for the positive path and black for ground. GPIO 18 is suitable as it is not reserved for boot or flash functions.
- **Power Considerations**: The 3.3V pin of ESP32 or USB supply (max ~500mA) powers the circuit. The 220Ω resistor limits current to ~6mA (I = (3.3V - 2V)/220Ω ≈ 0.0061A, accounting for the LED's ~2V drop), well within the 20mA limit of the pin. A 3.3V logic level matches the ESP32, avoiding the need for level shifters.

Programming Techniques with LEDC

The LEDC API of ESP32 provides flexible PWM control:

- **Setup**: Use `ledcAttachPin(pin, channel)` to assign a pin to a PWM channel (0–15), `ledcSetup(channel, frequency, resolution)` to configure the channel (for example: 1000Hz, 13-bit), and `ledcWrite(channel, duty)` to set the duty cycle (0 to `2^resolution - 1`).
- **Fade Logic**: Increment or decrement a `duty` variable in a `for` loop, applying it with `ledcWrite(channel, duty)`. A `delay(milliseconds)` controls the fade speed.
- **Direction Control**: Use an `if` statement to reverse the `fadeAmount` when `duty` hits the minimum (0) or maximum (for example: 8191 for 13-bit), ensuring a continuous cycle.

Optimization and Variations

The optimizations allow precise control over brightness transitions, responsiveness, and energy efficiency, which are few of the key considerations in professional IoT and embedded applications. By experimenting with the following variations, learners can gain deeper insight into how PWM parameters influence both the aesthetic and functional aspects of LED control on the ESP32 platform.

- **Speed Adjustment**: Reduce `delay(20)` to 10ms for a faster fade (16s cycle) or increase to 30ms for a slower one (49s cycle).

- **Step Size**: Lower `fadeAmount` to 100 for smoother transitions (8191 × 20ms ≈ 164s per direction) or raise to 1000 for coarser but quicker changes (~16s per direction).
- **Multiple LEDs**: Use channels 0–2 for GPIO 18, 19, and 21: `ledcAttachPin(19, 1); ledcAttachPin(21, 2);` with a loop to sync fades.
- **Frequency Tuning**: Increase `frequency` to 5000Hz for smoother visuals or decrease to 500Hz for power savings, adjusting via `ledcSetup()`.

Motor Speed Control

Motor speed control using PWM allows the ESP32 to regulate the rotational speed of a DC motor by modulating the duty cycle of the signal sent to the enable pin of a motor driver module. The L293D and L298N are popular dual H-bridge driver ICs that handle the higher currents and voltages (up to 36V and 1A for L293D, 46V and 2A per channel for L298N) required by motors, far exceeding the 3.3V/20mA GPIO limits of ESP32. By connecting the enable pin (for example: ENA for L293D) to a PWM pin and using the LEDC module, the ESP32 can smoothly adjust speed from 0% (stopped) to 100% (maximum speed), making it ideal for applications such as robotic vehicles or fan speed regulation. Let us explore this setup in detail.

Principles of Motor Speed Control with PWM

The speed of a DC motor is directly proportional to the average voltage across its terminals. PWM generates this average by rapidly switching the enable pin HIGH and LOW, with the duty cycle determining the effective voltage. For example, a 50% duty cycle on a 12V motor supply delivers an average of 6V, halving the speed. The ESP32's LEDC module supports configurable frequencies (for example: 1kHz) and resolutions (for example: 10-bit or 1023 levels), ensuring smooth speed transitions. The L293D/L298N also provides direction control via input pins (for example: IN1, IN2), but PWM focuses on speed via the enable pin, enhancing efficiency and reducing heat compared to linear voltage regulation.

Hardware Setup

A robust circuit is essential for safe and effective motor control:

- **Components**: Gather an ESP32 (for example: ESP32 DevKit V1), an L293D or L298N motor driver module, a DC motor (for example: 6V–12V), a breadboard, jumper wires, a 12V power supply (for example: battery or adapter), and a USB cable.
- **Wiring**:
  - Connect the 3.3V pin of ESP32 to the VCC of the driver (logic supply), and GND to GND.
  - Attach a PWM pin (for example: GPIO 18) to the ENA (enable A) pin on the driver for speed control.
  - Connect motor terminals to OUT1 and OUT2 on the driver.
  - Link the VS of the driver (motor supply) to the 12V positive, GND to the 12V negative.
  - Use direction pins IN1 and IN2 (for example: GPIO 19 and 21) to set rotation (HIGH/LOW combinations).
  - Add a 100µF capacitor across VS and GND to stabilize the motor supply.
- **Power Considerations**: Use a separate 12V supply for the motor to avoid overloading the 3.3V/500mA limit of ESP32. The L293D/L298N handles up to 1A/2A per channel, but ensures that the current draw of the motor matches the rating of the driver. A multimeter can verify voltage and current.

Programming Techniques with LEDC

The LEDC API of ESP32 enables precise PWM control:

- **Setup:** Use `ledcAttachPin(pin, channel)` to assign GPIO 18 to a channel (for example, 0), `ledcSetup(channel, frequency, resolution)` to configure (for example, 1000Hz, 10-bit), and `ledcWrite(channel, duty)` to set the duty cycle (0 to 1023).
- **Speed Logic:** Increment or decrement a `duty` variable in a `for` loop, applying it with `ledcWrite(channel, duty)`. A `delay(milliseconds)` controls the speed ramp.
- **Direction Control:** Use `digitalWrite()` on IN1 and IN2 to set forward (HIGH/LOW) or reverse (LOW/HIGH), with PWM adjusting speed independently.

Optimization and Variations

By adjusting timing parameters, duty cycle increments, and PWM frequency, you can fine-tune how smoothly the motor accelerates or decelerates, reduce audible noise, and even coordinate multiple motors in parallel. The following variations demonstrate how small modifications in code and configuration can significantly improve control precision and adaptability in motor-driven IoT applications:

- **Speed Adjustment:** Reduce `delay(50)` to 20ms for a faster ramp (20s cycle) or increase to 100ms for a slower one (102s cycle).
- **Step Size:** Lower `fadeAmount` to 10 for smoother transitions (1023 × 50ms ≈ 51s per direction) or raise to 100 for coarser changes (~10s per direction).
- **Multiple Motors:** Use channels 0–1 for two motors on GPIO 18 and 19 with L298N's ENA/ENB, syncing speed via an array.
- **Frequency Tuning:** Increase `frequency` to 5000Hz to reduce motor whine or decrease to 500Hz for power efficiency.

Servo Motor Control with PWM

Following our mastery of PWM applications for brightness and speed, we now explore servo motor control. This section delves into the mechanics of how servos operate using PWM and provides a detailed example using the Arduino Servo library on an Arduino Uno. Servo motors are pivotal in IoT for precise angular positioning, such as in robotics or automated systems, due to their ability to hold specific positions based on pulse width modulation. This comprehensive guide covers the working principles of servos, hardware setup, and programming techniques with the Servo library.

Servo Motor

Servo motors operate by interpreting the width of a PWM signal to determine their angular position, offering precise control within a typical range of 0° to 180°. The servo expects a pulse train with a period of approximately 20ms (50Hz), where the pulse width—ranging from 1ms to 2ms—dictates the position. This mechanism relies on an internal feedback system, typically involving a potentiometer and control circuit, to maintain the desired angle against load or external forces.

- **Pulse Width and Position**: A 1ms pulse corresponds to 0°, a 1.5ms pulse to 90° (neutral), and a 2ms pulse to 180°. The duty cycle of PWM signal (5% for 1ms, 7.5% for 1.5ms, and 10% for 2ms within a 20ms cycle) is generated by the microcontroller, with the electronics of the servo converting this into a precise shaft movement.
- **Feedback Mechanism**: The servo contains a DC motor, gearbox, and potentiometer. The control circuit compares the resistance of the potentiometer (indicating current position)

with the PWM pulse width, adjusting the motor to match the target angle. This closed-loop system ensures accuracy, even under varying loads.

- **Power Requirements**: Servos typically operate on 5V–6V, drawing 100mA–1A depending on size and load, necessitating a separate power supply to avoid overloading the microcontroller.
- **Frequency Consistency**: The 20ms period (50Hz) is standard, though some servos tolerate slight variations (for example: 19–21ms), making timing critical for reliable operation.

Arduino Servo Library Example

The Arduino Servo library simplifies PWM control for servos, abstracting the pulse width generation and allowing position control in degrees (0°–180°). Using an Arduino Uno, this example demonstrates sweeping a servo from 0° to 180° and back, showcasing the role of PWM in precise positioning. The library uses Timer1, limiting its use to 12 servos and certain pins (for example: 9, 10), but it handles the 20ms timing automatically.

Hardware Setup

A properly wired circuit ensures safe servo operation:

- **Components**: Gather an Arduino Uno, a breadboard, jumper wires, a standard servo motor (for example: SG90), a 6V battery pack or 5V power supply, and a USB cable.
- **Wiring**: Connect the signal wire of servo (usually yellow or white) to pin 9 (a Timer1 PWM pin), the red wire (VCC) to the 5V/6V supply positive, and the black/brown wire (GND) to the supply negative and Arduino GND (to share a common ground). Use a 100µF capacitor across the VCC and GND of the servo to reduce noise.
- **Power Considerations**: The 5V pin of Arduino can power small servos (for example: SG90 at ~150mA), but a separate 6V supply is recommended for larger loads or multiple servos to prevent voltage drops or resets. A multimeter can confirm 5V–6V at the servo.

Programming Techniques

The Servo library streamlines servo control:

- **Setup**: Include `<Servo.h>`, create a `Servo` object (for example, `myServo`), and use `attach(pin)` to link it to a pin (for example: 9).
- **Position Control**: Use `write(degrees)` to set the angle (0–180°), which the library translates into a 1–2ms pulse within a 20ms cycle. Add `delay(milliseconds)` to control sweep speed.
- **Sweep Logic**: Use a `for` loop to increment or decrement the angle, reversing direction at the limits (0° or 180°) with a conditional check.

Optimization and Variations

Fine-tuning parameters such as delay timing, step size, and angular position allows for precise and responsive movement control, which is essential in robotics, automation, and mechatronic systems. The following variations illustrate how adjusting these parameters can optimize servo performance and expand functionality for more advanced IoT and embedded applications

- **Speed Adjustment**: Reduce `delay(15)` to 5ms for a faster sweep (1.8s cycle) or increase to 30ms for a slower one (10.8s cycle).
- **Step Size**: Use `angle += 5` for coarser steps (36 steps × 15ms ≈ 0.54s per direction) or `angle += 0.5` for finer control (360 steps × 15ms ≈ 5.4s per direction, if supported).

- **Multiple Servos**: Attach up to 12 servos (for example: pins 9, 10, 11) with `Servo servo2; servo2.attach(10);`, syncing movements with arrays.
- **Position Hold**: Add a `delay(1000)` at 90° to pause, for example, `if (angle == 90) delay(1000);`.

Interrupts versus Polling

As we deepen our understanding of microcontroller programming introduces a critical comparison between interrupts and polling, two methods for handling input events, this section begins with an in-depth exploration of the polling method, focusing on its implementation, mechanics, advantages, limitations, and practical use cases using a microcontroller such as the Arduino Uno or ESP32. Polling involves continuously checking the state of a pin within the `loop()` function, offering a straightforward approach to detect changes, but at the cost of efficiency. This detailed guide covers the polling process, hardware setup, and programming techniques.

Polling Method

The polling method is a simple technique where the microcontroller repeatedly checks the state of a digital input pin (for example, HIGH or LOW) inside the `loop()` function to detect events or changes, such as a button press or sensor trigger. This approach relies on the program actively querying the status of the pin at regular intervals, making it easy to implement for beginners but inherently inefficient due to its continuous operation. As the microcontroller dedicates CPU cycles to this task regardless of whether an event occurs, polling can lead to wasted resources, especially in complex projects with multiple tasks. Understanding the mechanics of polling and trade-offs is essential before exploring the more responsive interrupt method in the next subsection.

Mechanics of Polling

Polling operates by embedding a conditional check within the `loop()` function, which executes repeatedly as fast as the microcontroller allows (for example, thousands of times per second on an Arduino Uno). The program uses `digitalRead(pin)` to sample the pin state and compares it against a desired condition (for example: HIGH). If the condition is met, an action is triggered, such as toggling an LED or recording a timestamp. The frequency of checks depends on the `loop()` execution speed and any added delays, but without optimization, it can consume significant processing power. This constant monitoring, contrasts with event-driven methods like interrupts, where the microcontroller responds only when triggered.

Hardware Setup

A basic circuit is sufficient to demonstrate polling:

- **Components**: Gather an Arduino Uno, a breadboard, jumper wires, a pushbutton, a 10kΩ pull-down resistor, an LED, a 220Ω current-limiting resistor, and a USB cable.
- **Wiring**: Connect the pushbutton between a digital pin (for example: pin 2) and 5V, with the 10kΩ resistor from pin 2 to GND to ensure a stable LOW state when unpressed. Attach the LED anode to pin 13 (or pin 9 for PWM) via the 220Ω resistor, cathode to GND. Use red wire for positive connections and black for ground to maintain clarity.
- **Power Considerations**: The 5V pin of Arduino or USB supply (maximum 500mA) powers the circuit. The pull-down resistor prevents floating inputs, while the 220Ω resistor limits LED current to ~15mA (`I = (5V - 2V)/220Ω ≈ 0.0136A`), within the 20mA limit of the pin.

Programming Techniques

Polling is implemented with a simple loop structure:

- **Setup**: Configure the input pin with **`pinMode(pin, INPUT)`** (for example: **`pinMode(2, INPUT)`**) and the output pin with **`pinMode(pin, OUTPUT)`** (for example: **`pinMode(13, OUTPUT)`**).
- **Polling Logic**: Use a **`while`** or **`if`** statement with **`digitalRead(pin)`** to check the button state. For example, **`if (digitalRead(2) == HIGH)`** triggers an action when the button is pressed.
- **Debouncing**: Add a small delay (like 50ms) or a state machine to handle button bounce, where mechanical switches create multiple false triggers.
- **Monitoring**: Use **`Serial.println()`** to log state changes, aiding debugging.

Optimization and Variations

Fine-tuning delay intervals, employing non-blocking techniques, and integrating threshold-based logic help enhance both performance and reliability—particularly in applications requiring real-time decision-making. The following variations demonstrate practical ways to optimize input detection, and expand functionality for more advanced and efficient embedded system designs:

- **Speed Adjustment**: Reduce **`delay(50)`** to 20ms for quicker response or increase to 100ms for heavier debounce, balancing speed and stability.
- **Multiple Inputs**: Poll pins 2, 3, and 4 with an array: **`int pins[] = {2, 3, 4}; for (int i: pins) if (digitalRead(i) == HIGH) { /* action */ }`**.
- **Non-blocking Polling**: Use **`millis()`** to check state changes without **`delay()`**, for example : **`if (millis() - lastTime >= 50 && digitalRead(2) == HIGH) { /* action */ lastTime = millis(); }`**.
- **Threshold Monitoring**: For analog inputs (for example: pin A0), use **`analogRead()`** with **`if (analogRead(A0) > 512)`** to trigger at half range (2.5V on 5V scale).

Interrupt Concept

Interrupts provide an event-driven mechanism where the microcontroller pauses its current execution to immediately handle a specific event by jumping to an Interrupt Service Routine (ISR), a dedicated function designed to manage that event. Unlike polling, which continuously monitors pin states and wastes CPU cycles, interrupts are triggered only when an event occurs, such as a pin changing from LOW to HIGH or a timer expiring, allowing the microcontroller to focus on other tasks until needed. This approach enhances efficiency, especially in multitasking environments, and is critical for time-sensitive operations in IoT systems. Understanding interrupts' operation and implementation is the key to optimizing microcontroller performance.

Mechanics of Interrupts

Interrupts work by leveraging the hardware capabilities of microcontroller to detect events and respond instantly. When an interrupt condition is met- for example: a rising edge on a pin or a timer overflow, the CPU saves its current context (program counter, registers) on the stack, disables further interrupts to prevent nesting (unless configured otherwise), and jumps to the ISR. The ISR executes the required action, such as toggling an LED or logging data, then restores the context and resumes the main program. Common interrupt sources include external pins (for example: INT0, INT1 on Arduino), timers, or internal peripherals. The ISR must be short and non-blocking to avoid delaying the main loop, typically avoiding **`delay()`** or complex operations.

Types of Interrupts

Interrupts enable microcontrollers to respond immediately to important events without constantly checking input states in the main loop. They form the backbone of responsive and efficient embedded systems, allowing real-time reactions to signals such as button presses, sensor triggers, or timed operations. Depending on the source and application, different types of interrupts can be utilized to handle various scenarios effectively. The following are the primary types of interrupts commonly used in microcontroller-based systems:

- **External Interrupts**: Triggered by changes on specific pins (for example: pins 2 and 3 on Arduino Uno), configurable for rising for example falling for example or both (change). **Example**: `attachInterrupt(digitalPinToInterrupt(2), ISR, RISING)`.
- **Timer Interrupts**: Generated by hardware timers at set intervals (for example: every 1ms), useful for periodic tasks such as PWM or sampling. **Example**: `Timer1.initialize(1000000); Timer1.attachInterrupt(ISR);` (using a library).
- **Pin Change Interrupts**: Available on most pins (for example: ESP32), detecting any state change, offering broader coverage but requiring careful filtering.

Hardware Setup

A simple circuit demonstrates external interrupts:

- **Components**: Gather an Arduino Uno, a breadboard, jumper wires, a pushbutton, a 10kΩ pull-down resistor, an LED, a 220Ω current-limiting resistor, and a USB cable.
- **Wiring**: Connect the pushbutton between an interrupt pin (for example: `pin 2`, `INT0`) and 5V, with the 10kΩ resistor from pin 2 to GND to ensure a stable LOW state when unpressed. Attach the LED anode to pin 13 via the 220Ω resistor, cathode to GND. Use red wire for positive and black for ground.
- **Power Considerations**: The 5V pin of Arduino or USB supply (max 500mA) powers the circuit. The pull-down resistor prevents floating inputs, while the 220Ω resistor limits LED current to ~15mA ($I = (5V - 2V)/220\Omega \approx 0.0136A$), within the 20mA limit of the pin.

Programming Techniques

Interrupts require careful setup and ISR design:

- **Setup:** Use `attachInterrupt(digitalPinToInterrupt(pin), ISR, mode)` to link a pin (for example: 2) to an ISR function with a mode (for example: `RISING`, `FALLING`, `CHANGE`). **Example**: `attachInterrupt(digitalPinToInterrupt(2), buttonISR, RISING)`.
- **ISR Definition**: Define the ISR as `void ISR() { /* action */ }`, keeping it minimal (for example: toggle a flag or variable). **Example**: `volatile bool ledState = false; void buttonISR() { ledState = !ledState; }`.
- **Main Loop**: Check the flag or variable in `loop()` to perform actions, avoiding direct I/O in the ISR. Use `volatile` for shared variables to prevent compiler optimization issues.
- **Disabling Interrupts**: Use `noInterrupts()` and `interrupts()` to manage critical sections, though this is rare with proper ISR design.

Optimization and Variations

Proper optimization ensures that interrupts execute efficiently without blocking other critical tasks, while variations such as debouncing, multiple interrupt sources, and timer-based triggers make the system more adaptable to complex real-world conditions. The following techniques highlight practical ways to enhance and extend interrupt-driven designs for robust IoT and embedded applications.

- **Debouncing**: Add a 50ms delay in `loop()` after toggling, for example : `if (millis() - lastToggle >= 50) { /* action */ lastToggle = millis(); }`, since ISRs cannot use `delay()`.
- **Multiple Interrupts**: Use pins 2 and 3 with separate ISRs: `attachInterrupt (digitalPinToInterrupt(3), secondISR, FALLING)`.
- **Timer Interrupts**: Use a library like `TimerOne` for periodic tasks: `Timer1.initialize(500000); Timer1.attachInterrupt(timerISR);`.
- **Edge Sensitivity**: Switch to `CHANGE` mode for both press and release detection.

Using Interrupts in ESP32/Arduino

Interrupts on the ESP32 and Arduino enable event-driven programming by allowing the microcontroller to pause its main execution and jump to an ISR when a specific condition is met, such as a pin state change or timer event. The ESP32, with its dual-core architecture and up to 22 interrupt-capable GPIO pins, offers advanced flexibility compared to the Arduino Uno, which supports external interrupts on pins 2 and 3 (INT0 and INT1) using the `attachInterrupt()` function. Both platforms leverage hardware interrupts to handle tasks such as button debouncing, motor control, or sensor monitoring with minimal CPU overhead. Mastering interrupt usage on these platforms enhances IoT project responsiveness and efficiency.

Interrupt Configuration

Each platform offers unique capabilities and constraints in terms of available interrupt pins, trigger modes, and hardware support. The following section compares how interrupts are set up and managed on the Arduino Uno and ESP32, highlighting their configuration methods, advantages, and limitations.

- **Arduino Uno**:
  - Supports two external interrupts on pins 2 (INT0) and 3 (INT1).
  - **Configurable modes:** `LOW` (trigger on LOW), `CHANGE` (any edge), `RISING` (rising edge), `FALLING` (falling edge).
  - **Setup:** `attachInterrupt(digitalPinToInterrupt(pin), ISR, mode)` links a pin to an ISR with the specified mode.
  - **Limitation:** Uses Timer1, restricting PWM on pins 9 and 10 when multiple servos are attached.
- **ESP32**:
  - Supports interrupts on any GPIO pin (0–39, excluding input-only pins like 34–39).
  - **Configurable triggers:** `RISING`, `FALLING`, `HIGH`, `LOW`, `CHANGE`, with edge or level sensitivity.
  - **Setup:** Use `attachInterrupt(digitalPinToInterrupt(pin), ISR, mode)` (Arduino core) or `gpio_isr_register()` (ESP-IDF) for advanced control.
  - **Advantage:** Dual-core support allows interrupt handling on one core while the main loop runs on the other, using `xTaskCreatePinnedToCore()`.

Hardware Setup

A consistent circuit works for both platforms:

- **Components**: Gather an ESP32 (for example: DevKit V1) or Arduino Uno, a breadboard, jumper wires, a pushbutton, a 10kΩ pull-down resistor, an LED, a 220Ω current-limiting resistor, and a USB cable.

- **Wiring**: Connect the pushbutton between an interrupt pin (for example: pin 2 on Arduino, GPIO 18 on ESP32) and 5V (Arduino) or 3.3V (ESP32), with the 10kΩ resistor from the pin to GND for a stable LOW state when unpressed. Attach the LED anode to pin 13 (Arduino) or GPIO 19 (ESP32) via the 220Ω resistor, cathode to GND. Use red wire for positive and black for ground.
- **Power Considerations**: 5V of Arduino or 3.3V of ESP32 (maximum 500mA) powers the circuit. The pull-down resistor prevents floating inputs, while the 220Ω resistor limits LED current to ~15mA (Arduino: I = (5V - 2V)/220Ω ≈ 0.0136A) or ~6mA (ESP32: I = (3.3V - 2V)/220Ω ≈ 0.0061A), within pin limits.

Programming Techniques

The techniques for managing interrupts vary slightly between microcontrollers such as the Arduino Uno and ESP32, primarily due to differences in architecture and multitasking support. The following examples outline how to define, attach, and manage ISRs on both platforms for optimal operation:

- **Arduino**:
    - **Define the ISR:** `void ISR() { /* action */ }`, for example : `volatile bool ledState = false; void buttonISR() { ledState = !ledState; }`.
    - **Setup:** `attachInterrupt(digitalPinToInterrupt(2), buttonISR, RISING)`.
    - **Main Loop:** Check `ledState` to update outputs, avoiding I/O in the ISR.
- **ESP32**:
    - **Define the ISR:** Similar to Arduino, but uses `gpio_install_isr_service(0)` for multiple pins if needed.
    - **Setup:** `attachInterrupt(digitalPinToInterrupt(18), buttonISR, RISING);` or use `gpio_config_t` for custom configurations.
    - **Dual-Core:** Assign ISR to core 0, main loop to core 1: `xTaskCreatePinnedToCore (loopTask, "loop", 2048, NULL, 1, NULL, 1);`.

Optimization and Variations

Optimization focuses on improving stability, handling multiple sources efficiently, and ensuring smooth multitasking without unintended triggers. The following techniques highlight key methods for refining interrupt-based designs on both Arduino and ESP32 platforms.

- **Debouncing**: Add a 50ms check in `loop()`: `if (millis() - lastToggle >= 50) { /* action */ lastToggle = millis(); }`.
- **Multiple Interrupts**: Arduino: Use pin 3; ESP32: Add GPIO 19 with `attachInterrupt (digitalPinToInterrupt(19), secondISR, FALLING);`.
- **Timer Interrupts**: Arduino: Use `TimerOne` library; ESP32: Use `hw_timer_t` for periodic tasks.
- **Priority**: ESP32 allows interrupt priority via `gpio_isr_handler_add()`, though rarely needed.

Edge Triggers

Edge triggers are a fundamental aspect of interrupt programming, determining the specific voltage transition on a pin that activates an Interrupt Service Routine (ISR). These triggers allow the microcontroller to respond only to defined events, optimizing resource use compared to level-sensitive interrupts. The three main edge trigger types are:

- `RISING`: Detects a transition from LOW to HIGH, typically when a button is pressed or a signal rises above a threshold (for example: 0V to 3.3V/5V).

- **`FALLING`**: Detects a transition from HIGH to LOW, often triggered by a button release or a signal dropping below a threshold.
- **`CHANGE`**: Detects either transition (LOW to HIGH or HIGH to LOW), offering flexibility for bidirectional event monitoring.

Mastering these triggers enhances the ability to design responsive IoT solutions, from simple input detection to complex real-time systems.

Mechanics of Edge Triggers

Edge triggers rely on the hardware of microcontroller to monitor pin voltage changes and generate an interrupt signal. The process involves:

- **`RISING` Trigger**: The ISR fires when the pin voltage shifts from below the logic threshold (for example: 1.5V on 5V systems) to above it, indicating the start of an event. This is ideal for detecting the initial press of a mechanical switch.
- **`FALLING` Trigger**: The ISR activates when the voltage drops from above to below the threshold, marking the end of an event, such as a button release or signal decay.
- **`CHANGE` Trigger**: The ISR triggers on any, for example, capturing both press and release or any signal fluctuation, useful for monitoring dynamic inputs like rotary encoders.

The microcontroller debounces these transitions internally or via software, ensuring a single interrupt per physical event. Timer synchronization may adjust for slight variations in edge detection timing.

Hardware Setup

A versatile circuit supports edge trigger testing:

- **Components**: Gather an Arduino Uno or ESP32 (for example: DevKit V1), a breadboard, jumper wires, a pushbutton, a 10kΩ pull-down resistor, an LED, a 220Ω current-limiting resistor, and a USB cable.
- **Wiring**: Connect the pushbutton between an interrupt pin (for example: pin 2 on Arduino, GPIO 18 on ESP32) and 5V (Arduino) or 3.3V (ESP32), with the 10kΩ resistor from the pin to GND to ensure a stable LOW state when unpressed. Attach the LED anode to pin 13 (Arduino) or GPIO 19 (ESP32) via the 220Ω resistor, cathode to GND. Use red wire for positive and black for ground.
- **Power Considerations**: 5V of Arduino or 3.3V of ESP32 (maximum 500mA) powers the circuit. The pull-down resistor prevents floating inputs, while the 220Ω resistor limits LED current to ~15mA (Arduino: $I = (5V - 2V)/220\Omega \approx 0.0136A$) or ~6mA (ESP32: $I = (3.3V - 2V)/220\Omega \approx 0.0061A$), within pin limits.

Programming Techniques

Edge triggers are configured with interrupt functions:

- **Setup**: Use `attachInterrupt(digitalPinToInterrupt(pin), ISR, mode)` with `mode` as `RISING`, `FALLING`, or `CHANGE`. **Example**: `attachInterrupt(digitalPinToInterrupt(2), buttonISR, CHANGE);`.
- **ISR Definition**: Define `void ISR() { /* action */ }`, for example: `volatile int edgeCount = 0; void buttonISR() { edgeCount++; }` to track transitions.
- **Main Loop**: Process ISR actions (for example: toggle LED) based on a flag or counter, avoiding direct I/O in the ISR.

- **Debouncing**: Implement a delay or timestamp check in `loop()` (for example : `if (millis() - lastEdge >= 50) { /* action */ }`) to filter bounce.

Optimization and Variations

Optimizing interrupt parameters allows smoother interaction, reduced false triggers, and better data handling across multiple input sources. The following approaches help refine and extend interrupt-driven systems for greater reliability and control:

- **Speed Adjustment**: Reduce debouncing to 20ms for quicker response or increase to 100ms for noisier switches.
- **Specific Triggers**: Use `RISING` or `FALLING` alone: `attachInterrupt (digitalPinToInterrupt(2), buttonISR, RISING);` to focus on presses.
- **Multiple Pins**: Monitor pins 2 and 3 (Arduino) or GPIO 18 and 19 (ESP32) with separate ISRs: `attachInterrupt(digitalPinToInterrupt(3), secondISR, FALLING)`.
- **Edge Logging**: Store timestamps in an array (for example: `unsigned long edges[10];`) for analysis.

Power and Timing Considerations

Following our exploration of interrupts and edge triggers, we now address critical power and timing considerations. This section delves into optimizing microcontroller performance for IoT projects using platforms such as the Arduino Uno and ESP32. Key factors include the limited current capacity of GPIO pins (approximately 20 mA on Arduino), the use of transistors or MOSFETs for higher loads, the addition of delay or debounce logic for mechanical switches, and the application of capacitors or RC filters for clean PWM output. These considerations ensure reliability, efficiency, and precision in power delivery and signal timing. This detailed guide covers the mechanics of each aspect, hardware setup, and programming techniques.

Power and Timing

Effective power and timing management are necessary for robust microcontroller-based systems. Each GPIO pin on an Arduino Uno can source or sink approximately 20 mA, a limit that restricts direct connection to high-current devices. For higher loads, transistors or MOSFETs act as switches to handle increased current while protecting the microcontroller. Mechanical switches require delay or debounce logic to filter noise from physical contact bounce, ensuring accurate event detection. Additionally, capacitors or RC filters smooth PWM output, reducing noise and improving signal quality for applications such as motor control or LED fading. Mastering these techniques enhances IoT project durability and performance.

Mechanics of Power and Timing

Each component—from current-driving capability to signal conditioning—plays a vital role in ensuring stable operation, especially when dealing with motors, relays, or mechanical switches. The following key principles highlight how to manage power safely and maintain accurate signal timing in practical IoT and embedded designs:

- **GPIO Current Limits**: Arduino Uno GPIO pins are rated for 20 mA per pin, with a total of 200 mA across all pins and 50 mA per port to avoid damage. Exceeding this requires external amplification. ESP32 pins handle ~20 mA at 3.3V, with similar total limits.
- **Transistors/MOSFETs**: These components amplify current, with NPN transistors (for example: BC547) or N-channel MOSFETs (for example: IRF540) switching loads up to several amps when controlled by a GPIO via a base/gate resistor (for example: 1kΩ).

- **Debounce Logic**: Mechanical switches create 5-20ms of bounce, triggering multiple false edges. Delay (for example: 50ms) or a state machine filters this, ensuring one event per press.
- **Capacitors/RC Filters**: A capacitor (for example: 0.1µF) across PWM pins or an RC filter (for example: 10kΩ resistor + 10µF capacitor) smoothens the square waves of PWM into a cleaner analog signal, reducing motor whine or LED flicker.

Hardware Setup

A practical circuit incorporates these considerations:

- **Components**: Gather an Arduino Uno or ESP32, a breadboard, jumper wires, a pushbutton, a 10kΩ pull-down resistor, an LED, a 220Ω resistor, an NPN transistor (for example: BC547), a 1kΩ base resistor, a 12V DC motor, a 0.1µF capacitor, a 10kΩ resistor, a 10µF capacitor, and a 12V power supply.
- **Wiring**:
  - Connect the pushbutton between pin 2 and 5V (Arduino) or 3.3V (ESP32), with a 10kΩ resistor from pin 2 to GND.
  - Attach the LED anode to pin 9 via a 220Ω resistor, cathode to GND.
  - For the motor: Connect the transistor collector to the motor, emitter to GND, and base to pin 3 via a 1kΩ resistor. Link the other terminal of the motor to 12V+, with a 0.1µF capacitor across motor terminals to reduce noise.
  - Add an RC filter: Place a 10kΩ resistor between pin 9 and the LED, with a 10µF capacitor from the resistor-LED junction to GND.
- **Power Considerations**: Use a 12V supply for the motor, with 5V of Arduino or 3.3V of ESP32 for logic. The transistor handles motor current (~200mA), while the 220Ω resistor limits LED current to ~15mA (Arduino) or ~6mA (ESP32).

Optimization and Variations

The following practical optimizations show how to safely increase current capacity, tune debounce behavior for different switch types, smooth PWM outputs for quieter operation, and drive multiple loads in parallel—each change balancing performance, responsiveness, and hardware complexity.

- **Current Boost**: Replace the transistor with a MOSFET (for example: IRF540) for loads up to 10A, adjusting the gate resistor to 100Ω.
- **Debounce Tuning**: Adjust delay to 20ms for faster response or 100ms for noisier switches.
- **PWM Smoothing**: Increase the RC filter capacitor to 100µF for slower PWM frequencies or add a 1kΩ series resistor.
- **Multiple Loads**: Use additional transistors for multiple motors, each on a separate pin.

Mini Projects

Following our detailed exploration of power and timing, we now move to hands-on applications. This section kicks off with a practical mini project: a touchless switch using interrupts. This project leverages an IR sensor or ultrasonic sensor, a relay, and an LED to create a hands-free switching system for IoT applications such as door automation or hygiene-focused controls. The logic involves triggering an interrupt when an object is detected, toggling the relay to control a load (for example, a light or fan), and providing visual feedback via the LED. This detailed guide covers the mechanics of the project, hardware setup, programming techniques, a comprehensive coding.

Touchless Switch Using Interrupts

The touchless switch project uses an interrupt-driven approach to detect objects without physical contact, enhancing safety and convenience. An IR sensor (for example: TCRT5000) or ultrasonic sensor (for example: HC-SR04) monitors the proximity of an object, triggering an interrupt when the distance falls below a threshold (for example: 10cm). This event toggles a relay, which switches a connected load (for example: 220V appliance), while an LED provides visual confirmation. The ESP32 or Arduino Uno handles the interrupt, ensuring an immediate response. This project demonstrates a real-world interrupt application in IoT, suitable for smart homes or public spaces.

Mechanics of the Touchless Switch

By leveraging sensors such as infrared or ultrasonic modules, it detects an approaching hand or object and responds instantly through an interrupt-driven mechanism. This design minimizes wear and tear, enhances hygiene, and delivers a seamless user experience ideal for smart appliances or automated environments. The following components and processes outline the core mechanics of a touchless switch system.

- **Sensor Operation**:
  - **IR Sensor**: Emits infrared light and measures reflection; a drop in output voltage indicates an object within range (typically 2–30cm).
  - **Ultrasonic Sensor**: Sends sound waves and calculates distance (for example: <10cm) using echo time; a LOW-to-HIGH transition on the echo pin triggers the interrupt.
- **Interrupt Trigger**: Configured for `RISING` or `CHANGE`, the ISR toggles a flag when the sensor detects an object, avoiding continuous polling.
- **Relay Control**: A 5V relay module, driven by a GPIO pin, switches the load when activated, isolated via an optocoupler for safety.
- **LED Feedback**: The LED blinks to confirm detection, synchronized with the relay state.

Hardware Setup

A well-designed circuit ensures safe operation:

1. **Components**: Gather an ESP32 (for example: DevKit V1) or Arduino Uno, a breadboard, jumper wires, an IR sensor (TCRT5000) or ultrasonic sensor (HC-SR04), a 5V relay module, an LED, a 220Ω current-limiting resistor, a 12V/5V power supply, and a USB cable.
2. **Wiring (IR Sensor)**:
   a. Connect the VCC of IR sensor to 5V, GND to GND, and output to an interrupt pin (for example: GPIO 18 on ESP32, pin 2 on Arduino).
   b. Attach the VCC of the relay module to 5V, GND to GND, and IN to GPIO 19 (ESP32) or pin 3 (Arduino).
   c. Link the LED anode to GPIO 21 (ESP32) or pin 13 (Arduino) via a 220Ω resistor, cathode to GND.
   d. Connect the COM and NO terminals of the relay to a 220V load (for example: lamp) and 220V supply, ensuring proper isolation.
3. **Wiring (Ultrasonic Sensor)**:
   a. Connect VCC to 5V, GND to GND, Trig to GPIO 5 (ESP32) or pin 9 (Arduino), and Echo to GPIO 18 (ESP32) or pin 2 (Arduino).
   b. Follow the same relay and LED wiring as earlier.

4. **Power Considerations**: Use a 12V/5V supply for the relay and sensor, with the microcontroller powered via USB (500mA max). The 220Ω resistor limits LED current to ~15mA (Arduino) or ~6mA (ESP32). A fly back diode across the relay coil prevents voltage spikes.

Programming Techniques

Implement interrupt-driven logic:

- **Setup**: Configure pins: `pinMode(18, INPUT); pinMode(19, OUTPUT); pinMode(21, OUTPUT);` (ESP32 example). Use `attachInterrupt(digitalPinToInterrupt(18), sensorISR, RISING)`.
- **ISR Definition**: `void sensorISR() { toggle = !toggle; }` sets a `volatile bool toggle` flag.
- **Main Loop**: Check the flag to control the relay and LED, for example: `if (toggle) { digitalWrite(19, HIGH); digitalWrite(21, HIGH); } else { digitalWrite(19, LOW); digitalWrite(21, LOW); }`.
- **Ultrasonic Logic**: Use `pulseIn(18, HIGH)` to measure echo time, converting to distance (distance = pulse/58 for cm), and trigger if <10cm.

Optimization and Variations

After implementing the basic touchless switch functionality, several refinements can enhance responsiveness, usability, and system reliability. Adjusting detection thresholds, timing intervals, and feedback mechanisms allows for smoother interaction and reduced false triggering. The following optimizations illustrate how to fine-tune sensing behavior, provide intuitive visual feedback, and expand functionality to support multiple sensors and controlled relay timing.

- **Distance Threshold**: For ultrasonic, add `long duration = pulseIn(sensorPin, HIGH); int distance = duration / 58; if (distance < 10 && millis() - lastToggle >= 50) { toggle = !toggle; }`.
- **Blink Feedback**: Add `if (toggle) digitalWrite(ledPin, (millis() / 500) % 2);` for a blinking LED.
- **Multiple Sensors**: Use GPIO 18 and 19 with separate ISRs for dual zones.
- **Relay Delay**: Add a 500ms ON delay: `if (toggle && millis() - lastToggle >= 500) digitalWrite(relayPin, HIGH);`.

Smart Lighting with PWM Brightness Control

The smart lighting system leverages an LDR to detect ambient light intensity, converting resistance changes into voltage variations read by an analog pin. The microcontroller (for example: Arduino Uno or ESP32) processes this data and uses PWM to adjust the brightness of LED strip, ensuring consistent lighting regardless of external conditions. The PWM duty cycle (0–255) maps to brightness levels, with lower ambient light triggering higher intensity and vice versa, optimizing energy use. This project exemplifies sensor-driven automation, enhancing comfort and efficiency in IoT setups.

Mechanics of Smart Lighting

The smart lighting system intelligently adapts brightness based on ambient light levels, combining sensor input with PWM-based LED control. Using an LDR (Light Dependent Resistor) as the primary sensing element, the circuit dynamically regulates illumination to maintain optimal visibility while conserving energy. The following points outline the working principles that govern sensor response, signal conversion, and brightness modulation in such systems.

- **LDR Operation**: The resistance of LDR decreases with increasing light (for example: 1kΩ in bright light, 100kΩ in dark), forming a voltage divider with a fixed resistor (for example: 10kΩ). The analog voltage (0–5V or 0–3.3V) reflects ambient levels, read via analogRead() (0–1023).
- **PWM Control**: The LED strip, driven by a PWM-capable pin, adjusts brightness based on the duty cycle. A 25% duty cycle (for example: 64/255) provides dim light, while 100% (255/255) offers full brightness, smoothed by an optional RC filter.
- **Mapping Logic**: The analog reading is mapped to a PWM range (for example: `map(sensorValue, 0, 1023, 255, 0)`), inverting the relationship so brightness increases as light decreases.
- **Power Management**: The LED strip (for example: 12V, 1A) requires a transistor or MOSFET for current amplification, as GPIO pins limit output to ~20 mA.

Hardware Setup

A robust circuit supports the smart lighting system:

- **Components**: Gather an Arduino Uno or ESP32 (for example: DevKit V1), a breadboard, jumper wires, an LDR, a 10kΩ resistor, an LED strip (12V, addressable or single-color), an NPN transistor (for example: BC547), a 1kΩ base resistor, a 12V power supply, a 0.1µF capacitor, and a USB cable.
- **Wiring**:
  - Connect the LDR and 10kΩ resistor in series between 5V (Arduino) or 3.3V (ESP32) and GND, with the junction to an analog pin (for example: A0).
  - Attach the ground of the LED strip to the transistor collector, the 12V+ to the positive of the strip, and the transistor emitter to GND. Connect the transistor base to a PWM pin (for example: pin 9 on Arduino, GPIO 18 on ESP32) via a 1kΩ resistor.
  - Add a 0.1µF capacitor across the LED strip terminals to reduce PWM noise.
  - Use red wire for positive and black for ground.
- **Power Considerations**: The 12V supply powers the LED strip, with the microcontroller powered via USB (500mA max). The 1kΩ resistor limits base current to ~5mA, while the transistor handles the load of the strip(for example: 1A). A fly back diode across the strip prevents voltage spikes.

Programming Techniques

Implement sensor-driven PWM control:

- **Setup**: Configure pins: `pinMode(A0, INPUT); pinMode(9, OUTPUT);` (Arduino example). Initialize PWM with `analogWrite(9, 0);`.
- **Reading Logic**: Use `int sensorValue = analogRead(A0);` to get the LDR voltage, applying a moving average (for example: `sensorValue = (sensorValue + lastValue) / 2;`) for stability.
- **PWM Adjustment**: Map the value: `int brightness = map(sensorValue, 0, 1023, 255, 0); analogWrite(9, brightness);` to adjust brightness inversely.
- **Smoothing**: Add a delay (for example: 100ms) or an exponential filter (for example: `brightness = (brightness * 0.9) + (newBrightness * 0.1);`) to reduce flicker.

Optimization and Variations

The core smart lighting circuit is functional, fine-tuning its behavior can significantly enhance responsiveness, stability, and adaptability to varying ambient conditions. Adjusting thresholds, transition speed, and calibration parameters allows the system to respond naturally to real-world lighting changes. The following refinements help optimize performance and expand the design for multiple lighting zones or custom brightness control:

- **Threshold Control**: Add `if (smoothedValue < 500) brightness = 255; else brightness = 0;` for on/off behavior.
- **Fade Speed**: Reduce `delay(100)` to 50ms for faster response or increase to 200ms for smoother transitions.
- **Multiple Strips**: Use pins 9 and 10 with separate transistors and `analogWrite(10, brightness)`.
- **Calibration**: Adjust the `map()` range (for example: 200, 800) based on LDR response in your environment.

Conclusion

This chapter has significantly expanded your expertis, building on the sensing foundations laid in the previous chapter by introducing real-time control techniques essential for IoT development. You have gained a comprehensive understanding of several key concepts and skills that empower you to create responsive, intelligent systems. You have learned how to effectively use GPIO pins for digital input and output, mastering the interaction between hardware and software through simple yet powerful circuits. The principles of Pulse Width Modulation (PWM) were explored, enabling you to control brightness and speed with analog-like precision, a critical skill for dynamic lighting or motor applications. You have also mastered manipulating servo motors using precise pulse signals, allowing for accurate angle positioning in robotic contexts. Additionally, the chapter introduced interrupts, teaching you how to implement event-driven, non-blocking code that enhances system efficiency by responding instantly to external triggers. Power and safety considerations were emphasized, ensuring that you can drive hardware reliably, while protecting both the microcontroller and connected devices from damage.

The mini-projects showcased in this chapter, such as the touchless switch, smart lighting, and servo-controlled systems, demonstrated the practical application of GPIO, PWM, and interrupts. These projects brought reactivity and intelligence to IoT devices, illustrating how sensors, actuators, and real-time control can transform a simple microcontroller into a smart, interactive solution. From automating lighting based on ambient conditions to creating touchless interfaces and precise robotic movements, you have seen how these techniques integrate to solve real-world problems. The practical exercises further solidified your skills, challenging you to handle digital I/O, simulate PWM fades, and command servo angles, preparing you for more advanced projects.

Looking ahead, *Chapter 8, Serial Communication and Data Transmission between Devices* will build on this foundation by exploring the most fundamental method of data exchange in embedded systems—serial communication. Before diving into Wi-Fi or cloud connectivity, IoT devices must communicate effectively with one another. This chapter will guide you through scenarios such as an Arduino sending data to a Raspberry Pi or a NodeMCU logging sensor values to a computer, all made possible by serial protocols. You will gain hands-on experience with UART, SPI, and I2C protocols, learning how to debug sensor data using the Serial Monitor, facilitate communication between boards, and transfer information to computers and cloud gateways. By the end, you will understand how information flows reliably and in sync within the hardware layer, setting the stage for networked IoT systems.

This chapter has equipped you with the tools to control hardware in real time, blending theory with practice to foster a deep, actionable understanding of IoT control systems.

Practical Exercises

Following the mini projects, we now transition to hands-on skill-building. This section introduces practical exercises to reinforce your understanding of microcontroller programming. We begin with Exercise 1: GPIO Ninja – Input/Output Challenge example, designed to help you master digital input and output handling using a button and an LED or buzzer on an ESP32 or Arduino platform. This exercise focuses on configuring GPIO pins, detecting state changes, and logging data, providing a foundational skill for IoT development.

Exercise 1: GPIO Ninja - Input/Output Challenge

The GPIO Ninja challenges you with creating a simple circuit to test digital input and output capabilities. The goal is to connect a button to a GPIO pin (for example: GPIO 15) with a pull-down resistor, link an LED or buzzer to another GPIO pin (for example: GPIO 2), and log state changes in the Serial Monitor. This exercise teaches you to handle button presses as inputs, control an output device (LED or buzzer), and monitor system behavior, laying the groundwork for more complex IoT projects. Mastering these basics is crucial for effective microcontroller programming.

Mechanics of the GPIO Challenge

- **Digital Input**: The button, when pressed, pulls GPIO 15 `HIGH` (for example: 3.3V on ESP32, 5V on Arduino), with a 10kΩ pull-down resistor ensuring a stable LOW state when unpressed. This binary input triggers state changes.
- **Digital Output**: GPIO 2 drives the LED (turning it `ON/OFF`) or buzzer (activating/deactivating a tone), with a current-limiting resistor protecting the circuit.
- **State Logging**: The Serial Monitor displays button states (`HIGH/LOW`) and corresponding output actions, providing real-time feedback for debugging and learning.
- **Timing**: Basic debounce logic ensures accurate detection, filtering mechanical switch bounce (typically 5–20ms).

Hardware Setup

A straightforward circuit supports the exercise:

- **Components**: Gather an ESP32 (for example: DevKit V1) or Arduino Uno, a breadboard, jumper wires, a pushbutton, a 10kΩ pull-down resistor, an LED, a 220Ω current-limiting resistor, a buzzer (optional, with built-in driver), and a USB cable.
- **Wiring**:
  - Connect the pushbutton between GPIO 15 and 3.3V (ESP32) or 5V (Arduino), with the 10kΩ resistor from GPIO 15 to GND to create a pull-down configuration.
  - Attach the LED anode to GPIO 2 via a 220Ω resistor, cathode to GND. (For a buzzer, connect its positive to GPIO 2 via 220Ω, negative to GND.)
  - Use red wire for positive and black for ground.
- **Power Considerations**: The 3.3V of ESP32 or 5V of Arduino (max 500mA via USB) powers the circuit. The 220Ω resistor limits LED current to ~15mA (Arduino: $I = (5V - 2V)/220\Omega \approx 0.0136A$) or ~6mA (ESP32: $I = (3.3V - 2V)/220\Omega \approx 0.0061A$), within pin limits. The buzzer (if used) draws ~10–20mA.

Programming Techniques

Implement input/output and logging:

- **Setup**: Configure pins: `pinMode(15, INPUT); pinMode(2, OUTPUT);` (ESP32 example). Initialize output: `digitalWrite(2, LOW);`.

- **Input Detection**: Use `int state = digitalRead(15);` to read the button state, applying debounce with a timestamp (for example: `if (millis() - lastPress >= 50 && state == HIGH)`).
- **Output Control**: Toggle the LED/buzzer with `digitalWrite(2, state);` or use `tone(2, 1000)` for a buzzer beep (Arduino only).
- **Logging**: Use `Serial.println("Button State: " + String(state));` to log changes.

Optimization and Variations

These optimizations refine timing accuracy, user response, and output diversity, making the design more responsive and feature-rich. The following variations demonstrate practical methods to expand functionality, enhance usability, and introduce audio-visual feedback mechanisms.

- **Buzzer Tone**: Replace `digitalWrite` with `tone(2, 1000, 100);` for a 1kHz beep lasting 100ms (Arduino only).
- **Debounce Tuning**: Adjust delay to 20ms for faster response or 100ms for noisier switches.
- **Multiple Outputs**: Add GPIO 4 for a second LED: `pinMode(4, OUTPUT); digitalWrite(4, !currentState);`.
- **State Counter**: Track presses: `static int pressCount = 0; if (currentState == HIGH) pressCount++; Serial.println(pressCount);`.

Exercise 2: Brightness Boss – PWM Fade Simulation

The Brightness Boss challenges you with mastering PWM to fade the brightness of an LED, mimicking analog control with digital signals. PWM adjusts the duty cycle (0-255) on a GPIO pin, creating the illusion of smooth brightness changes. The exercise connects an LED to GPIO 18 (ESP32) or pin 9 (Arduino Uno), configures the pin for PWM output, and implements a loop to fade the LED in and out by incrementally adjusting the duty cycle. This builds proficiency in timing and output modulation, essential for dynamic IoT projects. This exercise strengthens your control over microcontroller outputs.

Mechanics of PWM Fade Simulation

The microcontroller creates the illusion of gradual fading, even though the output remains purely digital. This technique effectively bridges the gap between binary control and analog-like behavior, offering fine-grained regulation of brightness, speed, or tone. The following points outline the operational principles that define PWM-based fade simulation:

- **PWM Basics**: PWM generates a square wave with a variable duty cycle, where a 50% duty cycle (127/255) produces half brightness, and 100% (255/255) yields full brightness. The LED appears to fade due to persistence of vision.
- **Fade Loop**: The program increments the duty cycle from 0 to 255 (fade-in) and decrements from 255 to 0 (fade-out), with a delay controlling the transition speed (for example: 10ms per step).
- **Pin Configuration**: ESP32 uses the LED Control library for precise PWM, while `analogWrite()` of Arduino simplifies the process, both leveraging hardware timers.
- **Timing**: The delay of the loop ensures visible fading, typically 5-20ms per step, balancing smoothness and responsiveness.

Hardware Setup

A simple circuit supports the PWM fade:

- **Components**: Gather an ESP32 (for example: DevKit V1) or Arduino Uno, a breadboard, jumper wires, an LED, a 220Ω current-limiting resistor, and a USB cable.
- **Wiring**:
    - Connect the LED anode to GPIO 18 (ESP32) or pin 9 (Arduino Uno) via a 220Ω resistor, with the cathode to GND.
    - Use red wire for the anode and black for the cathode.
- **Power Considerations**: The 3.3V of ESP32 or 5V of Arduino (max 500mA via USB) powers the circuit. The 220Ω resistor limits LED current to ~15mA (Arduino: I = (5V - 2V)/220Ω ≈ 0.0136A) or ~6mA (ESP32: I = (3.3V - 2V)/220Ω ≈ 0.0061A), within pin limits.

Programming Techniques

Implement PWM and fading logic:

- **Setup**: Configure the PWM pin. For ESP32: `ledcSetup(0, 5000, 8); ledcAttachPin(18, 0);` (Channel 0, 5kHz, 8-bit resolution). For Arduino: `pinMode(9, OUTPUT);`.
- **Fade Loop**: Use a `for` loop to increment/decrement the duty cycle: `for (int duty = 0; duty <= 255; duty++) { /* set duty */ delay(10); }`.
- **PWM Output**: For ESP32: `ledcWrite(0, duty);`. For Arduino: `analogWrite(9, duty);`.
- **Timing Control**: Adjust `delay()` to control fade speed, ensuring smooth transitions without overwhelming the processor.

Step-by-Step Breakdown

The following procedure walks through a practical, hardware-first approach to implement a PWM fade on an LED using either an **ESP32** or an **Arduino Uno**. It covers wiring, PWM initialization, and the fade loop so you can reproduce the visual effect reliably on real hardware. Follow the steps exactly, and you will have a smooth fade-in / fade-out running in minutes:

1. **Connect the LED to GPIO 18 (ESP32) or 9 (Uno)**: Assemble the circuit by linking the LED anode to the specified PWM pin via a 220Ω resistor, and the cathode to GND. This step ensures the LED is ready for PWM control, with the resistor protecting the pin from excessive current.
2. **Use `ledcAttachPin()` or `analogWrite()`**: For ESP32, initialize PWM with `ledcSetup(0, 5000, 8)` to set up Channel 0 at 5kHz with 8-bit resolution, then `ledcAttachPin(18, 0)` to assign the pin. For Arduino, simply use `pinMode(9, OUTPUT)` to prepare the pin for `analogWrite()`. This configures the hardware for PWM output.
3. **Create Fade-in/Fade-out Loop**: Implement two `for` loops: one increments the duty cycle from 0 to 255 (fade-in) and another decrements from 255 to 0 (fade-out). Use `ledcWrite(0, duty)` (ESP32) or `analogWrite(9, duty)` (Arduino) inside the loops, with a `delay(10)` to control the fade speed. This creates the smooth brightness transition.

Optimization and Variations

- **Fade Speed**: Reduce `delay(10)` to 5ms for a faster fade or increase to 20ms for a slower effect.
- **Custom Range**: Modify the loop to fade from 50 to 200: `for (int duty = 50; duty <= 200; duty++)`.

- **Dual LEDs**: Add GPIO 19 (ESP32) or pin 10 (Arduino) with a second LED: **`ledcAttachPin(19, 1); ledcWrite(1, 255 - duty);`**.
- **Smooth Transition**: Use an exponential curve: **`int newDuty = duty * duty / 255;`** for a non-linear fade.

Exercise 3: Servo Commander – Angle Positioning Game

The Servo Commander challenges you with mastering servo motor control using PWM, simulating a game where you adjust the angle of the servo. A servo motor, connected to GPIO 5, rotates to specific angles (0–180°) based on user input. You can use two buttons to increment or decrement the angle by 15°, or a potentiometer to map its analog output (0–1023) to the 0–180° range, providing interactive control. This exercise builds proficiency in actuator manipulation, a cornerstone of robotic systems such as robotic arms or camera mounts. This hands-on task prepares you for advanced IoT projects.

Mechanics of Servo Control

- **Servo Operation:** The servo motor uses PWM signals (typically 50Hz, 500–2500µs pulse width) to set angles, where 500µs corresponds to 0°, 1500µs to 90°, and 2500µs to 180°. The **`Servo`** library handles this timing.
- **Button Control**: Two buttons on GPIO 14 (increase) and GPIO 27 (decrease) trigger angle adjustments of 15° per press, with debounce to filter noise.
- **Potentiometer Control**: A potentiometer on an analog pin (for example: A0) provides a variable voltage (0–3.3V/5V), mapped to 0–180° for continuous angle adjustment.
- **Positioning**: The servo moves smoothly to the new angle, with limits (0–180°) to prevent damage.

Hardware Setup

A functional circuit supports the exercise:

- **Components**: Gather an ESP32 (for example: DevKit V1) or Arduino Uno, a breadboard, jumper wires, a servo motor (for example: SG90), two pushbuttons, a 10kΩ pull-down resistor (per button), a potentiometer, an LED (optional feedback), a 220Ω current-limiting resistor, and a 5V/3.3V power supply or USB cable.
- **Wiring (Button Option)**:
  - Connect the servo signal to GPIO 5, VCC to 5V, and GND to GND.
  - Attach the first button between GPIO 14 and 3.3V (ESP32) or 5V (Arduino), with a 10kΩ resistor from GPIO 14 to GND.
  - Attach the second button between GPIO 27 and 3.3V/5V, with a 10kΩ resistor from GPIO 27 to GND.
  - (Optional) Connect the LED anode to GPIO 2 via a 220Ω resistor, cathode to GND.
- **Wiring (Potentiometer Option)**:
  - Connect the servo as done earlier.
  - Wire the outer pins of the potentiometer to 3.3V/5V and GND, with the middle pin to A0.
  - (Optional) Add the LED as done earlier.

- **Power Considerations**: The servo (drawing ~100–300mA) may require a separate 5V supply, with GND connected to the microcontroller. The 220Ω resistor limits LED current to ~15mA (Arduino) or ~6mA (ESP32). Use a 0.1μF capacitor across the servo power pins to reduce noise.

Programming Techniques

Implement servo and input control:

- **Setup**: Include the `Servo` library: `#include <Servo.h> Servo myServo;`. Attach the servo: `myServo.attach(5);` (ESP32/Arduino). Configure pins: `pinMode(14, INPUT); pinMode(27, INPUT); pinMode(A0, INPUT);`.
- **Button Logic**: Read states: `int upState = digitalRead(14); int downState = digitalRead(27);`. Adjust angle with debounce: `if (upState == HIGH && millis() - lastPress >= 50) angle += 15;`.
- **Potentiometer Logic**: Read analog: `int potValue = analogRead(A0);`. Map to angle: `int angle = map(potValue, 0, 1023, 0, 180);`.
- **Servo Write**: Limit and set angle: `angle = constrain(angle, 0, 180); myServo.write(angle);`.

Step-by-Step Breakdown

This section explains how to control the angular position of a servo motor using either buttons or a potentiometer, built around an ESP32 (or Arduino). The setup demonstrates interactive motion control – perfect for projects like robotic arms, pan-tilt cameras, or smart mechanisms where precise, user-driven movement matters. You shall learn how to wire the servo, connect inputs, and write logic to adjust the position of the servo incrementally or smoothly.

1. **Servo → GPIO 5**: Connect the signal wire of the servo motor to GPIO 5, VCC to a 5V supply, and GND to the ground of the microcontroller. This step establishes the PWM channel for angle control, ensuring the servo is powered adequately.
2. **Increase/Decrease Angle by 15° with Buttons, or Map Potentiometer to 0–180°**: For buttons, wire GPIO 14 (up) and GPIO 27 (down) with 10kΩ pull-down resistors, reading their states to adjust the angle by 15° per press with debounce. For the potentiometer, connect it to A0, read the analog value, and map it to 0–180° using map(). This step enables interactive angle control.

Optimization and Variations

The servo control system is functioning; you can fine-tune performance and responsiveness through a few practical adjustments. These optimizations enhance movement smoothness, add user feedback, and allow more flexible input handling. The following variations help tailor the behavior to different applications – from precise robotic motion to simple interactive systems.

- **Smoother Movement**: Add `myServo.writeMicroseconds(map(angle, 0, 180, 500, 2500));` for finer control.
- **Potentiometer Hybrid**: Combine with buttons: `angle = map(analogRead(A0), 0, 1023, 0, 180); if (upState == HIGH) angle += 15;`.
- **LED Feedback**: Add `digitalWrite(2, angle > 90 ? HIGH : LOW);` to indicate angle direction.
- **Speed Control**: Adjust `delay(15)` to 5ms for faster response or 30ms for slower movement.

Chapter 8

Serial Communication and Data Transmission between Devices

Introduction

Chapter 7, Real-Time Control with GPIO, PWM and Interrupts, explored the fundamentals of real-time hardware control, focusing on using GPIO pins to manage digital inputs and outputs and applying techniques like PWM and interrupts to build responsive, event-driven IoT systems. This enabled the design of devices such as touchless switches and smart lighting systems that interact intelligently with their environments.

The module covered several key hardware control features, including the management of digital inputs and outputs through GPIO pins, and the use of PWM for analog-like control, such as adjusting LED brightness and motor speeds. Furthermore, it demonstrated the implementation of interrupts to create responsive, event-driven systems by immediately reacting to hardware events. Finally, the content examined controlling specific components, such as servo motors using precise pulse signals, and implementing safe power management for relays and larger motors.

This Chapter focuses on the next fundamental step in IoT development: enabling communication between devices through serial communication. This mechanism forms the backbone of embedded systems, allowing reliable data exchange between microcontrollers, sensors, computers, and cloud gateways. It lays the groundwork for networked and coordinated IoT systems. Serial communication involves transmitting data sequentially—bit by bit—over a single channel, making it an efficient approach for inter-device connectivity within IoT ecosystems. Before advancing to complex wireless protocols such as Wi-Fi or cloud-based systems, it is essential to understand serial communication, which underpins many local data exchange scenarios. Examples include an Arduino sending sensor readings to a Raspberry Pi, a NodeMCU logging temperature data to a computer, or multiple boards collaborating within a smart home network.

Structure

In this chapter, we will cover the following topics:

- Introduction
- Serial Communication and its Vital in IoT
- Serial and Parallel Communication
- Asynchronous and Synchronous Communication

- Universal Asynchronous Receiver and Transmitter (UART)
- Serial Peripheral Interface (SPI)
- Inter-Integrated Circuit (I2C)
- Using Serial Monitor for Debugging
- Parsing and Formatting Serial Data
- Cross-Device Communication (ESP32 to Arduino)
- Common Issues and Troubleshooting
- Mini Project: Temperature Logger
- Practical Exercises
- Conclusion

Serial Communication is Vital in IoT

Building on the foundational control techniques, where you harnessed GPIO pins for digital I/O, PWM for brightness and speed control, interrupts for event-driven programming, and power management for safe hardware operation, Chapter 8 shifts focus to enabling devices to communicate effectively, and introduces serial communication, which is the backbone of data exchange in embedded systems and IoT. This section explores the concept of serial communication, its mechanics, and its critical role in connecting microcontrollers, sensors, and computers. By sending data over a single channel, serial communication ensures reliable, efficient data transfer, forming the foundation for interconnected IoT ecosystems.

Serial Communication

Serial communication is the process of transmitting data sequentially, one bit at a time, over a single wire or communication channel, as opposed to parallel transmission, where multiple bits are sent simultaneously across multiple wires. This sequential nature makes serial communication simpler, cost-effective, and more reliable for long-distance or constrained environments, as it requires fewer connections and is less prone to timing errors. In IoT, serial communication is vital for enabling devices like Arduino, ESP32, or Raspberry Pi to exchange data with sensors, other microcontrollers, or computers, facilitating tasks such as logging sensor readings, coordinating multi-device systems, or transmitting data to cloud gateways. Protocols like UART, SPI, and I2C, explored later in this chapter, rely on serial communication to achieve synchronized, error-free data flow, making it indispensable for applications ranging from smart homes to industrial automation.Serial communication, by sending data bit by bit, is vital for IoT connectivity, enabling reliable data exchange. The next sections will dive into UART, SPI, and I2C protocols, building on this foundation.

Parallel Communication

Parallel communication is a method of data transmission where multiple bits are sent simultaneously through multiple data lines. Unlike serial communication, which sends data one bit at a time, parallel communication transfers an entire byte or group of bits at once, making it faster for short-distance communication. Each wire in the system carries one bit of data, and all bits are transmitted at the same time under a synchronized clock signal. This method was widely used in early computer systems for communication between processors, memory modules, and peripheral devices. However, parallel communication requires more wiring and can suffer from signal interference when used over longer distances. Because of these limitations, modern embedded and IoT systems prefer serial communication protocols. Nonetheless, parallel communication is still important for high-speed data transfer within computer hardware and internal buses.

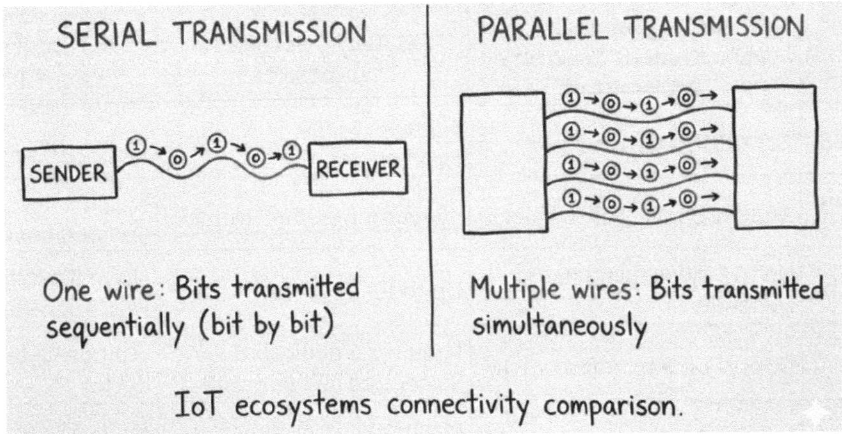

Figure 8.1: *Serial and Parallel Transmission*

This chapter introduces three fundamental serial protocols: UART (Universal Asynchronous Receiver-Transmitter), SPI (Serial Peripheral Interface), and I²C (Inter-Integrated Circuit). Each serves a distinct purpose; UART for simple point-to-point communication; SPI for high-speed data transfer; and I²C for multi-device communication over a shared bus, thereby providing the flexibility required for diverse IoT applications.

Through practical exercises, you will learn to configure these protocols, monitor and debug sensor outputs using the Serial Monitor, and establish communication between boards or external systems. Examples include configuring an ESP32 to transmit temperature data to another microcontroller or programming a NodeMCU to forward sensor readings to a cloud gateway for real-time analysis. The chapter emphasizes hands-on skills, such as setting up UART for direct data exchange, interfacing high-speed sensors using SPI, and managing multiple peripherals through I²C communication. Additionally, it covers debugging techniques, data integrity verification, and synchronization management to prevent transmission errors—all essential aspects of building robust IoT systems. By mastering serial communication, developers gain the ability to design interconnected devices that share data seamlessly, forming the foundation of intelligent IoT networks. Whether applied in a weather monitoring system or an industrial sensor network, these protocols ensure consistent, synchronized, and reliable information exchange.

This chapter provides the theoretical understanding and practical skills required to implement effective serial communication, bridging the gap between basic hardware control and fully networked IoT solutions. It establishes the foundation necessary for exploring wireless, cloud-integrated communication systems in subsequent chapters.

Comparison of Serial Communication Protocols

Serial communication protocols play a critical role in enabling microcontrollers and embedded systems to exchange data with sensors, actuators, and peripheral devices. Among the most widely used protocols in embedded and IoT systems are UART, SPI, and I²C, each designed to address different communication requirements such as speed, wiring complexity, and device scalability. While UART is commonly used for simple point-to-point communication, SPI and I²C support structured communication between controllers and multiple peripheral devices. The following table summarizes the key characteristics of these protocols to help developers understand their differences and select the most suitable option for a specific IoT or embedded application:

Feature	UART (Universal Asynchronous Receiver/ Transmitter)	SPI (Serial Peripheral Interface)	I²C (Inter-Integrated Circuit)
Wires Required	2 (TX, RX) + Ground	4 (MOSI, MISO, SCK, SS) + Ground	2 (SDA, SCL) + Ground
Communication Type	Asynchronous, Full-Duplex	Synchronous, Full-Duplex	Synchronous, Half-Duplex (Master-controlled)
Speed (Typical)	Up to 1 Mbps (Baud Rate Dependent)	Up to 10s of Mbps	Up to 3.4 Mbps (Standard, Fast, High-Speed Modes)
Addressing	None (Point-to-point only)	Requires a dedicated Slave Select (SS) line per slave	7-bit or 10-bit address per device
Topology	Point-to-Point	Master-Slave (Single Master, Multiple Slaves)	Multi-Master, Multi-Slave (Shared Bus)
Use Cases	Simple data logging, communication with PCs, Bluetooth modules, GPS modules, console debugging	Interfacing with high-speed peripherals like SD cards, displays, and ADCs	Interacting with multiple low-speed peripherals like EEPROMs, real-time clocks (RTCs), and sensors
Complexity	Low	Medium	Medium
Overhead	Start/Stop bits, Parity (optional)	Low	Address and R/W bits

Table 8.1: *Comparison of Serial Communication Protocols*

Importance in IoT

Serial communication is the cornerstone of IoT, enabling microcontrollers to exchange data efficiently with minimal resource overhead. By sending data bit by bit over a single channel, it reduces the need for complex wiring, making it ideal for compact, cost-effective devices. Most IoT modules—such as GPS for location tracking, GSM for cellular connectivity, Bluetooth for short-range communication, and Wi-Fi for internet access—rely on serial protocols like UART, SPI, or I2C to interface with microcontrollers like Arduino or ESP32. Furthermore, serial communication forms the foundation for transmitting data to cloud gateways, enabling real-time analytics and remote control in IoT applications. From smart agriculture to industrial automation, serial communication ensures seamless, reliable data flow, bridging the gap between local hardware and global networks, understanding its importance equips you to build scalable, interconnected IoT solutions.

Mechanics of Importance in IoT

- **Efficient Data Exchange**: Serial communication optimizes data transfer by using minimal pins (for example, 2 for UART, 4 for SPI), allowing microcontrollers to send sensor data (for example, temperature, humidity) to other devices or computers with low latency. For example, a baud rate of 9600 bps transfers ~960 bytes/second, sufficient for most sensor data, sufficient for most sensor data but too slow for applications like real-time image or audio transmission.
- **Reduced Wiring Complexity**: Unlike parallel communication, which requires multiple data lines (for example, 8 for a byte), serial protocols use 1–4 wires, simplifying circuit design and reducing costs in space-constrained IoT devices like wearables or smart sensors.
- **IoT Module Integration**: Modules like GPS (for example, NEO-6M, UART-based), GSM (for example, SIM800L, UART), Bluetooth (for example, HC-05, UART), and Wi-Fi (for example, ESP8266, UART/SPI) rely on serial communication to send commands and receive data, enabling features like location tracking or internet connectivity.

- **Cloud Connectivity**: Serial communication serves as the initial link in the data pipeline, transmitting local sensor data to a gateway (for example, Raspberry Pi) via UART or SPI, which then forwards it to cloud platforms like AWS IoT or Google Cloud for storage and analysis.

Asynchronous and Synchronous Communication

Following the foundational insights into the role of serial communication in IoT and the real-time control techniques mastered in *Chapter 7, Real-Time Control with GPIO, PWM and Interrupts*—such as GPIO manipulation, PWM for brightness and speed, interrupts for event-driven programming, and power management— dives into the key distinctions between asynchronous and synchronous communication , this section provides a comprehensive comparison of these two communication approaches, crucial for selecting the appropriate protocol (for example : UART, SPI, I2C) in IoT applications. By understanding their differences, you will be equipped to design efficient, reliable data exchange systems for interconnected devices like Arduinos, ESP32s, or sensors. Asynchronous and synchronous communication are two fundamental approaches to serial data transfer in embedded systems and IoT, each with distinct characteristics that impact their suitability for specific applications. Asynchronous communication transmits data without a shared clock signal, relying on predefined baud rates and framing bits to synchronize sender and receiver. Synchronous communication, in contrast, uses a dedicated clock signal to coordinate data transfer, ensuring precise timing between devices. These differences influence wiring complexity, speed, reliability, and use cases in IoT systems, such as sensor data logging or multi-device coordination

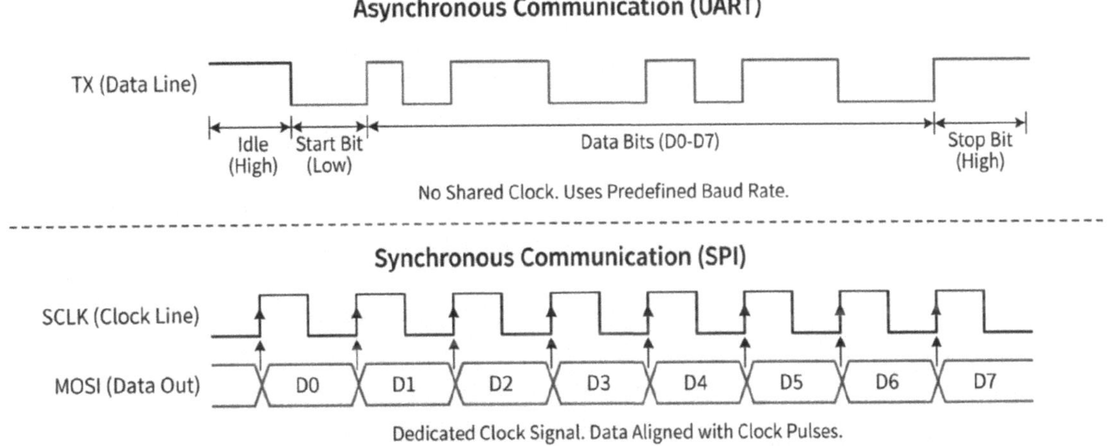

Figure 8.2: *Asynchronous and Synchronous Communication*

Key Differences

- **Clock Signal**:
  - **Asynchronous**: No shared clock signal; devices agree on a baud rate (for example, 9600 bps) and use start/stop bits to frame data. **Example**: UART sends data with a start bit, 8 data bits, and a stop bit, relying on matched timing settings.
  - **Synchronous**: Uses a dedicated clock line (for example, SCK in SPI) to synchronize data transfer, ensuring both devices operate in lockstep. **Example**: SPI sends data on clock edges, eliminating timing drift.

- **Wiring Complexity**:
  - **Asynchronous**: Requires fewer wires, typically two (TX, RX) plus ground for UART, making it simpler for point-to-point connections like Arduino-to-computer communication.
  - **Synchronous**: Needs additional wires for the clock and often chip-select lines (for example, 4–5 wires for SPI, 2 for I2C), increasing complexity but supporting multiple devices.
- **Data Transfer Speed**:
  - **Asynchronous**: Slower, typically 300–115200 bps for UART, limited by baud rate alignment and overhead from framing bits (for example, 10 bits per byte at 9600 bps = ~960 bytes/s).
  - **Synchronous**: Faster, with SPI reaching 1–10 Mbps because its dedicated clock and lack of addressing overhead allow for continuous, high-speed data transfer. I2C is slower, up to 400 kbps (Fast Mode), due to the addressing requirement for each transaction and the overhead associated with a shared bus.
- **Reliability and Synchronization**:
  - **Asynchronous**: Prone to timing errors if baud rates mismatch or clocks drift over long transmissions; suitable for short, simple data exchanges like sensor logging.
  - **Synchronous**: More reliable due to clock synchronization, ideal for high-speed, continuous data streams like display drivers or SD card interfaces.
- **Device Support**:
  - **Asynchronous**: Best for single-device communication (for example, Arduino to GPS module via UART), as it lacks addressing for multiple devices.
  - **Synchronous**: Supports multiple devices; I2C uses addresses to manage up to 127 peripherals, while SPI uses chip-select lines for multiple slaves.

Asynchronous communication, with its simplicity and minimal wiring, suits basic IoT tasks, while the speed of synchronous communication and multi-device support excel in complex systems.

Universal Asynchronous - Receiver and Transmitter

Following the comparison of asynchronous and synchronous communication and the real-time control foundations from *Chapter 7*—where you mastered GPIO for digital I/O, PWM for analog-like control, interrupts for event-driven programming, and power management for safe hardware operation—this section provides a comprehensive overview of UART, focusing on its core concepts, significance, and applications in IoT systems. UART enables reliable, point-to-point data exchange between devices using dedicated transmit (TX) and receive (RX) lines, with both devices agreeing on a baud rate to ensure synchronized communication. Common baud rates like 9600 and 115200 balance speed and stability, making UART a cornerstone for IoT applications such as sensor logging and module interfacing.

UART, or Universal Asynchronous Receiver/Transmitter, is a widely used serial communication protocol that facilitates data exchange between two devices over a simple, two-wire interface: one for transmitting data (TX) and one for receiving data (RX). As an asynchronous protocol, UART does not require a shared clock signal, relying instead on a mutually agreed-upon baud rate—such as 9600 or 115200 bits per second—to synchronize the sender and receiver. This simplicity makes UART ideal for connecting microcontrollers like Arduino or ESP32 to peripherals (for example, GPS, Bluetooth modules) or computers, enabling tasks like logging sensor data or sending commands. In IoT, ease of use of UART, compatibility with numerous modules, and support for direct communication make it a go-to choice for applications requiring reliable, low-complexity data transfer.

Core Concepts

- **TX and RX Lines**:
  - UART uses two dedicated lines: TX (transmit) sends data from one device, and RX (receive) accepts data on the other. For communication, the TX pin of one device connects to the RX pin of another, and vice versa, forming a full-duplex link where both devices can send and receive simultaneously.
  - **Example**: A TX pin of Arduino (for example, pin 1) connects to a RX of the computer via a USB-to-serial adapter, enabling data logging to the Serial Monitor.
- **Baud Rate Agreement**:
  - The baud rate defines the speed of data transmission in bits per second (bps). Both devices must use the same baud rate (for example, 9600, 115200) to ensure accurate data interpretation, as UART lacks a clock signal to synchronize timing.
  - Common baud rates include 9600 (slower, stable for long cables) and 115200 (faster, suited for high-speed modules like Wi-Fi). A mismatch results in garbled data, making configuration critical.
- **Data Framing**:
  - UART packages data with start and stop bits to mark the beginning and end of each byte, typically sending 8 data bits (1 byte) per frame. This framing compensates for the lack of a clock, ensuring the receiver recognizes the data sequence.
  - **Example**: Sending the letter 'A' (ASCII 65, binary 01000001) involves a start bit, 8 data bits, and a stop bit, totaling 10 bits per transmission.
- **Asynchronous Nature**:
  - Unlike synchronous protocols (for example, SPI, I2C), asynchronous operation of UART eliminates the need for a clock line, reducing wiring complexity but requiring precise baud rate alignment to avoid timing drift over long transmissions.

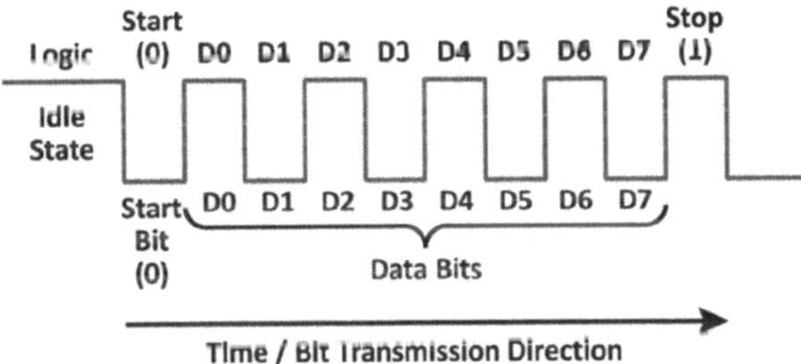

Figure 8.3: Serial Data Frame

Importance in IoT

- **Simplicity and Compatibility**: The minimal two-wire setup of UART (TX, RX, plus ground) makes it easy to implement on microcontrollers and compatible with a wide range of IoT modules, such as GPS (for example, NEO-6M), GSM (for example, SIM800L), Bluetooth (for example, HC-05), and Wi-Fi (for example, ESP8266).

- **Point-to-Point Communication**: UART excels in one-to-one connections, such as an ESP32 sending sensor data to a Raspberry Pi or a NodeMCU logging to a computer, making it ideal for direct, low-overhead data exchange.
- **Debugging and Logging**: The integration of UART with tools like the Arduino Serial Monitor allows real-time debugging of sensor values or system states, critical for IoT development and testing.
- **Gateway to Cloud**: UART often serves as the initial link in IoT data pipelines, transmitting local sensor data to a gateway device for further processing or cloud upload.

The simplicity, compatibility, and reliability of UART make it a vital protocol for IoT, enabling efficient point-to-point communication, Its use of TX/RX lines and agreed-upon baud rates supports a wide range of applications, from sensor logging to cloud connectivity.

Basic UART Connection

A basic UART connection involves linking two devices—an Arduino and an ESP32, for example—through their TX and RX lines, with a common ground to ensure signal integrity. The TX pin of Arduino connects to the RX pin of ESP32, and the RX pin of Arduino connects to the TX pin of ESP32, forming a full-duplex communication channel where both devices can send and receive data simultaneously. A shared GND line establishes a common voltage reference, critical for accurate signal interpretation. This simple setup enables point-to-point communication, allowing devices to exchange data like sensor readings or commands without complex wiring, understanding the concepts behind this connection is essential for building interconnected IoT systems, from sensor networks to debugging interfaces.

Core Concepts

- **TX to RX Connection**:
  - The TX (transmit) pin of one device sends data as a series of voltage pulses (representing bits) to the RX (receive) pin of another device. For example, connecting a TX (pin 1) of Arduino to a RX (GPIO 3) of ESP32 allows the Arduino to send data, such as a temperature value, to the ESP32.
  - This cross-connection (TX to RX, RX to TX) ensures bidirectional communication, enabling each device to both send and receive data in a full-duplex manner.
- **Common Ground (GND)**:
  - A shared ground line connects the GND pins of both devices, establishing a common reference voltage (0V) to ensure that HIGH (for example, 3.3V or 5V) and LOW (0V) signals are interpreted correctly. Without a common GND, voltage differences could lead to unreliable data transfer or hardware damage.
  - **Example**: An Arduino (5V) and ESP32 (3.3V) share a GND to align their signal levels, even if their logic voltages differ. Crucially, connecting a 5V signal directly to an ESP32 GPIO pin (rated for 3.3V) can permanently damage the ESP32. Always use a level shifter or a resistor divider circuit when interfacing 5V logic with the 3.3V-tolerant ESP32.
- **Baud Rate Synchronization**:
  - Both devices must operate at the same baud rate (for example, 9600 or 115200 bps) to synchronize data transmission. This agreed-upon speed determines how quickly bits are sent and received, ensuring the receiver interprets the incoming signal accurately.
  - **Example**: Both Arduino and ESP32 set to 9600 baud allow reliable exchange of sensor data, while a mismatch (for example, 9600 versus115200) results in garbled output.

- **Point-to-Point Simplicity**:
    - The basic connection of UART is designed for one-to-one communication, requiring only three wires (TX, RX, and GND), making it straightforward for IoT applications like connecting a microcontroller to a single peripheral or computer.

Importance in IoT

- **Device-to-Device Communication**: The TX-to-RX setup enables direct data exchange, such as an Arduino sending sensor data to an ESP32 for processing or forwarding to a cloud gateway, critical for multi-device IoT systems.
- **Debugging and Monitoring**: Connecting a TX of a microcontroller to a RX of a computer (via USB or serial adapter) allows real-time logging to tools like the Arduino Serial Monitor, aiding development and troubleshooting.
- **Module Integration**: Many IoT modules (for example, GPS, Bluetooth) use UART connections, leveraging the TX/RX/GND setup for seamless integration with microcontrollers.
- **Foundation for Complex Systems**: Basic UART connections form the building blocks for larger networks, where data from one device is relayed to others or aggregated for cloud transmission.

Serial Peripheral Interface (SPI)

Serial Peripheral Interface (SPI), a synchronous communication protocol pivotal for high-speed data transfer in IoT and embedded systems. Building on the understanding of serial communication from earlier sections, this overview explores the core concepts of SPI, focusing on its role as a master-secondary protocol that enables rapid, reliable data exchange between a single master device (for example, an Arduino or ESP32) and multiple slave devices (for example, sensors, displays). Unlike UART, SPI uses a clock signal to synchronize communication, offering superior speed and versatility for applications like SD card interfaces or LCD drivers.

Core Concepts

- **Master-Slave Architecture**:
    - SPI operates in a master-slave configuration, where a single master (for example, an Arduino) controls communication with one or more slaves (for example, an accelerometer). The master initiates data transfer, selects the slave, and provides the clock signal. Slaves only respond when addressed and can only send data when the master provides the clock signal, a key difference from asynchronous communication like UART.
    - **Example**: An ESP32 as the master communicates with an SD card (slave) to log sensor data, selecting it via a dedicated SS pin.
- **Synchronous Communication**:
    - Unlike asynchronous protocols like UART, SPI uses a clock signal (SCK) to synchronize data transfer, ensuring precise timing between master and slave. Data bits are sent or received on specific clock edges (rising or falling), minimizing timing errors.
    - **Example**: A master sends a byte on MOSI while simultaneously receiving a byte on MISO, synchronized by the SCK signal.
- **Four-Line Interface**:
    - SPI employs four lines: MOSI (data from master to slave), MISO (data from slave to master), SCK (clock signal), and SS/CS (to select a specific slave). Each slave has a dedicated SS pin, allowing the master to address multiple devices on the same bus.

    - **Example**: An Arduino uses three SS pins to control a sensor, display, and memory chip, sharing MOSI, MISO, and SCK.

- **Full-Duplex Capability**:
    - SPI supports simultaneous bidirectional data transfer, where the master sends data on MOSI and receives data on MISO in the same clock cycle, enhancing efficiency for real-time applications.
    - **Example**: A microcontroller reads sensor data while sending configuration commands to the same device in one transaction.

Importance in IoT

- **High-Speed Data Transfer**: The speed of SPI (1-10 Mbps) makes it ideal for applications requiring rapid data exchange, such as reading high-frequency sensor data or updating graphical displays in IoT devices.
- **Multi-Device Support**: The SS/CS line allows a single master to communicate with multiple slaves, enabling complex IoT systems like sensor arrays or networked peripherals.
- **Compatibility with Modules**: SPI is widely used by IoT modules like SD cards, TFT displays, and high-speed sensors (for example, gyroscopes), facilitating integration into projects like data loggers or smart wearables.
- **Reliability for Short Distances**: The clock-driven synchronization of SPI ensures reliable data transfer over short distances (for example,<1 meter), perfect for compact IoT setups like smart home controllers.

Pins

The Serial Peripheral Interface (SPI) relies on four key pins to orchestrate high-speed, synchronous communication between a master and multiple slave devices: MOSI, MISO, SCK, and SS. Each pin has a distinct role in ensuring data flows accurately and efficiently, supporting full-duplex, clock-driven architecture of SPI. MOSI carries data from the master to the slave, MISO returns data from the slave to the master, SCK provides the synchronization clock, and SS selects which slave is active. Together, these pins enable SPI to handle complex IoT applications, such as interfacing with SD cards, displays, or high-speed sensors, by providing a structured, scalable communication framework.

Core Concepts

COPI (Controller Out Peripheral In)

- COPI is the data line used by the controller to send information to a peripheral device. It carries commands, configuration data, or other payloads such as pixel data for a display or write instructions for a storage module.
- **Example:** An ESP32 acting as the controller sends pixel values to a TFT display (peripheral) through the COPI line to update a real-time IoT dashboard.

CIPO (Controller In Peripheral Out)

- CIPO is the data line that allows the peripheral device to send information back to the controller. This data may include sensor readings, device status, or memory responses.

  This communication allows SPI to operate in **full-duplex mode**, meaning that data can be transmitted and received simultaneously.

- **Example:** A temperature sensor acting as the peripheral sends temperature readings to an Arduino controller via the CIPO line while receiving configuration commands through COPI.

SCK (Serial Clock)

- SCK is the clock signal generated by the controller to synchronize data transmission. It provides a sequence of pulses that coordinate when bits are transmitted or sampled on the COPI and CIPO lines. This ensures accurate timing during communication between devices.
- **Example:** The SCK signal generated by an Arduino synchronizes rapid data exchange with an SD card module, ensuring that each bit is sampled at the correct clock edge.

CS (Chip Select)

- The **Chip Select (CS)** line allows the controller to choose which peripheral device should communicate on the SPI bus. When the CS signal is set **LOW**, the corresponding peripheral becomes active and responds to SPI commands. When the signal is **HIGH**, the device remains inactive. Multiple peripherals can share the same COPI, CIPO, and SCK lines while using separate CS pins for selection.
- **Example:** An ESP32 may use multiple CS pins to alternate communication between a sensor module, a display unit, and a memory chip connected to the same SPI bus.

Importance in IoT

- **Structured Data Exchange**: MOSI and MISO enable full-duplex communication, allowing simultaneous command and data transfer, critical for real-time IoT applications like sensor networks or display updates.
- **Precise Synchronization**: SCK ensures reliable timing, making SPI suitable for high-speed tasks like reading accelerometer data or writing to flash memory in IoT devices.
- **Multi-Device Scalability**: SS pins allow a single master to manage multiple slaves, supporting complex IoT systems with diverse peripherals, such as sensors and storage modules.
- **Module Compatibility**: Many IoT modules, like OLED displays or RFID readers, rely on the pin structure of SPI for fast, efficient communication, enhancing system integration.

Features

The SPI protocol is distinguished by its high data rate, capable of reaching several megabits per second (Mbps), and its ideal suitability for interfacing with displays, SD cards, and fast sensors. These features enable SPI to support data-intensive IoT applications where speed and responsiveness are critical. The high data rate ensures rapid transfer of large datasets, such as pixel data for displays or sensor readings, while its compatibility with performance-demanding peripherals makes it a go-to choice for real-time IoT systems like data loggers, robotic controllers, and smart interfaces.

Core Concepts

- **High Data Rate (Up to Several Mbps)**:
    - The ability of SPI to achieve data transfer rates of 1–10 Mbps (or higher in advanced implementations) far surpasses asynchronous protocols like UART (up to 115200 bps) and I2C (up to 400 kbps). This speed stems from the synchronous nature of SPI, where a master-generated clock signal (SCK) ensures precise, high-frequency data exchange without timing overheads like start/stop bits.

- **Example**: An ESP32 transfers a 1MB file to an SD card in seconds, leveraging multi-Mbps throughput of SPI, critical for real-time IoT data logging.

- **Ideal for Displays**:
  - SPI is well-suited for graphical displays (for example, TFT, OLED) due to its ability to quickly transmit large volumes of pixel data, enabling smooth updates for real-time visualizations like IoT dashboards or user interfaces.
  - **Example**: A microcontroller uses SPI to send pixel data to an OLED display, refreshing a temperature graph in milliseconds for a smart home system.
- **Ideal for SD Cards**:
  - The high-speed capability of SPI supports rapid read/write operations to SD cards, making it perfect for IoT applications requiring high-capacity data storage, such as logging environmental sensor data or storing configuration files.
  - **Example**: An Arduino logs sensor data to an SD card via SPI, enabling fast, reliable storage for a weather monitoring system.
- **Ideal for Fast Sensors**:
  - SPI excels in interfacing with high-speed sensors (for example, accelerometers, gyroscopes) that generate frequent or large datasets, ensuring real-time data acquisition for applications like motion tracking or industrial monitoring.
  - **Example**: An ESP32 reads high-frequency data from a gyroscope via SPI for precise robotic navigation in an IoT factory setup.

Importance in IoT

- **Real-Time Performance**: The high data rate enables SPI to handle time-sensitive tasks, such as updating a display with live sensor data or logging high-frequency readings, critical for responsive IoT systems like smart wearables or industrial controls.
- **Efficient Data Handling**: The speed of SPI supports large data transfers, making it ideal for IoT devices that process or store significant amounts of data, such as video feeds or multi-sensor arrays.
- **Peripheral Compatibility**: Displays, SD cards, and fast sensors are common in IoT, and the design of SPI ensures seamless integration, enhancing system scalability and functionality.
- **Enhanced User Experience**: Fast display updates and reliable sensor data acquisition improve the responsiveness and interactivity of IoT applications, such as smart home interfaces or autonomous systems.

Inter-Integrated Circuit (I2C)

Inter-Integrated Circuit (I2C) protocol, a cornerstone of synchronous serial communication in IoT and embedded systems. Building on the understanding of SPI, this overview focuses on the core concepts of I2C, emphasizing its two-wire, address-based architecture that enables efficient communication between a master and multiple slave devices. Using just two lines—SDA (Serial Data) and SCL (Serial Clock)—I2C supports up to 127 devices, each identified by a unique address, making it ideal for compact, multi-device IoT setups. The I2C protocol is a synchronous serial communication standard designed for efficient, short-distance data exchange between a master device (for example, Arduino, ESP32) and multiple slave devices (for example, sensors, EEPROMs) using only two wires: SDA for data transfer and SCL for clock synchronization. Each device on the I2C bus is assigned a unique address, allowing the master to select and communicate with specific slaves without additional control lines. Operating at speeds up to 400 kbps (Fast Mode), I2C is well-suited for IoT applications requiring compact, scalable communication, such as connecting multiple sensors or modules in smart homes or wearables.

Core Concepts

- **Two-Wire Interface**:
  - I2C uses two lines: SDA (Serial Data) for bidirectional data transfer and SCL (Serial Clock) for synchronization. Both lines are shared across all devices on the bus, minimizing wiring complexity.
  - **Example**: An Arduino communicates with a temperature sensor and an OLED display on the same SDA/SCL lines, using unique addresses to differentiate them.
- **Synchronous Communication**:
  - I2C is synchronous, with the master generating a clock signal on SCL to coordinate data transfer on SDA. This ensures precise timing, reducing errors in multi-device communication.
  - **Example**: A SCL signal of ESP32 synchronizes data exchange with a pressure sensor, ensuring accurate bit sampling.
- **Unique Addressing**:
  - Each slave device has a unique 7-bit or 10-bit address, allowing the master to select a specific device for communication. This addressing eliminates the need for dedicated chip-select lines, unlike SPI.
  - Example: A microcontroller addresses a sensor at 0x48 and an EEPROM at 0×50 on the same I2C bus, enabling targeted data exchange.
- **Multi-Device Capability**:
  - I2C supports up to 127 devices (7-bit addressing) on a single bus, making it ideal for IoT systems with multiple peripherals, such as sensor arrays or control modules, without requiring additional pins.
  - Example: A smart home system uses I2C to connect temperature, humidity, and light sensors to a single microcontroller.

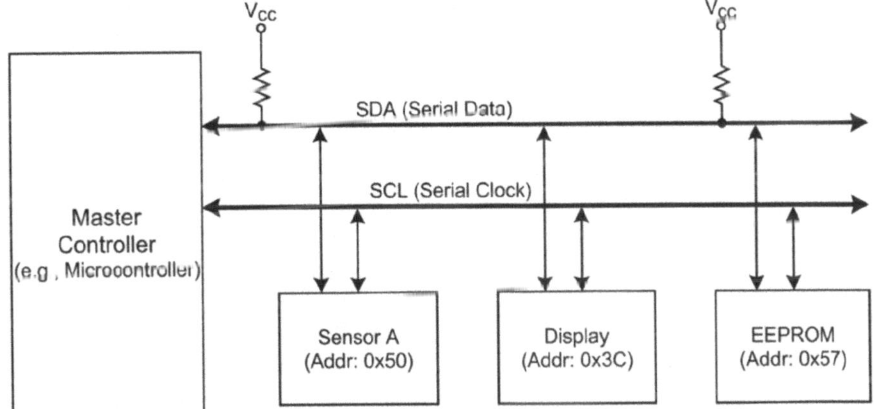

Multiple Devices on Shared I2C Bus with Unique Addresses.

Figure 8.4: SDA - SCL *Line*

Importance in IoT

- **Compact Design**: The two-wire interface reduces wiring complexity, making I2C perfect for space-constrained IoT devices like wearables or compact sensor nodes.
- **Scalable Multi-Device Communication**: Unique addressing allows a single master to manage numerous slaves, supporting complex IoT networks like environmental monitoring systems.
- **Peripheral Compatibility**: I2C is widely used by IoT modules, including sensors (for example, BME280), displays, and memory chips, ensuring seamless integration in projects.
- **Power Efficiency**: The low pin count of I2C and efficient addressing minimize power consumption, ideal for battery-powered IoT applications like remote sensors.

Pins

The I2C protocol relies on two essential pins—SDA (Serial Data) and SCL (Serial Clock)—to facilitate synchronous communication between a master and multiple slave devices in IoT systems. These pins form a shared bus that allows efficient, address-based data exchange, making I2C ideal for compact, multi-device setups like sensor networks or smart home systems. By minimizing the number of connections required, SDA and SCL enable scalable communication with low hardware overhead, supporting a wide range of IoT peripherals.

Core Concepts of Pins

- **SDA (Serial Data)**:
  - The SDA pin serves as the bidirectional data line, carrying both commands and data between the master and slave devices. It handles all data transfers, including addresses, read/write instructions, and payloads like sensor readings or display data.
  - **Example**: An Arduino sends a temperature reading command to a BME280 sensor via SDA, and the sensor responds with data on the same line, distinguished by addressing.
  - Conceptually, bidirectional nature of SDA allows a single wire to manage all data flow, reducing wiring complexity and enabling efficient communication in IoT applications.
- **SCL (Serial Clock)**:
  - The SCL pin provides the clock signal generated by the master to synchronize data transfer on the SDA line. This clock ensures that bits are sent and received at precise intervals, maintaining reliable communication across multiple devices.
  - **Example**: A SCL signal of ESP32 coordinates data exchange with an OLED display, ensuring pixel data is sampled accurately on clock edges.
  - Conceptually, the role of SCL as the timing backbone makes I2C a synchronous protocol, eliminating the need for baud rate agreements and supporting robust multi-device communication.

Importance of Pins in IoT

- **Minimal Wiring**: The two-pin interface (SDA, SCL) simplifies circuit design, making I2C ideal for space-constrained IoT devices like wearables or compact sensor nodes.
- **Shared Bus Efficiency**: Both pins form a shared bus, allowing multiple devices to connect without additional lines, supporting scalable IoT systems like environmental monitoring networks.

- **Synchronous Reliability**: The clock signal of SCL ensures precise data timing, critical for applications requiring consistent communication, such as real-time sensor data acquisition.
- **Versatile Integration**: SDA and SCL support a wide range of IoT peripherals, from sensors to displays, enabling seamless integration in diverse applications.

Characteristics

The defining characteristics of I2C—its master-slave model with addressing, requirement for pull-up resistors on both SDA and SCL lines, and widespread use in sensors like the MPU6050, OLED displays, and RTC modules—make it a versatile, efficient protocol for IoT. These features enable I2C to support complex, multi-device systems with minimal hardware, balancing simplicity and scalability. Its address-based communication, hardware requirements, and compatibility with common IoT peripherals position I2C as a go-to choice for applications requiring compact, reliable data exchange.

Core Concepts of Characteristics

- **Controller-Peripheral Model with Addressing**:
  - I2C operates in a master-slave architecture, where a single master (for example, Arduino) initiates and controls communication with multiple slaves (for example, sensors). Each slave has a unique 7-bit or 10-bit address, allowing the master to target specific devices on the shared bus.
  - **Example**: An ESP32 addresses an MPU6050 sensor at 0x68 to read motion data, then switches to an OLED at 0x3C to display it, all on the same bus.
  - Conceptually, the addressing system enables scalable, multi-device communication without additional control lines, unlike the slave-select pins of SPI.
- **Requires Pull-Up Resistors on Both Lines**:
  - SDA and SCL lines require pull-up resistors (typically 2.2kΩ–10kΩ) to maintain a HIGH state (3.3V or 5V) when idle. This open-drain configuration allows multiple devices to share the bus, with devices pulling the lines LOW to transmit bits.

    Common Mistake: Missing Pull-up Resistors

    If pull-up resistors are omitted, the SDA and SCL lines will remain in an indeterminate or stuck-LOW state. As a result, the bus will be unusable, and devices will be unable to communicate or send acknowledgements (ACKs).
  - **Example**: A 4.7kΩ resistor on SDA ensures reliable data signals when a microcontroller communicates with a Real-Time Clock (RTC) module.
  - Conceptually, pull-up resistors enable the bidirectional, multi-device functionality of the bus, ensuring stable communication.
- **Widely Used for Sensors Like MPU6050, OLEDs, RTC Modules**:
  - I2C is the protocol of choice for many IoT peripherals, including the MPU6050 (accelerometer/gyroscope), OLED displays, and RTC modules (for example, DS3231), due to its low pin count and addressing capabilities.
  - **Example**: An Arduino uses I2C to read motion data from an MPU6050 for a wearable device and updates an OLED display with the results.
  - Conceptually, the compatibility of I2C with these devices makes it a versatile standard for sensor networks, display interfaces, and timekeeping in IoT.

Importance in IoT

- **Scalable Device Management**: The master-slave model with addressing supports up to 127 devices, ideal for IoT systems with multiple sensors or modules, such as smart home networks.
- **Minimal Hardware Footprint**: Pull-up resistors and two-wire design reduce wiring and pin usage, perfect for compact IoT devices like wearables or IoT gateways.
- **Peripheral Compatibility**: The widespread use of I2C in MPU6050, OLEDs, and RTC modules ensures seamless integration in diverse IoT applications, from motion tracking to timekeeping.
- **Efficient Communication**: Addressing and pull-up resistors enable reliable, low-power data exchange, critical for battery-powered IoT systems.

Using Serial Monitor for Debugging

Serial communication protocols (UART, SPI, I2C), focusing on the critical role of the Serial Monitor in debugging IoT and embedded systems. This section explores the conceptual framework of opening and using the Serial Monitor, a tool within the Arduino IDE accessed via the Tools menu, to monitor and troubleshoot data exchanged over serial communication. A key aspect is ensuring the correct baud rate in the Serial Monitor matches the baud rate defined in the code of the microcontroller, enabling accurate data display.

Opening the Serial Monitor

The Serial Monitor is a built-in tool in the Arduino IDE, accessible through the Tools → Serial Monitor menu, that allows developers to view and interact with serial data sent or received by a microcontroller, such as an Arduino or ESP32, typically over a UART connection. It displays real-time data, such as sensor readings or system status, and enables users to send commands to the microcontroller, making it indispensable for debugging IoT applications. A critical concept is the need to match the baud rate of the Serial Monitor (for example: 9600, 115200) to the baud rate specified in the code of the microcontroller to ensure accurate data interpretation. This alignment ensures that the transmitted bits are correctly decoded, avoiding garbled output.

Core Concepts

- **Serial Monitor as a Debugging Tool**:
  - The Serial Monitor serves as a real-time interface for observing data sent from a microcontroller via serial communication, typically UART, allowing developers to monitor system behavior, log sensor values, or identify errors.
  - **Example**: An Arduino sends temperature data to the Serial Monitor, enabling a developer to verify sensor functionality during an IoT project.
- **Access via Arduino IDE**:
  - Located in the Tools → Serial Monitor menu, the Serial Monitor provides a user-friendly window to visualize incoming data and send commands, acting as a bridge between the microcontroller and the developer.
  - **Example**: A developer opens the Serial Monitor to view humidity readings from an ESP32, ensuring that the data aligns with the expected values.
- **Baud Rate Synchronization**:
  - The baud rate, measured in bits per second (bps), must match between the Serial Monitor and the code of the microcontroller (for example, set via `Serial.begin(9600)`. This

ensures that data bits are sampled at the correct intervals, preventing misinterpretation or corrupted output.

- **Example**: Setting the Serial Monitor to 9600 baud matches the configuration of the microcontroller, displaying clear sensor logs, while a mismatch (for example, 9600 versus115200) results in unreadable text.

- **Interactive Debugging**:
  - The Serial Monitor supports bidirectional communication, allowing developers to send commands to the microcontroller (for example, to toggle a sensor) while monitoring responses, facilitating interactive troubleshooting.
  - **Example**: A user types a command in the Serial Monitor to calibrate a sensor, observing immediate feedback from the microcontroller.

Importance in IoT

- **Real-Time Diagnostics**: The Serial Monitor provides immediate visibility into a data output of the microcontroller, crucial for verifying sensor readings or system states in IoT applications like environmental monitoring.
- **Error Identification**: By displaying raw serial data, it helps developers pinpoint issues, such as incorrect sensor values or communication failures, enhancing IoT system reliability.
- **Development Efficiency**: The ability to monitor and interact with data in real time streamlines the debugging process, reducing development time for IoT projects like smart home systems.
- **Module Integration**: The Serial Monitor is essential for testing communication with IoT modules (for example, GPS, Bluetooth), ensuring proper data exchange before deployment.

Tips

Effective debugging with the Serial Monitor relies on strategic practices to ensure reliable, clear, and timely data communication between a microcontroller (for example, Arduino, ESP32) and a computer or other device. The tips—initializing serial communication at the start, minimizing delays for uninterrupted output, and selectively using print functions—address common pitfalls in serial debugging, enhancing the development of IoT applications like sensor networks or smart home systems. By adopting these practices, developers can streamline data monitoring, reduce errors, and improve system responsiveness.

Core Concepts

- **Always Initialize Serial Communication in Setup**:
  - Initializing serial communication at the beginning of a program establishes the communication channel, typically via UART, between the microcontroller and the Serial Monitor or another device. This step sets the baud rate (for example, 9600, 115200 bps), ensuring the microcontroller is ready to send and receive data as soon as the program starts.
  - **Example**: A developer initializes serial communication to enable an Arduino to send temperature sensor data to the Serial Monitor immediately upon startup, ensuring no data is missed during debugging.
  - Conceptually, this practice ensures that the serial interface is active from the outset, preventing communication failures and enabling consistent data logging.

- **Avoid Long Delays for Smooth Serial Output**:
    - Long pauses in the execution of a program can disrupt the flow of serial data, causing delays in the display of the Serial Monitor or missing critical data points. By minimizing or avoiding extended delays, developers maintain a steady stream of data, crucial for real-time debugging of IoT systems.
    - **Example**: An ESP32 sending frequent sensor updates avoids long delays to ensure that the Serial Monitor displays continuous, real-time readings without gaps.
    - Conceptually, reducing delays keeps the serial output responsive, aligning with the need for timely data in applications like environmental monitoring.
- **Use Serial Print Functions Strategically**:
    - Selective use of print functions allows developers to output specific data (for example, sensor values, status messages) in a clear, organized format, avoiding clutter in the Serial Monitor. Choosing between functions that print data with or without a newline enables precise control over output readability and frequency.
    - **Example**: A NodeMCU prints sensor values without newlines for compact logs or adds newlines for readable, line-by-line debugging of an IoT state of the system.
    - Conceptually, strategic printing optimizes data presentation, making it easier to analyze system behavior or identify issues during development.

Importance in IoT

- **Reliable Debugging**: Initializing serial communication ensures a stable channel for monitoring IoT device data, critical for verifying sensor accuracy or system performance in applications like smart agriculture.
- **Real-Time Monitoring**: Avoiding long delays enables continuous data flow, essential for real-time IoT systems like weather stations where timely updates are crucial.
- **Clear Data Analysis**: Strategic printing organizes output in the Serial Monitor, simplifying the identification of errors or anomalies in IoT projects like home automation.
- **Development Efficiency**: These practices streamline debugging, reducing time spent troubleshooting communication issues in complex IoT networks.

Parsing and Formatting Serial Data

This section explores the principles of organizing and transmitting data in a clear, standardized format over serial protocols like UART, ensuring reliable interpretation by receiving devices or tools like the Serial Monitor of Arduino IDE. Structured data enhances the efficiency of data exchange, debugging, and integration in IoT applications, such as sensor networks or cloud-connected systems.

Sending Structured Data

Sending structured data involves organizing serial data into a consistent, well-defined format before transmission, enabling the receiving device—whether a microcontroller, computer, or cloud gateway—to easily parse and interpret the information. Unlike raw or unformatted data, structured data uses standardized formats, such as delimited strings, JSON, or key-value pairs, to convey multiple data points (for example, sensor readings, status flags) in a single transmission. This approach is critical in IoT for ensuring clarity, reducing errors, and facilitating interoperability between devices and systems. For example, a microcontroller might send temperature and humidity data in a structured format like "T:25.5,H:60" over UART, allowing the receiver to extract and process each value accurately.

Core Concepts

- **Structured Data Formats**: Structured data is organized into a predefined format, such as Comma-Separated Values (CSV), JSON, or custom delimiters (for example, "**`T:25,H:60`**"), to clearly delineate multiple data points or metadata within a single message.

Feature	Comma-Separated Values (CSV)	Custom Delimited Strings (such as "T:25,H:60")	JavaScript Object Notation (JSON)
Readability	Good (Simple, tabular structure)	Poor to Fair (Dependent on custom format)	Good (Hierarchical, self-describing)
Size	Smallest (Minimal overhead)	Small (Low overhead)	Larger (Requires keys and structural characters)
Parsing Complexity	Low (Standard library support)	High (Requires custom parsing logic)	Low to Moderate (Standard library support, more complex structure)
Best For	Simple tabular data, bulk transfer, legacy systems	Highly constrained, minimalist environments (including IoT, low-bandwidth)	Complex, hierarchical data, web APIs, inter-application communication

***Table 8.2**: Data Format Comparison*

  - **Example**: An Arduino sends "S1:23.5,S2:45.0" to represent readings from two sensors, allowing the receiver to distinguish between them easily.
  - Conceptually, structured formats ensure data is self-descriptive, simplifying parsing and reducing ambiguity during communication.

- **Data Clarity and Interpretability**:
  - By using consistent formats, structured data ensures the receiving device can reliably interpret the transmitted information, such as identifying which value corresponds to temperature or a specific sensor ID.
  - **Example**: A JSON string like **`{"temp":25.5,"humidity":60}`** sent via UART allows a cloud gateway to parse and store data systematically.
  - Conceptually, clarity enhances interoperability, enabling devices with different protocols or software to process the same data.

- **Error Reduction**:
  - Structured data minimizes errors by providing a predictable format, reducing the risk of misinterpreting raw bytes or unformatted streams, which is crucial for reliable IoT communication.
  - **Example**: A delimited string like **`"ID:01,VAL:42"`** prevents confusion compared to a raw number like **`"42"`** that lacks context.
  - Conceptually, structured formats act as a contract between sender and receiver, ensuring consistent data handling.

- **Support for Complex Data**:
  - Structured data allows multiple parameters, status codes, or metadata to be sent in a single transmission, supporting complex IoT applications like multi-sensor systems or device diagnostics.
  - **Example**: An ESP32 sends **`{"sensor":"BME280","temp":25.5,"pressure":1013}`** to convey sensor type and multiple readings in one message.

- Conceptually, this enables efficient transmission of diverse data, critical for IoT systems with multiple data sources.

Importance in IoT

- **Interoperability**: Structured data ensures compatibility between devices, such as a microcontroller and a cloud platform, by providing a universal format for data exchange, essential for IoT ecosystems like smart homes.
- **Efficient Debugging**: Clear, organized data displayed in tools like the Serial Monitor simplifies troubleshooting, allowing developers to verify sensor outputs or system states in IoT projects.
- **Scalable Systems**: Structured formats support complex, multi-device IoT networks by enabling the transmission of diverse data types, such as sensor arrays or configuration settings.
- **Cloud Integration**: Structured data, like JSON, aligns with cloud platforms' requirements, facilitating seamless data transfer from local devices to remote servers for analytics or control.

Receiving and Parsing on Another Device

Receiving and parsing serial data on another device involves capturing incoming data streams sent over a serial protocol (for example, UART) and extracting meaningful information by identifying patterns or structures within the data. Two key approaches include reading data until a specific delimiter, such as a newline character ('\n'), and extracting substrings to isolate individual values, or using a structured format like JSON to parse complex data systematically. These techniques enable a receiving device, such as an Arduino, ESP32, or Raspberry Pi, to interpret sensor readings, commands, or status updates sent from another device, ensuring reliable data processing in IoT systems. For example, a microcontroller might receive a string like `"T:25.5,H:60\n"` and parse it to extract temperature and humidity values, or process a JSON object like `{"temp":25.5,"humidity":60}` for cloud integration.

Core Concepts

- **Receiving Data Until a Delimiter**:
  - This approach involves capturing incoming serial data until a specific character, such as a newline ('\n'), is detected, marking the end of a message. The received data, typically a string, is then processed to extract meaningful values based on predefined separators (for example, commas, colons).
  - **Example**: An ESP32 receives `"S1:23.5,S2:45.0\n"` from an Arduino via UART, stopping at the newline and splitting the string at commas to retrieve sensor values.
  - Conceptually, this method ensures complete messages are captured, providing a simple way to handle structured data in IoT applications.
- **Extracting Substrings**:
  - After receiving a delimited string, the receiving device parses it by splitting the data into substrings based on separators (for example, commas, colons) to isolate individual data points, such as sensor readings or identifiers.
  - **Example**: A Raspberry Pi parses `"T:25.5,H:60\n"` to extract `"25.5"` as temperature and "60" as humidity, enabling separate processing of each value.
  - Conceptually, substring extraction allows precise data isolation, ensuring accurate interpretation of multi-value messages in IoT systems.

- **Using JSON for Structured Parsing**:
    - JSON (JavaScript Object Notation) provides a standardized, structured format for serial data, where key-value pairs (for example, **`{"temp":25.5}`**) enable complex data organization. A library like ArduinoJson simplifies parsing by mapping JSON objects to variables on the receiving device.
    - **Example**: An Arduino receives **`{"sensor":"BME280","temp":25.5}`** and uses JSON parsing to extract the temperature value for further processing.
    - Conceptually, JSON parsing supports complex, interoperable data exchange, ideal for IoT applications requiring integration with cloud platforms.
- **Reliable Data Interpretation**:
    - Both delimiter-based and JSON parsing ensure the receiving device accurately interprets incoming data, reducing errors by adhering to a predefined structure or format, critical for IoT systems like smart homes or industrial monitoring.
    - **Example**: A cloud gateway parses JSON data from a NodeMCU to store sensor readings, ensuring compatibility with external systems.
    - Conceptually, reliable parsing enables seamless communication between diverse devices, enhancing IoT system robustness.

Importance in IoT

- **Interoperable Communication**: Parsing structured data ensures compatibility between devices, such as microcontrollers and cloud gateways, enabling seamless data exchange in IoT ecosystems like environmental monitoring.
- **Accurate Data Processing**: Extracting specific values from delimited strings or JSON objects allows precise handling of sensor data or commands, critical for applications like smart agriculture.
- **Scalable Systems**: JSON parsing supports complex, multi-parameter data, facilitating scalable IoT networks with diverse devices, such as sensor arrays or control systems.
- **Debugging and Validation**: Parsing incoming data allows developers to verify correct data transmission, ensuring system reliability during IoT development.

Cross-Device Communication (ESP32 to Arduino)

This section explores the conceptual framework of linking microcontrollers for specialized tasks, such as one handling sensor data collection and the other managing cloud connectivity, focusing on the critical practice of cross-device communication between two microcontrollers, such as an Arduino and an ESP32, to enable efficient data transfer in IoT systems. Specifically, it covers the connection setup using UART (Arduino TX to ESP32 RX and a shared ground) and an example workflow where an Arduino reads DHT sensor data, sends it via UART every 2 seconds, and the ESP32 receives and uploads it to cloud platforms like Firebase or ThingSpeak. Cross-device communication involves linking two microcontrollers, such as an Arduino and an ESP32, to leverage their complementary strengths in an IoT system. By connecting the TX (transmit) pin of Arduino to the RX (receive) pin of ESP32 (for example, GPIO 16) and establishing a common ground (GND), data can flow reliably between the devices using UART, a simple and effective serial protocol. In a typical workflow, one microcontroller, like the Arduino, focuses on reading sensor data (for example, from a DHT sensor for temperature and humidity), transmitting it periodically (for example, every 2 seconds) to the other microcontroller, such as the ESP32, which handles advanced tasks like uploading data to cloud platforms (for example:

Firebase or ThingSpeak) for remote monitoring or analytics. This division of labor optimizes system efficiency, combining the robust sensor interfacing of Arduino with the Wi-Fi capabilities of ESP32.

Core Concepts

- **Linking Microcontrollers for Data Transfer**:
  - Cross-device communication enables two microcontrollers to collaborate by exchanging data, allowing each to perform specialized tasks. For instance, one device handles sensor interfacing, while the other manages network or cloud connectivity, creating a modular IoT system.
  - **Example**: An Arduino collects environmental data, while an ESP32 processes and uploads it to a cloud server, optimizing task distribution.
  - Conceptually, this approach enhances system modularity, allowing developers to assign roles based on the strengths of each microcontroller, such as processing power or connectivity features.
- **UART-Based Connection (Arduino TX → ESP32 RX, Shared GND):**
  - The connection uses TX and RX lines of UART to enable bidirectional data transfer, with the TX pin of Arduino sending data to the RX pin of ESP32 (for example, GPIO 16). A shared ground ensures a common voltage reference, critical for accurate signal interpretation.
  - **Example**: An Arduino sends temperature data to an ESP32, which receives it on GPIO 16, with both devices grounded to maintain signal integrity.
  - Conceptually, this simple two-wire (plus ground) setup provides a reliable, low-overhead channel for data exchange, ideal for IoT applications.
- **Task Specialization**:
  - Dividing responsibilities between microcontrollers leverages their unique capabilities. The Arduino, with its robust analog and digital I/O, excels at sensor data collection, while the ESP32, with built-in Wi-Fi, is ideal for cloud communication, enhancing overall system efficiency.
  - **Example**: An Arduino reads DHT sensor data, while an ESP32 handles Wi-Fi communication to upload data to Firebase, streamlining the workflow.
  - Conceptually, task specialization optimizes resource use, enabling complex IoT systems with minimal hardware.
- **Periodic Data Transmission**:
  - Data is sent at regular intervals (for example, every 2 seconds) to balance real-time updates with system stability, ensuring that the receiving device can process incoming data without overwhelming its buffer.
  - **Example**: An Arduino sends DHT readings every 2 seconds, allowing the ESP32 to process and upload data without missing updates.
  - Conceptually, periodic transmission ensures consistent data flow, critical for real-time IoT monitoring applications.
- **Cloud Integration**:
  - The receiving microcontroller (for example, ESP32) processes incoming data and forwards it to cloud platforms like Firebase or ThingSpeak, enabling remote access, storage, and analysis of IoT data for applications like smart agriculture or home automation.

- **Example**: An ESP32 uploads temperature data to ThingSpeak, allowing users to monitor environmental conditions remotely via a web dashboard.
- Conceptually, cloud integration extends local data collection to global accessibility, a cornerstone of IoT scalability.

Importance in IoT

- **Modular System Design**: Cross-device communication enables modular architectures, where microcontrollers handle specific tasks (for example, sensing, networking), improving scalability and flexibility in IoT systems like smart cities or industrial monitoring.
- **Efficient Resource Utilization**: By assigning roles based on microcontroller strengths, such as the sensor interfacing of Arduino and the Wi-Fi capabilities of ESP32, systems achieve optimal performance with minimal hardware.
- **Real-Time Data Flow**: Periodic UART transmission ensures timely data exchange, critical for real-time IoT applications like environmental monitoring or remote control systems.
- **Cloud Connectivity**: Linking local data collection to cloud platforms via cross-device communication enables remote access, analytics, and automation, essential for modern IoT ecosystems like smart homes or precision agriculture.
- **Debugging and Development**: The setup allows developers to test and validate data transfer between devices, ensuring reliable communication before deploying IoT systems.

Example Workflow in Context

The example workflow illustrates the power of cross-device communication:

1. **Arduino Reads DHT Sensor Data**: The Arduino interfaces with a DHT sensor to collect temperature and humidity readings, leveraging its robust analog and digital I/O capabilities for accurate sensor interfacing. This step ensures reliable local data collection, a foundational aspect of IoT systems.
2. **Sends Readings via UART Every 2 Seconds**: The Arduino transmits structured data (for example, `"T:25.5,H:60"`) to the ESP32 via UART, using a periodic interval to balance real-time updates with system stability. This ensures that the ESP32 receives consistent, manageable data streams.
3. **ESP32 Receives and Uploads to Cloud**: The ESP32 parses the incoming data and uses its Wi-Fi module to upload it to a cloud platform like Firebase or ThingSpeak, enabling remote access, visualization, or analytics. This step bridges local sensing with global connectivity, a hallmark of IoT.

This workflow demonstrates how cross-device communication combines the strengths of two microcontrollers to create a cohesive IoT system, from sensor data acquisition to cloudriver, ensuring robust, scalable, and cloud-integrated IoT solutions.

Broader Conceptual Insights

- **Modularity and Scalability**: The Arduino-ESP32 setup exemplifies modular design, where the role of each device (sensing, cloud connectivity) can be scaled to include additional microcontrollers or peripherals, supporting complex IoT architectures.
- **Data Pipeline Efficiency**: The workflow creates an efficient pipeline from local data collection to cloud storage, critical for IoT applications requiring real-time insights, such as smart agriculture or environmental monitoring.

- **Interoperability**: Structured data transmission (for example, `"T:25.5,H:60"`) ensures compatibility between devices and cloud platforms, enhancing system integration and flexibility.
- **Real-World Impact**: Cross-device communication enables practical IoT solutions, from remote health monitoring in Africa to industrial automation in North America, demonstrating its global relevance.
- **Error Mitigation**: Careful baud rate alignment and periodic transmission prevent data corruption, ensuring reliable communication critical for IoT reliability.

Common Issues and Troubleshooting

This section focuses on the critical topic of identifying and resolving common issues that arise in serial communication for IoT and embedded systems. By addressing problems such as baud rate mismatches, signal noise, address conflicts, and hardware-related issues, this guide equips developers to troubleshoot effectively, ensuring reliable data transfer in applications like sensor networks, cloud integration, or multi-device systems. Serial communication, encompassing protocols like UART, SPI, and I2C, is the backbone of IoT systems, enabling data exchange between microcontrollers (for example, Arduino, ESP32), sensors, and cloud platforms. However, issues such as incorrect baud rate settings, signal noise, address or slave-select conflicts, and hardware faults can disrupt communication, leading to data corruption, loss, or system failures. Troubleshooting these issues involves understanding their conceptual causes—such as timing mismatches or electrical interference—and applying systematic diagnostic strategies to restore reliable data transfer. This process is crucial for ensuring that IoT systems, from smart homes to industrial automation, operate seamlessly.

Core Concepts

- **Baud Rate Mismatches**:
    - In UART communication, both the sending and receiving devices must use the same baud rate (for example, 9600, 115200 bps) to ensure accurate data sampling. A mismatch results in garbled or unreadable data, as the receiver interprets bits at the wrong intervals.
    - **Example**: An Arduino set to 9600 baud sends data to an ESP32 set to 115200, causing corrupted output in the Serial Monitor.
    - Conceptually, baud rate mismatches disrupt timing synchronization, a common issue in asynchronous protocols like UART, requiring careful configuration alignment.
- **Signal Noise and Interference**:
    - Electrical noise, caused by long cables, electromagnetic interference, or poor grounding, can corrupt serial data, affecting UART, SPI, or I2C communication. This is particularly problematic in environments with high electrical activity or humid conditions.
    - **Example**: A long UART cable picks up noise, causing errors in sensor data sent from an Arduino to a computer.
    - Conceptually, noise introduces unwanted signal variations, necessitating strategies like shielding or shorter connections to maintain data integrity.
- **Address or Slave-Select Conflicts**:
    - In I2C, devices sharing the bus must have unique addresses to avoid conflicts, while in SPI, each slave requires a distinct Slave-Select (SS) pin. Misconfigured addresses or SS lines result in communication failures or incorrect device responses.

- **Example**: Two I2C sensors with the same address (for example, 0x68) cause bus contention, preventing data transfer.
- Conceptually, conflicts arise from improper device identification, disrupting multi-device communication in IoT systems.

- **Hardware and Connection Issues**:
  - Loose connections, incorrect wiring (for example, TX-to-TX instead of TX-to-RX), or hardware faults like damaged pins or corroded connectors can halt serial communication. These issues are common in humid or rugged environments.
  - **Example**: A loose ground connection between an Arduino and ESP32 disrupts UART data transfer.
  - Conceptually, hardware issues break the physical communication path, requiring verification of connections and component integrity.

Importance in IoT

- **System Reliability**: Troubleshooting ensures consistent data transfer, critical for IoT applications like environmental monitoring, where data accuracy is paramount.
- **Development Efficiency**: Identifying and resolving issues quickly reduces debugging time, accelerating IoT project development, such as smart home or industrial systems.
- **Scalability**: Effective troubleshooting supports multi-device communication, enabling scalable IoT networks like sensor arrays or cloud-integrated platforms.
- **Global Applicability**: Addressing common issues ensures robust communication in diverse environments, from humid agricultural fields to industrial factories.

Mini Project: Temperature Logger

This mini project demonstrates cross-device serial communication by building a Temperature Logger, where an Arduino Uno reads data from a DHT11 sensor and sends it via UART to an ESP32, which then prints it or uploads it to the cloud, such as UART setup, data framing, and structured parsing, to create a functional system. The objective is to showcase how serial communication enables task division—an Arduino for sensing and an ESP32 for processing or cloud integration—enhancing IoT efficiency.

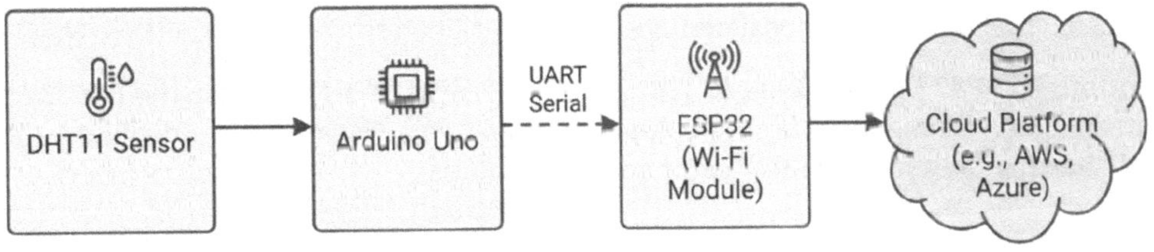

***Figure 8.5**: DHT System Flow*

Objective

The primary objective of the Temperature Logger is to create a modular IoT system where the Arduino Uno collects temperature and humidity data from a DHT11 sensor and transmits it serially to an ESP32, which receives, processes, and optionally uploads the data to a cloud platform like ThingSpeak. This project illustrates the power of UART for inter-device communication, allowing specialization: the

Arduino handles reliable sensor interfacing, while the ESP32 leverages its Wi-Fi for cloud connectivity. By achieving this, you gain practical experience in data exchange, parsing, and cloud integration, essential for scalable IoT applications like remote monitoring or smart environments.

Components

The project uses a minimal set of components to keep it accessible and focused on communication:

- **Arduino Uno**: Serves as the sensor-reading device, with its 5V logic and UART pins (TX: pin 1, RX: pin 0) for data transmission.
- **ESP32**: Acts as the receiver and cloud gateway, using its UART pins (for example, RX: GPIO 16, TX: GPIO 17) and Wi-Fi module for data handling and upload.
- **DHT11 Sensor**: Provides temperature (0–50°C) and humidity (20–80%) data, connected to the Arduino for initial reading.
- **Jumper Wires**: Facilitate connections between the TX of Arduino and the RX of ESP32, with a shared GND for signal reference.

These components, combined with the Arduino IDE, enable a simple yet effective demonstration of serial data flow.

Working

The workflow of Temperature Logger is divided into a step-by-step process that ensures smooth data collection, transmission, reception, and optional cloud upload, leveraging UART for reliable communication.

1. **Arduino Reads DHT Data**: The Arduino initializes the DHT11 sensor and periodically (for example, every 2 seconds) reads temperature and humidity values. It formats the data into a structured string (for example, `"T:25.5,H:60\n"`) to ensure clarity during transmission.
2. **Sends Temperature String via Serial**: The formatted string is sent over UART from the TX pin of Arduino to the RX pin of ESP32 at a predefined baud rate (for example, 9600 bps). This step ensures the data is transmitted reliably, with a newline delimiter ('\n') marking the end of each message for easy parsing.
3. **ESP32 Receives and Prints to Its Serial Monitor**: The ESP32 listens on its RX pin, receiving the string and parsing it to extract temperature and humidity values. It then prints the data to its own Serial Monitor for local debugging and verification.
4. **(Optional) ESP32 Uploads Data to ThingSpeak**: Using its Wi-Fi module, the ESP32 uploads the parsed data to ThingSpeak, a cloud platform for IoT data visualization, enabling remote access and charting of the temperature and humidity trends.

Practical Exercises

Introduces practical exercises to solidify the serial communication concepts covered in *Chapter* 8, including UART, SPI, I2C, Serial Monitor debugging, and cross-device data transfer. Exercise 1, titled *"Serial Spy – Debug Your Sensor,"* focuses on using the Serial Monitor of Arduino to view live data from a DHT11 (temperature and humidity sensor) or MQ-2 (gas sensor) in real time. The goal is to develop skills in real-time debugging and observation, enabling learners to monitor sensor outputs, verify system behavior, and troubleshoot issues in IoT applications.

Exercise 1: Serial Spy – Debug Your Sensor

Introduction

The *Serial Spy – Debug Your Sensor* exercise introduces learners to one of the most essential skills in IoT development: real-time data monitoring and debugging using serial communication. In this task, a sensor such as the DHT11 (for temperature and humidity) or MQ-2 (for gas detection) is connected to a microcontroller like the Arduino Uno. The system reads environmental data from the sensor and transmits it to the Arduino IDE's Serial Monitor via UART communication.

This exercise helps learners understand how sensor data is captured, formatted, and visualized in real time. By observing live readings, one can verify sensor accuracy, ensure proper connectivity, and quickly identify irregularities or errors in data output. Ultimately, it builds a strong foundation in serial debugging, a crucial aspect of developing reliable IoT systems and smart monitoring solutions.

Objective

The objective of the Serial Spy exercise is to connect a sensor—either a DHT11 (measuring temperature and humidity) or an MQ-2 (detecting gases like smoke or LPG)—to a microcontroller (for example, Arduino Uno) and use the Serial Monitor in the Arduino IDE to observe live sensor data. This exercise emphasizes real-time debugging and observation, allowing learners to verify sensor functionality, monitor environmental conditions, and identify anomalies in data output. By leveraging UART communication, the microcontroller sends sensor readings to the Serial Monitor, providing a practical introduction to serial data handling and debugging in IoT systems.

Working

The exercise involves a step-by-step process to collect, transmit, and display sensor data, ensuring learners understand the flow of real-time debugging using the Serial Monitor. The following is a detailed explanation of how the system works conceptually:

1. **Sensor Data Acquisition**:
    - The microcontroller interfaces with the chosen sensor (DHT11 or MQ-2) to collect environmental data. The DHT11 measures temperature (0–50°C) and humidity (20–80%), while the MQ-2 detects gas concentrations (for example, smoke, LPG, methane) as analog voltage levels proportional to gas presence.
    - **Example**: An Arduino reads temperature and humidity from a DHT11, producing values like 25.5°C and 60% humidity, or measures the analog output of MQ-2 to detect smoke levels.
    - Conceptually, this step involves the microcontroller querying the sensor periodically to capture real-time environmental data, forming the foundation of IoT monitoring systems.
2. **Data Formatting for Transmission**:
    - The microcontroller formats the sensor data into a structured string (for example, "`T:25.5,H:60`" for DHT11 or "Gas:450" for MQ-2) to ensure clarity when displayed in the Serial Monitor. This structured format aids in distinguishing multiple data points or sensor types.
    - **Example**: For a DHT11, the Arduino formats data as "**`Temp:25.5,Humidity:60\n`**" with a newline delimiter to mark the end of each reading.
    - Conceptually, formatting organizes raw sensor data into a human-readable and machine-parsable form, critical for effective debugging and observation.

3. **Serial Transmission via UART**:
   - The formatted data is sent over UART from the TX pin of the microcontroller to a computer running the Serial Monitor of Arduino IDE. The transmission occurs at a predefined baud rate (for example, 9600 bps), ensuring reliable communication between the microcontroller and the computer.
   - **Example**: An Arduino sends "`Gas:450\n`" every second to the Serial Monitor, allowing real-time tracking of MQ-2 gas levels.
   - Conceptually, UART provides a simple, reliable channel for streaming sensor data to a debugging interface, enabling live observation.
4. **Real-Time Display in Serial Monitor**:
   - The Serial Monitor, accessed via the **`Tools`** → **`Serial Monitor`** menu in the Arduino IDE, displays the incoming data in real time, allowing the developer to observe sensor readings, verify accuracy, and detect anomalies like erratic values or sensor failures.
   - **Example**: The Serial Monitor shows a continuous stream of "`Temp:25.5,Humidity:60`" updates, enabling the developer to confirm stable DHT11 performance.
   - Conceptually, the Serial Monitor acts as a window into the operation of the microcontroller, facilitating immediate feedback for debugging IoT applications.

Importance in IoT

- **Real-Time Debugging**: Observing live sensor data in the Serial Monitor allows developers to verify system functionality, critical for IoT applications like environmental monitoring or gas detection.
- **System Validation**: The exercise ensures sensors like DHT11 or MQ-2 are working correctly, validating their integration into larger IoT systems like smart homes or safety systems.
- **Skill Development**: Practicing serial data transmission and observation builds foundational skills for debugging complex IoT networks, such as those involving cloud integration or multi-device communication.
- **Error Detection**: Real-time monitoring helps identify issues such as sensor malfunctions or data inconsistencies, enhancing the reliability of IoT deployments.

Exercise 2: UART Talk - Arduino to ESP32 Communication

Introduction

The UART *Talk - Arduino to ESP32 Communication* exercise focuses on establishing seamless serial communication between two powerful microcontrollers: the Arduino Uno and the ESP32. In this setup, the Arduino serves as the data collector, interfacing with sensors like the DHT11 (temperature and humidity) or an LDR (light intensity), while the ESP32 acts as the data receiver and processor, handling visualization or further actions such as cloud integration or wireless transmission.

This exercise provides hands-on experience with UART (Universal Asynchronous Receiver-Transmitter) communication — one of the most fundamental and widely used serial protocols in embedded systems. Learners gain practical insight into how data flows between devices, how structured messages are transmitted and parsed, and how microcontrollers can collaborate to build scalable IoT systems. By mastering this setup, developers strengthen their understanding of cross-device communication, an essential concept for building interconnected and modular IoT architectures.

Objective

The objective of the UART Talk exercise is to create a system where an Arduino (for example, Arduino Uno) collects data from a sensor (for example : temperature, light, or other analog/digital sensor) and transmits it via UART to an ESP32, which receives and processes the data for display or further action. This exercise emphasizes the concept of cross-device communication, demonstrating how two microcontrollers can collaborate to leverage their strengths—Arduino for reliable sensor interfacing and ESP32 for advanced processing or connectivity. By mastering this, learners gain practical experience in UART-based data transfer, a foundational skill for building modular IoT systems like sensor networks or cloud-integrated platforms.

Working

The exercise involves a step-by-step process to collect sensor data, transmit it over UART, and process it on the receiving device, ensuring learners understand the flow of cross-device communication. Below is a detailed explanation of how the system works conceptually:

1. **Sensor Data Acquisition on Arduino**:
    - The Arduino interfaces with a sensor (for example, DHT11 for temperature/humidity, LDR for light intensity, or similar) to collect environmental or analog data. The sensor is queried periodically (for example, every 1–2 seconds) to capture real-time measurements, which are then prepared for transmission.
    - **Example**: An Arduino reads a DHT11 sensor, obtaining values like 25.5°C temperature and 60% humidity, or measures the analog output of an LDR to detect light levels.
    - Conceptually, this step leverages the robust I/O capabilities of Arduino to gather accurate sensor data, forming the starting point of the IoT communication pipeline.
2. **Data Formatting for UART Transmission**:
    - The Arduino formats the sensor data into a structured string (for example, `"T:25.5,H:60\n"` for DHT11 or `"Light:450\n"` for LDR) to ensure clarity and ease of parsing at the receiving end. A delimiter, such as a newline ('\n'), marks the end of each message to facilitate reliable data extraction.
    - **Example**: The Arduino formats DHT11 data as `"Temp:25.5,Humidity:60\n"` to clearly delineate temperature and humidity values for the ESP32.
    - Conceptually, structured formatting ensures the data is organized and interpretable, reducing errors during transmission and parsing.
3. **UART Transmission from Arduino to ESP32**:
    - The formatted data is sent over UART from the TX pin of Arduino to the RX pin of ESP32 (for example, GPIO 16) at a consistent baud rate (for example: 9600 bps). A shared ground (GND) connection ensures a common voltage reference for accurate signal interpretation.
    - **Example**: The Arduino sends `"Light:450\n"` every second via UART, with the ESP32 receiving it on GPIO 16, aligned by a shared GND.
    - Conceptually, UART provides a simple, point-to-point communication channel, enabling reliable data transfer between the two microcontrollers.
4. **ESP32 Receives and Processes Data**:
    - The ESP32 listens on its RX pin, capturing the incoming string until the newline delimiter. It parses the data to extract individual values (for example, temperature, light

level) and processes them, such as displaying them in its Serial Monitor, storing them, or preparing them for further actions like cloud upload.

- **Example**: The ESP32 receives "`Temp:25.5,Humidity:60\n`", parses it to extract 25.5°C and 60% humidity, and prints the values to its Serial Monitor for verification.
- Conceptually, this step demonstrates the ESP32's role as a data processor, leveraging its processing power to handle incoming sensor data in an IoT system.

Importance in IoT

- **Modular System Design**: The exercise illustrates how cross-device communication enables task specialization, with the Arduino handling sensing and the ESP32 managing data processing, critical for scalable IoT systems like smart homes.
- **Reliable Data Transfer**: UART ensures robust point-to-point communication, essential for IoT applications requiring consistent sensor data exchange, such as environmental monitoring.
- **Skill Development**: Practicing UART-based communication builds foundational skills for integrating multiple devices in IoT networks, preparing learners for complex projects like cloud-connected systems.
- **Debugging and Validation**: The exercise allows developers to verify data flow between devices, ensuring reliable communication before scaling to larger IoT deployments.

Exercise 3: I2C Device Scanner Mission

Introduction

The *I2C Device Scanner Mission* is designed to help learners explore and understand one of the most efficient communication protocols used in IoT and embedded systems — I2C (Inter-Integrated Circuit). In this exercise, the ESP32 acts as the I2C master, scanning the bus to detect connected slave devices such as sensors (similar to BME280, MPU6050) or displays (like OLED). The goal is to identify the unique I2C addresses of each device, which is necessary for establishing proper communication and avoiding address conflicts.

Through this exercise, learners gain hands-on experience with multi-device communication, I2C addressing, and bus scanning techniques. By observing detected addresses on the Serial Monitor, you will be able to verify device connections, troubleshoot wiring or configuration issues, and prepare the system for more advanced IoT applications. Ultimately, this mission strengthens your ability to set up, diagnose, and manage I2C-based networks, a crucial step in building scalable and reliable embedded systems.

Objective

The objective of the I2C Device Scanner Mission is to use an ESP32 as an I2C master to scan the I2C bus and detect the addresses of connected slave devices, such as sensors (for example, BME280, MPU6050) or OLED displays. This exercise emphasizes the concepts of I2C addressing and multi-device communication, enabling learners to identify and configure devices on a shared I2C bus. By mastering this, you gain practical skills in setting up and troubleshooting I2C-based IoT systems, ensuring proper device recognition and communication in applications like environmental monitoring or smart home networks.

Working

The exercise involves a step-by-step process to configure the ESP32, scan the I2C bus, and report detected device addresses, providing insight into multi-device communication. The following is a detailed explanation of how the system works conceptually:

1. **ESP32 as I2C Master Initialization**:
   a. The ESP32 is configured as the I2C master, initializing the I2C interface with its SDA (Serial Data) and SCL (Serial Clock) pins (for example, GPIO 21 for SDA, GPIO 22 for SCL). This step establishes the ESP32's role in controlling the I2C bus and generating the clock signal for synchronous communication.
   b. **Example**: An ESP32 sets up its I2C interface to communicate with connected devices like a BME280 sensor or an OLED display.
   c. Conceptually, initializing the ESP32 as the master prepares it to manage the I2C bus, coordinating data exchange with multiple slave devices.
2. **Scanning the I2C Bus for Devices**:
   a. The ESP32 systematically sends messages to all possible I2C addresses (typically 7-bit addresses from 0x03 to 0x77) to detect which devices respond. Each slave device with a unique address acknowledges the master's request, indicating its presence on the bus.
   b. **Example**: The ESP32 sends a message to address 0x68 and receives an acknowledgment from an MPU6050 sensor, confirming its connection.
   c. Conceptually, this scanning process identifies active devices, revealing their addresses for subsequent communication in a multi-device setup.
3. **Reporting Detected Addresses**:
   a. The ESP32 collects the addresses of devices that respond and outputs them to the Serial Monitor via UART. This provides a list of connected devices, allowing the developer to verify which peripherals are present and correctly configured on the I2C bus.
   b. **Example**: The Serial Monitor displays "Found device at address 0x3C" for an OLED display and "0x68" for an MPU6050, confirming their presence.
   c. Conceptually, reporting addresses enables developers to map the I2C bus, ensuring proper configuration and avoiding address conflicts.
4. **Interpreting Results for Multi-Device Setup**:
   a. The list of detected addresses is used to configure communication with each device, ensuring no address conflicts and enabling targeted data exchange. This step is critical for setting up multi-device IoT systems, where multiple sensors or modules share the same bus.
   b. **Example**: After detecting addresses 0x3C (OLED) and 0x68 (MPU6050), the ESP32 can communicate with each device individually, reading sensor data or updating the display.
   c. Conceptually, this step facilitates the design of scalable IoT systems by ensuring each device is uniquely addressable and accessible.

Importance in IoT

- **Multi-Device Configuration**: Scanning the I2C bus enables developers to identify and configure multiple devices, critical for IoT systems like sensor networks with diverse peripherals.

- **Address Conflict Prevention**: Detecting device addresses ensures unique assignments, avoiding communication failures in complex IoT setups like smart homes.
- **System Validation**: The exercise verifies the presence and functionality of I2C devices, ensuring reliable integration in applications like environmental monitoring.
- **Scalable Design**: Understanding I2C addressing supports the development of scalable IoT architectures, accommodating numerous sensors or modules on a single bus.

Conclusion

The I2C Device Scanner Mission uses an ESP32 to detect and report I2C device addresses, fostering skills in addressing and multi-device IoT setups, skills in debugging, cross-device communication, and multi-device setup. These projects showcased how serial protocols enable IoT devices to communicate efficiently, from monitoring sensor outputs to scanning I2C buses for connected devices. By applying UART, SPI, and I2C, you have seen how microcontrollers like Arduino and ESP32 can collaborate to handle tasks like sensor data collection and cloud uploads, transforming simple setups into intelligent, connected systems. These exercises provided hands-on experience in real-time data observation, structured data transmission, and device address management, preparing you for complex IoT architectures.

Looking ahead, *Chapter 9, Firebase, Blynk and Google Sheets*, will build on this foundation by introducing networked IoT systems. You will learn to stream sensor data from microcontrollers to cloud platforms like Firebase, Google Sheets, and Blynk, enabling real-time data visualization, remote monitoring, and control from anywhere in the world. This chapter will compare Firebase's database capabilities, Blynk's mobile UI, and Google Sheets' analytics, guiding you to select the right tool for specific IoT tasks. Projects will create real-time bridges between physical devices and digital platforms, supporting applications like remote climate monitoring and smart home control. By mastering cloud connectivity, you will extend local communication to global IoT ecosystems, enhancing system scalability and accessibility.

This chapter has equipped you with the tools to implement reliable serial communication, blending theory with practice to foster a deep, actionable understanding of data transfer in IoT systems. From debugging with the Serial Monitor to orchestrating cross-device communication, you are now prepared to build interconnected, efficient IoT solutions, setting the stage for networked systems in *Chapter 9, Firebase, Blynk and Google Sheets.*

CHAPTER 9

Firebase, Blynk, and Google Sheets

Introduction

In the previous chapter, you have learned how devices communicate locally using UART, SPI, and I²C – the hardware-level "heartbeat" of embedded systems. Those wired protocols allowed your Arduino or ESP32 to exchange data reliably, read sensors, and send commands with precision.

Now it is time to take your IoT project beyond the workbench and into the cloud.

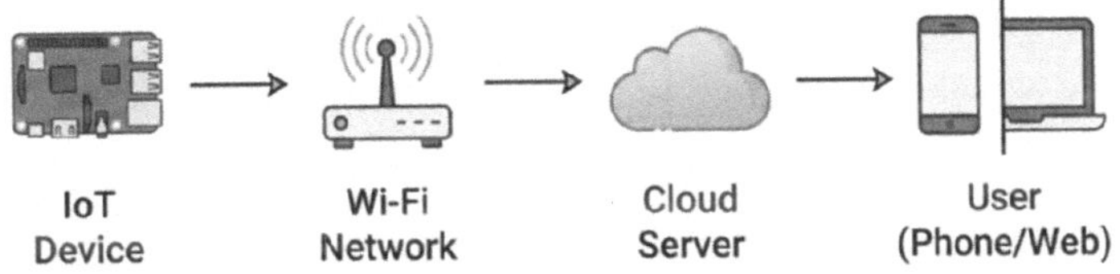

From Local to Global: Simple IoT Data Flow

From Local to Global: Simple IoT Data Flow

Figure 9.1: *IoT Data Flow*

This chapter connects your device to the digital world. Instead of data appearing only in the Serial Monitor, your sensor readings will stream across the internet, update on your phone in real time, and become accessible from anywhere. A temperature reading in your room becomes a cloud data point. A button press on your phone can toggle a device miles away.

You will explore three powerful cloud tools – Firebase, Blynk, and Google Sheets – each offering different strengths: real-time data, intuitive dashboards, and easy logging/analysis. Together, they form a complete toolkit for building connected, scalable IoT systems.

Tool	Primary Purpose	Real-time	User Interface	Analytics
Firebase	Real-time NoSQL Database & Backend	Excellent	Minimal built-in dashboard; focus on raw data	Requires integration with external tools
Blynk	Intuitive IoT Dashboard & Control	Very Good	Excellent customizable mobile/web dashboard	Basic logging and charting within the app
Google Sheets	Data Logging & Analysis	Moderate (via API)	Simple tabular interface	Excellent for advanced analysis and visualization

***Table 9.1:** Overview of Firebase, Blynk and Google Sheets*

You will learn how to stream live sensor data from your ESP32 to the cloud, build mobile dashboards that update in real time, and trigger actions remotely — turning a simple temperature logger into a smart, responsive system.

Structure

In this chapter, we will cover the following topics:

- Introduction to Real-Time Cloud Connectivity in IoT
- Firebase Setup: Rules, Structure, Read/Write Operations
- Sending Sensor Data to Firebase using REST APIs
- Reading Values Remotely for Actuation
- Visualizing Data in Google Sheets using IFTTT/Webhooks
- Logging Events for Analytics and Debugging
- Building Mobile Dashboards with Blynk
- Adding Buttons, Sliders, and Graphs to Control LEDs/Fans
- Using Tokens and Authentication for Secure Sync
- Cloud versus Local: Choosing the Right Approach
- Platform Comparison: Firebase versus Blynk versus Sheets
- Troubleshooting Real-Time Sync Issues
- Mini Projects

Introduction to Real-Time Cloud Connectivity in IoT

IoT was built on the serial communication foundation established in Serial Communication & Data Transmission Between Devices — where data flowed reliably between microcontrollers via UART, SPI, and I2C—to introduce the transformative power of real-time cloud connectivity in IoT systems. This section explores how cloud platforms elevate local, isolated prototypes into globally accessible, intelligent, and responsive smart solutions. For example, a simple prototype that measures room temperature can be transformed into a smart application allowing a user to check the temperature from their phone anywhere in the world. Instead of confining sensor data to the limited memory of a microcontroller or a local computer, information is pushed seamlessly to online platforms, where it can be stored indefinitely, analyzed in real time, and acted upon from anywhere in the world. This shift from local data silos to cloud-integrated ecosystems marks the evolution from basic embedded systems to true Internet of Things applications.

Core Concepts

- **Cloud Connectivity as the IoT Enabler:**
  - Cloud connectivity transforms IoT systems by connecting edge devices (microcontrollers, sensors) to centralized online platforms via the internet. This enables data to transcend physical boundaries, making systems accessible beyond the local network.
  - **Example**: A temperature sensor in a remote warehouse streams data to the cloud, allowing a manager in another city to monitor conditions in real time.
  - Conceptually, the cloud acts as a global nervous system (Sensors = Nerves, Cloud = Brain, Actuators = Muscles), linking distributed devices into a unified, intelligent network.
- **From Local Storage to Cloud Persistence:**
  - Instead of storing sensor data on the limited RAM of a microcontroller or an SD card, cloud platforms offer virtually unlimited, persistent storage. Data is preserved even if the device powers off, enabling long-term tracking and historical analysis.
  - **Example**: A solar-powered weather station logs years of environmental data to the cloud, surviving power cycles and enabling trend analysis.
  - Conceptually, cloud storage ensures data continuity, turning fleeting sensor readings into valuable, longitudinal insights.
- **Real-Time Data Push via Wi-Fi:**
  - Microcontrollers with Wi-Fi use HTTP or MQTT protocols to push data instantly to cloud APIs. This creates a live data pipeline where sensor values update online within seconds.
  - **Example**: An ESP32 sends a reading of soil moisture every 10 minutes to a cloud server, triggering irrigation alerts if levels drop.
  - Conceptually, real-time push enables immediate responsiveness, critical for time-sensitive IoT applications such as health monitoring or industrial control.

Typical Workflow of Cloud-Connected IoT

- **Sensor Collects Data:**
  - Physical sensors measure environmental or operational parameters and convert them into digital values.
  - **Example**: A BME280 sensor reads 25.5°C, 60% humidity, and 1013 hPa pressure.
- **Microcontroller Sends Data via Wi-Fi to a Cloud API:**
  - A Wi-Fi-enabled microcontroller formats the data and transmits it over the internet using HTTP POST or MQTT to a cloud endpoint.
  - **Example**: The ESP32 sends data every 30 seconds to the Realtime Database of Firebase.
- **Cloud Logs and Visualizes Readings:**
  - The cloud platform receives, stores, and updates the data in real time. It triggers visualizations (graphs, gauges) and analytics (averages, alerts) automatically.
  - **Example**: A Blynk dashboard shows a live temperature graph, while the Google Sheets appends a new row with a timestamp.

- **User Monitors or Controls Devices Using a Web or Mobile Dashboard:**
    - Authorized users access the data via intuitive interfaces—web portals, mobile apps, or spreadsheets—and issue commands that are relayed back to the device.
    - **Example**: A user taps a button in the Blynk app to activate a relay, and the command travels through the cloud to the ESP32.

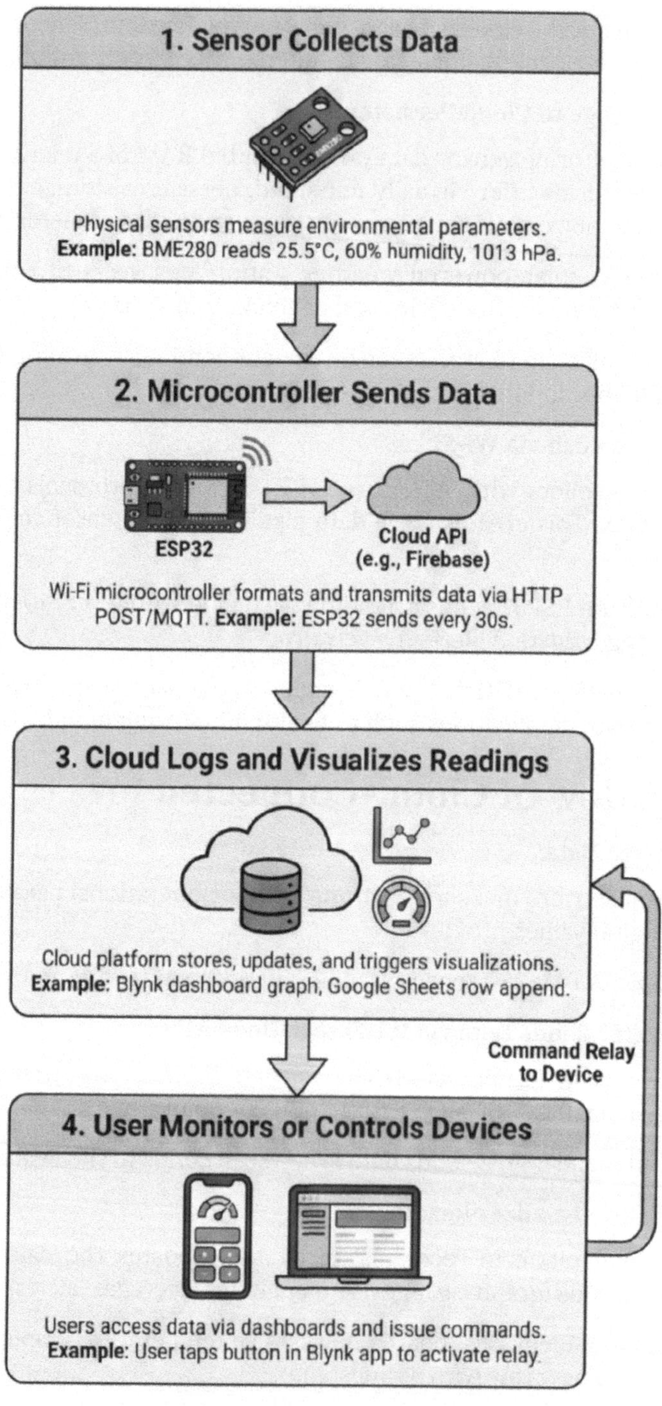

Figure 9.2: *Workflow of Cloud Connected IoT*

Importance in IoT Evolution

- **From Prototype to Product:** Cloud connectivity is what separates hobby projects from deployable, scalable IoT solutions. It enables mass deployment, fleet management, and over-the-air updates.
- **Data-Driven Intelligence:** By aggregating data from thousands of devices, cloud platforms power machine learning, predictive analytics, and AI-driven automation.
- **User-Centric Design:** Mobile and web dashboards make IoT accessible to non-technical users, expanding adoption in homes, offices, and public services.
- **Global Scalability:** A single cloud backend can support devices across continents, enabling international monitoring and cross-border control.

Firebase Setup: Rules, Structure, and Read, Write Operations

Firebase is a powerful, real-time NoSQL database and backend platform of Google. This section explores the conceptual foundation of Firebase as a real-time database that stores data in JSON format, enabling instant updates and bidirectional synchronization across all connected devices.

Firebase

Firebase is a Google-hosted, real-time NoSQL databases, unlike traditional SQL databases (which organize data into predefined tables and rows, similar to a spreadsheet), are more flexible. They often store data in formats like JSON (JavaScript Object Notation), which allows data to be structured more like a document or an object, making it easier to handle complex, evolving, or unstructured data. They also use Backend-as-a-Service (BaaS) platform designed to simplify IoT and mobile application development. At its core, it functions as a cloud-based data storage system that organizes information in JavaScript Object Notation (JSON) format — a lightweight, human-readable, and hierarchical structure that makes it ideal for representing sensor readings, device states, and user configurations. Unlike traditional databases that require polling or periodic refreshes, Firebase supports instant, bidirectional data synchronization: when data changes on one client, that change is immediately reflected on all connected devices — whether a mobile app, web dashboard, or another microcontroller. This real-time behavior transforms static data logging into a live, responsive system, enabling seamless interaction between the physical world and the digital cloud.

Firebase operates on a client-push, server-sync model. When a microcontroller sends new sensor data via Wi-Fi, it pushes the update directly to the Firebase cloud. The server then broadcasts this change to all subscribed clients in milliseconds, ensuring everyone sees the same truth. This is made possible through WebSocket-like persistent connections under the hood, eliminating the need for constant HTTP polling. Additionally, Firebase exposes a REST API, allowing devices to interact using standard HTTP methods such as `GET`, `PUT`, `PATCH`, and `DELETE` — making it accessible even to resource-constrained microcontrollers that cannot maintain persistent connections

Security is baked in through Firebase Security Rules, which is a declarative language that defines who can read or write which parts of the database. These rules act as a firewall, ensuring that only authenticated and authorized devices or users can access sensitive data. Finally, Firebase is scalable by design — starting free for small projects and automatically scaling to millions of users without infrastructure management.

- **Real-Time Database (RTDB):**
    - The flagship feature of Firebase: a NoSQL cloud database that syncs data in real time. When a node is updated, all listeners receive the new value instantly.
    - **Example**: An ESP32 writes `{"temp": 26.5, "time": 1729183200}` to Firebase; a Blynk app and web dashboard update simultaneously.
- **JSON Data Structure:**
    - Data is stored as nested key-value objects, not tables. This flexible hierarchy allows complex IoT data models.
- **Bidirectional Synchronization:**
    - Changes flow in both directions. A user toggles a virtual switch in a mobile app → Firebase updates → ESP32 receives the command and turns on a relay.
    - Conceptually, this creates a closed-loop control system over the internet.
- **REST API Access:**
    - Even without real-time listeners, devices can use **HTTP requests** (GET/PUT) to interact with Firebase, ideal for low-power or intermittently connected nodes.
    - **Example**: A battery-powered sensor wakes up, sends a PUT request with data, then sleeps.
- **Security Rules:**
    - Define access control at the **path level**. Rules can allow public reads but restrict writes to authenticated users or specific device IDs.
    - **Example**: `".write": "auth.uid === 'esp32_01'"` ensures only that device can update its node.
- **Scalability and Free Tier:**
    - Starts free (1 GB storage, 10 GB/month transfer), scales automatically. No server management required.

Database Structure and Rules

This single sentence unlocks the entire philosophy of Firebase Realtime Database. Unlike traditional SQL tables with rigid rows and columns, Firebase uses JavaScript Object Notation (JSON) – a tree-like, nested structure of key-value pairs that mirrors real-world IoT hierarchies: devices contain sensors, sensors produce readings, and readings have timestamps and values. This hierarchical model allows you to group, nest, and scale data intuitively, making it the perfect fit for dynamic, multi-device IoT systems.

Hierarchical JSON Structure:

- **Root Node**:
    - The top-level container – the home address of your database
    - All data lives under this root, organized into child nodes.
- **Nodes as Branches**:
    - Each key is a node (like a folder). Nodes can contain:
        - Primitive values (numbers, strings, booleans)
        - Objects (nested JSON)
        - Arrays (ordered lists)

Sending Sensor Data to Firebase Using REST APIs

The core concept of sending sensor data from a microcontroller (specifically the ESP32) to Firebase using REST APIs is explored . This section explores how the ESP32 pushes JSON-formatted sensor data directly to the cloud via standard HTTP methods (PUT, PATCH, POST) – thereby, enabling real-time, internet-based data streaming without requiring persistent WebSocket connections.

The ESP32, with its built-in Wi-Fi module, can push JSON-formatted sensor data directly to Firebase using Representational State Transfer (REST) APIs over HTTP. This method allows a microcontroller to act as an HTTP client, sending structured data to a specific Firebase database endpoint using standard methods such as PUT, PATCH, or POST. Unlike real-time listeners that require persistent connections, REST APIs enable lightweight, fire-and-forget communication, and are ideal for battery-powered or intermittently connected IoT nodes. This approach transforms the ESP32 from a local data collector into a cloud contributor, making sensor readings globally accessible in real time.

- **REST API as a Communication Bridge:** REST APIs allow the ESP32 to interact with Firebase using standard HTTP protocols. The microcontroller constructs a URL pointing to a specific database node and sends a request with a JSON payload.
- **HTTP Methods for Data Operations:**
    - `PUT`: Replaces the entire node with new data. Used when sending a complete sensor state.
    - `PATCH`: Updates only specific fields within a node. Efficient for partial changes.
    - `POST`: Appends data to a list. Firebase auto-generates a unique key.

Method	Purpose	Usage	Analogy
`PUT`	**Replace/Create:** Completely replaces the data at a specified path.	You want to send the **complete, current state** of an object or node (such as Setting *all* sensor values at once).	Replacing a whole document with a new version.
`PATCH`	**Update:** Modifies only specific fields within an existing node.	You only want to send **one or a few changes** to an existing object, leaving other fields untouched.	Making edits to specific sentences in a document.
`POST`	**Create/Append:** Adds a new item to a list and assigns it a unique ID.	You are **creating a new entry** in a collection or list (like adding a new log event or message).	Adding a new item to the end of a list.

Table 9.2: *Overview of Push, Patch and Post Methods*

- **JSON Payload Construction:**
    - Sensor data is packaged into **JSON format** before transmission. The ESP32 reads values, formats them into key-value pairs, and sends them as the HTTP request body.
    - **Example:** `{"temp": 26.5, "hum": 58, "time": 1729183200}` is compact, structured, and cloud-ready.
- **ESP32 as HTTP Client:**
    - The ESP32 uses its Wi-Fi stack to establish a connection, send the HTTP request, and receive a response. It does not need to maintain a persistent connection, making it suitable for low-power applications.

- **Real-Time Effect via Cloud Sync:**
    - Once data is written via REST, the real-time engine of Firebase instantly pushes the update to all listening clients (mobile apps, web dashboards) – even though the ESP32 uses a one-way HTTP call.

Reading Values Remotely for Actuation

Reading cloud-stored values triggers physical actuation. This section explores the conceptual framework of remote control, where a microcontroller continuously monitors a specific node in the Firebase Realtime Database and, upon detecting a change, activates an output – such as turning on a light, starting a motor, or opening a valve. This process transforms Firebase from a passive data logger into an active command center, enabling closed-loop, internet-mediated control of physical systems. Without delving into mechanics such as code, HTTP requests, or wiring, this guide expands the content to approximately 1000 words, focusing exclusively on core conceptual importance for your textbook – covering fundamental principles, data flow models, actuation logic, synchronization mechanisms, and system design implications – preparing learners for advanced IoT control paradigms.

IoT control is achieved by reading Firebase values and triggering outputs – a process that completes the bidirectional communication loop between the physical world and the cloud. While sending sensor data represents the input pathway, reading values for actuation forms the output pathway, enabling remote command execution. This is the essence of smart automation: a user in one location changes a value in the cloud (via app or dashboard), and a device in another location instantly responds by altering the physical environment.

At its core, this mechanism relies on the real-time synchronization property of Firebase. The microcontroller does not "pull" data periodically (polling); instead, it listens to a specific JSON node. When that value of the node changes, whether by a mobile app, web interface, or automated script, Firebase pushes the update to the listening device in milliseconds. The microcontroller then interprets the new value and maps it to a physical action via its GPIO pins.

The Command Node – A Virtual Switch in the Cloud

The foundation of remote actuation is the **command node** – a dedicated location in the Firebase JSON tree that stores the desired state of a physical actuator.

- A dedicated location in the Firebase JSON tree that stores the desired state of a physical actuator (`{"fan": "ON"}`).
- **Conceptual Role**: This node acts as a virtual control panel. Each key represents an actuator; each value represents its target state.
- **State Types**:
    - **Binary**: true/false, "`ON`"/"`OFF`" → for relays, LEDs, solenoids.
    - **Analog**: 0–255, 0–180 → for PWM dimming or servo angles.
    - **Enum**: "`AUTO`", "`MANUAL`", "`OFF`" → for mode selection.

The Listener – Real-Time Change Detection

The microcontroller establishes a persistent listener on the command node (or a specific child). This listener is a background process that waits for Firebase to signal a change.

- **How It Works**:
    1. ESP32 connects to Firebase and subscribes to `/controls/living_room_light`.
    2. The initial value is read and cached locally.

3. Any external write to this path triggers a callback.
4. The new value is compared with the previous state.
5. If different → actuation logic is executed.

- **Conceptual Advantage**: Event-driven, not time-driven. No wasted cycles polling every second. Response is near-instantaneous (typically <500 ms end-to-end).

Actuation Mapping — From Cloud Value to Physical Output

The microcontroller maintains a mapping function that translates cloud values into hardware signals.

- **Binary Mapping**:
  - Cloud: "`ON`" → GPIO HIGH → relay closes → bulb turns on.
  - Cloud: "`OFF`" → GPIO LOW → relay opens.
- **Analog Mapping**:
  - Cloud: 180 → PWM duty cycle 70% → LED brightness high.
  - Cloud: 90 → servo pulse width 1.5 ms → 90° angle.
- **State Machine Integration**:
  - Complex actuators use state validation:
    - Only allow OPEN if the current state is CLOSED.
    - Prevent rapid toggling (debouncing in software).

This mapping ensures safe, predictable behavior even over unreliable networks.

Feedback Loop — Closing the Control Cycle

True IoT control includes feedback — the device confirms execution back to the cloud. This critical feedback loop is what differentiates a command sent from a command actually executed, reinforcing reliability and trust in the system.

- **Workflow**:
  1. User sets **`garden_pump: true`**.
  2. ESP32 receives → activates pump → reads flow sensor.
  3. If flow detected → writes **`pump_status: "RUNNING"`** to Firebase.
  4. If no flow → writes **`pump_status: "FAILED"`**.
- **Conceptual Importance**: Creates a verified control loop. The user sees not just the command, but the actual outcome.

Synchronization and Conflict Resolution

Multiple users or automation rules may write to the same node simultaneously.

- **Last-Write-Wins Model**:
  - Firebase resolves conflicts by **`timestamp;`** latest write prevails.
  - Devices should **read-after-write** to confirm their command was accepted.

Fail-Safe and Default States

Network interruptions must not leave actuators in dangerous states.

- **Heartbeat Mechanism**:
  - Cloud writes a timestamp every 10 seconds.
  - Device checks: if no update in 30 seconds → revert to safe default
- **Local Override**:
  - Physical switch bypasses cloud → device writes current state back to Firebase.

Visualizing Data in Google Sheets using IFTTT and Webhooks

Google Sheets is a cloud-based data logger, leveraging If This Then That (IFTTT) and Webhooks to transform simple HTTP requests from a microcontroller into automatically appended rows in a spreadsheet.

Google Sheets acts as a free, online, real-time data logger that receives structured sensor data from IoT devices and organizes it into tabular rows and columns for visualization, analysis, and sharing. By integrating IFTTT — a no-code automation platform — with Webhooks, any HTTP POST request sent from an ESP32 is captured as a trigger event. IFTTT then executes a predefined action: appending a new row to a designated Google Sheet with values extracted from the request payload. This creates a seamless, serverless data pipeline from sensor → microcontroller → cloud → spreadsheet, enabling long-term logging, trend analysis, and team collaboration using a tool already familiar to millions.

Google Sheets as a Persistent Data Sink

At its foundation, Google Sheets serves as a cloud-hosted, versioned, structured database optimized for time-series IoT data.

- **Tabular Structure**:
  - **Columns** = data fields
  - **Rows** = individual logged events.
- **Conceptual Role:** Acts as a digital logbook where each sensor reading becomes a permanent, timestamped entry.
- **Key Property:** Append-only workflow — new data is added to the bottom; historical data remains intact.

Webhook — The Universal Trigger

A Webhook is a user-defined HTTP endpoint that receives POST requests and treats them as automation triggers.

- **Conceptual Model:**
  - ESP32 sends: **`POST`** `https://maker.ifttt.com/trigger/temp_log/with/key/abc123`
  - Payload: **`{"value1": "25.5", "value2": "60", "value3": "ESP32_01"}`**
- **Role in Pipeline:** Converts a network event (HTTP request) into an actionable signal within IFTTT.

- **Uniqueness:** The URL path (**`temp_log`**) and secret key ensure only authorized devices can trigger the applet. Exposing this URL publicly effectively compromises the system; ensure it remains confidential to maintain security.

Webhooks decouple the data source from the data destination, enabling one-to-many logging.

IFTTT Applet — The Automation Bridge

An IFTTT Applet is a conditional automation rule with one trigger and one action.

- **Structure**:
  - If: "Webhook receives a request named **`temp_log`**"
  - Then: "Add a row to Google Sheet **`IoT_Logger`**"
- **Payload Mapping**:
  - `value1 → Column B (Temperature)`
  - `value2 → Column C (Humidity)`
  - `value3 → Column D (Device ID)`
  - `{{EventTime}} → Column A (Timestamp)`
- **Conceptual Power**: Zero-code logic — the ESP32 only needs to send a properly formatted HTTP POST.

Event-Driven Logging Pipeline

The complete data flow forms an event-driven, push-based logging system:

- **Push Model:** Data is sent when ready, not polled.
- **Asynchronous:** ESP32 resumes operation immediately after POST; no waiting for a response.
- **Atomic:** Each request = one row, ensuring data integrity.

Timestamping and Data Integrity

Accurate timing is embedded at multiple levels:

- **IFTTT Event Time:** Automatically records when the webhook was triggered.
- **Optional Device Timestamp:** ESP32 can include **`millis()`** or NTP time in payload.
- **Sheet Formula:** =NOW() in a column for local edit time.

Logging Events for Analytics and Debugging

Event logging in Google Sheets is the practice of systematically recording every significant state change in an IoT deployment — not just sensor readings, but contextual metadata that tells the full story of system behavior over time. Each row becomes a digital footprint: *when* something happened, *what* the value was, and *why* it matters. This creates a persistent, queryable timeline that serves dual purposes: performance analytics (understanding normal behavior) and debugging (identifying and resolving abnormal behavior) — all without physical access to the device.

The Event Log as a System Journal

An event log is a chronological ledger of all meaningful occurrences in the IoT system. Extended Event Structure (for richer context):

- **EventType**: **`SENSOR_READ`**, **`ACTUATION`**, **`ERROR`**, **`BOOT`**
- **Message**: "Pump activated", "Wi-Fi reconnected"
- **Severity**: INFO, WARN, ERROR

Trend Analysis via Temporal Patterns

Trend analysis extracts long-term behavior from logged data to reveal system dynamics.

- **Key Metrics**:
  - **Daily Temperature Curve:** Min, max, average, rate of change
  - **Duty Cycle:** % time pump was ON over 24 hours
  - **Sampling Consistency:** Interval between logs (should be ~2 min)
- **Analytical Questions**:
  - Is the temperature rising faster in the afternoon? → Insulation issue?
  - Does humidity spike after pump activation? → Leak?
  - Are logs missing between 02:00–03:00? → Power or Wi-Fi dropout?
- **Conceptual Insight:** Patterns emerge only with time — a single reading is noise; 1000 readings are signals.

Anomaly Detection through Deviation Analysis

Anomalies are statistical or logical deviations from expected behavior, detectable via log inspection.

- **Types of Anomalies**:
  - **Spikes/Dips:** Temperature jumps from 25°C to 45°C in 2 minutes → sensor fault or fire.
  - **Gaps:** 10-minute silence after regular 2-minute logs → device crash or network loss.
  - **Drift:** Gradual increase in baseline humidity → calibration drift.
- **Detection Logic**:
  - **Threshold Rules:** Value > 30°C → flag as `HIGH_TEMP`
  - **Rate-of-Change:** ΔT> 5°C in <5 min → `RAPID_CHANGE`

    (Note: This is an example threshold and might vary based on application needs.)
  - **Sequence Violations:** `PUMP_ON` without prior `MOISTURE_LOW` → logic error

Fault Diagnosis via Log Correlation

Fault diagnosis uses multi-dimensional correlation across log fields to isolate root causes.

- **Correlation Examples**:
  - **WiFi_Status:** `DISCONNECTED` → followed by log gap → network issue
  - **Pump:** ON → no change in `Soil_Moisture` after 10 min → pump failure
  - **Battery_Voltage:** 3.1V → erratic sensor readings → power instability
- **Diagnostic Workflow**:
  - Filter logs by `DeviceID` and time window
  - Sort by Timestamp
  - Trace state transitions: `NORMAL` → `WARN` → `ERROR`
  - Identify the last known good state
- **Conceptual Insight:** One log is a data point; correlated logs are a story.

Post-Deployment Debugging without Physical Access

Remote debugging uses the event log as a virtual oscilloscope for field-deployed devices.

- **Debug Scenarios**:
  1. Device in a sealed greenhouse, 50 km away
  2. Sensor on factory roof, inaccessible after installation
  3. Fleet of 100 nodes in rural areas
- **Log-Enabled Debug Steps**:
  1. Add DEBUG event on boot: "Firmware v2.1 started".
  2. Log `WiFi_RSSI`, `FreeHeap`, Uptime every 10 min.
  3. On failure: log stack trace or error code.
  4. Developer views log → replicates issue locally

Log Granularity and Storage Strategy

Log granularity balances diagnostic richness with storage efficiency.

- **High-Granularity (every 10 sec)**:
  - Captures transients, ideal for lab testing.
  - Fills sheet quickly → use for short-term
- **Low-Granularity (every 15 min)**:
  - Focuses on trends, ideal for long-term field use.
  - Add SUMMARY events: daily min/max.
- **Hybrid Strategy**:
  - Normal: 15-min sensor logs.
  - On event: burst of 10-sec logs for 2 min.
  - Returns to normal after 120 seconds

From Logs to Actions — Closing the Analytics Loop

Actionable analytics convert log insights into system improvements

- **Feedback Loop**:
  - Log → Analysis → Insight
  - Insight → Firmware update or calibration
  - Update deployed → new logs validate fix
- **Example**:
  - Logs show pump runs 80% at night → add schedule
  - Logs show false motion triggers → adjust sensor threshold

Building Mobile Dashboards with Blynk

Blynk is a mobile IoT platform that allows developers to design, deploy, and interact with custom dashboards on smartphones, bridging the gap between embedded hardware and human users. It operates on a three-layered architecture: the microcontroller (edge), the Blynk Cloud (middleware), and the mobile app (interface). The platform abstracts complex networking and UI logic into visual components — enabling non-programmers to build functional IoT interfaces and engineers to focus on system logic. At its core, Blynk turns data streams into visual elements and user actions into device commands, creating a closed-loop, real-time control system accessible from anywhere.

Virtual Pins — The Universal Data Interface

Virtual Pins (V0, V1, V2 ...) are abstract data channels that decouple physical GPIO from cloud communication.

- **Conceptual Model**:
    - V0 → Temperature value
    - V1 → Light switch state
    - V5 → Pump runtime (minutes)
- **Bidirectional Flow**:
    - Device → Cloud: ESP32 writes `Blynk.virtualWrite(V0, 25.5)`
    - Cloud → Device: App writes to V1 → ESP32 receives in `BLYNK_WRITE(V1)`
- **Data Agnosticism**: A virtual pin carries any value — int, float, string, array.
- **Key Abstraction**: One pin, many widgets — V0 can feed a gauge, graph, and LCD simultaneously.

Cloud as Synchronization Backbone

The Blynk Cloud is a real-time message broker that ensures state consistency across all clients.

- **Synchronization Model**:
    - ESP32 writes to V0.
    - Cloud broadcasts to all connected apps.
    - User toggles button → Cloud sends to ESP32.
- **Persistent Connection:** WebSocket-based → sub-100ms latency.
- **Multi-Client Support:** 5 phones can view/control the same device simultaneously.
- **Offline Resilience:** Cloud queues last 10 values → syncs on reconnect.

Mobile Notifications — Event-Driven Awareness

Notifications push critical events from the device to the user, independent of open apps.

- **Trigger Types:**
    - **Value-based:** `if (temp > 30) →Blynk.notify("High Temp!")`
    - **State-based:** Pump failure, door opened
    - **Scheduled:** Daily summary
- **Delivery Model:** Push to all authenticated users

Dashboard as System State Mirror

The mobile dashboard is a real-time mirror of the internal state of the IoT system.

- **State Representation:**
    - Gauge = current temperature

  - LED = pump status
  - Graph = historical trend
- User Actions = state transitions
- **Consistency Guarantee:** Cloud ensures what you see is what the device sees.

This creates a digital twin interface — the phone becomes the control room.

Building Mobile Dashboards with Blynk

Blynk dashboard setup procedure is a system design workflow that transforms a bare microcontroller into a fully interactive, cloud-connected interface. This section focuses on core conceptual principles for your textbook — exploring template-based device modeling, authentication token architecture, widget-to-virtual-pin binding, and visual hierarchy design — without mechanics, screenshots, or code. The four steps are not mere instructions; they are architectural decisions that define data contracts, security boundaries, user experience, and system scalability in mobile IoT.

Setup Steps

The Blynk setup process is a structured design pipeline that moves from physical hardware to an abstract data model to secure connectivity to interactive visualization. Each step builds a layer of abstraction, ensuring the final dashboard is intuitive, secure, and maintainable.

1. **Install Blynk IoT App (Android/iOS):** This step establishes the human interface layer — the mobile client that will host all user interaction.
   a. **Conceptual Role:** The app is the control surface and display canvas — a portable operations center.
   b. **Platform Agnosticism:** Identical experience on Android/iOS → cross-platform consistency.
   c. **Offline Capability:** App stores dashboard layout locally → instant load on launch.
   d. **System Implication:** The phone of the user becomes the system console — no PC required post-setup.
2. **Create a New Template → Add Device (ESP32):** This is the device modeling phase — defining a reusable blueprint for all instances of a hardware type.

   Template Concept:
   - **A digital twin schema that specifies:**
     - Device type (ESP32 DevKit)
     - Firmware version
     - Virtual pin definitions (V0–V31)
     - Default widget layout
   - **Reusability:** One template → 100 identical greenhouse nodes
   - **Version Control:** Update template → push UI changes to all devices

   Add Device:
   a. Instantiates a unique runtime instance from the template.
   b. Assigns a device name (Greenhouse_01) and location.
   c. Generates a unique Auth Token.

3. **Copy the Auth Token:** The Auth Token is the cryptographic identity that binds a physical device to its cloud representation.
    - **Token Structure:** 32-character alphanumeric string Security Model:
        - One token per device → granular access control
        - Revocable → regenerate to disconnect compromised units
        - Never exposed in UI → transmitted only during initial setup
    - **Authentication Flow:**
        - ESP32 sends a token on boot.
        - Blynk Cloud validates against the template.
        - Connection authorized → virtual pins activated
    - **Conceptual Role:** The digital passport for cloud access.

Adding Buttons, Sliders, and Graphs to Control LEDs, Fans

The visual dashboard of Blynk into a fully interactive control system by integrating buttons, sliders, and graphs to command physical actuators (LEDs, fans) while monitoring their real-world impact in real time.

The integration of UI controls and data displays in Blynk creates a closed-loop, bidirectional interface where user intent (tap, slide) becomes physical action (LED on, fan speed), and system response (current draw, temperature) is immediately visualized. This section explores how buttons enable discrete control, sliders provide analog precision, and graphs deliver temporal context – forming a complete human-machine interaction cycle that is intuitive, verifiable, and adaptive.

Button Widget – Discrete State Control

The Button widget is a binary command interface that toggles a digital output between two states.

- **Control Model:**
    - **UI:** Button labeled "Living Room Light"
    - **Virtual Pin:** V1
    - **States:** 0 (**OFF**), 1 (**ON**)
    - **Actuator:** LED or relay
- **Interaction Flow:**
    - User taps → App writes 1 to V1
    - ESP32 receives → sets GPIO HIGH
    - LED turns **ON**.
    - ESP32 writes 1 back to V1 (optional echo).
- **Design Patterns:**
    - **Toggle Mode:** Single tap flips the state.
    - **Push Mode:** Hold to activate.
    - **Labeled Feedback:** Button color changes (gray → green).

Slider Widget – Analog Command Precision

The Slider widget maps a continuous user gesture to a proportional actuator output.

- **Control Model**:
    - **UI**: Slider 0–255, labeled "Fan Speed"
    - **Virtual Pin**: V2
    - **Output**: PWM duty cycle (%)
    - **Actuator**: DC fan via transistor/MOSFET
- **Mapping Function**:
    - Slider value **`S → PWM duty = S / 255 × 100%`**
    - Example: **`S = 128 → 50% speed`**
- **Interaction Flow**:
    - User drags the slider to 180
    - App writes 180 to V2
    - **`ESP32 receives → analogWrite(PWM_PIN, 180)`**
    - Fan spins at ~70% speed
- **Design Patterns**:
    - **Step Size**: 5-unit increments → smooth but controlled
    - **Default Position**: 0 on app launch
    - **Haptic Feedback**: Vibration on key values (0, 128, 255)

Graph Widget – Temporal Feedback and Verification

The Graph widget visualizes historical data to confirm actuation effectiveness and system behavior.

- **Data Model**:
    - **Virtual Pin**: V3
    - **Source**: Current sensor (for fan), light sensor (for LED)
    - **Time Base**: Last 1 hour, auto-refresh
- **Verification Use Cases**:
    - **Fan Activation**: Current spikes from 0 mA to 80 mA when slider > 0
    - **LED Dimming**: Light level increases proportionally with the slider.
    - **Thermal Response**: Temperature drops 2°C after the fan starts.
- **Graph Types**:
    - **Line Graph**: Continuous trend.
    - **Step Graph**: Discrete state changes.
    - **Dual Axis**: Speed (left) versus Temperature (right).

State Synchronization and Conflict Resolution

Blynk ensures the UI reflects reality through bidirectional sync.

- **Sync Mechanisms**:
    - **On Connect**: ESP32 pushes current states to all virtual pins.

    - **On Change**: Device writes to pin → cloud → all apps update.
    - **Periodic Heartbeat**: Every 10s to detect disconnect.
- **Conflict Resolution**:
    - **Last Write Wins**: Slider moved on Phone A → Phone B updates.
    - **Physical Override**: Manual switch on device → writes to V1 → apps reflect.

Adaptive Control via Feedback

Graphs enable intelligent automation by closing the perception-action loop.

- **Example Logic**:
    - If Graph(Temp) shows rise > 1°C in 5 min
    - And Slider(Speed) < 150
    - → Auto-increase slider to 200
- **Human-in-the-Loop**:
    - User sees graph → adjusts slider manually
    - System suggests: "Increase fan speed?"

Scalability to Multi-Actuator Systems

The pattern scales via **modular clusters** and **tabbed navigation**.

- **Multi-Zone Dashboard**:
    - **Tab 1**: Living Room (Light + Fan)
    - **Tab 2**: Kitchen (Exhaust + LED Strip)
    - **Tab 3**: Graphs (All sensors)
- **Virtual Pin Namespacing**:
    - V10–V19: Zone 1
    - V20–V29: Zone 2
- **Fleet View**: One app controls 10 ESP32s via device selector.

Using Tokens and Authentication for Secure Sync

Authentication and encryption is the security backbone of cloud-connected IoT systems. Secure synchronization in IoT relies on cryptographic identity, encrypted channels, and controlled access to prevent unauthorized monitoring, command injection, or data tampering. Authentication tokens and HTTPS form a trust boundary that protects the data-in-motion and data-at-rest, transforming open cloud platforms into fortified control systems.

Auth Token — The Digital Identity of the Device

Each Blynk device is assigned a unique Auth Token — a 32-character secret that proves its identity to the cloud.

- **Conceptual Model**:
    - **Token = Device Passport**

    - Generated at device creation → never reused
    - Stored in firmware → sent on connection

- **Authentication Flow**:
    - ESP32 → Blynk Cloud: Auth: a1b2c3d4...
    - Cloud validates against the template database.
    - Connection granted → virtual pins activated
- **Security Properties**:
    - **Uniqueness**: 1 token = 1 device
    - **Revocability**: Regenerate → instantly disconnect
    - **Non-recoverable**: Cannot be derived from device ID.

API Keys and HTTPS Endpoints — Gatekeepers of Firebase

Firebase uses **API keys** and **HTTPS URLs** to authenticate and encrypt data transactions.

- **API Key**:
    - 39-character string embedded in request URL.
- **HTTPS Endpoint**:
    - Enforces TLS 1.2+ encryption.
    - Protects payload confidentiality and integrity.
- **Dual-Layer Auth**:
    - **API Key**→ Project-level access
    - **Security Rules**→ Path-level access

Token Secrecy — The First Line of Defense

Never expose tokens publicly — in GitHub, tutorials, or screenshots.

- **Attack Surface**:
    - Public token → attacker connects as your device
    - Can read sensor data, inject commands, and deny service.
- **Exposure Vectors**:
    - Committed firmware with a hardcoded token
    - Shared tutorial video showing the dashboard
    - Unprotected serial monitor output
- **Defense Principle**:
    - **Tokens are passwords.** Treat them with the same rigor.
    - **Rotate on exposure,** like changing a breached password.

Secure Storage in Production — Environment Isolation

In production systems, store secrets in isolated, non-volatile memory.

- **Storage Strategies**:
    - ESP32 NVS (Non-Volatile Storage): Encrypted partition

- External Secure Element: ATECC608A chip
- OTA-Protected Flash: Write-once during manufacturing

- **Runtime Access**:
  - Load token into RAM at boot
  - Never log or transmit in plaintext
  - Wipe from memory on shutdown
- **Build Pipeline**:
  - Use environment variables in CI/CD
  - Inject token at compile/flash time → never in source

HTTPS – The Encrypted Transport Layer

Always use https:// – never http:// – for all cloud communication.

- **TLS Protection**:
  - **Confidentiality**: Eavesdroppers see only ciphertext.
  - **Integrity**: Tampered packets are rejected.
  - **Authenticity**: Server identity verified via certificate.
- **IoT Constraints**:
  - ESP32 supports TLS offloading.
  - Certificate validation prevents a man-in-the-middle.
- **Fallback Risk**:
  - http:// → data leaked, commands forged
  - Even on "trusted" networks.

Token Lifecycle Management

Treat tokens as **living credentials** with defined stages.

- **Phases**:
  - **Provisioning**: Generated during manufacturing.
  - **Activation**: First connection binds the token to the device.
  - **Rotation**: Scheduled or on suspicion.
  - **Revocation**: Immediate disconnect on compromise.
- **Fleet Operations**:
  - Central dashboard to revoke tokens.
  - OTA update to push new tokens.
- **Audit Trail**:
  - Log token usage: last seen, data volume

Cloud versus Local: Choosing the Right Approach

Cloud-based versus local-only IoT architectures as a strategic design decision that fundamentally shapes functionality, reliability, cost, security, and user experience. This section delivers core conceptual principles for your textbook — exploring data sovereignty, connectivity dependency, latency trade-offs, scalability models, operational autonomy, and failure modes — without mechanics, tools, or code.

Cloud and local processing represent two ends of a connectivity-control spectrum in IoT system design. Cloud-centric systems offload data storage, visualization, and control to internet-hosted platforms (Firebase, Blynk, and Google Sheets), while local-only systems keep all logic, storage, and interfaces within the physical boundary of the device or local network. The choice is not binary but contextual — driven by requirements, constraints, and risk tolerance.

Feature	Cloud Processing	Local Processing
Latency	Higher; dependent on internet connection and server response time.	Lower; near-instantaneous within the local network or device.
Availability	Dependent on continuous internet connectivity and cloud service uptime.	High; functions regardless of internet status, relying only on local power.
Security	Centralized, often robust security measures by the service provider; however, data is transmitted over the internet and stored off-site.	Data remains within the physical boundary of the system; security depends on local network configuration and device hardening.
Cost	Typically involves ongoing subscription fees or pay-as-you-go for service usage and data transfer.	Higher initial hardware cost for local storage and processing power, but lower ongoing service fees.

Table 9.3: *Difference between Cloud Processing and Local Processing*

Data Sovereignty and Ownership

Cloud transfers data custody to a third-party provider; local retains full ownership.

- **Cloud Model**:
  - Data resides in the servers of the providers.
  - Subject to terms of service, data retention policies.
  - **Risk:** Vendor lock-in, account suspension.
- **Local Model**:
  - Data stored on SD card, EEPROM, or local server.
  - Absolute control — no external access.
  - **Compliance:** Meets GDPR, HIPAA, government mandates.

Connectivity, Dependency, and Availability

Cloud requires continuous internet; local operates autonomously.

- **Cloud Failure Modes**:
  - Wi-Fi outage → no logging, no control
  - ISP downtime → global blackout
  - **Mitigation:** Local buffer + sync on reconnect
- **Local Resilience**:
  - Runs during internet apocalypse.
  - Control via Bluetooth, local web server, LCD.
  - **Limitation:** No remote access.

Latency and Real-Time Requirements

Cloud introduces network delay; local offers instant response.

- **Cloud Latency**:
  - **Typical:** 200–800 ms round-trip
  - Critical control → unacceptable
  - Monitoring (temp every 5 min) → negligible
- **Local Latency**:
  - <1 ms for GPIO, PWM
  - Ideal for safety loops, motor control.

Scalability and Maintenance

Cloud scales effortlessly; local scales manually.

- **Cloud Scaling**:
  - Add 1000 devices → same dashboard, same URL
  - Zero infrastructure — auto-backup, redundancy.
- **Local Scaling**:
  - 100 devices → 100 SD cards, 100 web servers
  - Manual firmware updates, physical access.

Cost Structure — CapEx versus OpEx

Cloud is subscription-based; local is an upfront investment.

- **Cloud Costs:**
  - Free tier → $5–50/month at scale
  - Data transfer, storage, API calls.
- **Local Costs:**
  - SD card, RTC, display → one-time
  - No recurring fees.
  - Higher initial complexity.

Security and Attack Surface

Cloud expands exposure; local minimizes external vectors.

- **Cloud Risks:**
  - Token leak → global compromise
  - DDoS, credential stuffing
  - **Mitigation:** HTTPS, token rotation
- **Local Security**:
  - Physical access = only threat
  - No internet → immune to remote hacks
  - **Risk:** Insider theft, firmware reverse-engineering.

User Experience and Accessibility

Cloud enables anywhere access; local requires proximity or VPN.

- **Cloud UX:**
  - Phone, laptop, tablet – same dashboard
  - Share link → instant collaboration
- **Local UX:**
  - Bluetooth range (~10m)
  - Local Wi-Fi + port forwarding/VPN → complex
  - On-device OLED → limited info

Hybrid Topology – Best of Both Worlds

Edge + Cloud combines local resilience with cloud visibility.

- **Architecture**:
  - **Local:** Critical control, buffering, fallback UI.
  - **Cloud**: Long-term storage, remote dashboard, alerts.
- **Sync Strategy**:
  - Push to the cloud when connected.
  - Run locally when offline.
  - Reconcile on reconnect.
- **Example**: Smart farm
  - **Local:** Pump runs on soil moisture.
  - **Cloud:** Logs data, sends SMS on failure.

Platform Comparison: Firebase versus Blynk versus Sheets

Firebase, Blynk, and Google Sheets represent three distinct paradigms in cloud-enabled IoT, each optimized for a different layer of the data-to-action pipeline. Firebase functions as a real-time, structured backend database that stores data in hierarchical JSON, enabling instant bidirectional synchronization across devices and apps. Its strength lies in programmable logic – developers define data models, security rules, and read/write paths, making it ideal for complex, multi-device systems where sensor data drives automation, mobile apps need live updates, or web dashboards require structured queries. The platform excels in scalable, stateful applications – a smart building with 50 sensors pushing temperature, occupancy, and HVAC status can maintain a single source of truth, with rules ensuring only authenticated nodes write to their paths. However, this power comes with a learning curve – security rules, REST endpoints, and JSON structuring demand planning, and costs rise with high-frequency updates.

In contrast, Blynk is a mobile-first, interaction-centric platform that prioritizes human control and visualization over data storage. It uses virtual pins as lightweight data channels, with pre-built widgets – buttons, sliders, graphs – that map directly to microcontroller GPIO or sensor values. The dashboard is the product: a user opens the app and immediately sees live gauges and toggles lights with a tap. Blynk abstracts away backend complexity – no database design, no API management – making it perfect for rapid prototyping, home automation, or field deployments where intuitive control trumps long-term analytics. Its cloud acts as a real-time message broker, not a database, so historical data is limited unless paired with external logging. This focus on UX makes Blynk the go-to for end-user-facing systems, but less suitable for data-heavy analytics or server-side processing.

Google Sheets, meanwhile, transforms a familiar spreadsheet into a low-barrier, collaborative data logger via IFTTT webhooks. An ESP32 sends an HTTP POST with sensor values, and IFTTT appends a new row — timestamp, temperature, status — in real time. The sheet becomes a living logbook: engineers filter for anomalies, plot trends, or share with teams via a link. It requires zero backend setup — no accounts beyond Google, no code beyond a URL — making it ideal for prototyping, educational projects, or small-scale monitoring where accessibility and visual analysis matter more than speed or scale. However, it is not real-time (1–3 second delay), not secure without complex workarounds, and not scalable beyond a few hundred rows per minute. Its power is in democratization — anyone with a browser can view, chart, or export data.

The choice between platforms hinges on the primary system goal. Use Firebase when you need structured, real-time data with programmable access control — think industrial telemetry, multi-zone climate systems, or apps with live leaderboards. Choose Blynk when the user interface is the product — smart lights, irrigation controllers, or robot arms operated from a phone. Opt for Google Sheets when logging and analysis are key, and ease of access outweighs performance — classroom weather stations, personal energy monitors, or proof-of-concept demos. In practice, hybrid approaches prevail: Blynk for control, Firebase for state, Sheets for audit — each platform playing its strength in a layered architecture.

Ultimately, these tools are not competitors but complements in the IoT ecosystem. Firebase is the brain, storing and syncing state. Blynk is the face, delivering interaction. Sheets are the notebook, recording history.

Troubleshooting Real-Time Sync Issues

Real-time synchronization in IoT involves a continuous chain — from sensor data acquisition to cloud update to user interface response. Any disruption in this chain can cause delayed data, missing logs, or inactive controls. Effective troubleshooting requires systematic analysis across five layers: connectivity, authentication, data integrity, timing, and client behavior.

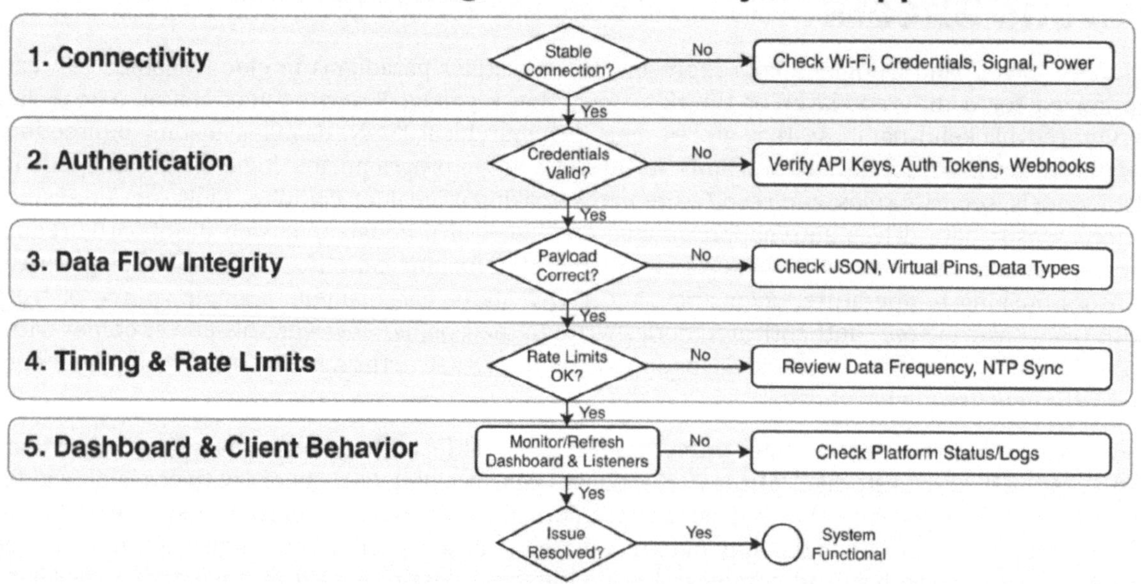

Figure 9.3: *Troubleshoot Flowchart*

1. **Connectivity:** The first step is ensuring that the edge device maintains a stable Wi-Fi connection with valid network credentials and adequate signal strength. Weak connections, interference, or power-saving modes may cause intermittent dropouts, preventing data from reaching the cloud.
2. **Authentication:** Expired or invalid credentials – such as Firebase API keys, Blynk Auth Tokens, or IFTTT webhook URLs – are common causes of silent sync failures. In these cases, devices appear connected but are rejected by the cloud, resulting in "offline" dashboards despite an active Wi-Fi indicator.
3. **Data Flow Integrity:** Malformed JSON payloads, incorrect virtual pin assignments, or mismatched data types often block cloud writes. For instance, Firebase rejects writes restricted by security rules, and Blynk may ignore updates when the firmware and app expect different data formats. IFTTT applets fail if event names or payload fields are incorrectly defined.
4. **Timing and Rate Limits:** Each platform enforces its own data rate constraints Firebase (≈1000 writes/s), Blynk (≈10 updates/s per virtual pin), and IFTTT (≈1 request/s). Exceeding these limits can silently drop updates. Time synchronization using NTP is recommended to maintain consistent timestamps and prevent out-of-order logs.
5. **Dashboard and Client Behavior:** Stale dashboards usually indicate listener detachment or caching issues. Reinitializing Blynk virtual pins or refreshing Firebase listeners ensures current values are displayed. Monitoring platform dashboards – such as Firebase usage metrics, Blynk server status, and IFTTT activity logs – helps identify server-side or regional delays.

By isolating each layer and analyzing logs – Wi-Fi RSSI, HTTP responses, webhook confirmations, and virtual pin echoes – engineers can trace the fault from symptom to source. This disciplined, layer-by-layer methodology transforms unpredictable sync issues into measurable, solvable engineering problems, ensuring reliable real-time IoT performance across Firebase, Blynk, and Google Sheets platforms.

Mini Projects

Project 1: Fire Alert System with Firebase Log

This mini project demonstrates real-time cloud alerting by building a Fire Alert System that detects flames, activates a buzzer, and logs alerts to Firebase. The objective is to create a safety-focused IoT system that senses fire, responds locally with an alert, and records events in the cloud for remote monitoring.

Objective

The objective of the Fire Alert System is to design an IoT prototype that uses an ESP32 to detect flames with a flame sensor, trigger a local buzzer for immediate alert, and log the event to Firebase for remote notification and record-keeping. This project emphasizes integrating sensor data with cloud storage, enabling real-time safety monitoring and historical analysis of fire incidents.

Components

The project uses a minimal set of components to keep it accessible and focused on communication:

- **ESP32**: The microcontroller handles sensor reading, buzzer control, and HTTP uploads to Firebase.
- **Flame Sensor**: Detects infrared light from flames, providing a digital output for threshold-based alerts.

- **Buzzer**: An active buzzer for audible warnings, connected to a digital pin.
- **Jumper Wires**: For connections between components.

These components, assembled on a breadboard with color-coded wires (red for VCC, black for GND), create a compact system. Challenges include power demands—plan for 200mA total—mitigated by external supplies, and component compatibility, ensured by matching pin logic (5V for Uno, 3.3V with level shifters for ESP32). This assembly, taking 20–30 minutes, forms the hardware backbone of the project.

Working

The working of the Fire Alert System is divided into a step-by-step process that ensures reliable detection, local response, and cloud logging, leveraging the Wi-Fi capabilities of ESP32.

1. **Flame Detection**: The flame sensor monitors for infrared radiation from flames. When a flame is detected, it sends a LOW signal (or HIGH, depending on configuration) to the digital pin of ESP32.
2. **Local Alert Activation**: Upon detection, the ESP32 sets the buzzer pin to HIGH, activating the audible alert to notify nearby users immediately.
3. **Data Preparation and Logging**: The ESP32 formats the event data into a JSON payload and sends it via HTTP POST to Firebase.
4. **Firebase Dashboard Update**: Firebase receives the data and updates the dashboard, showing the status "Fire Detected," enabling remote viewing and alerts.

Project 2: Moisture Monitoring System with Google Sheets

This mini project builds a real-time soil moisture monitoring system that logs sensor data directly into Google Sheets via IFTTT Webhooks, enabling long-term trend analysis, remote tracking, and collaborative agriculture.

Objective

The main objective of the Moisture Monitoring System is to design an IoT prototype using an ESP32 and a capacitive soil moisture sensor to continuously measure soil water content, send the data via IFTTT Webhook to Google Sheets, and create a live, shareable log that displays moisture trends over time. This project emphasizes serverless cloud logging, time-series data, and collaborative analytics, ideal for agriculture, education, and environmental monitoring.

Components

The project uses minimal, widely available components to keep it affordable and scalable:

- **ESP32 (DevKit V1 or similar):** Handles analog sensor reading, Wi-Fi connectivity, and HTTP POST to IFTTT.
- **Capacitive Soil Moisture Sensor (v1.2 or v2.0):** Non-corrosive analog sensor with 0–3.3V output (0V = dry, 3.3V = wet).
- **Jumper Wires:** For secure breadboard connections.
- **Breadboard (optional)**: For clean prototyping.

Working

The system follows a clear, event-driven pipeline from soil to cloud:

1. **Soil Moisture Sensing:**
   - The capacitive sensor outputs an analog voltage proportional to soil water content.
   - ESP32 reads this via ADC1 (GPIO 34–39) → converts to 0–4095 (12-bit).
2. **Data Processing:** Raw ADC value is mapped to percentage moisture using calibration: `Moisture % = map(ADC, dryValue, wetValue, 0, 100)`

   Example: **`dryValue`** = 2800, **`wetValue`** = 1200
3. **HTTP POST to IFTTT Webhook:**
   - ESP32 formats data into JSON: `{"value1": moisture%, "value2": timestamp}`
   - Sends via HTTPS POST to the IFTTT webhook URL.
4. **IFTTT Applet Trigger:**
   - Webhook receives request → triggers Google Sheets → Add Row action.
   - Appends new row: `Timestamp | Moisture (%) | Device: ESP32_Soil_01`
5. **Google Sheets Visualization:**
   - Sheet auto-updates every 5 minutes.
   - Users insert line chart → view daily/weekly moisture trends.

Project 3: Blynk-Based Smart Fan

This mini project transforms a regular electric fan into a remotely controllable smart device using mobile dashboard of Blynk, an ESP32, and a relay module.

Objective

The prime objective of the Blynk-Based Smart Fan is to design an IoT system where a mobile app button sends real-time commands via the Blynk Cloud to an ESP32, which toggles a relay module to control a 230V AC fan, working with 230V AC mains voltage, which is extremely dangerous and can be fatal. Strict electrical safety precautions are mandatory.

- **Isolation:** Ensure all high-voltage components are properly isolated from the low-voltage control circuitry. Use optocouplers, relays with sufficient voltage rating and clearance, and proper transformers.
- **Enclosure:** The entire high-voltage circuit, including wiring and connections, must be securely enclosed in a non-conductive, fire-resistant casing to prevent accidental contact and fire hazards.
- **Grounding:** Implement proper grounding for safety.
- **Handling:** Always disconnect the device from the mains supply before performing any inspection, modification, or maintenance. Do not touch any wires or components while the device is plugged in.

Professional Oversight: If you are not experienced with mains voltage electronics, seek guidance from a qualified professional.

Components

The project uses safe, reliable components for high-voltage control:

- **ESP32 (DevKit V1):** Processes Blynk commands and drives the relay.
- **5V Single-Channel Relay Module:** Electromechanical switch for 230V AC loads (rated 10A).
- **Electric Fan (Table/Pedestal):** Standard 230V AC appliance.
- **Jumper Wires:** For low-voltage connections.
- **Power Supply:** 5V 1A adapter for ESP32 + relay.

Working

The system follows a secure, real-time control loop:

1. **Blynk App Initialization:**

   User opens app → connects to Blynk Cloud → loads dashboard.

2. **Button Press:**

   The user taps the "Fan ON" button → app writes 1 to Virtual Pin V1.

3. **Cloud Sync:**

   Blynk Cloud instantly pushes V1 = 1 to ESP32.

4. **Relay Activation:**

   ESP32 receives 1 → sets GPIO HIGH → relay clicks → fan turns ON.

5. **Feedback Loop:**

   ESP32 confirms relay state → writes 1 back to V1 → app button turns green.

6. **Reverse Flow:**

   Tap "OFF" → V1 = 0 → relay opens → fan stops.

Conclusion

This chapter marked the transition of IoT systems from local, wired communication to globally connected, cloud-based architectures. Building upon the protocols introduced in Serial Communication & Data Transmission Between Devices, such as UART, SPI, and I²C, this chapter expanded the scope of IoT to include internet-driven communication and real-time data exchange. It demonstrated how microcontrollers evolve from isolated devices into intelligent, networked nodes capable of sensing, logging, and responding from anywhere in the world.

The chapter introduced three major platforms—Firebase, Google Sheets through IFTTT, and Blynk—that together create a complete cloud-based IoT ecosystem. Each platform serves a distinct purpose. Firebase provides a structured and scalable backend for storing and synchronizing data in real time. Google Sheets with IFTTT offers a simple, low-cost approach for data logging and visualization without the need for a dedicated server. Blynk delivers an intuitive mobile interface, enabling users to interact directly with devices through buttons, sliders, and real-time dashboards.

Security formed a vital part of this chapter. The importance of authentication tokens, HTTPS encryption, and secure key storage was emphasized as a foundation for trustworthy connectivity. Learners discovered that every cloud transaction must be protected, as a single leaked token or unsecured connection can compromise the entire system. Implementing encryption and access control was shown to be a mandatory step toward building production-grade IoT solutions.

Equally important was the analytical framework for selecting the right platform. Firebase was suited for structured, high-scale systems; Google Sheets offered simplicity and collaboration; and Blynk provided real-time interaction. The combination of these tools formed hybrid architectures that balanced performance, usability, and cost, preparing learners to make informed design choices based on application needs.

The chapter also established a clear method for troubleshooting real-time synchronization issues. Learners were guided through a systematic process of verification—checking connectivity, validating authentication, ensuring proper data format, monitoring timing, and confirming dashboard synchronization. This approach helps maintain reliable performance and reduces downtime in field-deployed systems. By learning to trace data from the sensor to the cloud and back to the user, engineers can diagnose problems efficiently and restore real-time communication with precision.

Three mini projects illustrated these principles in practice. The fire alert system used Firebase for real-time event logging, demonstrating how cloud databases can extend the reach of safety systems. The soil moisture monitoring project used Google Sheets and IFTTT to log environmental data collaboratively and visualize changes over time. The smart fan project implemented Blynk-based mobile control, showcasing instant actuation through a simple user interface. Each project reinforced theoretical knowledge with practical experience, helping learners connect cloud concepts with hardware implementation.

Ultimately, this chapter expanded the understanding of learners, of IoT from local circuits to global networks. It presented IoT as a digital ecosystem where sensors, actuators, cloud services, and users form an intelligent, responsive web of communication. By completing this chapter, students gained the ability to design systems that sense locally but act globally, integrating real-time data, secure connectivity, and user interaction into one cohesive architecture.

With the mastery of cloud connectivity achieved, learners are now prepared to explore more advanced topics. The following chapters will move toward long-range and low-power communication technologies such as LoRa and NB-IoT, introduce artificial intelligence at the edge using TensorFlow Lite, and explore MQTT-based architectures for industrial IoT. This chapter thus serves as both a milestone and a gateway, marking the point where IoT moves beyond experimentation to scalable, intelligent, and globally connected systems.

The next chapter will build upon this foundation by introducing the professional communication backbone of modern IoT—MQTT, REST APIs, and Webhooks. Unlike serial or basic Wi-Fi communication, these technologies enable secure, scalable, and lightweight messaging between devices and cloud servers. Readers will learn to transmit commands and data efficiently over HTTP and MQTT brokers, implement Webhooks to trigger external services, and integrate devices with advanced backend systems. Using platforms such as Adafruit IO, HiveMQ, and IFTTT, students will create cloud-synced devices capable of reliable, low-bandwidth communication across diverse networks. This next step transforms connected prototypes into robust, interoperable IoT systems capable of seamless communication across platforms and applications. By completing this chapter, you can now build cloud-connected IoT systems that log and visualize data by collecting sensor data and logging it securely to platforms like Google Sheets or Firebase in real time; enable global control of physical devices (like a fan or lights) from anywhere in the world using a mobile application like Blynk; implement real-time alerts by creating systems that monitor conditions (like fire or high moisture) and trigger instant, real-time alerts stored in a cloud database; design hybrid architectures by choosing the right combination of platforms (Firebase for structure, Google Sheets for logging, Blynk for UI) to balance performance, cost, and usability; ensure data security by integrating fundamental security measures, including authentication tokens and encryption, to protect cloud transactions; and troubleshoot connectivity by systematically diagnosing and resolving issues in the data path from the sensor, through the cloud, and back to the user interface.

Chapter 10
MQTT, REST APIs, and Webhooks for Device Communication

Introduction

In *Chapter 9, Firebase, Blynk and Google Sheets,* you learned how to push sensor data to cloud platforms such as Firebase, log information into Google Sheets using IFTTT, and control devices through a Blynk mobile dashboard. These tools provided quick connectivity and were ideal for prototypes, classroom experiments, and small-scale IoT deployments. However, most of those integrations relied on platform-specific or point-to-point connections. As IoT systems scale, devices must communicate through standardized communication layers that support reliable, secure, and large-scale data exchange across multiple platforms and services.

This chapter introduces the communication protocols and services that power modern IoT ecosystems. You will explore key technologies such as MQTT for lightweight real-time messaging, REST APIs for request–response communication with cloud services, and Webhooks for event-driven automation between systems. By the end of this chapter, you will understand how these communication mechanisms enable device-to-cloud, device-to-device, and cloud-to-cloud interactions, and how they are used to build scalable, interoperable, and production-ready IoT solutions.

Structure

In this chapter, we will cover the following topics:

- Understanding the Client–Server Model in IoT
- Push versus Pull versus Publish–Subscribe: Webhooks, REST, and MQTT
- MQTT Architecture: Broker, Publisher, Subscriber
- Installing and using MQTT Libraries on the ESP32
- Publishing Sensor Data to MQTT Brokers (HiveMQ, Adafruit IO)
- Subscribing to Control Commands (Turning a Fan ON/OFF)
- Setting up RESTful Endpoints on the ESP32
- Creating and Testing GET/POST Requests from Firmware
- Using Webhooks for Alerts, Logging, and Automation
- Example: Door Sensor Triggering an Email via Webhook

- Working with JSON: Serialization, Parsing, and Best Practices
- When to use MQTT versus REST versus Webhooks
- Sample Projects
    - MQTT-Based Smart Irrigation Controller
    - REST API–Based Home Automation System
    - Webhook-Based Gas Leak Alert System

Understanding the Client–Server Model in IoT

Everything you built in *Chapter 9, Firebase, Blynk and Google Sheets* — whether pushing temperature to Firebase, toggling a fan via Blynk, or logging soil moisture into Google Sheets – was running on top of this exact architecture.

- **Client**: The IoT edge device itself — ESP32, NodeMCU, Raspberry Pi Pico W, STM32 with NB-IoT module, or a solar-powered LoRaWAN sensor nodes. The client is the active initiator: it decides when to connect, what data to send, and what commands to request.
- **Server**: The always-on, always-listening central system — a cloud MQTT broker (HiveMQ, EMQX, Mosquitto on AWS), a REST API endpoint (AWS API Gateway, Azure Functions, own Node.js server), or a platform service (ThingSpeak, Blynk Cloud, Firebase). The server is passive but authoritative: it waits for clients, processes their messages, stores state, enforces security rules, and responds when asked.

The Request–Response Dance (Synchronous Communication)

The classic example you already know from *Chapter 9, Firebase, Blynk and Google Sheets*, is **REST over HTTP**:

1. **Client (ESP32)** wakes up → reads DHT22 → packages JSON → POST https://api.thingspeak.com/update
2. **Server (ThingSpeak)** receives, validates API key, stores in database, replies “200 OK”
3. **Client** sees success → goes back to sleep.

This is a synchronous **request–response**: the client blocks and waits for an answer. It is perfect for:

- Firmware OTA updates
- Device provisioning
- Fetching configuration
- Logging to Google Sheets via IFTTT webhook

Push Model

The moment something happens, the server immediately pushes a notification to a pre-registered URL without being asked.

How it works in practice:

Gas sensor on ESP32 detects LPG → sends HTTP POST to IFTTT webhook→ IFTTT instantly pushes email/SMS/Telegram/WhatsApp message → you get “ALERT: Gas Leak in Kitchen!” while sitting in a movie theatre in Mumbai.

Key characteristics:

- **Event-driven:** zero polling, zero delay.
- **One-way:** source → destination only.
- **No persistent connection** needed.
- **Perfect for alerts:** fire, intrusion, power failure, cold-chain breach.

Advantages: Instant, battery-friendly (device sleeps after one POST), easy to integrate with 5000+ services (Zapier, Make.com, n8n)

Disadvantages: No acknowledgement (fire-and-forget unless you add verification), destination must expose public URL, limited payload size

Pull Model

The client **actively polls** the server at regular intervals asking, "Anything for me"

How it works in practice:

Every 30 seconds ESP32 performs:

`GET` https://api.myfarm.in/devices/12345/config → receives `JSON {"pump":1, "threshold":40}` → turns pump ON

Key characteristics:

- **Request-response:** Client initiates everything.
- **Synchronous:** ESP32 waits for reply.
- **Predictable:** Easy to debug with `Serial.print`.

Advantages: Works behind NAT/firewalls, full control over timing, easy authentication (API keys), perfect for configuration and OTA

Disadvantages: Wastes battery and bandwidth (even when nothing changed), delay = polling interval (30 s → max 30 s latency), server load increases linearly with devices

Publish–Subscribe Model

Devices **publish** messages to named topics. Any subscriber to that topic receives the message instantly via the broker. No device ever knows who else is listening.

How it works in practice:

Temperature sensor publishes pune/factory42/line7/temp → 38.5

Node-RED dashboard, Grafana, mobile app, and factory PLC — all subscribed — receive it within 50 ms.

Key characteristics

- **Many-to-many:** one publisher → unlimited subscribers.
- **Decoupled:** publisher and subscriber never meet.
- **Broker-centric:** Mosquitto/EMQX/HiveMQ does all the heavy lifting.
- **Ultra-efficient:** 2-byte header versus 200+ bytes HTTP.

Advantages: Near-zero latency, battery life measured in years, scales to millions, works over unreliable networks (QoS 1/2), retained messages = instant state for new subscribers

Disadvantages: Requires always-on broker, more complex security (username/password + ACLs), learning curve for topic design

Feature	Push Model	Pull Model	Publish-Subscribe Model
Latency	Instant (zero delay)	High (up to polling interval)	Near-zero (milliseconds)
Battery Impact	Very Low (sleeps after POST)	High (wastes battery/ bandwidth)	Very Low (measured in years)
Scalability	Moderate (server must handle all POSTs)	Low (server load increases linearly with devices)	High (scales to millions via broker)
Typical Use Cases	Alerts (fire, intrusion, power failure)	Configuration updates, OTA (Over-The-Air) updates	Real-time sensor data, Decoupled systems

***Table 10.1:** Push, Pull and Publish Subscribe Model*

MQTT Architecture: Broker, Publisher, Subscriber

MQTT (Message Queuing Telemetry Transport) is the dominant protocol in large-scale IoT telemetry worldwide. Designed in 1999 by Dr. Andy Stanford-Clark of IBM and Arlen Nipper for monitoring oil pipelines over extremely low-bandwidth satellite links, MQTT today powers billions of devices. It is a brilliantly simple yet incredibly powerful three-component model: Broker, Publisher, and Subscriber – working together like an ultra-efficient postal system for the Internet of Things.

The Broker – The Central Nervous System

The MQTT broker is the always-on, intelligent server that receives, routes, filters, queues, and delivers every single message in the system.

The broker does **everything**:

- Accepts connections from thousands of devices.
- Enforces username/password, X.509 certificates, and ACLs (Authentication mechanisms can vary depending on the specific broker implementation.).
- Routes messages using topic hierarchy and wildcards.
- Queues messages when subscribers are offline (QoS 1/2).
- Sends retained messages so new subscribers instantly know the current state.
- Forwards Last Will and Testament (LWT) when a device dies unexpectedly.

The Publisher – The Voice of the Physical World

Any device that produces data is a publisher:

- ESP32 reading DHT22 in a Pune warehouse.
- LoRaWAN soil sensor in a Nashik vineyard.
- PLC monitoring motor current in a Bengaluru factory.
- Electric vehicle sending battery SoC every second.

The Subscriber – The Listener That Takes Action

Anything that needs data is a subscriber:

- Node-RED dashboard in a control room.
- Grafana live graph on the phone of a manager.

- Mobile app showing farm moisture.
- Another ESP32 that turns on a pump when moisture < 25%.
- Cloud Lambda that triggers SMS on fire alarm.

Installing and Using MQTT Libraries

Among several excellent options, one library has achieved near-universal adoption for MQTT on resource-constrained devices: **`PubSubClient`** by Nick O'Leary. A caution, however, is that **`PubSubClient`** is synchronous. For applications requiring high publish rates or non-blocking operation, an asynchronous alternative like **`AsyncMQTT`** might be preferred. First released in 2012 and continuously maintained ever since, **`PubSubClient`** is lightweight (under 15 KB flash usage), extremely stable, and supports the complete MQTT 3.1.1 specification including QoS 0–2.

Seamless Integration with Arduino IDE

The Arduino ecosystem has made library installation exceptionally user-friendly, eliminating the complex dependency management that once frustrated developers. To begin using **`PubSubClient`**, open the Arduino IDE and navigate to Sketch → Include Library → Manage Libraries. This opens the Library Manager – a curated repository containing thousands of verified libraries. In the search box at the top right, type "**`PubSubClient`**" and the official entry by Nick O'Leary will appear instantly. A single click on the Install button downloads, verifies, and places the library in the correct directory, ready for immediate use. The entire process typically completes in under ten seconds even on modest internet connections common in rural engineering colleges.

Several technical characteristics explain its dominance in real-world deployments. First, its memory footprint is remarkably small – crucial when you are running multiple sensors, OTA updates, and Wi-Fi stack simultaneously on an ESP32. Second, it implements non-blocking operation, **`loop()`** function never freezes while waiting for broker responses – a critical requirement for responsive user interfaces and time-critical control loops. Third, it gracefully handles network interruptions by automatically attempting reconnection and restoring subscriptions, behavior expected in industrial environments where 4G signals fluctuate or Wi-Fi access points reboot. Finally, its clean and well-documented API has remained stable for years, allowing firmware written in 2018 to compile and run perfectly on ESP32 boards in 2025.

Alternative Libraries for Specialized Needs

While **`PubSubClient`** remains the default choice, the ecosystem offers specialized alternatives for advanced scenarios. The **`AsyncMQTT`** library provides fully asynchronous operation using the native asynchronous TCP stack of ESP32, reducing CPU usage during high-frequency publishing – useful in energy-harvesting applications. The MQTT library by Joel Gaehwiler offers native support for MQTT 5.0 features such as user properties and enhanced authentication, increasingly required by enterprise brokers like HiveMQ and EMQX in large projects. However, for the vast majority of educational, prototype, and production deployments, **`PubSubClient`** strikes the perfect balance between capability and simplicity.

Preparing Development Environment

Before installing any MQTT library, ensure Arduino IDE is properly configured for ESP32 development. The ESP32 board package by Espressif Systems must be installed via the Boards Manager, providing access to all GPIO pins, dual-core operation, and the latest Wi-Fi drivers. Additionally, having a stable internet connection is essential, as the Library Manager downloads files directly from the content delivery network of GitHub.

The Installation Process in Practice

When you initiate the installation, the Library Manager displays version information and release notes. The latest stable version includes optimizations specifically for the ESP32-C3 and ESP32-S3 series, improving reconnection performance on low-power networks common in rural deployments. After installation completes, the IDE automatically includes example sketches demonstrating basic connection, publishing, subscribing, and reconnection logic. These examples serve as perfect starting points for both classroom exercises and real-world prototypes.

Publishing Sensor Data to MQTT

Publishing live sensor data from an ESP32 to a public MQTT broker, leveraging lightweight nature of MQTT for efficiency, often involves typical payload sizes of **<100 bytes**. This is the exact same action that occurs billions of times per second worldwide — when a smart meter in Lucknow reports energy consumption, when a cold-storage sensor in Bhiwandi records vaccine temperature, when a Tesla in California streams battery voltage, or when a solar-powered weather station in rural Rajasthan transmits rainfall data. The only difference between those industrial systems and what you are doing right now is scale — the underlying principle, protocol, and workflow are identical.

The DHT11 remains one of the most widely used sensors in education and prototyping because it is inexpensive, robust, and provides both temperature and humidity in a single package. Despite its modest accuracy (±2 °C, ±5% RH), it is perfectly adequate for learning telemetry concepts and for real applications such as classroom monitoring, home automation, greenhouse control, and warehouse comfort tracking. When connected to an ESP32 and combined with MQTT, a DHT11 becomes a globally accessible environmental monitor visible from any smartphone, laptop, or control room on Earth.

For immediate, zero-cost, no-installation testing, the industry has converged on public community brokers that allow anonymous connections with generous fair-use limits. Cluster maintained by HiveMQ GmbH in Germany, has been continuously available since 2014 and handles millions of messages daily from students, hobbyists, and enterprises testing new devices. Alternative public brokers such as **`broker.emqx.io`** and **`test.mosquitto.org`** serve the same purpose with similar reliability. These brokers require no account, no credit card, and no configuration — simply connect and publish.

The complete data flow from sensor to cloud is remarkably straightforward yet incredibly powerful. Every 10 to 30 seconds (the interval used by most real-world deployments), the ESP32 wakes its DHT11 sensor, initiates a reading, converts the raw values into meaningful numbers, packages them as compact strings, and publishes them to the appropriate topics. The public broker instantly routes these messages to every subscriber worldwide — a classmate in Kerala running MQTT Explorer, a teacher monitoring a Node-RED dashboard in Bengaluru, or a parent checking classroom comfort from Dubai. No polling, no delays, no central server to maintain — pure publish subscribe efficiency.

While many educational examples publish raw numbers as plain strings ("29.4"), systems increasingly adopt lightweight JSON payloads that travel well across languages and platforms.

Quality of Service (QoS) Selection for Sensor Data

MQTT offers three delivery guarantees, and sensor telemetry almost universally uses QoS 0 or QoS 1. QoS 0 ("fire and forget") is perfectly acceptable when publishing every 15 seconds because missing one reading out of 5760 daily messages has negligible impact. QoS 1 ("at least once") adds a lightweight acknowledgement ensuring that the broker received the message, and is preferred in medical cold-chain monitoring or energy metering where regulators demand evidence of delivery. QoS 2, with its four-message handshake, is reserved for financial transactions or safety-critical commands, not routine telemetry.

Rule-of-Thumb: For faster decisions, consider telemetry/data = QoS 0 or QoS 1, and commands/critical actions = QoS 1 or QoS 2.

The Callback Function

When ESP32 subscribes to a topic, the broker pushes every new message on that topic directly to the device. The `PubSubClient` library triggers a callback function the instant a message arrives — even if you're deep inside `delay()`.

***Important**: The logic inside the callback function must be lightweight and execute quickly. Avoid long delays, complex calculations, or blocking operations, as this can prevent the main loop() function from running, which is crucial for maintaining the MQTT connection and other device operations on the ESP32.*

Key Advantages of MQTT Subscription Over Traditional Methods

- **Zero polling:** Saves battery, reduces network traffic.
- **Instant response:** <500 ms end-to-end latency worldwide.
- **Works behind NAT/firewalls**: No port forwarding needed.
- **Scalable**: One topic can control 10,000 fans simultaneously.
- **Secure**: TLS + ACLs ensure only authorized users can command.

Setting up RESTful Endpoints

While MQTT excels at real-time telemetry and instant control, REST (Representational State Transfer) over HTTP/HTTPS remains the undisputed king for structured, transactional, and human-readable operations. Every major cloud provider — AWS IoT, Azure IoT Hub, Google Cloud IoT, Alibaba Cloud, and Indian platforms like T-Hub and NIELIT — exposes device management through REST endpoints.

What Makes an API "RESTful"

A truly RESTful API treats every resource (device, sensor, user, log) as a noun with a unique URL, and uses standard HTTP methods as verbs:

- `GET`: Retrieve current state (safe, idempotent, cacheable).
- `POST`: Create new resource or trigger action.
- `PUT/PATCH`: Update existing resource (idempotent).
- `DELETE`: Remove resource (rarely used with devices).

When discussing RESTful APIs, it is important to understand the difference between PUT and POST regarding idempotency.

- A `POST` request is **not idempotent**. Sending the same `POST` request multiple times will typically result in the creation of multiple resources (such as submitting the same sensor data repeatedly).
- A `PUT` request is **idempotent**. Sending the same `PUT` request multiple times will result in the *same* state on the server (it either creates the resource if it does not exist or completely replaces an existing one with the provided payload). This difference is crucial for IoT scenarios where network reliability can be an issue and repeated requests might occur.

Cloud-Native Platforms

- **Firebase Realtime Database/Firestore**: REST streaming + security rules
- **AWS API Gateway + Lambda**: Serverless, auto-scaling

- **Azure Functions + IoT Hub**: Enterprise integration
- **ThingSpeak**: MATLAB analytics + simple REST

Self-Hosted Servers

- **Node.js + Express.js**: Lightweight, runs on Raspberry Pi.
- **Python Flask/FastAPI**: Preferred in research labs.
- **NestJS (TypeScript)**: Enterprise favorite in Bengaluru startups.

Testing and Prototyping Endpoints

- `webhook.site`: Instant public URL for testing POSTs.
- `Mockbin/Beeceptor`: Simulate responses and inspect payloads.
- `Postman Mock Servers`: Full control over status codes and delays.

Advantages of REST

- Human-readable URLs and JSON payloads
- Works with any programming language and tool (curl, Postman, browser)
- Excellent tooling: Swagger/OpenAPI documentation, automatic SDK generation
- Built-in authentication (API keys, JWT, OAuth2)
- Caching, load balancing, and CDN support → handles millions of requests

Creating and Testing GET/POST from ESP32

Making ESP32 act as an **HTTP client** that can perform GET and POST requests exactly like a web browser or mobile app. This is how billions of devices worldwide talk to REST APIs.

HTTP GET/POST from ESP32

- Every cloud platform (Firebase, ThingSpeak, AWS, custom servers) uses HTTP.
- Firmware OTA updates are downloaded via HTTPS GET.
- Device provisioning and configuration happen over POST.
- Webhooks and alerts are triggered by POST.
- Even MQTT-only systems use HTTP for initial registration and OTA.

HTTP Client on ESP32

GET Request→ Retrieve data (no body, safe, cacheable)

POST Request→ Send data (has body, used for updates and triggers)

Key HTTP status codes you will see:

- 200 OK → Success
- 201 Created → Resource created
- 400 Bad Request → JSON malformed
- 401 Unauthorized → Wrong API key
- 404 Not Found → Wrong URL

- 429 Too Many Requests → Rate limited
- 503 Service Unavailable → Service temporarily overloaded or down

Required Libraries

- `WiFi.h`→ Built-in ESP32 Wi-Fi stack
- `HTTPClient.h`→ Lightweight, official Espress if HTTP client
- `WiFiClientSecure.h`→ For HTTPS (mandatory in 2025)

Using Webhooks for Cloud Alerts and Automation

While MQTT delivers real-time data and REST handles configuration, webhooks are the lightning-fast messenger that transforms a sensor reading into an immediate human action – without requiring any server, polling, or complex backend.

Webhook

A webhook is simply an HTTP GET or POST request that ESP32 sends the moment something important happens. Instead of waiting for a dashboard to refresh or a cloud function to run every minute, the device itself screams "ALERT!" directly to the internet, and the receiving service reacts instantly.

This is event-driven, serverless, zero-latency automation – the same mechanism that powers every emergency notification system.

Webhooks Work: The Complete Flow

ESP32 continuously monitors sensors → detects a critical condition → immediately fires an HTTP request → a cloud service receives it → triggers one or more actions (email, SMS, WhatsApp, Google Sheets entry, siren, phone call, Slack message).

Webhook Event Flow

ESP32 → [Wi-Fi] → Internet →Webhook Receiver (IFTTT / Make.com / n8n / Zapier / custom server) → Action (Email, SMS, Google Sheet, Telegram, Pushbullet, and so on.)

Webhooks Are Perfect for Critical Alerts

- **Instant**: No polling delay.
- **Battery-friendly**: Device sleeps until event occurs.
- **Zero infrastructure**: No server to maintain.
- **Reliable**: Uses same HTTPS stack as banking apps.
- **Massively scalable**: One webhook can trigger 50 actions simultaneously.

Example: Door Sensor Triggering Email via Webhook

An intelligent door sensor that instantly notifies you the moment someone opens a door – whether it is a home, a warehouse, a bank locker, or a cold room. Unlike temperature or humidity that changes gradually and can be sent every few minutes, a door opening is a binary, critical, time-sensitive event. You do not want to wait 30 seconds for the next MQTT publish cycle or dashboard refresh – you want to know right now. Webhooks deliver this instant notification using a single HTTP GET or POST the moment the reed switch changes state. In real deployments, however, careful debouncing is needed to filter out false positives from vibration or magnetic jitter.

Components of the System

- **ESP32 Development Board**: Brain of the system, always awake or in light-sleep.
- **Magnetic Reed Switch**: Simple ₹30 sensor with two states: closed (magnet near) or open (door opened).
- **Webhook Service**: IFTTT, `Make.com`, `webhook.site`, or custom server.
- **Notification Channel**: Email, SMS, WhatsApp, Telegram, phone call, or all combined.

The ESP32 continuously monitors the reed switch connected to a GPIO pin configured as input with internal pull-up. When the door is closed, the switch connects the pin to ground → GPIO reads LOW. The moment someone opens the door, the magnetic contact breaks → GPIO instantly goes HIGH. The ESP32 detects this rising edge (often using interrupt for sub-50ms response) and immediately fires an HTTP GET or POST request to a pre-configured webhook URL. The webhook service receives the request within 1–2 seconds and triggers the configured actions – sending an email titled "SECURITY ALERT: Front Door Opened at 09:22 PM", pushing a notification to phone, or even triggering a loud siren via another connected device.

JSON Formatting: Serialization and Parsing

JSON strikes the perfect balance between simplicity and power. It JSON strikes the perfect balance between simplicity and power. For ESP32 development, the ArduinoJson library is widely considered the de-facto standard for handling JSON parsing and serialization. JSONuses plain text that any human can read and debug, yet it can represent complex nested data structures that real-world sensors produce. Every major programming language – C++, Python, JavaScript, Java, Go – has rock-solid JSON libraries. Every cloud platform, mobile app framework, and database speaks JSON natively. When ESP32 sends temperature, humidity, GPS coordinates, battery level, and device status in one message, JSON is the only format that handles this gracefully without custom parsing code.

- **Key-value pairs** form the foundation. Each sensor reading or configuration has a name and value.
- **Objects** (curly braces) group related data. It is perfect for the complete state of one device.
- **Arrays** (square brackets) handle multiple readings or devices.
- **Nested structures** allow hierarchical data – location inside device inside factory
- **Data types** include strings, numbers, booleans, and null – exactly what sensors produce.

The Two Directions: Serialization and Parsing

Serialization (device → cloud)

ESP32 reads sensors → organizes data into structured key value pairs → converts to compact JSON string → sends via MQTT, HTTP POST, or webhook. This process is called serialization and happens millions of times per second across smart meters and factory sensors.

Parsing (cloud → device or device → device)

ESP32 receives a JSON command → breaks it into individual fields → extracts new setpoint or configuration → applies changes. This reverse process is called parsing and powers remote control of everything from street lights to irrigation pumps.

Use of MQTT, REST and Webhooks

In modern IoT systems, devices must exchange data reliably, efficiently, and often in real time. The challenge is that these devices vary widely – from tiny battery-powered sensors to cloud applications running massive analytics. To bridge these gaps, three core communication approaches dominate the IoT landscape today: MQTT, REST APIs, and Webhooks. Each of these technologies solves a different part of the communication puzzle and is chosen based on the nature of the device, the latency requirements, and the system architecture.

Use of MQTT in IoT

MQTT (Message Queuing Telemetry Transport) is purpose-built for devices that need to send small packets of data frequently, often over unreliable networks. Its ultra-lightweight design makes it ideal for low-power sensors, wearables, industrial monitoring systems, and remote devices deployed in environments with weak connectivity.

Instead of devices directly talking to each other, MQTT uses a broker that sits at the center.

- A device publishes messages to a specific topic.
- Other devices subscribe to that topic.

  This removes tightly coupled communication, allowing systems to scale easily as more devices join.

MQTT minimizes data overhead, making it efficient for:

- Rural IoT deployments
- Mobile devices
- Satellite communication
- Battery-powered sensors

  Even when connectivity drops, MQTT can queue data or deliver retained messages once the device comes back online.

MQTT supports three QoS levels:

- **QoS 0**: "At most once"; fastest, lowest guarantee.
- **QoS 1**: "At least once"; balances reliability and speed.
- **QoS 2**: "Exactly once"; maximum reliability.

These QoS levels let developers fine-tune reliability based on use case needs.

Use of REST APIs

Representational State Transfer (REST) APIs allow IoT devices and cloud applications to communicate using standard web protocols. REST is not limited to IoT – it is universally used across the web – making it easy for IoT platforms to integrate with the existing enterprise systems.REST treats every element of the system – devices, sensors, users, and data objects – as a resource that can be created, updated, retrieved, or deleted using simple HTTP methods like:

- `GET`
- `POST`
- `PUT`
- `DELETE`

This makes REST APIs intuitive, predictable, and easy for developers to work with.

Most IoT platforms use REST APIs to:

- Register devices
- Update firmware
- Fetch historical data
- Authenticate users
- Manage configurations

REST becomes the bridge between the IoT world and powerful cloud services like analytics, storage, dashboards, and ML pipelines.

REST is great for request-response operations. However, it is not built for real-time push-based communication. Devices must explicitly request updates, which adds latency and increases network cost. This is why REST is typically used for device management and configuration, rather than continuous data streaming.

Use of Webhooks in IoT

Webhooks work like "reverse APIs."

Instead of a device or application continuously requesting information, a webhook automatically pushes data to a URL whenever an event occurs.

This is highly efficient for systems that do not need continuous data transmission but require immediate response to certain triggers.

Webhooks are simple to set up:

1. Provide a callback URL.
2. Trigger an event.
3. Automatically receive the data in real time.

This makes them perfect for connecting IoT platforms to external services like dashboards, alerts, automations, and workflow engines. Because webhooks push data instantly, they eliminate the need for:

- Polling
- Periodic API calls
- Manual refresh

This reduces network load, and improves responsiveness.

Mini Projects

Each project demonstrates how MQTT, REST APIs, Webhooks, and JSON operate together inside a real-world IoT architecture. Students gain a clear, implementation-oriented perspective on device communication, cloud integration, and event-driven automation. Every project is intentionally scoped to be achievable within a short academic cycle while maintaining the structural integrity of an actual deployed system.

Project 1: MQTT Smart Irrigation Controller

Automatically water crops only when soil actually needs it, while allowing farmers or agronomists to remotely override from anywhere.

Complete System Flow

- A capacitive soil moisture sensor continuously reads percentage moisture (0–100%).
- ESP32 publishes the value every 30 seconds to an MQTT topic: India/Maharashtra/Nashik/farm42/plot7/moisture.
- A cloud dashboard (Node-RED, Grafana, or mobile app) subscribes and shows live graph.
- When moisture falls below 30%, the cloud (or the ESP32 itself) publishes "ON" to India/Maharashtra/Nashik/farm42/plot7/pump/command.
- The ESP32 subscribed to this command topic instantly activates a 12 V relay → water pump starts.
- When moisture reaches 60%, pump turns off automatically.
- Farmer receives daily summary via WhatsApp.

Features Included

- **Retained messages**: New dashboard instantly shows current pump state.
- **Last Will & Testament**: If ESP32 loses power, broker shows "offline".
- **QoS 1**: Guaranteed pump command delivery.
- **Deep-sleep mode**: Runs 6+ months on solar + 18650 battery.
- **Manual override**: Farmer sends "ON for 10 min" from phone.

Project 2: REST API Home Automation System

Allow complete home appliance control and monitoring using only REST API calls — no MQTT broker required for basic users.

Complete System Flow

- ESP32 hosts no server. It acts purely as HTTP client.
- At boot and every 15 minutes, it performs a GET request to:

  https://api.myhome.in/devices/livingroom/config
- Server returns a JSON payload containing the desired state of all appliances:

  `{ "fan": "ON", "light1": "OFF", "ac": 24, "tv": "ON" }`
- ESP32 parses the JSON and immediately sets relays and IR blaster accordingly.
- Optional: ESP32 also POSTs current sensor states (temperature, power usage) every 5 minutes.
- User changes state via mobile app or Alexa → app updates the central REST server → next GET cycle applies change within 15 seconds.

Features Included:

- Works behind any NAT/router — there is no port forwarding.
- Zero dependency on public MQTT brokers.
- There is an easy integration with Google Home, Alexa, and existing home automation platforms.
- Firmware OTA via REST endpoint

Project 3: Webhook-Based Gas Leak Alert System

Detect dangerous gas levels and instantly alert humans — no delay allowed.

Complete System Flow:

- MQ-2 or MQ-5 gas sensor continuously monitors LPG, methane, or CO levels.
- When concentration crosses safe threshold (1000 ppm), ESP32 instantly fires a webhook: https://maker.ifttt.com/trigger/gas_leak/with/key/xxxxxxxxxxxx with optional JSON payload containing location, ppm value, and timestamp.
- IFTTT instantly triggers multiple actions:
    - Sends SMS via linked phone number
    - Sends Email to family members
    - Posts message to Telegram group
    - Makes automated phone call saying "Gas leak detected in kitchen"
    - Optionally triggers buzzer and exhaust fan via another ESP32

Features included:

- Under 3-second alert delivery worldwide
- No polling — event-driven only
- Works even if main MQTT broker is down
- Battery backup ensures alert during power cut
- Anti-spam debounce — ignores brief spikes

Practical Exercises

Exercise 1: MQTT Scout – Real-Time Sensor Broadcasting

Create a tiny telemetry system:

- An ESP32 reads temperature and humidity from a DHT22 (or DHT11) sensor every 10 seconds.
- It connects to the free public HiveMQ broker (broker.hivemq.com) — used by millions of developers and companies worldwide.
- It publishes the sensor readings in clean JSON format to a public topic you own.
- Then use phone or laptop to subscribe to that exact topic and watch live data stream in real-time.
- Optionally, another ESP32 subscribes to the same topic and displays the data on an OLED screen.

This is exactly how real systems work: one device publishes, hundreds or thousands subscribe — no direct connection needed

Part 1: Hardware Setup – The Physical Sensor Node

- ESP32 Development Board (any model: DevKit, NodeMCU)
- DHT22 or DHT11 temperature & humidity sensor
- 4.7kΩ pull-up resistor (usually already on DHT modules)
- Breadboard and jumper wires
- Power via USB or 18650 battery pack for field testing

Part 2: Publishing Side – The Broadcasting Station

ESP32 becomes a publisher that:

- Connects to Wi-Fi (home or college network)
- Establishes a persistent MQTT connection to broker.hivemq.com:1883
- Uses `PubSubClient` library
- Every 10 seconds reads DHT sensor
- Creates a clean JSON payload

Part 3: Subscribing Side – Watching Live Data from Anywhere

Use HiveMQ Web Client

a. Open webclient.hivemq.com in any browser
b. Connect to broker.hivemq.com
c. Subscribe to `iotindia/classroom/esp32_07/dht`
d. Watch JSON messages appear live every 10 seconds

Exercise 2: MQTT Responder – Cloud-Controlled Fan/LED

You will create a complete cloud-controlled actuator system:

- ESP32 connects to the public HiveMQ broker.
- It continuously subscribes to a command topic: iotindia/home/livingroom/fan/command
- You publish "ON" or "OFF" (or even "SPEED:5") from phone or laptop.
- The instant the message arrives, ESP32 receives it via the callback function.
- A relay module or LED instantly turns ON/OFF.
- ESP32 publishes back current status to iotindia/home/livingroom/fan/status → creating a complete closed-loop system.

Part 1: Hardware Setup – The Controllable Device

- ESP32 Development Board (DevKit, NodeMCU, etc.)
- Single channel 5V relay module (₹80) or simple LED + 220Ω resistor
- Optional: 12V table fan or bulb connected via relay (for real demo)
- Jumper wires and breadboard
- Power supply (USB for testing, 18650 + TP4056 for battery operation)

Part 2: The Subscription Magic – Receiving Cloud Commands

ESP32 becomes a subscriber that:

a. Connects to `broker.hivemq.com` with a unique client ID
b. Subscribes to its command topic with QoS 1
c. Implements a callback function that triggers the moment any message arrives
d. Parses incoming payload ("`ON`", "`OFF`", or JSON like `{"state":"ON","speed":70}`)
e. Immediately controls the relay/LED
f. Publishes confirmation back to status topic with retained flag

Part 3: Publishing Commands – The Cloud Control Panel

a. Open **`webclient.hivemq.com`**
b. Publish to iotindia/home/livingroom/fan/command
c. Type **`"ON"`** → watch relay click instantly
d. Type **`{"state":"OFF"}`** → see status update

Exercise 3: REST POST Master – Push Data to API

Transform ESP32 into telemetry node that:

- It reads temperature and humidity from a DHT22 sensor.
- It creates perfectly formatted JSON payload with device ID, timestamp, location, and sensor data.
- It sends it via secure HTTPS POST to a real public API endpoint every 30 seconds.
- It receives and displays server response (success, new config, or error).
- It uses **`webhook.site`** (free, instant, public URL) data appear live in browser from anywhere.

Part 1: Hardware Setup – The Telemetry Node

- ESP32 Development Board (any variant)
- DHT22 or DHT11 sensor with 4.7kΩ pull-up
- Stable Wi-Fi connection (home, college, or mobile hotspot)
- USB power (or 18650 + TP4056 for field deployment)

Part 2: Creating the Perfect JSON Payload

ESP32 will generate enterprise-standard JSON

Part 3: Instant Testing with webhook.site – Zero Setup Server

a. Go to https://webhook.site→ get unique public URL instantly.
b. Example: https://webhook.site/abc123-def456-ghi789
c. ESP32 sends POST to this URL → you see live data in browser with headers, timestamp, IP.
d. No server setup, no hosting, no cost.

Exercise 4 :Webhook Trigger – Gas Leak Alert

Gas leak detection and instant notification system:

- MQ-2 or MQ-5 sensor continuously monitors LPG, methane, smoke, alcohol.
- When concentration exceeds safe threshold (1000 ppm), ESP32 instantly fires a webhook.
- Webhook goes to IFTTT Maker Webhooks service.
- IFTTT triggers multiple simultaneous actions.
- System works even during power cuts (with battery backup).

Part 1: Hardware Setup – The Life-Saving Detector

- ESP32 Development Board
- MQ-2 or MQ-5 gas sensor module
- Active buzzer for local alarm
- Optional: relay + exhaust fan for auto-ventilation

- 18650 battery + TP4056 for backup power

Part 2: Setting Up IFTTT

1. Go to https://ifttt.com→ create free account
2. Create new `Applet` →"`If This`"→ search "`Webhooks`"→"`Receive a web request`"
3. Event name: `gas_leak_emergency`
4. "Then That" → add multiple actions:
   i. SMS (via phone number linked)
   ii. Email
   iii. Telegram
   iv. Notifications
   v. Phone Call (via VoIP)
5. Finish → get unique key
6. webhook URL becomes:
   `https://maker.ifttt.com/trigger/gas_leak_emergency/with/key/your_secret_key`

Part 3: The Instant Trigger - Zero-Delay Alert

ESP32 will:

- Read MQ-2 analog value every 500ms.
- Apply calibration curve (preheat 24h for accuracy).
- When value > threshold (1000):
  - Sound local buzzer
  - Immediately fire HTTPS GET or POST to IFTTT URL
  - Include JSON with location, ppm, timestamp
  - Retry 3 times if network fails
  - Flash SOS pattern on LED

Conclusion

This chapter introduced the complete communication framework that enables modern IoT systems to operate reliably, securely, and at scale. You learned how MQTT supports real-time, low-power, publish-subscribe messaging for continuous device telemetry and control; how RESTful APIs provide structured, secure pathways for device provisioning, configuration, cloud integration, and data management; and how Webhooks enable event-driven automation by delivering instant notifications and triggering external workflows. Together, these technologies form the core of the current industrial, agricultural, smart home, and smart city deployments.

Through practical examples and mini projects, you saw how these protocols converge to create full end-to-end IoT solutions—from sensors publishing data to the cloud, to applications responding to critical events in real time. You also learned the role of JSON as the universal data format that maintains clarity and interoperability across all communication channels.

With this chapter, you have moved beyond local device communication into the world of scalable, cloud-connected IoT engineering. In the next chapter, you will advance into the security dimension—Encryption, Device Hardening & Authentication—ensuring that the systems you build are not only functional, but also safe and resilient in real-world environments.

Chapter 11
Encryption, Device Hardening, and Authentication

Introduction

In the preceding chapters, we have successfully established reliable communication channels for our Internet of Things (IoT) devices, connecting them to global cloud infrastructures using protocols such as MQTT, HTTP/REST APIs, and Webhooks. This connectivity empowered us to build sophisticated, real-time systems—from automated dashboards and remote actuation controls to intelligent, data-driven workflows. These foundational capabilities are what transform simple sensor nodes into transformative, internet-connected systems ready for deployment across diverse environments, from smart homes to industrial facilities and large-scale urban infrastructure.

Yet, this moment of successful connectivity also represents a critical inflection point, as every device joining the global network becomes a potential target. The unencrypted transmission of sensor data over public networks, the persistence of default or weak device credentials, and the potential for firmware compromise represent critical vulnerabilities that malicious actors actively exploit. High-profile incidents—such as the weaponization of Mirai botnet of millions of insecure devices, the deployment of ransomware on critical healthcare infrastructure, and global industrial espionage targeting compromised factory sensors—underscore the severe consequences of neglecting security. Connectivity without security is not merely insufficient; it is a profound liability, especially when considering the extended deployment longevity and unattended operation inherent in the IoT lifecycle.

This chapter fundamentally shifts our focus. Moving beyond mere functionality, our primary objective is to instill trust—encompassing confidentiality, integrity, availability, and auditability—and resilience into our IoT deployments, reinforcing the formal security model being applied. Security ceases to be an optional feature and becomes the indispensable foundation for any product intended for scalable, real-world deployment. We will undertake a comprehensive study of essential security paradigms: implementing robust end-to-end encryption for all communication channels, enforcing strong mutual authentication to ensure that only legitimate devices and servers interact, and hardening the device itself against both remote and physical tampering. Key topics will include secure boot processes, cryptographic signing of firmware for integrity, techniques for protecting sensitive cryptographic keys, securing Over-the-Air (OTA) updates, and practical methods for mitigating pervasive vulnerabilities in embedded systems.

Upon completion of this chapter, the student will possess the advanced knowledge required to design, develop, and deploy IoT systems that are not only functionally excellent but also engineered to withstand sustained compromise—even when operating within inherently untrusted networks or hostile operational environments. These critical security competencies distinguish professional, production-grade IoT solutions ready for global deployment—whether in major metropolitan areas, remote agricultural sites, or within the critical infrastructure of any nation. Security is the final, essential element that validates IoT technology for deployment on a global scale.

Structure

In this chapter, we will cover the following topics:

- Introduction
- The Foundation of Data Logging in Modern IoT Systems
- Cloud-based Logging Platforms: Firebase, Google Sheets, and Local SD Card Storage
- Real-Time Streaming and Batch Uploads
- Log Formatting Standards for Analytics using JSON and CSV
- The Foundation of Time: Synchronization Mechanisms in IoT Systems (RTC, NTP, and Internal Counters)
- Email Alerts Using SMTP Servers
- Blynk Notifications Setup
- IFTTT Multi-Platform Alert Workflows
- Logging Patterns in IoT: Rolling Logs and Circular Buffers
- Visualizing Logged Data using ThingSpeak and Google Data Studio
- Mini Project: Smart Temperature Logger with Multi-Channel Alerts
- Comprehensive Security Guidelines for IoT Logging
- Best Practices for IoT Data Logging: Timestamps, Retry Logic, and Batching

The Foundation of Data Logging in Modern IoT Systems

Data logging stands as a critical, systematic discipline defined by the scheduled capture and storage of raw sensor readings, dynamic device operational states, or high-priority system events over a defined period. For instance, in a smart manufacturing plant, data logging would involve continuously recording the temperature, vibration levels, and power consumption of critical machinery to enable predictive maintenance. In the contemporary landscape of the Internet of Things (IoT), this practice is fundamental, translating ephemeral physical world interactions into a persistent, verifiable historical record. Specifically, logging targets data originating from the Perception Layer of an IoT architecture—the interface with the physical environment. The robust implementation of data logging necessitates a reliable storage mechanism. This can be architected in two primary ways: local persistence or remote/cloud storage. It is also common to see a hybrid approach utilizing both. Local logging commonly involves using dedicated hardware like an SD card attached directly to the microcontroller unit, such as an ESP32 or Arduino. For microcontrollers with limited flash memory, utilizing the Serial Peripheral Interface Flash File System (SPIFFS) or LittleFS is an alternative. For remote persistence, the data is transmitted over the network to cloud databases—leveraging standardized IoT protocols such as MQTT (Message Queuing Telemetry Transport) for low-bandwidth, asynchronous communication, or HTTP/HTTPS for direct API-based ingestion. To guarantee data integrity and usability, implementations frequently employ specialized libraries (for example, SD.h of Arduino, the native file system libraries of ESP32). The essential steps in this process are precise timestamping of every data point to ensure chronological integrity, standardized formatting (often using human-readable CSV for simplicity or machine-parseable JSON for complex data structures), and preservation to facilitate subsequent, reliable retrieval. This transformation converts momentary sensor inputs into an accountable and trustworthy historical record. The significance of data logging in IoT environments cannot be overstated, as it is the critical link that transforms immediate, reactive operations into sophisticated, long-term analytical intelligence. An IoT device operating without logging capabilities is inherently blind to its own past. For example, a system designed to detect a gas leak using an MQ-2 sensor might successfully activate an auditory and visual alarm in real-time. However, without a logged record of the precise concentration readings, time of detection, and preceding environmental conditions, comprehensive root-cause analysis of the incident becomes impossible.

Logging enables sophisticated historical analysis, allowing stakeholders to move beyond simple fault detection and identify underlying critical patterns and operational trends. Examples include:

- **Predictive Maintenance:** In Industrial IoT (IIoT) settings, predictive maintenance can reduce unplanned downtime by up to 30%, logged data from vibration, acoustic, or temperature sensors on heavy machinery can reveal a progressive increase in signal anomalies over time. This trend analysis assists in the predictive determination of maintenance requirements (for example, replacing a bearing before catastrophic failure), documented to result in significant reductions in unscheduled downtime and maintenance costs.
- **Optimization and Yield Improvement:** In precision agriculture, tracking moisture levels, light intensity, and nutrient concentrations facilitates trend analysis. A progressive decrease in logged moisture levels within a smart greenhouse, for instance, predicts imminent crop stress, allowing the system to optimize irrigation schedules proactively, and improve the overall yield.
- **System Health Monitoring:** The progressive increase in temperature within an enclosed server rack or a critical equipment enclosure can be detected via logged data, signaling impending hardware failure or a breakdown in the cooling system.

Beyond Analysis: Debugging, Compliance, and Alerting

The utility of data logging extends into several other mission-critical areas:

- **Robust Debugging and Anomaly Tracing:** Logging provides developers with an indispensable tool for diagnostics. When an anomaly occurs—such as an ESP32-based home automation system failing to process a Bluetooth Low Energy (BLE) command—the log file offers a time-stamped chronological sequence of events. This allows developers to trace the failure back to the precise moment of execution, potentially revealing transient issues like a memory overflow, network instability, or an external power fluctuation that coincided with the command failure.
- **Regulatory Compliance and Auditing:** Data logging is often not optional but mandated across various highly regulated sectors, establishing accountability and adhering to legal frameworks:
    - **Healthcare:** Medical IoT devices, including continuous wearable heart monitors or remote patient monitoring systems, are required to log vital signs and device status to adhere to strict standards such as the Health Insurance Portability and Accountability Act (HIPAA) in the US or the General Data Protection Regulation (GDPR) in Europe, safeguarding patient data and ensuring treatment efficacy.
    - **Environmental Protection:** Systems used for monitoring air and water quality necessitate continuous, time-stamped logs of pollutant levels, which are critical for mandatory environmental audits and compliance with national and international pollution control standards.
    - **Industrial Safety:** Operational logs in industrial automation systems (for example, tracking valve positions, safety interlocks, and emergency stops) are required for mandatory safety certifications and forensic analysis following any industrial incident.

- **Foundational Mechanism for Effective Alerting Systems:** Log data provides the underlying context for effective and timely alerting. By establishing specific, predefined thresholds within the logging system – for example, programming the system to monitor if the temperature measurement from a smart sensor persistently surpasses – the logs can trigger immediate, real-time notifications. These alerts can be delivered through various channels, including electronic mail, SMS, or dedicated cloud-based notification platforms. This capability is paramount for mitigating potential catastrophic events, such as preventing server room overheating, stopping excessive irrigation in automated agricultural operations, or initiating emergency shutdowns in industrial processes.

Data Security and System Resilience

A final, non-negotiable consideration is the security of the log data itself. Logs often contain operational signatures (device IDs, locations, timings) that can be sensitive even without Personally Identifiable Information (PII). Within secure IoT architectures, logs are often highly sensitive and must be protected against tampering and unauthorized access. This requires implementing robust security measures such as:

- **Encryption** (both at rest and in transit) to safeguard the confidentiality of the data.
- **Authentication and Authorization** mechanisms to restrict access to authorized personnel only.
- **Integrity Checks** (for example, using cryptographic hashing) to ensure the logs have not been maliciously modified.

Maintaining log integrity and reliability is essential for both formal audits and critical forensic investigations following a system failure or security breach. Ultimately, the comprehensive mastery of data logging elevates IoT projects from simple, reactive prototypes—which only address the present moment—into resilient, secure, and sophisticated data-driven systems capable of reliable long-term analysis, robust operation, and global deployment. The decision of where to log data—a fundamental choice in any Internet of Things (IoT) deployment—ultimately balances the trifecta of reliability, accessibility, and complexity. IoT environments are too varied for a one-size-fits-all solution, spanning from perpetually connected smart homes to remote agricultural sensors battling intermittent cellular service. Therefore, the selection of a storage mechanism is a direct reflection of the mission of the system. At the highest level, the choice bifurcates into Cloud Logging and Local Logging.

The Cloud Advantage: Real-Time Access and Scalability

Cloud-based solutions prioritize accessibility and multi-user interaction. They are the ideal choice when data needs to be immediately available globally, often to power dashboards, notifications, or complex analytics.

- **Firebase Realtime Database / Firestore:** This is the choice of the professional for highly interactive applications. Its structured, JSON-based NoSQL architecture is engineered for real-time synchronization, meaning that as soon as a sensor records a temperature, every connected user sees the update instantly. Critically, it supports offline caching (for example, via the Firebase-ESP-Client library), allowing the device to continue logging data and then seamlessly synchronize the backlog once the network is restored. This combination offers both the speed of the cloud and a layer of local resilience.
- **Google Sheets (via Webhooks/IFTTT):** This option sacrifices advanced features for unparalleled simplicity and familiarity. It is the perfect entry point for quick prototyping, educational projects, or small-scale deployments where the stakeholders are more comfortable with a

spreadsheet interface than a database. The setup is fast, often requiring no custom code, but it lacks the real-time performance and robust security controls of dedicated databases.

- **ThingSpeak (by MathWorks):** Distinctly tailored for engineering and academic users, ThingSpeak is more than just a data logger; it is an analytical platform. By integrating built-in MATLAB analytics, it allows users to process and visualize data immediately, making it the de facto standard for research projects that require mathematical modeling and scheduled event triggers (for example, automatically tweeting an alert when a threshold is breached).

Cloud-Based Logging Platforms: Firebase, Google Sheets, and Local SD Card Storage

In IoT systems, where and how you store sensor data often determines whether your deployment succeeds or fails in the real world. A reliable logging strategy must balance three competing priorities:

- Zero data loss (even during network or power outages)
- Acceptable cost and bandwidth usage
- Timely visibility for monitoring and alerts

Different projects demand different solutions. Early prototypes favor instant cloud visibility, while remote, industrial, or high-frequency applications require bulletproof local storage.

- **SD Cards or MicroSD Modules:** These modules, connected typically via SPI, are the workhorses of remote deployments. Their primary strength is the ability to handle high-frequency logging (hundreds to thousands of samples per second) without the latency or bandwidth constraints of the internet. For remote weather stations, vibration monitoring on machinery, or long-term vehicle tracking where connectivity is a luxury, the SD card ensures zero data loss. The log files are either retrieved manually during maintenance or uploaded in large, efficient batches when a connection is briefly available.

Feature	Firebase / Firestore	Google Sheets	SD Card Logging
Primary Goal	Real-time multi-user access and security	Simplicity and familiar dashboarding	Reliability & high-frequency logging
Connectivity	Requires internet (but supports offline cache)	Requires internet (for immediate update)	Works completely offline
Latency/ Speed	Near-instant synchronization	Moderate (depends on webhook service)	Extremely fast (limited by card speed)
Best For	Smart homes, commercial dashboards, critical data	Quick prototypes, classroom projects, non-technical users	Remote locations, moving vehicles, high-speed sampling
Complexity	High (setup rules/data structure)	Low (often no code required)	Moderate (file system handling)

Table 11.1: *Comparison between Firebase, Google Sheets and SD Card Logging*

Real-Time Streaming and Batch Uploads

The fundamental decision in designing an Internet of Things (IoT) deployment often boils down to a critical trade-off: how frequently should the sensor data be transmitted This choice, between Real-Time Streaming and Batch Uploads, is not merely a technical detail; it is a strategic decision that governs the power consumption, operational cost, data utility, and reliability of the system. The Real-Time Streaming Paradigm in a real-time streaming model, data is transmitted to the cloud or edge server almost instantaneously upon measurement, typically within a window of 1 to 30 seconds. This approach prioritizes data freshness and immediate responsiveness.

Key Characteristics:

- **Best Suited For:** Applications where any delay could have significant safety, security, or financial implications. Examples include life-safety systems (smoke detectors, medical alerts), perimeter security, or critical manufacturing process monitoring.
- **Protocols:** Often utilizes persistent or guaranteed-delivery protocols such as MQTT with Quality of Service (QoS) level 1 or 2, WebSockets, or continuous, short-interval HTTP POST requests.
- **The Cost of Speed:** The continuous network connectivity and frequent radio wake-ups necessary for streaming result in significantly higher power consumption for the device and higher data/cloud ingestion costs for the operator.

The Batch Upload Paradigm

In contrast, batch uploading involves the device storing sensor readings locally for a period of time—minutes, hours, or even a full day—before waking up the radio to transmit all accumulated data in a single, aggregated payload.

Key Characteristics:

- **Best Suited For:** Remote, battery-powered, or solar-powered deployments where energy efficiency and extended battery life are the primary concerns. This model is ideal for logging environmental data (for example, periodic temperature, humidity, light levels) where a delay of an hour in data arrival is acceptable.
- **The Power Advantage:** By keeping the radio module in a deep-sleep state for the vast majority of its operational cycle, batch uploads dramatically reduce power consumption, allowing devices to operate for months or even years on a single battery pack. This also translates to lower cellular data costs.
- **The Trade-off:** The primary drawback is delayed visibility. Therefore, critical alerts must bypass batching, Alerts are not instantaneous, and should the device lose power or connectivity between uploads, the locally stored data is at risk of being lost.

Modern, professional IoT systems rarely adhere strictly to one model. A more robust, and often preferred, design utilizes a Hybrid Approach. The local intelligence (firmware) of the device is programmed to distinguish between routine and critical events:

- **Routine Data:** Non-urgent sensor readings (for example, every 5-minute temperature log) are batched and uploaded every hour.
- **Critical Events:** High-priority, safety-related events trigger an immediate, real-time transmission, overriding the batch schedule.

This strategy successfully balances the need for long battery life with the non-negotiable requirement for immediate response to emergencies.

Feature	Real-Time Streaming	Batch Uploads
Data Freshness	Immediate (1–30 seconds latency)	Delayed (Minutes to hours latency)
Primary Goal	Instant visibility and responsiveness	Energy efficiency and longevity
Power Consumption	High (Continuous radio activity)	Dramatically Reduced (Deep sleep cycles)
Operational Cost	Higher data bandwidth and cloud ingestion costs	Lower, optimized data transfer costs
Best Use Case	Life-safety, security alerts, fleet tracking, critical process control	Environmental monitoring, asset tracking, remote/utility metering
Data Reliability	High (Immediate acknowledgment/ retransmission)	Risk of data loss if power fails between uploads; requires local storage
Protocols	MQTT QoS 1/2, WebSockets, continuous HTTP POST	Periodic wake-up/upload cycle

Table 11.2: *Real Time Streaming versus Batch Uploads*

Log Formatting Standards for Analytics Using JSON and CSV

The structural organization of data prior to its storage or transmission fundamentally dictates the ease and efficacy of subsequent processing, visualization, and analytical endeavors. Within the Internet of Things (IoT) environment, two data formats are predominantly utilized for log recording: JSON (JavaScript Object Notation) and CSV (Comma-Separated Values). Each format presents distinct advantages, rendering it suitable for specific logging destinations and analytical applications. The selection between JSON and CSV is typically guided by criteria such as schema volatility, cloud ingestion compatibility, processing overhead, and storage efficiency.

JavaScript Object Notation (JSON) has been established as the industry standard for the majority of contemporary, cloud-centric IoT systems due to its inherent flexibility and extensive compatibility.

- **Structured and Hierarchical:** The principal advantage of JSON is its capacity to accommodate nested objects. This capability enables a single log message to encapsulate complex datasets, such as a primary device identifier, a precise timestamp, geographical coordinates (latitude/ longitude), and an encapsulated object or array containing multiple sensor readings (temperature, humidity, pressure) alongside ancillary metrics (battery level). This rich structure is optimally suited for organizing data exhibiting a one-to-many relationship.
- **Native Cloud Integration:** Virtually all major cloud platforms and middleware services—including Firebase, AWS IoT, Azure IoT Hub, ThingSpeak, and Node-RED—offer seamless, native support for the ingestion, parsing, and processing of JSON payloads.
- **Human-Readable and Efficiently Parsed:** While structurally compact, the key-value pair architecture ensures high readability for developers. Furthermore, on resource-constrained devices, such as the ESP32, highly optimized libraries (for example, ArduinoJson) facilitate rapid and memory-efficient serialization and deserialization processes.
- **Protocol Compatibility:** JSON serves as the standard payload format for modern web communications, making it the ideal choice for MQTT messaging and REST API endpoints used for data transmission across the network.

CSV Format

Comma-Separated Values (CSV) remains the most straightforward, lightweight, and universally compatible format, maintaining its relevance in specific IoT contexts, particularly for localized data logging.

- **Single-Line, Flat Structure:** CSV data is formatted as a plain text file where each distinct line constitutes a single data record, with individual fields within that record delineated by a separator (typically a comma). This planar structure is optimal for direct archival onto storage media such as SD cards and represents the native format for all principal spreadsheet applications (Google Sheets, Excel, and LibreOffice).
- **Minimal Overhead:** A CSV record comprises solely the data values and delimiters, precluding the repetition of field names in every line (a feature inherent to JSON). This attribute yields extreme byte efficiency, a critical factor for high-frequency logging applications where the maximization of storage capacity and the minimization of transmission bandwidth are paramount considerations.
- **Efficient Appending:** The process of recording new data is simplified to merely opening the file and appending a new line of text, which supports highly efficient, continuous, real-time logging operations on the device itself.

Analysis: Between JSON and CSV for IoT Log Management

Choosing the right payload format is crucial for efficient IoT data handling, especially when managing logs and telemetry at scale. JSON has become the de facto standard for cloud-bound MQTT payloads in enterprise IoT due to its flexibility, self-describing structure, and seamless integration with modern cloud services. It excels at representing complex, nested, or evolving sensor data without schema changes disrupting the pipeline.

CSV, while extremely compact and efficient for bandwidth-constrained scenarios, is better suited for local logging or high-frequency, fixed-schema data that feeds directly into tabular tools like spreadsheets or BI dashboards. Its simplicity reduces overhead on constrained devices but requires extra parsing or headers in the cloud, making it less ideal for dynamic IoT workflows.

Feature	JSON (JavaScript Object Notation)	CSV (Comma-Separated Values)
Structure	Hierarchical, capable of supporting nested objects	Planar, single-line record format
Overhead/ Size	Higher (Requires repetition of field names in each message)	Minimal (Comprises only data values and delimiters)
Complexity	Superior for handling complex, heterogeneous, or richly detailed datasets	Best suited for simple, fixed-schema datasets
Readability	High (Self-describing nature via key-value pairs)	Lower (Requires an explicit header or predefined schema for interpretation)
Cloud Integration	Established native standard for major cloud services (AWS, Azure, Firebase)	Frequently necessitates pre-processing or explicit configuration for parsing
Primary Application	Cloud data transmission (MQTT/REST), advanced analytical processing	Local data logging (SD Card), spreadsheet-based analysis, high-frequency data capture

Table 11.3: JSON *versus* CSV

The most resilient implemented IoT architectures frequently adopt a hybrid logging methodology. Data is initially logged locally in CSV format to ensure maximal speed and reliability on the embedded device. Upon establishing network connectivity, the stored CSV logs are retrieved, systematically converted into JSON batches, and subsequently uploaded to the designated cloud platform. This hybrid strategy achieves an optimal equilibrium: ensuring maximal storage efficiency and local fault tolerance on the embedded device, while simultaneously providing maximum flexibility, rich structural integrity, and native integration within the cloud environment for sophisticated analytics.

The Foundation of Time: Synchronization Mechanisms in IoT Systems (RTC, NTP, and Internal Counters)

In the rigorous environment of Internet of Things (IoT) deployments, where system integrity, data fidelity, and regulatory compliance are non-negotiable requirements, the availability of an accurate, highly synchronized time source is paramount. Time serves as the fundamental basis for establishing causality – it governs the precise sequence of operations, enables reliable execution of automated schedules, and validates the trustworthiness of all collected and recorded data points. Without this critical foundation, data logging loses its utility, and scheduled actions become inherently unpredictable. IoT devices achieve the requisite temporal reliability through the strategic integration of three primary and mutually complementary timing mechanisms. Rule of Thumb: Use NTP for global alignment, RTC for offline continuity, and `millis()` for internal scheduling.

The Three Core Pillars of Time: Detailed Mechanism and Application

Accurate time management is essential in IoT systems because it ensures proper data logging, event sequencing, and device synchronization. Without reliable time references, sensor data becomes difficult to analyze and automated operations may fail. IoT devices typically rely on three complementary mechanisms to manage time effectively: Real-Time Clock (RTC), Network Time Protocol (NTP), and internal timers such as `millis()` and `micros()`. Each of these mechanisms serves a unique role in maintaining time accuracy and system stability.

- **The Real-Time Clock (RTC):** The Essential Standalone Timekeeper
    - **Mechanism and Hardware:** The RTC is a dedicated Integrated Circuit (IC) featuring a high-stability crystal oscillator and a set of dedicated registers to continuously track the full calendar date and time (Year, Month, Day, Hour, Minute, Second). Industry-standard, high-precision models such as the DS3231 incorporate temperature compensation technology to restrict drift to within mere minutes per annum. Communication with the host microcontroller is typically facilitated via the I²C serial protocol.
    - **Crucial Role:** The distinguishing characteristic of RTC is its integrated battery backup circuit. This functionality ensures that the timekeeping process remains fully uninterrupted even if the main device power supply is disconnected for extended durations. Consequently, the RTC is deemed absolutely indispensable for remote, power-constrained, or intermittently connected assets (for example, environmental monitoring sensors, specialized meteorological stations, or long-term asset trackers) where immediate network access cannot be guaranteed upon system reactivation. It furnishes the device with an immediate, verifiable timestamp at the moment of power-on.

- **Network Time Protocol (NTP):** The Global Precision Synchronizer
    - **Mechanism and Protocol:** NTP is a standardized Internet protocol designed to acquire Coordinated Universal Time (UTC) from a global hierarchy of highly accurate clocks, including Stratum 1 (atomic) or Stratum 2 (server) sources (for example, pool.ntp.org). The protocol employs sophisticated algorithms to rigorously account for network latency and precisely calculate the current time.
    - **Crucial Role:** NTP delivers ultra-high precision time synchronization, typically achieving an accuracy level within tens of milliseconds across global networks. For platforms equipped with Wi-Fi or cellular connectivity, such as the ESP32 series, the integration of NTP is simplified, often requiring only a single library function call (configTime()) which also manages complex regional parameters like local time zones and automatic daylight saving time adjustments. NTP constitutes the industry standard for applications requiring high-fidelity, legally-traceable timestamps, including financial transaction logging, rigorous industrial process control, and comprehensive security event auditing, provided that continuous internet connectivity is maintained.
- **`millis()` and `micros()`:** The Local, Non-Blocking Time-Base
    - **Mechanism and Implementation:** These functions, fundamental to environments based on the Arduino framework (for example, ESP32), retrieve the current value of a continuous internal hardware counter (a simple 32-bit integer). This counter is continuously incremented by the internal clock source of the microcontroller and quantifies the number of milliseconds or microseconds elapsed since the most recent power-up or hardware reset of the device.
    - **Crucial Role:** The principal function of **`millis()`** is not the tracking of wall-clock time (Date/Time) but the enabling of non-blocking asynchronous code execution. In contrast to the detrimental delay() function, which completely stalls the central processing unit, comparing the current millis() value against a previously stored reference time allows for reliable task scheduling without impeding the primary execution loop. This mechanism forms the architectural backbone for responsive, computationally efficient IoT firmware, routinely utilized for executing periodic operations ("poll the pressure sensor every 10 minutes") or implementing sophisticated state machine transitions.

The Timing Strategy: Synthesis for Operational Resilience

The most advanced and robust IoT deployments never rely exclusively upon a singular time source. Instead, they meticulously implement a multi-layered, failover strategy that strategically leverages the distinct advantages of all three mechanisms:

Situation	Optimal Selection	Rationale and Professional Implementation Detail
Complete Power and Network Interruption	DS3231 RTC	The battery-backed hardware module guarantees uninterrupted temporal continuity, providing the system with an immediate, verified date/time reference upon restoration of primary power.
Global Reference Synchronization	NTP	Periodically (for example : on a 6-to-12-hour cycle), the device establishes an internet connection to acquire the global standard time, utilizing the superior precision of NTP to correct any minor temporal drift accumulated by the local RTC hardware.

Situation	Optimal Selection	Rationale and Professional Implementation Detail
Internal Task Management	`millis()`	Continuously employed within the main execution loop to manage all internal, local timing functions (for example : debouncing inputs, regulating LED states, executing software timers) without the detrimental effect of processor blocking.
The Ultimate Resilient Architecture	RTC + NTP Sync + `millis()`	**`millis()`** governs the internal workflow; the RTC provides the guaranteed, offline time baseline; and NTP functions as the ultimate global reference, periodically recalibrating the time of RTC to maintain perfect global temporal alignment. This 'trifecta' ensures accurate, auditable under *all* operational conditions.

Table 11.4: *Multi-Layered Timing Strategy for Operational Resilience in IoT Systems*

Email Alerts Using SMTP Servers

The integration of SMTP (Simple Mail Transfer Protocol) functionality fundamentally transforms a basic microcontroller—such as the ESP32, NodeMCU, or even advanced platforms like the Raspberry Pi Pico W—into a sophisticated, fully autonomous alerting device. This capability is a cornerstone of professional IoT deployment because it allows the device to bypass complex, often latency-ridden intermediate infrastructure, such as dedicated cloud platforms or intermediary message brokers. Instead, the device can directly send detailed, actionable notifications from the field the very moment a critical operational threshold is breached. This direct communication is absolutely vital for time-sensitive events—including a sudden fire detection, a dangerous gas leak, an unexpectedly high water level, or a critical system fault—effectively eliminating the dependence on a connected phone, a constantly running computer, or an external cloud platform to relay the message. The process is a direct, machine-to-server transaction, which is meticulously engineered to grant both high reliability and minimal transmission latency, ensuring the alert reaches the recipient in seconds, not minutes.

IoT Device (ESP32/NodeMCU) → Established Wi-Fi/Cellular Connection (Robust Connection Check) → Secure Handshake with SMTP Server (for example, smtp.gmail.com:587) → TLS/STARTTLS Encryption Layer Negotiation → Authentication & Credential Verification (App Password/API Key) → Mail Spooling & Transmission via the Relay Server → Inbox of the Recipient (Instant Alert).

In this flow, the microcontroller effectively acts as a full-fledged Mail User Agent (MUA). It initiates and establishes a secure, authenticated connection with the remote SMTP relay server. Once the message is successfully handed off, the relay server (for example, of Google or of SendGrid) takes full responsibility for routing and delivering the final email to the mailbox of the designated recipient, handling complex global email routing protocols.

Choosing the correct SMTP service is a critical design decision for ensuring maximum deliverability (guaranteeing the alert does not get mistakenly filtered into a spam folder) and efficiently managing the expected email volume and security requirements. The ability to send direct, autonomous email alerts unlocks significant operational value and safety improvements across diverse geographical and industry sectors:

- **Public Safety and Infrastructure:**
    - **Fire and Environmental Detection:** Immediate, targeted alerts for fire detection in large-scale warehouses or instant gas leak/high CO_2 level alerts in smart homes and commercial buildings.
    - **Water Management:** Proactive flood warning alerts from river/dam level sensors, or water tank overflow notifications in remote municipal water distribution systems.

- **Logistics and Cold-Chain Monitoring:**
  - **Critical Temperature Breaches:** Automated, time-stamped alerts for cold-chain temperature breaches during the transport or storage of sensitive materials like vaccines, pharmaceuticals, or high-value perishables.
- **IT and Server Room Monitoring:**
  - **Preventative Maintenance:** Instant notifications regarding server rack overheating, unforeseen power failure events (UPS battery state), or high humidity readings, ensuring IT personnel are alerted before catastrophic hardware damage or data loss occurs.
- **Agricultural and Environmental Management (AgriTech):**
  - **Resource Management:** Water tank overflow alerts in remote rural irrigation systems.
  - **Crop Protection:** Instant frost warnings or high-heat stress warnings sent directly to farm managers based on hyper-local sensor data, allowing for immediate protective measures.
- **Security and Access Control:**
  - **Tamper and Intrusion:** Instantaneous tamper alerts or unauthorized access notifications from battery-powered, deep-sleep perimeter security sensors that only wake up to transmit a critical event.

To successfully transition an SMTP alert system from a simple prototype to a reliable, industrial-grade operational system, several security and reliability measures are not just recommended, but mandatory:

- **Security First (TLS/STARTTLS Mandate):** Always use encrypted connections. This means utilizing port 587 (STARTTLS), which upgrades an initial connection to a secure one, or the older but still common port 465 (TLS). Never, under any circumstances, transmit login credentials or message content over plain text (Port 25 is obsolete for user-level sending).
- Modern providers often enforce additional security measures, requiring the use of OAuth2, app-specific passwords, or dedicated transactional email services instead of direct username/password authentication over standard SMTP.
- **Secure Credential Storage and Management:** Never hardcode sensitive credentials (SMTP username/password, App Password, or API key) directly into the main source code file (the `.ino` or `.cpp`). Instead, they must be stored in secure, non-volatile locations:
  - **SPIFFS (SPI Flash File System) / LittleFS:** Encrypted file storage on the flash memory of the microcontroller.
  - **EEPROM:** For very small data storage.
  - **Arduino Secrets.h:** A file specifically designed to be excluded from version control (.gitignore) to prevent accidental leaks.
- **Contextual Data Enrichment (The 5 W's of an Alert):** Every alert email must be rich in contextual data to facilitate immediate diagnosis and response. A mere "Error!" is useless. The alert must include:
  - **Device ID / Name:** Which specific sensor or unit triggered the alert (for example, "Fire Sensor 3A, Warehouse B").
  - **Exact Value:** The specific reading that breached the threshold.
  - **Timestamp:** The precise time the event occurred, synchronized with a reliable time server via NTP (Network Time Protocol).

    - **Location:** Physical location data (for example, "Warehouse B, Rack 4," or GPS coordinates if mobile).

- **Rate-Limiting and Debounce Implementation:** It is essential to implement a strict rate-limiting mechanism (for example, maximum 1 email per 10 minutes for the *same* continuous event). This critical step prevents two major issues: mailbox spamming the operator and, more seriously, preventing the IP address of the device from being temporarily blacklisted by the SMTP server during a prolonged fault condition (for example, a continuous power outage that triggers an alert every second).
- **Efficient Connection Management:** The microcontroller should establish the SMTP connection, transmit the email, and close the connection immediately after a successful send. This conserves precious network resources, frees up microcontroller memory, and minimizes the network presence of the device, improving security.

With robust SMTP alert integration and adherence to these best practices, an IoT device graduates from being merely a data-logging sensor to a truly autonomous entity: it continuously watches its environment, intelligently decides when a condition becomes critical, and instantly and securely informs the necessary human operator—operating reliably 24/7 from virtually any corner of the world.

Blynk Notifications Setup

Blynk fundamentally transforms how instant, real-time push notifications are implemented in Internet of Things (IoT) systems. It provides a highly efficient and simplified mechanism for generating alerts directly from an embedded device, such as an ESP32 or Arduino, and delivering them globally to the mobile phone of the user. This sophisticated process eliminates the complex and resource-intensive requirements traditionally associated with real-time alerting, offering a simple solution, often requiring only a single function call. Crucially, this system avoids the need to manage complex SMTP server configurations, rely on potentially unstable or costly external third-party messaging APIs (like Twilio or Pushover), or incur recurring monthly fees for standard, high-volume usage.

The seamless integration and functional reliability of the platform makes it a preferred professional choice for developing active, responsive IoT systems, moving beyond simple, passive data logging.

Adopting Blynk notifications is a strategic professional decision backed by significant technical and operational benefits that ensure high system reliability and a superior user experience:

- **Exceptional Low Latency and Guaranteed Delivery**: Notifications are characterized by their near-instantaneous delivery, often under a few seconds, consistently falling under two seconds. This is vital for time-sensitive, critical alerts like security breaches or equipment failure. The underlying MQTT-based architecture ensures a highly reliable connection, minimizing message loss through its Quality-of-Service (QoS) guarantees.
- **Universal Cross-Platform Compatibility:** The service is engineered to operate seamlessly across both dominant mobile operating systems, iOS of Apple and Android of Google. This inherent cross-platform design guarantees maximum user accessibility and simplifies the deployment process by removing the need for platform-specific development.
- **Exceptional Cost-Effectiveness and Scalability:** For prototyping and small to medium scale deployments, the legacy/free tier of the platform offers fully featured functionality, typically supporting up to five independent devices and an *unlimited* number of notifications. This positions it as an ideal, zero-operational-cost solution for proof-of-concept and personal projects. Higher, subscription-based tiers provide predictable, cost-effective scaling for commercial applications that require advanced features or greater device capacity.
- **Rich and Context-Aware Notification Support:** The system supports advanced features beyond simple text. Developers can customize the alert payload to include:

- Custom, descriptive text up to 100 characters for highly specific status or failure messages.
- Specific alert sounds (depending on mobile device settings) to differentiate urgent from standard messages, enhancing the perception of urgency of the user.
- Priority settings to influence how the operating system handles the alert (for example, waking the screen or overriding silent mode for critical alerts).
- Dynamic data inclusion, such as specific sensor readings, device uptime, or detailed diagnostic messages, providing immediate context to the user.

The Rapid Deployment and Configuration Protocol

The architecture is deliberately streamlined to enable rapid deployment, typically complete in under five minutes. The configuration follows a structured five-step protocol:

1. **Mobile Application and Project Initialization:** The process begins on the side of the user with installing the official Blynk mobile application. Within the app, the user creates a "New Project" and specifies the correct target hardware (for example, ESP32 Dev Board). This step defines the parameters of the project and ensures the correct communication libraries are used.
2. **Notification Widget Integration:** A dedicated Notification Widget must be explicitly placed onto the project canvas within the Blynk application interface. This widget acts as the necessary, active bridge/listener required by the Blynk cloud server to route the push alerts to the corresponding mobile device. Without this widget, the mobile app will not listen for the push notification event.
3. **Secure Authentication Token Retrieval:** Upon project creation, a unique Authorization Token (Auth Token)—a lengthy, secure string—is automatically generated and sent to the user via the registered email address. This Auth Token is the security credential the physical embedded device uses to securely authenticate with the Blynk cloud server, ensuring only authorized devices can send data.
4. **Integrated Development Environment (IDE) Preparation**: The developer must install the appropriate Blynk library within the Library Manager of Arduino IDE. This library, such as `BlynkSimpleEsp32.h`, exposes the necessary communication functions, including the core notification command and the connection handlers required to maintain the persistent link to the Blynk cloud.
5. **Minimal Firmware Implementation:** The final and most critical step involves integrating the retrieved Auth Token and the core notification command into the firmware/sketch of the device. The primary function for transmission is the Blynk.notify() command. This command is executed by the device to transmit the alert message, which can dynamically include text, numerical values (for example, temperature readings), and even standard or custom emoji characters for enhanced clarity.

Illustrative Real-World Applications across Industries

Blynk notifications are actively employed across a diverse range of industries and geographic locations for mission-critical monitoring and high-stakes alerting:

- **Safety, Security, and Compliance Monitoring:** Providing immediate, life-saving alerts for critical events such as fire, carbon monoxide, or gas leaks in residential, commercial (for example, data centers), and heavy industrial settings globally, ensuring rapid response times.
- **Automated Resource and Infrastructure Management:** Crucial for monitoring and preventing water tank overflow in large apartment complexes, municipal water systems, or

rural agricultural environments, thereby preventing costly water damage and resource waste through timely alerts.

- **Logistics and Cold-Chain Integrity:** Implementing continuous environmental monitoring systems in transportation. The notification system can trigger immediate, non-negotiable alerts in case of temperature breaches, vital during the transportation of sensitive goods such as medical vaccines, pharmaceutical products, or specialized food items, preserving product quality.
- **Perimeter and Asset Protection:** Forming the backbone of responsive intrusion detection systems for small businesses, retail shops, remote equipment enclosures, and secure garage facilities, providing instant alerts upon unauthorized access.

For robust, production-level deployments, system reliability, data integrity, and user experience can be significantly enhanced by adhering to established advanced techniques:

- **Contextual Data Inclusion for Diagnostics:** To ensure comprehensive logging, faster root-cause analysis, and easy troubleshooting, professional implementations must include precise contextual metadata within the notification text. This typically involves appending the unique device name or ID and a precise, real-time timestamp (for example, utilizing an NTP-synchronized time source). This contextual information is vital for clarifying the origin, timing, and specific state of the event, transforming a generic alert into an actionable diagnostic message.
- **Visual Status and Acknowledgment Feedback:** The notification system should be logically paired with a visual indicator, such as an LED widget or a styled Label widget, within the Blynk application dashboard. This synergistic approach allows operators to immediately see the current active alert status of a device *without* needing to open the mobile notification history, providing crucial at-a-glance status and a mechanism for the user to visually acknowledge the alert.
- **Sophisticated Spam Prevention Protocol (Rate Limiting):** The most crucial best practice is preventing the device from overwhelming the user with repetitive notifications—a common issue during transient sensor fluctuations or device reboots. It is highly recommended to combine the notification function with a controlled mechanism, such as using internal timers or state variables to manage a notification state machine. This ensures that the alert is only sent once per detected event cycle or only after a predefined "cooldown" period (for example, a 60-second lockout), thereby maintaining user trust and the credibility of the alerts. Frequent, redundant notifications lead to "alert fatigue," causing users to ignore critical warnings.

IFTTT Multi-Platform Alert Workflows: The Power of One Webhook

IFTTT is the Swiss army knife of IoT alerting and automation, providing a robust, low-code bridge between your simple hardware and the complex digital world.

The fundamental challenge in professional IoT deployments is routing a single, critical event—like a temperature breach or a gas leak—to multiple, disparate communication channels (for example, a phone notification for the manager, a logged entry for compliance, and a voice alert for on-site staff). IFTTT solves this elegantly. It allows your single, lightweight webhook from a constrained device, such as an ESP32 or Arduino, to simultaneously trigger dozens of tailored actions across diverse platforms—including phones, computers, smart speakers, and cloud services—without requiring any extra, complex, or resource-heavy code on the device itself.

Key Multi-Platform Actions and Real-World Use Cases

The true value of IFTTT lies in its vast network of integrations, transforming a simple web call into a sophisticated, multi-pronged response.

Action Category	Specific Service / Platform	Real-World Example and Professional Elaboration
Data Logging/ Auditing	Google Sheets	Append temperature breach to shared farm log: Crucial for compliance and post-incident analysis. Automatically maintains a centralized, time-stamped, and tamper-resistant record of every critical event, along with sensor data, for auditing and long-term performance tracking.
Formal Communication	Email	Send detailed report to maintenance team: Dispatches formal, structured reports containing sensor data (value1, value2) directly to professional inboxes. This ensures structured follow-up, ticketing, and integration with existing corporate helpdesk systems.
Instant Messaging	Telegram / WhatsApp	Instant group alert to field workers: Provides immediate, informal group notification in communication channels already used by on-site personnel. This is often faster and more direct than corporate email for time-sensitive issues.
Personal Alerts	Push Notification	Phone popup via IFTTT app (fastest for personal use): Delivers the quickest, most direct alert to a personal mobile device, bypassing SMS or email latency. Ideal for individual monitoring or primary alerts for managers on the go.
Critical Backup	SMS	Text message via connected phone (reliable backup): Serves as a critical, reliable communication fallback. Essential in areas with poor or intermittent data connectivity (3G/4G/Wi-Fi), ensuring the alert gets through even when internet services are spotty.
Local Environment	Google Home / Alexa	Voice announcement: "Gas leak detected in warehouse!" Provides hands-free, auditory notification in the local environment where staff may not be near a phone or computer. Ensures instant attention from nearby staff or residents.
Team Collaboration	Twitter / Slack	Post to factory channel (Japan): Integrates alerts directly into professional team collaboration software (like Slack) or public feeds (Twitter) for high-visibility incident management, real-time collaboration on response, and automatic archival of the event discussion.
Physical Response	Turn on/off devices	Trigger smart plug to activate siren or exhaust fan: This moves beyond mere notification to an immediate physical response. By controlling actuators (like Wi-Fi enabled plugs or switches), the alert system can automatically increase safety or mitigate the threat.

Table 11.5: *Multi-Platform Actions and Real-World Use Cases in IoT Systems*

When the condition is met, the ESP32 posts a JSON object containing dynamic data (the gas reading and location) to the IFTTT endpoint. IFTTT parses this data and makes it available to all linked actions using placeholders. This ability to pass context is vital for professional alerting.

Logging Patterns in IoT: Rolling Logs and Circular Buffers

In the demanding landscape of professional Internet of Things (IoT) deployments, the art of data management is centered not merely on collection, but on the strategic, responsible use of finite resources. Unlike the virtually limitless storage environments of traditional servers, IoT devices are defined by their constraints: persistent storage like SD cards has finite write cycles and physical capacity; microcontroller Random Access Memory (RAM) is measured in scarce kilobytes; and every byte transmitted to, and stored in, the cloud adds a measurable operational cost.

Note: *Circular buffers can be strategically stored in Real-Time Clock* (RTC) *memory for post-crash forensics.*

To guarantee continuous operation, prevent resource exhaustion, and ensure the long-term usefulness of collected data, professional IoT systems have adopted two robust, industry-standard logging patterns. These patterns form the core of data integrity: Rolling Logs for structured, long-term history, and Circular Buffers for high-frequency, immediate, transient event capture.

Rolling Logs represent the definitive standard for managing persistent, large-volume datasets where the total storage capacity is limited and the requirement is to maintain a *consistent* historicalwindow of data. This methodology is critical for any system utilizing non-volatile media such as SD Cards, eMMC flash, or micro-controller specific file systems like SPIFFS/LittleFS (on ESP32/ESP8266 platforms). The fundamental promise of Rolling Logs is that the storage medium will never fill up, thereby preventing system failure due to a lack of space.

The mechanism is a cycle of creation and deletion, strictly governed by a pre-defined policy:

- **Fixed Limit Policy Enforcement:** The system administrator defines a strict constraint. This limit can be specified in one of two ways:
  - **By File Count:** For example, the system must maintain exactly the last 30 log files.
  - **By Total Size:** For example, the total aggregated space allocated for all log files must not exceed 100 MB.
- **The Log Rotation Event:** When the logging activity triggers the fixed limit—either by needing to create a new file (and the file count limit is reached) or by the current file reaching its maximum size—the process of rotation or rolling is initiated.
- **Oldest File Deletion:** The core action of the roll is the identification and deletion of the oldest log file in the sequence. This is a deterministic process that frees up the necessary space for the new data to be safely written, maintaining the operational margin of the system.
- **File Naming Strategy for Ordering:** To facilitate the efficient identification of the "oldest" file, a systematic naming convention is essential:
  - **Sequential Numbering:** `log001.csv`, `log002.csv`, allows for easy arithmetic determination of the oldest index.
  - **Date/Timestamping:** `20251127.csv` (Year-Month-Day) provides a human-readable and chronologically accurate naming scheme.

Quick Decision Table

Resource Constraint	Best Logging Pattern	Typical IoT Use Case and Goal	Key Advantage
SD card / Flash storage	Rolling Logs	Long-term historical data (weeks/ months) for trends, compliance, and regulatory reporting.	Guarantees against resource exhaustion (storage filling up) and maintains a historical window.
Limited RAM (< 50 KB)	Circular Buffer	Pre-crash diagnostics, capturing high-frequency sampling data for transients, and capturing event sequences.	Unmatched speed, minimal processing load, and resilience against sudden power loss or system hangs.
Battery-powered + SD card	Rolling + Circular (Hybrid)	Best Practice: Use Rolling Logs for daily high-level history and a small, dedicated Circular Buffer in RAM (or RTC memory) for immediate crash forensics.	Offers the complete solution: long-term accountability combined with robust, high-resolution fault analysis.

Table 11.6: *A Quick Decision Table*

These two logging patterns are not merely options; they are the architectural backbone of data integrity in virtually every production-grade IoT device today.

Visualizing Logs Over Time: Transforming Data into Actionable Insight

The vast streams of raw data generated by IoT devices—often logged as simple numbers in CSV or JSON files—hold immense potential, but their sheer volume renders them functionally opaque to the human mind. Visualization is the critical step that converts thousands of disconnected data points into instant, intuitive insight, making complex patterns, critical anomalies, and subtle trends immediately visible and actionable.

The Power of Visual Transformation

Visualization fundamentally changes the relationship between an observer and the data:

- **From Abstract to Concrete:** Numbers become lines, bars, and gauges that tell a story.
- **Speed of Comprehension:** A person can identify a problem in a graph in seconds, a task that might take hours or days to achieve through manual review of log files.
- **Enhanced Collaboration:** Visual dashboards provide a common, easy-to-understand language for technical teams, management, and external stakeholders.

Popular Visualization Tools (Empowering Global IoT Deployments)

Access to powerful visualization does not require massive investment. Many of the most popular and effective tools offer robust free tiers, supporting projects from university research to massive industrial operations:

Tool	Core Strength and Best For	Global Application Examples	Key Features Beyond Basics
ThingSpeak	Quick line/bar/gauge charts; tightly integrated with the MATLAB ecosystem. Ideal for proof-of-concept and educational settings.	University labs (for sensor research), Indian weather stations (simple data sharing), personal smart home projects.	Built-in analytics functions, automatic code generation, easy integration with MATLAB analysis routines.
Google Sheets	Familiar spreadsheet interface with powerful, automatic chart generation. Best for ad-hoc analysis and simple data sharing.	Small farms (crop monitoring), classrooms (data science education), startups in Brazil (early-stage MVP tracking).	Real-time collaboration, basic formula-driven alerts, easy sharing via Google Drive infrastructure.
Looker Studio (formerly Google Data Studio)	Professional, interactive, and multi-source dashboards. Designed for aggregating data from various platforms (databases, cloud services, other Sheets).	Smart city projects in Singapore (public transport KPIs), large factory Key Performance Indicator (KPI) monitoring, logistics tracking.	Drag-and-drop report building, complex blending of data sources, robust permission controls for large organizations.
Grafana	The gold standard for advanced industrial and time-series dashboards. Highly configurable with powerful querying capabilities and integrated alerting.	German manufacturing (machine learning predictive maintenance), Japanese robotics (real-time telemetry), AWS IoT deployments.	Connects to nearly any data source, sophisticated templating, advanced alert routing (for example : Slack, PagerDuty).
Excel / LibreOffice	Essential for offline analysis and audit trails. Best when data is downloaded locally, often from SD cards or remote logging devices.	Remote African wildlife trackers (where connectivity is sparse), cold-chain audits for compliance, forensic analysis of failure events.	Powerful statistical functions, pivot tables for data summarization, widely accepted format for regulatory submissions.

Table 11.7: *Popular Visualization Tools*

The adoption of visualization is directly tied to measurable improvements in efficiency, yield, and safety:

- **Agricultural Yield Improvement:** A Brazilian farmer utilizing ThingSpeak dashboards successfully spotted recurring nighttime humidity drops that were stressing his crops. Adjusting the ventilation schedule based on this visualization led to an impressive 18% increase in overall yield.
- **Industrial Downtime Reduction:** A German factory implemented Grafana to visualize high-frequency vibration and temperature trends on critical machinery. By catching early signs of wear, they reduced unplanned operational downtime by 40%.
- **Regulatory Assurance:** Indian municipal corporations rely on Google Data Studio dashboards to present real-time and historical air-quality sensor data to pollution control boards, providing undeniable proof of sensor uptime and compliance efforts.

The Global Best Practice Workflow

The most successful and scalable IoT deployments worldwide follow a simple, four-step best practice pipeline:

1. **Log Everything:** Capture all sensor readings and events in a simple, standardized, and machine-readable format (CSV, JSON, or similar).

2. **Push to Cloud:** Securely transmit the raw data to a scalable cloud platform (for example, AWS IoT, Azure IoT Hub, dedicated database).
3. **Connect to Visualization Tool:** Establish a single point of connection between the cloud data store and a dedicated visualization tool (for example, Grafana, Looker Studio).
4. **Share Live Dashboard:** Distribute a live, interactive link to the dashboard with all relevant stakeholders, from field technicians to executive management.

This workflow, often requiring as little as five minutes of initial setup, provides continuous, weeks-long streams of actionable intelligence, With proper visualization, your IoT system moves beyond the mere task of collecting data and starts performing the vital function of telling stories—stories that save money, prevent catastrophic disasters, optimize resources, and ultimately improve lives.

Mini Project: "Smart Temperature Logger" with Multi-Channel Alerts

This comprehensive, hands-on mini project serves as the capstone for this chapter, integrating key IoT principles—specifically secure data logging, reliable time synchronization, multi-level threshold alerts, cloud integration, and essential device hardening—into a robust, real-world prototype. The goal is to construct an Internet of Things system capable of continuously monitoring ambient room temperature in an energy-efficient manner. The final product will be a self-sustaining logger that not only securely stores historical data but also instantly dispatches multi-channel alerts when critical environmental anomalies are detected.

This project is highly adaptable, making it suitable for a wide range of critical monitoring applications, such as ensuring optimal growth conditions in a controlled agricultural environment (for example, greenhouse monitoring), maintaining thermal stability in sensitive IT infrastructure (for example, server rooms), or guaranteeing the cold chain integrity for essential medical supplies (for example : vaccine storage). Upon completion, you will possess a fully functional, hardened prototype ready for deployment in a real-world scenario.

The project relies on a minimal yet powerful set of hardware and cloud services to achieve its objectives:

Component	Function/Purpose	Key Specifications/Details
ESP32 Microcontroller	The central processing unit. Manages all low-level tasks, including reading the sensor, establishing Wi-Fi connectivity, synchronizing time via NTP, and executing secure communication protocols (HTTPS/MQTT).	Integrated Wi-Fi/Bluetooth, Dual-Core Processor, Low-Power Capabilities, Built-in TLS/SSL Hardware Acceleration.
DHT11 Sensor	The primary environmental sensor. Measures both temperature and relative humidity.	Digital output, 3.3V–5V compatibility, Cost-effective, Temperature accuracy of ±2°C, Humidity accuracy of ±5%. Requires a single GPIO pin for data.
Cloud Service Layer	Facilitates secure data storage, visualization, and instant notification delivery.	Google Sheets: Used for simple, archival CSV-style logging via Webhooks. Firebase Realtime DB: Provides fast, real-time JSON storage for immediate analytics. Blynk: Serves as a user-facing dashboard and instant push notification service.

Component	Function/Purpose	Key Specifications/Details
Optional Components	Enhancements for production readiness and redundancy.	SD Card Module: Provides local, rolling storage capability to prevent data loss during Wi-Fi outages. CR2032 Battery/RTC: A real-time clock backup and battery for maintaining time synchronization during deep-sleep cycles, ensuring accurate timestamps even without constant NTP updates.

Table 11.8: *Quick Decision Table for Mini Project*

Implemented Features and System Specifications

The logger is engineered with the following critical operational parameters and security features:

- **Timed Logging Interval:** Data (temperature and humidity) is recorded and transmitted every 30 seconds. This interval provides a balance between data granularity and battery efficiency.
- **Time Synchronization:** All timestamps are synchronized using the Network Time Protocol (NTP) to ensure high accuracy and global consistency across all logged data.
- **Intelligent Alert Triggering:** An alert mechanism is triggered if the temperature reading exceeds a configurable high threshold of 38°C.
    - **Hysteresis Implementation:** It is a critical feature to prevent alert spamming (chattering) when the temperature hovers near the threshold. The alert will only be cleared (and subsequent alerts suppressed) once the temperature drops significantly below the threshold (for example, to 37°C).
- **Multi-Channel Alert System:** Alerts are simultaneously sent across three distinct channels for redundancy and reliability:
    - **Google Sheets Entry:** An additional row is appended to the spreadsheet with the alert timestamp and value.
    - **SMTP Email Alert:** A detailed email is sent via a reliable Simple Mail Transfer Protocol (SMTP) service (for example, SMTP2GO), providing an official record.
    - **Blynk Push Notification:** An instant, attention-grabbing phone popup is sent to the configured mobile device via the Blynk app.
- **Data Structure:** All data is consistently stored in a standard JSON (JavaScript Object Notation) format, ensuring easy parsing by cloud services and analytics tools.
- **Device Hardening and Security:** The system incorporates multiple layers of security to protect data and credentials:
    - **Disabled Debugging:** All `Serial.print` statements are permanently disabled in the production code to prevent unauthorized information leakage via the physical serial port.
    - **Secure Boot/Flash:** Utilizing the native features of ESP32 for secure boot and flash encryption protects the firmware and code from tampering or unauthorized reading.
    - **Secure Credential Storage:** Wi-Fi passwords, API keys, and server credentials are not hardcoded but are instead stored securely within the SPIFFS (SPI Flash File System) or the EEPROM/Preferences library.
    - **Encrypted Communication:** All data payloads are transmitted using TLS/SSL (Transport Layer Security), ensuring the data is encrypted via HTTPS or secure MQTT.

Step-by-Step Implementation

1. **Hardware Assembly and Power Management**

   The foundational step involves wiring the components.

   a. **Wiring:** Connect the DHT11 sensor to the ESP32

      i. **Crucial Note:** A 10kΩ pull-up resistor must be placed between the DHT11 Data line and 3.3V to ensure reliable digital communication.

   b. **Power:** Begin testing with USB power. For final deployment, integrate a deep-sleep circuit (for example, using a transistor and low-power regulator) to maximize battery life, allowing the ESP32 to wake up only for the 30-second logging/transmission cycle.

2. **Software Setup and Library Management**

   The programming environment must be configured to support the ESP32 and the necessary protocols.

   a. **IDE Setup:** Install the Arduino IDE and add the ESP32 board support package.

   b. **Required Libraries:** Install the following libraries via the Arduino Library Manager:

      i. DHT sensor library (Adafruit)

      ii. WiFi and HTTPClient (Standard ESP32 Libraries)

      iii. `NTPClient` (For time synchronization)

      iv. `ESP_Mail_Client` (A robust library for handling SMTP communication)

      v. `BlynkSimpleEsp32`

      vi. `Firebase_ESP_Client`

   c. **Credential Configuration:** Ensure a framework is in place to securely read Wi-Fi credentials from SPIFFS or preferences before initializing the connection.

3. **Cloud Services Configuration**

   Each cloud service requires specific setup to act as a logging and alerting endpoint:

   - **Google Sheets (Webhooks):**

     a. Create a new Google Sheet with columns (for example, Timestamp, Temperature, Humidity).

     b. Open the `Script Editor` (`Tools` -> `Script editor`).

     c. Write a Google Apps Script containing a `doGet()` or `doPost()` function that parses the incoming URL parameters and uses the `appendRow()` method to insert a new row.

     d. Deploy the script as a Web App to generate a unique Webhook URL (`SHEETS_URL`) for the ESP32 to POST data to.

   - **Firebase Realtime Database:**

     a. Create a new Firebase project and initialize the Realtime Database.

     b. Obtain the API Key and the Database URL.

     c. Configure the Security Rules to allow only write-only access from the device, preventing unauthorized reads or modifications.

   - **Blynk Platform:**

     a. Create a new project in the Blynk mobile app or web dashboard.

b. Add a Notification Widget to the dashboard.

c. Copy the unique Auth Token for the project.

- **SMTP Service (Email Alerts):**

  a. Register with a dedicated transactional email service (for example, SMTP2GO, SendGrid, or SMTP of Google).

  b. Obtain the necessary SMTP credentials: Host address, Port (typically 587 or 465), and the Login/Password for TLS communication.

4. **Code Implementation (Simplified Core Logic)**

   The main code utilizes non-blocking functions (`millis()`) to manage the timed logging and alerting cycle:

   The logic within the main loop() function is primarily driven by the time interval.

5. **Hardening and Deployment**

   The final stage involves rigorous testing and optimizing for long-term operation.

   - **Security Check:** Activate the hardware features of ESP32; Secure Boot (to verify firmware integrity) and Flash Encryption (to protect stored code and data). Verify that all sensitive keys are stored using the Preferences.h or SPIFFS libraries.
   - **System Testing:** Artificially manipulate the DHT11 sensor (for example, by holding it) to simulate a high temperature breach (for example: 40°C). Verify that the log entries are created in Google Sheets and Firebase, and that the email and Blynkpush notifications are received instantaneously.
   - **Data Visualization:** Integrate the Firebase data feed with a professional visualization tool like Grafana or ThingSpeak to analyze trends and monitor long-term stability.
   - **Low-Power Deployment:** Implement the `ESP.deepSleep()` function to put the device into an ultra-low-power state between logging cycles. The deep-sleep period should be set to 30 seconds, with the device waking up only to read the sensor, connect to Wi-Fi, transmit the data/alert, and immediately return to sleep.

This project successfully demonstrates the creation of a secure, scalable, and resilient IoT monitoring solution, adaptable for a wide variety of industrial and consumer applications.

Comprehensive Security Guidelines for IoT Logging

Production-grade rules used in every IoT deployment worldwide

Robust Input Validation and Sanitization of All Sensor Values Before Logging

The Principle: Never trust raw input, especially from physical sensors. Direct logging of unvalidated sensor strings or values can lead to data corruption, buffer overflows, or injection attacks if the log consumer is a web application or database. Consider adding a quick example: clamp temperature range, reject NaN, log an error event

Expansion:

- **Filter and Validate:** Always implement strict type checking and range validation. Define the expected minimum and maximum physical values for every sensor (for example, temperature, humidity, pressure).

- **Handle Errors Gracefully:** Check for sensor communication errors (I2C/SPI failure) and sensor-specific error values (like NaN or -999). Replace garbage data with a predefined, acceptable error value (for example, 0 or null) or, ideally, skip the log entry entirely and log a separate system error message.

Strict Minimization of Logged Sensitive Data (Data Pruning)

The Principle: The easiest way to secure sensitive data is not to store it in the first place. Adhere to the principle of "Data Minimization" required by global privacy laws (for example, GDPR).

Expansion:

- **Avoid PII and Credentials:** Do NOT log Wi-Fi passwords, private keys (for example, MQTT or API tokens), user email addresses, or specific personal identifiers unless absolutely required by compliance.
- **Geo-Fencing and Abstraction:** Instead of logging high-resolution coordinates (which can pinpoint a home or person), use data abstraction. Log a geographically generalized identifier.
    - **Bad Example:** `lat=12.9716`, `lon=77.5946` (Exact location of a device)
    - **Good Example:** Log "`zone=greenhouse`", "`site_id=SF_33`", or "`city=...`". This retains utility without revealing personal location.
- **Tokenization:** Replace actual sensitive identifiers with non-reversible tokens in the log files.

Encryption and Secure Storage for On-Device Credentials

The Principle: Credentials (passwords, keys) must never reside in plain text within the firmware or log files. If the device is physically compromised, the credentials must remain protected.

Expansion:

- **Flash Encryption:** Use hardware-backed encryption mechanisms. On platforms like ESP32, utilize the built-in Flash Encryption feature for storing configuration data and Wi-Fi credentials (often via the Preferences library).
- **Secure Headers/Secrets:** For compile-time secrets, use platforms like Arduino Secrets and the pre-processor to keep keys out of the main public code repository, or, for maximum security, inject keys at provisioning time, not compile time.
- **Key Derivation:** Avoid storing API keys directly. If possible, use Key Derivation Functions (KDFs) and store only a secure hash of a password required for local functions.

Mandatory Use of Secure Transport Protocols (HTTPS/TLS)

The Principle: All data transmitted over a network, especially the public internet, must be encrypted *in transit* to prevent eavesdropping and Man-in-the-Middle (MITM) attacks. Raw HTTP is unacceptable.

Expansion:

- **Web Services:** Always use HTTPS (HTTP Secure). Ensure the TLS library of the device is up-to-date and that certificate verification is enabled to check the identity of the server.
- **Google Sheets Integration:** Use a deployed Apps Script HTTPS endpoint as a secure proxy. Never try to post directly to a spreadsheet URL.
- **Firebase/Cloud Databases:** For cloud services, always enable Realtime Database secure rules or equivalent IAM (Identity and Access Management) policies to control who can read/write data, even if the connection is TLS-encrypted.
- **Email (SMTP):** If the device sends email alerts, use port 587 with STARTTLS or port 465 (SMTPS), ensuring the connection is encrypted before credentials are sent.

- **Webhooks/APIs:** Only use secure webhook services like maker.ifttt.com (HTTPS) or similar secure cloud functions.

Strict Application of Rate Limits and Throttling

The Principle: A runaway device or a malicious attacker should not be able to overwhelm the backend server, cloud platform, or local storage with a flood of logs (Denial-of-Service or DoS).

Expansion:

- **Prevent Log Flooding:** Implement a time-based check to limit the frequency of data submission. This saves battery/power, reduces cloud costs, and prevents DoS.
- **Alert Throttling:** Critical alerts (for example, "high temperature detected") must be subject to a much stricter, longer rate limit. This prevents users from being spammed and ensures the alert system remains effective.

Additional Production-Grade Security and Reliability Rules

These are non-negotiable rules for any robust, compliant, and trustworthy IoT product:

- **Accurate Time Synchronization:** Timestamp every log entry with NTP (Network Time Protocol) or RTC (Real-Time Clock), never with `millis()`. Milliseconds are unreliable across reboots and provide no global context. Accurate time is crucial for debugging, auditing, and legal compliance.
- **Data Integrity and Non-Repudiation:** For critical industrial or medical logs, Hash or digitally sign the log entry before transmission or storage. This proves the data has not been tampered with after it left the sensor (industrial compliance).
- **Secure Local Storage:** When using an SD card or flash storage, use append-only logging. Never allow random file overwrites, which can corrupt the integrity of historical data. Log files should be sequentially numbered and finalized (closed) to prevent tampering.
- **Firmware Hardening:** Disable `Serial.print()` completely in the final production firmware. Debug output can leak system state, memory addresses, or sensitive credentials to anyone physically connecting to the device. Use conditional compilation to strip it out.
- **Platform Security Features:** For advanced microcontrollers (for example, ESP32, STM32), Enable flash encryption and secure boot. Flash encryption protects the compiled firmware and configuration secrets at rest, while secure boot prevents unauthorized or malicious firmware from running on the device.

Best Practices for IoT Data Logging: Timestamps, Retry Logic, and Batching

The consistent inclusion of precise, human-readable timestamps is fundamental. This represents the initial, production-grade, and thoroughly validated technique employed across all reliable, long-lifecycle Internet of Things systems globally deployed.

Data without a reliable time reference is useless. For production IoT systems, simply using the internal uptime of the `device(millis())` or raw, un-zoned Unix epoch seconds is a major anti-pattern. These methods introduce ambiguity and complicate data analysis across different time zones and devices.

1. **The Approach: ISO-8601 Format:** The industry-standard requirement is to use a high-precision, globally consistent timestamp format, ideally sourced from a Network Time Protocol (NTP) server or a high-quality Real-Time Clock (RTC) chip.
   a. **Format to Use:** ISO-8601, including the time zone offset.

i. **Example (Local Time Zone):** 2025-11-27T14:30:22+05:30 (A specific moment in IST)

ii. **Example (UTC/ZULU Time):** 2025-11-27T09:00:22Z (Highly recommended for servers)

2. **Implement Robust Retry Logic:** The internet is unreliable, and wireless networks (Wi-Fi, Cellular, LoRa) drop packets and suffer from transient congestion. A device that attempts to send data once and gives up is guaranteed to lose data frequently, rendering the system unreliable. Professional IoT code never gives up easily; it retries intelligently.

3. **Batch Multiple Readings Before Upload:** Establishing a radio connection (Wi-Fi association, TCP handshake, TLS negotiation) is the single most power-intensive action an IoT device performs. This process typically consumes the majority of the duty cycle of the radio, often taking 2–5 seconds of high-power activity, even for a tiny 100-byte data payload.

Practical Exercises

These hands-on exercises reinforce the concepts of the chapter by guiding you through real implementations. Each builds on ESP32 hardware, assumes basic wiring knowledge from *Chapter 5, Getting Started with Arduino, NodeMCU, and ESP32*, and uses sensors from *Chapter 3, Sensor Technologies and Actuators*, (for example, DHT11 for temperature, MQ-2 for gas). Complete them in sequence for best results, testing in a safe environment.

Exercise 1: Smart Logger – Google Sheets Logging

Objective: Create a simple IoT logger that sends temperature data to Google Sheets every minute using IFTTT Webhooks, enabling easy visualization and historical analysis.

Components: ESP32 board, DHT11 sensor, Wi-Fi connection.

Step-by-Step Guide:

1. **Hardware Setup**
2. **Cloud Setup:** Prepare the online services for data logging.
3. **Code Implementation:** Write the Arduino sketch for the ESP32.
   a. **Libraries:** Install the necessary libraries in the Arduino IDE: WiFi, HTTPClient, and DHT sensor library.
   b. **Sensor Reading:** Write code to initialize the DHT sensor and read the temperature every 60 seconds (60000 milliseconds).
   c. **Webhook POST:** Construct the HTTP POST request. The URL should include the Webhook URL noted in Step 2, and the temperature reading should be passed as a query parameter to be recognized by IFTTT.
   d. **Logic:** Use the `millis()` function to ensure the sensor reading and data transmission happens only once every minute without blocking the main loop.
4. **Testing:** Upload the code and verify the entire data path.

Exercise 2: Threshold Watchdog – Email Alert

Objective: Build an alert system that sends an SMTP email when temperature exceeds a specified threshold (for example, 40°C), enhancing real-time monitoring.

Components: ESP32, DHT11, Wi-Fi.

Step-by-Step Guide:

1. **Hardware Setup**
2. **Cloud Setup:** Configure an external SMTP service to handle the email sending.
3. **Code Implementation:** Write the sketch using an SMTP client library.
    a. **Library:** Install the `ESP_Mail_Client` library (or similar) in the Arduino IDE.
    b. **Initialization:** Configure the SMTP session with the credentials obtained in Step 2.
    c. **Email Function:** Create a dedicated function (for example **:**`sendEmail()`) that constructs and sends the email message, including the sender, recipient, subject, and the body content (for example: the current temperature).
    d. **Loop Logic:** In the main `loop()`:
        i. Read the temperature from the DHT11 sensor.
        ii. Check if the temperature is above the alert threshold (for example: 40.0).
        iii. Implement a state variable (for example: `alertSent`) to ensure the email is only sent once when the threshold is crossed, preventing email spam.
        iv. Add a hysteresis condition. Reset the `alertSent` variable only after the temperature has dropped a few degrees below the threshold (for example: 38.0), ensuring the alert can be triggered again only after the danger has passed.
4. **Testing:** Upload the code and trigger an alert.

Exercise 3: Blynk Alert - Mobile Notification

Objective: Set up mobile push notifications via the Blynk platform when the MQ-2 gas level exceeds a critical value (for example :>450), for quick user alerts on a smartphone.

Components: ESP32, MQ-2 sensor, Wi-Fi.

Step-by-Step Guide:

1. **Hardware Setup**
2. **App Setup:** Configure the Blynk mobile application and project.
3. **Code Implementation:** Write the sketch to connect to Blynk and read the sensor.
    a. **Library:** Install the BlynkSimpleEsp32 library in the Arduino IDE.
    b. **Connection:** Include the Blynk library and use the Auth Token, Wi-Fi SSID, and Password to establish a connection using `Blynk.begin()`.
    c. **Main Loop:** Ensure `Blynk.run()` is called frequently within the `loop()` to maintain the connection.
    d. **Sensor Reading:** Read the analog value from the GPIO pin connected to the MQ-2 (for example: `analogRead(34)`). This value typically ranges from 0 to 4095.
    e. **Alert Logic:** Check if the read gas value exceeds the threshold (for example: 450).
    f. **Notification:** If the threshold is exceeded, call the `Blynk.notify()` function with an appropriate alert message (for example : "`Gas Leak! MQ-2 >450`").
    g. **Hysteresis/State:** Implement a simple state check (for example: `alertSentboolean`) to prevent continuous notifications. Reset the state when the gas level drops significantly below the threshold (for example: below 400).
4. **Testing:** Upload the code and expose the sensor to a gas source.

Exercise 4: Secure Logging – Sanitization and Structure

Objective: Log sensor data as valid JSON with timestamps, ensuring data security through sanitization and making it ready for analytics.

Components: An ESP32 microcontroller and a sensor (for example: DHT11 for temperature/humidity).

Step-by-Step Guide:

1. **Setup:** Set up your Arduino IDE environment for the ESP32.
2. **Sensor Reading and Data Sanitization:** In the main loop, read the data from your chosen sensor.
3. **JSON Formatting:**
   a. Create a function that is responsible for generating the log message.
   b. Inside this function, retrieve the current formatted timestamp from the NTPClient.
   c. Construct the log message as a standard JSON string. The JSON should minimally include:
      i. A key for the timestamp (for example: "`ts`") with the formatted time as its value.
      ii. A key for the sensor reading (for example: `"temp"`) with the sanitized sensor value as its value.
   d. Ensure proper JSON escaping for quotes when building the string in C++.
4. **Logging:**
   a. In the main loop, call your JSON generation function.
   b. Print the resulting JSON string to the Serial Monitor. For a more robust solution, this output could be logged to an SD card or sent to a cloud service.
5. **Testing:** Verify that the timestamps are accurate and that the sensor values are being logged correctly and are within the sanitized limits.

Exercise 5: Device Hardening Checklist

Objective: Systematically audit and modify an existing ESP32 project to secure it against common vulnerabilities.

Components: An existing, functional ESP32 project.

Step-by-Step Guide:

1. **Checklist Review and Security Policy Definition:** Review essential security measures for embedded IoT devices. The goal is to minimize the attack surface.
2. **Code and Configuration Implementation:**
   a. Modify your existing C++ code to remove all debugging output and initialize security features as defined in the review.
   b. Adjust the ESP32 board settings in the Arduino IDE (under Tools) to enable Flash Encryption and Secure Boot. Note that once these are enabled, the process for subsequent uploads changes, and unauthorized users will be unable to read or modify the firmware.
   c. Implement the NVS library functions to read and write stored credentials securely.

3. **Security Audit and Verification:** Compile and upload the hardened firmware.
4. **Functional Testing:**
    a. Deploy the hardened firmware.
    b. Ensure that despite the security modifications, the core functionality of the IoT device remains intact.

Conclusion

This chapter has delivered a practical, production-oriented security and reliability framework specifically tailored to resource-constrained IoT devices such as the ESP32. Rather than theoretical cryptography, the focus remained on what actually works in real deployments: eliminating debug leaks, protecting firmware through ESP32 Secure Boot and flash encryption, safely storing credentials, and disabling unnecessary interfaces and services. The chapter placed particular emphasis on robust data logging—covering local rolling logs on SD cards, cloud logging via Google Sheets, Firebase, and ThingSpeak, structured JSON/CSV formatting, accurate NTP and RTC timestamps, resilient retry mechanisms, and power-efficient batch uploads. Threshold-based alerting was explored through multiple real-world channels — SMTP email, Blynk push notifications, and IFTTT multi-platform workflows — ensuring critical events reach users instantly, even in remote locations.

The hands-on Smart Temperature Logger mini-project and five progressive exercises tied every concept together, transforming abstract best practices into working, auditable code. By strictly following the device-hardening checklist and logging patterns presented here, readers can now elevate simple prototypes into systems that survive years in the field—whether monitoring greenhouses in rural India, cold-chain transport across Africa, server rooms in Germany, or smart factories in Japan—without losing data, leaking secrets, or becoming part of the next botnet. These battle-tested techniques form the final bridge between "it works on my desk" and "it is trusted worldwide," preparing you confidently for the advanced cloud integration, edge processing, and large-scale deployment topics in the chapters ahead.

The next chapter introduces the foundational concepts, practical techniques, and industry best practices for implementing both local and cloud-based data logging, designing real-time alert systems, and integrating multi-platform notification services. You will learn how to capture sensor data in structured, timestamped formats such as CSV and JSON; implement threshold-based alerts with debouncing and hysteresis; and securely push data to cloud services including Firebase, Google Sheets via IFTTT, ThingSpeak, and Blynk for instant mobile notifications. You will also explore email gateways (SMTP), batch uploads, rolling log buffers, and time-windowed analytics that support dashboards, compliance reporting, and long-term trend analysis.

Chapter 12

Data Logging, Alert Systems, and Notification Integration

Introduction

In the previous chapter, we have explored how IoT devices establish secure and reliable communication with global cloud infrastructures.By introducing MQTT, HTTP/REST APIs, Webhooks, strong authentication, encrypted channels, firmware integrity checks, and secure OTA mechanisms, we learned how to transform basic embedded nodes into resilient, production-ready devices capable of operating safely in untrusted networks. Chapter 11 emphasized that connectivity alone is never enough—security must be foundational for any scalable IoT deployment, whether protecting industrial machinery, smart-home environments, or national-level infrastructure.

Building on this secure and trusted communication layer, we now shift our attention to what happens after a device is safely connected: how to continuously log meaningful data, detect critical events in real time, and deliver timely alerts across multiple platforms. This represents the next major milestone in the lifecycle of an IoT system—moving from secure communication to intelligent monitoring, historical analytics, and actionable notifications. As IoT systems mature from experimental prototypes into reliable, deployable solutions, the ability to record data, analyze trends, detect anomalies, and notify users instantly becomes indispensable. Whether monitoring temperature fluctuations in vaccine cold-storage units in rural clinics, tracking air-quality metrics in European laboratories, detecting soil-moisture drops in precision-agriculture systems in India, or identifying motion events in home-security installations in Japan, robust logging and alert mechanisms form the backbone of truly intelligent IoT deployments.

This chapter introduces the foundational concepts, practical techniques, and industry best practices for implementing both local and cloud-based data logging, designing real-time alert systems, and integrating multi-platform notification services. You will learn how to capture sensor data in structured, timestamped formats such as CSV and JSON; implement threshold-based alerts with debouncing and hysteresis; and securely push data to cloud services including Firebase, Google Sheets via IFTTT, ThingSpeak, and Blynk for instant mobile notifications. You will also explore email gateways (SMTP), batch uploads, rolling log buffers, and time-windowed analytics that support dashboards, compliance reporting, and long-term trend analysis.

Through hands-on exercises using familiar sensors like DHT11/22 and MQ-series gas detectors, and with guided code examples for ESP32 and Arduino platforms, you will progressively build the capability to construct IoT systems that not only collect and store data, but also interpret events, take intelligent actions, and notify users immediately through multiple channels. By the end of this chapter, you will be equipped to design IoT systems that maintain meaningful historical records, detect anomalies with confidence, communicate alerts in real time, and support data-driven decision-making across diverse real-world environments.

Structure

In this chapter, we will cover the following topics:

- Introduction to Data Logging in IoT
- Local Storage Options
- Cloud Logging Approaches
- Real-Time versus Batch Logging
- Formatting Logs for Analytics
- Alert System Fundamentals
- Cloud-Based Alert Techniques
- Mobile Notification Integration
- Event Logging Patterns
- Visualization of Logged Data
- Designing a Robust Alert Workflow

Introduction to Data Logging in IoT Systems

Logging data is the absolute backbone of pretty much any substantial Internet of Things (IoT) setup. It is the essential process that transforms fleeting, raw sensor readings into a solid, persistent historical record, allowing us to derive long-term meaning and context. While real-time data is excellent for immediate, reactive actions — such as automatically activating an air conditioning unit when a temperature threshold is exceeded — it is the *historical* data that provides the necessary foundation for true system intelligence. This accumulated data enables practitioners to uncover deep operational insights, spot recurring usage patterns, proactively identify anomalies, meet stringent compliance regulations, and ultimately make smart, informed strategic decisions. Without a robust logging mechanism, an IoT system is merely a collection of reactive components that lacks any real foresight or accountability. For instance, if a smart thermostat malfunctions and overheats a room, logging is the only way to determine if a software update, a sensor failure, or an external attack was the cause. Similarly, for Industrial IoT (IIoT), a lack of detailed logging would make it impossible to conduct a root cause analysis following an unplanned factory shutdown or a critical machinery failure. Conversely, with proper logging in place, the system transforms into a powerful tool for optimization, predicting future events, and ensuring system-wide accountability.

Data Logging: Local versus Cloud

IoT data logging generally falls into two primary architectural camps: local and cloud-based, each optimized for different operational requirements.

Logging Type	Best For	Typical Storage Medium	Key Advantages	Key Disadvantages
Local Logging	Remote/isolated deployments, high-rate sampling, intermittent connectivity.	SD cards, SPIFFS/LittleFS memory (on microcontrollers like ESP32).	Guarantees data capture during network outages, enables fully autonomous operation, conserves power and bandwidth.	Limited storage capacity, data not easily accessible for remote users, requires manual retrieval or delayed sync.
Cloud Logging	Global monitoring, multi-user access, complex analysis, long-term archival.	Platforms like Google Sheets, Firebase, ThingSpeak, AWS IoT, Azure IoT Hub.	Real-time, multi-user access; enables sophisticated visualization and integration with advanced analytical tools; offers massive scalability.	Requires a stable, continuous network connection; incurs ongoing service costs; reliant on external platform availability.

Table 12.1: *Local versus Cloud Data Logging*

Local Logging is executed directly on the IoT device using storage media such as SD cards or integrated memory (for example, SPIFFS, LittleFS) within microcontrollers. This is the optimal choice when network reliability is a concern or when an extremely high sampling rate is required. This approach ensures that data is not lost during connectivity interruptions, guarantees that systems can operate completely autonomously (as in remote wildlife tracking), and critically saves power and bandwidth—a vital consideration for battery-powered sensors or monitoring the "cold chain" in regions with nascent infrastructure, monitoring the "cold chain" in regions with nascent infrastructure, where local logging of temperature data is essential to ensure that sensitive products, such as vaccines, are not compromised even if network connectivity is intermittent or unavailable.

Cloud Logging involves offloading the storage and heavy processing to scalable, remote servers using platforms like Google Sheets, Firebase, ThingSpeak, or major cloud services (AWS IoT, Azure IoT). This method facilitates easy real-time, multi-user access, supports sophisticated data visualization, provides robust long-term archival, and connects seamlessly with enterprise analytical tools. It is the preferred method for city-wide data dashboards, global supply-chain tracking, and any research that demands immediate, location-independent data access.

Local Storage Options

Local storage plays an indispensable role in IoT deployments, particularly when internet connectivity is intermittent, expensive, or entirely unavailable. By writing sensor data directly to on-board or removable media attached to the microcontroller, the system guarantees zero data loss during network outages, supports high-frequency sampling that would otherwise overwhelm wireless links, and dramatically extends battery life by eliminating the need for constant radio transmission. In real-world applications ranging from solar-powered soil-moisture networks across thousands of Indian farms to wildlife tracking collars in African national parks and vibration monitoring on North Sea oil platforms, local storage is not a fallback option; it is the primary, trusted repository.

The most widely adopted local storage solution remains the microSD card module interfaced via SPI to ESP32, NodeMCU, or Arduino boards. With capacities routinely exceeding 32 GB and prices under $5, a single card can store years of minute-resolution data from multiple sensors. The built-in SDMMC host or standard SPI mode of ESP32, combined with the proven SD library (or the higher-performance SdFat library), delivers reliable read/write speeds of several hundred kilobytes per second, easily handling 100 Hz logging when required. Alternative on-chip options include SPIFFS and LittleFS filesystems in the flash of ESP32 (typically 1–4 MB partition) for smaller datasets and faster access, though they lack the removable, virtually unlimited nature of SD cards.

Three file structures dominate local logging: CSV (Comma-Separated Values), JSON (JavaScript Object Notation), and plain text CSV is often preferred for high-frequency local logs due to its minimal overhead, while JSON is better suited for cloud ingestion. Because of its minimal overhead, universal compatibility with Excel, Google Sheets, Python Pandas, and MATLAB, and simple line-by-line append behaviour. JSON offers richer structure—ideal when each record must include metadata, device IDs, GPS coordinates, or battery levels—and is natively parsed by cloud platforms upon later upload. Plain text is occasionally used for ultra-high-speed raw dumps or human-readable debug logs, but it sacrifices easy parsing and should be avoided for long-term storage.

The advantages of local storage are compelling: The advantages of local storage in IoT systems are significant. It provides complete independence from internet connectivity, consumes minimal power when idle, supports very high sampling rates that may not be feasible over wireless networks, and allows physical removal of storage media for forensic analysis or regulatory audits. These characteristics make local storage particularly useful in remote deployments and high-frequency data logging applications.

However, certain limitations must also be considered. SD cards have a limited number of write cycles per memory sector (typically around 100,000), although this can be mitigated using wear-leveling techniques provided by modern file systems and libraries. In addition, file systems must be designed to handle unexpected power loss safely, often by using synchronous writes or rolling log files. Since storage capacity is finite, systems typically implement strategies such as rolling logs, which automatically delete the oldest files when a storage limit is reached, or circular buffers in RAM to temporarily store critical data before it is written to persistent storage or transmitted to the cloud.

Cloud Logging Approaches

Cloud logging elevates IoT systems from isolated data collectors to globally accessible, collaborative intelligence platforms by offloading storage, processing, and visualization to remote servers. Unlike local storage, which excels in resilience and offline operation, cloud approaches provide virtually unlimited capacity, real-time multi-user access, automatic backups, and seamless integration with analytics, machine learning, and dashboard tools. This shift is essential for applications requiring stakeholder collaboration—such as farmers in India viewing soil data on mobile apps, factory managers in Germany monitoring production lines from anywhere, or researchers in Brazil analyzing environmental trends across thousands of nodes.

Among the most accessible and widely adopted cloud logging solutions for microcontroller-based projects is the Firebase Realtime Database of Google. This NoSQL database stores data as flexible JSON trees, synchronizing changes instantly across all connected clients with built-in offline caching support via the Firebase-ESP-Client library. Ideal for dynamic applications like smart home dashboards or multi-device fleets, it handles frequent updates efficiently and enforces security rules to control read/write access. ThingSpeak, developed by MathWorks, offers an IoT-specific alternative with dedicated channels containing up to eight data fields per device, native MATLAB analytics, and scheduled actions—making it a favorite in academic, research, and prototyping environments worldwide, from university weather stations to industrial proof-of-concept deployments. However, it is important to note the rate limits of the platform (1 update every 15 seconds for a free account), which directly influence the feasible data logging interval.

For ultimate simplicity, especially in educational and small-scale projects, Google Sheets combined with webhooks (often routed through IFTTT or direct Apps Script endpoints) remains unbeatable. A single HTTP POST from an ESP32 appends a new row containing timestamped sensor values, instantly updating shared spreadsheets with automatic charting capabilities. This approach requires minimal setup, leverages familiar tools used by non-technical stakeholders, and scales surprisingly well for low-to-medium data rates, powering community air-quality monitoring networks in urban India or classroom environmental projects across Europe.

The choice of logging interval profoundly influences system performance, power consumption, and cost. High-frequency logging (every 1–10 seconds) suits safety-critical or fast-changing scenarios—such as vibration monitoring in predictive maintenance or real-time patient vitals in wearable health devices—but demands constant radio activity, rapidly draining batteries and increasing cellular data charges. Low-power modes, common in remote agricultural or environmental sensors, extend intervals to minutes or hours, often combined with deep sleep cycles on the ESP32 to achieve months or years of operation from a single battery. designs frequently adopt adaptive strategies: high-frequency local logging during normal operation, with downsampled or event-triggered uploads to the cloud, ensuring both detailed records and efficient connectivity.

By carefully selecting the appropriate cloud platform and tuning logging intervals to match application constraints, developers create IoT systems that balance immediacy with longevity—delivering actionable insights to users worldwide while respecting the practical limitations of embedded hardware. These cloud logging approaches form the bridge between raw sensor data and intelligent, responsive applications explored in the remainder of this chapter.

Real-Time versus Batch Logging

The decision between real-time streaming and batch logging represents one of the most fundamental architectural choices in IoT system design, directly influencing responsiveness, resource consumption, data integrity, and overall system longevity. Real-time streaming involves transmitting each sensor reading—or groups of readings at very short intervals—immediately to the cloud or central server as soon as it is captured, while batch logging accumulates multiple readings locally before uploading them in consolidated packets at predetermined intervals or upon connectivity restoration. Both approaches have matured into industry standards, with deployments worldwide selecting or combining them based on application constraints and operational priorities.

Real-time streaming excels in scenarios demanding immediate visibility and rapid response, such as safety-critical monitoring in industrial plants, patient health telemetry in medical facilities, or intrusion detection in security systems. By maintaining an active connection and pushing data continuously via protocols like MQTT with QoS 1/2 or WebSockets, stakeholders gain instantaneous access to live dashboards, enabling split-second decisions—for instance, factory operators in Germany halting a production line upon detecting abnormal vibration, or caregivers in Japan receiving alerts for irregular heart rhythms in elderly patients. This model ensures minimal latency between event occurrence and awareness, making it indispensable where human lives, expensive equipment, or regulatory compliance are at stake.

Batch logging, conversely, prioritizes efficiency and resilience, particularly in constrained environments characterised by limited power, intermittent connectivity, or high data costs. Sensor data is stored locally on SD cards, SPIFFS, or in-memory buffers and transmitted in bursts—typically every few minutes to several hours—often during scheduled wake-up periods on low-power microcontrollers like the ESP32 operating in deep sleep. This approach dramatically reduces radio-on time, extending battery life from weeks to years in remote agricultural sensors monitoring soil conditions across vast Indian farmlands or environmental loggers tracking wildlife in African reserves. It also survives prolonged network outages without data loss and minimises cellular bandwidth expenses in LoRa or NB-IoT deployments common in smart metering.

The trade-offs are clear and often quantifiable. Real-time streaming consumes significantly more bandwidth and power—potentially 80–90 % higher than batch methods—and increases exposure to network-induced packet loss, though mitigated by reliable protocols and retries. Batch logging sacrifices immediacy, introducing delays that may prove unacceptable for urgent alerts, yet it offers superior reliability in unreliable networks and far greater energy efficiency, a critical factor for the billions of battery-powered edge devices projected globally. Hybrid strategies frequently emerge as the choice: critical events trigger immediate streaming, while routine telemetry is batched and uploaded periodically, balancing responsiveness with sustainability.

Selecting the appropriate model depends on careful analysis of use-case requirements. Choose real-time streaming when ultra-low latency is non-negotiable, stable connectivity is assured, and power/bandwidth constraints are minimal—typical in urban smart homes or continuously powered industrial settings. Opt for batch logging in remote, power-sensitive, or cost-constrained deployments such as precision agriculture, cold-chain logistics, or environmental monitoring. In many production systems worldwide, a thoughtful combination of both delivers the optimal outcome: timely alerts when needed and efficient, resilient data collection otherwise, ensuring IoT solutions remain practical, scalable, and economically viable across diverse global applications.

Formatting Logs for Analytics

Effective data logging extends far beyond mere storage; the format in which data is recorded profoundly influences its subsequent utility for analysis, visualization, and long-term insight generation. Poorly structured logs become opaque burdens, requiring extensive preprocessing before yielding value, whereas well-formatted logs integrate seamlessly with spreadsheets, databases, dashboards, and machine learning pipelines. In IoT systems—whether tracking energy consumption in European smart grids, monitoring crop health in Indian precision agriculture, or ensuring compliance in pharmaceutical cold chains worldwide—adopting standardized, machine-readable formats is not optional but a fundamental requirement for scalability and maintainability.

JSON (JavaScript Object Notation) has emerged as the dominant standard for cloud-bound and structured logging due to its hierarchical flexibility, human readability, and native support across virtually all modern platforms. JSON (JavaScript Object Notation) has emerged as the dominant standard for cloud-bound and structured logging due to its hierarchical flexibility, human readability, and native support across virtually all modern platforms.

Example JSON Log Payload:

```
{
  "timestamp": "2026-01-26T11:40:00Z",
  "level": "INFO",
  "service": "authentication-api",
  "message": "User login successful",
  "user_id": "pavanbr593",
  "session_id": "a1b2c3d4e5f6g7h8",
  "data": {
    "ip_address": "203.0.113.42",
    "latency_ms": 55
  }
}
```

A single JSON object can encapsulate timestamps, multiple sensor readings, device metadata, location coordinates, battery status, and even nested arrays of events, making it ideal for ingestion into Firebase, ThingSpeak, AWS IoT, or MongoDB. Libraries such as ArduinoJson on the ESP32 enable efficient serialization with minimal memory overhead, ensuring that even resource-constrained devices produce valid, parseable output.

Alert System Fundamentals

Alert systems elevate IoT deployments from passive data collectors to proactive, intelligent guardians that detect anomalies and initiate timely responses, often preventing minor issues from escalating into costly or dangerous failures. At their core, these systems rely on threshold detection, where sensor readings are continuously compared against predefined limits—triggering an action when conditions such as temperature exceeding a safe value, gas concentration surpassing a hazardous level, or motion detected in a restricted area are met. This simple yet powerful mechanism underpins countless real-world applications: refrigerators in pharmaceutical cold chains maintaining vaccine viability, gas sensors safeguarding homes and factories against leaks, and PIR motion detectors securing perimeters in residential and commercial properties worldwide.

While single-parameter thresholds form the foundation, alert logic frequently incorporates multi-parameter conditions to increase specificity and context awareness. For instance, a smart greenhouse might trigger an alert only when temperature rises above 35°C and humidity drops below 40 % simultaneously, indicating a combined risk of heat stress and dehydration rather than isolated fluctuations. Similarly, industrial machinery monitoring could combine vibration amplitude exceeding a limit with a sudden temperature spike, signalling bearing failure more reliably than either reading alone. Such Boolean combinations—using AND, OR, and NOT operators—allow developers to model complex real-world scenarios, as seen in predictive maintenance systems in German automotive plants or multi-sensor environmental monitors tracking air quality in densely populated Asian cities.

A critical challenge in alert system design is mitigating false positives, which erode user trust, drain resources through unnecessary notifications, and desensitise operators to genuine threats. Raw sensor data is inherently noisy, influenced by electrical interference, environmental transients, or brief mechanical disturbances. Debouncing techniques, borrowed from digital input handling, address this by requiring a condition to persist for a minimum duration—typically hundreds of milliseconds to several seconds—before registering as valid, effectively filtering out fleeting spikes common in PIR motion sensors or switch contacts. Averaging complements debouncing by smoothing readings over multiple samples; a moving average or exponential filter applied to temperature or gas sensor outputs reduces the impact of short-term noise, ensuring alerts reflect sustained trends rather than momentary aberrations.

Hysteresis introduces an elegant asymmetry to threshold logic, preventing rapid oscillation around a boundary point that would otherwise generate alert storms. Instead of triggering at exactly 35°C and clearing at the same value, the system might activate an overheating alert when temperature exceeds 35°C but only reset it once the reading falls below 32°C. This deadband approach is standard in HVAC controls across Japanese smart buildings, irrigation systems in Indian agriculture, and battery management in electric vehicles, where it maintains stability without sacrificing responsiveness. In practice, combining debouncing for event detection, averaging for noise reduction, and hysteresis for state stability yields robust, -grade alert behaviour—transforming potentially chaotic sensor streams into reliable decision triggers that operators worldwide can trust in mission-critical environments.

CSV (Comma-Separated Values), despite its simplicity, remains indispensable, offering minimal overhead in contrast to the schema flexibility of formats like JSON.for local storage and spreadsheet-centric workflows. Its line-based structure facilitates rapid appending on SD cards—critical when every byte and millisecond counts—and direct import into Google Sheets, Excel, LibreOfficeCalc, or Python Pandas without intermediate conversion. Each row typically begins with an ISO-8601 timestamp followed by sensor values, enabling immediate charting and basic statistical analysis by non-programmers such as farmers reviewing weekly trends or technicians auditing equipment performance. While lacking the nesting capability of JSON, CSV excels in minimal overhead scenarios and is often the format of choice for high-frequency local logs that are later transformed and uploaded.

Accurate timestamping forms the backbone of meaningful temporal analysis. Relying solely on the Arduino millis() function, which counts milliseconds since boot, risks ambiguity after power cycles or rollover events every 49 days. implementations therefore prioritize absolute time sources: Network Time Protocol (NTP) servers provide millisecond-accurate UTC when internet is available, automatically handling leap seconds and time zones, while hardware Real-Time Clock (RTC) modules such as the DS3231 maintain precise time offline using a coin-cell backup, essential for remote deployments in African environmental monitoring or offshore platforms. Every log entry must include an ISO-8601 formatted timestamp to enable correlation across devices and seamless merging of datasets.

Data integrity and sanitization represent the final critical layer. Raw sensor readings frequently contain anomalies—NaN values from failed DHT22 reads, out-of-range spikes due to electrical noise, or corrupted strings from communication errors—that can skew analytics or crash parsers. Best practice demands validation and cleaning before commitment to storage: check for numeric reasonableness, replace invalid readings with null markers, and escape special characters in text fields. On the ESP32, simple conditional checks during serialization prevent garbage propagation, while checksums or digital signatures on critical logs (common in regulated industries) ensure tamper detection. By rigorously applying these formatting principles, developers produce logs that are not only reliable and future-proof but also immediately actionable—transforming raw telemetry into the high-quality datasets that drive predictive maintenance, anomaly detection, and informed decision-making in IoT systems worldwide.

Cloud-Based Alert Techniques

Cloud-based alert techniques extend the reach and flexibility of IoT alert systems by leveraging internet-connected services to deliver notifications through diverse channels, ensuring that critical events are communicated promptly and reliably to users regardless of their location. Unlike on-device alerts limited to local buzzers or LEDs, cloud methods enable multi-channel delivery—email, instant messaging, push notifications, and even automated voice calls—transforming a solitary microcontroller into a globally coordinated emergency response system. This capability proves invaluable in applications such as remote agricultural monitoring in India, where farmers receive immediate warnings about irrigation failures.

Email alerts via SMTP (Simple Mail Transfer Protocol) services remain one of the most straightforward and universally accessible cloud notification methods. By configuring an ESP32 with libraries such as **`ESP_Mail_Client`**, the device can connect to free or low-cost SMTP providers like SMTP2GO, SendGrid, or Brevo to dispatch richly formatted messages containing sensor values, timestamps, device identifiers, and even attached images from cameras. These emails integrate seamlessly into workflows, triggering inbox rules, forwarding to teams, or archiving for compliance—widely employed in cold-chain logistics across Africa to report temperature excursions in vaccine transport or in server farms worldwide for immediate overheating notifications.

IFTTT (If This Then That) webhooks provide an exceptionally versatile platform for cross-channel alerts with minimal coding overhead. A single HTTP POST request from the microcontroller to a custom webhook URL can simultaneously activate multiple actions: appending event details to Google Sheets for audit trails, posting messages to collaboration tools like Slack or Discord, controlling smart home devices such as turning on sirens, or sending push notifications via the IFTTT mobile app. This orchestration capability shines in hybrid environments—for example, a greenhouse operator in Brazil might configure a webhook to log a frost warning to Sheets, illuminate warning lights via Philips Hue, and broadcast an announcement through Google Home speakers—all from one threshold breach detected by a remote ESP32 node.

While Google Sheets is primarily a logging tool, it effectively doubles as an alert mechanism when combined with Apps Script triggers: upon a new row appended via webhook (indicating an anomaly), automated emails or chat notifications can be dispatched to stakeholders. This approach suits small-to-medium deployments requiring visible, shareable records alongside alerts, such as community-based air quality networks in densely populated Asian cities where exceedance events automatically notify local authorities and residents through integrated Gmail alerts.

For instantaneous personal communication, messaging platforms like Telegram, WhatsApp, and SMS gateways offer compelling alternatives. Telegram bots, created freely and interfaced via simple HTTP APIs, deliver encrypted, media-rich notifications to individuals or groups—popular in European home automation circles for discreet yet immediate updates. WhatsApp Business API, though requiring more setup, enables official messaging in regions like Latin America and India where the platform dominates daily communication. Traditional SMS, routed through services such as Twilio or local providers, guarantees delivery even on feature phones without internet, making it indispensable for critical alerts in rural or developing areas where data connectivity remains unreliable.

Mobile Notification Integration

Mobile notification integration represents a pivotal advancement in IoT alert systems, delivering critical information directly to users' smartphones with the immediacy and convenience that modern lifestyles demand. Unlike traditional email or SMS, which require active checking, mobile push notifications appear instantly on lock screens, accompanied by sounds, vibrations, or banners, ensuring that anomalies—such as a freezer temperature breach in a remote clinic, a water leak in a smart home, or equipment failure in an industrial setting—delivered in seconds, enabling quicker acknowledgement. This direct-to-device paradigm has revolutionised user engagement in deployments worldwide, from urban home automation enthusiasts in Europe to field technicians monitoring agricultural sensors across vast rural landscapes in Asia and Africa.

The Blynk platform exemplifies an accessible yet powerful approach to mobile notifications for microcontroller-based projects. Its dedicated Notification widget, combined with the Blynk mobile app for iOS and Android, allows an ESP32 or similar device to send custom messages with a single line of code using the Blynk.notify() function. Messages can include dynamic content—current sensor values, timestamps, device identifiers, and even emojis for quick visual recognition—transforming raw alerts into informative, actionable updates. The cloud infrastructure of Blynk handles delivery reliably, supporting high-priority interruptions that bypass silent modes when configured, making it particularly effective for personal safety applications like gas leak detection in residential settings or health monitoring wearables alerting caregivers in real time.

Building comprehensive phone-based alert systems extends beyond simple notifications to create fully interactive mobile interfaces. Platforms like Blynk enable bidirectional communication: users not only receive alerts but can also view live dashboards, historical graphs, and remotely control actuators—all from the same app. This interactivity fosters proactive management, as seen in smart farming installations where a farmer receives a soil moisture alert and immediately activates irrigation pumps with a tap, or in home security systems where an intrusion notification prompts live camera viewing and siren activation. Advanced implementations often layer multiple services—combining instant push of Blynk with fallback email or SMS—for redundancy, ensuring delivery even if the primary app is offline or the device loses connectivity temporarily.

A fundamental distinction in mobile alerting lies between push and pull mechanisms. Push notifications, the preferred method for urgency, are server-initiated: the IoT device or cloud service actively sends data to the phone of the user via Apple Push Notification Service (APNS) or Firebase Cloud Messaging (FCM), appearing instantly without user intervention. This model minimises latency and battery drain on the mobile device, as the app remains dormant until alerted—ideal for critical events in industrial monitoring or medical alerts. Pull notifications, conversely, rely on the mobile app periodically polling the server or device for updates, consuming more battery and introducing delays but proving useful for non-urgent status checks or environments with restricted push permissions. systems overwhelmingly favour push for alerts while reserving pull for routine data refreshes, striking an optimal balance between responsiveness, reliability, and resource efficiency.

When integrated thoughtfully, mobile notifications transform IoT devices from silent observers into responsive companions that keep users informed and in control, regardless of distance. This capability has become a hallmark of consumer and IoT alike—empowering individuals in smart homes, technicians in factories, and operators in remote infrastructure to respond swiftly and effectively to the ever-changing conditions reported by their connected systems.

Rolling logs represent the standard approach for persistent storage media such as SD cards or flash file systems. This pattern maintains a fixed number of log files or a maximum total size, automatically deleting the oldest file when a new one is created or the limit is reached. For example, a security system might retain the last ten daily event files, ensuring weeks of history while capping storage at a predictable level—widely used in cold-chain monitoring to provide audit trails without requiring constant manual intervention. Circular buffers, in contrast, operate entirely in RAM or limited flash, overwriting the oldest entries once the buffer fills. Ideal for capturing high-resolution pre- and post-event data around faults—such as the seconds before a motor seizure in predictive maintenance—these fixed-size rings guarantee constant memory usage and rapid access, making them essential for crash forensics in battery-constrained devices deployed across global fleets.

Time-windowed logs offer a more selective refinement, retaining events only within defined periods such as the last hour, day, or week. This approach dynamically prunes older records while preserving complete detail for recent activity, proving particularly effective in applications requiring short-term granularity with long-term summarisation—for instance, a smart building system logging access control events for the past 24 hours to support immediate security reviews, or an agricultural node retaining detailed irrigation triggers from the last day to correlate with weather changes. Memory efficiency remains a paramount consideration throughout: structures must minimise overhead from metadata, favour compact binary or CSV formats over verbose JSON when space is tight, and implement wear-levelling on flash to extend media lifespan. On resource-limited microcontrollers like the ESP32, combining a small in-RAM circular buffer for immediate events with periodic rollover to SD card achieves optimal balance—delivering both rapid fault capture and durable long-term records in systems trusted worldwide for reliability and minimal maintenance.

Event Logging Patterns

Event logging patterns address the challenge of managing finite storage in long-running IoT systems, ensuring that critical historical data remains available without exhausting memory or media capacity. Unlike routine sensor logging, which may accumulate steadily over time, event logs capture discrete occurrences—threshold breaches, system faults, state changes, or user interactions—often at irregular intervals. implementations therefore employ strategies that prioritize recency, relevance, and efficiency, preventing overflow while preserving the most valuable information for diagnostics, compliance, and post-incident analysis in applications ranging from industrial machinery in European factories to remote environmental monitors in developing regions.

Rolling logs represent the standard approach for persistent storage media such as SD cards or flash file systems. This pattern maintains a fixed number of log files or a maximum total size, automatically deleting the oldest file when a new one is created or the limit is reached. For example, a security system might retain the last ten daily event files, ensuring weeks of history while capping storage at a predictable level—widely used in cold-chain monitoring to provide audit trails without requiring constant manual intervention. Circular buffers, in contrast, operate entirely in RAM or limited flash, overwriting the oldest entries once the buffer fills. Ideal for capturing high-resolution pre- and post-event data around faults—such as the seconds before a motor seizure in predictive maintenance—these fixed-size rings guarantee constant memory usage and rapid access, making them essential for crash forensics in battery-constrained devices deployed across global fleets.

Time-windowed logs offer a more selective refinement, retaining events only within defined periods such as the last hour, day, or week. This approach dynamically prunes older records while preserving complete detail for recent activity, proving particularly effective in applications requiring short-term granularity with long-term summarisation—for instance, a smart building system logging access control events for the past 24 hours to support immediate security reviews, or an agricultural node retaining detailed irrigation triggers from the last day to correlate with weather changes. Memory efficiency remains a paramount consideration throughout: structures must minimise overhead from metadata, favour compact binary or CSV formats over verbose JSON when space is tight, and implement wear-levelling on flash to extend media lifespan. On resource-limited microcontrollers like the ESP32, combining a small in-RAM circular buffer for immediate events with periodic rollover to

SD card achieves optimal balance—delivering both rapid fault capture and durable long-term records in systems trusted worldwide for reliability and minimal maintenance.

Visualization of Logged Data

Visualization transforms raw logged data into intuitive, actionable insights, enabling users to discern patterns, identify anomalies, and make informed decisions far more effectively than scanning rows of numbers. Caution: To prevent misinterpretation, dashboards should clearly include units, sampling frequency, and timestamp timezone for all displayed data. In IoT systems, where data accumulates rapidly from distributed sensors—whether monitoring factory equipment in Germany, crop conditions in Indian fields, or urban air quality in Singapore—effective graphical representation bridges the gap between complex telemetry and human understanding. Basic dashboards presenting bar, line, and time-series graphs convert historical and real-time logs into clear narratives, revealing trends such as gradual soil moisture decline, diurnal temperature cycles, or sudden spikes indicative of equipment faults.

ThingSpeak provides one of the most accessible platforms for IoT-specific plotting, offering built-in line, bar, and gauge charts directly tied to channel data feeds. With minimal configuration, multiple fields—temperature, humidity, pressure—can be plotted on shared time axes, supporting zoom, pan, and export features that facilitate detailed analysis. Its integration of MATLAB analytics further allows scripted trend detection and anomaly flagging within the same environment, making it a staple in educational institutions, research labs, and prototyping workflows worldwide. Google Sheets complements this with familiar, collaborative charting capabilities: once data is appended via webhooks or scripts, automatic line or column charts update in real time, complete with trendlines, annotations, and sharing options ideal for non-technical stakeholders such as farm managers reviewing weekly yields or facility supervisors tracking energy usage patterns.

Basic dashboards, whether constructed in ThingSpeak, Google Data Studio, or simple custom web pages, typically feature time-series graphs as the cornerstone—plotting values against precise timestamps to highlight temporal relationships. Line graphs excel at continuous variables like temperature or humidity, bar charts suit categorical comparisons such as daily averages across multiple nodes, and combination views overlay related parameters for correlation analysis. These visual tools empower proactive maintenance by making long-term degradation visible weeks in advance or support environmental studies by exposing seasonal cycles and outlier events.

Detecting trends and anomalies forms the ultimate value of visualization. A steadily rising baseline on a temperature plot might signal insulation failure in a cold-storage unit, while an abrupt deviation from established patterns could indicate sensor malfunction or genuine emergency—such as a gas leak in an industrial setting. By applying simple visual cues like threshold lines, moving averages, or colour-coded alerts, dashboards shift focus from raw data to meaningful intelligence, enabling operators in smart factories, precision agriculture systems, or urban monitoring networks to respond swiftly and accurately. When implemented effectively, visualization not only communicates the story hidden within logs but also drives the continuous improvement and reliability that define IoT deployments globally.

Designing a Robust Alert Workflow

A robust alert workflow ensures that the critical events in IoT systems are not only detected but also verified, recorded, and communicated reliably, minimising missed alarms and unnecessary disruptions in real-world operations. The standard sequence—event detection → verification → logging → notification—forms a disciplined pipeline that transforms raw sensor anomalies into trustworthy, actionable responses. This structured approach is employed in diverse deployments, from cold-chain monitoring in pharmaceutical transport across Europe to irrigation alerts in remote Indian farms and equipment fault warnings in Japanese manufacturing lines.

Event detection initiates the workflow through threshold comparisons or multi-parameter logic, as discussed earlier, identifying potential issues such as excessive temperature or detected motion. Verification immediately follows to confirm legitimacy, applying debouncing, averaging, or hysteresis to filter transient noise—preventing a brief power surge from triggering a false factory shutdown or a passing shadow from activating a security alert. Only after positive verification does the system proceed to logging, appending a detailed entry (with timestamp, sensor values, and event description) to local storage and, when possible, the cloud. This immutable record supports post-event analysis, regulatory compliance, and system improvement, ensuring that whether connectivity is present or not, evidence of the incident persists.

Notification constitutes the final stage, dispatching alerts via selected channels—push notifications, email, SMS, or messaging—prioritely for urgency. designs incorporate retry logic for network failures: upon transmission failure, the system queues the alert and attempts resends with exponential back-off (for example., 10 seconds, then 30, then 60), falling back to local storage if needed and resuming upon reconnection. This resilience prevents alert loss during outages common in rural or mobile deployments.

Acknowledgement cycles add an advanced layer of sophistication, all while maintaining idempotency to avoid duplicate acknowledgements or repeated escalation. Owing recipients to confirm receipt and resolution through app interactions or reply mechanisms—suppressing repeat notifications and updating system status. For instance, a maintenance engineer acknowledging a pump failure alert via Blynk might automatically log the response time and escalate to a supervisor if unaddressed after hours. By methodically implementing this detection-verification-logging-notification sequence with retries and acknowledgements, developers create alert workflows that operators worldwide can depend on—delivering precision, accountability, and peace of mind in safety-critical and resource-constrained environments, alike.

Practical Exercises

Exercise 1: Local Logger – Save Sensor Data to SD Card

Record temperature readings every 15 seconds and store them in a CSV file on an SD card. This teaches basic file handling, timestamps, and structured logging.

1. **Connect SD card module to ESP32/Arduino**
    a. Gather the required hardware: ESP32/Arduino board, SD card module, SD card, temperature sensor, and jumper wires.
    b. Wire the SD module using SPI pins. For ESP32: MISO–19, MOSI–23, SCK–18, CS–5.
    c. Connect the temperature sensor (for example, DHT11) to a digital input pin.
    d. Insert the SD card and power the board. Ensure the SD card is formatted as FAT32.
2. **Write code to append timestamp + temperature into a CSV file**
    a. Install required libraries: `SD.h` for storage and a sensor library (for example, `DHT.h`).
    b. Initialize the sensor, SD card, and serial monitor in `setup()`.
    c. In `loop()`, use a 15-second timer to read the temperature.
    d. Open (or create) a CSV file like `data.csv`.
    e. Append a new row containing the timestamp and temperature reading.
    f. Close the file after each write to prevent corruption.

3. **Validate data using Excel/Sheets**
    a. Remove the SD card after collecting data.
    b. Open the CSV file in Excel or Google Sheets.
    c. Verify that timestamps and temperatures are correctly logged at 15-second intervals.
    d. Inspect for missing values, incorrect formatting, or sensor noise.

Exercise 2: Cloud Logger – Streaming Data to ThingSpeak

Send temperature/humidity/gas readings to the ThingSpeak cloud every 20 seconds and visualize them using built-in graphs.

1. **Create a ThingSpeak channel**
    a. Create an account and open ThingSpeak.
    b. Create a new channel and enable desired fields (Field 1–Temperature, Field 2–Humidity, and so on.).
    c. Save the Channel ID and Write API Key — these will be used by ESP32.
2. **Use HTTP GET requests from ESP32 to update fields**
    a. Connect sensors to ESP32 and install WiFi + sensor libraries.
    b. In `setup()`, connect ESP32 to your WiFi network.
    c. Read sensor values every 20 seconds using a timer.
    d. Use HTTPClient to send data to ThingSpeak endpoint: `api.thingspeak.com/update?api_key=YOURKEY&field1=data`.
    e. Ensure ESP32 waits at least 15 seconds between uploads (ThingSpeak limit).
3. **View real-time graph on dashboard**
    a. Visit your channel page to see live graphs updating.
    b. Customize graphs (line plot, smoothing, time window).
    c. Observe trends and verify data is arriving consistently.

Exercise 3: Threshold Alert – Overheat Warning via Email

Monitor a temperature sensor and automatically send an email alert when the reading exceeds 40°C.

1. **Read sensor values every 10 seconds**
    a. Connect a temperature sensor to ESP32.
    b. Initialize WiFi and sensor libraries.
    c. Use a 10-second timer to sample temperature readings.
    d. Store values and print them to the serial monitor for debugging.
2. **If value exceeds threshold → send email (SMTP)**
    a. Create a free SMTP account (SMTP2GO or similar).
    b. Configure SMTP settings inside the ESP32 code (host, port, username, password).

   c. Use the ESP-Mail-Client library to send an email with subject **`"Overheat Alert! Temperature exceeded 40°C"`**
   d. Add a cooldown timer to prevent repeated email flooding.
3. **Test for multiple threshold events**
   a. Simulate high temperature using warm air or manual override.
   b. Check if email is received instantly.
   c. Ensure alerts are sent only when value drops and crosses threshold again.

Exercise 4: IFTTT Webhook – Gas Leak Notification

Detect high gas concentration using MQ-2 and trigger an IFTTT automation (email, Telegram, or notification) using a Webhook.

1. **Create IFTTT Applet: Webhook → Email/Telegram**
   a. Create an IFTTT account.
   b. Create a new applet where the trigger is a Webhook event (for example, **`"gas_leak"`**).
   c. Choose an action: Email alert, Telegram message, and the like.
   d. Copy the unique Webhook URL from IFTTT settings.
2. **ESP32 sends Webhook trigger when threshold is crossed**
   a. Read gas values using **`analogRead()`**.
   b. If reading exceeds threshold (for example, >450), send an HTTPS POST request to the IFTTT URL.
   c. Include JSON payload if needed (**`value1`**, **`value2`**).
   d. Add delays or flags to avoid multiple triggers per second.
3. **Validate real-time notifications**
   a. Expose MQ-2 to gas briefly to cross the threshold.
   b. Confirm that email/Telegram notifications arrive instantly.
   c. Adjust threshold to reduce false positives.

Exercise 5: Blynk Mobile Alert System

Use the Blynk mobile app to receive push notifications when gas levels rise or motion is detected.

1. **Add "`Notification`" widget in Blynk app**
   a. Create a Blynk project and add a Notification widget.
   b. Note the Auth Token sent to your email.
   c. Drag additional widgets (gauges, LEDs) if needed for visuals.
2. **Write logic: if gas > X or motion detected → `Blynk.notify()`**
   a. Connect MQ-2 or PIR sensor to ESP32.
   b. Initialize Blynk connection using the Auth Token.
   c. Continuously check sensor readings in **`loop()`**.
   d. If the threshold is crossed, call **`Blynk.notify("Alert: Gas/Motion Detected!")`**.
   e. Add minimum delay or hysteresis to avoid repeated alerts.

3. **Test alert response time**
    a. Trigger motion or gas event.
    b. Observe that mobile notification appears in under a few seconds.
    c. Repeat to test reliability and network performance.

Conclusion

Chapter 12, Data Logging, Alert Systems, and Notification Integration, has provided a comprehensive, practical framework for implementing reliable data logging, real-time alert systems, and multi-channel notification integration—essential capabilities that transform basic sensor networks into intelligent, responsive IoT solutions. From robust local storage on SD cards ensuring data persistence in remote or offline environments, to scalable cloud logging with platforms such asThingSpeak, Firebase, and Google Sheets enabling global access and visualization, students now possess the tools to capture and preserve meaningful historical records under diverse constraints. The exploration of real-time versus batch logging, structured formats such as JSON and CSV, precise timestamping, and event patterns like rolling logs has equipped readers to design systems that balance efficiency, power consumption, and data integrity. the chapter has demystified alert system design: from fundamental threshold detection with debouncing, averaging, and hysteresis to prevent false positives, to sophisticated cloud-based notifications via SMTP email, IFTTT webhooks, Blynk mobile push, and messaging integrations. The Smart Multi-Channel Alert System mini-project and progressive exercises have bridged theory with hands-on implementation, demonstrating how a single ESP32 node can monitor multiple sensors, log routinely, and instantly escalate critical events across channels—whether safeguarding homes in urban Japan, monitoring equipment in German factories, or protecting crops in Indian agriculture.

Thus, by mastering these techniques, readers can now build IoT deployments that not only collect data but actively watch over it, respond to anomalies without delay, and keep users informed through their preferred mediums. These skills form a critical pillar of IoT engineering, ensuring reliability and user trust in real-world applications where timely information can prevent loss, optimise operations, and even save lives. With this foundation in logging and alerting solidified, the stage is set for exploring more advanced topics in subsequent chapters, such as edge processing, machine learning integration, and large-scale fleet management. Well done—this chapter marks a significant milestone toward creating truly production-ready IoT systems, it marks the transition from standalone prototypes to fully cloud-powered, production-grade IoT systems. While the earlier chapters focused on building local sensor-actuator nodes, Chapter 13 unlocks the full potential of cloud computing—bringing scalability, remote access, analytics, secure data flow, and global system monitoring into the picture. Readers will explore how real-world IoT deployments operate at scale using platforms such as AWS IoT Core, Azure IoT Hub, and Ubidots, learning how these services handle device authentication, telemetry ingestion, real-time dashboards, serverless automation, and integration with enterprise BI tools.

Chapter 13

Cloud-Backed End-to-End Projects and Enterprise IoT Integration

Introduction

In the preceding chapters, learners have developed a solid foundation in IoT development: mastering GPIO control and sensor interfacing in the Perception Layer, exploring communication protocols such as MQTT, HTTP, LoRa, and BLE in the Network Layer, implementing secure data logging, threshold-based alerting, and multi-channel notifications in the Application Layer, and adopting best practices for device hardening and reliable operation. (Prerequisites: A working knowledge of C++ for microcontroller programming, basic networking concepts, and familiarity with MQTT and security fundamentals is assumed.) These skills have enabled the creation of robust, functional prototypes—capable of reading environmental data, processing it locally on microcontrollers like the ESP32, and delivering insights through cloud services such as ThingSpeak, Firebase, Google Sheets, and Blynk—ideal for educational projects, hobbyist applications, and small-scale deployments.

This chapter represents the pivotal transition from prototype-oriented designs to full-scale, cloud-backed enterprise IoT architectures , cloud platforms, including AWS IoT Core with its device shadow and rules engine, Microsoft Azure IoT Hub for bidirectional communication and digital twin support, Google Cloud IoT Core for seamless integration with BigQuery and AI services, as well as accessible enterprise-ready alternatives like Ubidots for rapid dashboard deployment and Blynk Pro for scaled mobile-first solutions. Key concepts will include secure device provisioning using X.509 certificates and JWT tokens, high-volume telemetry ingestion over MQTT with QoS guarantees, rule-based message routing to serverless functions (AWS Lambda, Azure Functions, Google Cloud Functions), automated storage in time-series databases, and the creation of sophisticated dashboards with tools like Grafana, Power BI, or platform-native visualization suites.

Hands-on sections will guide the secure connection of ESP32 devices to these platforms, implementation of over-the-air firmware updates, orchestration of serverless workflows for anomaly detection and actuation, and integration with external systems via webhooks and APIs. Through progressive exercises and end-to-end projects—such as a fleet-scale environmental monitoring system or an industrial predictive maintenance pipeline—learners will experience the complete lifecycle of enterprise IoT development.

By the end of this chapter, students will possess the knowledge and confidence to architect, deploy, and manage production-grade IoT solutions that operate reliably at scale, meeting the stringent requirements of modern industry while leveraging the power of cloud infrastructure to turn raw sensor data into strategic business value. This culmination of the three-layer IoT architecture prepares readers for advanced topics in edge intelligence, fleet management, and sustainable large-scale deployments in the global connected ecosystem.

Structure

In this chapter, we will cover the following topics:

- Limitations of Firebase and Blynk for Production-Scale IoT
- Introduction to AWS IoT Core, Azure IoT Hub, GCP (Overview and Evolution)
- Understanding Modern IoT Cloud Architecture
- Publishing Data to MQTT Topics from ESP32 (PubSubClient)
- Rule-Based Message Routing
- Serverless Compute: Using AWS Lambda / Azure Functions for Logic Handling
- Device Provisioning: Secure Authentication using TLS and X.509 Certificates
- Designing Scalable Topic Hierarchies (sensorID/Timestamp/Type)
- Payload Formatting for Analytics (JSON, CSV Standards)
- Using Cloud Dashboards
- Working with Lightweight Platforms (Ubidots, Blynk Pro, TuyaIoT)
- Cost Optimization: Free Tier Tips + Data Caps Management

Limitations of Firebase and Blynk for Production IoT

Firebase and Blynk have served admirably throughout earlier chapters as accessible, beginner-friendly platforms that dramatically accelerate prototyping and small-to-medium-scale deployments. Their generous free tiers, simple authentication models, and ready-made mobile apps and dashboards have allowed learners to connect ESP32 devices to the cloud, visualise data, and trigger alerts with minimal overhead. However, as IoT solutions transition from educational projects and proof-of-concept pilots to true production environments—managing thousands or millions of devices across industrial facilities, agricultural estates, logistics fleets, or smart-city infrastructure—these platforms reveal fundamental architectural constraints that make them unsuitable for enterprise-grade deployments.

Firebase Realtime Database and Firestore, while excellent for low-to-moderate data rates, were never designed as high-throughput time-series stores. High-frequency telemetry (≥1 Hz) from vibration sensors or GPS trackers quickly exhausts read/write limits, incurs steep overage costs, and suffers performance degradation due to document-size constraints and eventual consistency models. For example, 1,000 devices sending data at 1 Hz results in 86.4 million writes per day, a scale that quickly becomes prohibitively expensive and unmanageable on these platforms. Moreover, the security rules of Firebase, though powerful for small teams, become unwieldy at scale and lack native support for X.509 certificate-based mutual authentication—a non-negotiable requirement when provisioning tens of thousands of field devices securely. There is no built-in device shadow/twin capability, no native message-routing engine for MQTT topic wildcards, and no straightforward path to cold storage or advanced analytics integration without expensive third-party middleware.

Blynk, even in its paid Blynk Pro incarnation, remains primarily a visualisation and remote-control platform rather than a full-fledged IoT device-management backbone. It excels at beautiful mobile dashboards and instant push notifications for dozens or hundreds of units, but enterprise features such as fine-grained Role-Based Access Control (RBAC), device lifecycle management (provisioning, decommissioning, grouping), audit trails, firmware-over-the-air at scale with rollback, and integration into existing IT/OT governance frameworks are either rudimentary or entirely absent , deployments demand platforms engineered from the ground up for massive device fleets, certificate-based identity, guaranteed message delivery (QoS 1/2), rule engines that route millions of messages per minute to serverless functions or data lakes, digital twins for state reconciliation, and seamless integration with enterprise identity providers (Azure AD, AWS IAM) and compliance frameworks.

This reality motivates the migration to dedicated enterprise IoT cloud platforms—AWS IoT Core, Microsoft Azure IoT Hub, and Google Cloud IoT Core—each purpose-built to address the exact shortcomings outlined above. The remainder of this chapter will demonstrate how these industrial-strength services, along with accessible enterprise alternatives like Ubidots Enterprise, enable the secure, scalable, and maintainable architectures required when IoT moves from the workbench to the world. Understanding these limitations is not a criticism of Firebase or Blynk; rather, it is a recognition that different tools serve different phases of the IoT lifecycle, and engineers must know precisely when to graduate to the next tier of infrastructure.

Introduction to AWS IoT Core and Azure IoT Hub

As enterprise IoT deployments scale beyond the capabilities of prototyping platforms, the need for robust, fully managed cloud services becomes paramount. Leading the field are AWS IoT Core from Amazon Web Services and Microsoft Azure IoT Hub, two mature, battle-tested platforms specifically engineered to handle the demands of production environments: secure ingestion of telemetry from millions of devices, reliable bidirectional communication, advanced device management, and seamless integration with broader cloud ecosystems for processing, storage, analytics, and actuation. These services represent the gold standard for industrial-gradeIoT, powering applications from predictive maintenance in European manufacturing plants to remote asset tracking in Australian mining operations and real-time patient monitoring in Asian healthcare networks.

Choosing Between AWS IoT Core and Azure IoT Hub: The decision often hinges on your existing cloud strategy. AWS IoT Core is typically the preferred choice if your organization is already heavily invested in the AWS ecosystem, or if your solution requires robust edge computing capabilities like those offered by AWS Greengrass. Conversely, Azure IoT Hub is a strong fit for organizations using Microsoft products (such as heavily invested in the Microsoft stack, Power BI for visualization, or require deep integration with industrial protocols like OPC UA via specific offerings of Azure).

AWS IoT Core stands out as a comprehensive, highly scalable managed service that enables devices to interact securely with cloud applications and other devices. At its heart is a fully managed MQTT broker supporting both MQTT v3.1.1 and the advanced MQTT v5 standards, complete with features like shared subscriptions, user properties, and session expiry for sophisticated fleet management. All communications are protected by mutual TLS authentication, with support for X.509 certificates, custom authorizers, and fine-grained IAM policies. The powerful Rules Engine allows SQL-like queries to filter, transform, and route messages to over 20 AWS services including Lambda for serverless processing, S3 for storage, DynamoDB for NoSQL persistence, or Kinesis for real-time streaming—without managing any infrastructure. Device Shadows provide a persistent virtual representation of the state of each device, enabling reliable command delivery even during intermittent connectivity, while fleet provisioning supports just-in-time registration and bulk onboarding at massive scale. Additional capabilities, such as Device Advisor for automated connectivity testing and integration with AWS Greengrass for edge computing, make it ideal for heterogeneous deployments requiring low-latency decision-making at the edge.

Microsoft Azure IoT Hub, meanwhile, offers a similarly enterprise-focused solution with particular strengths in bidirectional communication and deep integration within the Azure ecosystem. It supports multiple protocols—including MQTT, AMQP, and HTTPS—with built-in support for MQTT over WebSockets to navigate restrictive firewalls. Security is paramount, featuring per-device authentication via symmetric keys, X.509 certificates (including recent enhancements for Microsoft-managed PKI), and integration with Azure Active Directory for enterprise identity management. The standout Device Twins feature maintains a JSON document representing the reported and desired state of each device, facilitating configuration management, remote commands, and synchronization across unreliable networks. Message routing provides flexible, query-based forwarding to endpoints like Azure Blob Storage, Event Hubs, Service Bus, or directly into Stream Analytics for real-time processing. Azure IoT Hub excels in industrial scenarios through native support for protocol gateways seamless visualization via Power BI, and Device Update for IoT Hub, which enables secure over-the-air firmware deployments with staged rollouts and rollback. Recent preview features, such as Azure Device Registry for unified cross-hub management, further simplify operations at extreme scale.

Both platforms eliminate the operational burden of managing brokers, registries, or scaling infrastructure, offering pay-as-you-go pricing based on message volume and device connections while providing high availability across global regions. While Google Cloud once offered IoT Core as a comparable service—with managed device registries, an MQTT bridge, and tight BigQuery integration—it has been fully retired since 2023, with users now directed toward partner solutions or other cloud providers. This shift underscores the dominance of AWS and Azure in the enterprise IoT space.

In the sections ahead, learners will explore hands-on connectivity from ESP32 devices to these platforms, certificate-based provisioning, rule-driven workflows, and end-to-end projects that leverage serverless computers and dashboards—equipping them to design IoT architectures that meet the rigorous demands of real-world production systems worldwide.

Understanding Modern IoT Cloud Architecture

Modern enterprise IoT systems are built upon a layered, modular cloud architecture that efficiently handles the complexities of massive device fleets, diverse data streams, and demanding operational requirements. This generalized pipeline—often referred to as the enterprise IoT stack—extends the three-layer model introduced in *Chapter 2, IoT Architecture and Ecosystem*, (Perception, Network, and Application) into a more sophisticated, cloud-centric framework. It ensures secure, reliable data flow from edge devices to advanced analytics and actuation, supporting applications such as predictive maintenance in Japanese automotive plants, smart grid management in European utilities, precision irrigation across Indian farmlands, and remote patient monitoring in global healthcare networks.

The architecture begins at the **Device Layer**, where resource-constrained nodes like ESP32-based sensor stations collect raw environmental, industrial, or health-related data. These devices run lightweight firmware that samples sensors, performs basic preprocessing and packages readings into structured payloads—typically JSON—while conserving power through deep-sleep cycles and selective transmission.

Secure communication is managed in the **Connectivity Layer**, where devices publish telemetry using MQTT over TLS (port 8883) or MQTT over WebSockets. Mutual TLS authentication with X.509 certificates ensures that only provisioned devices can connect, preventing unauthorized access even in hostile environments. This layer leverages QoS levels (0–2) to balance reliability with bandwidth, critical for intermittent cellular or LoRaWAN links in remote deployments.

Data arrives at the **Cloud Ingestion Layer** via fully managed services such as AWS IoT Core or Azure IoT Hub. These platforms act as scalable message brokers, authenticating devices, decrypting payloads, and providing high-availability endpoints across global regions. They handle millions of concurrent connections and billions of messages daily without infrastructure management, automatically scaling to accommodate seasonal spikes—such as harvest-time telemetry surges in agriculture.

The **Routing Layer** applies intelligent, rule-based filtering using SQL-like queries on message topics, payloads, or metadata. For example, high-priority alerts can be routed immediately to notification services, while routine telemetry is forwarded to storage or analytics.

Processing occurs in the **Compute Layer** through serverless functions (AWS Lambda, Azure Functions). Triggered by routing rules, these lightweight, auto-scaling code snippets perform tasks such as data validation, unit conversion, anomaly detection via simple thresholds or statistical models, and actuation commands sent back to devices via Device Shadows or Twins. Serverless execution eliminates server management and charges only for actual compute time, making it cost-effective for sporadic industrial events.

Persisted data flows into the **Storage Layer**, where time-series databases or general-purpose stores (DynamoDB, Azure Blob Storage, Cosmos DB) provide durable, queryable archives. Hot data remains in fast-access tables for real-time needs, while cold paths automatically tier older records to low-cost object storage, supporting years of historical analysis required for compliance or trend forecasting.

The **Analytics Layer** unlocks deeper insights using managed services like AWS IoT Analytics, Azure Stream Analytics, or integration with external tools such as Apache Kafka and machine learning platforms. Here, data is cleaned, aggregated, enriched with external sources (weather APIs, market prices), and fed into models for predictive maintenance, demand forecasting, or optimisation—transforming raw telemetry into strategic business intelligence.

Finally, the **Dashboard and Alert Layer** delivers actionable information through visualisation tools (Grafana, Power BI, QuickSight) and notification pipelines (email, SMS via Twilio, push via Firebase Cloud Messaging, or enterprise messaging like Slack/Teams). Custom dashboards aggregate fleet-wide KPIs, while automated alerts escalate issues to on-call engineers, ensuring rapid response in mission-critical scenarios.

This end-to-end architecture exemplifies the maturity of modern enterprise IoT: resilient, secure, cost-efficient, and highly extensible. By decoupling concerns across layers, it enables independent scaling, rapid iteration, and integration with existing IT/OT systems—forming the backbone of production deployments worldwide. The following sections will guide readers through implementing key components of this pipeline using ESP32 devices and leading cloud platforms, bridging theoretical design with practical, scalable engineering.

Publishing Data to MQTT Topics from ESP32

Publishing telemetry from ESP32 devices to enterprise cloud platforms marks a significant step toward production-grade IoT systems, where secure, reliable, and scalable communication replaces the simpler HTTP-based approaches used in prototyping. While platforms like ThingSpeak and Blynk rely on HTTPS POST requests, AWS IoT Core and Azure IoT Hub are built around the MQTT protocol—lightweight, publish-subscribe messaging optimized for constrained devices and unreliable networks. When secured with TLS and mutual authentication, MQTT provides end-to-end encryption, low overhead, and efficient bidirectional communication, making it the standard choice for industrial monitoring in European factories, agricultural sensor networks in India, and asset tracking across global supply chains.

Connecting an ESP32 to AWS IoT Core requires certificate-based authentication rather than simple username/password schemes. The process begins with device provisioning: creating a thing in the AWS console, generating an X.509 certificate and private key pair, attaching a policy granting publish/subscribe permissions on a specific topic and downloading the root CA certificate (Amazon Trust Services or similar). These files—device certificate, private key, and root CA—are then stored securely on the ESP32 filesystem (LittleFS or SPIFFS) to prevent exposure in source code.

The `PubSubClient` library, combined with `WiFiClientSecure`, forms the foundation for TLS-secured MQTT on ESP32. The client connects to the custom endpoint on port 8883, sets the certificate chain for server verification, and loads the device certificate and key for client authentication. Once connected, the device publishes structured JSON payloads to hierarchical topics, enabling fine-grained routing via wildcards in cloud rules. QoS 1 ensures at-least-once delivery—critical for billing-grade energy metering or compliance logging—while retained messages can update Device Shadow states for synchronization.

This approach ensures encrypted, authenticated communication with minimal bandwidth—typically under 1 KB per message—while supporting thousands of devices per account. Similar patterns apply to Azure IoT Hub using symmetric keys or certificates with libraries like Azure SDK for C. By mastering secure MQTT publishing, readers gain the capability to integrate ESP32 nodes into enterprise pipelines, where cloud rules can immediately route telemetry to storage, analytics, or actuation—forming the critical link between edge perception and cloud intelligence in IoT architectures worldwide.

Rule-Based Message Routing

Rule-based message routing forms the intelligent core of enterprise IoT cloud platforms, enabling automated, conditional processing of incoming telemetry without requiring custom servers or constant human oversight. Once devices publish data to MQTT topics in services like AWS IoT Core or Azure IoT Hub, the built-in rule engines evaluate each message against user-defined queries – similar to SQL `SELECT` statements – filtering, transforming, and directing payloads to appropriate downstream destinations. This capability transforms raw sensor streams into orchestrated workflows, powering applications from real-time anomaly alerts in German manufacturing lines to automated irrigation decisions in Australian farms and predictive maintenance triggers in Japanese automotive plants.

In AWS IoT Core, the Rules Engine supports expressive queries that inspect topic structure, JSON payload fields, metadata, and even nested objects. For instance, a rule might select only messages where temperature exceeds 40°C from greenhouse devices, extracting device ID, timestamp, and value before routing. Supported actions span the AWS ecosystem: inserting structured records into DynamoDB for fast querying, archiving raw payloads in S3 for long-term compliance storage, invoking Lambda functions for custom processing or publishing notifications via Amazon SNS for SMS, email, push alerts, or integration with collaboration tools like Slack. Additional destinations include time-series databases like Timestream, real-time streaming with Kinesis, event buses, or third-party endpoints via HTTP.

The message routing of Azure IoT Hub offers comparable power with query conditions based on message properties, system properties, or body content. Routes can forward to built-in endpoints or custom ones such as Azure Blob Storage for immutable archives, Event Hubs for high-throughput streaming, Service Bus queues for decoupled processing, or directly into Stream Analytics jobs. Critical alerts might bypass storage entirely, routing straight to Logic Apps for multi-step workflows—sending SMS through Twilio, escalating via Microsoft Teams, or updating a Power BI dashboard in real time. Both platforms support multiple concurrent rules per message, enabling fan-out patterns where routine data goes to storage while exceptions trigger immediate notifications.

This declarative approach dramatically reduces operational complexity and cost: rules execute at massive scale with pay-per-action pricing, automatically handling retries, dead-letter queues for failed deliveries, and monitoring via CloudWatch or Azure Monitor. Deployments leverage routing to enforce data governance—separating high-value events from bulk telemetry, applying retention policies, and ensuring compliance with regional regulations such as GDPR in Europe or industry standards in healthcare and energy.

Serverless Compute: AWS Lambda and Azure Functions

Serverless compute represents a cornerstone of modern enterprise IoT architectures, allowing custom business logic to execute automatically in response to incoming messages without the overhead of provisioning or managing servers. A key architectural decision in an IoT solution involves choosing the right mechanism for processing incoming data. [Use direct IoT Rule → storage/actions for simple, one-step flows]. Use a serverless function (like AWS Lambda or Azure Functions) when you need multi-step logic, data enrichment, or calls to external APIs. Platforms like AWS Lambda and Azure Functions provide fully managed environments where short-lived functions—written in languages such as Python, Node.js, or Java—run on demand, scaling instantly from zero to thousands of concurrent executions. Triggered directly by cloud IoT rule engines, these functions process telemetry in real time, enabling sophisticated workflows that would otherwise require dedicated backend infrastructure. This paradigm proves particularly powerful in production deployments, from smart agriculture systems in vast Indian fields automatically adjusting irrigation based on soil data, to industrial monitoring in German factories detecting equipment anomalies, and healthcare networks in Japan processing wearable vitals for immediate clinical alerts. The use cases for serverless functions in IoT pipelines are diverse and transformative. One primary application is the automatic generation of alerts: a function can evaluate sensor readings against dynamic thresholds—factoring in time of day, historical baselines, or external data like weather forecasts—and dispatch notifications via SMS, email, or enterprise messaging systems when conditions warrant. Another critical role involves cleaning and formatting sensor data upon ingestion: functions can parse inconsistent payloads, convert units validate ranges to filter out erroneous readings from electrical noise, enrich records with metadata such as device location or firmware version, and restructure data for optimal storage. This preprocessing ensures downstream analytics receive high-quality, standardized inputs, essential for accurate predictive maintenance in automotive plants or yield forecasting in precision farming.

Serverless functions also excel at database operations, directly inserting processed records into relational or NoSQL stores—such as Amazon DynamoDB, Aurora, or Azure Cosmos DB—while applying indexing, partitioning, or aggregation logic to support efficient querying. In more complex scenarios, they orchestrate multi-step workflows: upon detecting a temperature excursion in a cold-chain logistics container traversing Africa, a function might log the event, trigger an SMS to the driver via Twilio, update a dashboard in real time, and initiate a remedial actuation command back to the device through Device Shadow or Twin mechanisms. Similarly, functions can invoke machine learning models hosted on the same cloud platform to classify anomalies—distinguishing genuine gas leaks from sensor drift in urban safety networks—or aggregate data for compliance reporting in regulated industries like pharmaceuticals.

The inherent advantages of this serverless model—pay-per-execution pricing (often free for moderate volumes), automatic scaling to handle traffic spikes during events like harvest seasons, built-in fault tolerance with retries and dead-letter queues, and seamless integration with the broader cloud ecosystem—make it indispensable for cost-effective, maintainable enterprise IoT. By offloading logic from edge devices (preserving battery life) and eliminating server management, serverless compute empowers engineers to focus on innovation rather than operations. As readers progress through hands-on examples in subsequent sections, they will configure Lambda and Azure Functions to process real ESP32 telemetry, experiencing firsthand how this layer adds intelligence and responsiveness to cloud-backed IoT systems operating reliably at global scale.

Device Provisioning and Secure Authentication

Device provisioning and secure authentication represent the cornerstone of trust in enterprise IoT systems, ensuring that only authorised devices can connect to the cloud, publish telemetry, or receive commands—even in untrusted networks spanning remote agricultural fields in India, industrial zones in Germany, or urban infrastructure in Singapore. Unlike prototyping platforms that often rely on simple API keys or username/password credentials, production-grade services such as AWS IoT Core and Azure IoT Hub mandate mutual TLS authentication using X.509 certificates. This cryptographic approach provides robust identity verification, end-to-end encryption, and protection against common threats like eavesdropping, replay attacks, and impersonation, making it indispensable for deployments where data integrity and system security are paramount. The provisioning process begins with generating or obtaining three essential components: a unique private key, a corresponding device certificate signed by a trusted Certificate Authority (CA), and the root CA certificate for verifying the identity of the server. The private key—never shared or exposed—remains securely stored on the device, while the device certificate contains the public key and metadata such as the device's unique identifier. During manufacturing or deployment, devices are registered in the cloud platform's device registry, associating the certificate with access policies that define permitted operations (publish to specific topics, subscribe to command channels). Fleet provisioning templates in AWS or Device Provisioning Service (DPS) of Azure automate bulk registration, enabling just-in-time activation of thousands of units without manual intervention—critical for large-scale rollouts in logistics or smart metering. Mutual TLS authentication elevates security beyond server-only verification. When an ESP32 connects to the cloud endpoint (port 8883), it presents its device certificate, and the server validates it against the registered public key and CA chain. Simultaneously, the device verifies the certificate of the server using the stored root CA, preventing connection to rogue brokers in man-in-the-middle scenarios. This bidirectional trust ensures that only provisioned devices can establish a session, while all subsequent MQTT traffic is encrypted with session keys negotiated during the TLS handshake—rendering intercepted packets useless to attackers.

The benefits extend far beyond access control. Encrypted channels protect sensitive telemetry—such as location data from delivery vehicles or health metrics from wearables—complying with regulations like GDPR in Europe or HIPAA in healthcare. Certificate Revocation Lists (CRL) or Online Certificate Status Protocol (OCSP) support allow immediate decommissioning of compromised devices, while short-lived certificates and automated rotation further harden the system against long-term key exposure. In practice, this framework scales seamlessly: a single CA hierarchy can manage millions of unique device identities, with policies enforcing least-privilege access. By embedding strong cryptographic identities from the outset, engineers create resilient IoT ecosystems that withstand evolving threats, ensuring confidentiality, integrity, and availability as systems grow from prototypes to global fleets.

Designing Scalable Topic Hierarchies

Effective topic hierarchy design is essential for maintaining organization, security, and scalability in enterprise MQTT-based IoT systems, where thousands or millions of messages flow daily from distributed devices. Poorly structured topics lead to chaotic routing, excessive wildcard subscriptions straining brokers, bloated access policies, and difficulties in debugging or auditing large fleets. In contrast, a thoughtful, consistent hierarchy—leveraging inherent publish-subscribe flexibility of MQTT—enables precise message filtering, granular access control via cloud policies, efficient rule engine queries, and seamless scaling as deployments grow from dozens of nodes in a single greenhouse to tens of thousands across global agricultural cooperatives or industrial parks. Best practices begin with adopting a logical, multi-level structure that reflects real-world organization: typically starting with a top-level category, followed by geographic or logical grouping, device identification, and message type and aligns with enterprise governance—allowing policies to grant read access to analytics teams on telemetry topics while restricting command topics to authorised operators. Incorporate clear separation between data flows: use distinct subtrees for telemetry, commands, events and configuration. For example, a predictive maintenance system might publish vibration readings, critical faults and receive firmware update commands. This segregation prevents cross-contamination, enables targeted routing rules and supports QoS variation—higher reliability for commands than bulk data.

Versioning future-proofs the hierarchy: prefix topics with a version indicator to allow non-breaking changes as payload formats evolve, avoiding costly fleet-wide migrations. Keep topics concise yet descriptive, avoiding unnecessary depth that increases payload overhead, and use lowercase letters with hyphens for readability and consistency across platforms. Device identifiers should be unique and meaningful—combining serial numbers, MAC addresses, or logical names—to facilitate troubleshooting and integration with digital twins or asset management systems. Security considerations are integral: design hierarchies to align with least-privilege policies in AWS IoT Core or Azure IoT Hub, where certificates grant publish rights only to specific paths. Wildcards in subscriptions must be carefully managed to prevent unintended data exposure, especially in multi-tenant environments like shared smart-city platforms , deployments worldwide demonstrate these principles in action: logistics companies structuring topics by container ID and shipment route for real-time tracking, energy utilities organizing by substation and meter for regulatory compliance, or healthcare networks grouping by hospital ward and patient device for privacy-protected monitoring. By adhering to these best practices, engineers create MQTT topic hierarchies that not only scale efficiently but also enhance operational clarity, security enforcement, and long-term maintainability—forming a critical foundation for the sophisticated, cloud-orchestrated IoT workflows explored throughout this chapter.

Payload Formatting for Analytics (JSON, CSV)

Payload formatting plays a pivotal role in enterprise IoT systems, determining how efficiently data flows through the pipeline—from edge devices publishing to MQTT topics, through rule-based routing and serverless processing, to storage and analytics layers. Well-structured payloads ensure seamless parsing by cloud services, accurate time-series alignment, effective querying in databases, and meaningful visualization in dashboards. In production environments—whether monitoring manufacturing equipment in German factories, tracking soil conditions across Indian farmlands, or managing refrigerated assets in global logistics chains—choosing the appropriate format balances flexibility, overhead, interoperability, and analytical readiness.

JSON (JavaScript Object Notation) has emerged as the overwhelmingly recommended standard for IoT telemetry payloads due to its hierarchical structure, human readability, and native support across virtually all cloud platforms and programming languages. A typical JSON payload encapsulates multiple sensor readings, metadata, and context in a single, self-describing object—for example, including device identifiers, precise ISO-8601 timestamps, location coordinates, battery levels, and nested arrays for multi-value sensors like accelerometers. This richness enables rule engines in AWS IoT Core or Azure IoT Hub to perform sophisticated queries directly on fields while serverless functions can easily extract, transform, or enrich specific attributes without fragile string parsing. The flexibility of JSON accommodates evolving schemas—adding new fields without breaking existing consumers—and integrates effortlessly with NoSQL stores like DynamoDB, document databases, or analytics tools that expect structured data. In practice, compact JSON payloads keep message sizes under a few hundred bytes, minimising bandwidth costs in cellular deployments while providing the context needed for advanced applications such as predictive maintenance or anomaly detection.

CSV (Comma-Separated Values), while simpler and more compact, remains valuable in specific scenarios, particularly when targeting direct integration with business intelligence tools or legacy systems. A CSV payload might represent a single line of values—timestamp, temperature, humidity, pressure—suitable for high-frequency logging where every byte counts, or when appending to blob storage for later batch import into Power BI, Google Data Studio, or Excel-based reporting common in small-to-medium enterprises. Its flat structure excels in straightforward time-series ingestion into tools that natively parse tabular data, enabling rapid charting and pivoting by non-technical stakeholders such as farm managers reviewing daily averages or facility supervisors auditing compliance logs. However, CSV lacks built-in metadata support, requiring separate documentation for field order and making it prone to errors during schema changes; escaping commas in values or multilevel data further complicates implementation on constrained devices, guidelines strongly favour JSON for most enterprise use cases due to its robustness and extensibility, reserving CSV for bandwidth-critical or BI-direct pipelines where simplicity outweighs flexibility. Best practices include using consistent key naming (lowercase with underscores), including high-resolution UTC timestamps, avoiding unnecessary nesting to reduce parsing overhead, and validating payloads on the device when possible, to prevent malformed messages from propagating. By standardising on well-formatted JSON payloads from the outset—often serialised efficiently with libraries like ArduinoJson on ESP32—engineers ensure that data remains analytics-ready throughout the pipeline, empowering downstream machine learning, forecasting, and decision-making in scalable IoT deployments worldwide. This attention to payload design, though sometimes overlooked in prototyping, proves essential for maintaining data quality and operational efficiency as systems mature to enterprise scale.

Using Cloud Dashboards

Visualization through cloud dashboards completes the enterprise IoT pipeline, transforming processed telemetry into intuitive, actionable insights accessible to engineers, managers, and executives alike. In production systems—whether overseeing vast solar farms in Australia, monitoring production quality in Japanese automotive lines, or optimizing water distribution in European smart cities—effective dashboards provide real-time fleet overviews, historical trend analysis, anomaly highlighting, and KPI tracking across global operations. Leading cloud platforms offer native or tightly integrated visualization tools that eliminate the need for custom front-end development, while open-source alternatives like Grafana provide flexible, high-performance options for demanding environments.

AWS IoT Analytics serves as a fully managed solution specifically tailored for IoT time-series data, automating the creation of sophisticated data pipelines that clean, enrich, and prepare telemetry for visualization. It ingests messages directly from IoT Core rules, applies transformations such as filtering outliers or interpolating missing values, and stores results in optimized datasets. Built-in machine learning inference enables advanced features like containerized models for anomaly detection—flagging unexpected sensor deviations in industrial equipment—or predictive forecasting of asset failure probabilities. Time-series visualizations include interactive charts, heatmaps, and notebooks that support ad-hoc exploration, with scheduled reports and Jupyter integration for deeper investigative analysis. Dashboards built on QuickSight or integrated third-party tools then render these insights, allowing stakeholders to drill down from fleet-wide metrics to individual device performance seamlessly.

Grafana has become a de-facto standard for real-time IoT monitoring due to its exceptional flexibility and performance in handling high-cardinality data. It connects natively to time-series databases such as InfluxDB, Prometheus, or cloud-managed stores like Amazon Timestream, and can subscribe directly to MQTT topics for live streaming when paired with brokers like EMQX. Panels support a vast array of visualizations—line graphs for temperature trends, gauge widgets for current battery levels, heatmaps for spatial sensor distributions, or geomaps for asset tracking—updated in sub-second intervals. Alerting integrates tightly with notification channels, while role-based access control and provisioning via Terraform ensure enterprise governance. Industrial deployments worldwide favorGrafanaGrafana for its ability to unify disparate data sources into single-pane-of-glass views, such as combining vibration, pressure, and environmental readings from factory floor machinery with external weather feeds to correlate production anomalies.

Microsoft Power BI excels in enterprise analytics scenarios, offering drag-and-drop chart creation that empowers non-technical users to build compelling reports and interactive dashboards. Deep integration with AzureIoT Hub enables direct streaming datasets for real-time tiles—displaying live device counts, alert rates, or geographic distributions—while historical data flows from Blob Storage or SQL databases for comprehensive analysis. The natural language query of Power BI, AI visuals (key influencers, decomposition trees), and automated insights uncover hidden patterns, such as identifying underperforming nodes in a precision agriculture network or correlating downtime with specific operating conditions in manufacturing. Row-level security, on-premises data gateways, and integration with Microsoft Teams or Power Apps facilitate secure sharing across organizations, making it particularly prevalent in corporate environments where IoT data informs broader business intelligence.

These cloud dashboard solutions—whether platform-native like AWS IoT Analytics and Power BI, or versatile open-source tools like Grafana—deliver far more than static charts: they enable proactive decision-making through customizable alerts, collaborative annotations, and mobile access. By presenting complex telemetry in contextually relevant formats, they bridge the gap between raw data and operational excellence, ensuring that enterprise IoT investments translate into measurable improvements in efficiency, safety, and profitability across global deployments.

Lightweight Platforms (Ubidots, Blynk Pro, TuyaIoT)

While major cloud providers like AWS and Azure dominate large-scale enterprise IoT deployments, a category of lightweight, user-friendly platforms fill an essential niche for startups, small-to-medium businesses, educational institutions, and rapid prototyping efforts worldwide. Platforms such as Ubidots, Blynk Pro, and TuyaIoT Core strike an effective balance between powerful functionality and accessibility, enabling teams with limited resources to deliver production-capable solutions in weeks rather than months. These services are particularly valuable in emerging markets—such as precision agriculture startups in India, smart home product developers in Southeast Asia, or environmental monitoring initiatives in Latin America—where speed to market, low development overhead, and affordable scaling are critical success factors.

Ubidots stands out for its intuitive, engineering-focused environment, offering drag-and-drop dashboard builders, rich widget libraries for real-time charts, maps, gauges, and tables, and seamless integration with ESP32 devices via MQTT or HTTP. Its device templates accelerate onboarding by predefining data structures, variables, and derived metrics, while built-in alerting supports multi-condition triggers with email, SMS, webhook, or Telegram notifications. Ubidots excels in industrial and STEM applications, providing synthetic variables for custom computations, event engines for automated actions, and scheduled reports—features that enable small teams to deploy reliable monitoring systems for factories, solar installations, or research projects without deep cloud expertise.

Blynk Pro evolves the familiar mobile-first experience of its free tier into a scalable commercial platform, emphasizing beautiful, responsive apps and dashboards accessible from smartphones, tablets, or web browsers. It supports unlimited devices in paid plans, white-label branding for customer-facing products, organization hierarchies for team collaboration, and advanced features like map-based asset tracking, QR-code provisioning, and over-the-air firmware updates. Startups building consumer or commercial smart devices—such as connected appliances in European markets or irrigation controllers in African agriculture—benefit from the rapid UI prototyping of Blynk, push notification reliability, and bridge to hardware via simple library calls on ESP32, allowing focus on product differentiation rather than backend infrastructure.

TuyaIoT Core targets the consumer and smart-home ecosystem with a comprehensive, end-to-end solution that includes device-side SDKs, cloud connectivity, and a vast library of pre-certified modules for Wi-Fi, BLE, and Zigbee. Its strength lies in accelerating time-to-market for OEMs and brands: developers select from thousands of product templates, customize firmware with no-code tools, and instantly gain access to mobile apps, voice assistant integrations (Alexa, Google Home), and global cloud regions. Small businesses launching connected lighting, security cameras, or environmental controllers leverage the marketplace of Tuya for rapid certification and distribution, while retaining control over data flows and branding making it a preferred choice for hardware startups in China and expanding globally.

These lightweight platforms share common advantages that make them ideal for specific use cases: dramatically faster development cycles through visual programming and pre-built components, charting and alerting without custom coding, device templates that enforce consistency across fleets, and pricing models that scale predictably from pilot to thousands of units. They are particularly well-suited for deployment pilots validating business models, small businesses managing hundreds of installations, or startups iterating quickly before potentially migrating to heavier cloud providers. By lowering barriers to sophisticated IoT functionality, Ubidots, Blynk Pro, and Tuya empower innovators worldwide to bring reliable, connected products to market efficiently—bridging the gap between prototype and commercial success in resource-constrained environments.

Cost Optimization Strategies

Cost optimization is a critical discipline in enterprise IoT deployments, where even modest per-message or per-connection fees can accumulate rapidly across thousands or millions of devices—potentially turning a viable project into an unsustainable expense. In applications ranging from precision agriculture monitoring vast fields in India and Australia, to industrial sensor networks in European factories, and smart metering infrastructures in urban Asia, effective strategies ensure long-term financial viability without compromising reliability or performance. The challenge must balance operational needs with cloud billing models—typically charged on message volume, connection minutes, rule executions, and data transfer—while leveraging platform features to minimize waste and maximize value.

Impact of Optimization:

Implementing optimization techniques can dramatically alter the economics. For instance, in the Large-Scale Operation (1,000 devices):

- **Batching:** If devices switch from sending 1 message per minute to batching data and sending one larger message every 10 minutes (reducing message count by 90%), the total monthly messages drop from 43.2 million to 4.32 million. The rough monthly messaging cost falls from ~$194.40 to ~$19.44, saving over $170 per month on messaging alone.
- **Adaptive Sampling:** Applying an adaptive strategy where a sensor only sends a message when the temperature reading changes by more than 0.5 degrees Celsius—rather than every minute—could reduce the effective message rate to, say, once every 5 minutes on average. This would reduce the total monthly messages to around 8.64 million, cutting the rough monthly messaging cost to approximately $38.88, a significant saving compared to the fixed-rate approach.

Maximizing free-tier usage forms an excellent starting point, particularly during development, pilots, and low-volume production phases. Major providers like AWS IoT Core and Azure IoT Hub offer generous free tiers—often millions of messages and connection minutes per month—sufficient for testing hundreds of devices or running small commercial fleets. By staying within these limits through careful monitoring via cloud dashboards, teams can defer costs entirely in early stages, as seen in startups validating environmental monitoring solutions in developing regions before scaling.

Data batching represents a powerful technique for reducing message counts: instead of publishing individual readings every few seconds, devices aggregate multiple samples into a single JSON array or compacted payload transmitted periodically—perhaps every few minutes. This approach dramatically lowers billing in high-frequency scenarios, such as vibration monitoring in machinery, while preserving data integrity through timestamped entries. Reduced message frequency complements batching by adjusting sampling intervals based on application requirements: critical alerts trigger immediate transmission, but routine telemetry can be scheduled less often, conserving both bandwidth and cost in battery-powered or cellular-connected nodes. Using retained MQTT messages strategically eliminates redundant transmissions for slowly changing values. By setting the retain flag on status or configuration topics—such as device location, firmware version, or current operating mode—subsequent subscribers receive the last known value instantly upon connection, avoiding polling loops that generate unnecessary traffic. This proves especially valuable in fleet management systems where dashboards need immediate state synchronization without querying each vehicle individually. Offloading cold data to cheaper storage tiers prevents escalating costs from long-term retention in hot databases. Enterprise pipelines route frequently accessed recent telemetry to fast stores like DynamoDB or Azure Table Storage, while automatically archiving older records—via lifecycle policies—to low-cost options such as AWS S3 Glacier or Azure Cool Blob. This tiered approach supports years of historical analysis for compliance or trend forecasting in regulated industries like energy or pharmaceuticals, at a fraction of the price.

Additional strategies include compressing payloads, implementing edge preprocessing to filter irrelevant data before transmission, and rightsizing provisioned resources through regular cost audits using tools like AWS Cost Explorer or Azure Cost Management. By combining these techniques—free-tier leverage, intelligent batching and scheduling, retained messages, and storage tiering—engineers achieve sustainable economics that scale gracefully from pilot projects to global deployments. This disciplined approach not only controls expenditure but also encourages efficient system design, ensuring that enterprise IoT delivers maximum return on investment in diverse, real-world applications worldwide.

Practical Exercises

Exercise 1: Firebase versus AWS versus Azure (Cloud Reality Check)

Push a simple payload to three cloud platforms (Firebase Realtime Database, AWS IoT Core, Azure IoT Hub) and compare **latency**, **authentication flow**, and **dashboard experience**.

Required materials:

- ESP32 (or any Wi-Fi microcontroller)
- Wi-Fi credentials
- Accounts on Firebase, AWS, and Azure (free tiers are fine)
- Basic HTTP/MQTT client libraries for ESP32 (`HTTPClient`, `PubSubClient`/`WiFiClientSecure`)

Step-by-step

1. **Prepare cloud accounts and projects**
    a. **Firebase:** Create a Firebase project →Realtime Database → enable (test mode or secured rules). Note the database URL and REST endpoint.
    b. **AWS:** Create an AWS account → AWS IoT Core → create a thing (device). Note endpoint URL.
    c. **Azure:** Create Azure account →IoTHub → create an IoT Hub and get the Hub hostname.
2. **Set up authentication for each platform**
    a. **Firebase (REST):** Create a database secret or generate a short-lived token (for testing you can use open rules, but note production security).
    b. **AWS IoT Core (MQTT):** Create a thing, generate and download X.509 certificates, attach an IoT policy allowing `iot:Connect`, `iot:Publish`.
    c. **Azure IoT Hub:** Create a device identity under IoT Hub → get the device connection string (SAS token or X.509 in prod).
3. **Prepare ESP32 code templates**

    Firebase (HTTP REST):

    a. **AWS IoT Core (MQTT over TLS):**
        i. Use `WiFiClientSecure` with device cert/key, `PubSubClient` for MQTT.

    ii. Publish to **`topic/test`** with payload.

  b. **Azure IoT Hub (MQTT or HTTPS):**

    i. Use SAS token or X.509. Publish to **`devices/<id>/messages/events/`** or use REST.

4. **Deploy and run tests**

  a. Upload respective sketches to ESP32 (one at a time).

  b. For each platform, record:

    i. Time when payload is sent (local millis or timestamp).

    ii. Time when it appears on the dashboard or in cloud logs.

    iii. Number of steps required in auth (certs, tokens, SAS).

    iv. Complexity of getting a readable dashboard.

5. **Measure latency and auth complexity**

  a. Latency = (cloud timestamp or observed arrival time) - (device send time). Repeat 10 times and compute average and standard deviation.

  b. Note auth steps: how many files/keys, renewals, client library complexity.

6. **Observe dashboards**

  a. **Firebase:** Realtime DB viewer updates.

  b. **AWS:** Use AWS IoT Core Test client or CloudWatch logs, or route to DynamoDB and view.

  c. **Azure:** Use IoT Hub metrics / Azure Storage / Stream Analytics output.

7. **Document results**: Create a small table: Platform | Avg latency | Auth complexity | Dashboard ease | Notes (cost limits, quotas).

Validation / Testing

- Repeat sends at 5s and 20s intervals. Check for throttling or rejected requests.
- Test auth failure cases (invalid token, expired cert) to observe error messages.

Troubleshooting

- HTTP 403/401 → invalid token or insufficient permissions.
- MQTT connect fails → certificate wrong format, root CA missing.
- Dashboard not updating → check cloud-side routing / rules.

Exercise 2: Publish Soil Moisture to AWS IoT Core (MQTT + TLS)

Publish soil moisture readings from an ESP32 to AWS IoT Core over TLS to topic: **`agri/moisture/device1`**. Learn certificate-based device provisioning and secure MQTT publishing.

Required materials

- ESP32 with Wi-Fi
- Soil moisture sensor (analog)
- AWS account with IoT Core access
- **`WiFiClientSecure`**, **`PubSubClient`** libraries

Step-by-step

1. **Register device in AWS IoT Core**
    a. In AWS Console →IoT Core → Manage → Things → Create things.
    b. Create a new certificate for the thing; download the **device certificate**, **private key**, and **root CA** (Amazon Root CA 1).
    c. Attach a policy that allows **`iot:Connect`**, **`iot:Publish`**, **`iot:Subscribe`**, **`iot:Receive`** on the appropriate resources (or use resource wildcard for the lab).
2. **Prepare ESP32 with certificates**
    a. Convert cert/key to suitable format (PEM) and embed them as **`const char*`** strings or store on SPIFFS if large.
    b. Use **`WiFiClientSecure`** and set the CA and client cert/key.
3. **Write MQTT publish code**: Initialize **`WiFiClientSecure`** and **`PubSubClient`** to point to AWS IoT endpoint (found in AWS Console).
4. **Security considerations**
    a. Protect private keys – in a production build use secure element or hardware secure storage.
    b. Rotate certificates as per policy; tests that revoked certs cannot connect.
5. **Test publishing**
    a. Use AWS IoT Core → Test → Subscribe to agri/moisture/# to observe messages.
    b. Publish at a reasonable interval. Check message payloads.
6. **Optional: route messages**: Create an IoT Rule to route messages to DynamoDB, S3, or Lambda for storage/processing.

Validation/Testing

- Observe successful **`MQTT CONNECT`** and PUBLISH (AWS test client).
- Simulate network loss and ensure reconnect and publish-once-after-reconnect or queueing.

Troubleshooting

- TLS handshake fails → root CA missing or time on device incorrect (secure TLS needs correct time).
- Auth errors → policy not attached or certificate inactive.
- MQTT publish returns error → topic forbidden by policy.

Exercise 3: Serverless Rule-Based Cloud Logic (AWS Lambda)

When a published moisture message indicates **`moisture < 30%`**, route that message via an AWS IoT Rule to an AWS Lambda function which writes an alert record to DynamoDB and/or sends an email.

Required materials

- AWS account with IAM permissions for IoT/Lambda/DynamoDB/SNS
- Existing IoT messages flowing from Exercise 2

Step-by-step

1. **Create DynamoDB table**
   a. **Table name:** `SoilAlerts` with primary key `alertId (string)` and attributes such as `deviceId`, `moisture`, `timestamp`.
2. **Create an AWS Lambda function**
   a. **Runtime:** Node.js / Python (choose what students are comfortable with).
   b. **Lambda role:** Attach policy allowing `dynamodb:PutItem` and `sns:Publish` (if sending emails via SNS).
3. **Create an IoT Rule**
   a. **Configure action:** Invoke Lambda function (select the Lambda created).
   b. Optionally add a DynamoDB action directly (simple put) or SNS action.
4. **Test end-to-end**
   a. Publish a test message.
   b. Monitor CloudWatch logs for Lambda invocation.
   c. Check DynamoDB table for new item.
   d. Check email (if SNS) for alert.
5. **Implement**
   a. In Lambda, consider preventing duplicate alerts within short windows (store `lastAlertTimestamp` in DynamoDB and check).

Validation / Testing

a. Publish multiple low-moisture events and verify DynamoDB entries created and email notifications delivered.

b. Test non-triggering messages (`moisture = 50`) ensure no Lambda invocation (or no DB write).

Troubleshooting

a. IoT Rule not triggering → Rule SQL mismatch or rule disabled.

b. Lambda permission errors → add `iot:Publish` / `lambda:InvokeFunction` policies as needed.

c. DynamoDB write fails → insufficient IAM permissions.

Exercise 4: Enterprise Dashboard Drill: MQTT →Grafana / Power BI

Stream MQTT sensor data into a time-series database (InfluxDB or Azure Stream Analytics) and create dashboards in Grafana or Power BI to visualize trends.

Required materials:

- MQTT broker (cloud HiveMQ, EMQX, or local Mosquitto)
- InfluxDB (cloud-hosted or local) or Azure Stream Analytics → Power BI
- Grafana (cloud or local) or Power BI account
- Connector service or bridge (Telegraf / MQTT subscriber)

Step-by-step

1. **Provision MQTT broker**
   a. Use a cloud-hosted broker (HiveMQ Cloud free plan) or install Mosquitto locally.
   b. Ensure devices publish to a known topic
2. **Set up data ingestion into a time-series DB**
   a. Option A — InfluxDB + Telegraf:
      i. Install Telegraf and enable the MQTT consumer plugin to subscribe to topics and write to InfluxDB.
      ii. Configure `Telegraf[[inputs.mqtt_consumer]]` with broker URL and topics; configure `[[outputs.influxdb_v2]]`.
   b. Option B — Azure Stream Analytics:
      i. Configure IoT Hub or MQTT ingestion → Stream Analytics job → output to Power BI or Azure Data Explorer.
3. **Publish sample data**
   a. Ensure timestamps in ISO 8601 or include device timestamp fields.
4. **Create dashboards**
   a. **Grafana:**
      i. Add InfluxDB as a data source.
      ii. Build panels: time-series line graphs for temp/humidity, gauge for current value, threshold alert panel.
   b. **Power BI:**
      i. Connect to Azure Stream Analytics output or import CSV from time-series DB.
      ii. Create visuals: line charts, slicers (time range), cards for current metrics.
5. **Add alerts and annotations**
   a. **Grafana:** Set alert rules to notify via email/Slack.
   b. **Power BI:** Use real-time streaming dataset + alerts (if supported in workspace).
6. **Test visualizations**
   a. Publish continuous data and watch graphs update.
   b. Validate time alignment, smoothing options, and retention windows.

Validation / Testing

- Verify data freshness (latency from publish to panel).
- Confirm accuracy: compare raw MQTT payloads with displayed values.

Troubleshooting

- No data in DB → check Telegraf logs and MQTT subscriptions.
- Time skew → ensure payload timestamps are in UTC and time-synced.
- Missing fields → ensure consistent JSON schema across devices.

Conclusion

This chapter has guided learners through the critical evolution from prototype-focused IoT development to robust, cloud-backed enterprise architectures capable of supporting thousands or millions of devices in real-world production environments. By examining the inherent limitations of beginner-friendly platforms like Firebase and Blynk, exploring the capabilities of industrial-strength services such as AWS IoT Core and Azure IoT Hub, and delving into foundational concepts—including secure device provisioning with X.509 certificates, scalable MQTT topic hierarchies, rule-based routing, serverless compute with Lambda and Azure Functions, structured payload design, and sophisticated visualization through tools like Grafana and Power BI—readers have gained the knowledge and practical skills to architect, deploy, and optimize end-to-end IoT systems that deliver reliability, security, and business value at scale.

Through hands-on exercises, such as securely publishing sensor data to AWS IoT Core, implementing threshold-based alerting via serverless functions, and building enterprise dashboards, learners have experienced the complete lifecycle of production-grade IoT: from edge perception and secure connectivity to intelligent cloud processing, storage, and visualization. Cost-optimization strategies and lightweight alternatives like Ubidots and Blynk Pro further equip readers to make informed architectural decisions tailored to project scale, budget, and timeline.

Mastering these enterprise principles completes the foundational three-layer IoT stack while preparing engineers to design systems that meet the stringent demands of industry—whether monitoring vast agricultural networks, optimizing manufacturing processes, or enabling smart infrastructure worldwide. With a solid grasp of cloud-backed integration, readers are now ready to elevate their IoT solutions from reactive data collection to proactive, intelligent decision-making through the power of machine learning at the edge.

The next chapter marks an exciting progression into the realm of intelligent IoT systems, where devices evolve from passive sensors into smart, autonomous agents capable of local reasoning and decision-making. While previous chapters focused on reliably collecting, transmitting, and processing sensor data in the cloud, Chapter 14 introduces Edge AI—the practice of running lightweight machine learning models directly on resource-constrained microcontrollers. This shift dramatically reduces latency, minimizes dependence on constant connectivity, lowers cloud bandwidth costs, and enables real-time responses even in offline or remote environments.

Chapter 14
Introduction to ML with Sensor Data

Introduction

In *Chapter 13, Cloud-Backed End-to-End Projects and Enterprise IoT Integration*, we moved from prototype-level IoT systems to enterprise-grade cloud architectures. Readers learned how ESP32 devices publish data securely using MQTT with TLS, how cloud platforms like AWS IoT Core and Azure IoT Hub scale real-world systems, and how serverless computers and dashboards bring automation and analytics to life. That chapter established how IoT devices can send data to powerful cloud engines that store, process, and visualize information at scale. This chapter, however, shifts the focus from moving data to the cloud to extracting intelligence from that data, both in the cloud and at the edge, which is why Machine Learning (ML) is the natural next step in the IoT stack.

The Internet of Things has grown explosively: more than 15 billion connected devices today are projected to exceed 30 billion by 2030. This enormous, continuous stream of data makes human review of raw sensor feeds infeasible, necessitating automated machine learning approaches. Each device—whether a smart sensor in a factory, a soil monitor on a farm, or a wearable health tracker—generates continuous streams of time-series data from accelerometers, microphones, temperature, humidity, pressure, gas, or optical sensors, for years, the default architecture was simple: collect raw samples, packetize them, and push everything to the cloud. Powerful servers running deep learning models would then classify events, detect anomalies, or trigger actions, sending results back to the device. This worked well at small scale, but as deployments reach millions of nodes and real-time requirements tighten, the limitations of cloud-only intelligence have become critical bottlenecks.

Round-trip latency often exceeds 200–500 ms on cellular networks and can stretch to seconds during congestion—far too slow for safety-critical tasks like motor fault shutdown, fall detection in elderly care, or collision avoidance in drones. Constant data transmission also drains batteries rapidly (radio transmission typically consumes 50–100× more power than local computation) and incurs high cellular or satellite bandwidth costs. In remote or congested environments, connectivity is unreliable or absent altogether. Most importantly, sending raw audio, vibration patterns, or movement data to the cloud raises serious privacy and regulatory concerns under frameworks such as GDPR and CCPA.

Edge AI fundamentally changes this paradigm by embedding machine learning inference directly into the sensor node itself. Using only a few tens to hundreds of kilobytes of RAM and flash, modern microcontrollers can now execute optimized neural networks or decision trees in real time, often in under 10 ms and at microjoule energy cost per inference. Devices no longer stream gigabytes of raw sensor data; they transmit only high-level events ("person detected," "machine overheating," "keyword spoken") or act autonomously without any network traffic. As a result, Edge AI delivers near-instant response, drastic reductions in data traffic (often >99%), true offline capability, stronger privacy by design, and battery life measured in years rather than days.

This chapter introduces the principles, tools, and workflows that make Edge AI practical today. You will learn how to turn raw sensor streams into intelligent, autonomous behavior on devices costing just a few dollars—unlocking a new generation of scalable, responsive, and sustainable IoT systems.

Structure

In this chapter, we will cover the following topics:

- Edge AI and How it is Transforming IoT
- Introduction to TinyML and Low-Power Model Inference
- Differences between Cloud ML versus Edge ML
- Basics of ML: Data, Training, Inference
- Collecting Real-Time Sensor Data for Model Training
- Data Labeling and Preprocessing (Noise Filtering, Normalization)
- Training ML Models on Edge Impulse (No-Code and Low-Code)
- Deploying ML Models on Microcontrollers (ESP32, Arduino Nano 33 BLE Sense)
- Real-World Use Cases
- Testing and Evaluating Edge ML Models
- Limitations and When to Offload to the Cloud
- Tips to Optimize Performance: Quantization, Pruning, Memory Handling

Edge AI and How it is Transforming IoT

Edge AI, also known as TinyML or on-device machine learning, is the practice of executing trained machine learning models directly on resource-constrained edge devices—typically 32-bit microcontrollers, digital signal processors, or low-power application processors—rather than relying exclusively on remote cloud or data-center servers for inference. These edge devices include battery-powered sensor nodes, wearables, industrial controllers, smart cameras, and gateway modules that reside at or near the physical source of data.

In a traditional cloud-centric IoT architecture, raw sensor samples are continuously transmitted to the cloud, where high-capacity GPUs or TPUs run large deep-learning models to produce classifications, predictions, or control decisions. The result is then sent back to the device. By contrast, Edge AI moves the inference stage onto the local microcontroller itself: the device captures data, runs a compact, optimized model (often just 20–500 KB in size), produces a high-level result locally, and either acts on it immediately or transmits only a tiny event message when necessary.

The practical advantages of performing machine learning at the edge are profound and address nearly every major pain point of large-scale IoT deployments.

- **Ultra-Low Latency for Real-Time Applications:** Inference on modern microcontrollers typically completes in 1–50 milliseconds, compared to 100–2000 ms round-trip delays when using the cloud. This difference is decisive in time-critical scenarios: detecting an impending bearing failure in a motor and stopping it before catastrophic damage, recognizing a fall event in the wearable of an elderly person and triggering an alert, identifying a "stop" hand gesture in a collaborative robot, or classifying gunshots versus fireworks in acoustic urban monitoring systems.

- **Dramatic Reduction in Bandwidth and Communication Costs:** A single 9-axis IMU sampling at 100 Hz generates approximately 3.6 KB/s of raw data. Streaming this continuously over cellular networks is expensive and quickly exhausts data plans. An Edge AI model performing gesture recognition or anomaly detection on the same device can reduce transmitted payload by more than 99%, sending only a one-byte event ("wave detected," "abnormal vibration") a few times per minute instead of kilobytes per second. In LoRaWAN, NB-IoT, or satellite-connected deployments, this often determines whether an application is economically feasible at all.
- **Reliable Offline and Intermittent-Connectivity Operation:** Many IoT devices operate in basements, mines, ships, remote agricultural fields, or moving vehicles where internet access is unreliable or completely unavailable. Edge AI enables full autonomous functionality under such conditions: a soil-moisture sensor node with a TinyML model can still classify pest infestations from hyperspectral signatures, a wildlife camera can identify protected species without ever connecting to the network, and a cold-chain logger can flag temperature excursions even during multi-day transport outages.
- **Privacy and Regulatory Compliance by Design:** Raw sensor data frequently contains sensitive personal or proprietary information—voice recordings, precise location traces, vibration signatures that reveal industrial processes, or health metrics from wearables. When inference occurs locally, raw data never leaves the device, eliminating exposure to man-in-the-middle attacks, cloud breaches, or third-party data sharing. This architecture greatly simplifies compliance with GDPR, CCPA, HIPAA, and emerging IoT cybersecurity regulations.
- **Reduced Cloud and Operational Expenditure:** Processing terabytes of raw sensor streams in the cloud incurs significant compute, storage, and egress costs. Edge AI offloads the vast majority of inference workload to the device, shrinking cloud bills by orders of magnitude. For a fleet of one million vibration monitors, moving from cloud-based to edge-based anomaly detection can reduce annual cloud expenses from millions to thousands of dollars while simultaneously extending battery life from months to years.
- **Energy Efficiency and Extended Battery Life:** Radio transmission remains the dominant power consumer in most wireless sensor nodes—often 50 to 100 times more expensive than local computation. By eliminating continuous data streaming, Edge AI routinely extends battery life from weeks or months to 5 to 10 years on the same coin cell or AA batteries, making maintenance-free, "deploy-and-forget" sensors a practical reality.

Taken together, these benefits are driving Edge AI from research prototypes to mainstream industrial, consumer, agricultural, and medical products. What began as academic demonstrations on Arduino boards in 2018–2019 has matured into commercial deployments by companies such as Bosch, ABB, Arm, STMicroelectronics, and thousands of startups. The result is a new class of intelligent, autonomous, and sustainable IoTdevices that operate faster, cheaper, more reliably, and more privately than was previously thought possible.

Introduction to TinyML and Low-Power Model Inference

TinyML represents the most extreme and exciting frontier of Edge AI: the deployment of machine learning models on battery powered microcontrollers that possess less than 1 MB of flash memory, fewer than 512 KB of RAM, and active power consumption often below 1 mW. Coined in 2019 by researchers at Harvard University and Google, the term "TinyML" has rapidly evolved from an academic curiosity into a practical engineering discipline that is redefining what ultra-low-power embedded systems can achieve.

At its core, TinyML is not a new class of algorithms but rather a confluence of hardware, software, and model-optimization techniques that together make deep learning feasible under constraints previously considered prohibitive. A typical TinyML system can perform dozens to hundreds of inferences per second while drawing only a few microjoules per inference—energy levels comparable to, or even lower than, traditional fixed-function signal-processing code written in C.

Key Technical Characteristics of TinyML

As the Internet of Things (IoT) continues to expand, the need for edge-based Artificial Intelligence (AI) solutions grows increasingly important. TinyML, the field of deploying Machine Learning (ML) models on extremely resource-constrained devices, is central to the evolution of IoT applications. By enabling sophisticated ML algorithms to run directly on microcontrollers with minimal memory and computational power, TinyML allows IoT systems to process data locally, making them faster, more reliable, and less dependent on cloud infrastructure. The following key technical characteristics highlight the cutting-edge capabilities and trade-offs that define TinyML, making it a powerful tool for IoT applications, from real-time sensor processing to predictive maintenance.

- **Extreme Resource Constraints:** Target devices include Arm Cortex-M0+, M4, M7, M33, M55, RISC-V RV32, and EspressifXTensa LX7 cores with 32–1024 KB RAM and 128 KB–2 MB flash. Some production deployments run useful models in as little as 16 KB RAM and 64 KB flash.
- **Optimized Inference Engines:** The dominant framework is TensorFlowLite for Microcontrollers (TFLM), a sub-100 KB interpreter specifically designed for bare-metal environments with no dynamic memory allocation. Alternative runtimes include Edge Impulse EON, uTensor, Neuton, and STM32 Cube.AI, all offering static memory usage and deterministic execution time.
- **Model Size and Precision:** Models are aggressively quantized to int8 or even binary/ternary weights. A complete Convolutional Neural Network (CNN) for keyword spotting may occupy only 20–80 KB, while person-detection or anomaly-detection models typically fit within 100–400 KB.
- **Supported Task Categories:** Despite the constraints, TinyML routinely solves real commercial problems: multi-class classification (gesture, sound, activity recognition), binary and one-class anomaly detection (motor health, structural integrity), regression (battery state-of-health, temperature forecasting), and basic time-series forecasting using tiny recurrent or convolutional architectures.
- **Real-Time and Deterministic Performance:** Inference latency ranges from 0.5 ms to 50 ms depending on model complexity and clock frequency, easily meeting the requirements of 50–1000 Hz sensor pipelines. Execution is fully deterministic—no operating system, no preemption, no garbage collection.

Representative TinyML Use Cases in Production and Research

TinyML has rapidly transitioned from a research concept to a key enabler of real-world IoT applications. Its ability to perform machine learning tasks on microcontrollers with minimal resources—often without the need for a cloud connection—opens up a wealth of possibilities across various domains. From voice-triggered devices to predictive maintenance in industrial settings, TinyML is making an impact where low power, low latency, and local processing are crucial. Below are some representative use cases, demonstrating how TinyML is being implemented across different industries, solving complex problems with resource-constrained devices and contributing to advancements in both production and research.

- **Wake-Word and Keyword Spotting:** Devices such as battery-powered voice remotes, earbuds, and smart intercoms use <100 KB models to detect trigger phrases while sipping <50 μA average current in always-listening mode.
- **Human Activity and Gesture Recognition:** Wearables and hearables classify walking, running, cycling, or complex gestures (double-tap, wrist-flick, air-drawing of digits) using 6–9 axis IMU data, enabling touchless user interfaces in watches, rings, and industrial gloves.
- **Industrial Predictive Maintenance:** Wireless vibration sensors attached to motors, pumps, gearboxes, and conveyor belts run 1D CNNs or autoencoders to detect bearing wear, misalignment, cavitation, or imbalance months before failure, reducing unplanned downtime by 30–50 %.
- **Smart Agriculture and Environmental Monitoring:** Soil, weather, and livestock nodes perform on-device classification of insect sounds, animal distress calls, or plant stress from hyperspectral and gas sensors, operating for 5 to 10 years on solar or primary batteries in remote fields.
- **Health and Elderly Care:** Fall detection, abnormal gait analysis, respiratory rate estimation from accelerometers, and seizure onset detection from wrist-worn devices—all performed locally to protect patient privacy and guarantee response even without connectivity.
- **Smart Buildings and Appliances:** TinyML enables refrigerators to detect compressor anomalies, washing machines to classify load imbalance, and HVAC systems to identify dirty filters—all without cloud dependency.
- **Wildlife Conservation and Security:** Camera traps and acoustic monitors deployed in rainforests run lightweight CNNs to distinguish endangered species calls or gunshots from background noise, transmitting only high-value events over expensive satellite links.

The rapid maturation of TinyML has been accelerated by open-source hardware, public datasets and especially by cloud-native development studios such as Edge Impulse and SensiML that lower the entry barrier to the point where students and small teams can create production-grade models in days, rather than months.

Cloud ML versus Edge ML: Understanding the Fundamental Trade-Offs

In IoT systems, the decision of where to perform machine learning inference—on a remote cloud server or directly on the edge device—is one of the most important architectural choices. Both approaches are valid and often complementary, but they solve very different problems under very different constraints.

Cloud-Based Machine Learning (Cloud ML)

Cloud ML follows the traditional centralized intelligence model that dominated IoT from approximately 2010–2020.

Characteristics

- Models are large (tens of megabytes to many gigabytes), typically 32-bit floating-point deep neural networks with millions to hundreds of millions of parameters.
- Training and inference exploit massive GPU/TPU clusters offering teraflops to petaflops of compute.

- Virtually unlimited storage permits retention of years of historical sensor data for retraining and forensics.
- Inference latency is dominated by network round-trip time (50 ms–several seconds) plus queueing and load-balancing delays.
- Continuous internet connectivity is mandatory for real-time decisions; intermittent connectivity forces buffering or loss of intelligence.
- Raw sensor data leaves the device, creating potential privacy, security, and regulatory issues.

Best Suited for

- Applications where maximum possible accuracy is paramount and latency is not critical (for example: monthly energy-disaggregation reports, fleet-level predictive maintenance using data from thousands of machines, video analytics on archived footage).
- Complex multimodal problems requiring fusion of data from many sources (factory-wide optimization, smart-city traffic modeling).
- Scenarios with abundant bandwidth and power (mains-powered gateways, industrial PCs, 5G-connected cameras).

Edge-Based Machine Learning (Edge ML / TinyML)

Edge ML pushes inference to the sensor node itself, using models specifically engineered for microcontrollers and low-power processors.

Characteristics

- Models are tiny (typically 10–500 KB) and heavily quantized (int8, int4, or binary weights). Parameter counts rarely exceed 500 000 and are often below 50 000.
- Compute is limited to tens to a few hundred kilo-operations per inference, executed on 32-bit or even 16-bit fixed-point cores running at 8–240 MHz.
- RAM budget is measured in tens to hundreds of kilobytes; flash in hundreds of kilobytes to 2 MB.
- End-to-end inference latency is usually 1–50 ms and fully deterministic.
- No network required for inference; the device remains intelligent even when completely disconnected.
- Raw sensor data never leaves the device, providing inherent privacy and security.

Best Suited for

- Latency-critical applications (<100 ms response required).
- Battery-powered or energy-harvested nodes where radio transmission must be minimized.
- Environments with poor, expensive, or nonexistent connectivity (remote agriculture, underground mining, ocean buoys, wilderness monitoring).
- Privacy-sensitive domains (health wearables, in-home voice assistants, worker-safety monitors).

Hybrid Approaches: The Best of Both Worlds

- Modern production systems increasingly adopt tiered or hybrid intelligence.
- Edge devices run fast, lightweight models for immediate local actions and filtering (for example: wake-word detection, anomaly flagging).
- Only interesting events or aggregated features are forwarded to the cloud for heavier re-scoring, retraining, or global optimization.
- The cloud periodically pushes improved quantized models back to the edge via Firmware-Over-the-Air (FOTA) updates.
- This cooperative architecture delivers low latency and privacy at the edge while retaining the ability of the cloud to learn from fleet-scale data and gradually increase on-device accuracy over time.
- Understanding these trade-offs early in the design phase is critical. A well-architected IoT solution rarely relies exclusively on cloud ML or edge ML; instead, it strategically places each workload where it makes the most technical and economic sense. The remainder of this chapter focuses on the tools and techniques that make Edge ML practical, reliable, and surprisingly accurate on even the smallest microcontrollers.

Basics of Machine Learning: From Sensor Data to Embedded Intelligence

Although the mathematics behind modern machine learning can be sophisticated, the fundamental workflow remains remarkably straightforward and consists of three distinct phases: data collection, model training, and inference. Mastering these phases with sensor-generated time-series data is the foundation of every successful Edge AI project.

Phase 1: Data Collection and Labeling

All machine learning begins with data. In the context of IoT and TinyML, the raw material is almost always time-series data produced by physical sensors: accelerometers, gyroscopes, magnetometers, microphones, temperature/humidity/pressure sensors, gas sensors, optical/ToF sensors, current/voltage monitors, or radar modules.

- **Vibration-based Motor Monitoring:** 3-axis Accelerometer + Current Sensor + Temperature Sensor
- **Smart Door Lock:** Time-of-Flight (ToF) Sensor + Magnetometer + Gyroscope
- **Air Quality Monitor:** Gas Sensor (VOC/CO2) + Temperature/Humidity/Pressure Sensor
- **Wearable Activity Tracker:** Accelerometer + Gyroscope + Heart Rate Sensor (Optical)
- **Predictive Maintenance on Industrial Equipment:** Microphone (Acoustic) + Accelerometer + Temperature Sensor
- **Smart Lighting/Occupancy Sensing:** Passive Infrared (PIR) or Radar Module + Ambient Light Sensor
- **Water Leak Detection:** Conductivity/Moisture Sensor + Temperature Sensor
- **Asset Tracking:** GPS (often paired with) + Accelerometer (for movement/impact detection)

Key Principles for High-Quality Datasets

- **Real-world representativeness:** Data must be recorded on the exact hardware (or identical sensor suite) that will eventually run the model. Differences in sensor noise, mounting orientation, sampling rate, or analog front-end can dramatically degrade performance.
- **Diversity and coverage:** Capture samples across all operating conditions the device will ever encounter—different users, speeds, orientations, backgrounds, lighting levels, temperatures, noise environments, and disturbance sources.
- **Balanced classes:** For classification tasks, each class should have roughly equal representation to prevent bias toward the majority class.
- **Sufficient volume:** While TinyML models can achieve useful accuracy with only a few hundred to a few thousand windows per class (thanks to transfer learning and data augmentation), more data almost always helps.
- **Accurate labeling:** Time-aligned ground-truth labels are essential. Tools such as the mobile phone app of Edge Impulse, Arduino Serial Studio, or custom smartphone BLE applications make real-time labeling practical during collection.

Phase 2: Training and Validation

Training is the process by which a model adjusts its internal parameters (weights) to minimize prediction error on labeled training data. For most student projects, this phase will be handled by a cloud-based tool (like Edge Impulse or SensiML) rather than by writing raw TensorFlow/PyTorch code, which is a perfectly acceptable approach.In practice, this phase almost always occurs in the cloud or on a powerful workstation for three reasons:

- Exploration of hundreds of architectures and hyper-parameters is computationally expensive.
- Training benefits from GPU/TPU acceleration and large batch sizes.
- Advanced techniques such as quantization-aware training, pruning, and neural architecture search require frameworks (TensorFlow/Keras, PyTorch) that are not available on microcontrollers.

The training pipeline for sensor data typically includes:

- **Preprocessing and feature extraction:** Windowing (usually 0.5 -- 2 seconds), overlap (50–75%), filtering, normalization, and optional transformation to frequency domain (FFT, Mel-spectrogram, MFCC).
- **Model selection:** Classical algorithms (k-NN, SVM, decision trees, random forests) or neural networks (MLPs, 1D/2D CNNs, depthwise separable convolutions, tiny LSTMs/GRUs, or Transformer-inspired blocks).
- **Training objective:** Categorical cross-entropy for classification, mean-squared error for regression, contrastive or reconstruction loss for anomaly detection.
- **Validation and early stopping:** A held-out validation set (typically 20%) prevents over-fitting.
- **Quantization-Aware Training (QAT):** Simulates int8 inference during training to minimize accuracy loss after conversion.

Modern TinyML platforms (Edge Impulse, SensiML, Neuton, QeexoAutoML) automate most of these steps, testing dozens or hundreds of pipelines and returning the smallest model that meets a user-defined accuracy target.

Phase 3: Inference on the Edge Device

Inference is the deployment phase: the trained and optimized model is converted into efficient C/C++ code and executed on the microcontroller whenever new sensor data arrives. It is important to note that typical edge devices have severe constraints, including limited RAM and flash memory budgets, strict latency targets, and specific duty cycle requirements. Therefore, the size and complexity of the model must be carefully planned and constrained against these device limitations.

Steps Performed Automatically by Current Toolchains:

- **Post-training quantization:** 32-bit floating-point weights → int8 (or lower) with minimal accuracy degradation (typically < 1% drop).
- **Operator fusion and kernel optimization:** Multiple layers are collapsed into single highly optimized functions.
- **Static memory allocation:** The entire model, input/output buffers, and interpreter fit into fixed RAM and flash regions.
- Generation of a complete firmware project (Arduino sketch, ESP-IDF component, Zephyr module, or Mbed library) that reads sensors, manages windows, runs inference, and exposes results via serial, BLE, or GPIO.
- **During real-time operation:**
  - The microcontroller continuously fills a sliding window buffer from sensor interrupts or DMA.
  - When the buffer is full, the inference engine is invoked (usually taking 1–50 ms).
  - The output (class probabilities, anomaly score, regression value) drives local actions: LED indicators, motor shutdown, buzzer activation, BLE advertisement, or queued LoRa transmission.

Because inference is lightweight and deterministic, it easily coexists with other embedded tasks (communication, sensing, power management) without requiring a real-time operating system.

Collecting Real-Time Sensor Data for Model Training

In Machine Learning for IoT, the quality and relevance of the training dataset determine the upper bound of achievable performance.

Critical Insight: Data quality sets the upper bound on model performance.

No amount of architectural sophistication or hyper-parameter tuning can compensate for poorly collected, unrepresentative, or incorrectly labeled sensor data. For TinyML and Edge AI applications, data collection is simultaneously the most time-consuming and most critical phase of development. Therefore, project planning should allocate a significant majority (often 60-80%) of the initial development timeline to rigorous data collection, cleaning, and labeling, with the remaining time focused on model architecture and tuning.

Unlike image or text datasets that can often be sourced from public repositories, high-quality sensor datasets almost always must be recorded in-house using the exact hardware, firmware, and physical deployment conditions the final product will experience.A model trained on laboratory bench data collected with perfect orientation and no background noise will invariably fail when deployed on a vibrating machine, worn on a moving person, or exposed to wind and temperature extremes. As a rough rule of thumb, expect 50–70% of project effort in a first TinyML project to be data collection, cleaning, and labeling.

Principles of Effective Sensor Data Collection

High-quality sensor data is the foundation of every successful TinyML system. Because TinyML models operate within extremely tight computational budgets and often lack the capacity to compensate for noisy or inconsistent inputs, the quality of the training dataset becomes even more critical than in conventional machine learning. Effective data collection must therefore be intentional, repeatable, and closely aligned with real deployment conditions. The following principles outline the essential practices for gathering reliable, representative, and well-labeled data—ensuring that TinyML models trained in the lab behave predictably and accurately in the field.

- **Hardware Fidelity:** Data is collected using the identical microcontroller, sensor part number, and analog front-end that will ship in production. Even minor differences in sensor gain, filtering, noise floor, or mounting rigidity introduce domain shifts that degrade accuracy.
- **Sampling Consistency:** A fixed, known sampling frequency is maintained throughout each recording session (typically 10–104 Hz for inertial sensors, 16 kHz for audio, 1–10 Hz for environmental sensors). Jitter, dropped samples, or variable rates complicate windowing and frequency-domain features.
- **Environmental and Operational Coverage:** It maintains a record keeping in consideration the full range of real-world conditions: different users, speeds, orientations, temperatures, humidity levels, background noise sources, lighting conditions, and interference. For a gesture-recognition system, this means dozens of people performing each gesture in multiple orientations and clothing types; for predictive maintenance, it means capturing healthy operation plus early, mid, and late-stage fault progression.
- **Class Balance and Duration:** Aim for roughly equal representation of each target class and at least several minutes of continuous recording per class. Short, fragmented captures increase the risk of accidental correlations (for example, confusing a gesture with the sound of a chair moving).
- **Precise Time:** Aligned Labeling Labels must be synchronized to the exact sensor windows they describe. Manual post-hoc labeling on waveforms is error-prone; real-time labeling during collection (via button press, mobile app, voice command, or automated trigger) is strongly preferred.

Practical Data Acquisition Workflows

Two mainstream approaches have emerged as the most efficient for students and professional teams alike:

Direct Ingestion into Cloud Studios

Platforms such as Edge Impulse, SensiML, and Neuton provide firmware daemons for popular development boards (Arduino Nano 33 BLE Sense, Nordic nRF52/53, ESP32, ST SensorTile, and so on). The board streams timestamped sensor samples over USB Serial or BLE directly into the cloud project. Users label data in real time using keyboard shortcuts, a smartphone app, or automated triggers. This method eliminates intermediate files, ensures perfect timestamp integrity, and is the fastest path from hardware to training.

Local Capture with Subsequent Upload

When internet access is limited during field collection, firmware can log raw or pre-processed samples to on-board flash, SD card, or stream to a laptop/phone as CSV or binary files. After collection, files are uploaded manually to the chosen ML platform. This approach offers maximum flexibility in remote locations but requires careful attention to timestamp preservation and file format compatibility.

Recommended Sensor Sampling Guidelines by Application

- **Motion and gesture recognition:** 50–100 Hz, 6–9 axis IMU, ±4–16 g accelerometer range, ±500–2000 dps gyroscope.
- **Vibration-based predictive maintenance:** 1–10 kHz (often using dedicated piezoelectric or MEMS accelerometers), high dynamic range (±50 g or more).
- **Audio keyword spotting and acoustic event detection**: 16 kHz, 16-bit PCM, digital PDM or analog MEMS microphone.
- **Environmental anomaly detection:** 1–10 Hz for temperature, humidity, pressure, gas; higher rates only when monitoring fast transients.
- **Optical and proximity gestures:** 50–200 Hz time-of-flight or ambient light sensors.

Dataset Structure and Typical Size

A well-structured dataset for a moderate-complexity TinyML project usually contains:

- 10–60 minutes total recording time.
- 2,000–20,000 labeled windows (after segmentation with 50–75 % overlap).
- CSV or JSON lines format with columns for Unix timestamp or sample index, all sensor axes/channels, and ground-truth label.

Each recording session should be stored as a separate file with clear metadata (device ID, firmware version, user, environmental conditions, sensor orientation) to enable traceability and future debugging.

Data Labeling and Preprocessing: Turning Raw Sensor Streams into Training-Ready Features

Raw sensor data, as collected from microcontrollers, is rarely suitable for direct input into machine learning models. Time-series signals from accelerometers, microphones, environmental sensors, or current monitors are typically corrupted by electronic noise, mechanical vibration, temperature drift, sampling jitter, and irrelevant background activity. Moreover, neural networks and classical algorithms require fixed-size input vectors, whereas sensors produce continuous streams of variable length.

The preprocessing and labeling stage bridges this gap. Performed either on-device during inference or in the cloud during training, these operations clean the signal, extract discriminative patterns, and assign meaningful ground-truth annotations. When executed properly, preprocessing can improve final deployed accuracy by 20–50 percentage points and dramatically reduce the model complexity required to reach a given performance target.

Core Preprocessing Techniques for IoT Sensor Data

Transforming raw sensor readings into reliable machine-learning inputs is one of the most critical steps in any IoT or TinyML workflow. Because microcontroller-based models typically operate with limited computational capacity and tight latency budgets, they depend heavily on well-structured, noise-reduced, and informative data. Effective preprocessing not only improves model accuracy but also reduces model size, simplifies training, and ensures consistent behavior in real-world deployments. The techniques below outline the core methods used by practitioners to clean, normalize, segment, and enrich sensor streams, forming the essential bridge between physical signals and efficient on-device inference.

Signal Conditioning and Noise Reduction: Real-world sensors exhibit high-frequency noise, 50/60 Hz power-line interference, and low-frequency drift. Common filtering approaches include:

- Moving-average or exponential smoothing for gentle denoising.
- Butterworth or Chebyshev low-pass, high-pass, or band-pass Finite Impulse Response (FIR) or Infinite Impulse Response (IIR) filters implemented either on the microcontroller or in the cloud pipeline.
- Outlier removal using median filters or simple threshold clipping.

Normalization and Scaling: Most machine learning algorithms perform best when inputs are zero-centered and scaled to a consistent range. Typical strategies:

- Min-max normalization to [0,1] or [–1,1] per axis or per sensor type.
- Z-score standardization (subtract mean, divide by standard deviation) computed over the entire training set.
- Robust scaling using median and interquartile range when outliers are common.

Windowing and Overlapping: Because events have duration (a gesture lasts 0.5–2 seconds, a machine fault produces a characteristic 100–500 ms vibration burst), raw streams must be segmented into fixed-length windows. Standard practices:

- **Window duration:** 0.5–2 seconds for human motion and voice, 50–500 ms for industrial vibration, 10–30 seconds for slow environmental phenomena.
- **Overlap:** 50–80% to increase dataset size and provide multiple views of the same event.
- The resulting windows become individual training examples.

Feature Extraction: Instead of feeding raw samples directly to the model (which demands larger networks and longer training), engineers often compute hand-crafted or automatically derived features that capture the essence of the signal:

- **Time-domain:** Mean, RMS, peak-to-peak, zero-crossing rate, skewness, kurtosis, crest factor.
- **Frequency-domain:** Power spectral density via FFT, dominant frequency bins, spectral centroid, spectral entropy, Mel-frequency cepstral coefficients (MFCCs) for audio.
- **Time-frequency:** Spectrograms, wavelet coefficients, continuous wavelet transform scalograms. Modern TinyML platforms increasingly allow raw or lightly preprocessed windows to be fed directly into convolutional neural networks, which learn optimal features automatically, often outperforming manual engineering.

Data Augmentation: To improve robustness and reduce overfitting on small datasets, synthetic variations are injected during training:

- Time warping, magnitude scaling, random cropping.
- Addition of realistic noise, rotation of IMU axes, pitch/speed shifting for audio.
- Sensor-specific augmentations such as background mixing for sound or vibration overlay for machinery.

Data Labeling Strategies

Labeling assigns semantic meaning to each window or sample. Inaccurate or inconsistent labels are the fastest way to destroy model performance—even perfect features cannot overcome systematic labeling errors.

Best practices include:

Real-time labeling during collection (preferred): the person or system performing the action presses a physical button, mobile app trigger, or speaks a marker phrase at the exact moment the event begins and ends. This produces sub-100 ms timing accuracy.

Post-collection annotation using visual tools: waveforms are displayed in Edge Impulse, SensiML, or custom Jupyter notebooks, allowing precise drag-and-drop region labeling.

Hierarchical and multi-label schemes: many real applications require more than simple single-class labels. Examples:

- **Primary activity:** "idle," "walking," "running," "cycling," "fall."
- **Secondary context:** "indoors/outdoors," "holding phone," "in pocket."
- **Anomaly scoring:** continuous "health index" from 0 (failed) to 100 (perfect) rather than binary pass/fail.

One-class and negative sampling for anomaly detection: normal operation is labeled extensively; rare faults are either collected when possible or synthesized via simulation.

Common labeling taxonomies encountered in IoT projects:

- **Motion and human activity:** "still," "walking," "jumping," "falling," "waving," "circle gesture," "punch."
- **Acoustic events:** "silence," "speech," "dog bark," "glass break," "machine running," "keyword: open," "keyword: close."
- **Industrial health:** "healthy," "bearing fault," "misalignment," "imbalance," "cavitation," "belt slip."
- **Environmental:** "light on," "light off," "door open," "door closed," "person present," "no person."
- **Biomedical:** "normal breathing," "cough," "wheeze," "arrhythmia," "seizure onset."

Rigorous labeling discipline, combined with thoughtful preprocessing, transforms noisy, continuous sensor streams into compact, informative feature vectors that even the smallest microcontrollers can interpret with remarkable accuracy. The next stage—model training and optimization—builds directly upon this foundation.

Training Machine Learning Models with Edge Impulse: A Complete End-to-End TinyML Platform

Among the numerous tools that have democratized Edge AI, Edge Impulse stands out as the most widely adopted development environment for professional and educational TinyML projects. Launched in 2019, it provides a complete, browser-based, end-to-end workflow that enables engineers, data scientists, students, and even domain experts with minimal programming experience to transform raw sensor data into optimized, production-ready microcontroller firmware in hours, rather than weeks.

Unlike traditional machine learning frameworks that require separate tools for data management, preprocessing, training, validation, quantization, and deployment, Edge Impulse integrates every stage into a single unified studio. This integration dramatically reduces friction and errors, making it the de facto standard for IoT-focused TinyML development worldwide.

Core Capabilities and Differentiating Features

Seamless Hardware Integration: Official firmware images and libraries exist for more than 300 development boards, including Arduino Nano 33 BLE Sense, all ESP32 variants, Nordic nRF52/53/91, STMicroelectronics STM32 series, Raspberry Pi Pico, Himax WE-I Plus, and many others. Connecting a supported board via USB or BLE instantly enables live data streaming into the cloud project.

Real-Time Data Ingestion and Labeling: The studio receives timestamped sensor streams at native sampling rates and displays them live. Users label data in real time using keyboard shortcuts, a companion mobile app, or automated triggers, achieving sub-100 ms timing accuracy without manual alignment.

Automated and Expert-Mode Signal Processing: The platform offers two parallel paths:

- "Impulse Design – Auto" generates complete spectral feature pipelines (filtering, FFT/Mel spectrograms, MFCCs) with sensible defaults for motion, audio, and vibration data.
- "Expert Mode" exposes every parameter (window size, overlap, filter cutoffs, axis combination, augmentation) for fine control.

Flexible Learning Blocks:

- **Classification:** Fully connected neural networks, 1D/2D convolutional networks, MobileNetV2 variants, and transfer learning from public datasets.
- **Anomaly detection:** k-means clustering, Gaussian mixture models, and autoencoder-based reconstruction error.
- **Regression:** For continuous value prediction (temperature forecasting, battery SoH). The system automatically runs neural architecture search across dozens of configurations and returns the smallest model that meets the user-defined accuracy target.

Quantization-Aware Training and Model Optimization: All training is performed with int8 quantization awareness from the first epoch, ensuring that the accuracy displayed in the studio is nearly identical to what will be observed on the microcontroller after deployment.

Comprehensive Model Validation:

- Live classification testing directly from connected hardware.
- Confusion matrices, per-class F1 scores, on-device performance estimates (RAM, flash, latency).
- Sensitivity analysis showing which features contribute most to decisions.

One-Click Deployment Options:

- Fully optimized TensorFlowLite for Microcontrollers (`.tflite`) binary.
- Complete C++ library (static model array + inference code) ready for Arduino, ESP-IDF, Zephyr, Mbed, or plain CMake projects.
- Pre-compiled Arduino sketches, WebAssembly for browser-based testing, and firmware binaries for supported boards platforms.

Standard Edge Impulse Training Workflow

The typical path from idea to deployed intelligent device follows seven reproducible stages:

- **Project Creation**: Select target hardware and application type (motion, audio, vibration, multimodal). The studio pre-configures sensible sampling rates and processing defaults.
- **Data Acquisition:** Record diverse, real-world samples using live ingestion or file upload. Aim for balanced classes and broad coverage of operating conditions.

- **Labeling and Dataset Splitting:** Assign accurate ground-truth labels to time regions. The platform automatically splits data into training (70–80%), validation (10–15%), and test (10–15%) sets while preserving temporal integrity.
- **Impulse Design:** Build the processing pipeline: choose raw data, spectral features, or hybrid blocks. Configure windowing parameters and enable data augmentation as needed.
- **Model TrainingX:** Launch training (usually 10–60 minutes depending on dataset size). Monitor training/validation loss curves and early-stopping behavior in real time.
- **Model Evaluation and Live Testing:** Review test-set accuracy, confusion matrix, and feature importance. Connect the physical device and perform live classification to verify on-device performance matches studio predictions.
- **Deployment:** Download the optimized library or binary, flash it to the target microcontroller, and integrate inference results into the application logic (LED feedback, BLE notifications, LoRa transmission, actuator control).

Because every step is visual, version-controlled, and shareable via public or private project links, Edge Impulse excels in both educational settings and enterprise teams. Entire classrooms can collaborate on the same dataset, and industrial teams can maintain strict audit trails for regulatory certification.

The ability of the platform to deliver production-grade accuracy (>95 % on many benchmark tasks) with models that fit in <300 KB flash and execute in <30 ms on a Cortex-M4 has made it the tool of choice for thousands of commercial products in predictive maintenance, consumer electronics, agriculture, and healthcare.

In the practical sections that follow, we will walk through multiple complete Edge Impulse projects—gesture recognition, keyword spotting, and vibration anomaly detection—demonstrating how quickly a functional intelligent sensor can be created, validated, and deployed using this powerful yet accessible environment.

Deploying Machine Learning Models on Microcontrollers: From Cloud Training to Real-Time Embedded Inference

The final and most rewarding step in any Edge AI project is deployment: transforming a trained, optimized model into firmware that runs autonomously on a real microcontroller, powered by a coin cell or small battery, often in harsh or remote environments. Modern TinyML toolchains have reduced this once-daunting process to a few clicks followed by standard embedded development practices, making production-quality intelligent devices accessible to students and professional teams alike.

Deployment is Now Straightforward

Until 2020, deploying neural networks to microcontrollers required manual conversion of weights, custom memory management, hand-written fixed-point kernels, and weeks of debugging. Today, platforms such as Edge Impulse, TensorFlowLite for Microcontrollers, and STM32 Cube.AI automate every difficult step:

- Full int8 (and lower) quantization with calibrated scaling factors.
- Static memory allocation (no heap, no dynamic allocation).
- Optimized operator implementations for every major MCU family.
- Automatic generation of complete buildable projects.
- Accurate on-device performance estimators (RAM, flash, latency, energy).

The result is that the model you validate in the cloud behaves almost identically when flashed to hardware—typically within 0.5–2% accuracy of the quantized validation score.

Widely Supported Target Platforms

Virtually all modern 32-bit development boards and production modules are first-class citizens in the TinyML ecosystem. The most frequently used platforms include:

- Espressif ESP32, ESP32-S3, ESP32-C3, and ESP32-C6 families (240 MHz dual-core Xtensa or RISC-V, integrated Wi-Fi/BLE, 520 KB SRAM, up to 16 MB flash)
- Arduino Nano 33 BLE Sense and Nano 33 BLE Sense Rev2 (Arm Cortex-M4F @ 64 MHz, built-in 9-axis IMU, digital microphone, multiple environmental sensors)
- Raspberry Pi Pico and Pico W (RP2040 dual Cortex-M0+ @ 133 MHz, very low cost)
- Nordic nRF52840, nRF5340 (Cortex-M33 + M4, excellent BLE power efficiency)
- STMicroelectronics STM32L4, STM32H7, STM32U5 series (ultra-low-power to high-performance Cortex-M33/M7)
- Silicon Labs EFM32, NXP i.MX RT, Renesas RA, and many RISC-V boards

New boards are added monthly; most projects begin with an Arduino-compatible or ESP32 development kit and later migrate to custom PCBs with the same processor.

Standard Deployment Workflow

Regardless of the training platform, the deployment process follows the same robust pattern:

- Model Export From Edge Impulse (or similar), download either:
  - An Arduino library (ZIP file containing the complete model as a C array, inference runner, and example sketch), or,
  - A quantized `.tflite` file plus a platform-specific inference engine.
- Project Integration In Arduino IDE, PlatformIO, ESP-IDF, Zephyr, or Mbed:
  - Add the library or `.tflite` file to the project.
  - Include the generated header that exposes a simple `run_classifier()` or `run_inference()` function.
  - Configure sensor drivers to fill the same input buffer shape used during training (window length, sampling rate, axis order).
- Firmware Build and Flash Compile with the standard toolchain (no special flags required in most cases). Flash via USB, SWD, or OTA.
- Real-Time Inference Loop At runtime, the firmware continuously:
  - Appends new sensor samples to a circular buffer.
  - Triggers inference when a full window is available.
  - Receives an array of class probabilities or an anomaly score in < 50 ms.
  - Executes local actions based on confidence thresholds (turn on LED, assert GPIO, send BLE notification, queue LoRa packet, enter low-power mode, and so forth).

Validation and Debugging Results are streamed over Serial, BLE characteristic, or OLED display. Typical debug output includes raw inference scores, predicted class, confidence, and timing/energy metrics.

Practical Considerations for Robust Deployment

- **Deterministic timing:** Use timer interrupts or sensor FIFO watermarks to guarantee fixed sampling rates.
- **Power management:** Place the MCU in deep sleep between windows; wake on sensor interrupt or RTC.
- **Over-the-air updates:** Reserve flash partitions for new model versions; many teams use MCUboot or OTA mechanisms of Espressif.
- **Safety and fallback logic:** Never rely solely on ML output for critical actuation; implement watchdog timers and fail-safe states.
- **Confidence thresholding:** Only act when the maximum probability exceeds a tuned threshold (commonly 75–95%) to reduce false positives.

When these practices are followed, deployed TinyML applications routinely achieve > 99 % uptime, multi-year battery life, and field accuracies that match or exceed laboratory results.

The transition from a blinking "Hello World" LED to a battery-powered sensor that autonomously recognizes human activities, detects machine faults, or responds to spoken keywords—all without ever connecting to the internet—represents one of the most empowering achievements in modern embedded systems education and industry. The hands-on laboratories in the following chapters will guide you through complete deployment cycles on real hardware, giving you the confidence to ship intelligent IoT products that operate reliably at the true edge of the network.

Real-World Edge Machine Learning Use Cases in IoT Systems

Edge Machine Learning (Edge ML) represents a paradigm shift in IoT deployments by moving intelligence from the cloud to device-local or gateway-level processing. This approach dramatically reduces latency, preserves bandwidth, protects privacy-sensitive data, and enables operation in disconnected or low-connectivity environments. The following sections explore practical, field-proven Edge ML applications that are already deployed at scale in consumer, industrial, and healthcare IoT ecosystems.

Fall Detection Using Inertial Sensors

One of the most mature and life-critical Edge ML applications is real-time fall detection for the elderly and patients with mobility impairments. Modern wearable devices (pendants, smartwatches, wristbands) and fixed home sensors are equipped with 3-axis accelerometers and gyroscopes (collectively called Inertial Measurement Units or IMUs). A lightweight machine learning model—typically a decision tree, SVM, or a tiny convolutional neural network—continuously analyzes the IMU data stream for characteristic patterns: a rapid free-fall acceleration spike (>3–6 g) followed by a period of near-zero movement (indicating the person is lying motionless) and is often preceded by an abnormal orientation change.

Because the inference must occur within milliseconds to trigger an immediate alert, the model runs entirely on the microcontroller (for example, STM32, nRF52, or ESP32-S3 series) without cloud dependency. Power consumption is kept extremely low (<50 μA average) by using threshold-based pre-filtering that wakes the ML model only when acceleration exceeds a safe baseline. Commercial systems from companies such as Philips Lifeline, Apple Watch (Fall Detection feature), and numerous medical-alert vendors have demonstrated that edge-based fall detection achieves >95 % sensitivity and drastically reduces false alarms compared to traditional threshold-only methods. The privacy benefit is equally important: no raw movement data ever leaves the device unless an actual fall is confirmed.

On-Device Voice Command Recognition

Voice interfaces have become ubiquitous in battery-powered and privacy-sensitive IoT products, yet continuously streaming audio to the cloud is impractical and often unacceptable. Edge-based keyword spotting solves this by running a highly compressed deep neural network (typically <100 KB) directly on low-power audio MCUs such as the Syntiant NDP series, Arm Cortex-M55 with Ethos-U NPU, or GAP8/GAP9 processors.

The model is trained to detect a small, user-defined vocabulary—usually 5–20 command words such as "turn on," "turn off," "increase," "decrease," "help," or custom wake words—while rejecting background speech, music, and noise. State-of-the-art accuracy now exceeds 97 % even in noisy environments, thanks to techniques like depthwise separable convolutions, quantization to 8-bit integers, and temporal convolution layers that capture phonetic dynamics. Because only the detected keyword (a few bytes) is transmitted, bandwidth drops by orders of magnitude and user conversations never leave the device. This technology powers always-on voice control in true wireless earbuds, smart speakers with local mode, hearing aids, and industrial headsets operating in high-noise factories.

Electrical Anomaly and Outage Detection at the Edge

Smart plugs, energy monitors, and industrial motor drives increasingly embed Edge ML to detect electrical anomalies in real time without relying on constant cloud connectivity. By sampling current and voltage waveforms at 1–8 kHz using integrated ADCs or external current transformers, tiny ML models can identify signatures of impending failures: arcing (high-frequency noise), lamp flickering, motor bearing wear (specific harmonic patterns), or sudden load disconnection.

For residential and small-commercial applications, anomaly detection models (often one-class classifiers or autoencoders sized <30 KB) run on Wi-Fi/Thread-enabled smart plugs and immediately cut power via an integrated relay when dangerous conditions are detected—preventing electrical fires before smoke even appears. In larger facilities, sub-metering devices use Edge ML to detect partial discharge detection in medium-voltage equipment, achieving detection latencies under 100 ms and eliminating the need for expensive dedicated monitoring hardware. The same principles apply to outage detection: the device distinguishes between intentional switch-off and grid failure by monitoring residual voltage decay characteristics, enabling automatic failover to backup power or rapid notification even when the internet is down.

Predictive Maintenance through Vibration Analysis

Rotating machinery (pumps, fans, compressors, conveyor motors) generates distinctive vibration patterns long before catastrophic failure. Edge ML nodes equipped with MEMS accelerometers sample vibration at 1–10 kHz and execute spectral analysis combined with classification models to detect imbalance, misalignment, bearing wear, and cavitation. Models are typically trained in the cloud on historical failure data and then compressed and deployed to the sensor node (for example: using TensorFlowLite Micro or Edge Impulse runtime).

Because vibration signatures are highly equipment-specific, modern workflows support on-site "few-shot" learning: the node operates in a baseline mode for a few days, then fine-tunes its model locally when the maintainer confirms healthy operation. This eliminates the need for identical training fleets and achieves >90 % early-detection rates weeks or months before breakdown, dramatically reducing unplanned downtime in factories, wind turbines, and HVAC systems.

Gesture Recognition in Wearables and Human-Machine Interfaces

Beyond simple tap detection, advanced wearables and industrial gloves now recognize complex hand gestures using only IMU data or flexible strain sensors. A small recurrent or temporal convolutional network running on the device can distinguish between gestures such as swipe, circle, fist clench, or pinch with >98 % accuracy while consuming only a few microjoules per classification.

Applications range from touch-free control in sterile medical environments and AR/VR controllers to silent command interfaces for soldiers and divers. The fully local processing ensures sub-20 ms latency—critical for responsive user experience—and prevents gesture data from being intercepted or stored remotely.

Occupancy and People-Counting with Low-Resolution Thermal or mmWave Sensors

Privacy regulations (GDPR, CCPA) and user comfort have driven adoption of non-camera sensors for occupancy detection. Low-resolution 8×8 or 16×16 thermal arrays (for example, Grid-EYE) and 60 GHz mmWave radar modules now embed Edge ML models that classify room occupancy, count people, and even detect forgotten infants in vehicles.

These models run comfortably on Cortex-M4/M7 cores and distinguish between humans, pets, and inanimate heat sources by analysing movement dynamics and micro-Doppler signatures. The resulting data is limited to simple metrics (0–5 persons, zone occupancy) rather than identifiable images, satisfying the strictest privacy requirements while enabling intelligent lighting, HVAC optimization, and security alerting.

Soil and Environmental Condition Monitoring in Precision Agriculture

Battery, or solar-powered soil sensors deployed in remote fields cannot afford continuous cellular transmission. Edge ML enables multi-year operation by executing classification directly on sensed parameters (moisture, temperature, electrical conductivity, NPK estimates via low-cost spectroscopy). Models predict irrigation need, detect fungal infection risk, or identify nutrient deficiency days before visible symptoms appear.

By transmitting only high-level decisions ("irrigate zone 3 tomorrow") instead of raw time-series, data volume reduced by 99 %, allowing LoRaWAN or satellite backhaul in areas without cellular coverage and bringing precision agriculture to smallholder farmers in developing regions.

These examples illustrate the maturing ecosystem of Edge ML frameworks (TensorFlowLite Micro, Edge Impulse, STMicroelectronics NanoEdge AI, Arm Ethos-U, Syntiant Core) and hardware accelerators that make sophisticated intelligence feasible on devices costing just a few dollars and consuming microwatts in sleep mode. As model compression, hardware acceleration, and automated training pipelines continue to advance, virtually every connected sensor will evolve from passive data collector to autonomous decision maker—ushering in a new generation of resilient, private, and ultra-efficient IoT systems.

Testing and Evaluating Edge Machine Learning Models in Resource-Constrained IoT Environments

The successful deployment of Edge ML models on microcontrollers, digital signal processors, and low-power application processors demands a rigorous evaluation methodology that extends far beyond the traditional accuracy metrics used in cloud-based machine learning. In evaluating an Edge ML model, engineers must simultaneously optimize for classification performance, real-time responsiveness, energy efficiency, memory footprint, and long-term robustness under varying environmental conditions.

Performance Metrics Tailored for Edge Use Cases

While overall accuracy provides a quick sanity check, it is often misleading in edge scenarios where classes are heavily imbalanced (for example, fall events occurring <0.1 % of the time, or motor failures being extremely rare). Standard tools from supervised learning therefore remain indispensable:

- **Confusion matrix**: Essential for visualizing true positives, false positives, true negatives, and false negatives across all classes. In safety-critical applications such as fall detection or gas leakage detection, the cost of false negatives is dramatically higher than false positives, making the confusion matrix the primary evaluation artifact during development.
- **Precision, Recall, and F1-score**: Precision measures the reliability of positive predictions (critical when false alarms drain battery or annoy users), whereas recall (sensitivity) measures the ability of the model to capture all actual events of interest. The harmonic mean of precision and recall—the F1-score—becomes particularly valuable when an optimal balance between the two is required. Many edge deployments target >95 % recall for critical classes even if precision drops moderately, accepting occasional false alerts rather than missing a single dangerous event.
- **Receiver Operating Characteristic (ROC) and Area Under Curve (AUC)**: When adjustable detection thresholds are available (common in anomaly detection), ROC curves help select an operating point that satisfies product requirements.

Real-Time and On-Target Validation

Laboratory validation using recorded datasets is necessary but insufficient. Edge models must be evaluated under realistic streaming conditions:

- **Live sensor testing**: The final model is flashed onto the target hardware and exposed to real sensor inputs in the actual deployment environment. This reveals problems invisible in offline evaluation, such as sensitivity to temperature-induced accelerometer drift, acoustic reverberation in voice commands, or electromagnetic interference affecting current waveforms.
- **Latency measurement**: Inference time is measured cycle-accurately using GPIO toggles or hardware timers. Acceptable latency varies by application—<50 ms for fall detection, <200 ms for voice commands, and <1 s for predictive maintenance alerts. End-to-end latency including pre-processing, inference, and post-processing must be reported.
- **Power profiling**: Using precision current measurement tools (for example, Nordic Power Profiler, Otii Arc), average and peak current during inference are recorded. Deep-sleep current, wake-up transient, and inference burst must all stay within the energy budget of coin-cell or energy-harvesting designs.

Memory and Binary Size Constraints

Microcontrollers typically offer 128 KB–1 MB of flash and 32 KB–512 KB of RAM. Evaluation therefore includes:

- Static memory footprint (flash usage for model weights, runtime, and application code).
- Peak RAM usage during inference (input buffers, activations, and stack).
- Quantized model size versus floating-point baseline—8-bit integer quantization routinely reduces model size by 4× with <1 % accuracy loss, often making the difference between fitting and not fitting on the target device.

Tools such as TensorFlowLite Micro Analyzer, STM32Cube.AI Analyzer, and the deployment reports of Edge Impulse provide automated breakdown of memory consumption before physical deployment.

Overfitting and Generalization Assessment

Tiny datasets collected in controlled settings frequently cause severe overfitting. Common validation strategies include:

- **Hold-out test set** from different devices, users, environments, and seasons than the training data.
- **k-fold cross-validation** adapted to time-series (non-shuffled folds to preserve temporal structure).
- **On-device fine-tuning validation**: After initial cloud training, a portion of devices in the field collect new labeled samples and perform lightweight transfer learning, verifying that the model can adapt without catastrophic forgetting.

Robustness and Corner-Case Testing

Edge devices operate in harsh, variable conditions:

- **Environmental robustness**: Models are tested across temperature (–20 °C to +70 °C), humidity, mechanical shock, and supply voltage brown-outs.
- **Sensor degradation simulation**: Gradual offset or noise injection mimics aging accelerometers or contaminated gas sensors.
- **Adversarial and out-of-distribution testing**: Deliberately corrupted inputs (loud impulsive noise during keyword spotting, magnetic interference on current sensors) verify graceful degradation rather than confident misclassification.

Continuous Post-Deployment Evaluation

Leading deployments implement Over-the-Air (OTA) model updates combined with silent telemetry that reports confusion matrix statistics, inference latency distribution, and memory utilization back to the development team (while fully anonymized and only for correctly authenticated devices). This closed-loop approach enables fleet-wide monitoring for concept drift—such as changing acoustic environments in smart homes or evolving vibration patterns as machinery wears—and triggers retraining when degradation exceeds predefined thresholds.

Limitations of Edge Machine Learning and Strategic Decision: When to Offload to the Cloud

Although Edge ML has transformed the capabilities of battery-powered and disconnected IoT devices, it operates under severe physical and architectural constraints that fundamentally limit the complexity and performance of models that can be deployed. Understanding these limitations is essential for system architects when deciding whether intelligence should remain fully on the edge, be partitioned between edge and cloud (hybrid approach), or be offloaded entirely to cloud or gateway servers.

Fundamental Resource Constraints on the Edge

Modern high-end microcontrollers used for Edge ML (STM32H7, nRF54, Maxim MAX78000, GAP9, ESP32-S3 with NPU) typically provide 512 KB to 2 MB of flash memory and 128 KB to 1 MB of RAM, of which only a fraction is available after reserving space for the application firmware, communication stack, and real-time operating system. Specialized AI accelerators such as Ethos-U55, Syntiant Core 3, or Cadence Tensilica Vision even when present, support only a few hundred Giga-operations per second at sub-milliwatt power—orders of magnitude below smartphone NPUs or desktop GPUs.

These restrictions directly translate into severe limitations on model capacity. Even aggressively quantized (8-bit or binary) neural networks rarely exceed 500 KB in weight storage on true edge nodes, restricting practitioners to models with fewer than roughly 300 000 parameters. Consequently, only shallow architectures—tiny convolutional networks, depthwise separable convolutions, decision trees, boosted ensembles, or heavily pruned transformers—can be executed within real-time and energy budgets. State-of-the-art mobile-scale models such as MobileNetV3, EfficientNet-Lite, or modern vision transformers (several million to hundreds of millions of parameters) are simply infeasible without unacceptable latency or memory overflow.

Accuracy on complex perceptual tasks therefore suffers dramatically. For example, keyword spotting on edge routinely achieves >97% accuracy on 10–20 commands, but speaker identification, continuous speech recognition, or natural language understanding remain far below usable performance. Similarly, image classification on 224×224 RGB images rarely exceeds 70–75% top-1 accuracy on challenging datasets such as ImageNet subsets when restricted to <250 KB models, compared to >90 % from cloud-scale models.

Another critical limitation is the inability to train or fine-tune on large datasets directly on the device. Edge devices lack both the storage and computational capacity to handle gigabytes of training data or perform backpropagation at scale. While techniques such as federated learning and tiny on-device transfer learning are emerging, they remain limited to minor weight adjustments rather than full retraining. This makes edge-only solutions brittle when environmental conditions drift significantly from the original training distribution (for example, new accents, new machinery types, or seasonal changes in agricultural fields).

Power and thermal constraints further exacerbate these issues. Sustained high utilization of AI accelerators rapidly depletes coin-cell batteries and can cause thermal throttling in sealed industrial sensors, forcing designers to duty-cycle inference and accept blind periods.

Scenarios Where Cloud or Gateway Processing Remains Mandatory

Despite rapid progress in edge compression techniques, several classes of IoT applications continue to demand cloud or near-edge (gateway/fog) processing:

- **High-Resolution Vision and Video Analytics:** Object detection, instance segmentation, facial recognition, license-plate reading, and defect inspection on megapixel images or video streams require models with tens to hundreds of millions of parameters (YOLOv8, EfficientDet, Vision Transformers). Even with aggressive pruning and quantization, such models demand gigabytes of RAM and multiple watts of power—impossible on battery-powered edge nodes. These tasks are therefore typically performed on AC-powered gateways, industrial PCs, or directly in the cloud after secure video streaming.
- **Multimodal Sensor Fusion Involving Large Modalities:** Applications combining high-bandwidth sensors—such as simultaneous processing of 1080p video, multi-channel audio, LiDAR point clouds, and inertial data (autonomous drones, advanced driver-assistance systems, robotic manipulation)—generate data rates of tens to hundreds of megabits per second. Fusion models that jointly reason across modalities (for example, audio-visual speech recognition, video + IMU action recognition) are far too large and data-hungry for edge deployment and must execute on powerful edge servers or cloud instances.
- **Continuous Learning and Large-Scale Personalization:** When models that must adapt to thousands of users, languages, or environments (voice assistants learning new commands over months, recommendation systems, medical diagnostics refined per patient) require centralized training on massive datasets followed by periodic model update distribution. Pure edge learning cannot achieve comparable personalization quality or convergence speed.

- **Complex Time-Series and Anomaly Detection over Long Windows:** Predictive maintenance systems monitoring weeks or months of multi-sensor data, fraud detection in smart meters, or network intrusion detection frequently employ recurrent architectures or transformers with attention over thousands of time steps. Such models exceed edge memory capacity and are better suited to cloud execution with occasional summary statistics transmitted from sensors.
- **Regulatory or Audit Requirements for Full Data Access:** In certain healthcare, financial, and legal applications, regulations mandate that raw data or full inference traces be stored centrally for audit trails. Edge-only processing that discards raw data immediately after inference cannot satisfy these requirements.

Hybrid Edge–Cloud Architectures as Practical Compromise

In practice, most production IoT systems adopt tiered intelligence: simple, frequent, privacy-sensitive, or latency-critical decisions (fall detection, keyword spotting, basic anomaly flagging) execute fully on the edge, while rare, complex, or accuracy-critical tasks trigger compressed data upload to a gateway or cloud for heavyweight processing. Confidence thresholding is commonly used—when edge model confidence falls below a calibrated threshold, raw or lightly processed data is transmitted for re-evaluation. This approach delivers the best trade-off among latency, bandwidth, privacy, and accuracy.

In conclusion, while Edge ML continues to expand the frontier of on-device intelligence each year, physical laws and economic realities ensure that cloud-scale models will remain indispensable for the foreseeable future. Successful IoT architects master not only model compression, but also the disciplined partitioning of intelligence across the edge-to-cloud continuum according to application constraints and business objectives.

Practical Optimization Techniques for TinyML and Edge ML Deployments

Deploying machine learning models on microcontrollers with only a few hundred kilobytes of RAM and flash requires aggressive, systematic optimization at every layer of the stack. The goal is not merely to make the model "fit," but to achieve the best possible accuracy within strict real-time, energy, and memory budgets. The following techniques, when applied in combination, routinely reduce model size and energy consumption by 5–20× while preserving >98 % of original floating-point accuracy.

Post-Training Quantization (PTQ) and Quantization-Aware Training (QAT)

The single most effective optimization remains quantization of weights and activations from 32-bit floating point to 8 bit integers (int8), and in extreme cases to 4-bit or even ternary/binary representations.

Post-training quantization analyzes the dynamic range of each layer after full-precision training and selects optimal scaling factors. Modern tools (TensorFlowLite Converter, STM32Cube.AI, Edge Impulse) routinely achieve 3.5–4× reduction in model size and 2.5–4× faster inference with typically <1% accuracy drop on classification tasks.

Quantization-aware training inserts fake quantization nodes during the training process itself, allowing the optimizer to learn robustness to reduced precision. QAT is essential when pushing below int8 or when the task is highly sensitive (for example, audio event detection, anomaly detection), and can recover nearly all lost accuracy.

For ultra-low-power devices, 8-bit weight / 8-bit activation (W8A8) is now considered the standard baseline, with many vendors providing dedicated int8 matrix-multiply accelerators.

Structured and Unstructured Pruning

Pruning systematically removes parameters with the least impact on output.

Magnitude-based unstructured pruning zeros individual weights and is combined with quantization to produce sparse models that can be compressed further using sparse storage formats.

Structured pruning (channel-wise, filter-wise, or layer-wise) removes entire filters, rows, or neurons, preserving dense matrix operations and yielding direct speedups on standard CPU/NPU hardware without special sparse libraries.

Iterative pruning followed by fine-tuning (prune → retrain → repeat) can eliminate 80–95 % of parameters in convolutional and fully connected layers with negligible accuracy degradation. When combined with quantization, total model compression routinely exceeds 10–20×.

Knowledge Distillation

A large, highly accurate teacher model (trained in the cloud) is used to generate soft labels that guide a much smaller student model during training. The student learns not only the correct class lessons but also the confidence distribution of the teacher, achieving significantly higher accuracy than if trained directly on hard labels. Distillation is especially valuable when the compressed model must operate far from its natural accuracy-capacity curve.

Architecture Selection and Neural Architecture Search (NAS) for TinyML

Starting with an inherently efficient backbone is often more effective than heavy compression of a large model. Proven tiny-friendly architectures include:

- MobileNetV2/V3, EfficientNet-Lite, and TinyML-specific variants (ProxylessNAS, Once-for-All networks, and MCUNet series explicitly optimize for MCU constraints during search.
- Depthwise separable convolutions, inverted residuals, squeeze-and-excitation blocks, and 1×1 pointwise convolutions dramatically reduce computation at minimal accuracy cost.

Many commercial tools now ship pre-optimized architecture templates that already respect target MCU memory limits.

Feature Engineering and Pre-processing Optimization

Raw sensor data is rarely fed directly into neural networks on microcontrollers.

- Hand-crafted lightweight statistical features (mean, variance, RMS, zero-crossing rate, spectral centroid, peak-to-peak, FFT bins) often outperform learned features on tiny datasets and execute orders of magnitude faster.
- Fixed-point signal processing pipelines (decimation, filtering, windowing) are implemented with integer arithmetic and look-up tables.
- Dimensionality reduction via Principal Component Analysis (PCA) or manual band selection is performed offline, and only the reduced feature vector is computed on-device.

Memory Management Discipline

Dynamic memory allocation (malloc/free) is strictly forbidden in most production TinyML firmware due to fragmentation risks and non-deterministic timing.

- All tensors, activation buffers, and intermediate results are pre-allocated as static arrays or placed in CCM (Core-Coupled Memory) on supported MCUs.

- Tensor arenas are carefully sized and aligned; the TensorFlowLite Micro interpreter requires a single contiguous arena that must accommodate the largest activation set during inference.
- Input pipelines reuse the same buffer (in-place processing) wherever possible to minimize RAM usage.

Operator Fusion and Kernel Optimization

Framework-level optimizations automatically fuse consecutive operations (Conv2D + BiasAdd + ReLU→ single kernel) to eliminate temporary buffers and memory traffic. Vendor-specific libraries (CMSIS-NN, Ethos-U NPU driver, STM32 AI runtime) provide highly optimized int8 kernels that exploit SIMD instructions, DMA and achieve >90% of theoretical peak MAC utilization.

Inference Scheduling and Duty Cycling

Even an optimized model can drain a battery if run continuously. Practical systems employ:

- Event-triggered wake-up (accelerometer threshold, always-on audio detector).
- **Multi-stage cascades:** An ultra-low-power always-on model detects candidates, waking the main MCU only when necessary.
- Adaptive sampling rates based on context (higher rate during motion, lower when stationary).

Toolchain-Assisted Deployment Workflow

Modern TinyML platforms automate most of the above steps, delivering fully optimized C libraries that integrate seamlessly with MCU IDEs and RTOSes. These tools also provide accurate pre-deployment estimates of RAM, flash, latency, and energy per inference on the exact target hardware.

By methodically applying quantization, pruning, distillation, efficient architectures, and disciplined memory handling, engineers routinely deploy models that achieve cloud-grade accuracy while consuming only a few kilobytes of RAM and a few microjoules per inference—enabling a new generation of truly intelligent, decade-lasting, battery-powered IoT devices.

Hands-On Practical Exercises for Edge Machine Learning in IoT

To reinforce the concepts of data collection, model training, and deployment discussed in previous sections, this chapter includes three guided practical exercises. These activities are designed for learners with basic familiarity with microcontroller programming (for example: Arduino IDE) and require affordable hardware such as an ESP32 board, sensors like DHT11 (temperature/humidity), LDR (light-dependent resistor), or a 3-axis accelerometer (for example: ADXL345 or MPU6050). The exercises use free tools like Edge Impulse for model development, ensuring accessibility for educational and hobbyist settings. Each exercise builds on the previous one, starting from raw data gathering and culminating in a fully operational edge inference system. Safety note: Always handle electronics with care, ensuring proper voltage levels and avoiding short circuits.

Exercise 1: Building a Sensor Logging System for Dataset Creation

The primary objective of this exercise is to assemble a simple IoT sensor node that collects time-series data from environmental or motion sensors, labels it appropriately, and exports it in a structured format suitable for machine learning training. High-quality, labeled datasets are the foundation of effective Edge ML models, and this hands-on activity teaches the importance of real-world data variability, noise handling, and manual annotation.

Step 1: Connecting the Sensors to the Microcontroller

Begin by assembling the hardware setup. Select a microcontroller board such as the ESP32 or Arduino Nano 33 BLE Sense, which offers built-in analog/digital pins and sufficient processing power for basic logging. Connect the DHT11 sensor to a digital pin (for example, GPIO 4 on ESP32) for temperature and humidity readings, the LDR to an analog pin (for example : GPIO 34) via a voltage divider circuit to measure light intensity, and the accelerometer to I2C pins (for example : SDA on GPIO 21 and SCL on GPIO 22) for motion detection. Use jumper wires and a breadboard for prototyping. Power the setup via USB or a battery pack, and verify connections using a multimeter to ensure no loose wires or incorrect pin assignments. This step establishes the physical interface between the sensors and the processor, allowing raw analog or digital signals to be captured.

Step 2: Implementing Periodic Data Logging

Program the microcontroller to read sensor values at regular intervals. Using the Arduino IDE or PlatformIO, write a firmware sketch that initializes the sensors in the setup function and, in the main loop, queries each sensor every 500 milliseconds (half a second) to simulate real-time monitoring without overwhelming the system. For the DHT11, use a library to retrieve temperature and humidity floats; for the LDR, read the analog voltage and convert it to a lux approximation; for the accelerometer, fetch x, y, z acceleration values in g units. Store each reading in a timestamped structure, including the current `millis()` time or an RTC-derived timestamp for chronological accuracy. This logging frequency balances data density with power efficiency, capturing enough samples to represent dynamic events like motion, while avoiding excessive storage demands.

Step 3: Manual Labeling of Sensor States

As data is collected, introduce manual labeling to create supervised training examples. During operation, observe the sensor behavior and annotate states in real time or post-collection. For instance, shake the accelerometer to simulate "motion" and leave it stationary for "still," or vary light exposure for "bright" versus "dim" with the LDR. Use a serial monitor or a connected app to input labels via button presses or keyboard commands, associating each data sample or window (for example, 10 consecutive readings) with a categorical label. This step highlights the human effort required for ground-truth annotation, teaching how imbalanced classes (for example, more "still" than "motion") can arise naturally and affect model performance.

Step 4: Exporting the Dataset for Further Use

Once sufficient data is gathered (aim for at least 1,000–5,000 labeled samples per class), export it in a machine-readable format. Serialize the timestamped readings and labels into a CSV file stored on an SD card module connected to the microcontroller or transmit them wirelessly via Wi-Fi/Bluetooth to a computer or directly to Google Sheets using an API integration. Structure the CSV with columns for timestamp, sensor values (for example, temp, hum, light, `accel_x`, `accel_y`, `accel_z`), and label. Review the exported file for completeness, removing any corrupted entries due to sensor glitches. This final step prepares the dataset for upload to ML platforms, emphasizing data hygiene practices like normalization previews and outlier detection.

Exercise 2: Training a Classifier Model Using Edge Impulse

Building on the dataset from Exercise 1, this activity focuses on cloud-assisted model training tailored for edge devices. Edge Impulse is a user-friendly platform that handles data preprocessing, feature extraction, and model optimization without requiring deep ML expertise, making it ideal for IoT prototyping. The goal is to create a classifier that can distinguish states like "motion" versus "still" with high accuracy.

Step 1: Uploading the Collected Dataset to Edge Impulse

Create a free account on the Edge Impulse website and start a new project classified as "time-series" or "sensor data." Upload the CSV file from Exercise 1 directly via the data acquisition tab of the dashboard, ensuring the file is parsed correctly with timestamps aligned. Split the dataset automatically into training (70–80%), validation (10–15%), and test (10–15%) sets. This step integrates your real-world data into the ML workflow, allowing the platform to visualize distributions and identify any upload errors early.

Step 2: Preprocessing the Data for Model Readiness

In the preprocessing stage, apply filters to clean the raw signals: use a low-pass filter to remove high-frequency noise from accelerometer data, normalize values to a standard scale (for example, 0–1 or mean-zero unit variance) to handle sensor variability, and segment the time-series into fixed windows (for example: 2–5 seconds) with overlap for feature extraction. The blocks of Edge Impulse like spectral analysis (FFT for frequency-domain features) or statistical summaries (mean, variance, and kurtosis) can be chained here. Experiment with different configurations and preview the processed data to ensure artifacts like sensor drift are mitigated, preparing a robust input representation for training.

Step 3: Training the Classifier Model

Select a neural network architecture suitable for tiny devices, such as a 1D convolutional neural network or a fully connected classifier, from the impulse design tab of Edge Impulse. Initiate training with default hyperparameters (for example: 100 epochs, Adam optimizer), monitoring progress via the live dashboard. The platform automatically handles class balancing if needed. This step demonstrates how cloud resources accelerate training that would be infeasible on the edge, resulting in a model optimized for accuracy while respecting MCU constraints.

Step 4: Evaluating Model Accuracy and Performance

After training, review the confusion matrix, precision, recall, and F1-score on the validation and test sets to assess generalization. Use live classification mode to feed new unlabeled data and check for misclassifications. If accuracy is below 90 %, iterate by adjusting preprocessing or adding more data. Export performance metrics and consider on-device estimates for latency and memory. This evaluation reinforces the iterative nature of ML development, ensuring the model is reliable before deployment.

Exercise 3: Deploying the Trained Model to a Microcontroller

The final exercise shifts focus to edge deployment, where the model from Exercise 2 is integrated into firmware for autonomous inference. This bridges the gap between cloud training and real-world operation, highlighting optimization for low-power hardware.

Step 1: Exporting the Model as an Arduino-Compatible Library

In Edge Impulse, navigate to the deployment tab and select "Arduino Library export", which generates a ZIP file containing quantized model weights, inference engine, and example sketches. Choose optimizations like int8 quantization to minimize size. Download and extract the library, then import it into the Arduino IDE via the library manager. This step converts the abstract ML model into embeddable C++ code, ready for microcontroller integration.

Step 2: Flashing the Model and Firmware to the Device

Open the provided example sketch in the Arduino IDE, modify it to interface with your sensors from Exercise 1 (for example, replace placeholders with DHT11/LDR/accelerometer reads), and compile for your target board (ESP32 or Nano 33 BLE Sense). Connect the device via USB, select the correct port and board type, and upload the firmware. Monitor the serial console for boot messages confirming model loading. This flashing process embeds the ML intelligence directly onto the hardware, enabling offline operation.

Step 3: Testing Inference with Live Sensor Inputs

Power the device and expose it to real scenarios: for motion detection, move the board and observe serial outputs or LED indicators showing predicted labels like "motion" or "still." Measure inference latency (typically <50 ms) and compare predictions against manual observations. Debug any discrepancies by checking sensor calibration or model confidence scores. Iterate by reflashing updated models if needed. This hands-on testing validates the end-to-end pipeline, demonstrating how Edge ML delivers low-latency, privacy-preserving decisions in IoT applications.

These exercises provide a complete workflow from data to deployment, encouraging experimentation and troubleshooting. Advanced variations could include multi-sensor fusion or OTA updates, but mastering these basics equips you to tackle real-world Edge ML challenges in smart homes, wearables, and industrial monitoring.

Conclusion

This chapter has provided a comprehensive introduction to the transformative field of Edge Machine Learning and TinyML—the practice of executing fully functional machine learning models directly on resource-constrained IoT endpoints such as microcontrollers, sensor nodes, and battery-powered embedded devices. Rather than merely collecting raw measurements and forwarding them to distant servers, modern IoT systems can now interpret sensor data locally, make informed decisions in milliseconds, and act autonomously while preserving bandwidth, privacy, and energy. The core philosophy of Edge AI is simple yet powerful: move the intelligence to where the data is born, not the data to where the intelligence resides.

Through detailed examination of production-grade use cases—elderly fall detection using IMU patterns, always-on keyword spotting in voice interfaces, predictive vibration monitoring for industrial assets, privacy-preserving occupancy detection, and electrical anomaly detection in smart plugs—students have seen how these techniques are already saving lives, preventing equipment failures, reducing energy waste, and enabling new product categories that were previously impossible due to latency, cost, or privacy constraints. The chapter also candidly addressed the current boundaries of Edge ML: severe memory and compute limitations, reduced accuracy on complex perceptual tasks, and the continued necessity of hybrid edge-cloud architectures for high-resolution vision, multimodal fusion, and large-scale continuous learning. Understanding when to keep processing local and when to strategically offload remains a key architectural skill.

By completing the hands-on exercises, students have gained practical proficiency in the entire TinyML pipeline—from breadboard to deployed intelligent device. These skills are immediately applicable to domains as diverse as wearable health monitors, smart agriculture sensors, home automation controllers, environmental monitoring networks, and industrial condition-based maintenance systems. Equipped with the foundations presented in this chapter, readers are now prepared to design the next generation of truly smart, resilient, and autonomous IoT ecosystems that do not merely observe the physical world but truly understand and respond to it in real time. Thus, the era of passive data collectors is over; the age of perceptive, decision-making devices has begun.

The next chapter builds on these foundations by moving from intelligent prototypes to industry-ready IoT products. *Chapter 15, Deployment, Testing, and Scaling*, covers essential skills for real-world deployment—testing strategies, version control, OTA updates, monitoring, scalability planning, and long-term device maintenance. It also provides practical career guidance and professional workflows to help students transition from classroom projects to robust, production-grade IoT systems.

Chapter 15
Deployment, Testing, and Scaling

Introduction

The preceding chapters have equipped readers with the essential building blocks of modern IoT systems: sensor interfacing, embedded firmware development, secure communication protocols, cloud integration, data analytics, and the incorporation of Edge AI and TinyML capabilities. These tools enable the creation of sophisticated prototypes that demonstrate core functionality – whether monitoring environmental conditions, controlling actuators, detecting anomalies, or making autonomous decisions at the edge. However, the transition from a laboratory prototype to a reliable, field-deployed product represents, one of the most challenging and often underestimated phases in the IoT development lifecycle. While initial prototyping may consume only 20–30% of project time, the critical process of hardening for production – covering security, reliability, scalability, and certification–often consumes 50–70% of the overall effort.

In real-world deployments, IoT devices must operate continuously for years in harsh environments, withstand power fluctuations, cope with intermittent connectivity, recover gracefully from failures, receive secure updates without physical access, and scale seamlessly from a handful of units to tens or thousands, or even millions. A single unpatched vulnerability, a poorly managed firmware update, or an unscalable cloud architecture can lead to catastrophic consequences, including safety risks, costly recalls, or complete project failure.

Upon completing this chapter, readers will possess the knowledge required to bridge the critical gap between innovation and industrial deployment. They will be prepared not only to build intelligent devices but also to operate, secure, update, and scale them profitably at scale. This final stage of the IoT lifecycle marks the true maturity of any IoT practitioner and opens doors to career opportunities in product engineering, DevOps for embedded systems, fleet operations, and strategic roles in leading IoT companies.

Structure

In this chapter, we will cover the following topics:

- Understanding Production-Level Deployment Needs in IoT Systems
- Firmware Versioning and OTA Update Pipelines
- Managing Configuration Remotely (JSON Files, Secure Tokens)

- Platform IO and Continuous Integration/Continuous Deployment (CI/CD)
- Functional Testing: Sensors, APIs, Dashboards
- Regression Testing and Version Rollback Plan
- Secure Device Provisioning for Fleets
- Power Optimization for 24×7 Deployments
- Field Readiness Checklist
- Basics of Fleet Management
- Cost Considerations for Scaling IoT Projects
- Common Failure Modes and Recovery Strategies
- Final Project Checklist Template
- Career Pathway: Skills to Become an IoT Developer and Architect,
- Future of IoT: LEO Satellites, 5G, Federated Learning, Zero-Trust Security

Understanding Production-Level Deployment Needs in IoT Systems

The transition from a working prototype to a production-grade IoT deployment represents one of the most significant leaps in the development lifecycle. While a prototype demonstrates feasibility and proves core functionality in a controlled laboratory environment, a production system must operate reliably, securely, and economically at scale across thousands or millions of devices in unpredictable real-world conditions. The differences between these two stages are profound and often underestimated, leading to costly rework or outright project failure when prototypes are prematurely deployed to the field.

Prototypes are inherently designed for rapid iteration and developer convenience. Firmware is typically flashed manually via USB or JTAG using development tools such as the Arduino IDE, PlatformIO, or vendor-specific flashers. Security credentials—such as Wi-Fi passwords, cloud API keys, or TLS certificates—are often hardcoded directly into the source code for simplicity. Testing occurs on a single device or a handful of units under ideal conditions, with debug logging enabled continuously to aid troubleshooting. Power supplies are stable, connectivity is reliable, and human intervention is expected and frequent. These characteristics accelerate development but introduce practices that are fundamentally incompatible with long-term field operation.

Prototype	Production
Update Method: Typically flashed manually via USB or JTAG	**Update Method:** Over-the-Air (OTA) or automated production line flashing
Credential Storage: Hardcoded or simple, non-secure storage	**Credential Storage:** Secure Element, Hardware Security Module (HSM), or secure encrypted storage
Testing Rigor: Functionality testing, limited stress/long-term testing	**Testing Rigor:** Comprehensive stress testing, regulatory compliance testing, long-term reliability
Power Source: Bench power supply, battery intended for temporary use	**Power Source:** Final regulated power supply, optimized for long-term efficiency and reliability
Logging Strategy: Verbose debugging logs, often sent over serial/USB	**Logging Strategy:** Minimal, efficient logs focused on errors and critical events, often sent to a remote server
Bill of Materials (BOM): May use expensive or non-optimized components	**Bill of Materials (BOM):** Cost-optimized, supply-chain robust, and mass-market components

Table 15.1: *Difference between the Prototype and Production*

In contrast, a production IoT system must be engineered from the outset to minimize human intervention, withstand harsh environments, and survive inevitable failures. Devices are deployed in remote locations—industrial plants, agricultural fields, urban infrastructure, or consumer homes—where physical access is expensive or impossible. Firmware updates must occur remotely Over-the-Air (OTA) to deliver security patches, new features, or bug fixes without recalling devices. Credentials must be stored securely using hardware-protected mechanisms such as secure elements, Trusted Platform Modules (TPM), or MCU-integrated secure storage, and never exposed in source code or firmware binaries.

Testing shifts from manual single-device validation to fully automated pipelines that simulate real-world variability: temperature cycling, power brown-outs, network dropouts, electromagnetic interference. Typical qualification runs involve testing 10 to 50 units over 30 to 90 days of accelerated life testing to generate statistically significant reliability data and accelerated aging. Reliability becomes paramount, with systems designed for multi-year operation on limited power sources, often with Mean Time between Failures (MTBF) measured in decades. Logging is minimized or encrypted to preserve bandwidth and battery life, while diagnostic telemetry is transmitted only when necessary and under strict privacy controls.

A core principle of production IoT design is the assumption that failure is inevitable. Connectivity will drop, power will fail, sensors will drift, memory will corrupt, and attackers will probe vulnerabilities. Therefore, the system must incorporate robust fault tolerance: automatic recovery from crashes via watchdog timers, graceful degradation when sensors fail, redundant communication paths (for example, cellular fallback for Wi-Fi failures), and self-healing mechanisms such as configuration rollback or firmware reverts. Devices should be capable of operating in degraded modes—reporting critical alerts even when full functionality is unavailable—and support zero-touch provisioning so that newly manufactured units can join the fleet securely without manual configuration.

Firmware Versioning and Over-the-Air (OTA) Update Pipelines

In production IoT deployments, the ability to update device firmware remotely—known as Over-the-Air (OTA) updates—is not merely a convenience but a fundamental requirement for long-term viability, security, and competitiveness. Once devices are installed in remote locations, embedded in infrastructure, or deployed in consumer products, physical access for manual flashing becomes prohibitively expensive, logistically impractical, or entirely impossible. OTA enables manufacturers and operators to deliver critical security patches, resolve functional bugs, introduce new features, optimize performance, and even extend product lifespan without ever touching the hardware again.

The primary motivations for OTA are rooted in the realities of connected devices operating over extended periods. Security vulnerabilities discovered post-deployment—whether zero-day exploits, cryptographic weaknesses, or protocol flaws—must be addressed immediately to prevent widespread compromise. Regulatory frameworks increasingly mandate timely patching for consumer IoT and industrial systems (IEC 62443). Beyond security, OTA allows continuous improvement: adding support for new cloud services, improving energy efficiency, enhancing AI models via updated TinyML weights, or adapting to changing network conditions. Feature rollouts can be staged gradually, starting with beta cohorts and expanding based on field performance, minimizing risk to the entire fleet.

Effective OTA pipelines must be robust, secure, and user-friendly. At minimum, they require a secure communication channel (typically HTTPS/TLS 1.3 with mutual authentication), a verifiable firmware binary (signed with cryptographic keys), and a mechanism for the device to check for updates periodically or on demand. Critical safeguards include integrity verification before installation, rollback capability in case of failed updates, and a failsafe boot mechanism that reverts to the previous working version if the new firmware does not boot correctly. This safety is often enabled by dual-partition architectures, where MCUs like the ESP32 reserve two firmware slots (active and backup) to enable safe, atomic Over-The-Air updates successfully. Differential updates—transmitting only the changes since the last version—dramatically reduce bandwidth usage, making OTA feasible even over constrained networks such as NB-IoT, LoRaWAN, or cellular with low data plans. Advanced versioning practices include channel-based strategies: stable channels for production devices, beta channels for early adopters, and development channels for internal testing. Rollout policies can enforce gradual deployment (for example, 5 % of devices first, then 20 %, then 100 %) with automatic pause or rollback if error rates exceed thresholds. For high-security applications, updates may require multi-factor approval or staged key rotation.

By implementing disciplined versioning and a secure, resilient OTA pipeline, IoT operators ensure that devices remain secure, functional, and valuable throughout their operational life—often spanning five to ten years or more. This capability transforms static hardware into living, evolving products and forms the foundation of modern IoT fleet management.

Managing Configuration Remotely

One of the most common mistakes in transitioning from prototype to production IoT devices is hardcoding critical parameters directly into the firmware. Thresholds for alerts (for example, temperature limits, acceleration spikes for fall detection), timing constants (sampling intervals, watchdog periods, OTA check frequency), operational modes (debug versus production logging, Wi-Fi credentials, cloud endpoints), and feature flags are all examples of values that may need adjustment after deployment. Embedding these as compile-time constants forces developers to reflash every device for even minor tweaks, making the system brittle, slow to iterate, and expensive to maintain at scale. For example, a fleet of 10,000 units with hardcoded 5-minute data polling may cost $X/ month in cloud resources; changing to adaptive 15-minute intervals requires reflashing all devices (potentially days of downtime) versus instantly updating a cloud configuration (takes 5 minutes).

Remote configuration management addresses this limitation by treating configuration as dynamic, external data rather than static code. The device fetches its configuration from a remote source at boot time and periodically thereafter, applying changes immediately without requiring a firmware update. This approach enables operators to tune behavior across the entire fleet in minutes, respond to field conditions (such as seasonal environmental changes or new regulatory requirements), conduct A/B testing of features, and roll back problematic settings—all while the devices remain in the field.

A typical remote configuration architecture stores settings in a structured, human-readable format such as JSON. The configuration file might reside on a cloud-hosted service that provides high availability, low latency, and strong access controls. The device implements a lightweight configuration client that runs on boot and at configurable intervals (for example, every 6–24 hours, or on demand via a cloud-triggered signal). Upon connection, it sends its device ID, current firmware version, and optionally a hash of the last known configuration to the server. The server responds with the full or delta configuration payload. The device parses the JSON, validates its schema (to prevent malformed data from causing crashes), and applies the new values to runtime variables, persistent storage (for example, NVS on ESP32, EEPROM emulation, or filesystem), or feature flags.

Advanced implementations support hierarchical configuration: global defaults overridden by device-group settings (for example, per-region or per-model), and individual device overrides for troubleshooting. Changes can be scheduled (for example, activate power-saving mode at night) or conditional (for example, enable verbose logging only if battery level is above 80 %). For high-security applications, sensitive parameters (such as encryption keys) may be delivered via a separate secure channel or derived on-device using a hardware security module. By decoupling configuration from firmware, remote management transforms static embedded systems into adaptable, living products. Operators gain the agility to optimize performance, fix misconfigurations, and deploy new behaviors without the overhead of OTA firmware updates. This practice is a cornerstone of mature IoT fleets, enabling cost-effective operation at scale while maintaining the flexibility needed to evolve with changing requirements and environments.

Platform IO and Continuous Integration/ Continuous Deployment (CI/CD)

As IoT projects mature from single-device prototypes to multi-model product lines, the development workflow must evolve to support collaboration, repeatability, quality assurance, and rapid iteration across diverse hardware targets. Traditional Arduino IDE workflows, while excellent for beginners and quick experiments, quickly become limiting when managing large codebases, multiple board variants, library dependencies, and automated testing. This is where PlatformIO emerges as the professional-grade tool of choice for embedded IoT development.

PlatformIO is an open-source, cross-platform build system and Integrated Development Environment (IDE) extension that runs on top of Visual Studio Code, CLion, or as a standalone command-line tool. It addresses the pain points of embedded development by providing a structured, professional project layout that separates source code, libraries, tests, and configuration files in a consistent, version-control-friendly manner. Unlike the flat sketch structure of Arduino IDE, PlatformIO enforces a clean directory hierarchy—src/ for application code, lib/ for custom libraries, test/ for unit tests, and a platformio.ini manifest file that declares all dependencies and build targets. While PlatformIO requires initial setup (VS Code extension, platformio.ini syntax), the payoff in team collaboration and automated workflows becomes clear within days. One of the most powerful features of PlatformIO is its library dependency management. Developers specify libraries and their exact versions (or ranges) in the platformio.ini file, and PlatformIO automatically downloads, installs, and updates them from the global registry or private repositories. This eliminates the library hell common in Arduino projects where mismatched versions cause cryptic compile errors. PlatformIO supports thousands of libraries, including popular IoT frameworks such as ESPAsyncWebServer, PubSubClient, ArduinoJson, and TinyML runtimes, ensuring consistent builds across team members and CI servers.

Integrating PlatformIO with Continuous Integration/Continuous Deployment (CI/CD) pipelines brings the same DevOps rigor to embedded firmware that software teams have enjoyed for years. GitHub Actions is the most popular choice for IoT projects due to its native integration with GitHub repositories, generous free tier, and extensive marketplace of pre-built actions. A typical CI/CD workflow for an IoT project includes:

- **Automated builds:** On every push or pull request, the pipeline triggers PlatformIO to compile the firmware for all defined environments, catching compile errors or dependency conflicts early.
- **Static analysis and linting:** Tools such as cpp check, clang-tidy, or custom scripts run automatically to enforce code quality and security best practices.
- **Unit and integration testing:** The native test runner of PlatformIO executes host-based unit tests (using frameworks like Unity or GoogleTest) and simulated integration tests, reporting results back to the pull request.
- **Firmware artifact generation:** Successful builds produce binary files (.bin, .elf, .uf2), size reports, and memory usage summaries that are stored as release artifacts.
- **Release automation:** On tagged commits (for example: v1.2.3), the pipeline creates GitHub Releases with signed binaries, changelog summaries, and OTA update packages ready for deployment.

This workflow mirrors industry-standard DevOps practices adapted for resource-constrained embedded systems. It ensures that every code change is validated against the exact target hardware configurations, reduces human error, accelerates release cycles, and provides full traceability from commit to deployed firmware. For larger teams, the pipeline can extend to automated OTA deployment to staging devices, security scanning of binaries, and notifications to Slack or email on failures.

By adopting PlatformIO and CI/CD, IoT developers achieve the same level of professionalism and velocity as their cloud-native counterparts. The combination enables scalable, collaborative development of reliable, maintainable firmware—essential for delivering secure, high-quality IoT products that can evolve over years of field operation.

Functional Testing: Sensors, APIs, Dashboards

Functional testing forms the cornerstone of validation for any production IoT system, ensuring that every subsystem performs its intended purpose reliably under realistic conditions before devices are committed to the field. Unlike unit testing, which focuses on isolated code modules, functional testing evaluates the integrated behavior of the complete device—from sensor input through processing, communication, actuation, and cloud interaction—to confirm that the system delivers the expected end-to-end results. This stage is critical because a single undetected flaw, such as intermittent connectivity drops or sensor drift under temperature variation, can cascade into widespread operational failures, data loss, or safety risks once deployed at scale. Production IoT systems typically aim for 80–90% functional test coverage of user-facing features and safety-critical paths.

Functional tests must be comprehensive, covering all key subsystems and their interactions. A well-designed test suite includes:

- **Sensor accuracy and stability validation:** Calibrate each sensor against reference standards (for example, using a controlled temperature chamber for DHT22 or BME680, a known light source for photodiodes, or a shaker table for accelerometers). Record multiple readings across the operating range and compare against expected values, calculating metrics such as mean error, standard deviation, hysteresis, and long-term drift. Test under environmental extremes—temperature cycling, humidity swings, vibration, and electromagnetic interference—to verify robustness and detect anomalies like offset errors or non-linearity.
- **Wireless connectivity and reconnection reliability:** Simulate real-world network conditions by intentionally introducing packet loss, signal attenuation, and access point outages. Measure time-to-connect, reconnection success rate after power cycles or network failures, and maximum outage tolerance. For Wi-Fi devices, test roaming between access points and fallback to cellular or LoRaWAN when available. For low-power protocols like BLE or Thread, verify pairing stability and low-latency data transfer in the presence of interference from other 2.4 GHz devices.
- **Cloud upload success rate and data integrity:** Transmit large volumes of data (for example, 10,000 samples) over extended periods while monitoring upload latency, packet loss, and retransmission behavior. Verify that payloads are received correctly at the cloud endpoint by comparing hashes or checksums. Test edge cases such as partial uploads during network interruptions, buffer overflow during bursts, and graceful handling when the cloud service is temporarily unavailable (for example, queueing messages and retrying with exponential backoff).
- **Actuator response timing and consistency:** For devices with relays, motors, LEDs, or solenoids, measure the delay between command issuance and physical action, ensuring it meets real-time requirements (for example,<100 ms for lighting control). Cycle actuators thousands of times to detect wear, sticking, or power-consumption drift. Validate safety features such as timeout protection to prevent stuck states and confirm that actuators return to a known safe position after power loss.
- **Dashboard and user interface update latency:** From the moment a sensor value changes or an event occurs, measure the end-to-end time until the update appears on the cloud dashboard or mobile app. Test under varying network conditions and server loads to ensure responsiveness remains acceptable (typically <2–5 seconds for near-real-time monitoring).

Verify that historical data visualization, alarms, and notifications trigger correctly and that user commands (for example, remote relay toggle) are executed reliably.

By rigorously validating functional behavior before deployment, teams significantly reduce the risk of field failures, accelerate time-to-market, and build confidence in the long-term reliability of the system. Functional testing is not a one-time activity but an ongoing discipline, with automated suites run on every build and manual exploratory tests performed on representative hardware batches to catch subtle issues that automated checks might miss. This commitment to validation ensures that the IoT system performs as intended, even under the unpredictable realities of the real world.

Regression Testing and Version Rollback Plan

In the context of IoT systems that evolve continuously through over-the-air updates, adding new features, security patches, and performance improvements, the risk of introducing unintended regressions—where previously working functionality breaks—becomes a critical concern. A single regression in a field-deployed device can affect thousands or millions of units, leading to widespread service disruptions, customer dissatisfaction, or even safety hazards. Regression testing and rollback planning are therefore indispensable disciplines that ensure updates enhance rather than degrade the overall system reliability and user experience.

Regression testing systematically verifies that existing features and core behaviors remain intact after every code change, firmware build, or OTA release. Unlike functional testing, which focuses on validating new capabilities, regression testing targets the vast surface of legacy functionality that users already rely upon. To support rapid and confident releases, teams maintain a library of known-good firmware images—golden binaries that have passed all regression tests and been validated in staged field rollouts. These images serve as the baseline for comparison during testing and as the immediate fallback target during rollback procedures. Versioning these images clearly (for example, v1.2.3-stable) and storing them securely in a release repository ensures traceability and quick recovery.

A robust rollback strategy is essential for large device fleets, where even a 1 % failure rate translates to thousands of affected devices. The cornerstone of rollback is the dual-bank or multi-partition firmware architecture supported by modern microcontrollers such as the ESP32, STM32, or nRF52 series. In this design, the device maintains at least two firmware slots: the active slot and one or more inactive slots. During an OTA update, the new firmware is written to the inactive slot, verified for integrity, and marked as the next boot target. The device then reboots into the new version. Rollback planning also extends to configuration changes. When remote configuration updates are applied, devices should store the previous configuration locally and provide a mechanism to revert to it if the new settings cause instability. This can be achieved by versioning configuration payloads and including rollback hooks in the configuration handler of the device.

By combining rigorous automated regression testing with bulletproof rollback mechanisms, IoT teams achieve the confidence required to deploy updates frequently and at scale. These practices minimize downtime, protect user trust, and enable the continuous improvement that defines successful long-lived IoT products. In an ecosystem where devices must operate reliably for five to ten years or more, mastering regression testing and rollback planning is not optional—it is a fundamental requirement for operational excellence.

Secure Device Provisioning for Fleets

Provisioning—the process of securely onboarding and registering new devices into an IoT fleet—is one of the most critical yet often overlooked stages in scaling from prototypes to production deployments involving hundreds, thousands, or even millions of units. Insecure or manual provisioning practices expose the entire system to risks such as unauthorized device impersonation, man-in-the-middle attacks, credential theft, or denial-of-service through rogue devices. To underscore the stakes, in

2016, the Mirai botnet compromised millions of IoT devices using default credentials—a catastrophic failure of secure provisioning. Enterprise-grade provisioning must therefore ensure that each device is uniquely identifiable, cryptographically authenticated, and seamlessly integrated into the cloud backend from the moment it powers on for the first time, all with zero-touch or minimal human intervention.

The foundation of secure provisioning lies in assigning each device a unique, immutable identity during manufacturing. This identity typically takes the form of a globally unique serial number, a hardware-generated unique ID (such as the eFuse-based MAC-derived ID of ESP32), or a manufacturer-assigned device ID. This ID serves as the primary key for all subsequent interactions and must be stored in tamper-resistant memory, ideally within a Hardware Security Module (HSM), Secure Element (SE), or Trusted Platform Module (TPM) to prevent extraction or cloning. For added security, many manufacturers employ secure token injection during the production line. Using automated test fixtures, a factory server injects a unique device certificate and private key into the secure element before sealing the device. Alternatively, devices can generate their own key pairs during first boot and use a secure enrollment protocol (such as Device Attestation with DICE or TPM-based attestation) to prove the integrity of their firmware and hardware state to the cloud before receiving operational credentials.

Cloud platforms provide comprehensive native support for these flows. The Fleet Provisioning feature of AWS IoT Core allows template-based registration with custom lambda hooks for business logic. Azure IoT Hub offers Enrollment Groups and Individual Enrollments with symmetric keys or X.509 certificates. Google Cloud IoT Core supports device registries with public key management. These services handle device shadowing, policy enforcement, and lifecycle management, ensuring that newly provisioned devices are immediately discoverable, monitorable, and controllable. By implementing secure, automated provisioning, organizations achieve true zero-touch deployment: devices ship from the factory, connect to Wi-Fi or cellular networks, and join the fleet without human intervention or exposure of sensitive credentials. This capability is necessary for cost-effective scaling, rapid market entry, and maintaining a strong security posture across the entire device lifecycle—from manufacturing to end-of-life decommissioning.

Power Optimization for 24×7 Deployments

In deployments where devices must operate continuously for months or years on limited energy sources—such as coin cells, primary batteries, rechargeable packs, or energy harvesting—power consumption becomes the single most critical design constraint. A device that draws excessive current will exhaust its power source prematurely, leading to frequent replacements, increased maintenance costs, reduced reliability, and ultimately shortened product lifespan. Achieving true 24×7 operation in remote or inaccessible locations requires a holistic approach to power optimization, combining hardware selection, firmware architecture, and system-level strategies to minimize average current draw down to microampere levels while preserving essential functionality.

The cornerstone of power efficiency is aggressive use of deep sleep modes available on modern microcontrollers. High-end MCUs such as the ESP32 series, STM32L series, nRF52/53, and SAM L10/11 feature ultra-low-power deep sleep states where the CPU is powered off, most peripherals are disabled, and only a Real-Time Clock (RTC). Deep sleep typically adds 1–5 ms wake-up time; for most IoT applications (such as periodic sensing), this is negligible versus battery gains, or ultra-low-power coprocessor remains active. In these modes, current consumption drops to 1–10 μA or less, compared to tens of milliamperes when the core is running. The device enters deep sleep immediately after completing its tasks (for example, sampling sensors and transmitting data) and remains there until awakened by an external interrupt, timer, or wake-up pin.

To maximize the time spent in deep sleep, systems should adopt an event-driven wake-up architecture rather than periodic polling. Instead of waking every few seconds to check for activity, the device uses hardware triggers to wake only when meaningful events occur. Examples include accelerometer motion interrupts for activity detection, capacitive touch or PIR sensor triggers for occupancy monitoring, or external comparators for threshold-based environmental events. This approach reduces average power by orders of magnitude, as the device may spend 99.9 % of its time asleep, waking only a few times per hour or day.

Data transmission is one of the most power-hungry operations in IoT devices. Batch data transmission minimizes radio-on time by accumulating multiple sensor readings or events locally and sending them in a single, compact packet at infrequent intervals (for example, every 10–60 minutes instead of continuously). Techniques such as delta encoding (transmitting only changes since the last report) and lossy compression further reduce payload size. For protocols like LoRaWAN, NB-IoT, or LTE-M, which support long sleep cycles, aligning transmission windows with network availability windows maximizes efficiency. Wi-Fi and Bluetooth devices benefit from connectionless modes or periodic association to avoid the high overhead of frequent reconnections. Reduced sensor sampling frequency is another powerful lever for power savings. In monitoring applications, high-frequency sampling is rarely necessary. For example, temperature and humidity changes occur slowly, so readings every 5–15 minutes suffice; vibration or acceleration monitoring can drop to 1–10 Hz when idle, ramping up only on motion detection. Adaptive sampling—where the device increases frequency during detected events and decreases it during quiescence—strikes an optimal balance between responsiveness and energy use. Power gating unused sensors or peripherals via MOSFETs or dedicated low-dropout regulators further eliminates quiescent current leakage.

Thus, by combining deep sleep, event-driven operation, batched transmission, and adaptive sampling, production IoT devices routinely achieve average currents below 10 μA, enabling multi-year operation on small batteries. These techniques are indispensable for remote deployments in agriculture, environmental monitoring, asset tracking, smart metering, and industrial sensing, where replacing batteries is logistically challenging or cost-prohibitive. Mastering power optimization transforms battery-powered IoT from a short-lived novelty into a sustainable, long-term solution that delivers reliable value over the full lifecycle of the device.

Field Readiness Checklist

Deploying IoT devices into real-world environments demands far more than flawless firmware and cloud integration. The field exposes devices to extremes of temperature, humidity, vibration, dust, electromagnetic interference, and physical abuse that no laboratory simulation can fully replicate. Neglecting the physical and logistical aspects of field readiness is one of the most common causes of premature failure—even when the software performs perfectly in controlled tests. A comprehensive field readiness checklist ensures that devices are not only functionally capable but also mechanically robust, environmentally resilient, and operationally self-sufficient.

This checklist focuses on the critical physical and low-level operational preparations that must be completed before any production deployment.

Physical and Environmental Protection

- **Protective Casing:** The enclosure must shield internal electronics from mechanical damage, dust ingress, and accidental tampering. Use ruggedized materials such as ABS, polycarbonate, or aluminum alloys with sufficient wall thickness. For industrial or outdoor applications, incorporate reinforced mounting points, impact-resistant corners, and tamper-evident seals. Ensure that the casing allows adequate heat dissipation for power components while maintaining structural integrity.
- **Weatherproofing and Ingress Protection (IP Ratings):** Devices exposed to the elements require a minimum IP65 rating (dust-tight and protected against water jets) for general outdoor

use, IP67 for submersion tolerance, or IP68 for prolonged underwater operation. Verify seals around cable glands, connectors, and openings using O-rings, gaskets, or potting compounds. Conduct accelerated environmental testing (temperature cycling, salt fog, UV exposure) to validate long-term performance.

- **Stable Power Supply or Battery Backup:** Reliable power is the lifeblood of field devices. For mains-powered units, include surge protection, wide-input voltage regulators, and reverse polarity protection. For battery-operated devices, select high-quality lithium-thionyl chloride (Li-$SOCl_2$) or lithium-iron phosphate ($LiFePO_4$) cells for long shelf life and temperature stability. Implement low-battery detection with early warning telemetry and graceful shutdown logic to prevent data corruption.
- **Offline Data Buffering:** Intermittent connectivity is inevitable in remote locations. Implement non-volatile storage (EEPROM, FRAM, or external flash) to buffer sensor readings, events, or logs during outages. Use a circular buffer or FIFO queue with timestamps and prioritize critical data for retransmission upon reconnection. Ensure the buffer survives power cycles and has sufficient capacity for days or weeks of operation.
- **Secure Mounting:** Devices must withstand wind, vibration, and thermal expansion. Use vibration-dampening mounts, anti-tamper screws, and UV-resistant cable ties. For pole or wall mounting, provide brackets with anti-theft features. In agricultural or industrial settings, ensure mounting allows for easy cleaning and inspection without compromising seals.

Neglecting these physical design elements often leads to catastrophic failures despite perfect software. Water ingress corrodes boards, vibration loosens connections, power glitches corrupt flash memory, and poor mounting causes devices to fall or overheat. By rigorously addressing the field readiness checklist, engineers ensure that IoT deployments achieve the reliability and longevity demanded by real-world applications.

In summary, treat field readiness as a non-negotiable gate in the deployment process. Conduct a formal review with hardware, firmware, and operations teams before signing off on production runs. Only devices that pass this checklist should be released to the field—where they will operate autonomously for years without intervention.

Basics of Fleet Management

Once IoT devices are deployed at scale—whether dozens, hundreds, or millions—manual management becomes impossible. Manual management works up to ~50–100 devices; beyond that, centralized fleet tooling becomes mandatory to avoid operational chaos. Fleet management refers to the centralized oversight, monitoring, maintenance, and orchestration of an entire population of connected devices. It transforms a collection of individual nodes into a cohesive, observable, and controllable system. Without robust fleet management, even the most sophisticated devices can suffer from undetected failures, inconsistent performance, security vulnerabilities, and escalating operational costs. The primary goal of fleet management is to maintain high availability, ensure security compliance, minimize downtime, and maximize the return on investment for the deployed hardware. This is achieved through a combination of device-side capabilities (telemetry reporting, OTA support, secure provisioning) and cloud-side infrastructure (dashboards, analytics engines, automation workflows). Cloud platforms serve as the central nervous system for IoT fleets. Leading services such as AWS IoT Core, Azure IoT Hub, Google Cloud IoT Core, Particle, and ThingsBoard provide native fleet management tools, while specialized platforms like Cumulocity, Ayla Networks, and DeviceHive offer advanced features tailored for specific industries. These platforms aggregate data from thousands of devices, process it in real time, and present actionable insights through intuitive web dashboards and APIs.

Key Components of Fleet Management

Fleet management in IoT systems involves monitoring, maintaining, and controlling large numbers of connected devices deployed across different locations. To ensure reliability, scalability, and security, several essential components work together to track device health, manage connectivity, and respond to operational issues in real time.

- **Device Health Monitoring:** Every device in the fleet reports periodic telemetry – battery voltage, temperature, CPU usage, memory pressure, sensor status, signal strength (RSSI), and uptime counters. The cloud platform visualizes these metrics in real time. Health dashboards typically use color-coded indicators—green for health, yellow for warnings (for example: low battery or high temperature), red for critical alerts (for example: device offline for >15 minutes). Threshold-based alarms trigger notifications via email, SMS, Slack, or PagerDuty. Advanced systems employ anomaly detection to spot unusual patterns, such as sudden spikes in power consumption that might indicate a failing sensor.

- **Firmware Status Tracking:** With OTA updates being frequent, fleet managers must know exactly which firmware version is running on each device. Cloud platforms maintain a device shadow or twin – a digital representation of the current state of the device – including firmware version, last update timestamp, and update success/failure status. Dashboards display version distribution histograms, allowing operators to see adoption rates of new releases (for example: 85 % of devices on v1.3.2). This visibility enables safe, staged rollouts and rapid identification of problematic versions.

- **Remote Diagnostics and Troubleshooting:** When a device malfunctions, physical access is rarely feasible. Fleet management tools support remote diagnostics: on-demand log retrieval (with configurable log levels), live command execution (for example: reset sensor calibration), and configuration inspection. Some platforms allow device twin debugging, where operators can query or modify runtime parameters. For critical systems, remote console access or packet capture from the device can be enabled temporarily. Diagnostic data is stored with timestamps and device IDs for post-mortem analysis.

- **Bulk Updates and Orchestration:** Updating thousands of devices simultaneously is risky. Fleet management platforms support bulk OTA campaigns with granular controls: target by device group, model, region, or firmware version; set rollout speed (for example: 1,000 devices per hour); enforce mandatory updates for security patches; and automatically pause or rollback if error rates exceed a threshold. Differential updates minimize data usage. Platforms also support bulk configuration changes (for example: update Wi-Fi credentials for all devices in a factory) and scheduled operations (for example: enable power-saving mode at night).

Cloud Dashboards and Analytics

The heart of fleet management is the cloud dashboard—a unified interface that provides at-a-glance visibility into the entire fleet. Key views include:

- **Online/Offline Status:** Real-time map or table showing which devices are connected, with last-seen timestamps and connection history. Offline devices are flagged for investigation.

- **Error Rates and Alerts:** Aggregated metrics on failed OTA attempts, connection drops, sensor errors, and application crashes. Heatmaps highlight problem clusters by geography or device type.

- **Data Throughput and Latency:** Monitor the volume of data flowing into the cloud, peak usage, and end-to-end latency from device to dashboard. This helps detect bottlenecks or cost overruns.

- **Usage Analytics:** Track active users, device utilization, battery life trends, and feature adoption to inform product improvements.
- **Security Posture**: Display certificate expiration dates, authentication failures, and detected anomalies (for example: unexpected IP changes).

Advanced dashboards integrate machine learning for predictive maintenance—forecasting battery depletion or hardware failures days in advance—and automated remediation workflows (for example : auto-reboot unresponsive devices or trigger OTA on detected vulnerabilities). Fleet management turns a distributed collection of IoT endpoints into a manageable, intelligent asset. By leveraging cloud platforms for monitoring, diagnostics, updates, and analytics, organizations achieve operational excellence, enhanced security, and sustained value from their deployments. Mastering these basics prepares engineers to operate IoT systems at enterprise scale—where the difference between success and failure often lies not in the devices themselves, but in the centralized intelligence that keeps them running smoothly.

Cost Considerations for Scaling IoT Projects

An absolutely critical topic— Cost considerations — although are often ignored until it is too late. A smart agriculture startup, for instance, saw monthly cloud bills balloon from $500 (1,000 devices) to $25,000 (20,000 devices), forcing a painful and expensive architecture redesign. Planning for cost scaling upfront prevents such crises.

Scaling an IoT system from a proof-of-concept with a few dozen devices to a production fleet of thousands or millions introduces significant cost escalations that can threaten project viability if not managed proactively. While hardware costs often stabilize or decrease with volume, cloud and operational expenses grow non-linearly with the number of devices, data volume, and interaction frequency. Understanding and controlling these costs is critical for building sustainable IoT businesses, where profitability depends on keeping lifetime operational costs well below the value delivered to customers. Manual management works up to ~50–100 devices; beyond that, centralized fleet tooling becomes mandatory to avoid operational chaos.

The Critical Cost of Scale

A smart agriculture startup saw monthly cloud bills balloon from $500 (1K devices) to $25K (20K devices), forcing a painful architecture redesign. Planning for cost scaling upfront prevents such crises.

Scaling an IoT system from a proof-of-concept with a few dozen devices to a production fleet of thousands or millions introduces significant cost escalations that can threaten project viability if not managed proactively. While hardware costs often stabilize or decrease with volume, cloud and operational expenses grow non-linearly with the number of devices, data volume, and interaction frequency. Understanding and controlling these costs is critical for building sustainable IoT businesses, where profitability depends on keeping lifetime operational costs well below the value delivered to customers.

Major Cost Drivers in Scaling IoT Deployments

As IoT deployments grow from a few prototype devices to thousands or even millions of connected nodes, operational costs become a critical consideration. Understanding the major cost drivers helps organizations design efficient architectures, optimize resource usage, and prevent unexpected expenses during large-scale deployments.

- **Cloud Messaging and Connectivity**: Each device maintains a persistent connection to the cloud (typically via MQTT, HTTP, or WebSocket), sending periodic telemetry and receiving commands. As fleet size grows, the number of concurrent connections and messages per second increases dramatically. Cloud providers charge for connected devices (for example, AWS IoT Core bills per million minutes of connection), published/subscribed messages, and data transfer. A fleet of 100,000 devices sending 10 messages per minute can generate millions of messages daily, quickly exceeding free tiers and incurring substantial bills.

- **Data Storage and Retention**: Raw sensor data, logs, and metadata accumulate rapidly. Storing everything indefinitely in hot storage (for example :DynamoDB, Firestore, or S3 Standard) becomes prohibitively expensive. A single temperature sensor logging every minute produces ~1.5 GB per device per year; at 10,000 devices, that is 15 TB annually. Cold storage (S3 Glacier, BigQuery) is cheaper but still adds up, and egress fees for analytics or backups further inflate costs.
- **Analytics and Processing**: Real-time dashboards, alerting, machine learning inference, and batch reporting consume compute resources. Serverless functions (Lambda, Azure Functions) scale automatically but charge per invocation and duration. Running complex analytics on large datasets (for example: anomaly detection across time-series) can trigger high costs in data warehouses or streaming platforms (Kinesis, IoT Analytics).
- **OTA Firmware Updates and Bandwidth:** Delivering full firmware binaries (often 1–4 MB) to thousands of devices simultaneously can generate massive data egress charges. Differential updates help, but initial deployments and frequent patches still contribute significantly. Cellular or satellite connectivity adds per-device subscription fees, and bandwidth-heavy protocols (for example: continuous video streaming) can dominate the budget.

Cost Control Strategies for Sustainable Scaling

Effective cost management requires intentional design decisions from the architecture phase onward. The following strategies, when combined, can reduce operational expenses by 50–80%, while maintaining functionality:

- **Batching Instead of Streaming**: Replace continuous streaming with periodic batch uploads. For example, instead of sending sensor readings every second, accumulate data locally for 5–15 minutes and transmit a compressed summary or full batch in one message. This reduces message count by 300–900×, cuts connection overhead, and lowers both messaging and compute costs. Use efficient serialization formats (Protobuf, CBOR, or MessagePack) to minimize payload size.
- **Smart Data Storage Policies:** Implement tiered storage: keep raw data in hot storage for only 7–30 days (for real-time diagnostics), then move it to cold storage for longer-term archiving or analytics. Aggregate data at the edge (for example: compute daily averages or histograms) and transmit only summaries to the cloud. Use time-series databases (InfluxDB, Timestream) optimized for IoT data, which are far cheaper than general-purpose stores. Set retention policies that automatically delete or archive old data based on business needs.
- **Optimize MQTT Message Frequency and Payload:** Tune MQTT keep-alive intervals, QoS levels, and topic structures. Use QoS 0 for non-critical telemetry and QoS 1 only for commands. Consolidate multiple values into a single JSON or binary message. Implement adaptive reporting: increase frequency during alerts or anomalies and reduce it during stable operation. Avoid unnecessary subscriptions and use shared subscriptions for load balancing
- **Leverage Free Tiers and Cost-Optimized Services:** Most cloud providers offer generous free tiers (for example, AWS IoT Core free for 500,000 messages/month, Azure IoT Hub 8,000 free messages/day). Use these strategically during early scaling phases. Choose serverless architectures to pay only for actual usage. For storage, prefer S3 Intelligent-Tiering or Glacier Instant Retrieval for infrequently accessed data. Monitor usage with cost allocation tags and budgets to prevent surprises.

- **Edge Computing and Local Processing:** Offload computation to the device or gateway whenever possible. Perform filtering, aggregation, and basic analytics at the edge to reduce cloud-bound data. TinyML models can detect events locally and transmit only alerts or summaries. This approach dramatically cuts messaging and storage costs while improving latency and privacy.
- **Predictive Cost Modeling:** Before scaling, build a cost model spreadsheet or use cloud pricing calculators to forecast expenses at different fleet sizes, message rates, and retention periods. Identify cost hotspots early and redesign accordingly. Regularly review bills and usage reports to optimize configurations.
- **Alternative Connectivity Choices:** For low-data-rate applications, switch from cellular to LoRaWAN, Sigfox, or satellite (for example: Swarm, Orbcomm) where available. These often have lower per-device fees and better coverage in remote areas. Use Wi-Fi where possible and implement failover to cheaper networks.

Cost-aware design is not an afterthought—it is a foundational requirement for sustainable IoT businesses. Projects that ignore scaling costs often face a harsh reality: rapid growth leads to unsustainable bills, forcing price increases, feature cuts, or project abandonment. Conversely, companies that architect for cost efficiency from day one can scale profitably, reinvest in innovation, and deliver competitive pricing. In practice, successful IoT enterprises treat cost management as a core engineering discipline. They conduct quarterly cost audits, run A/B tests on data strategies, and continuously refine edge-cloud partitioning. By embedding cost consciousness into every decision—from protocol choice to data retention—teams ensure their IoT solutions remain viable and profitable at any scale.

Common Failure Modes and Recovery Strategies

In any real-world IoT deployment, failures are not exceptions—they are inevitable. Devices operate in harsh environments with unreliable power, intermittent connectivity, environmental stressors, and potential security threats. The most prevalent failure modes encountered in field deployments, by approximate frequency, are Network outages (~70% of incidents), power issues (~15%), firmware/ bugs (~10%), and physical damage (~5%).

The key to building resilient systems is anticipating these failure modes and designing automatic recovery mechanisms that restore normal operation without human intervention. This section examines these failure modes and the proven recovery strategies that ensure high availability and minimal downtime, helping teams prioritize which mechanisms to implement first based on their impact frequency.

Common Failure Modes

- **Network Outages:** Connectivity loss is the most frequent issue, especially in remote or mobile deployments. Wi-Fi signals fade, cellular coverage drops in rural areas, LoRa gateways go offline, or ISP failures occur. Devices may become unreachable for minutes, hours, or days, halting cloud reporting, command execution, and OTA updates. Prolonged outages can also cause buffered data to overflow or battery drain from repeated reconnection attempts.
- **Power Loss or Brownouts:** Battery-powered devices face depletion, especially in cold temperatures that reduce capacity. Mains-powered units suffer from grid fluctuations, surges, or outages. Sudden power cuts can interrupt writes to flash memory, leading to partial firmware corruption or corrupted configuration data. Voltage drops below the minimum operating level of MCU cause erratic behavior, resets, or complete lockup.
- **Firmware Corruption:** OTA updates can fail midway due to network interruptions, power loss, or transmission errors, leaving the device with an incomplete or corrupted image. Flash wear

from excessive writes, cosmic ray-induced bit flips (rare but real), or malicious tampering can also corrupt firmware. A corrupted binary prevents normal boot, resulting in a bricked device.

- **Sensor Drift and Degradation:** Over time, sensors experience calibration drift due to temperature cycling, humidity exposure, chemical contamination, or mechanical wear. This leads to inaccurate readings that propagate errors through analytics, alerts, or control loops. Degraded sensors may also consume excessive power or fail entirely, causing silent data loss.
- **Software Bugs and Resource Exhaustion:** Memory leaks, unhandled exceptions, infinite loops, or stack overflows can freeze the application. High-priority interrupts starving lower ones or race conditions in multi-threaded code (common in FreeRTOS) can cause deadlocks. These issues manifest as frozen devices that appear responsive to pings but fail to process sensor data or send updates.
- **Security Incidents:** Unauthorized access, credential compromise, or denial-of-service attacks can disrupt operation. Malicious firmware injection or configuration changes may force the device into unsafe states.

Recovery Strategies

Resilient IoT systems incorporate multiple layers of defense to detect, isolate, and recover from failures automatically.

- **Watchdog Timers (Hardware and Software):** The most fundamental recovery mechanism is the hardware watchdog timer built into nearly all modern MCUs (ESP32, STM32, nRF52). It must be periodically kicked (reset) by the application. If the firmware hangs or loops indefinitely, the watchdog triggers a full system reset. Configure the timeout to be slightly longer than the worst-case legitimate execution time. Software watchdogs can monitor specific threads or subsystems for finer-grained recovery.
- **Auto-Restart Logic and Safe Boot Modes:** On reset, implement a boot counter in non-volatile storage. If the device fails to boot successfully multiple times (for example: three consecutive failures), automatically revert to the previous firmware partition or enter a minimal safe mode that only reports status and waits for OTA recovery. OTA API of ESP32 supports this natively with rollback partitions.
- **Local Data Caching and Queuing:** During network outages, store sensor readings, events, and logs in non-volatile memory (external flash, FRAM, or filesystem). Use a persistent queue with timestamps and priority levels. On reconnection, transmit queued data with backoff to avoid overwhelming the server. This ensures no data loss and graceful recovery from connectivity gaps.
- **Health Heartbeat Messages:** Devices send periodic heartbeat messages to the cloud, containing status summary: uptime, battery level, firmware version, sensor health, and recent error codes. The cloud monitors these heartbeats and detects anomalies (for example: missed beats indicate a crash or outage). If a device is unresponsive, the cloud can trigger actions such as OTA recovery, configuration reset, or alerting operators.
- **Sensor Self-Diagnostics and Calibration:** Periodically run self-tests on sensors (for example, check for stuck values, out-of-range readings, or noise levels). Implement drift compensation algorithms or periodic recalibration using reference points. For critical sensors, maintain redundant units and switch automatically when degradation is detected.
- **Power Management and Brownout Protection:** Use voltage supervisors or brownout detectors to trigger clean shutdowns before voltage drops too low. Implement low-power recovery logic: on power restoration, validate flash integrity, restore last known state, and resume operation. For battery devices, predict depletion and enter ultra-low-power hibernation mode with minimal telemetry.

- **Security Recovery Mechanisms:** Use secure boot to verify firmware integrity on every start. Implement certificate revocation lists or short-lived credentials. If compromise is detected (for example, via anomaly detection), force a factory reset or enter quarantine mode that only allows OTA recovery.
- **Fail-Safe Defaults and Graceful Degradation:** Design systems to fall back to safe states: relays open, actuators stop, alerts default to conservative thresholds. Allow partial functionality during failures (for example: local control when cloud is unavailable).

By embedding these recovery strategies, IoT systems achieve high resilience. A device may experience a brief reset or data delay, but it recovers autonomously, reports the incident via heartbeat, and continues operation. This never fail silently principle minimizes downtime, reduces field service calls, and builds trust in the system.

In summary, resilient IoT design assumes failure at every layer and counters it with layered, automatic recovery. Watchdogs, heartbeats, caching, and safe modes turn inevitable failures into minor, self-healing events—ensuring that the fleet remains operational and reliable for years.

Final Project Checklist Template

Before any IoT project transitions from development to full-scale production deployment, a rigorous final review is essential to ensure the system is robust, secure, reliable, and maintainable. Declaring a project deployment-ready is not a casual milestone—it is a formal gate that protects against costly field failures, regulatory non-compliance, and reputational damage. Industry-leading teams treat this as a Release Readiness Review (RRR), often involving cross-functional sign-off from firmware, hardware, security, operations, and product stakeholders. In mature organizations, the RRR typically includes the firmware lead, hardware engineer, security officer, QA lead, operations specialist, and product manager—ensuring comprehensive cross-functional sign-off.

The following comprehensive checklist serves as a structured template that mirrors professional practices used by companies deploying IoT at scale. Each item must be demonstrably completed, with evidence (test reports, logs, signatures) documented in a release package. Passing this checklist confirms that the project is prepared for real-world operation over years, not just weeks.

- **Firmware and Update Readiness:** Firmware must be versioned, reproducible, securely signed, and include recovery support. OTA updates and rollback mechanisms must be fully tested under realistic failure and network conditions.
- **Logging and Monitoring:** Devices should generate minimal structured logs with defined severity levels. Health monitoring and alerting must reliably report failures, anomalies, and device status to cloud dashboards.
- **Security and Compliance:** Secure boot, encrypted communication, and unique device credentials are mandatory. Provisioning, credential management, and compliance with relevant security and data protection standards must be verified.
- **Power and Environmental Reliability:** Power consumption must meet battery or energy targets, with safe recovery from low-power conditions. Devices must tolerate expected environmental stresses in real deployments.
- **Data and Connectivity Resilience:** Systems must handle network outages through local buffering and reliable retransmission. Connectivity recovery and failover logic should ensure continuous operation.
- **Documentation and Support:** Installation, operation, and maintenance documentation must be complete. Support procedures, escalation paths, and release notes must be clearly defined.

- **Final Validation and Approval:** End-to-end testing, regression validation, and limited fleet trials must confirm system stability. Formal sign-off from all stakeholders is required before deployment.
- **Outcome:** Completion of this checklist confirms the transition from prototype to a production-ready IoT system capable of sustained field operation.

This checklist is not exhaustive but represents the minimum bar used in commercial IoT deployments. Each item should be accompanied by verifiable evidence (screenshots, test logs, signed reports). Passing this review shifts the project from prototype to production-ready, ensuring the system can operate reliably in the field for years with minimal intervention. By adopting this disciplined approach, teams avoid the common pitfalls of premature deployment—costly recalls, security breaches, and loss of customer trust—and set the foundation for scalable, profitable IoT products.

Career Pathway: Skills to become an IoT Developer and Architect

The Internet of Things has evolved into a large global industry spanning smart homes, industry, healthcare, agriculture, transportation, and energy. As deployments scale, demand for skilled IoT professionals continues to grow, offering diverse, well-compensated, and high-impact career opportunities.

- **IoT Developer**: Focuses on firmware development, sensor integration, communication protocols, OTA updates, and power-efficient embedded design. Requires skills in embedded C/C++, RTOS, hardware interfaces, wireless connectivity, and basic device security. Career growth typically progresses from junior developer to lead firmware architect.
- **IoT Solutions Architect**: Designs end-to-end IoT systems spanning devices, gateways, edge, and cloud. Responsibilities include architecture definition, protocol and cloud selection, scalability planning, security compliance, and cost optimization. This is a senior role with progression toward principal architect or technology leadership positions.
- **TinyML Engineer**: Combines embedded systems with machine learning to deploy AI models directly on devices. Work includes model optimization, on-device inference, and hybrid edge-cloud design. Requires TinyML workflows, model compression, and performance-power trade-off expertise.
- **Fleet Operations Engineer**: Manages large-scale device fleets after deployment. Responsibilities include CI/CD for firmware, OTA campaigns, monitoring, automation, and reliability engineering. Skills span embedded tooling, cloud DevOps platforms, and monitoring systems.
- **IoT Security Engineer**: Ensures device and system security through secure boot, cryptography, penetration testing, compliance enforcement, and incident response. This role is critical in protecting large IoT deployments against cyber threats.
- **IoT Product Manager**: Bridges technology and business by defining product roadmaps, aligning engineering efforts with market needs, and driving go-to-market strategies. Requires technical literacy combined with strong business and communication skills.
- **Emerging and Specialized Roles**: Includes IoT data scientists, hardware engineers, consultants, and academic researchers focusing on analytics, hardware design, strategic advisory, or advanced research.
- **Building a Career in IoT**: Career development is supported by hands-on projects, open-source contributions, professional certifications, industry networking, and continuous learning in areas such as Edge AI, 5G, and next-generation IoT protocols.

The IoT industry is still in its early growth phase. Professionals who master both the technical depth (embedded systems, AI, security) and the system-level thinking (architecture, scaling, operations) will be in extremely high demand for decades. This book has given you the foundational skills—now it is time to apply them, build, deploy, and innovate. Your career in IoT is just beginning, and the opportunities are virtually limitless.

Future of IoT: LEO Satellites, 5G, Federated Learning, Zero-Trust Security

The Internet of Things has already transformed industries, but the next decade will see it evolve from a network of connected sensors into a truly intelligent, autonomous, and resilient global fabric. By 2035, projections estimate over 75 billion connected devices worldwide, generating zettabytes of data annually. This explosion will be driven by converging technologies that address the contemporary limitations—coverage gaps, latency, privacy concerns, security vulnerabilities, and operational complexity. The future of IoT lies in seamless integration, extreme efficiency, and intelligence that operates at every layer of the stack.

- **LEO Satellites and Global Ubiquitous Connectivity:** Low Earth Orbit (LEO) satellite constellations—led by Starlink, OneWeb, Amazon Kuiper, and emerging players—are eliminating the connectivity divide. Traditional cellular and terrestrial networks struggle in remote, oceanic, or polar regions, leaving billions of potential IoT endpoints underserved. LEO satellites provide low-latency (20–50 ms), high-throughput coverage across the entire planet, enabling truly global deployments.
- **5G Advanced, 6G, and NB-IoT Evolution:** 5G has already delivered massive Machine-Type Communication (mMTC) through NB-IoT and LTE-M, but Release 18 (5G-Advanced) and the emerging 6G standards will push capabilities further. Ultra-Reliable Low-Latency Communication (URLLC) will drop latency below 1 ms, enabling real-time control for industrial robotics, autonomous vehicles, and remote surgery.
- **Federated Learning and Privacy-Preserving Intelligence:** As privacy regulations tighten (GDPR, CCPA, emerging global laws), sending raw sensor data to the cloud becomes untenable. Federated Learning (FL) allows models to train collaboratively across devices without ever sharing raw data. Only model updates (gradients) are exchanged, keeping sensitive information local.
- **Zero-Trust Security Models and Quantum-Resistant Cryptography:** The perimeter-based security of the past is obsolete when billions of devices are exposed. Zero-trust architectures assume no device is inherently trustworthy—every request is authenticated, authorized, and continuously verified. Device identity is tied to hardware roots of trust (secure elements, TPMs). Micro-segmentation limits lateral movement in case of compromise. Continuous monitoring detects anomalies in real time. By 2030, quantum-resistant algorithms (post-quantum cryptography) will replace vulnerable RSA and ECC, protecting IoT from future quantum attacks.
- **Autonomous, Self-Healing IoT Ecosystems:** The ultimate vision is IoT systems that manage themselves. AI-driven orchestration will monitor fleet health, predict failures, and autonomously trigger OTA updates, reconfiguration, or component isolation. Self-healing networks reroute traffic around failed gateways; digital twins simulate failures and test recovery strategies in the cloud before applying them. Swarm intelligence will emerge in dense deployments—drones or robots coordinating via local mesh networks without central control. Blockchain and distributed ledgers may enable decentralized trust for peer-to-peer IoT interactions, such as energy trading in microgrids.

The future of IoT is not just about more devices—it is about creating ecosystems that are intelligent, distributed, secure, and sustainable. Professionals entering the field today will shape this transformation, building systems that are as reliable as electricity and as pervasive as the air we breathe.

Practical Exercises

Exercise 1: Firmware Versioning and OTA Simulation

This exercise focuses on implementing semantic versioning for firmware, setting up an OTA update mechanism, and simulating rollback to handle failed updates. The goal is to create a resilient firmware pipeline that mimics production OTA without risking device bricking.

Step 1: Setting Up Version Control and Initial Firmware

Begin by initializing a new project in PlatformIO or Arduino IDE for your ESP32 board. Write a simple base firmware that blinks an LED and prints the version number (for example: v1.0.0) to the serial monitor. Use semantic versioning: tag this initial code as v1.0.0 in your Git repository (for example: via `git tag v1.0.0` and `git push --tags`). Compile and flash this version to the device, confirming it runs correctly by observing the LED and serial output.

Step 2: Implementing OTA Update Functionality

Modify the firmware to include OTA support using the native OTA library of ESP32. Add code to periodically check a cloud-hosted server (use a free GitHub repository or HTTP server) for a new binary file named after the next version (for example: v1.1.0.bin). Implement integrity checks with MD5 or SHA-256 hashing. Flash this updated code (still tagged v1.0.0 for now) and test a manual OTA update by uploading v1.1.0 (a minor change, like faster LED blinking) to your server. Verify the device downloads, installs, and reboots into the new version.

Step 3: Simulating Rollback for Failed Updates

Enable dual-partition support in the partition table of ESP32 (via platformio.ini or the partition scheme of Arduino). Add rollback logic: after update, the firmware runs a self-test (for example: check if LED blinks as expected or connect to Wi-Fi). If the test fails (simulate by introducing a deliberate bug in v1.1.1), mark the partition invalid and revert to v1.1.0. Test by triggering an OTA to the faulty version, observing the automatic rollback via serial logs.

Step 4: Documentation and Iteration

Document the process with screenshots of serial output, version tags, and server files. Iterate by simulating network interruptions during OTA (for example : unplug Wi-Fi) to ensure partial updates trigger safe aborts. This exercise demonstrates how versioning and rollback prevent deployment disasters.

Exercise 2: Remote Configuration Loader

In this activity, you will implement a system to load dynamic configurations from a cloud-hosted JSON file, allowing runtime changes without firmware reflashing. The objective is to make your IoT device adaptable to field adjustments, such as changing LED blink rates or thresholds.

Step 1: Preparing the Cloud-Hosted Configuration

Create a simple JSON file (for example, `{blink_rate: 500, threshold: 25}`) and host it on a free platform like GitHub (raw file URL), Firebase Realtime Database, or AWS S3 with public read access. Ensure the file is versioned or timestamped to prevent caching issues. Test accessibility by curling the URL from your computer.

Step 2: Integrating Configuration Fetching in Firmware

In your ESP32 firmware from Exercise 1, add Wi-Fi connection code and an HTTP client (for example: using HTTPClient library). On boot and every 30 minutes, fetch the JSON from the cloud URL. Parse it with ArduinoJson, validate the schema (for example: check for expected keys and value ranges), and apply the settings to runtime variables (for example: update LED blink interval). Flash this code and verify it loads the initial config by monitoring serial output.

Step 3: Handling Edge Cases and Security

Add fallback logic; if fetching fails (network error or invalid JSON), revert to locally stored defaults in NVS (Non-Volatile Storage). Implement basic security by signing the JSON with a HMAC key and verifying on-device. Test by modifying the cloud JSON (for example: change blink_rate to 100) and observing the device update without rebooting. Simulate failures by disconnecting Wi-Fi or corrupting the JSON to confirm graceful degradation.

Step 4: Testing and Documentation

Run the device for an hour, changing the cloud config multiple times, and log application times. Document the flow with code snippets (no full code), JSON examples, and observations. This exercise highlights how remote config enables agile post-deployment tuning.

Exercise 3: Functional and Regression Testing Suite

Here, you will develop and execute a suite of tests to validate functionality and prevent regressions, ensuring your system remains reliable after changes. The aim is to create repeatable tests that cover key subsystems.

Step 1: Defining Test Cases

Document a suite of 10–15 test cases in a spreadsheet or Markdown file. Include functional tests (for example: Verify LED blinks at config rate, Test OTA success under stable Wi-Fi) and regression tests (for example, Confirm sensor reading accuracy after config change). Each case should have: objective, preconditions (for example: firmware version), steps, expected results, and pass/fail criteria.

Step 2: Setting Up Automated and Manual Testing

For automated tests, use the unit test framework of PlatformIO (for example: Unity) to script checks like config parsing or LED timing via GPIO mocks. For manual tests, connect the ESP32 and run scenarios: flash v1.0.0, apply a config, perform OTA to v1.1.0, and re-run all tests to catch regressions. Use tools like Serial Monitor or Python scripts to automate input/output validation.

Step 3: Executing and Iterating Tests

Run the full suite twice: once on the base firmware and again after an OTA update with intentional bugs (for example, `brokenconfig` fetch). Log results, including failures (for example, Regression: Blink rate not updating). Fix issues and retest until 100% pass rate.

Step 4: Reporting and Best Practices

Compile a test report with metrics (for example: 95% coverage) and lessons learned. This exercise teaches the importance of structured testing in maintaining system integrity during scaling.

Exercise 4: Field Readiness Audit

This final exercise evaluates a fully assembled device against a real-world checklist, simulating pre-deployment inspection. The goal is to identify physical and operational gaps before actual field use.

Step 1: Assembling the Device for Audit

Build or use your ESP32 setup from previous exercises, enclosed in a protective case (for example: 3D-printed or off-the-shelf IP65 box). Add a battery or power supply, sensors (for example: DHT11), and secure mounting (for example : brackets).

Step 2: Applying the Field Readiness Checklist

Reference the checklist from Section 15.10: Check protective casing for durability (drop test from 1m), (Disclaimer: Drop test should be done with unpowered device or USB power only (no Li-Po battery) to avoid fire risk if casing cracks. drop test from 1m),weatherproofing (spray water test for IP rating), power stability (simulate brownouts with variable supply), offline buffering (disconnect Wi-Fi and verify data queues), and secure mounting (vibrate on a shaker or table). Document each with photos and notes.

Step 3: Simulating Field Conditions and Fixes

Test in harsh environments: place in a freezer (cold test), near fan (vibration), or outdoors (weather). Identify failures (for example : water ingress) and iterate fixes (for example : add seals). Verify recovery strategies like auto-reboot after power loss.

Step 4: Final Audit Report

Compile findings into a report, rating readiness (for example, 85% compliant) and recommending improvements. This exercise underscores that software excellence alone is insufficient—physical resilience is key to long-term success.

Conclusion

This chapter has provided a comprehensive guide to the final, critical phase of the IoT lifecycle: deployment, testing, and scaling. Learners have explored the professional practices that transform experimental prototypes into reliable, maintainable, and economically viable products capable of operating at scale in real-world conditions. Key topics included rigorous firmware versioning and secure over-the-air (OTA) update pipelines, remote configuration management for dynamic adaptation, automated functional and regression testing suites, secure fleet provisioning, power optimization techniques for 24×7 battery-powered deployments, and cost-aware strategies to prevent runaway cloud expenses. The chapter also emphasized resilient architectures that assume failure is inevitable—incorporating watchdog timers, automatic rollback, health heartbeats, and self-healing mechanisms to ensure high availability with minimal human intervention. The chapter concluded with a forward-looking perspective: an overview of career pathways in IoT—from embedded developers and Edge AI engineers to solutions architects and fleet operations specialists—along with emerging trends that will shape the field in the coming decade. By mastering these final elements, readers are now equipped not only to build intelligent devices but also to deploy, secure, operate, and evolve them at enterprise scale.

The next chapter of the textbook paints a clear roadmap of where the Internet of Things is headed over the next 10–15 years. Moving beyond the foundational technologies covered in previous chapters, *Chapter 16, The Future of IoT*, explores the convergence of IoT with artificial intelligence, advanced connectivity, and digital transformation. Readers will gain awareness of current industry trends, enterprise-grade architectures, and the growing role of AI at both edge and cloud layers. The chapter delves into emerging paradigms such as digital twins, autonomous industrial ecosystems, and smart city platforms, while highlighting opportunities in Industrial IoT (IIoT), predictive maintenance, remote factory operations, and sustainable energy systems.

CHAPTER 16

The Future of IoT

Introduction

The preceding fifteen chapters have guided readers through a complete journey—from the basics of microcontrollers, sensors, and embedded programming to advanced topics such as secure cloud integration, Edge AI and TinyML, production-grade deployment, rigorous testing, fleet management, and cost-aware scaling. Together, they have provided a robust foundation for building, securing, and operating IoT systems as they exist today: reliable, intelligent, and increasingly autonomous devices that collect data, make local decisions, and integrate seamlessly with cloud platforms. Yet the field of IoT is not static. What we consider cutting-edge in 2025 will be baseline infrastructure by 2035. Technologies discussed here range from production-ready today (IIoT, digital twins) to emerging 2027–2030 (6G, planetary-scale swarms) to visionary beyond 2030 (self-evolving systems). The Internet of Things is rapidly evolving from a collection of smart devices into large-scale, interconnected, and deeply intelligent ecosystems capable of powering entire factories, cities, energy grids, transportation networks, healthcare systems, and critical national infrastructure. This transformation is being driven by converging forces: the maturation of Industrial IoT (IIoT), the widespread adoption of 5G and emerging 6G connectivity, the rise of digital twins, the pervasive embedding of artificial intelligence at both edge and cloud layers, and the growing demand for sustainability and resilience in the face of global challenges such as climate changes and supply-chain disruptions.

This chapter shifts the focus from how IoT works today to where IoT is going tomorrow. It offers a strategic roadmap of the technologies, architectures, and business models that will define the next decade of connected systems. Readers will explore the shift toward fully autonomous industrial ecosystems, the role of digital twins in virtualizing physical assets, the impact of ultra-low-latency and global satellite connectivity. (**Note**: *Understanding these trends is essential not just for technical excellence but for strategic roles—IoT architects, product managers, and technical leaders who shape roadmaps 3–5 years out.*) The emergence of privacy-preserving machine learning, and the rise of zero-trust security models will become mandatory in a world of billions of endpoints. By the end of this chapter, readers will not only understand the technological trajectory of IoT but also recognize the strategic, economic, and societal implications of this transformation. While earlier chapters equipped you to build the systems of today, this chapter prepares you to lead the innovations of tomorrow, thereby giving you the strategic lens to recognize emerging opportunities and architect solutions that will remain relevant for years. You will be prepared to contribute meaningfully to the next wave of innovation—shaping not just smarter devices, but truly intelligent, resilient, and sustainable systems that underpin the future of industry, society, and the planet.

Structure

In this chapter, we will cover the following topics:

- Industrial IoT
- Role of PLCs, Gateways, and Real-Time Protocols in Factories
- Edge Intelligence: AI is Moving Closer to Sensors
- Intro to Digital Twins: Modeling Physical Systems Virtually
- Examples of Industrial Deployments: Manufacturing, Logistics, Power Grids
- Role of 5G in High-Throughput, Low-Latency IoT Systems
- Data Lifecycle in IIoT
- Role of IoT in Sustainability (Smart Grids, Smart Farming, Energy Monitoring)
- Trends:
    - Hyperautomation
    - Swarm robotics
    - TinyML growth
    - Self-healing networks
- Certifications in IoT + AI (Azure, AWS IoT, Edge AI)
- Final Motivation: Building a Future-Ready Mindset for the IoT Age
- Practical Exercise

Industrial IoT

Industrial IoT (IIoT) represents the specialized application of Internet of Things technologies within industrial and critical infrastructure environments. Unlike consumer IoT, which focuses on convenience, personalization, and user experience in homes, offices, or public spaces, IIoT is engineered to deliver mission-critical performance in harsh, high-stakes settings such as manufacturing plants, power generation facilities, oil and gas refineries, chemical processing sites, large-scale logistics and warehousing operations, mining operations, and smart energy grids.

The Stakes: In consumer IoT, a device failure inconveniences a user; in IIoT, a single sensor failure in a refinery can trigger a $1M+/hour production shutdown or safety incident. This difference drives every architectural decision, making IIoT systems prioritize reliability, security, and low-latency performance above all else. At its core, IIoT deploys networked sensors, actuators, controllers, and edge gateways to collect, process, and act upon operational data in real time. The goal is not merely to monitor equipment but to optimize processes, predict failures, enhance safety, reduce downtime, improve energy efficiency, and ensure regulatory compliance. IIoT systems are typically integrated with existing Industrial Control Systems (ICS), Programmable Logic Controllers (PLCs), SCADA networks, and Enterprise Resource Planning (ERP) platforms, creating a seamless bridge between Operational Technology (OT) and Information Technology (IT).

Key Characteristics of IIoT

IIoT deployments are distinguished by a set of demanding technical and operational requirements that set them apart from consumer-grade systems:

- **High Reliability and Uptime**: Industrial processes cannot tolerate unplanned downtime. IIoT systems are designed for 99.99 % or higher availability (often referred to as five-nines or better), with redundant power supplies, dual communication paths, and fault-tolerant architectures to ensure continuous operation even during component failures.

- **Deterministic and Real-Time Communication**: Many industrial applications require precise timing and guaranteed delivery of data. Protocols such as OPC UA, PROFINET, EtherCAT, and Time-Sensitive Networking (TSN) over Ethernet or 5G provide deterministic latency in the sub-millisecond range, enabling closed-loop control of robotic arms, conveyor belts, or power distribution.
- **Long Device Lifecycles**: This lifecycle mismatch is a major challenge: IoT devices deployed in 2026 must still be secure, supported, and functional in 2046, while communication protocols (5G→6G) and cloud platforms will evolve multiple times. Design for adaptability (OTA, modular firmware) is essential.
- **Strict Safety and Compliance Requirements**: IIoT systems must comply with rigorous standards such as IEC 61508 (functional safety), IEC 62443 (cybersecurity for industrial automation), ISO 13849 (machine safety), and industry-specific regulations (for example: ATEX for explosive atmospheres, FDA for pharmaceutical manufacturing). Safety is non-negotiable—failure can result in injury, environmental damage, or catastrophic loss.
- **Integration with Legacy Industrial Systems**: Most industrial facilities rely on decades-old equipment (PLCs, DCS, fieldbus systems). IIoT solutions must seamlessly interface with these legacy systems via protocols such as Modbus, Profibus, HART, and OPC UA, often through gateway devices that translate between old and new communication standards.

IIoT and Consumer IoT

Consumer IoT focuses on user experience, convenience, and cost-effectiveness. Devices such as smart thermostats, cameras, speakers, and wearables prioritize ease of setup, attractive design, frequent feature updates, and low purchase price. Uptime is important but not critical — users tolerate occasional reboots or app refreshes. Connectivity is typically Wi-Fi or Bluetooth, and security is improving but often secondary to usability. Data is primarily used for personalization and analytics, not for controlling physical processes. In contrast, IIoT prioritizes reliability, safety, determinism, and long-term operational integrity over cost and user-friendliness. Downtime can cost millions per hour in lost production; a security breach can halt operations or cause environmental disasters. Devices are ruggedized, protocols are deterministic, and security is designed from the ground up. Updates are carefully managed to avoid disrupting production, and systems must operate for decades with minimal maintenance. The value lies not in individual devices but in the optimization of entire processes and the prevention of costly failures.

Dimension	Consumer IoT	IIoT	Why It Matters
Primary Focus	User experience, convenience, cost-effectiveness	Reliability, safety, determinism, operational integrity	Downtime is tolerable vs. downtime costing millions/hr
Uptime/ Reliability	Important, but occasional reboots/ failures are tolerated	Critical; near 100% required	Ensures continuous production and prevents environmental disasters
Latency/ Determinism	Best-effort (Wi-Fi, Bluetooth); non-deterministic	Low-latency, highly deterministic (such as Time-Sensitive Networking)	Guarantees real-time control over physical processes (like robotics)
Operational Lifecycle	Short (1–5 years); frequent replacements/ upgrades	Very long (10–50 years); must operate for decades	Justifies higher upfront cost and complex maintenance procedures

Dimension	Consumer IoT	IIoT	Why It Matters
Security	Often secondary to usability; improving	Designed from the ground up; multi-layered, critical	Protects physical assets, prevents catastrophic failures, maintains IP
Update Cadence	Frequent feature updates; often automated/forced	Carefully managed; infrequent; heavily tested and scheduled	Avoids disruption to production and ensures system stability
Environment/ Ruggedness	Standard indoor environments; aesthetic design	Ruggedized enclosures; must withstand extreme heat, vibration, dust	Ensures functionality in harsh industrial settings
Value Proposition	Personalization, convenience, lifestyle improvements	Optimization of entire processes, preventative maintenance, failure avoidance	Shifts focus from individual product to enterprise-level efficiency and risk mitigation

Table 16.1: *IIoT and Consumer IoT*

While consumer IoT improves daily life, IIoT drives economic productivity, energy efficiency, and industrial safety. As these two worlds converge—through shared technologies like 5G, Edge AI, and cloud platforms—the lessons learned in industrial environments are increasingly informing the design of next-generation consumer systems, and vice versa. IIoT is not simply IoT in factories—it is a distinct discipline that demands extreme reliability, real-time performance, safety certification, and seamless integration with legacy industrial infrastructure. Understanding these differences is essential for engineers, architects, and decision-makers working at the intersection of operational technology and digital transformation.

Role of PLCs, Gateways, and Real-Time Protocols in Factories

Industrial IoT systems rarely operate in isolation. They must integrate seamlessly with decades-old industrial control infrastructure while simultaneously connecting to modern cloud platforms and edge intelligence. This integration is achieved through three foundational elements: Programmable Logic Controllers (PLCs), industrial gateways, and real-time communication protocols. Together, they form the operational backbone of IIoT, ensuring deterministic behavior, safety, and interoperability across legacy and new systems.

Programmable Logic Controllers (PLCs)

PLCs are the workhorses of industrial automation and have been the standard for controlling machinery since the 1970s. These ruggedized, purpose-built controllers are designed to operate reliably in harsh environments—high vibration, extreme temperatures, dust, and electromagnetic interference—where consumer-grade computers would fail quickly. The defining characteristic of a PLC is deterministic execution. Unlike general-purpose processors, PLCs run a fixed scan cycle (typically 1–20 ms) in which they read inputs, execute logic (ladder diagrams, structured text, or function blocks), and update outputs. This cycle repeats indefinitely, guaranteeing that control actions occur at precise, predictable intervals. This determinism is critical for safety-critical applications such as emergency shutdowns, robotic motion control, or conveyor synchronization.

PLCs handle real-time I/O directly through fieldbus connections or integrated modules, ensuring sub-millisecond response times for sensors and actuators. Modern PLCs (for example: Siemens SIMATIC S7, Rockwell Allen-Bradley ControlLogix, Schneider Modicon) also include built-in Ethernet ports,

OPC UA servers, and edge computing capabilities, allowing them to participate in IIoT architectures while maintaining their core real-time responsibilities.

Industrial Gateways

Industrial gateways act as the vital bridge between legacy OT systems and modern IT/cloud environments. They sit at the boundary of the factory floor and the enterprise network, performing protocol translation, data normalization, edge analytics, security enforcement, and data aggregation. Legacy industrial systems often use proprietary or non-IP protocols such as Modbus RTU, Profibus, or HART, which are incompatible with cloud platforms that expect MQTT, HTTP, or OPC UA. Gateways translate these protocols in real time, enabling legacy equipment to participate in IIoT without requiring costly rip-and-replace upgrades. For example, a Modbus-enabled temperature transmitter can send its readings to a cloud dashboard via MQTT after passing through a gateway. Beyond translation, gateways perform edge processing to reduce latency and bandwidth usage. They can run local analytics (for example: anomaly detection, threshold alarming) and only forward summarized data or alerts to the cloud. Gateways also enforce security policies: segmenting OT from IT networks, implementing firewalls, authenticating devices, and encrypting traffic. They often include local storage for buffering data during network outages and support OTA updates for themselves and downstream devices. Common examples include Siemens Scalance, Moxa, Advantech, and Cisco industrial routers/gateways, which are built with industrial-grade components and support multiple protocols simultaneously.

Real-Time Industrial Protocols

To ensure deterministic, low-latency communication in industrial environments, IIoT relies on specialized real-time protocols that provide timing guarantees, fault tolerance, and high reliability.

- **Modbus**: The oldest and most widely deployed protocol, Modbus (both serial and TCP/IP variants) is simple and reliable but lacks built-in real-time guarantees or advanced security. It remains ubiquitous due to its simplicity and backward compatibility.
- **PROFINET**: A leading Ethernet-based standard from PROFIBUS and PROFINET International (PI), PROFINET offers Real-Time (RT) and Isochronous Real-Time (IRT) classes, with cycle times as low as 31.25 µs. It supports distributed clock synchronization and is widely used in high-speed motion control.
- **EtherCAT**: Developed by Beckhoff, EtherCAT achieves cycle times below 100 µs by using a single Ethernet frame that circulates through all slaves, enabling extremely fast and deterministic communication. It is dominant in high-precision applications like robotics and CNC machines.
- **OPC UA (OPC Unified Architecture)**: A platform-independent, secure, and interoperable standard that has become the backbone of modern IIoT. OPC UA provides real-time data access, historical data, alarms and events, security (including certificates and encryption), and information modeling. It is increasingly used for cloud connectivity and vendor-neutral integration.

These protocols ensure that critical control loops remain stable even under network load, while also providing the security and interoperability needed for modern IIoT deployments. PLCs provide deterministic, real-time control at the machine level; gateways bridge legacy OT systems with cloud and IT infrastructure; and real-time protocols ensure precise, reliable communication across the entire industrial network. Together, they form the operational foundation of IIoT, enabling factories and critical infrastructure to achieve high availability, safety, and efficiency while integrating with modern digital technologies. Understanding these components is essential for engineers designing or deploying IIoT solutions in industrial environments.

Edge Intelligence: AI Is Moving Closer to Sensors

The concept of Edge AI, introduced in *Chapter 14, Introduction to ML with Sensor Data*, has evolved from an interesting optimization technique into a fundamental requirement for modern Industrial IoT (IIoT) systems. Five years ago, Edge AI was a novelty demo; today, it is mandatory for applications like collision avoidance (automotive), real-time quality control (manufacturing), and privacy-sensitive medical devices. The question is no longer 'if' but 'how much intelligence at which layer.' In industrial environments, where processes are fast, safety is non-negotiable, and connectivity can never be guaranteed, running artificial intelligence directly on or near the sensors—rather than in distant cloud data centers—is no longer optional. Edge intelligence transforms sensors from passive data collectors into active, autonomous decision-makers capable of interpreting their surroundings and acting in real time.

Edge AI Is Critical in Industrial Environments

Several converging factors make edge intelligence indispensable in IIoT:

- **Ultra-Low Latency Decision-Making:** Many industrial applications demand response times in the millisecond or even microsecond range. A robotic arm adjusting its path based on a vision system, a conveyor belt stopping to prevent a collision, or a safety interlock reacting to a human entering a hazardous zone all require near-instantaneous decisions. Cloud-based inference introduces unavoidable round-trip latency (50–500 ms or more), which can render the system unsafe or inefficient. By executing AI models directly on the device or at the local gateway, edge intelligence eliminates this delay, ensuring deterministic and safe control.
- **Reduced Dependency on Cloud Connectivity:** Industrial facilities often operate in remote locations, underground mines, offshore platforms, or areas with intermittent or expensive connectivity. Relying on constant cloud access for decision-making introduces unacceptable risk. Edge AI enables devices to continue functioning autonomously even during network outages, performing critical tasks such as fault detection, emergency shutdowns, or local control loops without interruption. For instance, during Hurricane Katrina, cellular networks failed but local edge systems with satellite fallback continued operating. Edge autonomy is a disaster-recovery requirement, not just a cost optimization.
- **Lower Bandwidth Usage and Cost Savings:** Continuous streaming of high-resolution video, vibration waveforms, or multi-sensor data to the cloud can quickly overwhelm network capacity and incur high data transfer costs. Edge AI processes raw data locally, extracting only high-level insights (for example: bearing fault detected or product defect classified) and transmitting compact summaries or alerts. This reduces bandwidth consumption by 90–99 % in many cases, making deployments economically viable on constrained networks such as LoRaWAN, NB-IoT, or legacy fieldbus.
- **Increased System Resilience and Fault Tolerance:** Distributed intelligence at the edge means the system is not vulnerable to a single point of failure in the cloud. If a central server or wide-area network fails, edge nodes can continue operating in degraded mode, maintaining production and safety. This resilience is especially important in continuous-process industries (chemicals, oil and gas, power generation) where stopping operations can cost millions per hour.
- **Improved Data Privacy and Regulatory Compliance:** Certain industries (pharmaceuticals, food and beverage, defense) face strict data sovereignty and privacy regulations. Edge AI allows sensitive information to remain on-site, reducing exposure and simplifying compliance with standards such as GDPR, FDA 21 CFR Part 11, or ITAR. Only aggregated or anonymized results are sent to the cloud, minimizing the risk of data breaches.

Real-World Examples of Edge Intelligence in IIoT

- **Vibration-Based Fault Detection on Motors and Pumps:** A TinyML model running on an edge gateway or directly on a vibration sensor analyzes accelerometer data in real time to detect bearing wear, misalignment, or imbalance. When a fault is identified, the system can automatically slow down the machine, schedule maintenance, or trigger an alarm—all without sending gigabytes of raw waveform data to the cloud.
- **Vision-Based Quality Inspection on Assembly Lines:** High-speed cameras paired with lightweight convolutional neural networks (for example, MobileNet or EfficientDet variants) inspect products for defects such as scratches, missing components, or incorrect labeling. The model runs on an edge device (for example: NVIDIA Jetson, Intel Movidius, or even STM32 with an AI accelerator), rejecting faulty items instantly and logging only statistics to the cloud.
- **Safety Monitoring in Hazardous Zones:** In oil refineries or chemical plants, edge AI processes camera feeds and thermal imaging to detect unauthorized personnel entering restricted areas, gas leaks, or abnormal heat signatures. The system can trigger immediate shutdowns or activate sprinklers without waiting for cloud confirmation, ensuring compliance with functional safety standards (SIL 2/3).

Edge intelligence is not merely a performance optimization—it is a strategic necessity in industrial IoT. By moving AI closer to the sensors, IIoT systems achieve the ultra-low latency, independence, resilience, and privacy demanded by mission-critical operations. Sensors evolve from passive observers into intelligent agents that understand their environment, make decisions, and act autonomously. This shift marks a fundamental change in how industrial automation is designed, deployed, and maintained, paving the way for the next generation of smart factories, energy grids, and critical infrastructure.

Intro to Digital Twins: Modeling Physical Systems Virtually

A Digital Twin is a dynamic, virtual replica of a physical asset, process, or system that mirrors its real-world counterpart in near real-time. Think of a digital twin as a video game version of your factory: it mirrors the real world in real time, but you can pause, rewind, fast-forward, or test 'what-if' scenarios without risking the physical asset. It is continuously updated with data from embedded sensors, actuators, and operational systems, creating a living digital model that evolves alongside the physical entity throughout its lifecycle. Coined by NASA in the early 2000s and popularized by industry visionaries, the digital twin concept has matured into one of the cornerstone technologies of Industry 4.0, enabling unprecedented levels of visibility, prediction, and optimization in manufacturing, energy, transportation, healthcare, and infrastructure.

Unlike traditional simulation models that are static or updated periodically, a true digital twin maintains a bidirectional connection with its physical counterpart. Data flows from the physical asset to the twin for monitoring and analysis, while insights, control commands, or optimized parameters can flow back to influence the physical system. This closed-loop interaction transforms the twin from a passive representation into an active tool for decision-making and autonomous operation.

Core Components of a Digital Twin

A functional digital twin architecture comprises several interconnected elements:

- **The Physical System**: This is the real-world entity being twinned—ranging from a single component (for example, a motor, pump, or turbine blade) to an entire process (for example, an assembly line, a wind farm, or a complete factory). The physical asset must be instrumented with sufficient sensors and actuators to provide comprehensive operational data.

- **Sensors and Data Acquisition Layer**: High-fidelity sensors (vibration, temperature, pressure, flow, acoustic, vision, and the like) continuously capture the state, behavior, and environmental conditions of the physical asset. In IIoT deployments, this data is often pre-processed at the edge to filter noise, aggregate readings, and reduce transmission overhead before being sent to the twin.
- **The Virtual Model**: Hosted on cloud platforms, edge servers, or hybrid environments, the digital model is a high-fidelity simulation that replicates the geometry, physics, kinematics, and behavioral characteristics of the physical asset. It may incorporate 3D CAD models, finite-element analysis, thermodynamic simulations, or reduced-order models derived from machine learning. Building a full-physics twin requires specialized expertise (CFD, FEA) and can take months. For many applications, a 'data-driven twin' using ML to predict behavior from historical data delivers 80% of the value at 20% of the cost and time. Leading platforms include Siemens MindSphere, GE Predix, Microsoft Azure Digital Twins, and AWS IoT TwinMaker.
- **Analytics, Prediction, and Control Logic**: Advanced analytics—combining physics-based modeling, statistical methods, and machine learning—process incoming data to detect anomalies, forecast degradation, and recommend or autonomously execute actions. This layer enables predictive maintenance, performance optimization, and scenario simulation.

Digital Twins in Modern Industry

The value of digital twins extends far beyond visualization; they deliver tangible economic and operational benefits that are reshaping industrial practices:

- **Predicting Failures Before They Occur**: By continuously comparing actual sensor data against expected behavior modeled in the twin, anomalies can be detected weeks or months in advance. For example, subtle changes in vibration signatures can signal bearing wear long before catastrophic failure, shifting maintenance from reactive or scheduled to truly predictive. Traditional scheduled maintenance: replace bearings every 5,000 hours (over-maintenance). Digital twin: predict failure at 7,200 hours based on actual vibration (optimal). Result: 40% longer component life and fewer unnecessary shutdowns. Timelines clarify the value proposition.
- **Simulating What-If Scenarios**: Engineers can test operational changes—new production schedules, material variations, or extreme weather conditions—on the virtual twin without risking the physical asset. This capability accelerates design iterations, validates process improvements, and supports compliance testing in regulated industries.
- **Optimizing Performance and Maintenance**: Digital twins enable real-time tuning of operating parameters (for example, adjusting pump speed for maximum efficiency under current load) and optimization of maintenance schedules across entire fleets. Organizations routinely report 15–30% reductions in unplanned downtime and 10–20% improvements in energy efficiency.
- **Reducing Downtime and Operational Costs**: By minimizing unexpected failures and optimizing resource use, digital twins deliver rapid ROI. In capital-intensive sectors like oil and gas, aviation, and power generation, even small improvements translate into millions of dollars saved annually.

Digital twins are increasingly recognized as central to Industry 4.0 and the broader vision of smart manufacturing. They close the loop between the physical and digital worlds, enabling autonomous factories where machines self-optimize, supply chains self-correct, and entire production systems adapt dynamically to demand, disruptions, or sustainability goals. As computing power, sensor density, and AI capabilities continue to advance, digital twins will evolve from asset-level representations to system-of-systems models encompassing entire value chains and cities. For engineers and organizations embracing IIoT, mastering digital twin concepts is no longer optional—it is essential for remaining competitive in an increasingly data-driven industrial landscape.

Examples of Industrial Deployments: Manufacturing, Logistics, Power Grids

The true power of Industrial IoT (IIoT) is best understood through real-world deployments that demonstrate how connected sensors, edge intelligence, and cloud analytics transform operational efficiency, safety, and sustainability in high-stakes industrial environments. The following examples highlight deployments across three critical sectors: manufacturing, logistics, and power grids. Each case illustrates the integration of physical assets, real-time data, and intelligent decision-making to achieve measurable improvements in uptime, cost, and performance.

Manufacturing

In modern smart factories, IIoT enables predictive maintenance, automated quality control, and dynamic production optimization.

- **Predictive Maintenance of Motors and Rotating Equipment:** Vibration, temperature, and acoustic sensors are embedded in motors, pumps, gearboxes, and compressors. TinyML models running on edge gateways continuously analyze signatures to detect early signs of bearing wear, misalignment, imbalance, or lubrication failure. When anomalies are identified, the system automatically schedules maintenance during planned downtime, alerts technicians with root-cause analysis, and adjusts machine speed to prevent catastrophic failure. Leading manufacturers report 20–40% reductions in unplanned downtime and 15–30 % lower maintenance costs.
- **Vision-Based Quality Inspection on Assembly Lines:** High-speed industrial cameras paired with lightweight convolutional neural networks inspect products for defects such as scratches, incorrect labeling, missing components, or dimensional variations. Edge processing ensures sub-millisecond decisions, rejecting faulty items instantly and logging only statistics to the cloud. This approach achieves >99 % detection accuracy, eliminates human error, and supports 100 % inspection at line speeds previously limited to sampling.
- **Production Optimization and Digital Twins:** Real-time data from machines, robots, and environmental sensors feeds digital twins of entire production lines. The twsimulates process changes (for example: increasing conveyor speed or altering material feed rates) and recommends optimal parameters to maximize throughput, minimize energy use, and reduce scrap. This approach is most effective for complex production lines (including lines with >10 process steps or >50 major machines). Manufacturers using this approach have achieved 10–25% productivity gains and significant energy savings.

Logistics and Supply Chain

Logistics operations benefit from IIoT through precise asset visibility, route optimization, and condition monitoring across global networks.

- **Asset Tracking in Warehouses and Distribution Centers:** RFID tags, Bluetooth beacons, and ultra-wideband (UWB) anchors provide real-time location accuracy down to centimeters. Edge gateways aggregate location data and integrate it with Warehouse Management Systems (WMS) to optimize picking routes, reduce search time, and prevent misplaced inventory. Large distribution centers have reported 30–50 % faster order fulfillment and near-zero inventory discrepancies.

- **Route Optimization for Fleets:** Connected vehicles equipped with GPS, telematics, and environmental sensors transmit real-time data on location, fuel consumption, driver behavior, and traffic conditions. Cloud-based AI platforms analyze this data alongside weather forecasts and delivery constraints to generate dynamic, fuel-efficient routes. Fleet operators using IIoT-enabled route optimization achieve 10–20% fuel savings and improved on-time delivery rates.
- **Cold-Chain Monitoring for Perishables:** Battery-powered sensors continuously track temperature, humidity, and shock levels inside refrigerated trailers, containers, and storage facilities. Edge intelligence detects excursions (for example: door left open) and triggers immediate alerts. Blockchain integration ensures tamper-proof records for regulatory compliance. Pharmaceutical and food companies report near-100 % product integrity and drastically reduced spoilage losses.
- **Supply Chain Integration:** Supply chain integration refers to the seamless coordination and sharing of data between different stakeholders involved in the supply chain, including manufacturers, suppliers, logistics providers, warehouses, and retailers. In IIoT-enabled environments, connected sensors, tracking systems, and cloud platforms allow real-time visibility of goods, inventory levels, shipment conditions, and delivery status across the entire supply chain. This integration improves decision-making, reduces delays, minimizes inventory discrepancies, and enhances overall operational efficiency by ensuring that all participants operate with synchronized and accurate information.

  Note: *Modern logistics IoT integrates with* ERP (SAP, *Oracle*) *and* TMS (*transportation management*) *systems, not just standalone dashboards. API-first design and standard data formats* (EPCIS *for* RFID) *are essential for enterprise deployments.*

Power Grids and Utilities

IIoT is revolutionizing the management of electrical grids, enabling smarter, more resilient, and more sustainable energy systems.

- **Smart Meters and Advanced Metering Infrastructure (AMI):** Millions of smart meters transmit consumption data in near real-time, enabling dynamic pricing, demand-response programs, and theft detection. Edge processing at the meter level identifies tampering or abnormal usage patterns, while cloud analytics forecast demand and optimize load distribution. Utilities achieve 5–15% reductions in non-technical losses and improved customer satisfaction through accurate billing.
- **Load Balancing and Grid Stability:** Distributed sensors monitor voltage, current, and frequency across transmission and distribution networks. Edge AI at substations detects imbalances and automatically adjusts capacitor banks, transformers, or demand-response loads to maintain stability. This capability is critical for integrating intermittent renewable sources (solar, wind) while preventing blackouts.
- **Fault Isolation and Rapid Recovery:** Sensors and Intelligent Electronic Devices (IEDs) detect faults (for example, downed lines, short circuits) within milliseconds. Edge logic isolates the faulted section and reroutes power through alternative paths, minimizing outage scope and duration. Modern grids using IIoT achieve self-healing capabilities, reducing average outage times from hours to minutes.

These deployments demonstrate the transformative impact of IIoT across industries. By combining real-time visibility, edge intelligence, and cloud-scale analytics, organizations gain unprecedented control over complex, mission-critical systems. The result is higher reliability, lower costs, improved safety, and the ability to respond dynamically to changing conditions—hallmarks of the next generation of industrial infrastructure.

Role of 5G in High-Throughput, Low-Latency IoT Systems

The fifth-generation mobile network (5G) represents one of the most significant enablers of the next decade of IoT, unlocking capabilities that were previously constrained by the limitations of 4G/LTE, Wi-Fi, and legacy cellular technologies. While 4G had delivered broadband connectivity to billions of smartphones, 5G is fundamentally designed for massive-scale machine-to-machine communication, ultra-reliable low-latency applications, and the seamless integration of billions of IoT devices. Its technical advancements directly address the long-standing pain points of industrial, critical, and consumer IoT deployments.

Key Capabilities of 5G for IoT

5G introduces four transformative features that redefine what IoT systems can achieve:

- **Ultra-Low Latency:** 5G achieves end-to-end latency as low as 1 millisecond (and sub-millisecond in some configurations) through advanced radio access techniques (for example: short transmission time intervals, massive MIMO, and beamforming). This is orders of magnitude faster than the typical 20–50 ms latency of 4G, enabling real-time control loops that were previously impossible over wireless networks.

  5G supports up to 1 million devices per square kilometer (equivalent to approximately one device per square meter), making it feasible to deploy dense sensor networks in factories, ports, smart cities, or agricultural fields without overwhelming the network. This massive connectivity (mMTC) is critical for applications requiring thousands of sensors per site. To visualize this density: it enables smart cities to sensor every parking space, streetlight, and trash bin—a level of granularity previously impossible. For context, an area the size of Manhattan (~60 km^2) could support up to 60 million sensors on 5G, compared to an estimated 3–5 million on 4G.

- **Network Slicing:** Operators can create virtual, isolated network slices tailored to specific use cases. A single physical 5G infrastructure can simultaneously support a low-latency slice for robotic control, a high-bandwidth slice for video surveillance, and a massive IoT slice optimized for low-power, infrequent sensor reporting—all with guaranteed Quality of Service (QoS).

- **High Throughput and Reliability:** Peak data rates exceed 20 Gbps, while Ultra-Reliable Low-Latency Communication (URLLC) provides packet delivery reliability up to 99.9999%. This combination supports bandwidth-intensive applications such as 4K/8K video streaming from drones or cameras, as well as mission-critical control in hazardous environments.

Impact of 5G on Key IoT Applications

The capabilities of 5G enable entirely new classes of IoT systems that operate at human-perception timescales or faster.

- **Autonomous Vehicles and V2X Communication:** Vehicle-to-everything (V2X) communication requires sub-millisecond latency for real-time coordination between cars, infrastructure, and pedestrians. 5G enables cooperative sensing, platooning, and emergency collision avoidance at highway speeds—capabilities that 4G could not guarantee.

- **Remote Robotic Control and Teleoperation:** Heavy machinery, surgical robots, or drones can be operated remotely with near-zero perceptible delay. This enables applications such as remote mining operations, disaster response robotics, and telesurgery, where operators control equipment as if they were physically present.

- **Augmented Reality (AR) and Virtual Reality (VR)-Assisted Maintenance:** Field technicians wearing AR headsets can receive real-time overlays of schematics, torque values, or remote expert guidance. The high bandwidth and low latency of 5G ensures smooth, lag-free AR experiences, significantly reducing repair times and improving first-time-fix rates.
- **Smart City Infrastructure:** Dense deployments of traffic cameras, environmental sensors, smart lighting, and public safety systems can operate seamlessly on a single network. Network slicing ensures that emergency services receive priority while routine monitoring remains cost-effective.
- **Industrial Automation and Private 5G Networks:** Factories are increasingly deploying private 5G networks to guarantee deterministic performance for robots, Automated Guided Vehicles (AGVs), and real-time process control. These networks eliminate the interference and latency variability of Wi-Fi, enabling fully wireless production lines.

5G is not merely an incremental upgrade for IoT; it is a foundational enabler that removes the last major barriers to truly real-time, massive-scale, and mission-critical connectivity. By delivering ultra-low latency, extreme reliability, massive device density, and flexible network slicing, 5G allows IoT systems to operate at human-perception timescales or faster—making applications such as autonomous mobility, remote teleoperation, and fully wireless factories a practical reality. As 5G deployment accelerates and 6G begins to emerge, it will further amplify the intelligence, autonomy, and pervasiveness of connected systems across industries and societies. For IoT professionals, understanding and leveraging 5G is no longer optional – it is essential for designing the next generation of intelligent, responsive, and resilient infrastructure.

Data Lifecycle in Industrial IoT

In Industrial IoT (IIoT) systems, raw sensor readings are transformed into actionable intelligence through a carefully orchestrated data lifecycle. This lifecycle spans multiple stages, from the physical edge to the cloud and back, ensuring that data is collected efficiently, processed intelligently, transmitted securely, and ultimately drives precise, timely decisions. Each stage is designed to balance latency, bandwidth, reliability, security, and cost—critical requirements in industrial environments where downtime or errors can have severe consequences. This 'data reduction funnel' is the key to economical IIoT. Visualizing the volume reduction clarifies the architecture.

- **Edge Sensing: Data Acquisition at the Source:** The journey begins at the physical asset itself. Sensors embedded in machines, motors, valves, pipelines, or environmental monitoring points continuously capture high-fidelity data: vibration waveforms, temperature profiles, pressure readings, acoustic signatures, electrical current, flow rates, video frames, or gas concentrations. These sensors operate in harsh conditions and must provide high accuracy, stability, and robustness. Modern IIoT deployments often use multi-sensor fusion, combining several measurement types to create a richer picture of the state of the asset. At this stage, the focus is on high-resolution sampling, precise timestamping, and minimal data loss.
- **Local Preprocessing and Filtering at the Edge:** Immediately after acquisition, data undergoes local preprocessing on the edge device or nearby gateway. This stage is critical for reducing volume and extracting value. Common tasks include noise filtering, downsampling, feature extraction (for example : RMS vibration levels, FFT frequency peaks, statistical summaries), anomaly detection, and event triggering. TinyML models running on resource-constrained edge nodes can classify events (for example: bearing fault versus normal operation) or reject irrelevant data, transmitting only meaningful insights or alerts. This step dramatically reduces bandwidth usage (often by 90–99%) and enables real-time decisions even during network outages.

- **Secure Transmission to the Cloud or On-Premises Systems:** Processed data is securely transmitted to the next layer. Industrial protocols such as OPC UA, MQTT over TLS, or HTTPS with mutual authentication ensure confidentiality, integrity, and authenticity. Many deployments use private 5G networks, industrial Ethernet, or dedicated fiber links to guarantee reliability and low latency. Data is often encrypted end-to-end, with device certificates and zero-trust principles enforced. During transmission, buffering and retry mechanisms handle temporary connectivity disruptions, ensuring no critical data is lost.
- **Cloud or On-Premises Storage and Management:** Once received, data is stored in time-series databases (for example: InfluxDB, TimescaleDB, Azure Time Series Insights) optimized for high-velocity industrial data. Hot storage retains recent, high-value data for immediate analysis, while cold storage (for example: object storage like S3 or Azure Blob) archives historical data for long-term trends and compliance. Data lakes integrate structured and unstructured sources, enabling advanced analytics across multiple assets. Governance policies enforce retention periods, access controls, and audit trails to meet regulatory requirements.
- **AI Inference and Advanced Analytics:** This stage transforms raw or preprocessed data into actionable intelligence. Cloud-based or on-premises AI platforms run complex models—deep learning for fault classification, reinforcement learning for process optimization, or physics-informed neural networks for simulation. Digital twins receive real-time data streams to update their virtual models, enabling predictive maintenance, anomaly detection, and performance forecasting. The results are scored for confidence and severity, with thresholds triggering alerts or automated actions.
- **Decision-Making and Actuation:** The final stage closes the loop. Insights are delivered to operators via dashboards, mobile apps, or AR interfaces, or fed directly into control systems for automated actuation—adjusting machine speeds, scheduling maintenance, or initiating emergency shutdowns. Feedback from actuation flows back to the physical asset, updating the digital twin and refining future predictions. This bidirectional flow creates a closed-loop system where data continuously drives optimization and safety.

The IIoT data lifecycle is a highly engineered process that turns billions of sensor readings into high-value intelligence while respecting the constraints of industrial environments: determinism, security, reliability, and cost. By intelligently distributing computation between edge and cloud, IIoT systems achieve the speed, resilience, and efficiency required for real-time control, predictive maintenance, and autonomous operation. This lifecycle is the foundation of smart factories, intelligent grids, and resilient infrastructure, ensuring that data is not merely collected, but actively harnessed to improve safety, efficiency, and sustainability.

Role of IoT and Sustainability

The Internet of Things has emerged as one of the most powerful enablers of sustainability in the 21st century. By providing real-time visibility, precise control, and data-driven decision-making, IoT systems help industries and societies reduce resource consumption, minimize waste, lower greenhouse gas emissions, and transition toward circular and low-carbon economies. In an era of climate urgency and resource scarcity, IoT transforms sustainability from an aspirational goal into a measurable, operational reality.

Smart Grids and Energy Systems

Smart grids represent one of the most impactful applications of IoT for sustainability. Distributed sensors and smart meters monitor electricity generation, transmission, and consumption in real time. Dynamic energy balancing algorithms adjust supply and demand instantaneously, reducing the need for fossil-fuel peaker plants. IoT enables seamless integration of intermittent renewable sources—

solar, wind, and hydro—by forecasting generation and shifting loads accordingly. Demand-response programs use connected appliances and industrial loads to shed non-critical usage during peak times, flattening demand curves and avoiding costly infrastructure upgrades. These capabilities collectively reduce energy waste, increase grid efficiency, and accelerate the decarbonization of power systems.

Smart Farming and Precision Agriculture

In agriculture, IoT delivers precision farming techniques that optimize resource use while maximizing yields. Soil moisture, temperature, and nutrient sensors guide targeted irrigation systems that deliver water only where and when it is needed, reducing water consumption by 20–50% in many cases. Variable-rate fertilizer application, controlled by IoT-enabled spreaders, applies nutrients precisely based on real-time soil and crop data, minimizing runoff and chemical pollution. Drone-mounted multispectral cameras and satellite imagery, integrated with IoT platforms, monitor crop health and detect pests or disease early, reducing the need for broad-spectrum pesticides. Yield optimization models combine historical data with weather forecasts to recommend planting schedules, seed varieties, and harvest timing, increasing food production while lowering environmental impact.

Industrial Energy Monitoring and Carbon Footprint Tracking

In manufacturing and heavy industry, IoT enables continuous energy audits and carbon accounting. Sub-metering devices track electricity, gas, steam, and compressed air usage at the machine level, identifying inefficiencies and leaks. Real-time dashboards highlight high-consumption processes, allowing operators to adjust settings, schedule maintenance, or shift production to off-peak hours. Carbon footprint tracking systems aggregate data from energy meters, fuel usage, and supply-chain inputs to calculate Scope 1, 2, and 3 emissions in real time. This transparency supports compliance with ESG reporting requirements, carbon pricing schemes, and corporate net-zero commitments. Many facilities have achieved 10–30% reductions in energy intensity through IoT-driven optimization.

Broader Impact

Beyond these examples, IoT contributes to sustainability in waste management (smart bins and recycling optimization), transportation (traffic flow management and electric vehicle charging networks), and buildings (smart HVAC and lighting control). The common thread is data-driven decision-making: IoT turns invisible inefficiencies into visible opportunities for conservation and efficiency.

IoT is not just a technology for connectivity—it is a foundational tool for building sustainable systems. By providing granular visibility, predictive intelligence, and automated optimization, IoT empowers industries and governments to achieve more with less, aligning economic growth with environmental responsibility in a resource-constrained world.

Emerging Trends in IoT

The Internet of Things is entering a new phase of maturity, moving beyond connectivity and basic intelligence toward fully autonomous, adaptive, and self-managing ecosystems. Several powerful trends are converging to shape this future, each building on the foundations of edge computing, AI, and advanced networking. These developments will enable IoT systems to operate with minimal human intervention, respond dynamically to changing conditions, and scale to planetary levels.

Hyperautomation

Hyperautomation integrates IoT, Artificial Intelligence, Robotic Process Automation (RPA), and low-code platforms to automate entire end-to-end workflows across physical and digital processes. For clarity, we shall distinguish it from traditional automation: "**Traditional:** Automate a single task (robotic welding). **Hyperautomation:** Automate the entire process—from quality inspection (vision AI) to defect routing (RPA) to supplier notification (NLP chatbot) to production schedule adjustment (optimization AI)—with no human in the loop. It is end-to-end versus point solutions."

In a factory, for example, sensors detect a quality issue, AI classifies the defect, RPA triggers a service ticket, and an autonomous robot reroutes the part—all without human involvement. Hyperautomation extends beyond traditional automation by combining structured data from IoT devices with unstructured data (for example: maintenance logs, video feeds) and orchestrating actions across multiple systems. This trend is accelerating digital transformation in manufacturing, logistics, and utilities, driving efficiency gains of 30–50 % in complex operations.

Swarm Robotics

Swarm robotics enables large groups of simple, low-cost robots to collaborate intelligently without centralized control. Each robot operates using local rules and communication with nearby units, mimicking biological swarms such as ant colonies or bird flocks. In industrial settings, swarms of drones or ground robots can perform warehouse inventory, search for leaks in pipelines, or clean solar panels in large arrays. The absence of a single point of failure makes swarm systems highly resilient—individual robots can fail or be replaced without disrupting the mission. Swarm intelligence, powered by edge AI and mesh networking, is poised to transform inspection, logistics, and hazardous environment operations.

TinyML Growth

TinyML—the deployment of machine learning models on ultra-low-power microcontrollers—continues to expand rapidly. Advances in model compression, hardware accelerators (for example: Arm Ethos-U, Syntiant NDP, Google Coral Edge TPU), and automated optimization tools have made it possible to run sophisticated neural networks on devices with less than 1 mW of power. TinyML is now embedded in wearables, industrial sensors, smart agriculture probes, and consumer products for tasks such as anomaly detection, keyword spotting, and gesture recognition. The trend is accelerating as costs drop and accuracy improves, enabling intelligence to move even closer to the physical world.

Self-Healing Networks

Self-healing networks automatically detect, diagnose, and recover from failures without human intervention. In an IIoT context, this means a sensor node that loses connectivity can reroute through neighboring devices via mesh networking, a gateway that detects a fault can failover to a backup, or a fleet management system that identifies degraded performance can autonomously trigger OTA updates or reconfiguration. Self-healing is achieved through AI-driven monitoring, redundancy, and predictive maintenance at the network level. This capability is essential for critical infrastructure such as power grids, transportation systems, and remote industrial sites where downtime is unacceptable.

These emerging trends—hyperautomation, swarm robotics, TinyML growth, and self-healing networks—collectively point toward a future of autonomous, adaptive IoT ecosystems. Systems will not only collect and analyze data but also act, collaborate, learn, and recover with minimal human oversight. This evolution will drive unprecedented efficiency, resilience, and scalability, redefining industrial processes, urban infrastructure, and environmental monitoring. For engineers and organizations, mastering these trends is essential to remain competitive in an increasingly intelligent and connected world.

Certifications in IoT + AI (Azure, AWS IoT, Edge AI)

The convergence of IoT, artificial intelligence, 5G connectivity, digital twins, and industrial automation is creating a new generation of high-impact, high-demand career opportunities. As organizations across industries accelerate digital transformation, professionals who can design, deploy, secure, and optimize connected systems are in unprecedented demand. Certifications validate expertise and are highly regarded by employers. The following are among the most recognized in the IoT and IIoT fields:

- **AWS Certified IoT Specialty:** Demonstrates proficiency in designing and deploying IoT solutions on AWS, including device provisioning, OTA, security, and analytics.
- **Microsoft Azure IoT Developer Specialty:** Covers Azure IoT Hub, Digital Twins, Edge modules, and integration with Azure services.
- **Google Cloud Professional IoT Engineer:** Focuses on Cloud IoT Core, Pub/Sub, and edge computing with Google Cloud.
- **Arm Embedded Systems Developer:** Validates embedded programming and optimization skills for Arm-based processors.
- **TinyML / Edge AI Certifications:** Offered by Edge Impulse, Arm, and the TinyML Foundation, these credentials prove expertise in deploying ML on resource-constrained devices.
- **Cisco Certified Internet of Things Specialist:** Covers IoT networking, security, and industrial connectivity.
- **IEC 62443 Cybersecurity Certifications:** Essential for industrial roles, focusing on securing OT environments.

The IoT job market is growing faster than most other technology sectors. Organizations need professionals who can bridge Operational Technology (OT) and Information Technology (IT), implement secure and scalable systems, and extract value from massive data streams. Roles that combine embedded development with AI, cloud, and cybersecurity command the highest salaries and offer the greatest influence on business outcomes.

For students and early-career professionals, the message is clear: build hands-on experience with real hardware, master both edge and cloud technologies, and pursue certifications that validate your skills. The next decade will belong to those who can design intelligent, resilient, and sustainable connected systems. The IoT revolution is creating career opportunities that are not only lucrative but also deeply meaningful—shaping the factories, cities, energy systems, and critical infrastructure of tomorrow.

Final Motivation: Building a Future-Ready Mindset for the IoT Age

The IoT landscape is evolving so rapidly that technical knowledge alone is no longer sufficient. By the time a student graduates, many of the contemporary advanced tools and protocols will be considered legacy. To thrive in this dynamic field, learners must cultivate a mindset that emphasizes adaptability, holistic understanding, and lifelong curiosity. This section outlines the four core mental habits that will separate successful IoT professionals from the rest.

- **Systems Thinking:** IoT is never about a single device. A smart thermostat is meaningless without its cloud backend, mobile app, energy provider integration, and regulatory compliance. Future engineers must train themselves to see the entire system: how a change in sensor sampling rate affects battery life, cloud costs, network congestion, and user experience. Practice drawing architecture diagrams that span hardware, firmware, edge, cloud, security, and business value. Ask repeatedly: What happens if this component fails? How does this decision impact the whole ecosystem? System thinking prevents siloed designs and prepares you for troubleshooting complex, interdependent failures. Practice: For your next project, create a Failure-Modes and Effects Analysis (FMEA) table. For each component, ask: What if this fails? How does it cascade? What is the recovery path? This discipline trains systems thinking and is standard in automotive/aerospace IoT.

- **Security-First Design (Shift-Left Security)**: In the IoT era, every connected device is a potential attack surface. The mindset shift is to treat security as a foundational requirement, not an afterthought. Embed security considerations from day one: unique device identities, secure boot, encrypted communication, minimal attack surface, regular OTA patching, and privacy-by-design.
- **Continuous Learning and Comfort with Uncertainty:** The half-life of IoT knowledge is short. New protocols (Matter, 6G), frameworks (Zephyr RTOS), chip families (RISC-V boom), and AI techniques emerge constantly. Adopt a habit of deliberate learning: follow key voices on X/Twitter, read IEEE papers, experiment with new dev boards quarterly, and contribute to open-source projects. Accept that you will never know everything—and that is okay. The valuable skill is to know how to learn quickly: read a datasheet, prototype a proof-of-concept, search for community solutions, and iterate. Comfort with uncertainty is the superpower in a field that reinvents itself every 18–24 months.
- **Cross-Domain Knowledge (T-Shaped Professional)**: Gone are the days when an IoT engineer could specialize only in firmware. The most impactful professionals are T-shaped: deep expertise in one area (the vertical bar) combined with broad knowledge across domains (the horizontal bar). A strong IoT engineer today understands:
    - Hardware basics (PCB layout, power electronics, RF considerations)
    - Embedded software (RTOS, drivers, memory management)
    - Networking (TCP/IP, 5G slicing, mesh protocols)
    - Cloud platforms (AWS IoT, Azure Digital Twins)
    - AI/ML (TinyML, federated learning)
    - Cybersecurity (zero-trust, secure provisioning)
    - Business ontext (ROI, compliance, sustainability)

Even if you never design a PCB, understanding signal integrity helps you debug noisy sensor readings. Even if you never train a model, knowing TinyML limitations helps you decide what belongs at the edge versus the cloud.

The IoT engineers of the future will not merely build devices. They will design connected, intelligent ecosystems that sense, reason, act, self-heal, and evolve while respecting safety, security, privacy, and sustainability. Cultivating the four mindsets above—systems thinking, security-first, continuous learning, and cross-domain fluency—prepares you not just to follow trends, but to anticipate and shape them.

Start small: Build one complete project end-to-end, break it on purpose, fix it, document your decisions, and explain the trade-offs to someone else. Repeat. Over time, this practice rewires your brain for the complexity and velocity of the IoT world. The tools and platforms will change constantly, but the mindset you build now will carry you through decades of innovation.

Practical Exercises

Exercise 1: Industry Deep Dive – IIoT versus Consumer IoT

This exercise explores the key differences between Industrial IoT (IIoT) and Consumer IoT, focusing on architecture, reliability, and real-time requirements. The goal is to analyze how these factors vary across sectors, helping learners understand why industrial systems demand higher rigor.

Step 1: Research and Select Sectors

Begin by selecting two sectors: one from IIoT (for example, manufacturing, energy grids, or logistics) and one from Consumer IoT (for example, smart homes, wearables, or connected vehicles). Use online resources or textbooks to gather basic information on typical applications in each. For IIoT, note examples such as predictive maintenance in factories; for Consumer IoT, consider voice-activated assistants.

Step 2: Compare Architectures

Create a side-by-side comparison table or diagram outlining the architectures. For IIoT, highlight ruggedized hardware (for example: PLCs, industrial gateways), deterministic protocols (for example, PROFINET, OPC UA), and hybrid edge-cloud setups with on-premises redundancy. For Consumer IoT, describe consumer-grade devices (for example, Wi-Fi-enabled sensors), cloud-centric models (for example, AWS IoT or Google Home), and simpler protocols (for example, MQTT over Wi-Fi). Discuss how IIoT architectures prioritize fault tolerance and integration with legacy systems, while Consumer IoT emphasizes ease of use and scalability for mass markets.

Step 3: Analyze Reliability and Real-Time Requirements

Evaluate reliability: For IIoT, explain the need for >99.99 % uptime, long lifecycles (10–30 years), and certifications (for example: IEC 61508 for safety). Contrast with the tolerance of Consumer IoT for occasional downtime and shorter product lifecycles (2–5 years). For real-time aspects, describe the sub-millisecond latency needs of IIoT(for example, robotic control) versus acceptable delays of Consumer IoT(for example : 100–500 ms for smart lighting). Use sector-specific examples to illustrate risks: a factory shutdown versus a delayed home notification.

Step 4: Synthesize Insights and Report

Write a short report (500–1,000 words) summarizing your analysis, including recommendations for when to apply IIoT principles to consumer applications (for example: in critical home health monitoring). This step develops your ability to adapt designs across contexts.

Exercise 2: Digital Twin Simulator

This conceptual exercise involves designing a digital twin for a physical system and mapping its data flow. The objective is to understand how digital twins enable prediction and optimization, preparing learners for roles in smart manufacturing or asset management.

Step 1: Choose a Physical System

Select a simple yet realistic physical asset, such as a wind turbine, conveyor belt, or HVAC system. Describe its key components (for example, blades, sensors, motor) and operational parameters (for example, rotation speed, temperature, vibration).

Step 2: Define the Virtual Model

Outline the structure of the digital twin: a virtual simulation mirroring the physical asset. Specify software tools (for example, conceptual use of Siemens MindSphere or Microsoft Azure Digital Twins) and model elements (for example: 3D geometry, physics equations for wind flow, or ML models for wear prediction). Identify bidirectional links: sensor data updates the twin, while twin insights (for example, optimized blade angle) feed back to the asset.

Step 3: Map the Data Flow

Create a flowchart showing the data lifecycle: edge sensing (for example, vibration data collection), local preprocessing (for example, filtering noise), secure transmission to the cloud, storage and analysis (for example, anomaly detection), and actuation (for example, alert for maintenance). Highlight feedback loops and potential bottlenecks (for example, latency in remote locations).

Step 4: Simulate Scenarios and Evaluate

Test the twin conceptually by simulating scenarios (for example, high winds causing fatigue). Predict outcomes (for example, failure in 3 months) and propose optimizations (for example, reduce speed). Document your design in a report, discussing benefits like reduced downtime and challenges like data accuracy.

Exercise 3: Edge versus Cloud AI – Use Case Mapping

This exercise requires deciding the optimal placement of AI (edge, cloud, or hybrid) for various IoT applications. The aim is to develop judgment on trade-offs like latency, privacy, and cost, essential for future Edge AI roles.

Step 1: Identify Use Cases

List 5–7 diverse IoT applications (for example: fall detection in wearables, defect inspection in manufacturing, traffic prediction in smart cities, or crop monitoring in agriculture). For each, note key requirements: latency tolerance, data volume, privacy needs, and connectivity reliability.

Step 2: Evaluate Trade-Offs

For each use case, analyze pros/cons of edge AI (for example: low latency but limited compute), cloud AI (for example, powerful models but high bandwidth), and hybrid (for example, edge for real-time, cloud for training). Consider factors like power constraints (edge suits battery devices) and scalability (cloud for massive data).

Step 3: Map Optimal Placement

Create a decision matrix: rows for use cases, columns for placement options, with justifications. For example, edge for fall detection (needs <50 ms response, privacy-sensitive), cloud for traffic prediction (requires city-wide data aggregation), hybrid for crop monitoring (edge anomaly flagging, cloud yield forecasting).

Step 4: Justify and Reflect

Write a explaining your mappings, including edge tools (for example, TinyML) or cloud platforms (for example, AWS SageMaker). Reflect on how 5G might shift mappings toward the edge. This builds strategic thinking for AI deployment.

Exercise 4: Swarm Robotics Simulation

This design-focused exercise involves creating decentralized coordination logic for multiple IoT devices acting as a swarm. The goal is to conceptualize swarm intelligence, preparing learners for trends in collaborative robotics and distributed systems.

Step 1: Define the Swarm Scenario

Choose a scenario (for example, warehouse inventory robots, environmental monitoring drones, or search-and-rescue bots). Specify 5–10 devices, each with capabilities (for example, movement, sensing, local communication) and constraints (for example, limited battery, no central controller).

Step 2: Design Local Rules

Outline simple, decentralized rules for each device. For example, If low battery, move to charging station; otherwise, explore unvisited areas. Use concepts like attraction (group cohesion), repulsion (collision avoidance), and alignment (shared direction). Ensure rules rely only on local data (for example, neighbor broadcasts via BLE mesh).

Step 3: Simulate Coordination

Sketch a flowchart or state diagram showing how rules lead to emergent behavior (for example, flocking to cover an area efficiently). Simulate manually: describe step-by-step how the swarm responds to events like an obstacle or target discovery. Highlight resilience (for example, one failure does not halt the swarm).

Step 4: Evaluate and Document

Assess pros/cons (for example: scalability versus complexity) and suggest improvements (for example: add AI for adaptive rules). Document it in a report with diagrams, discussing real-world applications like the warehouse bots of Amazon. This fosters understanding of distributed autonomy.

Conclusion

This chapter has taken readers beyond the current state of IoT and into its rapidly emerging future. We explored the critical evolution from consumer-focused devices to large-scale, mission-critical industrial ecosystems powered by Industrial IoT (IIoT). We examined the indispensable role of edge intelligence in enabling ultra-low-latency decisions, the transformative power of digital twins in virtualizing physical assets, and the foundational impact of 5G and emerging 6G connectivity in delivering deterministic, massive-scale, and real-time communication. Emerging trends such as hyperautomation, swarm robotics, TinyML proliferation, and self-healing networks were highlighted as key drivers of autonomous, adaptive IoT ecosystems that operate with minimal human intervention. The chapter also provided a clear view of the data lifecycle in IIoT, emphasizing how raw sensor data becomes actionable intelligence through intelligent edge–cloud partitioning. We discussed the vital contribution of IoT to sustainability—through smart grids, precision agriculture, and industrial energy optimization—and outlined the high-demand career paths that await professionals who master these technologies. Finally, we encouraged the development of a future-ready mindset: systems thinking, security-first design, continuous learning, and cross-domain fluency. By the end of this chapter, readers are no longer just equipped to build the contemporary IoT systems—they are prepared to anticipate, design, and lead the next generation of connected, intelligent, and sustainable infrastructure.

The next chapter brings together all the concepts covered throughout the textbook in a comprehensive, real-world capstone project. Learners will design, build, test, and deploy a fully functional IoT system from the ground up—integrating hardware, firmware, edge intelligence, cloud connectivity, security, and fleet management. The project will simulate a complete industrial or smart-city use case, requiring students to apply every major topic from Chapters 1 through 16: sensor interfacing, embedded programming, real-time protocols, Edge AI, OTA updates, digital twins, sustainability considerations, and production-grade deployment practices. Through this hands-on capstone, readers will experience the entire IoT development lifecycle—from requirements gathering and architecture design to testing, scaling, and future-proofing.

Plan 20–40 hours for the capstone project—comparable to a real-world sprint. Use project management tools (Trello, GitHub Projects), document your architecture decisions, and create a 5-minute demo video. These artifacts become your portfolio, proving to employers that you can deliver end-to-end IoT solutions, not just complete tutorials.

CHAPTER 17

Applied IoT with Edge AI and Vision

Introduction

The preceding chapters have provided a comprehensive foundation of the core principles and technologies of the Internet of Things: from sensor interfacing and embedded firmware development to secure cloud connectivity, Edge AI with TinyML, industrial protocols, fleet management, and sustainable design. Readers have learned how to build reliable, intelligent, and scalable IoT systems using resource-constrained microcontrollers such as ESP32, STM32, and nRF52 series. However, certain high-value IoT applications demand significantly more computational power than traditional microcontrollers can provide. Tasks such as real-time image classification, object detection, video analytics, facial recognition, license-plate reading, defect inspection, and advanced gesture recognition require deep neural networks, high-resolution processing, and parallel computation—capabilities that exceed the limits of 8-bit or even high-end Cortex-M devices.

This final chapter explores the frontier of applied IoT where powerful edge-computing platforms bridge the gap between low-power microcontrollers and full cloud processing. We introduce single-board computers such as the Raspberry Pi family and NVIDIA Jetson series, which run full Linux operating systems, support Python, OpenCV, TensorFlow, PyTorch, and ONNX, and deliver GPU-accelerated inference at the edge. These platforms enable vision-based IoT systems that can visually interpret the physical world, make complex decisions in real time, and operate autonomously in environments where latency, bandwidth, or privacy constraints prohibit cloud dependency. The second half of the chapter shifts focus from technology to real-world adoption. Through detailed case studies drawn from agriculture, energy, logistics, and manufacturing, readers will see how complete IoT + AI systems are deployed at scale. Each case highlights architectural decisions, communication protocols, security strategies, edge–cloud partitioning, and measurable business impact—illustrating how the concepts learned throughout the textbook are applied in production environments.

For students approaching the job market, adding: "Mastering vision-based IoT sets you apart: only ~20% of IoT engineers have hands-on CV experience, yet vision applications represent 40–50% of high-value industrial IoT projects. This skill combination—embedded systems + computer vision—makes you highly competitive for roles at companies like Amazon Robotics, Tesla, John Deere, or manufacturing automation providers." Career context motivates deeper engagement.

This chapter serves as both a technical extension and a practical capstone. It bridges the gap between theory and deployment, demonstrating how advanced edge platforms unlock new categories of IoT applications and inspiring learners to think creatively about the next generation of intelligent, vision-enabled systems. By the end of *Chapter 17*, readers will not only understand the tools and techniques but also recognize the strategic value these systems deliver in real-world industries.

Structure

In this chapter, we will cover the following topics:

- Introduction to Raspberry Pi, Jetson Nano, and Edge AI boards
- Use cases for Computer Vision in IoT
- OpenCV Basics for Vision-Based IoT
- Sample Task: Motion Detection Alert via MQTT
- Integrating Vision Systems with Microcontrollers
- TinyML/Edge Impulse Overview (Basic Model Deployment)
- Siemens: MQTT for Real-Time Factory Analytics
- AWS IoT Core in Smart Farming: The Punjab Case Study
- Flipkart Warehousing: LoRa-Based Inventory Tracking
- Tata Power: Smart Grid with ZigBee and NB-IoT
- Key Industry Takeaways
- Mini Project: Vision-Triggered Smart Security System

Introduction to Raspberry Pi, Jetson Nano, and Edge AI Boards

While low-power microcontrollers such as the ESP32, STM32, and nRF52 series excel at simple, real-time tasks and TinyML inference, many vision-based IoT applications demand significantly more computational resources. Image processing, object detection, semantic segmentation, and video analytics require high memory bandwidth, floating-point performance, parallel computation, and full operating system support—capabilities that lie beyond the reach of traditional microcontrollers. This is where powerful single-board computers (SBCs) and edge AI platforms come into play. For instance, the Raspberry Pi 4B (4GB): ~$55; Pi 5 (8GB): ~$80. At this price point, the Pi is often cheaper than designing a custom board with comparable peripherals, which is why it appears in production systems, not just prototypes. These devices bridge the gap between resource-constrained embedded systems and full cloud processing, enabling sophisticated vision and AI workloads to run locally with low latency and high privacy.

Raspberry Pi: The Versatile Prototyping Powerhouse

The Raspberry Pi family has become the de facto standard for affordable, Linux-based single-board computing. Since its introduction in 2012, the Raspberry Pi has evolved from a basic educational tool into a robust platform for IoT prototyping, industrial gateways, and edge vision applications.

Key strengths may include its full Linux operating system (typically Raspberry Pi OS, based on Debian), support for Python and other high-level languages, and extensive peripheral connectivity such as USB ports, HDMI output, Ethernet, Wi-Fi, Bluetooth, GPIO pins, and the official Camera Module interface. The latest models (Raspberry Pi 5 and earlier 4B) offer quad-core ARM Cortex-A processors, up to 8 GB of RAM, and hardware video encoding/decoding. These features make the Pi ideal for running OpenCV for classical computer vision tasks (for example: edge detection, color segmentation, motion tracking) as well as lightweight deep learning frameworks such as TensorFlow Lite or ONNX Runtime.

Its low cost, large community, and vast ecosystem of libraries and accessories make it the first choice for rapid prototyping of vision-enabled IoT systems.

NVIDIA Jetson Nano: The AI-First Edge Platform

The NVIDIA Jetson Nano is purpose-built for edge AI workloads, delivering GPU-accelerated deep learning performance in a compact, low-power form factor. Unlike the Raspberry Pi, which is a general-purpose SBC, the Jetson Nano is optimized for running Convolutional Neural Networks (CNNs) and other AI models with high throughput and low latency.

At its core is a 128-core NVIDIA Maxwell GPU capable of delivering up to 472 GFLOPS of half-precision (FP16) performance—enough to run modern vision models such as YOLO, MobileNet, or EfficientDet in real time. The Nano supports full TensorFlow, PyTorch, and NVIDIA's optimized TensorRT inference engine, enabling developers to deploy complex vision pipelines with minimal code changes. It also includes a quad-core ARM Cortex-A57 CPU, up to 4 GB of RAM, and multiple camera interfaces (MIPI CSI and USB). These capabilities make the Jetson Nano the preferred platform for demanding applications such as robotics, autonomous drones, industrial inspection, and smart surveillance.

Microcontrollers are Not Sufficient for Vision Tasks

Microcontrollers such as the ESP32 or STM32 are engineered for low-power, deterministic, real-time control. They excel at handling simple scalar data, running TinyML models, and maintaining long battery life. However, vision processing imposes fundamentally different requirements:

- **High Memory and Bandwidth Needs**: A single 640×480 RGB image requires nearly 1 MB of storage; processing multiple frames per second demands fast memory access and large buffers.
- **Floating-Point and Parallel Computation**: Deep neural networks rely on floating-point matrix operations and massive parallelism—tasks that GPUs handle orders of magnitude faster than Cortex-M cores.
- **Full Operating System and File System**: Vision libraries (OpenCV, TensorFlow) require Linux-style file systems, process management, and multitasking—the features which are absent in bare-metal RTOS environments.
- **Development Productivity**: High-level languages (Python) and mature frameworks are essential for rapid iteration on vision algorithms; microcontrollers are typically programmed in C/C++ with limited debugging tools.

In practice, vision tasks cannot be effectively executed on microcontrollers without severe compromises in accuracy, speed, or model complexity. Edge AI boards complement rather than replace microcontrollers: the microcontroller handles low-power sensing and control, while the SBC or Jetson manages compute-intensive vision and AI workloads. Raspberry Pi and NVIDIA Jetson Nano represent two complementary classes of edge AI platforms that unlock the full potential of vision-enabled IoT. The Raspberry Pi offers affordability, versatility, and ease of use for prototyping and moderate workloads, while the Jetson Nano delivers GPU-accelerated performance for demanding deep learning applications. Together, they extend the reach of IoT beyond scalar data into the rich, contextual world of images and video, enabling intelligent perception at the edge. Understanding when and how to deploy these platforms is essential for building the next generation of vision-driven IoT systems.

Use Cases for Computer Vision in IoT

Computer vision transforms IoT systems from passive data collectors into active observers capable of interpreting the physical world through images and video. By processing visual data at the edge or in the cloud, these systems can detect objects, recognize patterns, track movement, and classify scenes with human-like accuracy—all in real time. This capability unlocks a wide range of applications across industries, where traditional scalar sensors (temperature, pressure, vibration) cannot provide sufficient context or granularity. Regulatory note: Face recognition in public spaces is restricted or banned in several jurisdictions (EU AI Act, San Francisco, Boston). Always check local laws and consider privacy-preserving alternatives like silhouette detection or anonymized analytics. Legal awareness is critical for real deployments. The following use cases illustrate how vision-based IoT delivers measurable value through enhanced perception, automation, and decision-making.

Surveillance and Security

Vision-enabled IoT systems have revolutionized surveillance. Smart cameras equipped with edge AI detect and classify intruders, vehicles, or animals, reducing false alarms from simple motion sensors. Facial recognition (anonymized for privacy compliance) or license-plate reading identifies authorized personnel or vehicles, enabling access control without physical keys. In public spaces, cameras monitor for suspicious behavior, crowd density, or abandoned objects, triggering real-time alerts to security teams. These systems operate continuously, even in low-light conditions with infrared or thermal imaging, and integrate with cloud dashboards for live monitoring and forensic review.

Smart Traffic Management

In urban environments, vision-based IoT improves traffic flow and safety. Cameras at intersections count vehicles, classify them (car, truck, bicycle, pedestrian), and detect violations such as running red lights or illegal turns. A single intersection typically generates 5–20 GB/day of video (4 cameras, 1080p). Edge processing reduces cloud transmission to <100 MB/day of metadata and event clips, cutting bandwidth costs 50–200×. Quantified savings show ROI. Real-time analytics feed adaptive traffic signals that adjust timing based on current demand, reducing congestion and emissions. In parking facilities, cameras identify available spaces and guide drivers, while license-plate recognition enables seamless payment and enforcement. These deployments often use 5G for low-latency communication, ensuring rapid response to incidents.

Warehousing and Logistics

Vision systems automate inventory and logistics operations. Fixed or mobile cameras (on robots or drones) track packages, pallets, and forklifts in real time. Object detection models identify items by shape, color, or barcode, updating warehouse management systems instantly. Vision-guided robots navigate aisles, pick items, and avoid obstacles, while overhead cameras monitor stock levels and flag misplaced goods. This reduces manual counting errors, speeds up order fulfillment, and improves safety by detecting unsafe behavior such as blocked aisles.

Manufacturing and Quality Assurance

In production lines, vision-based IoT performs 100 % quality inspection at high speeds. Cameras capture images of products exiting the assembly line, and deep learning models detect defects—scratches, misalignments, incorrect labels, or missing components—with greater accuracy than human inspectors. Rejected items are diverted automatically, and production data is logged for traceability and process improvement. These systems integrate with PLCs and SCADA for closed-loop control, adjusting machine parameters to prevent recurring defects.

Precision Agriculture

In agriculture, vision-enabled IoT enhances crop monitoring and resource efficiency. Drones or fixed cameras capture multispectral images to detect plant stress, disease, or nutrient deficiency weeks before visible symptoms appear. AI models classify issues and recommend targeted interventions—

pesticides, fertilizers, or irrigation—reducing chemical usage and environmental impact. Livestock monitoring uses vision to track animal health, detect abnormal behavior, or count heads, improving welfare and farm efficiency.

Common Architectural Elements

Vision-based IoT systems typically combine several core components:

- **Cameras**: High-resolution industrial or consumer-grade cameras (MIPI CSI, USB, or IP) with wide-angle, zoom, or thermal capabilities.
- **Edge AI Boards**: Raspberry Pi for prototyping or NVIDIA Jetson for GPU-accelerated inference, running OpenCV and deep learning frameworks.
- **Communication Protocols**: MQTT or HTTP for transmitting metadata, alerts, or video clips to cloud platforms; RTSP for live streaming.
- **Cloud Dashboards**: Centralized interfaces (AWS IoTSiteWise, Azure IoT Central, or custom web apps) for monitoring, historical analysis, and remote management.

Computer vision elevates IoT from monitoring discrete parameters to understanding entire scenes. By enabling perception, classification, and real-time decision-making, vision-based systems deliver transformative value in safety, efficiency, quality, and sustainability across diverse industries. As camera costs continue to fall and edge AI hardware becomes more powerful, vision-enabled IoT will become the default for any application requiring contextual awareness—marking a new era where devices not only sense but truly see and understand the world around them.

OpenCV Basics for Vision-Based IoT

Open Source Computer Vision Library (OpenCV) is the most widely adopted OpenCV is an open-source framework for image and video processing. Originally developed by Intel in 1999 and now maintained by a global community, OpenCV provides a comprehensive set of tools for real-time computer vision tasks. It is written in C++ with bindings for Python, Java, and other languages, making it accessible to both embedded developers and data scientists. Its performance, portability, and extensive ecosystem have made it the de facto standard for vision-enabled IoT applications, especially on resource-constrained edge platforms like Raspberry Pi.

Getting Started

Recommendation for Beginners: Start with image capture and simple transforms (grayscale, blur, thresholding) before attempting detection. The learning curve of OpenCV is steep; budget 10 to 20 hours of hands-on practice to gain fluency.

Core Capabilities of OpenCV

OpenCV offers a rich set of functions tailored to the needs of IoT vision systems:

- **Image and Video Capture:** OpenCV provides seamless integration with USB cameras, Raspberry Pi Camera Modules, IP cameras (via RTSP), and other video sources. It handles frame grabbing, timestamping, and buffering, enabling continuous video streams for real-time analysis.
- **Image Transformations and Preprocessing:** Essential operations include color space conversion (RGB to grayscale, HSV), resizing, blurring, thresholding, edge detection (Canny, Sobel), and geometric transformations (rotation, perspective correction). These steps prepare raw camera input for more complex algorithms by reducing noise and normalizing data.
- **Object and Face Detection:** OpenCV includes pre-trained classifiers (Haar cascades, HOG + SVM) for detecting faces, eyes, pedestrians, and common objects. It also supports

deep learning-based detectors (DNN module) that can load models from frameworks like TensorFlow, PyTorch, or ONNX, enabling accurate detection of custom objects such as defects or machinery parts.

- **Motion Detection and Tracking:** Frame differencing, background subtraction (MOG2, KNN), and optical flow algorithms allow OpenCV to detect movement, track objects across frames, and identify anomalies. These techniques are critical for surveillance, intrusion detection, and activity monitoring.
- **Additional Tools:** OpenCV provides contour detection, shape analysis, text recognition (Tesseract integration), barcode/QR code reading, and calibration functions for multi-camera systems. Its DNN module accelerates inference on compatible hardware (for example: Raspberry Pi with Coral USB Accelerator).

Typical OpenCV Pipeline in IoT Applications

A standard vision-based IoT pipeline using OpenCV follows a clear, repeatable structure:

1. **Frame Capture:** The system continuously grabs frames from a connected camera (USB, CSI, or network stream) at a defined frame rate (for example: 15–30 FPS).
2. **Preprocessing:** Each frame is converted to grayscale, resized to reduce computational load, and filtered to remove noise or enhance contrast. This step ensures subsequent algorithms operate efficiently and reliably.
3. **Detection and Analysis:** The preprocessed frame is passed to detection logic: classical methods (for example: Haar cascades for faces) or deep learning models (for example: YOLO for objects). Results include bounding boxes, class labels, confidence scores, or motion vectors.
4. **Action and Communication:** Based on detection results, the system triggers actions: sending MQTT alerts, logging events, activating relays, or streaming annotated video to a cloud dashboard. Only relevant metadata or low-resolution snapshots are transmitted to conserve bandwidth.

This pipeline runs in a continuous loop, typically within a Python script using the cv2.VideoCapture class and threaded processing to maintain real-time performance.

OpenCV is Ideal for Vision-Based IoT

OpenCV is lightweight enough to run efficiently on Raspberry Pi (even older models) while being powerful enough for real-time processing on more capable platforms like NVIDIA Jetson. It requires no proprietary licenses, supports hardware acceleration (for example, OpenGL, CUDA on Jetson), and benefits from a massive community that provides pre-trained models, tutorials, and optimized builds for edge devices. Its cross-platform nature ensures portability across Linux, Windows, and embedded systems. OpenCV is the cornerstone of vision-based IoT development. It provides the tools to capture, process, and interpret visual data with high performance and flexibility, enabling IoT systems to move from simple sensing to true environmental understanding. Mastery of OpenCV is essential for anyone building intelligent, vision-enabled IoT applications in the real world.

Sample Task: Motion Detection Alert via MQTT

Face detection is one of the most widely recognized and practical applications of computer vision, serving as a foundational building block for numerous IoT and IIoT systems. It involves identifying the presence and location of human faces within images or video frames, typically by drawing bounding boxes around detected regions. In IoT contexts, face detection enables a wide range of intelligent, real-time applications—from access control and attendance tracking to enhanced security and human-machine interaction—while maintaining low latency and privacy when processed at the edge.

The Face Detection Workflow

The standard workflow for implementing face detection with OpenCV on an edge platform such as Raspberry Pi or NVIDIA Jetson follows a clear and repeatable sequence:

1. **Capture Live Video Feed:** The system continuously acquires video frames from a connected camera (USB, Raspberry Pi Camera Module, or IP camera via RTSP). Frames are grabbed at a controlled frame rate (typically 15–30 FPS) to balance responsiveness and processing load.
2. **Apply Face Detection Algorithm:** OpenCV provides two primary methods for face detection:
    a. **Haar Cascade Classifiers**: A classic, lightweight approach using pre-trained XML models (for example, `haarcascade_frontalface_default.xml`). These are fast and suitable for resource-constrained devices but less accurate under varying lighting, angles, or occlusions.
    b. **DNN-Based Detection**: Using DNN module of OpenCV, the system loads a deep learning model (for example, MobileNet-SSD or YOLO trained on face datasets) for higher accuracy and robustness. This method leverages GPU acceleration on platforms like Jetson Nano.
3. **Draw Bounding Boxes and Annotate:** Once faces are detected, the system draws rectangles around each face, optionally displaying confidence scores, tracking IDs, or additional metadata. These annotations can be overlaid on the video stream for live monitoring or saved as images for logging.
4. **Trigger Events and Communication:** Detection results drive actions – logging timestamps and face counts, sending MQTT alerts for unauthorized access, integrating with access control systems (for example, unlocking doors), or streaming annotated video to a cloud dashboard. Only relevant metadata or low-resolution snapshots are transmitted to minimize bandwidth usage.

Extending Face Detection in IoT Applications

Face detection serves as a powerful starting point that can be extended into sophisticated, production-grade IoT solutions:

- **Attendance and Time-Tracking Systems:** Cameras at entry points detect and recognize employees or students (using face recognition models such as DeepFace or FaceNet), automatically logging arrivals and departures. This eliminates manual check-ins, reduces errors, and provides real-time workforce visibility.
- **Access Control and Security:** Face detection and recognition replace keycards or PINs for secure entry. Systems can enforce "one-person-at-a-time" rules, detect tailgating, or flag unauthorized individuals. Edge processing ensures privacy by keeping biometric data local, while cloud integration enables centralized policy management.
- **Smart Surveillance and Behavior Monitoring:** Cameras in public spaces or workplaces use face detection to track crowd density, identify loitering, or detect abnormal behavior. Thermal cameras can combine face detection with temperature measurement for health screening. In retail, face detection enables anonymized customer counting and dwell-time analysis for business intelligence.

When deploying face detection in IoT systems, privacy and ethics must be addressed from the outset. Use anonymized processing (for example : detect faces without storing images), implement opt-in consent where possible, and comply with regulations such as GDPR or CCPA. Edge-based detection (processing on-device rather than in the cloud) significantly reduces privacy risks by keeping sensitive data local. Best practice: Post visible signage ('Video surveillance in use'), obtain informed consent where feasible, and conduct a Privacy Impact Assessment (PIA) before deployment. Documentation protects both users and deployers legally.

Face detection with OpenCV is a practical and accessible introduction to vision-based IoT. Its straightforward workflow—capture, detect, annotate, and act—demonstrates how edge platforms can transform raw video into intelligent, actionable insights. As a foundational skill, face detection opens the door to more advanced applications such as facial recognition, emotion analysis, and human activity understanding. Mastering this task equips learners with the confidence to design and deploy the next generation of intelligent, vision-enabled IoT systems that truly perceive and respond to the human world.

Motion Detection Alert via MQTT

Motion detection is one of the most common and practical applications of computer vision in IoT. Unlike traditional Passive InfraRed (PIR) sensors, which detect changes in infrared radiation and are prone to false triggers from heat sources or sunlight, vision-based motion detection analyzes actual changes in the field of view of the camera. This approach offers greater accuracy, flexibility, and context awareness—enabling systems to distinguish between meaningful movement (for example, a person entering a restricted area) and irrelevant changes (for example, shadows, leaves, or animals). When integrated with MQTT, motion detection becomes a powerful, event-driven automation trigger that can notify other devices, cloud services, or human operators in real time.

Motion Detection Logic with OpenCV

The core logic for vision-based motion detection relies on comparing consecutive video frames to identify regions of change. The process is straightforward yet highly effective:

1. The system continuously grabs frames from the camera at a steady frame rate (typically 10 30 FPS). Each frame is stored temporarily for comparison with the previous one.
2. The absolute difference between the current frame and the previous frame is calculated pixel by pixel. This produces a different image where moving objects appear as bright regions against a dark background. To improve robustness, the frames are often converted to grayscale and blurred (Gaussian smoothing) to reduce noise from lighting variations or camera jitter.
3. The difference image is thresholded to create a binary mask—pixels with significant change are marked white, while static areas remain black. Contours (boundaries of white regions) are then detected. If the size of any contour exceeds a predefined threshold, motion is confirmed. This step filters out small noise artifacts such as camera shake or minor lighting fluctuations.
4. When motion is detected, the system publishes an MQTT message to a designated topic (for example: **`iot/motion = 1`**, **`iot/motion_zone/living_room`**, or **`iot/motion_alert`** with a timestamp). The message can include metadata such as the location of the motion, number of moving objects, or a low-resolution snapshot (cropped to the moving region) for verification.

Integration with MQTT for Automation

MQTT's lightweight, publish/subscribe model makes it ideal for event-driven IoT. Upon detection, the vision system acts as an MQTT client and publishes the event to a broker (for example: Mosquitto running locally or on a cloud server). Subscribers—such as a microcontroller (ESP32), smart home hub, cloud dashboard, or mobile app—receive the message instantly and respond accordingly:

1. A microcontroller can activate a buzzer, turn on lights, or trigger a relay to lock doors.
2. A cloud service can log the event, send push notifications, or record a short video clip.
3. A smart home system can arm/disarm security zones or adjust lighting based on occupancy.

This architecture creates a loosely coupled, scalable system where the camera is responsible only for detection, while other devices handle actuation or notification.

Advantages over Traditional PIR Sensors

Vision-based motion detection offers several advantages:

- **Contextual Awareness:** It can distinguish between types of motion (human versus animal versus vehicle) using additional AI models.
- **Reduced False Positives:** PIR sensors trigger on heat changes (sunlight, HVAC, pets), while vision detects actual scene changes.
- **Zonal Detection:** Cameras can define multiple zones with different sensitivity or response rules.
- **No Additional Hardware:** One camera can replace multiple PIR sensors, reducing cost and wiring complexity.

Since motion detection involves video processing, privacy must be addressed. Edge-based detection (processing on the device) ensures no raw video leaves the premises unless an event is triggered. When transmitting images or clips, use encryption (TLS over MQTT) and anonymization techniques (for example, blurring faces). Compliance with regulations such as GDPR or CCPA is essential. Vision-based motion detection with OpenCV and MQTT transforms cameras into intelligent, event-driven sensors. By analyzing frame differences and publishing alerts, IoT systems gain the ability to react to real motion with high accuracy and context. This approach enables camera-driven automation across security, smart homes, industrial monitoring, and more—demonstrating how vision can replace or enhance traditional sensors in modern IoT deployments.

Integrating Vision Systems with Microcontrollers

In real-world IoT deployments, it is rare for a single device to handle all tasks efficiently. Vision-based systems require significant computational power for image processing and AI inference, while control tasks—such as driving actuators, managing low-power sensors, or handling real-time I/O—demand deterministic timing, low energy consumption, and robust hardware interfaces. The most effective architectures therefore divide responsibilities between a high-performance edge AI board (for example: Raspberry Pi or NVIDIA Jetson Nano) and a low-power microcontroller (for example: ESP32, STM32, or nRF52 series). This hybrid approach leverages the strengths of each platform, creating a system that is both intelligent and efficient.

Typical Architecture

The standard division of labor is as follows:

- **Edge AI Board (Raspberry Pi or Jetson Nano):** This platform handles compute-intensive tasks: capturing and processing video frames, running OpenCV or deep learning models for detection and classification, and making high-level decisions. It runs a full Linux operating system, supports Python and high-level libraries, and provides ample memory and GPU acceleration for vision workloads.
- **Microcontroller (ESP32 or similar):** The microcontroller manages low-level, real-time control: interfacing with actuators (relays, buzzers, motors, LEDs), reading simple sensors (temperature, motion, switches), and handling local I/O. It excels at low-power operation, deterministic timing, and direct hardware access via GPIO, PWM, I^2C, or SPI.
- **Communication Link:** The two devices communicate via a lightweight protocol. MQTT is the most common choice due to its pub/sub model, low overhead, and reliability over unreliable networks. Alternatives include REST/HTTP for simpler setups or serial communication (UART) when the microcontroller is physically close to the edge board.

Example Flow: Motion Detection and Alarm Trigger

A practical example illustrates the synergy:

- The Raspberry Pi or Jetson Nano continuously captures video from a connected camera and processes frames using OpenCV. When motion is detected (via frame differencing or a lightweight AI model), the board publishes an MQTT message to a topic such as **`iot/motion/alert`** with payload **`{ "event": "motion_detected", "location": "front_door", "timestamp": "2025-12-21T14:30:00" }`**.
- An ESP32 microcontroller, running on battery or low-power supply, subscribes to the same MQTT topic via its built-in Wi-Fi. Upon receiving the message, it triggers a connected buzzer, activates a relay to turn on floodlights, or sends a local signal to a secondary system (for example : a siren).
- The ESP32 can optionally publish a confirmation back to the broker (iot/motion/acknowledged), allowing the Pi to log the event or deactivate the alarm after a timeout.

This flow ensures that the compute-heavy vision processing runs on the powerful edge board, while the low-power microcontroller handles actuation and maintains system responsiveness even if the Pi temporarily loses power or network connectivity.

Benefits of This Division of Responsibility

Separating responsibilities between the edge AI processing unit and the microcontroller-based control layer offers several architectural advantages in modern IoT systems. This division allows each component to perform tasks best suited to its capabilities while improving efficiency, maintainability, and scalability.

- **Efficient Resource Usage:** The edge AI board is optimized for parallel computation and memory-intensive tasks, while the microcontroller consumes far less power and can remain in deep sleep until needed. This extends battery life in portable or remote deployments.
- **Clean System Design:** Separating vision/AI from control logic creates a modular, maintainable architecture. Each component can be developed, tested, and updated independently, reducing complexity and improving reliability. Separation also enables independent OTA updates: update vision model on Pi without touching ESP32 firmware, or fix a buzzer timing bug on ESP32 without redeploying OpenCV. In 24/7 systems, this modularity minimizes downtime.
- **Scalability and Flexibility:** Multiple microcontrollers can subscribe to the same MQTT topics, enabling distributed actuation (for example: multiple alarms or lights). The edge board can be upgraded to a more powerful model (for example: Jetson Orin) without affecting the control layer. MQTT brokers can also bridge multiple sites or connect to cloud platforms for centralized monitoring.

Integrating vision-capable edge AI boards with low-power microcontrollers creates a balanced, high-performance IoT architecture. The edge board handles the intelligence—seeing, understanding, and deciding—while the microcontroller executes precise, real-time control. MQTT provides the glue that ties these components together, enabling clean, scalable, and efficient designs. This hybrid model is the standard approach in production vision-based IoT systems, from smart security cameras to industrial inspection robots, and it exemplifies the power of combining complementary platforms to solve complex real-world problems.

TinyML and Edge Impulse Overview

While powerful edge platforms like Raspberry Pi and NVIDIA Jetson excel at compute-intensive vision tasks, many IoT applications require intelligence on extremely resource-constrained devices—

microcontrollers with only kilobytes of RAM, limited flash memory, and microwatt-level power budgets. This is the domain of TinyML: the practice of deploying lightweight machine learning models directly on microcontrollers such as ESP32, STM32, nRF52, or Arduino Nano 33 BLE Sense. TinyML enables always-on, battery-powered intelligence for tasks where low latency, privacy, and energy efficiency are paramount, and where cloud connectivity may be unreliable or unavailable.

TinyML models are aggressively optimized—quantized to 8-bit or lower precision, pruned of redundant weights, and distilled from larger teacher models—to fit within tens or hundreds of kilobytes while maintaining high accuracy. This allows inference to run in microseconds with power consumption in the microwatt range, making it ideal for wearable devices, industrial sensors, and remote environmental monitors.

Edge Impulse: The Leading TinyML Development Platform

Edge Impulse is the industry-standard, cloud-based platform for building, training, and deploying TinyML models. It simplifies the entire workflow, making TinyML accessible even to developers without deep machine learning expertise.

The Edge Impulse platform guides users through a structured pipeline:

- **Data Collection**: Ingest time-series data from accelerometers, microphones, or other sensors. Users can upload existing datasets or collect live data directly from connected devices.
- **Preprocessing and Feature Extraction**: Apply filters, windowing, and transformations to extract meaningful features (for example, spectral analysis for audio, statistical summaries for acceleration).
- **Model Training**: Automatically select and train lightweight neural networks or classical ML algorithms (decision trees, SVMs). The platform handles hyperparameter tuning and model compression.
- **Deployment**: Generate optimized C++ libraries or Arduino sketches for target microcontrollers. The resulting model runs entirely on-device, with no cloud dependency during inference.

Edge Impulse supports a wide range of hardware, including ESP32, Arduino Nano 33 BLE Sense, STM32, and Nordic nRF52 series. It also provides continuous integration for Over-the-Air (OTA) model updates and performance benchmarking on real hardware.

Typical TinyML Tasks

TinyML shines in applications where low power, privacy, and real-time response are critical:

- **Gesture Recognition**: Accelerometers in wearables detect hand motions (for example: swipe, shake, tap) to control devices or trigger alerts.
- **Audio Keyword Spotting**: Microphones listen for wake words ("`OK Google`," "`Hey Siri`") or industrial sounds (machine faults, alarms) with sub-milliwatt power consumption.
- **Anomaly Detection**: Vibration sensors on motors or pumps identify unusual patterns indicating wear or failure, enabling predictive maintenance without continuous cloud connectivity.

Complementary Roles: TinyML and Vision Systems

TinyML and vision-based systems are not mutually exclusive—they form complementary layers in multi-tiered IoT architectures. A typical setup might include:

- **TinyML on Microcontroller**: Always-on, low-power detection of simple events (for example: motion or keyword spotting) to wake the system from deep sleep.

- **Vision on Edge AI Board**: When triggered, the microcontroller activates a Raspberry Pi or Jetson Nano to perform complex visual analysis (for example: face recognition or object classification).
- **MQTT Coordination**: The microcontroller publishes events to an MQTT broker, which the vision board subscribes to, enabling seamless collaboration.

This layered approach achieves the best of both worlds: ultra-low power for standby operation and high-performance intelligence for critical decisions. TinyML brings machine learning to the extreme edge, enabling intelligence on battery-powered microcontrollers that would otherwise be too resource-constrained for AI. Edge Impulse democratizes TinyML development, providing an end-to-end platform for data collection, model training, and deployment. Together with vision-capable edge boards, TinyML forms the foundation of multi-layer intelligent IoT systems—where low-power detection triggers high-performance analysis, creating responsive, efficient, and privacy-preserving applications. Understanding both paradigms is essential for designing the next generation of truly autonomous IoT devices.

Siemens: MQTT for Real-Time Factory Analytics

Siemens, one of the global leaders in industrial automation and digitalization, has pioneered the use of MQTT as the core messaging protocol for real-time data pipelines in smart factories. Through its MindSphere cloud platform and industrial IoT solutions, Siemens leverages MQTT to stream high-volume machine telemetry from production lines, robots, CNC machines, PLCs, and sensors directly to cloud-based analytics engines. This approach enables predictive maintenance, process optimization, and factory-wide visibility with unprecedented speed and scalability.

MQTT's lightweight publish/subscribe model is ideally suited for industrial environments where thousands of devices generate continuous data streams. Siemens deploys MQTT brokers (often Mosquitto or proprietary implementations) at the edge or in the cloud to handle massive message throughput with minimal overhead. Each machine or sensor publishes telemetry data—vibration readings, temperature profiles, current draw, cycle times, and fault codes—to structured topics organized in a hierarchical namespace.

The key benefits Siemens realizes with MQTT include:

- **Low-Latency Analytics**: MQTT's pub/sub architecture ensures near-real-time delivery of data from edge devices to analytics engines. Siemens uses this to run continuous monitoring and anomaly detection models that identify impending failures (for example: bearing wear in motors) before they cause downtime. Latency is typically in the millisecond range, enabling predictive maintenance that reduces unplanned stops by 30–50% in many deployments.
- **Scalable Topic Hierarchies:** The topic-based routing of MQTT scales effortlessly across thousands of machines. Siemens structures topics to reflect factory organization (plant → line → machine → component), allowing operators to subscribe to specific subsets of data (for example : all robots in Line 3) or aggregate data across the enterprise. This flexibility supports both local edge dashboards and global enterprise views without requiring complex custom routing logic.
- **Security via TLS and Certificates:** Siemens enforces end-to-end security using MQTT over TLS 1.3 with mutual authentication via X.509 certificates. Each device receives a unique certificate during provisioning, ensuring that only authorized machines can publish or subscribe. This zero-trust approach protects sensitive production data from interception or tampering, meeting the stringent cybersecurity requirements of IEC 62443 and other industrial standards.

In practice, Siemens MindSphere ingests MQTT streams from factory devices, applies machine learning models for predictive analytics, and delivers actionable insights through factory-wide dashboards. Operators view real-time key performance indicators (KPIs), receive automated alerts for anomalies, and access historical trends for root-cause analysis. The platform also supports closed-loop control: insights from the cloud can trigger MQTT commands back to devices, such as adjusting machine speed or scheduling maintenance. Siemens' adoption of MQTT demonstrates its maturity as the messaging backbone for modern industrial IoT. By enabling low-latency, scalable, and secure data pipelines, MQTT empowers factories to move from reactive to predictive and ultimately autonomous operation. For IoT engineers, Siemens' approach serves as a blueprint for building resilient, real-time analytics systems that integrate edge devices with enterprise-scale intelligence. The combination of MQTT's simplicity, performance, and security makes it the protocol of choice for Industry 4.0 deployments worldwide.

AWS IoT Core in Smart Farming: The Punjab Case Study

Agriculture in Punjab, one of India's most productive regions, faces mounting challenges from water scarcity, unpredictable weather, and the need to maintain high yields with shrinking margins. To address these issues, several large-scale smart agriculture projects have deployed IoT solutions built on AWS IoT Core, demonstrating how cloud-native IoT platforms can transform traditional farming into data-driven, resource-efficient operations.

At the heart of these deployments are networks of soil moisture sensors, temperature and humidity probes, and weather stations installed across fields. These low-power devices, often powered by solar panels and connected via LoRaWAN or cellular gateways, continuously monitor critical parameters: soil moisture at multiple depths, air temperature, relative humidity, and localized rainfall. The sensors transmit data at regular intervals (typically every 15–60 minutes) to edge gateways that forward the telemetry to AWS IoT Core.

AWS IoT Core serves as the central ingestion and routing layer. It authenticates each device using unique X.509 certificates, securely accepts MQTT messages from thousands of field sensors, and routes them to downstream services. AWS Lambda functions process incoming data in real time: calculating evapotranspiration rates, comparing current soil moisture against crop-specific thresholds, and determining whether irrigation is required. If conditions warrant action, Lambda triggers commands back through AWS IoTCore to field controllers—actuators that open solenoid valves or activate drip irrigation pumps.

The benefits of this architecture are measurable and significant:

- **Reduced Water Usage:** Automated, precision irrigation based on actual soil and weather data has reduced water consumption by 30–50 % in participating farms. Farmers previously relied on fixed schedules or visual inspection, often overwatering. The system applies water only when and where needed, conserving groundwater and lowering electricity costs for pumping.
- **Improved Crop Yields and Quality:** By maintaining optimal soil moisture levels, the system prevents both under- and over-watering stress, leading to healthier plants, higher yields, and better-quality produce. In some cases, farmers have reported yield increases of 15–25% for water-intensive crops like rice and wheat.
- **Data-Driven Farming Decisions:** All sensor data is stored in Amazon Timestream or S3, enabling historical analysis and machine learning models that predict future water needs based on weather forecasts and crop growth stages. Farmers access real-time dashboards via mobile apps, receiving actionable recommendations and alerts, transforming farming from intuition-based to evidence-based decision-making.

Security is a cornerstone of architecture. Each sensor and gateway uses mutual TLS authentication with unique certificates provisioned through AWS IoT Core's Just-In-Time Registration. Data in transit and at rest is encrypted, and fine-grained IAM policies control access to Lambda functions and storage buckets.

The Punjab smart farming projects illustrate how AWS IoT Core can scale to thousands of devices across geographically dispersed fields, providing reliable, low-latency data ingestion and processing. By integrating low-cost sensors with cloud-native analytics, these initiatives demonstrate that IoT can deliver sustainability and profitability to smallholder and large-scale farmers alike. The success in Punjab has become a model for smart agriculture initiatives across India and other water-stressed regions worldwide. AWS IoT Core enables smart farming by securely connecting field sensors to powerful cloud analytics, automating irrigation, reducing resource waste, and empowering farmers with actionable insights. This case exemplifies how cloud IoT platforms can address real-world agricultural challenges, making precision farming accessible and economically viable at scale.

Flipkart Warehousing: LoRa-Based Inventory Tracking

Flipkart, one of India's largest e-commerce platforms, operates some of the most advanced warehousing and fulfillment centers in the country. To manage inventory in massive, multi-story warehouses spanning hundreds of thousands of square feet, Flipkart has deployed a LoRa-based Real-Time Location System (RTLS) that tracks the movement and precise location of goods, pallets, carts, and assets throughout the facility. This deployment exemplifies how long-range, Low-Power Wide-Area Network (LPWAN) technology can solve scalability and cost challenges in large-scale logistics environments.

The system uses battery-powered LoRa tags attached to inventory items, picking carts, forklifts, and storage bins. These tags periodically transmit their unique identifiers and location data to a network of LoRa gateways strategically placed throughout the warehouse. The gateways, connected via Ethernet or Wi-Fi to the backend, forward the messages to a central server where location is calculated using Time-Difference-of-Arrival (TDoA) or fingerprinting techniques. The system achieves location accuracy of 1–5 meters, sufficient to track items down to the aisle and bay level, even in environments with metal racking and high interference.

LoRa is the Ideal Choice for Large Warehouses

Flipkart selected LoRa over alternatives such as Wi-Fi, Bluetooth, or UWB for several compelling reasons:

- **Long Range and Penetration:** LoRa provides coverage of several hundred meters to kilometers indoors, easily spanning multi-story warehouses with thick concrete floors and metal shelving. Unlike Wi-Fi, which requires dense access point deployment and suffers from signal blockage, a single LoRa gateway can cover tens of thousands of square meters, reducing infrastructure costs significantly.
- **Ultra-Low Power Consumption:** LoRa tags operate for years on small coin-cell batteries due to their low transmission power and adaptive data rate. This eliminates the need for frequent battery replacement or wired power, making the system practical for tagging millions of inventory items or mobile assets like carts and forklifts.
- **Scalability and Cost-Effectiveness:** LoRa supports thousands of devices per gateway with minimal network congestion. The low cost of LoRa modules and gateways (often under $10 per tag) makes it economically viable to tag individual packages or pallets, a scale that would be prohibitive with more expensive technologies like UWB or RFID readers.
- **Robustness in Harsh Environments:** Warehouses are filled with metal racks, moving forklifts, and electromagnetic interference. The chirp spread spectrum modulation of LoRA provides excellent resistance to multipath fading and interference, ensuring reliable communication even in challenging RF environments.

Operational Benefits

The LoRa-based system delivers tangible improvements in warehouse efficiency:

- Real-time visibility of inventory location reduces "search time" for pickers, accelerating order fulfillment.
- Automated alerts for misplaced or misplaced goods prevent stock discrepancies.
- Tracking of material handling equipment (forklifts, carts) improves safety and utilization.
- Integration with the Warehouse Management System (WMS) of Flipkart enables dynamic slotting, reducing travel distance for pickers and optimizing space utilization.

Security is maintained through end-to-end encryption and device authentication, ensuring that location data and inventory information remain protected. The LoRa-based inventory tracking system of Flipkart demonstrates how LPWAN technology can solve the unique challenges of large-scale warehousing: coverage, power, cost, and scalability. By enabling precise, battery-powered tracking of millions of assets, LoRa empowers e-commerce giants to achieve faster fulfillment, higher accuracy, and lower operational costs. This deployment serves as a benchmark for modern logistics operations, illustrating that the right connectivity choice—long-range, low-power, and low-cost—can transform warehouse efficiency at scale. For IoT practitioners, The approach of Flipkart highlights the strategic value of selecting the appropriate network technology for the physical and economic realities of the deployment environment.

Tata Power: Smart Grid with ZigBee and NB-IoT

Tata Power, one of largest integrated power companies in the Indian subcontinent, has deployed a hybrid IoT architecture in its smart grid initiatives to enhance monitoring, fault detection, and overall grid reliability. The system combines ZigBee for local, low-power mesh networking at the consumer and distribution level with NB-IoT for wide-area, long-range backhaul to the utility's central control center.

ZigBee forms robust, self-healing mesh networks among smart meters, distribution transformers, and local sensors in neighborhoods and apartment complexes. These networks aggregate meter readings, voltage data, and tamper alerts from hundreds of endpoints and forward them to a ZigBee gateway, which acts as the bridge to the wide-area network. The low power consumption of ZigBee and mesh topology ensures that there is a reliable coverage in dense urban areas with buildings and interference, while its short range keeps deployment costs manageable.

NB-IoT provides the long-range, deep-indoor penetration link from gateways to Tata Power's cloud platform. The narrowband design of NB-IoT and low data-rate profile make it ideal for infrequent, small-packet telemetry from remote substations, pole-mounted transformers, and feeder points. It operates over existing cellular infrastructure, reducing the need for dedicated towers or fiber, and supports massive device density with excellent battery life for field devices.

The combined architecture delivers:

- **Real-Time Energy Monitoring:** Continuous visibility into consumption patterns, load profiles, and power quality across the distribution network.
- **Faster Fault Detection:** Smart meters and sensors detect anomalies (for example: voltage dips, outages) and report them instantly, reducing fault localization time from hours to minutes.
- **Improved Grid Reliability:** Predictive maintenance of transformers and feeders, reduced technical losses, and quicker restoration during outages, resulting in higher uptime and customer satisfaction.

The deployment of Tata Power demonstrates a practical, cost-effective hybrid approach: ZigBee for dense, low-power local connectivity and NB-IoT for reliable, wide-area backhaul. This layered strategy has become a model for utilities modernizing aging grids while managing capital expenditure and operational complexity.

Key Industry Takeaways

The real-world deployments examined in this chapter—Siemens factories, Flipkart warehouses, Tata Power smart grids, Punjab smart farming, and others—reveal consistent patterns that define successful industrial and enterprise IoT implementations. These lessons transcend specific technologies and industries, serving as universal principles for building scalable, secure, and profitable IoT systems.

Scalability is the most prominent requirement. Successful projects routinely manage tens of thousands to millions of devices across large geographic areas or dense facilities. This is achieved through hierarchical architectures, efficient protocols (MQTT, LoRa, NB-IoT), and cloud-native platforms that handle massive message throughput without performance degradation. The ability to add devices seamlessly without redesigning the entire system is non-negotiable.

Design Rule: Build systems that scale from 100 to 100,000 devices with configuration changes, not architecture rewrites. Use cloud-native platforms (managed brokers, and auto-scaling ingestion), stateless edge processing, and hierarchical data aggregation from day one.

Security is non-optional. Every production deployment enforces certificate-based authentication (X.509), mutual TLS encryption, and zero-trust principles. Device provisioning, firmware signing, and secure OTA updates are standard practices to protect against unauthorized access and tampering. Privacy-preserving edge processing is increasingly common, especially in regulated sectors.

Reliability is measured in years of uninterrupted 24×7 operation. Redundant communication paths, self-healing networks, edge autonomy during outages, and robust power management ensure systems remain operational even under harsh conditions. Downtime is measured in minutes, not hours, and fault tolerance is designed in from the start.

Return on Investment (ROI) is the ultimate driver. Every deployment focuses on quantifiable outcomes: reduced water usage in agriculture, lower maintenance costs in manufacturing, faster fault detection in utilities, or improved fulfillment speed in logistics. For Engineers: When designing systems, always ask: "What business metric improves?" (downtime, waste, labor cost, safety incidents). If you can't quantify value, the project may not get funded. Engineers who speak ROI become architects and leaders. The architecture is chosen to maximize efficiency gains and cost reduction, not just to deploy technology for its own sake.

The overarching takeaway is clear: industry IoT success depends far more on thoughtful architecture than on the devices themselves. The best hardware fails without the right connectivity, security, data pipeline, and business alignment. Conversely, modest hardware can deliver extraordinary value when integrated into a well-designed, scalable, secure, and ROI focused system. For IoT professionals, mastering architecture—how components interact, how data flows, and how value is created—is the true differentiator in the real world.

Practical Exercises

To culminate the concepts of vision-based IoT, edge AI integration, and real-world deployment discussed in this chapter, the following three practical exercises and a capstone mini project provide structured, hands-on activities. These exercises require a Raspberry Pi (model 4 or 5 recommended for better performance), a compatible camera module, an ESP32 microcontroller, basic electronics (for example: buzzer, relay), and free software tools like OpenCV, Python, and Mosquitto MQTT broker. They build progressively: starting with standalone vision tasks, moving to cross-device communication, analyzing industry cases, and finally integrating everything into a complete system. Safety note: Handle electronics with care, ensure proper voltage levels to avoid damaging components, and test in a controlled environment.

Exercise 1: Face Detection with OpenCV on Raspberry Pi

The goal of this exercise is to introduce vision-based automation through real-time face detection, demonstrating how a Raspberry Pi can process video streams and apply basic computer vision algorithms. This builds foundational skills for more complex vision-enabled IoT applications.

Step 1: Set up the Hardware and Software Environment

Begin by assembling your Raspberry Pi setup: connect the Raspberry Pi Camera Module (or a USB webcam) to the appropriate port. Power on the Pi and install Raspberry Pi OS if not already done. Use the terminal to install OpenCV and its dependencies via pip install opencv-python (or opencv-contrib-python for additional modules). Also install Python if needed. Test the camera by running a simple script to capture and display a frame, ensuring the video feed works without issues.

Step 2: Implement the Face Detection Algorithm

Download a pre-trained Haar Cascade classifier for faces (available from the OpenCV GitHub repository as an XML file). In a Python script, use OpenCV's cv2.VideoCapture to access the camera feed. In a loop, read frames, convert them to grayscale, and apply the cascade classifier to detect faces. Draw bounding boxes around detected faces using cv2.rectangle. Display the annotated video in a window with cv2.imshow. Add basic thresholding or size filtering to reduce false positives.

Step 3: Test and Optimize

Run the script and test in various lighting conditions and with multiple faces. Measure frame rate (aim for 15–30 FPS) and adjust parameters like scale factor or minimum neighbors to improve accuracy. Experiment with DNN-based detection (using OpenCV's DNN module with a pre-trained model like Caffe or TensorFlow) for better robustness. Log detection events to a file for later analysis.

Step 4: Reflect and Extend

Document your observations: accuracy under different scenarios, computational load on the Pi, and potential improvements (for example: adding facial recognition). Extend by triggering a simple action, like printing a message when a face is detected, to preview integration with IoT elements.

Exercise 2: Motion Detector with MQTT Trigger

This exercise focuses on enabling cross-device communication by building a motion detector on the Raspberry Pi that publishes alerts via MQTT. The goal is to demonstrate how vision systems can trigger events in a distributed IoT network, bridging computer vision with messaging protocols.

Step 1: Configure the MQTT Environment

Install an MQTT broker like Mosquitto on the Raspberry Pi or a separate computer. Start the broker and test it with a simple client tool. On the Pi, install the Paho MQTT library via `pip install paho-mqtt`. Ensure your camera is connected and functional from Exercise 1.

Step 2: Implement Motion Detection Logic

In a Python script, capture consecutive frames from the camera using OpenCV. Compute the absolute difference between frames, apply Gaussian blur and thresholding to create a binary mask, and find contours. If a contour's area exceeds a threshold (for example: 500 pixels), classify it as motion. To reduce noise, use dilation and erosion morphological operations.

Step 3: Integrate MQTT Publishing

When motion is detected, create an MQTT client in the script, connect to the broker (localhost or IP address), and publish a message to a topic like `iot/motion/alert` with a payload such as `{"event":`

`"motion_detected", "timestamp": current_time}`. Include optional metadata like motion intensity or frame coordinates. Draw bounding boxes on the video feed for visual confirmation.

Step 4: Test and Debug

Run the script and simulate motion (for example: wave your hand). Use an MQTT client tool (like MQTT Explorer) to subscribe to the topic and verify messages arrive. Measure latency from detection to publish (aim for <100 ms). Debug false positives by adjusting thresholds or adding background subtraction (for example: using MOG2 of OpenCV). Extend by saving a snapshot of the motion frame and including its path in the MQTT payload.

Exercise 3: Industry Case Study Breakdown

This analytical exercise requires breaking down a real-world IoT deployment (for example : Siemens factory analytics, Flipkart warehousing, or Tata Power smart grid from earlier sections). The goal is to analyze architecture, protocols, and business impact, fostering systems thinking for future IoT designs.

Step 1: Select and Research a Case Study

Choose one case from the chapter (or an external example like fulfillment centers of Amazon). Gather details from online resources, company whitepapers, or videos: identify key components (sensors, gateways, cloud platforms), protocols used (for example : MQTT, LoRa), and objectives (for example : efficiency gains).

Step 2: Map the Architecture

Create a diagram or written description outlining the system layers: edge devices (sensors/microcontrollers), gateways (data aggregation), communication (protocols and networks), cloud processing (analytics/AI), and actuation (outcomes). Highlight edge vs. cloud decisions and scalability features.

Step 3: Evaluate Protocols and Impact

Analyze why specific protocols were chosen (for example :LoRa for long-range in warehousing) and their role in reliability/security. Assess business impact: quantify benefits (for example : 30% cost reduction) and challenges (for example : integration with legacy systems). Discuss sustainability or ethical aspects.

Step 4: Synthesize and Propose Improvements

Write a report (500–1,000 words) summarizing your breakdown, including lessons learned and proposed enhancements (for example : adding 5G for lower latency). This step develops critical evaluation skills for industry deployments

Mini Project: Vision-Triggered Smart Security System

This capstone mini project integrates vision detection, MQTT communication, and microcontroller actuation into a complete end-to-end IoT system. The goal is to build a smart security setup that detects motion via camera, alerts via MQTT, and triggers a response on an ESP32—demonstrating separation of AI, control, and communication layers.

Step 1: Assemble Hardware and Set Up Environment

Connect a camera to your Raspberry Pi and a buzzer/relay to the GPIO pins of ESP32. Install OpenCV and Paho MQTT on the Pi; program the ESP32 with Arduino IDE or PlatformIO, including Wi-Fi and MQTT libraries. Set up a local MQTT broker on the Pi or a computer.

Step 2: Implement Motion Detection on Pi

On the Pi, write a Python script using OpenCV for motion detection (from Exercise 2). When motion is detected, publish an MQTT message to iot/security/alert with details like timestamp and severity.

Step 3: Configure ESP32 as MQTT Subscriber and Actuator

On the ESP32, write firmware to connect to Wi-Fi, subscribe to the MQTT topic, and trigger the buzzer/relay (for example : high for 5 seconds) upon receiving an alert. Add LED feedback for connectivity status.

Step 4: Integrate and Test the System

Run both devices on the same network. Simulate motion to verify: Pi detects, publishes, ESP32 receives and acts. Add optional cloud logging by forwarding MQTT messages to AWS IoT or a similar service. Measure end-to-end latency (<500 ms) and debug issues like network drops.

Step 5: Document and Extend

Create a report with an architecture diagram, workflow description, challenges faced, and outcomes. Extend by adding features like email alerts, video snapshots, or integration with a mobile app. This project showcases a production-like IoT system, highlighting multi-device collaboration.

Conclusion

This chapter has bridged the foundational concepts of earlier chapters with the practical realities of advanced, vision-enabled IoT systems. Readers have explored how powerful edge platforms—such as Raspberry Pi for versatile prototyping and NVIDIA Jetson Nano for GPU-accelerated AI—unlock the ability to process rich visual data directly at the edge. Through OpenCV, the chapter demonstrated real-time capabilities like face detection, motion detection, and object tracking, showing how cameras transform passive sensors into active observers capable of interpreting complex scenes.

The integration of vision systems with low-power microcontrollers via MQTT highlighted a key architectural principle: divide responsibilities for maximum efficiency. High-computer tasks run on edge AI boards, while deterministic control and actuation remain on microcontrollers, creating modular, scalable, and power-optimized designs. Industry case studies—from Siemens' MQTT-driven factory analytics and LoRa-based warehousing of Flipkart to ZigBee/NB-IoT of Tata Power smart grid and AWS-powered precision agriculture of Punjab —illustrated how these technologies are deployed at scale, delivering measurable outcomes in efficiency, reliability, and sustainability.

Therefore, by combining vision, edge AI, and robust communication, this chapter equips learners with a practical, future-oriented perspective. Readers now understand not only how to build intelligent IoT devices but also how to design systems that see, reason, and act in real-world environments—preparing them to create impactful solutions in manufacturing, agriculture, logistics, security, and beyond. The journey from scalar sensing to visual intelligence marks the next frontier of IoT, where perception and autonomy converge to drive the next wave of innovation.

Index

Symbols

E

J

L

M

N

O

P

Q

R

S

T

U

V

W